HEIDEGGER ON BEING
AND ACTING:
FROM PRINCIPLES TO
ANARCHY

Studies in Phenomenology and Existential Philosophy

GENERAL EDITOR
JAMES M. EDIE

HEIDEGGER ON BEING AND ACTING: FROM PRINCIPLES TO ANARCHY

REINER SCHÜRMANN

TRANSLATED FROM THE FRENCH BY CHRISTINE-MARIE GROS
IN COLLABORATION WITH THE AUTHOR

INDIANA UNIVERSITY PRESS • BLOOMINGTON

To the memory of Hannah Arendt

This book was brought to publication with the aid of a grant
from the Andrew W. Mellon Foundation.

Translated and enlarged from *Le Principe d'anarchie: Heidegger et la question
de l'agir* (Paris: Editions de Seuil, 1982).

Manufactured in the United States of America

Library of Congress Cataloging-in-Publication Data
Schürmann, Reiner, 1941–
Heidegger on being and acting.

(Studies in phenomenology and existential philosophy)
Translation of: Le principe d'anarchie.
Bibliography: p.
Includes indexes.
1. Heidegger, Martin, 1889–1976.   I. Title.
II. Series.
B3279.H49S35513   1986   193   85-45072
ISBN 0-253-32721-0

1   2   3   4   5   90   89   88   87

Hoc enim proprie vivit quod est sine principio.

Only that which is without a principle
properly lives.

MEISTER ECKHART

CONTENTS

PART THREE

The Origin Is Said in Many Ways

PART FOUR

Historical Deduction of the Categories of Presencing

PART FIVE

Action and Anarchy

ACKNOWLEDGMENTS

While working on the original French edition of this study, I published several sections in the English language. These pieces not only suffered from being taken out of their systematic context, but all of them were also preliminary versions, later reworked. Nevertheless I wish to thank the directors of the following publishing houses and journals for their permission to resettle in its native habitat material first printed in diaspora: The Columbia University Press, *Human Studies, Man and World,* Precedent Publishing, *Social Research,* and The State University of New York Press.

R. SCH.

INTRODUCTION

The argument that I would like to develop in these pages can easily be summarized. It consists in raising the inherited question of the relationship between theory and practice, but considered under Heidegger's hypothesis that metaphysical rationality produces its own closure. That inherited question is to be raised anew, then, from a perspective that forbids couching it in opposites such as 'theory and practice'.

I would like to show what happens to the old problem of the unity between thinking and acting once 'thinking' no longer means securing some rational foundation upon which one may establish the sum total of what is knowable, and once 'acting' no longer means conforming one's daily enterprises, both public and private, to the foundation so secured. The hypothesis of closure entails more than the obsolescence of any such speculative base upon which life is to find its steadiness, its legitimation, and its peace: it entails the necessity of a deconstruction. In its rigorous, not its inflated sense, this term denotes the dismantling of what Kant called dogmatic philosophy. Deconstruction interrupts, throws out of gear, the derivations between first philosophy and practical philosophy. It was because of such derivations that ontology used to be called first philosophy: it provided the founding and legitimating discipline in relation to the body or system of the specialized disciplines. This, then, is the argument: in the answers that they have traditionally brought to bear on the 'special' question "What is to be done?" philosophers have relied, in one way or another, on some standard-setting first whose grounding function was assured by a 'general' doctrine, be it called ontology or something else. From this doctrine, theories of action received their patterns of thought as well as a great many of their answers. Now, the deconstruction of metaphysics situates historically what has been deemed to be a foundation. It thus closes the era of derivations between general and special metaphysics, between first philosophy and practical philosophy. As one of its consequences, deconstruction leaves the discourse on action suspended in a void. It deprives such discourse of the schemata that properly belonged to speculations on sensible or divine substance, on the subject, on spirit, or on 'being'. But it follows further that action itself, and not only its theory, loses its foundation or *archē*.

§1. Deconstructing Action

It is a decisive question for me today how a
political system, and what kind of one, can at
all be coordinated with the technological age.
I do not know the answer to this question. I
am not convinced that it is democracy.

"Only a God Can Save Us Now"[1]

It is the nature of this "I do not know," of the ignorance admitted in
these lines—feigned? sincere? or perhaps *necessary?*—which is of interest
here. I am not treating this avowal of ignorance as a signifier that would
refer to some state of consciousness or some event in Martin Heidegger's
life; one that would be the symptom, in other words, of some psychologi-
cal, political, or moral signified. Whether the avowal of ignorance is pretended or sincere, whether it refers to political longings and leanings or
not, is not my subject. But perhaps this avowal is not accidental. Perhaps it
directly concerns the single question that never ceased to preoccupy Heidegger. In any case, it can be paralleled with other 'confessions' of ignorance: "The greater the work of a thinker—which is in no way measured by
the extent and number of his writings—all the richer is what remains
unthought in that work, that is, what emerges for the first time thanks to it,
as having not yet been thought."[2] "The fact that the real has been showing
itself in the light of Ideas ever since Plato, is not a fact brought about by
Plato. The thinker only responded to that which addressed itself to him."[3]
"The plurivocity of the essence of reality at the beginning of modern metaphysics is the sign of an authentic [epochal] transition."[4] "What Kant,
beyond his express formulation, brought to light in the course of his laying
the foundation . . . Kant himself was no longer able to say anything about.
Generally, whatever is to become decisive in any philosophical knowledge
is not found in the propositions enunciated, but in that which, although
unstated as such, is brought before our gaze through these propositions."[5]
Like the works of Plato, Descartes, and Kant, *Being and Time* itself is
traversed by something unthought or unsaid that is not due to chance: "Do
not our own efforts, if we dare compare them with those of our predecessors, ultimately evidence a hidden avoidance of something which we—
certainly not by accident—no longer see?"[6]

A very distinct ignorance, then, seems to prevail at the moments of
transition between epochs, at the 'decisive' moments (*decidere*, 'to cut off,'
'to set apart'). It remains to be seen what this ignorance bears upon and
what is the source of its necessity. Perhaps it has nothing to do with the
opinions and convictions of an individual, with his sense of political responsibility or with the sagacity of his analyses of power. What if the avowal of
ignorance were integral to the body of writings which circulate, operate,

put people to flight, or make them think—that is, which function—under the name of 'Heidegger'? What if this ignorance were so necessary to his discourse that without such a confession it would no longer quite be a text, a fabric governed by internal laws? Can it be said that the Heideggerian corpus is structured according to rules that are few in number, one of which directly concerns this ignorance? That this ignorance is closely woven into the texture of his thinking? If this is so, 'to read Heidegger' will mean to inscribe that other individual, called the interpreter, into the same textual fabric and to advance solely within the written word. Such an approach is modest. Indeed, it deprives itself of the very possibility of verifying or invalidating through experience what is read. It is modest as is 'thinking', which cannot avail itself of the prestige of knowledge. But to approach Heidegger in this fashion is also violent: if it is possible to exhibit a few general rules of procedure in his writings, it may also be possible to steer what is said in a direction the man Martin Heidegger would not have wished to be led.

'Heidegger', then, will take the place here of a certain discursive regularity. It will not be the proper name, which refers to a man from Messkirch, deceased in 1976. We might say 'with Heidegger', but in all strictness we must say 'in Heidegger'.

We know that 'being' was his obsession, his first and final word—or at least nearly so. For it is true that toward the end even he could no longer hear it and would rather speak of 'presencing', of 'world', or of 'event'. What would be more tempting then, more deserving perhaps, than to develop, after Heidegger, what his obsession with that single question prevented him from accomplishing, and to 'derive' a 'practical philosophy' from his 'philosophy of Being'? It may be regrettable that he did not take this step himself. But after all we have the first philosophy, and a little ingenuity may suffice to extract from it a "Politics," an "Ethics," or even a "Second Critique." It could be argued that Heidegger, concerned solely with the lofty problem of 'being', would not have had such an acute sense for more concrete, more earthbound, or at least more philosophically traditional questions: so much so that in his life he stumbled at one of these concrete particulars that was more perilous than Thales' well. His obsession would be embarrassing especially when measured against his predecessors since Socrates, who consistently repeated that "virtue is knowledge," that practical reason receives its architecture from pure reason, and that *theōria*, since it is what is most noble within our reach, prescribes the routes to *praxis*. In short, Heidegger's obsession would simply have made him forget that *agere sequitur esse*, action follows being. He turned the question of being over and over—to us to translate it in terms of action.

I would like to show on the contrary that Heidegger does not at all dissociate 'being and acting'. He does not overlook the latter to the advantage of the former. To speak of presencing as he does is to speak of acting.

He does not disjoin the ancient unity between theory and practice, but he does much worse: he raises the question of presencing in such a way that the question of acting is already answered; he raises it in such a way that action can no longer become a separate issue; in such a way that to seek an enduring standard for answering the question, 'What is to be done?' is to search in the vacuum of the place deserted by the successive representations of an unshakable ground; in such a way, finally, that the epochal constellations of presencing have always already prescribed not only the terms in which the question of action can and must be raised (ousiological, theological, transcendental, linguistic terms), but also the ground from which it can and must be answered (substance, God, cogito, discursive community) as well as the types of answers that can and must be adduced (hierarchy of virtues, hierarchy of laws—divine, natural, and human—hierarchy of imperatives, and hierarchy of discursive interests, that is, cognitive or emancipatory). The Heideggerian deconstruction (*Abbau*—the term only turned into a catchword once translated into French, fifty years after it was coined) of the historical constellations of presencing shows that one can speak of the closed unity of the metaphysical epoch at least in one respect: the concern with *deriving* a practical philosophy from a first philosophy. 'Metaphysics' is then the title for that ensemble of speculative efforts with a view to a model, a canon, a *principium* for action. In the light of the deconstruction, that ensemble appears as a closed field. The hypothesis of the closure of the metaphysical field is the point of departure for everything that will follow. This hypothesis functions doubly (even though the opposition between system and history will eventually fall victim to that same hypothesis): it is a *systematic* closure, inasmuch as the norms for action formally 'proceed from' the corresponding first philosophies; and it is a *historical* closure, since the deconstructionist discourse can arise only from the boundary of the era over which it is exercised. The hypothesis of closure determines the deconstruction at each step of its progress. It confers its ambiguity on the Heideggerian enterprise: still enclosed in the problematic of presence, but already outside the fief where presencing functions as constant presence, as identity of self with self, as unshakable ground.

The hypothesis of closure also confers its radicality on the deconstructionist move: action bereft of *archē* is thinkable only at the moment when the problematic of 'being'—inherited from the closed field of metaphysics but subject on its threshold to a transmutation, to a passover—emerges from ontologies and dismisses them. If in the epoch of post-modernity (in short, since Nietzsche) the question of presence no longer seems capable of articulating itself as a first philosophy, and if the strategy of the concept of 'presencing' in Heidegger annihilates the quest for a complete possession of self by self, it is in the epochal constellation of the twentieth century that the ancient procession and legitimation of *praxis* from *theōria* comes to exhaustion. Then, in its essence, action proves to be an-archic.

'Anarchy' is only the complement of the two premises that have just been advanced, namely: (1) traditional doctrines of praxis refer this concept to an insurpassable science from which proceed the schemata that are applicable to a rigorous reasoning about action; (2) in the age of metaphysics' closure, this procession from or legitimation by a first science proves to be *epochal*—regional, dated, finite, and 'finished' in both senses of the word: complete as well as terminated.

Correlatively, here 'anarchy' means: (1) The prime schema which practical philosophy has traditionally borrowed from first philosophy is the reference to an *archē*, articulated according to the attributive πρὸς ἕν or the participative ἀφ' ἑνός relation. Theories of action not only depend in general on what prevails as ultimate knowledge in each epoch but, furthermore, they reproduce the attributive-participative schema as if it were a pattern. In this way, these theories have their origin in first philosophy, and they borrow from it the very design of seeking an origin for action, a first instance on which the manifold is to rest. The attributive-participative schema, when translated into the doctrines of praxis, results in the ordering of acts to one focal point. This focal point is continually displaced throughout history: ideal city, heavenly kingdom, the happiness of the greatest number, noumenal and legislative freedom, "transcendental pragmatic consensus" (Apel), etc. But none of these transferences destroys the attributive, participative, and therefore normative, pattern itself. The *archē* always functions in relation to action as substance functions in relation to its accidents, imparting to them sense and *telos*. (2) In the epoch of closure, on the other hand, the regularity of the principles that have reigned over action can be laid out. The schema of reference to an *archē* then reveals itself to be the product of a certain type of thinking, of an ensemble of philosophic rules that have their genesis, their period of glory, and that today perhaps are experiencing a decline. What we read, then, in Heidegger is that the principial function has been assured by numerous firsts over the course of the centuries; that the regularity of this function is formally reducible to the Aristotelian πρὸς ἕν (of which the ἀφ' ἑνός is but the symmetric counterpart); and that, with the closure of the metaphysical era, the epochal principles (metaphysical "stamps," *Prägungen*) that have ordered thoughts and actions in each age of our history are *withering away*. Anarchy in this sense does not become operative as a concept until the moment when the great sheet of constellations that fix presencing in constant presence folds up, closes in upon itself. For Western culture, things manifold have been frozen—diversely, of course, according to the epochs—around a first truth or a rational *principium*. Since the attributive schema has moreover been exported into practical philosophy, these rational principles delineate the structure in which is located the *princeps*, the authority to which all that is feasible in an era is referred. The first philosophies furnish power with its formal structures. More precisely, 'metaphysics' then designates that disposition where action requires a principle to which words, things, and deeds can be related. Action appears without principle in the age of the turning, when presence as ultimate identity turns into presencing as irreducible difference (or reducible only categorially). If these are the contours of the program of deconstruction, the necessity of an avowal of ignorance begins to be glimpsed: the very question of a "political *system* coordinated with the technological age" is one of principial constructs.

The most adequate expression to cover the whole of these premises would be 'anarchy principle'. The word 'anarchy', though, clearly lends itself to misunderstanding as does the juxtaposition of the two nouns which, for the professionals of speculative contradiction, inevitably suggests redemption through sublation. 'Anarchy' here does not stand for a program of action, nor its juxtaposition with 'principle' for dialectical reconciliation. With this twofold caveat, the paradox of the expression is nonetheless instructive, dazzling. Is not the backbone of metaphysics—whatever the ulterior determinations by which this concept would have to be specified— the rule always to seek a first from which the world becomes intelligible and masterable, the rule of *scire per causas*, of establishing 'principles' for thinking and doing? 'Anarchy', on the other hand, designates the withering away of such a rule, the relaxing of its hold. This paradox is dazzling because in two words it points within and beyond the closure of metaphysics, thus exhibiting the boundary line of that closure itself. The paradox that the expression 'anarchy principle' articulates locates the Heideggerian enterprise, it indicates the place where it is situated: still implanted in the problematic of τὶ τὸ ὄν; ("What is being?"), but already uprooting it from the schema of the *pros hen*, which was connate to that problematic. Retaining presence, but dislocating it from the attributive schema. Still a principle, but a principle of anarchy. It is instructive to think this contradiction. The principial reference then appears to be counteracted, both in its history and in its essence, by a force of dislocation, of plurification. The referential *logos* becomes "archipelagic speech," "pulverized poem" (*"parole en archipel," "poème pulvérisé,"* René Char). The deconstruction is a discourse of transition. By putting the two words 'anarchy' and 'principle' side by side, one prepares oneself for this epochal transition.

Needless to say, here it will not be a question of anarchy in the sense of Proudhon, Bakunin, and their disciples.[7] What these masters sought was to *displace* the origin, to substitute the 'rational' power, *principium*, for the power of authority, *princeps*—as metaphysical an operation as has ever been. They sought to replace one focal point with another. The anarchy that will be at issue here is the name of a history affecting the ground or foundation of action, a history where the bedrock yields and where it becomes obvious that the principle of cohesion, be it authoritarian or 'rational', is no longer anything more than a blank space deprived of legislative, normative, power. Anarchy expresses a destiny of decline, the decay of the standards to which Westerners since Plato have related their acts and deeds in order to anchor them there and to withdraw them from change and doubt. It is *the rational production of that anchorage*—the most serious task traditionally assigned to philosophers—that becomes impossible with Heidegger.

The deterioration of foundations is hardly an explicit theme in Heidegger insofar as it affects action. Rather, he recognizes it in an oblique way. Yet Heidegger says more about the uprooting, the rootlessness, of action than repeated declarations such as "thinking changes the world" lead one to suspect. Indeed, from *Being and Time* through the last of his writings he curiously inverts the relationship between 'thinking' and 'acting' as viewed retrospectively from the borderline of metaphysical closure. He articulates the inversion of the transcendental status proper to the ancient distinction between theory and praxis in ever new ways. This inversion will appear as the factor that *begins* to render the distinction in question anachronistic. Heidegger *makes action deprived of* archē *the condition of the thought which deconstructs the* archē. Whether this is expressed in terms of 'authentic temporality', of 'releasement', of 'dwelling' in language, or of 'letting things come to presence in their world', a practical determination, and one that determines all action, always appears as the a priori for the 'thought of being'. This is more than a simple inversion of the relationship between being and acting; it is the subversion of that classical relation, its overturn (*vertere*) from the base (*sub*-). Heidegger actually inscribes himself here in a tradition entirely different from that of Aristotle. Plotinus and Meister Eckhart teach that practice, rather than issuing as a consequence from an operation through which the mind grasps being, functions as the condition of the mind's presence to itself. Heidegger, however, transmutes these sources, since the practical a priori becomes dissociated from presence as the ideal possession of self by self.

In the age when 'principles' expire, presence can no longer denote anything noumenal. The deconstruction of action can be measured by the yardstick of Kant, the champion of the specific preeminence proper to practical reason: no practical philosophy without a noumenal a priori. Heidegger would subscribe to this discovery. But since presencing—being—is not a noumenon for him, the entire enterprise of devising a practical philosophy must fall. This is Kant turned against himself. Presencing is not a noumenon, nor is it the contrary of a noumenon, an empirical phenomenon or a positive given. Between the Scylla of an ideal, principial, ontological, noumenal understanding of presence and the Charybdis of its positive understanding, Heidegger traces the middle line of the categorial, subverting Kant as well. Presencing is one, but simply as the unity of the formal traits that link the epochs. Hence the impossibility of a practical philosophy drawn from the 'thought of being'. Hence, too, the importance of a table of the categories of presencing which establishes this impossibility. Such a table should put an end to all readings of Heidegger that, whether openly or not, tend to reduce 'being' to some version of the absolute. There is no manifestation of the absolute to be found in Heidegger's phenomenology of presencing, which is to say, in his deconstruction. If the identity in difference is of a purely categorial order, this phenomenology has broken with idealities, with the whole enterprise of construing some identity of self with self. Similarly, if manifestation is only another name for presencing and not its appearing, not the manifestation *of* presence, then the possibility of an epiphany of an in-itself in history vanishes (together with the possibility of a regulation explainable through a deductive-nomological model). One may add: if *logos* designates the structure of the constellation in and by which beings are near one another at any moment of the synchronic cut, and not the 'reason' enduring beyond all breaks and ruptures, it seems difficult to insert Heidegger within onto-theo-teleological logocentrism. Finally, if 'presencing' is the name for the synchronic constellation in which present beings circulate, and only that, it is entirely impossible to fit his thought into some philosophy of otherness, be it the divine Other or human others. The categorial solution that is brought to bear on the old problem of identity and difference, or of the one and the many, directly affects the discussion of action: there is no unity of action except that which characterizes an epoch. For, as I will attempt to show, 'in principle' all men do the same things. . . .

The avowal of ignorance concerning the political system best adapted to the technological age now appears as a consequence of another radicalized Kantian topic, enlightenment. "Enlightenment is man's release from his self-incurred tutelage."[8] For radical phenomenology, Western man has *incurred* his tutelage by endowing some of his representations with ultimacy. *Release* from such self-incurred tutelage can only come from reason's undoing what it has itself set up. To submit to a critique the measure-giving figments it has imposed on itself is to exhibit their origin. This cannot be done, however, by inquiring once again into the makeup of the subject, since it is precisely the transcendental I that Kant ends up instituting as yet another first. Critical phenomenology has therefore to turn to the history of presencing if it is to lay bare the conditions of self-incurred tutelage and complete the business of enlightenment—emancipation—left unfinished by Kant. Metaphysical thinking sets up systems of wardship under the guise of rationality; it is speculative inasmuch as its rationalization of bondage is held to mirror an a priori order that can be known through contemplation or reflection. Phenomenological thinking, on the other hand, points out the mechanics of those systems as well as the interests they support. But contrary to what contemporary critics (particularly from so-called Critical Theory) have charged, dethroning the transcendental subject as the modern ultimate referent in no way amounts to celebrating irrationality and dismissing the struggle for enlightenment. Heidegger sharpens that struggle as he turns 'thinking' polemically against 'reason', the originator of speculative custodial agencies. His avowal of ignorance only indicates that radical phenomenology has no such supreme guarantor to turn to.

The avowal of ignorance now also appears more coherent, better inscribed, at least, in the general unity of the texture which is the deconstructionist discourse. If the question of political systems can become an issue only within epochal and principial organizations, and if, furthermore, the epochal-principial modality of presencing comes to an end in the age of closure, then weighing the advantages and inconveniences of the different systems is a bad way of raising the political question. This can be shown in several ways.

First, and most obviously, by the opposition between thinking and knowing. In Heidegger, no dialectic links thought and knowledge; no synthesis makes it possible to pass from one to the other: "Science does not think." This opposition, also inherited from Kant (although in spite of the consistent use Heidegger makes of it, he never recognizes the debt), establishes two territories, two continents, between which there is neither analogy nor even resemblance. "There is no bridge that leads from science to thought."[9] We "think being" and its epochs, but we "know entities" and their aspects. There is a generalized ignorance, then, that strikes thought in all its advances. If Heidegger invokes this necessary poverty of philosophy so persistently it is perhaps because it is the placeholder of a necessity even closer to the very matter of thinking.

Furthermore, on the boundary line that encloses a long history the matter of thinking is to "repeat" or retrieve presencing itself, to "win back the originative experiences of metaphysics through a deconstruction of representations that have become current and empty."[10] If that long history actually reaches its end (and Heidegger's confident affirmation in this regard, as well as that of others after him,[11] may leave one perplexed), then in the crisis the structure of its field lapses out of order; its principles of cohesion lose their efficacy; the νόμος of our οἶκος, the economy that encloses us, produces fewer and fewer certainties. The moment when an epochal threshold is crossed is inescapably one of ignorance.

Finally, the necessary ignorance concerning political systems and their respective merits results from the constellation of presencing whose dawn is described to us as a cessation of principles, a deposing of the very principle of epochal principles, and the beginning of an economy of passage, that is, of anarchy. In the epoch of transition, then, words, things, and actions would come to presence in such a way that their public interaction is irreducible to any systematicity. It is through a historical deduction of the categories of "the other beginning" that action deprived of a unifying *pros hen* will become thinkable. The same deduction will establish the possibility of thinking an identity within manifold praxis that will consist only of "guiding traits." Since these traits apply to 'theory' and 'practice' alike, that distinction loses its pertinence.

This said and understood, nonetheless it must be added that the avowal of ignorance is, of course, a feint. And one that is more than strategic—unless the word 'strategy' is understood, not in relation to human actions and the art of coordinating them, but in relation to the economies of presencing. Then one sees that there are strong reasons for feigning. Indeed, after having outlined the withering away of principles, how could one avoid questions of the following type: What is your theory of the State? And of property? And of law in general? What will become of defense? And of our highways? Heidegger makes himself scarce. After one of the most direct developments of what could be called ontological anarchy—expressed at this juncture by the concept of "life without why," borrowed from Meister Eckhart (via Angelus Silesius)—Heidegger concludes: "In the most hidden ground of his being, man truly is only if in his way he is like the rose—without why." The "without why" points beyond the closure; therefore it cannot be pursued. The brusque halt of the development—"We cannot pursue this thought any further here"[12]—as well as the feigned ignorance, are inevitable when "another thought" is attempted. To strengthen this point a little further: a life "without why" certainly means a life without a goal, without *telos*; also it is said that "in the most hidden ground of his being"—hence, totally—man must be deprived of *telos*. For man to be "in his way like the rose" would be to abolish practical teleology. It is clear that the objections rebound: But without *telos* action would no longer be action. . . . Indeed. Whence the necessity of the feint.

To deconstruct action is to uproot it from domination by the idea of finality, the teleocracy where it has been held since Aristotle. A deconstruction, then, is not the same as a destruction. At the end of the Introduction to *Being and Time* Heidegger announced a "phenomenological *destruction* of the history of ontology."[13] By that he meant a way of rereading the philosophers. The subject matter of destruction is made up of philosophical systems, of books. With the help of that method Heidegger hoped to retrieve the thought experiences from which each of the inherited ontologies was born. The subject matter of deconstruction, on the other hand, is provided by the constellations of presencing that have succeeded one another throughout the ages. If the closure must be understood as it has been sketched here, if it is that disturbance of the rules whereby the general unity of the constellation called culture rearranges itself, then deconstruction is necessarily all-inclusive, indivisible. The *Abbau* cannot contain itself within a 'region', within a determinate science, or a discipline. Action is not deconstructible in isolation. This is why the first task is that of a phenomenology of the epochal principles.[14]

The point of departure of this entire enterprise is not really innovative. It is the very traditional wonder before the epochs and their slippages: How is it possible to account for the fact that, in the heart of an epochal enclosure (those enclosures called *polis,* Roman Empire, Middle Ages, etc., or, according to a scarcely more discriminating division, seventeenth, eighteenth, or nineteenth centuries) certain practices are possible and even necessary, while others are not? How does it happen that a Revolution was impossible in the Middle Ages, just as an International was during the French Revolution, and a Cultural Revolution was at the moment of the First International? Or, according to a perspective that is less alien to the questions of the 'principles' than it may seem: How does it happen that a Duns Scotus, although surnamed *Doctor subtilis,* could write neither a critique of pure reason nor a genealogy of morals? How does it happen, in other words, that a domain of the possible and the necessary is instituted, endures for a time, and then cedes under the effect of a mutation? 'How does it happen?' This is a descriptive question, not to be confounded with the etiological question, 'Why is it that . . . ?' The causal solutions brought to bear on these phenomena of mutation, whether they are 'speculative', 'economist', or whatever, leave one unsatisfied for the very reason of the causal presupposition which they cannot question—which they cannot *situate,* for this presupposition is only an epochal incidence of the *pros hen* schema.

To situate the epochal principles in the history of the modalities of presencing is to draw a genealogy of these principles. This entails a double task: on one hand, such a genealogy will trace the ancestral line of the last of these principles, technology; by so doing, it will establish the filiation that leads from "the Greek dawn" to "the night of the world" in which—according to Hölderlin—modernity is engulfed. On the other hand, the genealogy of principles will show how this lineage itself was born; how, with a certain radical turn, the Socratic turn, the constellations of presencing *began* to be dominated by principles; how, at last, with another no less radical turning, which announces itself in the technological reversal, these constellations can *cease* to be dominated by principles. But this thought of a possible withering away of the principles is only progressively articulated in Heidegger. It has been clear from the start that the question, "When are you going to write an ethics?"[15] posed to him after the publication of his major work, arose from a misunderstanding. But it is only in Heidegger's last writings that the issue of action finds its adequate context: the genealogy of a finite line of epochal principles.

When one considers the sufferings that men have inflicted and inflict on one another in the name of the epochal principles, there can be no doubt that philosophy—or "thinking"—is no futile enterprise: a phenomenology that deconstructs the epochs "changes the world"[16] because it reveals the withering away of these principles.

§2. Theory of the Texts

> After *Being and Time*, [my] thinking replaced
> the expression 'meaning of being' with 'truth
> of being'. And so as to avoid any
> misapprehension about truth, so as to exclude
> its being understood as conformity, 'truth of
> being' has been elucidated as 'locality of
> being'—truth as the locus-character of being.
> That presupposes, however, an
> understanding of what a locus is. Hence the
> expression *topology of being*.
>
> Seminar in Le Thor, 1969[17]

These lines indicate how Heidegger should be read.

Only in his last writings does he raise the question of presencing as that of "loci." These loci are the historical economies. In each moment they constitute a field of presencing. Across the epochs presencing articulates itself differently, sets itself to work (ποιεῖν) differently. The 'poietic' character of presencing is what Heidegger calls *Dichtung*, "poetry." "Poetry that thinks is in truth the topology of being." Needless to say, this has nothing to do with the art of composing verse, or even with human language. "The poietic character of thinking"[18] is only the echo, the reverberation of presencing and *its* poietic character. Presencing crystallizes (*dichten* means "to thicken," to render dense) into successive orders. Conversely, these epochal crystallizations determine the kind of words we speak and write in. The self-ordering of presencing thus must be understood as the primordial language. Throughout his texts, the essential concern of Heidegger's thinking remains the same: to understand 'being' phenomenologically as presencing, and to understand it through the manifold modes that entities have of rendering themselves "dense," of ordering themselves, of constituting a text or 'poem'. When the guiding idea of Heideggerian phenomenology is "the meaning of being," this manifold is one of regions: entities 'given for handling', entities 'given as objects', and 'being-there'. When its guiding idea is "the truth of being," the manifold is one of epochs: Greek, Latin, Modern, Technological. Finally, when the guiding idea is "the topology of being," the manifold is no longer a matter of regions or epochs, but is the "coming-to-presence" itself: an event of multiple origination which, as a transcendental condition, renders the spatial, temporal, linguistic, and cultural "loci" possible.

Only with this last form of multiplicity does the thrust of the problematic appear which has moved Heidegger throughout the trajectory of his polymorphic writings with their shifting vocabularies: to grasp presencing as a force of plurification and of dissolution. From the genealogical perspective, the historical constellations of entities appear as orders arranged under an ordering first. But once the phenomenological gaze moves back from the quality and interplay of things present toward their presencing, the line of descent in which these constellations were put into place by figures of an epochal first proves to have itself sprung from an initial concealment: from the forgottenness of the event of presencing and the inability to sustain its manifold. The genealogy, then, which calls attention to the multiplicity of historical orderings, discovers at this line's start the incapacity to stand or bear, and hence to understand or grasp, the "poietics" in those orderings, the plasticity of their making and unmaking. The quest for principles springs from a lack of stature.[19] Heidegger's last writings could therefore be read as the attempt to elaborate the chief traits of an economy of presencing that is not reducible to one *archē*—the traits of a plural economy.

If this is the case, it is clear that the "phenomenological destruction of the history of ontology" promised in *Being and Time,* can be fully understood—and carried out—as a deconstruction only from the standpoint of Heidegger's last writings. Only then does it become apparent how time can be *"der Sinn des Seins"*: not the "meaning" of being, but its directionality; the "sense" as the direction in which something, e.g., motion, takes place (this acceptation of both the English 'sense' and the French *sens*—'sense' of a river, or of traffic—stems, not from Latin, but from an Indo-European verb that means to travel, to follow a path). Not the "signification" of being for a man and hence "a human accomplishment"[20] (a misunderstanding that Heidegger says threatened the deconstruction in its first phase, that of a destruction in *Being and Time*), but the directionality of the orderings by which constellations of presencing produce themselves. Not the *sens unique,* the one-way street of the epochs unfolding across the ages either (a misunderstanding that threatened during the phase of "the history of being"), but the multiple presencing in which things present emerge from absence. These distinctions are what is most difficult in Heidegger. The point here is that the correct understanding of his early writings is obtained only if he is read backward, from end to beginning.

The hermeneutical dilemma of whether Heidegger should be read forward or backward appears most clearly in connection with praxis. Much has been written on the possible political implications of *Being and Time.* According to some, the pronouncement to follow the Führer, made six years after its publication, could already be seen in germ in that book. The address delivered by Heidegger at the inauguration of his university rectorship, with its call for triple mobilization in the service of labor, arms, and knowledge,[21] would show the outcome of a direction taken by him ever since the Existential Analytic. The key term which supposedly indicates this continuity of thinking is that of resolve, *Entschlossenheit.* The same themes are said to reappear still later with the praise of the great statesman (compared to other "creators" like poets, artists, and thinkers) in the late thirties. Heidegger's early writings are thus supposed to constitute the

framework that his political speeches would only have had to fill out as
rallying cries to a leader capable of walking alone and resorting to violence.
Hence the themes of the *Rektoratsrede* and other speeches of that period,
focusing on "the battle community of teachers and students," would be
neither accidental nor isolated in Heidegger.[22] Later, his hands burned by
politics, Heidegger is said to have chosen less compromising subjects for
his publications, notably Hölderlin's poetry. It would be all too understandable that on several subsequent occasions he declared himself incapable of seeing any practical implications of his thinking. Thus, if Heidegger is read from beginning to end, Karl Jaspers's judgment seems to have
bearing: not only did he never renounce his nostalgia for a certain past, but
"the fundamental constitution of that way of philosophizing must lead, in
praxis, to total domination."[23]

When read backward, from the last writings to the first, Heidegger
appears in a different light. Once again, his texts alone are at issue. From
the viewpoint of the topology, *praxis*—just like *theōria*, it should be
added—is only the response that the actors in history give, and cannot but
give, to the constellations of presencing that enclose them. If there is a
'normative' aspect to this phenomenology of the epochal constellations, it
consists in the possibility of a withering away of the principles and a plurification of action. Under different titles—the "fourfold" or "quadrate" is only
one of many—Heidegger then attempts to think presencing explicitly as
plural. The action that responds to presencing so understood, will be dia-
metrically opposed to the *Führerprinzip;* it would be a type of action
irreconcilably alien to all reduction to the uniform, an action hostile to the
standard.

The hermeneutical dilemma is noteworthy here: in reading Heidegger
forward, that is, from the Existential Analytic to the Topology, an "ideal-
ization of unity to the detriment of plurality"[24] may be construable out of
a few sparse texts of his. But in reading Heidegger backward, from the
Topology to the Existential Analytic, the evidence is to the contrary.
Presencing then appears more Nietzschean, deprived of metaphysical
principles, "chaotico-practical."[25] Instead of a unitary concept of ground,
we then have the "fourfold"; instead of praise for the firm will,[26] detachment; instead of the integration of the university into the civil service,
protest against technology and cybernetics; instead of a straightforward
identification between Führer and right,[27] anarchy.

Heidegger's treatment of the traditional opposition between theory and
practice shows most clearly that his texts must be read in reverse order.
Indeed, in *Being and Time*, this relation is still ambiguous. Commentators
hold various opinions: either that in that work practice takes precedence
over theory, or that theory takes precedence over practice, or finally, that
their distinction is altogether abolished.[28] In the later works, the more the
"truth of being" comes to be understood in its historical essence, the more

the terms 'theory' and 'practice' disappear, and must disappear. If theory as well as practice turn into ways of responding to the constellations of unconcealment, to aletheiological constellations, then their distinction is subsumed within the broader notion of 'thinking'. "Thinking acts insofar as it thinks."[29] The genesis of theoretical knowledge from the circumspective concern that accompanies all manipulation of entities given for handling[30] tells us little about thinking. Manipulation, from which theory may be born, is technical. In the Analytic this is dissociated from projects of existence and later comes to be viewed as the natural outcome of Greek θεωρία. "The characterization of thinking as θεωρία and the determination of knowing as 'theoretical' attitude, occur already within the 'technical' interpretation of thinking."[31]

The rudimentary character of the notions of theory and practice in Heidegger's early writings, and consequently the necessity of completing them with the later writings, is the result specifically of the still entirely insufficient conception of technique in *Being and Time*. In the only passage in which Heidegger speaks of technique,[32] it is limited to the handling of instruments in research: the installation of a measuring dial in physics, the preparation of a substance on a microscope slide in chemistry, etc. Here the concept of technique stands for the sum of procedures employed in conducting scientific research. As yet it in no way designates technology as transformative of nature. Even though certain traits that become part of the latter concept are not entirely absent from *Being and Time,* they nevertheless enter into it from an angle that has nothing to do with a reflection on action. The project of quantification results from an inauthentic totalization of existence. In such an existenti*ell* project, the distinctions between what is given for handling or available (*zuhanden*), objectively given or subsistent (*vorhanden*), and there-with-others (*mitdaseiend*) disappear.[33] Only retrospectively can it be held that the descriptions of the 'mathematical project' as an existentiell a priori contain in germ the later descriptions of technology as *Gestell,* enframing, and of the total control it exercises over the modern world. And retrospectively, we can—and should—wonder that these descriptions of technology seem to derive from a priority of the inauthentic over the authentic in *Being and Time* rather than from the few scattered remarks concerning the techniques of scientific research.[34]

Further evidence that Heidegger ought to be read backward results from his most compromising declarations in favor of Nazism. As is well known, in a course given in 1935 Heidegger praised "the inner truth and greatness" of National Socialism, which resides, the text says, in "the encounter between global technology and modern man."[35] This statement stands indeed in direct line with the thinking of *Being and Time*—but only in what it says about technology. How could a political movement be supposed capable of bearing up against global technology, unless the latter was still viewed as a force that might be stemmed and modified? Consequently, in the mid-thirties technology is still seen as an inauthentic project that an authentic project could in some way redress. What is new in this affirmation, when compared to *Being and Time*, is that the inauthentic project is now identified with "Russia and America, which are metaphysically the same, namely in regard to their world character and their relation to the spirit."[36] It is only toward the end of the thirties that Heidegger discovers the understanding of technology that will remain his: the force of totalitarian and monolithic enframing, to which he will continuously oppose a manifold thinking of presencing as manifold. Then, "the global imperialism of technologically organized man" will encompass "Americanism" as well as "man who wills himself as a people, breeds himself as a race and finally empowers himself as lord of the earth."[37] From the viewpoint of such an encompassing notion of technology, the preceding works appear in their true function, as trailmarks. "*Wege, nicht Werke.*"[38]

Here, then, is how in such a theory of the texts the an-archic, anti-teleocratic element can be traced back as far as *Being and Time*. Authenticity is described there as anticipatory resolution. Existence is freed for its own finitude by the resolute anticipation of its death. "Anticipation turns out to be the possibility of understanding one's ownmost and uttermost potentiality-for-being, that is to say, the possibility of authentic existence."[39] If our ownmost potentiality-for-being reveals itself in the anticipation of our death—and Heidegger was always to maintain that it is a change in attitude toward our death that would produce a new experience of presencing—then it is my total negativity that will totalize my existence. Is this not an odd "potential" if it projects me toward my negation? It is as if what is "most originarily"[40] myself projects me nowhere, toward nothing. Indeed, what is it that my existence makes its own in becoming authentic? My possibility of not being at all. Nothing, then, is made my own. Since he retains 'potential' and the 'possible' as the decisive marks of authenticity, it is clear that the concept of authentic existence contains no teleological structure. Higher than *archē* and *telos* stand an-archy and a-teleocracy since "higher than actuality stands possibility."[41] It is true that, as the horizon of anticipation, death is certainly a concretization of the teleological structure that characterizes 'care' in general. But to speak of death as one's ownmost possibility, a possibility that has to be appropriated ever anew, is already to introduce an element of non-finality into authenticity that is absent from the descriptions of care. Authentic temporality—not linear, but ecstatic—abolishes the representations of a 'terminus a quo' and a 'terminus ad quem' in the understanding of existence. The ecstatic potential is thus anticipatory of death while devoid of relations, *unbezüglich*. Death is "one's ownmost possibility, non-relational and unsurpassable."[42] In this way, Heidegger thinks the authentic as ecstatic fullness of one's potential, ontologically exempt from all relations to entities, including the relation to death represented as an entity. All entities convey a 'why': those that are subsistent or given as objects yield knowledge, and those that are available or given for handling are there for use. Knowing and using constitute the two ways the real or the actual imparts its teleological structure. "But higher than actuality stands possibility." Why higher? Because the possible is never either subsistent or available. Possibility, and consequently potential, thus never fall within the coordinates of *archē* and *telos*, that is to say, within the coordinates of causality. The understanding of time through which Heidegger reverses all metaphysics since Aristotle is so innovative because it undermines these representations. Ecstatic time is opposed to linear time—the Aristotelian "number of becoming" as well as the Augustinian "extendedness of the soul"—as the possible is opposed to the unity of act and potency, as thinking is to knowing, and as the principle of anarchy is to the principle of causality.

From what has been said, the following consequences can be drawn for a theory of Heidegger's texts:

1) If periods or articulations are to be distinguished in these texts, it is advisable to renounce once and for all the opposition between "Heidegger I" and "Heidegger II"[43] and instead to retain the three moments I have mentioned: the first in which the question of presencing is raised as that of the "sense of being," the second in which it is raised as the "truth of being"—more precisely as the history of that truth, *alētheia*—and the third in which it is raised by the "topology of being."

2) Situated on the boundary line of metaphysics' closure, Heidegger is not, cannot be, a systematic thinker. Nevertheless, what he says about Nietzsche—that we must learn to read him with the same rigor as we read Aristotle—applies even more to himself. It is obvious what we stand to gain and lose by a rigorous reading of his texts. We gain a precise and sustained strategy of thinking, directed against withering principial referents, against the illusion of any legitimating first that could function as a rule for thinking and as an authority for conduct. We lose the Heidegger that has become a boon to the market of poetic and religious tranquilizers. However, the rigorous reading of his texts requires a starting point and a method.

3) The starting point is the hypothesis of "the end of the history of being," the end of that history of presencing in which "being lies in destiny."[44] Its ending is technology, understood not as a set of tools for some people's material culture—as one would speak of Roman or medieval technology—but as the phenomenal configuration of the twentieth century. From Plato through our own age, Western civilization has been placed under the control of metaphysical "stamps" (*Prägungen*), under the control of what I call the epochal principles. But if the history of epochs is drawing to a close, it can no longer simply be held that "the history of being, alone, is being itself,"[45] for another shape of presencing then takes over from *epochal* unconcealment.[46] The "stamps" or principles belong to the epochs and wither away with them. Heidegger calls the other shape of

presencing or of being the *Ereignis,* the event of appropriation. But, and this is crucial, "the *Ereignis* is not a new stamp of being belonging to the history of being."[47] That is my starting point.

4) As for the method, it consists in reading Heidegger backward. The notion of "sense" in *Being the Time* (first moment) can be freed from its neo-Kantian overtone—"meaning"— and be correctly understood as directionality only through the historical-destinal conception of "truth" (second moment), which casts off the subjectivist, neo-Kantian inflection; likewise, "truth" can be clearly understood as epochal unconcealment only through the still later notion of *"topos,"* site or locus (third moment). The topology brings the epochs to their end. In other words, the reason why *ecstatic temporality* does not yet allow Heidegger to think of presencing "as time"[48] appears only with the *destinal temporality* of the history of presencing; this destinal temporality in turn is located, situated, by the *temporality of event,* by the topology.

5) When looked at in the light of the history of presencing, human practice appears as a response to the epochal constellations of truth. This discovery, made after *Being and Time,* inaugurates the *Kehre,* "turning," in Heidegger's thinking. From the still later point of view of the topology, human practice is not sufficiently described by this character of response. If the epochs are drawing to their close, presencing is deprived of any principle, that is, of any *archē* and *telos.* Human practice, then, can and must be thought of as likewise "without why." Retrospectively, goalless practice is in no way absent from *Being and Time.* As was said, the very word 'potential'—*Möglichkeit*—stands for a power (*Macht,* from *mögen*—all words of the same root as 'making', *machen,* as well as 'mechanic' and 'magic'), a sheer power potential, a sheer superabundance with no purpose or end, be it intrinsic or extrinsic. In reading Heidegger from end to beginning, then, the practical implications of his thinking leap into view: the play of a flux in practice, without stabilization and presumably carried to the point of an incessant fluctuation in institutions, is an end in itself. The turn beyond metaphysics thus reveals the essence of praxis: exchange deprived of a principle.

These five rules for reading Heidegger allow for preliminary answers to a few objections. The proposed theory of the texts separates some pertinent from some pointless questions about deconstruction.

Here is one possible objection: *By putting so much emphasis on the economies of presencing—economies of epochs, first, and then of the event—you cannot but lose sight of all that Heidegger has to say about language. Now if there is a question today that generates unanimity at least as a question, it is certainly that of language. Therefore, you are denying Heidegger entry into the most lively debates of our time.*—Not so. In its ultimate topological form, the deconstruction *situates* language as it can be spoken in a given epoch: "Man's relation to language could transform itself analogously to the change of the relation to being."[49] Hence, there is a certain identity between language and being. Incidentally, the topology also makes it possible to situate the ideal of scientificity that predominates in contemporary preoccupations with language.

One might also raise the following objection: *It is understood that our relation to being and its metamorphoses follows no rational necessity, no progression toward more and more conscious, free, logical, universal forms of life in society. Granted. But you go overboard to the other extreme. The emphasis on the economies merely amounts to a positivism of historical periods. Hence the Heideggerian waitfulness: "We are to do nothing but wait."[50] Wait for an era of presencing more favorable to thinking? As one waits for a sunny day to go to the beach? If that is not historicist positivism!*—The text cited does treat, in an oblique way, the possibility of a shift toward something new in history, toward what "as yet has never been experienced." Heidegger asks how we are to gain access to radical novelty. We must think about that place, he says, "from whence alone such a transition can happen." The transition from one historical economy to another can thus be accomplished only if thinking locates itself *in another place*, a place other than the succession of the given economies. A place other than the given: the place of what "gives" the given. This is the "step backward" through which Heidegger adopts and modifies the transcendental tradition. To put it differently: the place to be gained is one where "the essence of thinking" and presencing understood as an event arise together, inseparably. A place that can be determined only by categorial traits. The unity of thinking and presencing results from an appropriation and anti-subjectivist transformation of what Kant called the highest synthetic principle,[51] but it is not epochal positivism.

It would furthermore be mistaken to view the deconstruction as no more than a provisional discipline, auxiliary to phenomenology, and thus to object: *You make a great case for the deconstruction, but does the topology of the later Heidegger not simply make it obsolete?*—The question is mistaken inasmuch as the *topoi* of being are to be construed "without regard for a foundation of being in entities,"[52] construed, that is, precisely by deconstructing such foundations. During the period of *Being and Time*, there can be no projection without facticity and no construction of a fundamental ontology without deconstruction of the foundational ontologies. In those early writings, the deconstruction is an integral part of the construction, just as the essential structure that is to be *projected* belongs to the matrix of *facticity*. The phenomenological reduction wrests the structure of being from this matrix. Reduction, construction, and deconstruction then are the three parts of hermeneutical phenomenology.[53] Later, in *On Time and Being*, there can be no "understanding of what a locus is" without a distancing. This is to say that according to the last texts the analysis retrogresses first from the situated or manifest entities (from the given, or again, from the present, *das Anwesende*) toward their site or their being-manifest (being-given or the mode of presence, *die Anwesenheit*); then it retro-gresses further to the self-situating, the self-manifesting as such (the giving, *Es gibt*, or presencing, *das Anwesen*). This double step backward[54] is one of the ways Heidegger, in his later writings, dismantles the ancient philo-sophical quest for a stable and credible foundation on which to rest our knowing as well as acting. Manifestation founds nothing. It is therefore gained at the cost of deconstructing historical presence or 'being manifest'. From the situated entities, to their site, then to the situating—the emerg-ing into the open, presencing—the transcendental retrogradation is decon-structive *essentially*.

Here is another unfounded question: *Is the hypothesis of closure not pure utopia? Indeed, if the truth of being*, alētheia, *has "as yet never been experienced," "renouncing the transmitted ways of thinking" strongly re-sembles the imaginary barter in which a dim present is exchanged for a bright future. In fact, "the step back from the one thinking to the other thinking"[55] seems to correspond exactly to the equivocal idea of a utopia: on one hand the thinking to come would be the excellent place* (εὖ-τόπος) *where truth radiates, since the historical concealment of presencing, the* epochē, *would cease. But on the other hand, this future thinking would accentuate* lēthē, *the essential concealment or absence in the heart of pre-sencing; therefore it would also be Nowhere, the no-place* (οὐ-τόπος) *of truth, a forever unattainable radiance. Does Heidegger not put forward* the other thinking *as a salvation, opposed to the prospect of a future run by "demonic"[56] technology? The demonic is the technological enterprise as it tightens its grip, making the future the age of horror; it is the victory of knowing over thinking, consequently of a knowing that whirls in mere accumulation of information; it is total administration, the ideal of order for the sake of order, without specific content, reifying the political appar-ently beyond recourse. Does Heidegger not challenge such a prospect of the future with the help of the beneficial* exeat *called "closure" quite as Thomas More challenged the England of Henry VIII with the blissful isle of Nowhere?*—Here, the answer has to follow the same line as my earlier remark regarding anarchists: Utopianism, whether conceived as the theory of the perfect city or as the philosophy of history attaining its future culmi-nation in some universal harmony, is as 'metaphysical' as theoretical anarchism.[57] In either case, political thinking consists in weighing the ad-vantages and drawbacks of one theory or another. Nothing of the kind occurs in Heidegger. The pertinent question is therefore not of knowing whether technology may be counteracted, mastered, surpassed, subli-mated; whether nature, given over to the rule of reason for two millennia and summoned to surrender its energies to the reign of comfort for two centuries, may be 'restored', whether man can be 'reconciled' with it. About matters such as these the deconstruction has nothing to say. If it did, the double step backward, carefully elaborated by Heidegger, would—for better or worse—once again amount to a "transmitting" between theory and practice.[58] One would disengage oneself from practice in order to step back and occupy some vantage point, some theoretical Sirius from which to ascertain ethical and political criteria. One would return to the πρὸς ἕν of the *Nichomachean Ethics*, where actors are related theoretically to the ideal of the prudent man,[59] and of the *Politics*, where citizens are measured theoretically against the ideal of the perfect city. These are just so many principial relations that, as will be shown, are parasitic on the *Physics*. Utopia is the most fanciful and imaginary instance of the substantialist relation to the One. Consequently, one Sirius is not enough. The retrogression has to be twofold, from practice to theory of practice, and from theory to thinking.

Here, then, are what I consider to be the pertinent questions inscribed in the Heideggerian texts. They concern (1) the epochal principles and their withering away; (2) the reversals between epochs (*Wenden*) and the closing turn (*Kehre*), as well as the way in which these shifts affect action; (3) the "origin" of action; (4) the categorial unity of the economies of presencing as the location of the 'one' and the 'many' in history; (5) the practical a priori required in order to think presencing, and with it several concrete consequences of the deconstruction for action. In the five corresponding parts of this work, I want to show how these still rudimentary notions yield a coherent picture of Heidegger's thinking about practice and politics, and how they allow him to maintain that the epoch of closure is also that in which the ancient derivation of action from being exhausts itself.

To do this, I will have recourse to an assortment of terms not all of which are to be found in Heidegger, and some of which he expressly rejects. In order to develop an argument, it seems inevitable to me to reinstate certain words excluded from his vocabulary because they were too heavily overdetermined, such as 'term' (excluded in order to keep thinking on the way, in a certain indeterminacy without reaching any 'terminal'), 'category' (too integral to a "logic of things"), 'transcendental' (too closely connected to subjectivism) and many other standard locutions from the tradition. Words such as these need to be converted, to be deconstructed, so as to make them say both more and less than they are expected, or allowed, to say within the closure. The key notions not found in Heidegger just enumerated will be elucidated along the way. If expressions like 'epochal principles' and 'economies of presence' are not literally Heideggerian formulations, these concepts are no less strictly operative in his texts. The demand for a fairly liberal attitude toward the words he uses is again a result of the hypothesis of closure. This hypothesis imposes on the deconstruction a vocabulary and a reading that remain philosophical, but whose extreme edge already plunges beyond that 'archeological' layer where they invariably guaranteed for the mind a first principle. The terms we have inherited no longer fulfill this architectonic function. Taken up within deconstruction, they occur as though in quotation marks.

Part One
Genealogy of Principles

I

UNDERSTANDING HISTORY THROUGH ITS REVERSALS

When the turning comes to pass in the
danger, this can only happen abruptly.

"The Turning"[1]

As an epoch comes to an end, its principle withers away. The principle of an epoch gives it cohesion, a coherence which, for a time, holds unchallenged. At the end of an epoch, however, it becomes possible to question such coherence. In withering away, the supreme referent of an age becomes problematic. As long as its economy dominates, and as long as its order disposes the paths that life and thought follow, one speaks otherwise than when its hold loosens, giving way to the establishment of a new order. The principle of an epoch is a matter both of knowing and of acting; it is both the *principium*, the foundation that provides reasons, and the *princeps*, the authority that dispenses justice. The justificatory reason of an epoch has its time: it establishes itself, reigns, and eventually founders. Its rise, the regime it imposes, and then its peril show that it is essentially precarious. Ultimate reasons are unquestionable, but only temporarily so. They have their genealogy and their necrology. They are epochal. They establish themselves without a blueprint and collapse without warning. Thus, the principle of an epoch rules over it; but such a principle, too, has a beginning. Its birth, its *archē*, occurs in the crises of history. Understood in terms of epochal history, the origin appears to be plural: *archē*, insofar as it designates what begins and rules an epoch; *princeps-principium* inasmuch as it functions as its foundation and as its authority; finally, the arising or coming forth, *Ursprung*, itself, by which an entity enters into presence within any given epochal order.

Is it possible to draw up the genealogy of epochal principles? And will such a genealogy allow one to oppose the reversals in history (*Wenden*) to one single turning (*die Kehre*) in which *the lineage of these principles itself comes to an end*? When the habitat which has transitorily become ours decays and falls, questions previously unheard of, questions hitherto incapable of being asked, surge forth: if such is its end, what might its origin have been? But in the reversals of history the origin of the field in which the most familiar things appear shows itself to be complex—*archē, princeps-principium,* and *Ursprung.* As to the breaks or transitions, some are mere passages from one epoch to the next, while the other—the one other crisis—is the unmediated egress, "in the danger," from epochal history as such.

§3. The Puma-Shaped City

The *principia* occupy the first place, stand in the first row. The *principia* refer to a series and an order. . . . We observe them without meditating.

Der Satz vom Grund[2]

   The fortress, encircled by three concentric walls, overhangs the city. The ramparts forming the palisade are built in a zigzag design. They are con-structed of granite polygonal stones, some up to thirty feet high and weigh-ing three hundred tons. An esplanade, where the troups were reviewed, extends from one side of the fortress. On the other side the terrain falls abruptly to the roofs of the capital. The descent is made by precipitous trails. The oxygen is rarified, breathing is difficult. At this altitude almost nothing grows except steppe grass and some shrubs. Terrace cultures sub-sist on other slopes. The city is encased between two mountain ranges which rise to twenty thousand feet. Formerly the houses were made of adobe and covered with straw, later they were built of regularly cut stone. The buildings stretch without much order around a vast plaza that re-sembles two trapezoids adjoining at their smaller bases. This plaza is said to have been filled with life-size animals made of solid gold and silver. It is also reported that a hundred llamas were sacrificed there each month. Apparently this plaza was much too spacious for the commercial needs of the natives, and this city lacked ordinary markets and afforded housing only for priests. It abounded however in lodgings for pilgrims. When seen from the surrounding slopes, the fortress and the city describe the clear outline of an animal: the great arteries of Cuzco, together with the Tullumayo River, form the body, and the Sacsayhuaman fortress, the head of a puma.
   Cuzco bears its principle inscribed within it. Given the absence of com-mercial areas and the hypertrophy of governmental and ceremonial monu-ments, its principle leaps out at the eye: the centralization of the Inca empire under the domination of the class symbolized by the puma. 'Cuzco' means navel, and 'Inca' is the name of the ruling class. It can also designate the leader of that class, the emperor. His insigne is the puma. It represents the principle in its function as authority, *princeps.* Paved roads ran from the central plaza, following the ridge lines. Along them couriers transmit-

ted the summonses, directives, decrees, and verdicts as far as what is today Argentina, to the south, and Quito, to the north. The principle of the Inca system made it possible to subject heteroclite tribes to the central power. Across the one-time empire, urbanism still testifies to this autocracy. Throughout the conquered provinces, plazas similar to that at Cuzco were used for celebrations, the administration of justice, the call to arms, and payments of tribute. Towns seem to have been conceived less as conglomerations of dwellings than as relays of power for the central authority, and the people were considered above all as manual labor, detachable according to the requirements of the rational organization of the economy.

But what is the principle of intelligibility, the *principium*, of this, the most centralized empire ever? The population, the animals, the labor, the soil itself, were parcelled into decimal units. The cacique of ten heads of families oversaw the agricultural work and distributed the provisions. Other duties were incumbent upon the leaders of fifty, one hundred, five hundred, one thousand, and ten thousand families. The ages were grouped into units of ten. The public officials, recognizable by ear perforations that varied according to their rank, constituted cells of ten. The corps of craftsmen, the plots of land, even the sexes were organized in the same way. According to the chronicle of Huaman Poma, who claimed to have been the grandson of the Inca Tupac Yupanqui, there were ten groups of men and ten groups of women. For the pleasure of it I quote *in extenso:*

1. *Auca camayoc.* The warriors, or more precisely, those who could be mobilized. The whole male population from twenty-five to fifty.

2. *Puric macho.* From fifty to eighty years. Servants of the noblemen, carrying out light duties.

3. *Rocto macho.* From eighty to one hundred years and over. "Old men hard of hearing, only able to eat and sleep, plait ropes and raise rabbits and ducks." But they were feared and honoured because of their sharp tongues.

4. *Unoc runa.* The sick, deaf, dumb, blind, hunchbacked, dwarfs, and maimed. They gave what service they could and "were the butts of the rest."

5. *Sava panac.* From eighteen to twenty years. They carried the messages and tended the herds. Practiced poverty and abstinence, and were not entitled to women.

6. *Macta cona.* From twelve to eighteen years. They kept the flocks, caught birds with a net and offered the feathers to the *curaca.*

7. *Tocilacoc namracona.* From nine to twelve years. They protected the small birds, sown seeds and harvests.

8. *Pucllacoc namracona.* "Those who play," from five to nine years. Their favorite toy was a spinning top, but it was agreed that they should be "taught and punished for the good of the realm."

9. *Llullo vamracona.* From first steps to five years. The law permitted parents two years to care for their children, to enjoy them, and "to save them from falling or being burned."

10. *Uaua quiro-picac.* Infants in the cradle.

The women's classification was in line with the men's:

1. *Auca camayoc pa varmi*. The warrior's wife. In between times she wove cloth for garments.

2. *Pavacona*. They wove cloth and cooked. Chastity was enforced on widows of a certain age.

3. *Punoc paya*. They helped to bring up the children if they had the strength.

4. *Uncoc cumo*. The cripples. They married other cripples. Dwarfs married dwarfs, blind married blind, and so on.

5. *Cipascona*. Young girls ripe for marriage. These were destined for the temple of the Sun, for the king, for the chiefs and warriors, according to a method of division drawn up by officials of the Empire. "No one could choose a wife according to his own wishes." Any infraction of this rule was punished by death. The age limit for marriage was fixed at thirty years.

6. *Corotasque*. "The little shavelings." With short skirts and bare feet, they learned to cook, to spin and weave. They prepared the fermented drink, *chicha*. They were forbidden "to know woman or man on pain of death." They were depilated.

7. *Pauau pallac*. "The little girls who gathered flowers." They also helped their parents.

8. *Pucllacoc uarmi namra*. "The little girls who played as they went." They looked after their little brothers and fetched water for cooking.

9. *Llucas uarmi uana*. "Those learning to walk."

10. *Chillo uaua uarmi quiraupicac*. As we say, babies.[3]

What is remarkable in these two lists is the ease with which their thoroughness accommodates the arbitrary. The number ten, imposed on all conceivable matters, was the delight and the strength of the empire. The architectonic of the Inca system allowed for the subjection of tribes, for equal allocation of food supplies, for public works like the transportation of monoliths for distances of over two thousand miles. It can still be perceived today in the Peruvian vestimentary codes, especially in the types of hats. The headgear indicated the clan of provenance so that the social position of each was exposed to the eyes of all.

The *archē*, as the 'beginning' of this system, was the grandiose imperial project devised by the first Inca, Pachacuti (or, according to the legend, the birth of Manco Capac and of his sister and wife, Mama Ocllo, from the waters of Lake Titicaca). The *archē*, understood as 'rule', was the autocracy. The principle of this civilization is also apparent: as the first in the order of authority, the *princeps* was the political apparatus with the supreme cacique exercising vertical control at its head; as the first in the order of intelligibility or rationality, the *principium* was the decimal system. Every detail of daily life was subject to arithmetic laws for the sake of pacification, expansion, agricultural growth, defense, public works. The Inca empire could be pan-Andean because it was a system, a pyramid with a decagonal base. The origin of the system, 'origin' both as *archē* and as *princeps-principium,* allows one to understand this society and its achievements.

And yet we must admit that we understand almost nothing about it. This is not due solely to the absence of writing in Inca civilization. *Archē* and principle do not tell everything about the origin, not the entire origin. They do not allow us to understand how things entered into presence in everyday experience. The origin both as *archē* and as principle conceals presencing. How did things come to presence, how did they appear, before the arrival of the conquistadores? That is what will forever escape us. Everything is not told about the rise of the Inca civilization once its conquests, its superb usage of the decimal system, its disdain for the particular and the individual have been described. Another type of arising remains to be understood, the uprise as coming forth to presence, as presencing: the origin as *Ursprung*.

In the order of authority as in the order of intelligibility, principles occupy the first rank in the field opened to an epoch. These principles lay out the paths to be assumed by the course of exploitations and the discourse of explications. As such they are observed without question in a given epoch. When questions are raised about principles, the network of exchange that they have opened becomes confused, and the order that they have founded declines. A principle has its rise, its period of reign, and its ruin. Its death usually takes disproportionately more time than its reign.

As to presencing, it requires a type of thought other than that which traces the reversals of historical principles. We observe the principles unwittingly, without meditation ("*ohne Besinnung*"). The turning in history at which the origin manifests itself as presencing may require a comparable turning in the way of thinking. And perhaps this new *Denkungsart*, the phenomenology of presencing, will teach us something about the manifold origin of epochal principles, as Nietzsche's new mode of thinking taught us something about "the origin of our moral prejudices." The difficulty encountered in the genealogy of principles stems from its scope. It will have to decipher much more than "the hieroglyphic script of men's moral past."[4] The genealogies of morals, of the scientific mind, of the democratic ideal, etc., will all be only instantiations of the genealogy of epochal principles.

§4. The Rise and Decline of Principles

In the history of Western thought, which began in the sixth century B.C., 2,300 years were required before the familiar representation, "Nothing is without reason," was expressly posed as a principle and known as a law. . . . Until the present day we have hardly meditated on the phenomenon that this little phrase required such an extraordinarily long period of incubation.

Der Satz vom Grund[5]

Is a principle not something that inspires awe,[6] something that is recognized as prevailing against all historical contingencies? Is it not 'worthy', ἄξιος—an axiom, therefore—because untouchable by chance? On the contrary, with Heidegger, we will have to speak of the establishment of a principle: its establishment in the double sense of its founding at the beginning of an epoch and of its reign during that epoch. We will have to think the *archē* of a principle as its beginning and its rule. An epoch will have to be viewed as determined by a code that is unique every time—not a convention, but a law of regional application, in the sense in which the French speak of the *code de la route*. The instatement of a code to the rank of principle opens a field of intelligibility. It establishes a first, a reference. This code regulates the 'establishment' of a regional or epochal order in the sense of putting it in place, and it regulates its 'establishment' in the sense of an institution of public utility, of a regime. Thus the little phrase "nothing is without reason" attains to such a principial rank at the beginning of the modern era after a long period of incubation.[7] This accession of the so-called principle of sufficient reason and its subsequent reign allow one to understand the *archē* of modernity, its genesis from one type of origin. The modern era is that period in which, in thought as well as in action, the principle of sufficient reason is reputed to "occupy the first place, to stand in the first row." To think is to render reason, *rationem reddere*, and to act is to impose rationality upon nature. Retrospectively, we understand an epoch as the opening, by such an accession and estimation, of a bygone field of presencing.

The establishment of a principle is its institution at the beginning of the period for which it will serve as ultimate point of reference, of recourse, thus dominating that era. Such a first becomes thinkable however only when its grip begins to loosen. The establishments bequeathed us are talked about and questioned as they collapse, so that we know history primarily by its reversals.

The reversals of history[8] are what makes it intelligible. The focus that an epoch ranks supreme—the code that holds together the activities and the words in which it recognizes itself—comes into sight in the crises that are fatal to its rule. What is held to be ultimate in a given age thus enters the critical-genealogical discourse once its law is overturned. The reversals of history are its 'crises' in the full sense of the word: they 'separate' one epoch from the other. Properly speaking, they are the crises of each *principle* which for a while establishes a given civilization in a finite field where it can attend to its needs. Access to these fields will be gained through the phenomenology of the reversals of history.

The point of impact of such a phenomenology does not lie, however, in the past. Indeed, if the reversals of history are best circumscribed by the retreat of a referent which until then encoded the order of things, then what potential do things, words, and actions yield at those rare moments of *interregnum* among which our own times may have to be counted? The establishment in which a collectivity abides for a while has its order, but what about the very sequence of these establishments? Do the thresholds between epochs have an *archē* which they rationally articulate? Are they the joints where a Reason can be cognized, a Reason still more reasonable than the order that the phenomenologist reads in the finite clearing of a given culture? Or will these transitions, on the contrary, prove to be bereft of order, literally anarchic?[9]

What we are attempting to understand is the caesura that marks the end of the metaphysical epoch.[10] It may well be that in these decades of ours, the principle is reversing that hitherto has managed a long epoch; that therefore as a principle, it becomes thinkable because it is already farther away; and that in this our interstice, an absence reveals itself that is soon forgotten when laws and order obtain without question under the unsuspected dominion of a referent held supreme. It may be that in the divide between one era and the next anarchism appears, the absence of an ultimate reason in the succession of the many principles that have run their course in the West. It may be that as this absence becomes apparent, human practice, notably political action, becomes thinkable in a way that it is not when life and thought obey the order made for them between two reversals.

How can a principle appear transitory? This is the first question to be raised. It concerns the type of analysis that leads to the concept of anarchy. Analysis will have to be taken literally as the dissolution or dislocation, as the de-construction of the edifices of intelligibility transmitted to us. It will also have to be shown how this analysis, this genealogy of the formations or economies of presence, is phenomenological (Part II). The *difference* between presence and presencing, with which I have already been working, will then have to be drawn for its own sake.

Next, the three senses of origin—*archē, princeps-principium, Ursprung*—will have to be disentangled (Part III). A concrete sequence of epochal principles will thus pass before the phenomenological gaze, the sequence wherein the era of representation gives way to that of consciousness, then to nihilism, then to technology, to speak only of the modern age.[11]

That sequence of principles will furthermore have to be interrogated according to its inner conditions. If it can be read prospectively, onward from a certain datable turn in antiquity, as well as retrospectively, backward from another turn which is also datable and equally decisive, what is the status of identity and difference in history? That status will prove to be *categorial* (Part IV).

The terms in which the question of *acting* can be raised will finally prove to be the very terms of the "question of being." The two questions can only be solved as one (Part V). How is their conjunction possible? Both being and acting—more generally, practice—are understood by the later Heidegger through what he calls "the turning." The inquiry I am attempting into what Heidegger may have to teach us about politics in particular would condemn itself to outright failure if its access were sought elsewhere than in the phenomenon he calls *die Kehre*. However, since this concept lends itself to mystification, its clarification must be attempted first. Unless the phenomenon it designates is recognized, one would not even be able to examine the fate the question 'What is to be done?' suffers at the end of metaphysics, let alone to ask: what is to be done at the end of metaphysics?

II

UNDERSTANDING PRACTICE
THROUGH THE "TURNING"

> The essence of the framing (*Gestell*) is the
> danger. . . . In the essence of this danger lies
> hidden the potential for a turning in which
> the forgetfulness about the essence of being
> will so turn itself that, with *this* turning, the
> truth of the essence of being will expressly
> turn in—turn homeward—into all that there
> is. . . . The danger is the epoch of being
> coming to presence as the framing.
>
> "The Turning"[1]

The first element of the genealogy of principles is provided by the reversals (*Wenden*) between epochs. The second key element is that of the
turning (*die Kehre*). The lines quoted above clearly indicate the general
premise of the deconstruction, that with "the turning" the epochs in our
history come to an end. This end of epochal history is the starting point for
everything Heidegger has to say about both thinking and acting. One may
call it his hypothesis of closure.

§5. Practical Philosophy and the Hypothesis of Closure

> One essential way in which truth establishes
> itself in the entities that it has opened up is
> truth setting itself into work. Another way in
> which truth comes to presence is the deed
> that founds a political state.
>
> "The Origin of the Work of Art"[2]

The phrase 'practical philosophy' can designate two things: either the
special discipline that deals with human practice or the practical nature of
philosophy in general. Paradigmatic for the first of these two meanings is

the corpus of Aristotelian treatises entitled *Ethics, Politics,* and *Economics.* These treatises essentially borrow their rational schemata from the more 'theoretical' disciplines dealt with by the *Metaphysics,* the *Organon,* and the *Physics.* They examine human action according to structural relations, above all the *pros hen* relation. In practical philosophy as a 'discipline' descriptive and prescriptive discourse remain closely intertwined. The sum of what is knowable appears organized like a tree whose stem is ontology and whose branches are the applied sciences. This kind of organic derivation of an ideal pattern does not allow one to disentangle what is descriptive from what is prescriptive in practical discourse.

It is the nature of the prescriptive element that changes when the phrase 'practical philosophy' comes to mean that the very content of philosophy is practical. Such diverse authors as Plotinus, Meister Eckhart, Marx, and Kierkegaard would agree on this coincidence of the theoretical and the practical. As Heidegger understands 'the truth of being' instituting itself epochally in entities, in all entities, he renders any derivation of the practical from the ideal impossible. The lines quoted above give testimony to this encompassing essence of *alētheia.* Whether truth comes about in an artwork or in a political deed, these are but modalities in which it orders itself for awhile in a given area. It is useless, then, even to attempt a delineation between practical and theoretical philosophy. The relation between description and prescription changes because theory no longer consists in gathering up determinant idealities. A philosophy that describes the 'epochal institutions' of truth is, as a whole, both theoretical and practical. The practical is no longer measured by the theoretical. Thus the very terminology of prescription loses its pertinence. Instead, both theory and practice appear as *regulated* by the way presencing arranges itself for a time. This is not to deny any phenomenal distinctness between thinking and acting. It is however no longer thinking that spells out the paths to be followed by acting. Both are equally subject to aletheiological regulation. Thus presencing articulates itself today according to the principle called 'framing' or 'im-posing'. As such, it uniforms thinking, artistic creation, the terms in which political issues are raised and solved, as well as all other regions of possible experience. The aletheiological modulations in history stamp theory and practice with their *epochal* marks, but it is no longer the theoretical that stamps the practical with its *ideal* and *normative* marks.

Now "the turning" contains the hypothesis that guides this entire genealogy of epochal stamps, this genealogy of principles. In the turn of times which may have set in quite a while ago, "the forgetfulness about the essence of being so turn[s] itself that, with *this* turning, the truth of the essence of being expressly turn[s] in—turn[s] homeward—into all that there is." This is a clear enunciation of the hypothesis of closure. With the technological turning, being may eventually be thought of in itself, for its own sake—as the event of presencing. The lineage of ideal entities promoted to the rank of principles would reach its end. The turning is only a potential, a hypothesis; compliance with presencing, in both thinking and acting, is only a possibility, an eventuality. Nevertheless the turning allows us to speak of metaphysics as a closed field. Consequently, it allows us to speak of practice as undergoing a transmutation. Because of this transmutation practice can free itself from the principles for whose sake presencing remained "forgotten."

What, then, is "the technological danger" mentioned in the epigraph above? It is primarily neither the danger of suffocation with which industry threatens life, nor the danger of stultification with which total planification threatens the mind. "The danger is the epoch," the *epochē*, the withholding or oblivion of presencing, its obfuscation by the principles. Such obfuscation, hence such danger, is ancient. However, it reaches its greatest opacity in the technological age.

If practical philosophy designates a discipline that is based on a theory, on a first science or even a first critique, then the hypothesis of closure signifies the impossibility of a foundational reflection on human practice. Furthermore, if with the technological turning, the obfuscation (of which 'disciplinary' discourse is only one sequel) of presencing as such may reach its end, then the essence of human practice will no longer consist in realizing, applying, deriving prescriptions for action from any norm-providing foundation.

In addition to this function within the history of being, the "turning" plays a more modestly heuristic role: viewed from the contemporary site that it designates, historical epochs appear retrospectively as constituted each by a *preponderant* referent, that is to say, one 'weighing more heavily' for a time upon the life and intelligence of men. As norm-providing in the order of authority (the puma) and norm-providing in the order of intelligibility (the decimal system), the principle spreads open a "clearing"[3] in which a given community can live. A historic community is recognizable by the rise of an epochal first. Its principle can be observed in any domain whatsoever: Inca urbanism, the tattoos, the hats, the aide-memoires made of small cords called *quipu*—each speaks in its own way of the referent that gives coherence to that culture. But not all cultural facts have an equally revelatory value. For Heidegger, the most revealing traces of past historical fields are preserved in philosophical works.[4] This priority is not something that goes without saying. It may even seem debatable once it is understood how culturally encompassing such historical fields are, constituting an order of all phenomena present to a community, a manifest order.[5] Perhaps philosophical works are themselves like tattoos: executed in order to embellish, heavy with meaning for the clan members, signifying a truth to which one dedicates oneself, but using decidedly formalized figures, and therefore mediated by abstractive spirit. Perhaps the order of an historical field is even less legible in the philosophical works that emanate from it than in tattooed faces. In that case, where is such an order to be read most plainly? It would have to be in a domain where multiple conducts come together; where things, actions, and words join to become accessible to all; at the strategical intersection of thought and practice; where the collectivity is witness to dealings and proceedings while also being their protagonist: in what is at the same time both communal and noticeable, that is, public. The arena where an epochal constellation most obviously displays its principle is the political.[6]

The political is that domain, that *dominium*, which most clearly marks an epochal principle's scope of rule. Each of "Western man's various fundamental positions among entities"[7] produces its own particular economy, which first imposes itself upon entities and then disposes them during its period of sway. A principle's initial imposition and subsequent disposition together spell out the *archē*—beginning and commanding—of those fundamental positions. Put differently, the "deed that founds a political state" inaugurates the field of possibles in which that community will live. Such an initial deed thus rules the polity by legitimating its *princeps* and its *principium*. The inaugural deed—the founding of the Inca empire by Pachacuti or of modern nations by their founding fathers—decrees the original code that will remain in effect throughout that civilization. It is the visibility of the origin as *archē, princeps,* and *principium* in the political domain that is important here. To act in public is to join words and things in action. The modality of epochal presencing becomes obvious when in the midst of his fellow men a man speaks up about a certain state of affairs.

Speaking cannot, by itself, fully reveal the code that rules the way things are present to one another at a given epoch. Such a code stands in league with power. Speech alone, without reference to a state of affairs and without a call to action, constitutes a domain other than the political: taken by itself, it constitutes the region of the text.[8] Likewise, if action remains deprived of speech and of reference to other actions, a new domain opens itself: not that of action but of activity with utensils.[9] Neither the presence of other actors, nor speech are required for the handling of tools. If other actors join in, the activity becomes work, and if speech makes the work public, it becomes political. The exchange among men, finally, can also occur in a pure state. A true hatred nourishes itself without words and without action on things. It belongs to yet another domain, that of the modalities of 'being-with'.[10] But when these three regions interact, which undoubtedly is the usual case, the principle of an epoch manifests itself. The political is the correlation in broad daylight of speech, of acting, and of a state of affairs. This correlation produces the order into which the code obeyed by an epoch concretely translates itself.

The reversals of history are its crises, but also its reverse, its netherside. As a new strategy of presencing comes upon us, it holds back (*epechein*) its essence. It remains epochally concealed within the new mode of unconcealment, and we do not quite understand how life is changing. But when acting, things and speech have settled into their new economy, then the reversals, though past, show themselves. It is the owl of Minerva that retrieves them, *ex post facto*.[11] The political appears as the domain in which the fixed order of an era[12] reveals itself, while the epochal underside of history is shifting. It is in this hidden layer that the displacements of order occur—of orders, rather, since the genealogy does not allow the phenomenologist to postulate some primordial order prior to the successive or contemporaneous economies of unconcealedness and concealment. Only on the premise of the plurality of historical orders can Heidegger the phenomenological genealogist claim that times of transition uproot political acting.[13] The *obverse* of an epoch is the disposition of the political reticulum, which remains the same for as long as its mode of presencing endures. But the *reverse* of an epoch is a profound, concealed ordering, the excavation of which requires its own method.[14] The decisive hinges, when a new field of intelligibility and life establishes itself, at first go unnoticed quite as, for Heidegger, the decisive philosophers are the least aware of what is given them to think.[15] At the thresholds between epochs the orders intermingle and become confused. In retrospect, their confusion proves highly revelatory: at these transitions, when the obvious is troubled, the origin appears different from *archē* and *princeps-principium*. These intermittent ways of its being different must be wrested from the origin. To do so, it will not suffice to lay out the archaeology of political forms as they have run their course in the West, although the phenomenological destruction of ontologies does indeed require, as a counterpart, a comparable deconstruction of the regimes and their typic schemes. This deconstruction of the political fields has been carried out elsewhere, and admirably so, by Hannah Arendt.[16] But the question we are raising is different: At the moment when "the turning" becomes a historical possibility, how does the origin show itself? "At bottom"[17] it appears, paradoxically, as an-archic. Its patent expression, the political, will then be deprived of its foundation.

What had first to be shown was, as I have done, the identity between the manifest order of an epoch and the political. From the point of view of epochal history, the political is characterized less by the exercise of power in a society (the state) or the interaction of the groups that compose it (civil society) than by that society's code made patent by the genealogist. The political is the surface where the code that rules a historical field becomes visible. This visibility can be described as the emergence from the private: when speech becomes public persuasion instead of merely private expression, when doing becomes action instead of mere activity, and when things become products instead of mere artifacts, then each time the political order is constituted. This threefold emergence in sight happens differently for each epoch. In the Greek *polis*, such emergence means that one has freed oneself from domestic labor and from its ties based on necessity in order to rally men of equal condition, free men, and accomplish noble deeds, thereby attaining excellence. In Roman society, this emergence into the public occurs through taking power rather than through taking the *rostrum* (the pulpit for orations which progressively came to serve the display of victories, cf. the *columna rostrata*), so much so that the relations of domination, confined as they were in Greece to the household, now make up the political fabric itself.[18] This fabric, whether Greek or Roman, is always the visible ordering, the *eidos* or aspect of an epoch.[19] The political exhibits the epochal principle.

With the hypothesis of closure, however, the principial reference as such, the *pros hen*, withers away.

§6. The Closure as the Withering of the *Pros Hen* Relation

> In the most hidden ground of his essence,
> man truly is only when in his way he is like
> the rose—without why. We cannot however
> pursue this thought any further here.
>
> *Der Satz vom Grund*[20]

What is noteworthy in remarks like this is, to be sure, the subversion of teleocratic representations: under the label, here, of life "without why." But still more noteworthy is perhaps the implied construction of an historical site for such subversion. *When* is it that man, in his way, can be like the rose? No doubt, he can be so only when the "why" withers. The question "Why?" is as old as metaphysics. It may well be the very question that gave birth to metaphysics. Aristotle answers it by pointing to substance as the ground or foundation for accounts that provide reasons. All instances of being, becoming, and knowing are referred to *ousia*. To this all-embracing *pros hen*, to substance as the focal point for each and every occurrence, Heidegger opposes his "without why."

It seems that "stepping back from the question, Why?"[21] entails consequences more extreme than Heidegger would wish. Hence his attempt at mitigation: "We cannot however pursue this thought any further here." Any further? What is it that is to be avoided? Heidegger is eluding, it seems, a threefold consequence, namely, the contestation of teleocracy, the historical moment where such contesting becomes possible, and its political character. He dodges these issues while at the same time pointing them out to us. Indeed, if the history made of end-assigning principles is to terminate, then his very discovery of epochal history amounts to contesting teleocracy. Furthermore, the moment when that discovery becomes possible is the turning, the era of metaphysical closure. The essentially political character of subverting the representations of end follows from the fact that in and with this turning the *pros hen* can no longer serve as the chief model for social life. With the turning, a certain way of understanding the political becomes impossible, and another way becomes inevitable. Let us begin with this third point.

With Heidegger, the political has to be described as the manifest constellation of things, actions and speech. This understanding of the public
realm differs from the schemes of thought rooted in Attic philosophy. For
Heidegger the political is a "site" of interaction. The German word for
"site," *Ort*, he observes, originally signified the iron point of a lance where
everything joins together.[22] In the political the force of a principle collects
into a transient order all that is phenomenally present.

It is clear how a description of epochs "steps back" from the principles that
rule over them. The principles answer the question, Why? Why do people
in a given epoch speak about, act upon, suffer from phenomena the way they
do? The principles, which are arch-present in their respective epochal
orders, provide the reasons for all that is the case, whether lofty or lowly,
within that order. But the "step backward" retrogresses from what is present
to presencing as such. The site, then, answers instead the question, Where?
Where do things, actions and words join within the *alētheia*—unconcealment—of presencing? They join in that particular type of disclosure which is
the political. In such an approach to the political, the question of a first that
begins and commands public undertakings and of an end that guides and
completes them no longer even arises. In its stead arises the question of the
difference between what is present and its presencing.

For the ancients, at least according to the way they have been received
by the vast majority of their followers, reflection on the political endeav-
ored to translate an ahistorical order, knowable in itself, into public organization, for which that order served as an a priori model and as a criterion
for a posteriori legitimation. The categories for understanding the body
politic were derived from the analysis of sensible bodies and were transposed into practical discourse from speculative or 'ontological' discourse.
Aristotle's *Physics*, the *Grundbuch*, "foundational book,"[23] of Western philosophy, provided practical philosophy with its elementary vocabulary
worked out in the context of movement and its causes. From physics this
vocabulary has penetrated all other disciplines.[24] To justify such transposition, the scholastics invoke the axiom "acting follows being."[25] Speculative
philosophy serves as patron and pattern (both words deriving from *pater*,
father) for practical philosophy. What does practical philosophy inherit
from its father, speculative philosophy? Precisely the reference to a first. In
order that there be knowledge of the sensible there must be a first to which
the multiple can be referred and thus be made true or verified. Likewise,
in order that there be action and not merely activities there must be a first
that provides action with sense and direction. Political philosophies differ
in the way they articulate this relation to the one, *pros hen*. Without such
reference, however, the commonwealth would cease to be accessible to
metaphysics. This first, in reference to which the commonwealth becomes
conceivable, need not be a supreme power. Aristotle compares the constitution of a principle for action to an army in full retreat, propelled by fear,
but in which first one, then several soldiers stop, look to the rear where the

enemy is approaching and regain their courage. The entire army does not
stop because two or three master their fear, but suddenly it obeys orders
again and the activities of each become again the action of all.[26] Aristotle
views command (archē) imposing its order on the runaways just as he views
substance, as archē, imposing its unity upon the accidents. Such is the
filiation between ousiology and practical philosophy. Both observations are
construed in relation "to the one." This formal identity between speculative and practical philosophy maintains itself until the rise of what today is
called political theory.[27] From Plato's philosopher-king to Machiavelli's
prince, this pros hen reference defines the relations of the many subjects to
the one leader as it defines the relations of the many accidents to substance
and, in general, of the secondary analogates to prime analogates.[28] It is
instructive in this regard that Aristotle first analyzed "proportion," the
identity of relation between two terms, in the political context,[29] well before the Metaphysics. Political philosophy is not the same, to be sure,
when the first to which acting is referred is a man, or a collectivity, or the
common good, or duty. But these are all archai, and the point is to notice
the structural similarity between what the tradition calls ontology and political philosophy. Political action originates in rule (of a commander or of
law), quite as movement originates in cause. The analysis of the political
domain can no more do without a principle of legitimation than that of
becoming can do without a principle of movement, or that of sensible
substance without a principle of unity. Each of these domains is conceived
according to the schema of relation to a first; hence the categories of
politics are not sui generis, but borrowed from ousiology. The deconstruction of ontology in Heidegger cuts short such transpositions.[30]

The phenomenological deconstruction of this metaphysics of the body
politic[31] shifts the question. Heidegger seeks, not to ground but to locate
the political. He attempts to think of the political domain as a locus, a
site.[32] From the point of departure so displaced, the political realm becomes thinkable as the manifestation of an epochal principle. Phenomenological "situating"[33]—as a gathering, a recollection—of this manifestation
allows Heidegger to grasp how such a principle prevails. Objects of science
have their site, tools have their site,[34] works of art have their site, and so,
too, has politics. The site of politics is 'the political', which is to say, the
public conjunction of things, actions, and speech. The political makes public, literally exposes, the epochal principle which life otherwise obeys tacitly. As long as a principle holds sway, it affects the assemblies of the many
as it affects intimate reveries, the deeds and feats of the mighty, as well as
the voice of God and the voice of the people. But the site that manifests an
epochal order is the political. Nowhere else does what a given community
holds highest appear as clearly. Nowhere else does the manner in which it
orders all things toward this first, pros hen (Incan decimal system or medieval terrestrial and celestial hierarchies), become accessible in its scope.

To situate or locate the principles that have held sway over our history is to objectify them. Such objectification is a therapeutic exercise. One of its goals is to work through the figures that have ordered Western history as through so many obsessions. To situate or locate these figures is to show how phenomena are phenomena *for* epochal principles; how our world functions around them. "Everything functions. What is uncanny is that it all functions and that this functioning pushes ahead to further functioning."[35] The task (and the good fortune) of thinking is to extricate itself from this generalized functioning by inquiring into its conditions. Such inquiry becomes possible, and most urgent, at the moment where the functioning reaches its peak and where expectations formerly placed in some first philosophy are now vested, as Heidegger observes, in cybernetics.

"The turning" also designates this step backward that we take in thinking. It is a step that leads from the ontologies of the body politic to the topology of the political site. But if the turning were merely an *Erörterung*, the methodical step back to the phenomenal *Ort*, Heidegger's contesting the principles would amount to little. It would merely indicate the space where a phenomenon unfolds its essence,[36] the region where it comes to presence. But it would not call into question the machinalization of presencing, the generalized functioning around the epochal principles. What "the turning" in thinking achieves is precisely this calling into question. Phenomenological thinking asks about the origins of presencing as machine, and it discovers that presencing has had a history. At the juncture of generalized functioning, the understanding of being becomes evident that has brought us where we are. 'Being' has functioned as the imaginary hub legitimating ever wider control by means of epochal principles. It is on these principles represented as ultimate referents, that men have based their actions, their things, and their words. In order to center universal functioning—incipient with the Greek animate *kosmos* and complete with the modern cybernetic system—some focal point must be constantly available, arch-present. "The turning" is the attempt at de-centering the network of phenomena by seeking its condition not in ultimate grounds, but in the simple event of coming to presence and its historical modalities.

Of the two types of thinking so discriminated by this break—grounding constant presence and complying with presencing as an event—the first is operative within the metaphysical closure, the second, outside that closure. Constant presence of the principles "is due to the destiny" that transmits the epochs encompassed by the closure. To step beyond that closure, then, is to "enter into the event." "For the thinking within the event of appropriation . . . the [epochal] history of being is at an end."[37] This is the end of indubitably first referents. It is the alternative to generalized functioning. One might say that the word of Nietzsche comes true here: "I belong to those machines that can *explode.*"[38]

Heidegger's discovery, with the *Kehre*, of the history of presencing does not entail an abandonment of phenomenology as transcendental. The "step backward" from what is ontic to its ontological conditions however reaches structures that are no longer immutable (and which are certainly not subjective). This methodical step retrogresses toward the historical zone of belonging where we are implicated in, 'folded in', the phenomena. Their φαίνεσθαι, appearing or coming forth, remains as the one ultimate condition we belong to as one belongs to one's ownmost concerns. The ontologies of the body politic *theorize* about the practical, that is, they consider it and refer it to some ideality. But one thinks correctly only that to which one *belongs*: the economies of presencing. We belong to the technological era only because, more originally, we belong to the event through which any economical constellation comes about. The step back toward topological phenomenology is thus an "abrupt entry into belonging."[39] It is abrupt since the resistances may suddenly vanish by which the 'rational animal', the metaphysical animal, defends itself against polymorphous presencing as against its death. The rational animal, we will hear, has yet to become mortal. Its resistances, its defense mechanisms, have made all epochal principles. With their dissolution, Heideggerian transcendentalism turns historical. When presencing is understood to have a history, Heraclitus is rehabilitated. Under the hypothesis of closure only a certain slice of history is *destinal*—that which withers away with the entry into the event. But presencing is always *historical*, dispensing itself like a child. "The dispensation of being: a child that plays. . . . Why does it play, that great child of the world-play seen by Heraclitus? It plays because it plays. The 'because' perishes in play. The play is without 'why.' "[40]

From this perspective, the last of the three points enunciated earlier, the concept of teleocracy, finds its solution. The destiny of presencing is that history where the *principia* set themselves up as *telē*, as the ends for man, for his doing and his speculating. However, if being is to be thought of not as constant availability but as presencing, as the play of the event, then it is hostile to any domination by ends (in Aristotle the usage of the verb *kratein*, "to dominate," indicates the incipient link between metaphysics of reason or mind and mastery over nature: "*mind, in order to dominate*, that is, to know, must be free from all admixture"[41]). The subsumption of things 'given as stock' under a principle of order has its opening and its closing moment. The opening moment is Aristotle's discovery that the *pros hen* can be applied to the whole of human phenomena and therefore to all branches of philosophy. Man's central position in the constellation of presencing is the epochal condition for such a sweeping relation-to-one. Aristotle's theoretical discovery can thus be viewed as a mere prosopopoeia of Socrates' interest in man: by imposing upon each and every philosophical issue the schema that rightfully pertains only to the *Physics*, Aristotle has Socrates speak with the voice of a physicist. The Socratic turn toward man, toward the question of the good life, now solidifies as the doctrine of a legitimizing ultimate center of reference.

With the *Physics*, the *pros hen* becomes systematized. This totalitarian sweep of the relation-to-one exhausts its powers at the closing moment of subsumption under principles. The opening moment and the closing moment of epochal history provide the framework for the genealogy of principles. These are born with the Socratic turn and they wither with the Heideggerian turn. Heidegger is however not alone in having sensed this exhaustion of referential history. Marx and Nietzsche felt it before him. And the French poet René Char writes: "*Amont éclate*" (Upstream bursts), "*Poème pulvérisé*" (Pulverized poem), and "*Cette part jamais fixée, en nous sommeillante, d'où jaillira DEMAIN LE MULTIPLE*" (That part never fixed, asleep in us, from which will spring TOMORROW THE MANIFOLD).[42]

III

GENEALOGY OF PRINCIPLES
AND ANTI-HUMANISM

Should thinking, through an open resistance
to "humanism," risk an impulse . . . ?

"Letter on Humanism"[1]

The anti-humanism enunciated by Heidegger in these lines is not unheard
of in the twentieth century. For the following reasons, I should like briefly
and schematically to parallel one definite experience in Heidegger with one
in Marx and in Nietzsche. For Heidegger, "the beginning of metaphysics in
Plato's thinking is at the same time the beginning of 'humanism.' "[2] Therefore the end of metaphysics may indeed signify the end of a certain humanism. Moreover a methodical disinterest in the concept of man characterizes
contemporary developments in the human sciences as much as in philosophy. In addition, the relevance of the "turning" for reconsidering the nature
of action can be grasped only if it designates a shift in the general constellation of presence rather than in just an individual attitude of thought. Lastly,
Marx and Nietzsche have, each in his way, experienced what in the preceding chapter has appeared as the de-centering of phenomena. I wish to show,
then, how in these three writers an isomorphic reversal takes place through
which the operative concept of origin ceases to be humanistic and becomes
plural; how in late modernity, in other words, the origin becomes dispersed.

To be sure, these three writers are not saying the same things. But all
three speak *from* a reversal in the coordinates of their historical locus
which is functionally comparable. Their respective situations are structurally alike due to the experience of a break. What is the consequence of this
break for a genealogy of epochal principles? If it could be shown that with
it the very quest for an ultimate referent becomes impossible, then their
threefold experience of rupture would by the same token be the experience
of the end of principial history. Each of them would have sensed an incipient plurification. And if it could be shown that the referent dismissed in
each of these three cases is man as the point of reference, as the 'center',
for what is knowable about entities, then their experience would anticipate

a constellation of presence where such a cognitive center fails entirely. What would make their experiences alike is the move away from man.

My point of departure lies in the observation that "the concern for human being and for the position of man in the midst of entities dominates metaphysics throughout."[3] The main perspectives from which this genealogy will reveal the end of the metaphysical lineage, then, are the *break* (or turning), *plurification,* and the de-centering of man or *anti-humanism*.

To show how these three concepts operate within the genealogy, I will take recourse in a fourth, namely 'economy of presence'. Let us say for now, that 'economy' refers to what Heidegger calls the constellations of concealing-unconcealing, i.e., to aletheiological constellations, and 'presence' (*Anwesenheit*) to being as it appears in a given context, i.e., to what he also calls beingness. Presence is a historical mode of 'presencing' (*Anwesen*, but this distinction is not rigorous in Heidegger). There are, then, a great many economies of presence. As metaphysical, they are ruled by an epochal principle, and as post-metaphysical they are an-archic. The argument I am proposing here is that the same transition from a principial economy to an anarchic economy of presence is reflected in Marx, Nietzsche, and Heidegger. Even if the hypothesis of closure were in this way confirmed by further testimony, it would remain a hypothesis nonetheless. Unlike knowledge, thinking does not rest on proofs or accumulated evidence. But the shifts experienced by Marx and Nietzsche may be treated as indices. They will indicate a fundamental reversal in the exchange of actions, things, and words and so suggest the incipient transition from the modern to the post-modern era. (Just like the term 'deconstruction', that of 'post-modernity' has suffered the fate Western mass culture inflicts on its most pertinent conceptualizations: turned into slogans, they lose their savor like styrofoam peaches. In speaking of the possible transition toward a post-modern economy I wish to *counter the counter-revolution* currently in full swing, according to which all that is left for us today is to plunder the past and reshuffle bits and pieces of it in a carnival of quotations and collages. For such flashcard historicism no novel arrangement of actions, things, and words is thinkable. But just this novelty is at stake in the hypothesis that modernity may be the last epoch in principial history).

The concept of anti-humanism is of Marxist origin. As used by Althusser, it denotes Marx's polemic refusal of a metaphysics of man. It connotes the rejection of the program derived from such a metaphysics, a program that aims at restoring "integral man."[4] It was Feuerbach's project to conceive the reconciliation between individual and total Man by the individual's appropriating the totality of human predicates. But the concept of anti-humanism is more than a weapon simply in the polemic against idealist anthropology. It refers in several ways to an attempt at surmounting representations centered on the epochal figure of man. Here are a few of these representations:

Cultural individuality. In this sense, the subject that anti-humanism relegates to the background of philosophy is the subject of inwardness, of the *mémoires intérieurs*. It is the inner self whose complexities fascinate Western man and which he has learned to refine through educational ideals inspired by the Renaissance, by von Humboldt and Winckelmann—or by Napoleon's *Memorial of Saint-Helena*. In a first approach, anti-humanism is a useful strategy for conceptualizing how, in a society moving toward cultural isomorphism, the individual is threatened with spiritual homelessness.

Reflective subjectivism. Anti-humanism offers itself as a critique of reflection. Reflectivity presupposes that man can somehow draw meaning out of his own ground, that the mind only needs to take its spontaneous acts as objects of thought in order to know the truth. "Reflection is nothing but an attention to what is in us,"[5] says Leibniz. This conception of subject has been contested by transcendental criticism. Since then, it is scarcely maintained anymore that reflection grasps a thinking thing or eternal essences, but rather that it reaches a mere functional pole within a system of forms. The Kantian formal subject, understood as an ordered a priori multiplicity of functions, can in this sense be considered the forefather of 'structure'.

Transcendental subjectivity. Kant's understanding of man as a merely functional unity of a priori forms has indeed, in its way, prepared man's elimination, proclaimed today, from the central position in the field of knowledge and discourse. Inasmuch as with Kant the subject of the predicate 'thinking' retreats into unknowability, transcendental criticism is not the counter-position to deconstruction but rather its antecedent. The exposition of the paralogisms in the inference from thinking to thinker must be viewed as the first step in the direction of this economic deconstruction, except that today the ego itself becomes 'subject to' a system of functions. In this way the formalism discovered with the help of the Cogito is turned against the Cogito. The radical transcendentalism of what I call the economies of presence also dislodges transcendental subjectivity from its sovereign position.

The practical subject. "History is a process, and a process without a subject."[6] "What is bewailed with such vehemence is not the disappearance of history, but the eclipse of that form of history that was secretly, but entirely, referred to the synthetic activity of the subject."[7] Whether considered from the viewpoint of the relations of production or from that of discursive regularities, man appears as a public object rather than as a private or transcendental subject. He appears even less as history-making, as a person responsible for his acts, as the initiator of a new order of things, in short, as a moral agent. The old Socratic unity between knowledge and virtue comes apart the moment the subject of that unity is no more than one variable within a vast exchange of functions. It is finally the subject in this sense of an actor in history that disappears with the hypothesis of closure.

These four senses of subjectivity—individuality, reflectivity, transcendentality, and morality—blend in many ways. Their unity constitutes "humanism" in the sense of "the characteristic feature of all metaphysics, which is that it is 'humanistic.' "[8] It is this very broad notion of humanism that Marx, Nietzsche, and Heidegger (as well as their epigones Foucault and Althusser) criticize. The element common to these three masters of anti-humanism lies in their experience of a reversal—or rather, in their experience that a reversal is articulating itself through them. I am attempting a cross-section through the contemporary economy of words, things, and actions, and comparing twentieth-century closing modernity with nineteenth-century late modernity. If with the possible shift *beyond* modernity our economy of presence ceases to be centered on man, then we will have an ontological reason for saying with Lévi-Strauss that man has been "the insufferable spoiled child that has occupied the philosophical scene far too long and has hindered all serious work by its demands for exclusive attention."[9]

§7. A Threefold Break with "Humanism"

—I hardly know anymore who and where I
am.
—None of us knows that as soon as we stop
fooling ourselves.
—But don't we still have the path we have
come?
—To be sure. But forgetting it too quickly
we give up thinking.

"Conversation on a Country Path
about Thinking"[10]

Marx, Nietzsche, Heidegger: three moments in a single epochal crisis (κρίνειν, to separate) from late to closing modernity.

1. The concept of epistemological break has been developed from Marx's writings by Louis Althusser: "Beginning in 1845, Marx broke radically with every theory that based history and politics on an essence of man."[11] This is to say that beginning with the *German Ideology,* the entire language of human essence borrowed directly from Feuerbach and indirectly from Hegel—although paradoxically used by the young Marx to stand Hegel on his feet—disappears from Marx's thinking. According to Althusser, the break produces a scientific theory of history and politics based on radically new concepts, such as "productive forces, relations of production, superstructure, ideology, determination in the last instance by economy," etc.

Furthermore, since that break, theory can no longer be confused with philosophy, which as philosophy of consciousness is humanistic through and through. Finally, not only does philosophy appear humanistic, but both philosophy and humanism are at the same time defined as ideology. Together they are opposed to "Marx's scientific discovery" as one field of inquiry (Althusser also says one "continent") is opposed to another. The technical term for designating this opposition is "problematic." A problematic is a "typical systematic structure unifying all the elements of thought."[12] Basically, there are two problematics: the one Marx turned away from in 1845, namely humanism, philosophy, and ideology, and the one he turned toward, namely theory (political, historical, economic), science, knowledge. The path that leads from ideology to Marxist science appears as the transition from myth to knowledge. "It is impossible to *know* anything about people except on the absolute precondition that the philosophical myth of man is reduced to ashes."[13] Any discourse about man will retain a mythical cast as long as it does not rest on the new concepts of class struggle, division of labor, possession of the means of production. . . . And with these concepts what is at stake is precisely not man. Mythical discourse is opposed to science as thinking is opposed to knowing. After the break of 1845, the point for Marx is no longer to *think* man's essence, but to *know* people's practices. The leading representation is no longer man as the root ("To be radical is to grasp matters at the root. But for man the root is man himself"[14]). Rather, the leading representation is practice as strewn.

The epistemological break is thus to be understood as the continental divide between two problematics, ideology and science. As such, it appears once and for all. The Marxian experience of the epochal reversal from modern humanism to incipient post-modern anti-humanism draws the line between thinking and knowing. This does not mean that the new economy of things, actions, and words has no room for pure thinking, but that henceforth thinking belongs to the ideological field. Non-scientific thinking will remain with us forever. It is even necessary, not only because it allows Marxist science to demarcate its own field of validity, but also because it provides this science with its contents. I shall show later that nothing compels us to blunt the Marxian reversal by qualifying the break as merely epistemological. But whether its ontological import is recognized or not, Marx's discovery of the anti-humanist viewpoint in 1845 remains a fact. Viewed in this new perspective, his earlier manuscripts appear in their true light: as variations on idealist and humanist themes. If Marx did not publish them, it is because they preceded his literally "critical" discovery of the heterogeneity between thinking and knowing.

2. Nietzsche describes a similar crisis: "Now I shall relate the history of my *Zarathustra*. The fundamental conception of this work, the idea of the eternal recurrence, this highest formula of affirmation that is at all attainable, belongs in August 1881: it was penned on a sheet with the notation

underneath: 'Six thousand feet beyond man and time'. That day I was walking through the woods along the lake of Silvaplana; at a powerful pyramidal rock not far from Surlei I stopped. It was then that this idea came to me."[15] Six thousand feet *beyond man*, "it" came to Nietzsche; "it invaded me," he says. The very first mention of the thought Zarathustra teaches, the eternal recurrence, situates it above "man," outside the human. The content of this teaching is as follows: "That everything recurs is the closest approximation of a world of becoming to a world of being—high point of the meditation."[16] In the discovery of the eternal recurrence, described here as the convergence between becoming and being, between flux and form, "meditation"—not *theōria* but *thinking*—culminates.

Prior to being invaded by something that addresses itself to thinking alone, Nietzsche's philosophy had a decidedly humanist cast. Witness his first writings on "the metaphysics of the artist." These texts describe an ideal of genius, of creation of values, of self-assertion in the face of corrosive asceticism. After the great discovery of 1881, these can no longer be the highest formula of affirmation. From the self-assertion of the subject it is necessary to climb "six thousand feet beyond man." Only the thought of the eternal recurrence does justice to becoming and affirms it. The subject appears as a fiction, an artificial immobilization of the flux. "The 'subject' is the fiction that many similar states in us are the effect of one substratum." "My hypotheses: the subject as multiplicity."[17] This great discovery of 1881 as well as the "proofs" that Nietzsche attempted of it are *thought* experiments. As knowledge claims about what nature really is, they would simply be misconstrued. This discovery is neither meant nor fit to assume the status of knowledge. It is an attempt and a temptation, says Nietzsche, rather than the result of some demonstration. It is a possible thought of a possibility. But nevertheless, a decisive thought, 'cutting off' (*de-caedere*) one epoch from another; a thought that is *entscheidend* because it *scheidet*, separates. Since then, much remains for us to think but little for us to know. There are "only multiplicities in any case; but 'unity' is nowhere present in the nature of becoming." There are only "complex forms of relative life-duration within the flux of becoming,"[18] only configurations of forms and forces for thought but no truth in and for itself. Truth as the correlate of knowing is itself a fiction. "Truth is that kind of error without which a certain species of living beings could not live."[19]

In this second experience of the epochal reversal, knowing and thinking are no longer assigned their respective fields, as in Marx. Knowing follows the fictions of thinking. "There would be nothing that could be called knowledge if thought did not first re-create the world." To "know" is to create the fictions that we hold as objective and true. But in the perspective acquired in 1881, truth too is only a thought creation, hence untrue. "Only because there is thought is there untruth."[20] And the first of these untruths or fictions is man understood as knowing and acting subject, as self.

3. The third experience of the epochal shift from a humanist economy into the anti-humanist one is dated shortly before 1930. In that year, writes Heidegger, a development culminates in which "everything is turned around." *"Hier kehrt sich das Ganze um."*[21] Throughout his later writings he refers to this *Kehre*—"the turning"—as the response in thinking to the *Kehre* in the economy of presence. When the constellation of things, actions, and words mutates into a new era, understanding finds itself unsettled. For the economy that expires in such a reversal, this shift constitutes the supreme danger. Nevertheless, thinking can then give itself over to its sole and unique task: gathering up the economic traits of presence so as to retrieve presencing as such. For Heidegger, the type of thinking he experienced in 1930 put an end to a previous type of thinking as old as the Western love of wisdom. Philosophy as a whole appears as "one thinking," to which "the other thinking" is now opposed. Strictly speaking, the latter is no longer philosophic. It is entirely a response, namely, to the nascent economy. How does one respond to the crisis of modernity? By "stepping back from the thinking that merely represents, that is, from explanatory thinking, toward the thinking that attends. This step back which leads us from *one* thinking to *the other* is no mere shift in attitude."[22]

Heidegger's thinking is critical inasmuch as it steps back from things present to the economy in which they 'presence'. Such a step proves to be so radical that it endangers the understanding man has of himself. "Should thinking, through an open resistance to 'humanism', risk an impulse that could cause perplexity about the *humanitas* of *homo humanus* and its basis?"[23] Still more, it threatens man's central position in the modern economy: " 'Humanism', should we decide to retain the word, henceforth means: the essence of man is essential for the truth of being, but in such a way that, as a matter of consequence, what is at stake is precisely not man merely as such."[24] The step backward from phenomena to their epochal condition may even imperil civilization and culture: "the other thinking," that which gathers up the withering away of principles at the end of the genealogy of epochal economies, is urgent, "but not for the sake of man so that his creations may vindicate civilization and culture."[25]

Marx, Nietzsche, and Heidegger all begin with at least a methodical interest in man. The humanism of the young Marx, the "metaphysics of the artist," and the existential analytic share this trait. In each of them a reversal is felt which has multiple effects: as the contemporary age establishes its order, man retreats from the scene as that which is most intensely present, and thinking acquires its independence from knowing. Following the same threefold guiding thread, let us see how the end of the humanist genealogical lineage affects the respective understanding of origin. Man as decentered can no longer be the origin of objectivity as he was in anthropocentric criticism. If our place in history is indeed that of a dawning era in which man is driven from his principial position, how will the 'origin' of that economy of presence have to be understood?

§8. A Threefold Break with Principial Origins

> In accordance with the intrinsically manifold
> state of affairs which is that of being and
> time, all words giving it utterance—like
> "turning," "forgottenness," and "mittence"—
> remain multivocal. Only a manifold thinking
> will succeed in an utterance that corresponds
> to the very issue of that state of affairs.
>
> "Preface"[26]

As we have seen, an epoch is dominated by what is 'first caught' in it, by its *primum captum*, its principle. When the modern epoch is described by the triumph of subjectivity, this means that at least since Descartes, but more profoundly since Plato, philosophy has systematically inquired about man 'in the first place', and of everything else in relation to him. Man is the theoretical origin from which objects receive their status of objectivity. Nothing is more revealing in this respect than the project of a universal *mathēsis:* for the moderns knowledge is protected from the onslaught of doubt only when it rests on a first that renders *mathēsis* 'universal', that is, 'turned toward the one', turned toward man. The modern cognitive project consists in establishing the subject as the unshakable, indubitable foundation of knowledge. Not so for *thought* projects. If, with the closure, thinking achieves its emancipation from knowing, it is also freed from domination by the One. To thinking, as opposed to knowing, the origin does not offer itself as a *principium*. Within thinking, the word 'origin' recovers its etymological meaning: *oriri,* coming forth. For thinking, and incipient with the closure, origination means multiple presencing.

1. The humanism of the young Marx is best understood as concomitant to the dialectic of consciousness. The essence of man exteriorizes and estranges itself and, by a process of "naturalization of man and humanization of nature," recovers the fullness of its attributes. As has frequently been observed, the young Marx has by no means shed the idealist realism of universals. Only this time it is derived from a speculative principle called, following Feuerbach, "generic being." However—and it is here that Althusser's presentation of the epistemological break oversimplifies things—within the problematic of universals for consciousness, another inflection rings through which anticipates later developments in Marx. A well-known text, written before the break, describes the task of emancipation in Germany in these terms: "A class must be formed with radical chains . . . a sphere that can no longer claim any traditional title but only a human title, a sphere that does not stand partially opposed to the consequences, but totally opposed to the premises of the German political system . . . a sphere, in short, that is the complete loss of humanity and that can therefore redeem itself only by the complete redemption of humanity. This dissolution of society as a particular

class is the proletariat."[27] The proletariat as the contradiction to the prevailing German political system *must be formed!* The class struggle is here taken
out of the realm of the dialectics of consciousness in order to provide an
answer to the question of what must be done. What is to be done in Germany? Form the proletariat. This is so because it does not exist there yet.
Michel Henry calls that formation "the a priori construction of the proletariat."[28] Even more, not only is contradiction not described as a universal law
in this text, but Marx also speaks of man otherwise than in terms of a specific
essence: the "total redemption" of what is human is also a practical, political
goal. The necessary conditions for conflict do not exist in Germany, Marx
observes, as they do in France and England. "Here, then, is our reply," he
writes in the introduction to this text. The status of the entire Hegelian
vocabulary of essence, opposition, self-alienation, universals, suddenly
topples. Once metaphysical, it becomes strategic. Marx has recourse to this
vocabulary only to make himself heard by the Germans who understand only
dialectic. This transference of contradiction and its resolution into strategy
announces nothing less than an egress from metaphysical principles. It is an
indicator of the shift in what is held to be originary.

Beginning with the *German Ideology*, Marx's understanding of the origin
explicitly turns away from any realism of universals as well as from any
essence, any speculative referent to which individual phenomena would
stand as predicates. Here, too, the key text is well known, although not
always interpreted in this sense: "The premises from which we begin are
not arbitrary ones, not dogmas; they are real premises from which we can
abstract ourselves only in imagination. *They are the real individuals*, their
activity and the material conditions of their lives. . . . [Individuals] begin
to distinguish themselves from animals as soon as they begin to produce
their means of subsistence. . . . What they are, therefore, coincides with
their production."[29] The new standpoint gained in 1845 is the realism of the
laboring individual. It is expressed by the equation between reality and
individual practice. It requires that we relocate originary being in the
activity through which people sustain their lives. What happens, then, in
the so-called epistemological break is primarily not of an epistemological
order at all. Something more fundamental than the constitution of 'Marxist
science' occurs. The way the *origin* is understood undergoes a transmutation such that Marx can indeed claim to have put an end to all philosophies
that refer the phenomenal to some noumenal in-itself, to a metaphysical
principium.

Beginning with this break there is, properly speaking, no origin as *one*,
that orders the late modern economy of things, actions, and words. There
is no origin, but only a profusion of originary actions by which individuals
satisfy their basic needs. The origin becomes fragmented, monadic, in
accordance with a monadic understanding of practice in the *German Ideology*. Therefore, we must understand the break of 1845 not only as the
separation of one epistemological "continent" from the other, as the rift

between ideology and science, but more decisively as the splintering, the plurification of the origin. Within Marx's texts, the epochal reversal appears as the inversion of two problematics: the realism of universal essences, which constituted the major problematic before 1845, recedes only to reappear later in limited theoretical fields, namely, historiography, political theory, economy, and the critique of ideology. The notion of "value" in *Capital* may be viewed as one example of such a return of universalist realism. At the same time, the realism of individual practice, which constituted the minor problematic in the early writings, comes to the fore in 1845 and remains the major problematic in all the philosophical works to come. More precisely, it remains the philosophical background that alone makes all the later writings fully intelligible. Whenever Marx speaks of universals, such as classes, he does so within the framework of what would have to be called regional theories, which derive their intelligibility from originary practice, the practice of the individual working in order to satisfy physical needs. Such originary practice is as irreducibly manifold as individual practices are, and it cannot be *known*. The subject matter (such as means of production, forms of property, classes, the state, ideologies, party strategies) of regional theories yields knowledge, whereas originary practice can only be *thought*. When Marx reduces thinking to ideology, this is understandable given his polemic against the philosophy of consciousness. Ideology constitutes the farthest refraction of originary practice. Marx's discovery of the plural origin and the way it relates to theory and ideology can indeed be represented as a series of refractions. In the medium of knowledge, originary practice appears as theory; in the still farther removed medium of imagination, it appears as ideology. Marx limits the role of thought to its ideological refractions, and so reduces thought to imagination. Structurally, however, the proper issue for thinking is originary practice itself. To think is to gather up the multiple originary acts prior to the constitution of theoretical or imaginary universals. At any rate, at the level of originary practice no appeal is made, can be made, to the humanistic quest for self-identity, self-possession, resolution of alienation, etc. Marx's anti-humanism results, not from the discovery of a new "scientific continent" (Althusser), but from that of originary practice and its monadic, atomistic allotropism.

2. A comparable but not identical fragmentation of the origin occurs in Nietzsche's experience of thinking. Here, too, man is dislodged from his principial position as a consequence of a more radical displacement, namely, the transmutation of the origin as a single principle into the origin as polymorphous activity. This is the transmutation of an ultimate speculative in-itself, e.g., Schopenhauer's "will," into the "will to power" as a mere differential factor among forces. Again the monistic origin is atomized. After this fragmentation, no force or value will any longer play the role of an enduring first principle. In the order of thinking, the transmuta-

tion of all values only responds and corresponds to the epochal reversal, to the reversal that Nietzsche experienced as having already placed us in a different economy. The incursion on the origin as *one* is carried out by a historical deconstruction that reveals "how the 'true world' finally became a fable"[30] (in one page, this text provides the pattern for all the destructions, desedimentations, archaeologies, and deconstructions that have emerged in the twentieth century). The correlative attempt to understand the origin as *multiple* is articulated for instance by the expression already mentioned, "complex forms of relative life duration within the flux of becoming." If there is some kinship between Marx's and Nietzsche's thinking, I see it in this plurification of the origin.

The Nietzschean notion of complex forms within the flux of becoming is explicitly atomistic. "Our way of thinking is to a great extent Heraclitean and Democritean," he says.[31] However, instead of "atoms," he speaks of "forces." These include cultural entities such as good and evil, as well as natural ones: "I am wary of speaking of chemical 'laws': that savors of morality. It is far more a question of the absolute establishment of power relationships."[32] The origin as manifold, then, consists in the ever new formation of complex forces within the flux of becoming. Nietzsche calls these configurations of forces "formations of domination." For instance: "In place of 'sociology', a theory of the formations of domination."[33] It is this concept of formations of domination, *Herrschaftsgebilde*, which allows one to think becoming and the dissolution of the subject. "The sphere of a subject constantly growing or decreasing, the center of the system constantly shifting; in cases where it cannot organize the appropriate mass, it breaks into two parts."[34] In this way, phenomena of split personalities as well as social or chemical phenomena are thought—but not 'explained', known—by these constellations of forces. "Formations of domination: the sphere of that which dominates continually growing or periodically increasing and decreasing according to the favorability or unfavorability of circumstances."[35]

These formations appear as aggregates of forces temporarily realized by a stronger force: "The individual itself as a struggle between parts (for food, space, etc.): its evolution tied to the victory or predominance of individual parts, to an atrophy, a 'becoming an organ' of other parts."[36] In Nietzsche's thought, the concept of eternal recurrence is the one that allows him best to affirm the radical fluidity of inorganic, organic, social, and cultural forces. All these forces struggle on equal footing so long as one of them does not impose its temporary order on all others. The eternal recurrence is the affirmation of these countless onsets.

An epochal economy, made of such finite formations of domination, is by definition precarious. It corresponds entirely to the Aristotelian notion of the contingent: that which can be or not be. And if any necessity stands opposed to these formations it is none other than that of chance, of play, of throwing dice. They are not derived from anything that might resist change. Nietzsche's program of transvaluation subverts all representations of a first, be it man, God, a principle for reasoning or acting, or an ideal

such as scientific truth. Nietzsche is assuredly entitled to the various epithets of Anti-Christ, Anti-Socrates, Immoralist (or rather Amoralist).
Strictly speaking, however, these are titles of incipient closure. They express, not some doctrine on the subject of Christ, Socrates, or morality,
but the foundering of any epochal principle at the end of modernity. They
are titles for the transmutation of the origin understood as *primum captum*
into the origin as unseizable aggregation and disaggregation of forces. In
opposition to the Christian, Socratic, or moral principles, the configurations of forces perpetually change. They give birth to the economies and
they prompt their death. The Nietzschean origin is the economy of meta-
morphic formations of domination. Their epochal reversals occur through
the weight of a new force. Nietzsche understands his thought of the eternal
recurrence as having already placed us in a new order: this thought "comes
first to one, then to many, and finally, to all."[37] It "comes," it is not the
product of a creative act of genius. Thinking assumes the very anonymity of
the economy that Nietzsche sees ahead of us.

To speak of the end of the humanistic epoch therefore not only implies
that man is no longer the referent in relation to which all things are known.
This end entails another consequence: man is by no means the master of
the epochal economies. They unfold and fold up again. They articulate
themselves in us in unforeseeable ways, and once they have had their time,
the mode according to which they render things present is irretrievably
lost. The Nietzschean genealogy of values and typology of the will therefore
do not revive past modes of dominant presence. They merely trace their
progressive extenuation. Values and forms of will have their origin in the
formations of domination and fade with them, as do the laws of thinking.
When actions, things, and words arrange themselves in a new pattern,
thinking changes. What gives rise to thinking escapes it. Such is the discovery made by Nietzsche in that crucial summer of 1881. The anthropocentric economy which has ruled Western culture since antiquity reveals its
perspectival nature. Accordingly, any epochal principle turns out to be no
more than a perspective projected on the chaos of forces. I take him
literally when he says of his discovery: "This is *my* experience of inspira-
tion; I do not doubt that one has to go back thousands of years in order to
find anyone who could say to me, 'It is mine as well'."[38] Thousands of
years—indeed, two thousand. Such is the interval that must be crossed in
order to rejoin that other caesura which instated man as the referent and
measure for Western theory and praxis.

3. As the text cited in the epigraph to this section indicates, the Heideggerian plurification of the origin is the result of multiple relations between
being and time. In this—and even if "today everyone thinks and poetizes
in the light and the shadow of Nietzsche, with his 'for him' or 'against
him' "[39]—Heidegger's *deconstructing* differs irreconcilably from both
Marx's and Nietzsche's *dismantling* (taking away dissimulating mantles).
They had a foreboding of the closure, but they did not think "the turning."

The origin becomes multiple in Heidegger only with the passage from existential or ecstatic temporality to destinal or epochal temporality.

In *Being and Time*, it is indeed *Dasein* that is originary. "The ontological site" of phenomena is determined there by their "originary rootedness" in existence.[40] Because it is systematically linked to the transcendentalism of the existential analytic, fundamental ontology cannot produce what Heidegger later calls a "multivocal" concept of being. A fundamental ontology conceived in view of the existential analytic cannot but trace everything that appears back to man, *for whom* it appears. The origin is man understood as "that entity for which . . . , in its being, that being itself is *at issue.*"[41] And in what way is being an issue for man? "The meaning of *Dasein* is temporality."[42] Being is the issue as always ahead of the project which man is, always before him, still to come and to be grasped. The ecstases are rooted in this to-come. "The essence of temporality is the process of temporalizing in the unity of the ecstases." More precisely, "the having-been arises from the future, and in such a way that the future which has been (or better, which unfolds as having been) releases the present from itself. This unitary phenomenon of a future that unfolds as having been and as rendering itself present is what we call temporality."[43] Being is the issue for man, temporally. In this projective and ecstatic issue, phenomena have their origin.

"The turning" puts an end to such a radical, radicular relation between time and being. The ecstatic rootedness of time in man can no longer be originary once presencing is understood as having a history. From then on, the origin is no longer singular. It designates, on one hand, the rise or inception (*Anfang*) of an epochal economy, and on the other, the mutual entry into presence of things, words, and actions, that is, their springing forth (*Ursprung*), their coming to presence within such an economy. Henceforth, the origin is epochal and eventlike. As epochal or diachronic, it inaugurates an age; as eventlike or synchronic, it opens the mercurial play of presencing which—each time, here and now—plays us quite as Heraclitus's "playing child" plays the world. This is no longer a 'radical' play, but rather a rhizomatic one.[44]

Thinking, too, becomes historical-ahistorical. On one hand, to think means to remember: to recall the birth of an epoch and the sequence of ancestors that establish its filiation. When a historical world falls in place, its beginning assigns us a new dwelling. A new arrangement produces a new *nomos* of our *oikos*, a new economy. The thinking that recalls our beginnings is best described as *economic thinking*. On the other hand, to think means to gather. The event to be grasped here is not history-founding; it is not a setting to work that makes an epoch. The event to be gathered synchronically is rather the presencing by which phenomena appear *within* a given arrangement, the way each component has of rendering itself present in an order. Keeping in mind the literal sense of *legein*, to gather, one may call this *logical thinking*. 'Economic thinking' can be illustrated by the example of the Parthenon: within the network of actions, things, and words, the way an entity like the Acropolis is present epochally assumed a well-defined, although complex character—when rhapsodes prepared for the Panathenaean festival, when the Parthenon served as a Byzantine church, when the Turks used it as a powder magazine. Today, when it has become a commodity for tourist consumption and when UNESCO plans to protect it from pollution with a plastic dome, it is present in an epochal economy in yet another fashion—a mode of presence certainly inconceivable for its architect, Ichtynos. At each moment of this history, the edifice was present according to finite, unforeseeable, uncontrollable traits. And each reversal entailed the irremediable disappearance of such an epochal physiognomy. As for 'logical thinking', it steps back from *epochē* and attempts to retrieve presencing as such. The disparity between the two will yield the *temporal difference*.

The issue of both the genealogy of epochal principles and the phenomenology of presencing as such—economic as well as logical thinking—is the origin as multiple. Heidegger's attitude after the turning is therefore necessarily anti-humanistic. This is so since the hypothesis of closure makes him look toward an *oriri* that belongs to "being as time,"[45] and no longer to human temporality. The "intrinsically manifold state of affairs which is that of being and time" prohibits referring the epochs and their closure, let alone the "event," to some figure of root, of the One, of man. It is because of this anti-humanism that Heidegger's concept of *epochē* has nothing to do with Husserl's. The phenomenology of the reversals in history follows the trail of the regimes to which unconcealment gave "sudden birth," but which have folded up their order to withdraw again into concealment. The genealogist seeks to understand this phenomenon of an encompassing, although precarious arrangement as it comes about and recedes. The birth of such an arrangement is "epochal," since in it presencing as such 'withholds' (*epechein*) itself. Thus what establishes us in our precarious dwellings is not some thing, it is nothing—a mere coming to pass. In the deconstruction of the texture or text of Western history, phenomenology remains transcendental in that it looks for the context which is the world; it is however dissociated from all a priori reference to the subject as text-maker. The principle of an epoch is a factual a priori, finite and of a non-human facticity. It exhibits the paradox of an "ontological fact."[46] What bequeaths the historical epochs and their principles, the 'event', is itself nothing, neither a human nor a divine subject,[47] nor an available or analyzable object.[48] Presencing reserves itself. But by its withdrawal, by withholding itself, it keeps things present, as if in a preserve. Heidegger borrows the word *epochē* not from Husserl, but from the Stoics.[49] Hence, this word does not here mean objectivation or systematic bracketing by a thetic act of consciousness. The word is taken in the broader sense of an act of interruption, a halting place, a stopping point. To speak of an "epoch" in presencing means two things:

presencing itself *withholds* itself in what is present; and presencing marks or stamps the stopping points that found the ages. The first meaning of the word becomes inoperative with 'the turning'; the second defines intra-metaphysical 'reversals'. Thus the age of metaphysical closure is the end of epochal history. The halting places of the differences between presencing and modes of presence are ascribable to no other condition than presencing itself.[50] Therefore, it is still the event of presencing that the genealogist strives to uncover, if indirectly. Furthermore, even though the epoch is an anti-humanist notion in Heidegger, it nonetheless entails an imperative for thinking. The deconstruction sets presencing free in its arrival and its withdrawal; to this issue for thought, so retrieved, thinking responds and corresponds by "reserving" (*an sich halten*) in its turn "all usual doing and prizing, knowing and looking."[51]

In whatever way it is articulated—by the transcendental materialism of the laboring individual, by the typology of the formations of domination, or by the phenomenology of the difference between presencing and modes of presence—the closure requires that man renounce the role of chief focal point in the genealogical depositions and dispositions. Without anti-humanism, there can be no metaphysical closure. And only anti-humanism authorizes Heidegger's saying that it is "the mittence of being"—not man or Spirit—that opens and closes the epochs: "In every phase of metaphysics a portion of a way becomes visible each time that the mittence of being clears for itself in sudden epochs of truth upon whatever is."[52] An epoch is not an era, but the self-establishing of an era. The arrangement that orders everything present, stops or punctuates its way through the ages. Our history, then, will count as many origins as it will admit thresholds. Whether these are discovered in following the revolutions in the modes of production or, as Heidegger sometimes does, in following the transitions between natural languages (Greek, Latin, modern vernacular), the formal description of these breaks need not vary. What counts is the *diachronical* atomization of the origin that the genealogy of the epochal principles reveals.

The atomization of the origin, however, attains its true profusion only with the *synchronical* 'event'. This will be described later by the temporal difference between the original and the originary.

Thinking, "more sober than scientific technology," has its own necessity, which comes to it from the principles and their genealogy. This necessity was recognized and mocked at the same time by Marx when he paraphrased Proudhon in these words: "Each principle has had its own century in which to manifest itself. The principle of authority, for example, had the eleventh century, and the principle of individualism, the eighteenth. Consequently, it was the century that belonged to the principle, and not the principle to the century. In other words, it was the principle that made the history, and not the history that made the principle."[53] If we extract these formulations from the context of the polemic against idealism—that is, if we do not conceive these principles in the form of idealities—we can retain a double genealogical truth from these lines. On one hand, they suggest how a principle, as it governs a temporary network of exchanges, emerges, reigns, and founders. They indicate the essential precariousness of epochal principles. On the other hand, they suggest that an order of things can be thought of only *ex post facto*, retrospectively. Furthermore, perhaps we may conclude from the raillery underlying this passage that for Marx idealist concepts of history have had their time and that with the "real" premises of the materialist conception of history, the lineage of hypostatized principles passes away. Marx, Nietzsche, and Heidegger have, each in his way, experienced such extinction. We will see that technology is the place where this lineage comes to an end. The non-humanistic language of epochal economies will thus make it possible to hold an alternative discourse on technology: from a Marxian viewpoint, the alternative to summary labels such as 'late capitalism' would be the transcendentalism of originary practice and its irreducible diversity; from a Nietzschean viewpoint, the alternative to the denunciation of technology as the global reach of the overman's power (an entirely erroneous interpretation of Nietzsche in any case) would be the phenomenology of the will to power and its infinite modulations in the formations of domination; and from a Heideggerian viewpoint, the alternative to a summary rejection (impossible anyway) of the *Gestell*, technological "enframing," would lie in the transcendental phenomenology of the economies of presence.

Before proceeding to the manifold senses of the origin (Part III), it has to be shown how the discovery of the epochal principles and the anti-humanism that results from their genealogy displaces *die Sache selbst,* the very issue, of phenomenology. This displacement emancipates thinking from knowing. I have tried to describe a few traits of this "other thinking": its inability to produce knowledge; its essential dependence on the economies of presence which, in turn, provide its 'matter'; its inability to secure a ground on which to rest metaphysical speculation or scientific research; its uselessness as a predicate of the subject 'man' and as an indicator of his nature; and finally, its plural essence. The "multivocity of utterance" is only the echo of "the all-playing conjunction of never-resting transmutation."[54]

Unscientific Postscript to Anti-Humanism

It will be objected:

—*The alliance between anti-humanism and anarchy is only too clear. We have seen sufficiently in the twentieth century where that kind of doctrine ultimately leads. Lofty praise of 'thinking' does nothing to mitigate the case. Under the pretext of alleviating the grip of technology, you end up eliminating all checks on violence. Granted, the purpose of the genealogy is not to return to ancient Greece. But it promotes a far more ill-starred regression*. Qui veut faire l'ange fait la bête, *and whoever wants to return to the origins of civilization runs the risk of trading it in for unbridled power. In fact, you lead us back to what in the eighteenth century was called the state of nature.*

—How could there be a regression to or an apology for naked violence when the sole criterion of epochal transition is thinking? At Eichmann's trial in Jerusalem, it occurred to Hannah Arendt that the evils of our century to which you allude resulted from thoughtlessness.[55] And Heidegger's case against technology stands and falls with the claim that it is dangerous because *gedankenlos*, thoughtless. This charge is accompanied by a conviction: thinking changes the world. How can a call for thoughtfulness be mistaken for a call for brutal force?

—*This does not tell us why anti-humanism is not dangerous, particularly if the phrase is meant to inform us of what is to be done at the end of metaphysics. It sounds as if Heidegger's project were to do away somehow with 'man', at least with the concept.*

—A systemic inquiry into epochal economies (about which more in the following Part II) *does not encounter* 'man' as that issue to which all statements must ultimately be referrable if they are to make sense. In the so-called soft sciences initial resistances against considering activities such as myth-telling (Lévi-Strauss) and laboring (Althusser) structurally rather than referentially have largely been quelled today. Heidegger's anti-humanism enjoins one likewise to think of practice otherwise than in terms of determinations affecting an actor. As will be shown, the name for men in his anti-humanist strategy is 'mortals'. As 'rational animal', man rules supreme over the economies, but as 'mortal' he is one variable within them. The difficult question will be: What is the practice—and the politics—of mortals? But the difficulty is not to distinguish between systemic and referential strategies. That distinction has already been legitimized by Kant when he established that "causality in accordance with the laws of nature" *does not encounter*, either to affirm or deny, the issue of "another causality, that of freedom."[56]

—*What then can 'thinking' do against the institutionalization of violence—against the brutality that is precisely 'without principles' and indifferent to man as ultimate referent?*

—Institutionalized violence is visible to all today in the catatonic state that is the gift of generalized production and administration. Measured against these, much of contemporary violence amounts instead to counterviolence. If there is a regression in denouncing thoughtlessness, it is an analytical step backward from oppressions to the economies that make them possible. Pointing out the representations fictitiously endowed with ultimacy is the apogee of the Enlightenment. It is in no way an apology for obscuration and coercion. What needs to be analyzed are the principles born of epochs whose economy called for them. Genealogical analysis can show that these principles are not only deadly but also mortal.

Part Two
The "Very Issue" of Phenomenology: The Economies of Presencing

Thinking corresponds to a truth of entities
that has already happened.

"The Origin of the Work of Art"[1]

To understand the later Heidegger is to understand why the question of being, which is the very issue of his thinking, must divaricate into the question of two economies of presence—one epochal and principial, the other eventlike and anarchic—once the phenomenology of man, of subjectivity, of consciousness, proves to be lodged in the philosophy of subsistent being and linear time.

Already in *Being and Time* the phenomenology of consciousness is denounced as inadequate to the "question of being." And yet Heideggerian anti-humanism constitutes itself fully only with "the turning" subsequent to *Being and Time*. Hence the transitional status of that work; hence also the necessity of retracing briefly the path by which the "very issue," *die Sache selbst*, of thinking progressively concretizes in Heidegger's writings, transforming the question of being into that of the economies of presence and their *difference* from the event of presencing. (Note: I use the subjective genitive, 'economy of presence', to speak of the systemic constellations that make up an era and the objective genitive, 'economy of presencing', to include the event. This second expression is the shortest phrase for addressing what I will call the temporal difference).

The development in Heidegger can be summarized by the conceptual shift from *Dasein* to 'thinking'. *Dasein* is man insofar as being is an issue for him. For 'thinking', on the other hand, being is no longer an issue that belongs to man; thinking is not the attempt to discover the 'meaning' of this issue. Thinking is simply the echo—response and correspondence—to any aletheiological constellation as it has already established itself, each time.

61

"Thinking corresponds to a truth of entities that has already happened."
Therefore, the matter of phenomenology is the destinal precedence of
being that the existential analytic lacked all tools to retrieve.[2] The aletheiological constellations in which being precedes thinking are the economies
of presence. The later the date of Heidegger's publications, the more explicitly the economies are described as the way a given totality of things
"enters *of itself* into presence" (*von sich aus anwesen*). This is a "new
location" for thinking in which it finds itself constrained to "give up the
primacy of man."[3]

IV

MUTATIONS OF PHENOMENOLOGICAL TRANSCENDENTALISM

> In what is its ownmost, phenomenology is
> not a trend. It is the potential of thinking, at
> times changing and only thus persisting, to
> correspond to the address and claim of what
> is to be thought.
>
> "My Way to Phenomenology"[1]

From the beginning, phenomenology is more than a method for Heidegger. He retains it as a possibility, a "potential." Husserl had set free a capacity for investigation that still needed to be developed and radicalized. "Higher than actuality stands possibility. We can understand phenomenology only by seizing upon it as a possibility."[2] To learn how the 'very issue' toward which Husserl redirected our gaze could finally come to be sought in the economies of presence, a line of segregation must be drawn through the "rigorous science" conceived by Husserl. If Heidegger adopts phenomenology as a potential for thinking, there has to be something to preserve and something to be left behind in that science. " 'A priorism' is the method of any scientific philosophy that understands itself."[3] It is the transcendental step back (*Rückgang*, regress, retreat) toward an a priori that is to be retained. But what a priori and what transcendental step back? And what is to be left behind? Following the guiding thread of temporality, we shall see that the a priori undergoes a transmutation as Heideggerian phenomenology reaches its 'issue' proper.

To trace this progressive constitution of the affair for thinking, the best approach is to ask, What is the time notion which, according to Heidegger, prevails in Husserl?[4] I will then oppose this received notion to the various determinations of time in Heidegger—existential (according to which the concern of phenomenology is the 'meaning' or 'sense' of being), historical (according to which that concern is the epochal 'truth' of being), and event-like (according to which it is the 'topology' of being). For a thinking entirely devoted to the relations between being and time, there can be no other criterion for segregating the potential from the actual in phenomenology, for bringing into focus the disciple's ambivalence toward the master, and especially for directing phenomenology toward its chosen ground—the economies of presence. Following these transmutations, it is possible to sketch briefly the trajectory that "leaves the dimension of consciousness" and moves toward "what is wholly different from man, namely, the clearing of being."[5]

§9. From Subjectivity to Being-There

> I tried to think the essence of
> phenomenology in a more originary manner,
> so as to fit it in this way back into the place
> that is properly its own within Western
> philosophy.
>
>   "A Dialogue on Language"[6]

The way phenomenology belongs to Western philosophy results from complex interlacings that affect not only the kind of statements possible within phenomenological discourse, that is, the manner and the vocabulary in which it raises its questions, but also the interests that underlie its various steps, as well as the problems it excludes from its investigations. However, these webs of connection with the tradition are tied to certain initial orientations in the European way of philosophizing since antiquity, orientations that are easy enough to identify. In broad strokes, if phenomenology is connected to Greek philosophy, it is through the quest for an a priori that conditions and renders possible any and every experience. And if it is tied to modern philosophy, it is because it seeks those conditions in the transcendental knowing subject. The question arises whether a priorism and transcendentalism do not proceed from a common source that would precisely determine "the essence of phenomenology." This source from which ancient, modern, and contemporary philosophies proceed can be for Heidegger only a certain conception of time. To fit phenomenology "back into the place that is properly its own within Western philosophy" can only amount to inserting it into the one enduring cadre of metaphysics: an understanding of time that—again, in broad strokes—has predominated from ousiology through egology without ever really being challenged (at least within the mainstream of that tradition).

1. "Husserl considers decidedly metaphysical questions."[7] Gauged by the discovery of ecstatic temporality, this verdict of Heidegger's is undeniable. A closer examination can only substantiate it by stressing the linear

continuity of time in Husserl against its existential discontinuity in Heidegger; the preeminence of the present against that of the future; retention and protention against "having-been" and "to-come"; the temporal flow (*Zeitstrom*) against the threefold "outside oneself," the ecstases. And yet, at first sight there is nothing metaphysical in the Husserlian attempt to reduce the natural everyday attitude to a description of essences, whether these descriptions are of objects or of experiences in the world. Husserl's is a retrogression from the known toward its subjective possibilities, toward acts of generative and formative thinking, into which the quest for a world μετὰ τὰ φυσικά, beyond sensible things, does not and cannot enter. It is however a retrogression that guarantees knowledge a stable origin. But what kind of stability? And why is the natural attitude qualified as prephilosophical if not because it is ignorant of its own origin, because it lacks solid grounding? It is bracketed so that one can discover how the objects of understanding arise, how they can at the same time be actively constituted and given in evidence. What does time have to be so that such a bracketing as well as the reduction of the natural attitude can be performed and that we can intuit essences at all? To analyze the constitution of objects, Husserlian thinking distances itself from the empirical in order to more readily view the a priori contents. Does this analysis escape what in *Being and Time* is called the domain of subsistent entities (*vorhanden*, "given as objects")? Does the phenomenology of object constitution provide an alternative to the specific temporality of that domain, to constant presence?

The primacy Husserl accords *sight* already indicates that the answer must be negative. The eidetic contents are given to be seen (to be sure, by a productive vision, not a simple and direct one). They subsist opposite the gaze and for the gaze. This remains true even though Husserl frequently describes the perceiving subject as assuming different positions with respect to the perceived objects, looking at them from various angles. Within Western philosophy, there is nothing new about the primacy Husserl gives sight. Ever since Aristotle, sight has remained the privileged metaphor for the activity of the mind. Even more, since the classical Greeks, to think is to see.[8] To know is to have seen, and to attain evidence is, as the word indicates, 'to have seen well'. We only see well what is given to us, and we see best what remains immobile. Hearing, on the other hand, is the sense attuned to time: the ear perceives movements of approach and retreat better than the eye. A sound is not yet, then it approaches, it is there, and already it fades and is no more. For the gaze there is only the either-or of the present and the absent. To look is to strive to see what is the case. It is an act that requires distantiation. We are unable to read signs printed on a page with the eye 'glued' to it.[9] Not so for hearing. The closer a sound is the better I perceive it. Hence 'belonging' has the connotation of 'hearing'. The German *gehören* derives from *hören*. In the Greek, Latin, and Germanic languages, to be capable of hearing is to be capable of obeying; *horchen* means *gehorchen*. The eye is the organ of distance and the con-

stantly present. The ear is the organ of involvement and of disclosure in
time.

The Husserlian concept of consciousness, too, points toward *Vorhanden-heit*. The eidetic contents produce evidence by and for the life of consciousness. This is an objectifying life since as ground-providing context it
is objectively subsistent. Do not both the eidetic reduction and the Husserlian transcendental step back from experience amount, then, to deepening
once more the ancient opposition between ἐπιστήμη and δόξα, between
science and belief? For Husserl, this step toward the transcendental origin
of cognition constitutes a knowledge, whereas the attitude that is bracketed
is precisely a mere belief, the belief that the world of things is as we
ordinarily experience it. The theater of the essences, the subject, *subsists*
as it already subsisted for Descartes and as the theater of the ideas subsisted for Plato. It is this mode of temporality, subsistence, that inserts
Husserl into the mainstream of Western philosophy. What is it indeed that
the universal *epoché* makes us see? How is the origin behind the contents
of natural experiences conceived, the origin from which the species and
types instantiated by those contents arise? What is 'seen' is primarily the
very subject of the natural belief in the world. It is on this point that
Husserl remains loyal to Descartes and Kant. At the end of the reduction,
the objects in the world as well as the subject itself show themselves as part
of the solid universe of the transcendental subject. The constitution of an
essence as a particular object, elaborated from real or imaginary experiences, establishes transcendental subjectivity as the arena for intentional
experiences. From the perspective of time, this subjectivity could not function or 'live' without the kind of permanence already essential to the ancient *hupokeimenon*. Described in this manner, the step backward is the
constitution of an epistemological field where a rigorous knowledge of the
life of transcendental subjectivity is procured. Is the ancient 'rational animal' not recognizable again in the life of the cogito? Is the insertion into
Western metaphysics not obvious? In Husserl, too, "the ζῷον's mode of
being is understood in the sense of being-subsistent [*Vorhandensein*] and
of occurring. The λόγος is some superior endowment; the kind of being
which belongs to it, however, remains quite as obscure as that of the entire
entity thus compounded."[10]

But is Husserl not rightfully renowned for having overcome the conception of an atemporal I? He distinguishes in subjectivity between the substrate and the monad. The I is "the identical substrate of lasting prop-
erties,"[11] the substrate of habitual possessions, of acquired modalities of
consciousness. This construct makes it possible to understand how the world
of variably determined objects becomes enriched through experiences. The
I to which every new object must relate is the 'monad'. And indeed, the
monad has a past and a future. The substrate, however, although it is no
longer an entity as it was for the metaphysicians, does not change. It is
removed from relations to the world and to others. This is what remains

stable. It is the I as the identical pole of given experiences. From the point of view of temporality—the only one that matters here—the substrate is thus assimilated to the world of facts. It is the subjective, abstract pole of the world, but it is not being-in-the-world. It is as constantly present as the objects. Such limitation of temporal modes to one of them, constant presence, is what in Heidegger's view assigns Husserl the "place that is properly [his] own within Western philosophy." It is fatal for the understanding of "world." Constant presence blocks any access to being-in-the-world. Heidegger therefore comes to surmise that the self-donation of objects is a delusion. From the standpoint of being-in-the-world and ecstatic temporality, he can say that the self-giving of the I is a "seduction," "leading one astray."[12] The Heideggerian starting point cuts short the very possibility of fixing the subject in subsistence and time in permanence. The temporal continuum must collapse when "for the first time in the history of philosophy, being-in-the-world appears as the primordial mode of encountering entities."[13]

However, the relations between the phenomenology of being-in-the-world and that of consciousness are more ambiguous. Husserl struggles against the natural attitude inasmuch as it consists in believing the contents of my consciousness to be available to me, there before my eyes. Therefore it is the notion of natural attitude that prefigures the Heideggerian *Vorhandenheit*.[14] Both designate what the transcendental move must step beyond. Consequently, does Heidegger not climb through the breach already opened by his master's works? He recognizes that Husserlian phenomenology prepared the "soil"[15] for the question of being. The equation between self-givenness, constant presence, and subsistent being is, then, not so simple. There is one 'datum' in the phenomenology of consciousness whose characteristics lay bare both the thread that runs from subjectivity to being-there and the irremediable break that separates them.

"Husserl touches on, grazes, the question of being in the sixth chapter of the sixth *Logical Investigation* with the notion of 'categorial intuition.' "[16] An intuition is the corollary of donation, as receiving is the corollary of giving. What is given in a categorial intuition? A category—for example, substance. But how can a category be intuited, seen, *angeschaut*? "I see before me this book. But where is the substance in this book? I do not in any way see it in the same manner that I see the book. And yet, this book positively is a substance that I must 'see' in some way, since otherwise I could not see anything at all."[17] Unlike Kant, Husserl treats the categories as intuitively received. In the narrow sense, says Husserl, "being is nothing that can be perceived." "But it is well known that one speaks of perception, and notably of vision, also in a much wider sense," i.e., of *Einsehen*, intuiting.[18] This intuition is *analogous* to the intuitions of inner or outer sense. In seeing 'substance' or 'being' at the same time as the book, I always see more than this book. The chief category, 'being', thus is *seen* in each and all perceptions. It exceeds every perception. Substance and being are "nothing *in* the object, they are not part of it, they do not constitute an inherent moment. . . . Nor is being something added upon the object. . . ."[19] Hence the splitting of intuition into two simultaneous acts, sensible and categorial. In treating it as an object of intuition, Husserl "grazes" the question of being. A pre-understanding of being as a category accompanies any act of sense perception.

However, this doctrine of being's intuitive status falls far short of a phenomenological ontology. It does not make it possible to determine by what mode of being consciousness stands in relation to the natural world opposite it. What is the crucial deficiency here? The temporality of the perceiving subject is not distinguished from that of perceived objects. Existential time is not distinguished from that of perceived objects. Existential time is not distinguished from constant presence. There is no way to pass from the categorial intuition of substance to the determination of subsistence as a way of being—as one way of being among others. When 'being' is sought for in perception, worldliness and *Vorhandenheit* necessarily remain unthought. The analysis proceeds entirely within these two and cannot thematize them. Furthermore, as life world, the world still receives its status of being from consciousness, from 'man' as the grounding representation.

Husserl thus made it possible for Heidegger to think being no longer out of the copula's function in a judgment, but as intuitively manifest and in that sense as a priori. "With these analyses of categorial intuition, Husserl has freed being from its fixation in judgment."[20] Husserl has worked out the phenomenality of being in the category. But he has not questioned the identification of being with consciousness, nor, consequently, that of time with constant presence. By methodically falling back on the cogito, the phenomenology of transcendental subjectivity accomplishes a step backward that leads from the immediately and naturally given world to the world given for and by consciousness. Everything that 'is', and notably the object of intentionality, is in consciousness, present to consciousness. To be is to be represented.

The 'very issue' or 'matter itself' of Husserlian phenomenology thus turns out to be representation. From this point of its insertion into Western philosophy, the restrictive understanding of time in that *Sache selbst* leaps into view. What is temporal about the object is that it maintains itself before the subject. "Here to represent means to bring subsistent being [*das Vorhandene*] before oneself as something standing over against [*Entgegenstehendes*] oneself, to relate it to oneself, to the one representing it, and to force it back into this relation to oneself as the normative realm."[21] By forcing the object back into the subjective normative realm, the subject constitutes itself as guarantor and guardian of the object and its permanence.

It is clear that, in order to show how Husserl belongs to the metaphysical tradition of linear time conception, Heidegger has recourse not to the notions of flux and flow (*Zeitstrom*) but to those of subsistent being and

representation. The framework of the philosophy of subjectivity he uncriti-
cally adopts prevents Husserl from questioning the understanding of being
as objective presence.

2. Heidegger turns away from this phenomenology of transcendental
consciousness in three stages: first, by passing to existential phenomenology as fundamental ontology,[22] then by passing to the phenomenology of
historical *alētheia*,[23] and lastly by attempting a topology of the 'event'. The
first metamorphosis of phenomenological transcendentalism leads to the
replacement of the 'subject' by *Dasein,* the second to that of *Dasein* by
Menschentum, the third to its replacement by an even less subjectivistic,
humanistic, existential word: 'thinking'.

The phenomenology of *Dasein* or of "being-there" may appear to be a
concretization of the phenomenology of intentional consciousness.[24] Transcendental subjectivity would then be the condition for the possibility of
existential analysis. But as is indicated by the reference to the question of
being contained in the very word *Dasein,* the foundational relation is rather
the inverse: the existential analysis does not 'fill in' a posteriori the more
formal concept of the transcendental I, but, on the contrary, it designates
the a priori stratum that makes possible any philosophy of the I, of the
subject's consciousness.[25] Regarding the transcendentalism of consciousness, the phenomenology of *Being and Time* takes a new step backward.
Through its ontological essence, "being-there" is an origin more originary
than consciousness. The mutation of transcendentalism from Husserl to
Heidegger thus has to do with the role of man: the condition of our knowing and experiencing is no longer sought purely in man, but in his relation
to the being of entities in their totality.[26] The origin is no longer sought in
the formal structures of consciousness through which indubitable representations are obtained, but in the ontological structures through which the
entity we are is said to belong to being as such.

This transformation would still not be radical if it simply consisted in
tracing phenomena to our *ontic* involvement with them[27]—if it amounted
to declaring that sciences and ontologies are activities that proceed from
concrete man. Viewed in this manner, phenomenology would reveal a twin
origin, epistemological and existential, *cogito* and *Dasein.* However, this
way of understanding the two phenomenological projects would gloss over
the heterogeneity of the matter that each strives to see. The origin appears
as subjectivity when this matter is representation. It appears as being-there
when this matter is the being of entities.[28] The priority of existential transcendentalism over the transcendentalism of subjectivity is established by
retreating from objective essences to the being of entities. Once that step is
taken, Husserl's own starting point appears as a "delusion."

The same methodic retreat makes it necessary to dismiss the dualism of
subject and object; to construe phenomenology as interpretation rather

than reflection; to follow the arrival and withdrawal of things in the horizon of the world instead of remaining riveted to entities constantly present; to sap the prestige of seeing over hearing;[29] finally, to deconstruct the theories of the constitution of universals for consciousness. In such theories the origin functions as the *archē* of the contents of the understanding, but not as *Ursprung*, the emergence, the springing forth, of the "there" of being.

The overcoming of subjective transcendentalism does not put an end to the transcendental method as such. To question the "there" that we are instead of the I, and to disengage from being-there the structures of its performance in the world instead of the I's a priori structures of objective knowledge, is still to seek the origin of phenomena. The starting point, to be sure, is no longer perception but rather our being's involvement with things and with others. The origin as epistemological demands an analytic of the understanding, and the origin as existential, an analytic of being-in-the-world. The shift from one to the other discloses "the originary meaning" of the transcendental, so that even the Kantian critique is now exposed in "its proper tendency, possibly still hidden from Kant."[30] The proper tendency of transcendentalism becomes apparent when the a priori is recognized no longer in the acts by which the understanding gives itself totalities, but in the possibility of totalization proper to our being. Nevertheless, it is still a matter of coming back to ourselves in order to inventory conditions of possibility—of knowledge and experiences in one case, of the modalities of involvement and belonging in the other. In this way, the transcendentalism of the period of *Being and Time* retreats doubly from immediate experience: not only from the perceived to the structures of perception, but further, toward "that which renders possible perception, position, as well as the cognitive faculties . . . as so many attitudes of that entity to which they belong."[31] Subjective transcendentalism, from Kant to Husserl, retrogresses from the objects of experience to our a priori modes of knowing them; Heidegger in turn retrogresses from these a priori modes to their rootedness in the entity that we are.[32]

In this way, recourse to the I as the origin of knowledge is led back to "being-there" as the origin of the possible determinations of existence in the world. The transcendentalism of phenomenological ontology consists in this double regress. In *Being and Time*,[33] Heidegger distinguishes three senses of the term "phenomenology": formal, ordinary, and—this qualificative, which may be surprising, is found in another text—scientific.[34] In *Being and Time*, this third sense is properly called "phenomenological." The three senses are derived from three ways a thing may be said to appear.[35] "Formal" phenomenology is the discourse about a thing that shows itself as it is in itself, that appears as such to the gaze by entering the horizon of the 'there'. "Ordinary" phenomenology considers the thing as it seems to be, what it looks to be. But an entity can seem to be something only because it first always and essentially appears. Therefore, this second sense of φαίνεσθαι is dependent on the first. The third sense of appearing applies to something whose self-manifestation is only concomitant with phenomena in the formal or the ordinary sense. It does not show itself at first sight and for itself, but is "the meaning and the ground of . . . what shows itself."[36] Such an appearing must be wrested from phenomena, and that is the work of "scientific" phenomenology, "the science of the being of entities."[37] It is scientific because radically transcendental: it steps back from entities in such a manner that what shows itself is the other of entities, an 'other' that conceals itself in them as much as it reveals itself therein—not any noumenal 'other', but the 'sense of being'. Understanding this sense is the very way to be of human *Dasein*. The a priori understanding of the sense of being makes possible all comportment toward this or that entity. So rephrased, transcendentalism has abandoned the problematic of the constitution of universal essences.

By disclosing *another time* it has also abandoned the neo-Kantian problematic of meaning. The expression "*Sinn des Seins*" in *Being and Time* can be understood in several ways. On the first page of that book, Heidegger cites a text from Plato about θαυμάζειν, the wonder that generates philosophy. Heidegger asks: "Are we today even perplexed at our inability to understand the expression 'to be'?"[38] 'Sense', *Sinn*, means, first of all, a sensibility for the question of being, as one may say of someone that he has a sense of fairness. *Being and Time* is to revive in us this sense of being as the sensibility for an issue. In the second place, 'sense' designates whatever can be understood. Something makes sense, i.e., has meaning, only within the domain of existential projection, the domain that is *Dasein*. In this perspective, the sense of being is being insofar as it enters into the opening constituted by *Dasein*. The limits of such an acceptation of the word *Sinn* are obvious: "The inadequateness of this starting point is that it all too easily makes the 'project' understood as a human performance."[39] In other words, *Sinn* as 'meaning' too spontaneously evokes subjectivist transcendentalism. Once this misunderstanding is eliminated, the third acceptation appears: 'sense' is direction. This usage, derived as I have said not from the Latin *sensus* but the German *sinno*, is rare in English. Still, one may speak of a body that moves in one sense or the other, as the French speak of the *sens* of a river. A one-way street is *une rue à sens unique*. In German, "*sinnan* or *sinnen* means to follow the direction that is the way something has, of itself, already taken."[40] In the context of *Being and Time* such bearing or directionality of being is not at all linear. "To think being as time"[41] is to bring to light what *Dasein* never ceases to do, namely, to ec-sist, to be ecstatically. 'Sense' in this third acceptation, then, designates the threefold bearing of the temporal ecstases.

The metamorphosis by which 'sense' is disengaged from the acts of consciousness and engaged in temporality best shows the path that stretches from Husserl to *Being and Time*, the path from subjectivity to being-there.

§10. From *Menschentum* to "Thinking"

Having given up the preeminence of consciousness for the sake of a new domain, the
domain of *Dasein,* man has but one
possibility left to attune himself to this new
domain, namely, to enter into it. . . . Those
who believe that thinking is capable of
changing man's place still represent it
according to the model of production.—What
then?—Then we say with all due caution
that thinking begins preparing the conditions
for such an entrance.

Seminar in Zähringen, 1973[42]

The first mutation of phenomenological transcendentalism, that from
subjectivity to being-there, does not entirely leave the ground of man.
Indeed, the trend of Heidegger's thrust beyond Husserl appears only retrospectively. Consciousness as producing eidetic contents ultimately is
abandoned for a domain where man finds his place *assigned* to him, where
he is no longer the master of disclosure. The task that then remains for him
is to follow the movement of coming-to-presence as it occurs around him
and to turn his thinking resolutely toward that historical economy. The line
that leads Heidegger from *Dasein* to its latest offspring, 'thinking', is drawn
in two strokes: from *Dasein* to *Menschentum,* a collectivity as situated by
an epoch of truth, and from there to *Denken* as pure obedience to presencing understood as event.

In *Being and Time,* to be present still means to be present to 'man'. The
being that we are *is* presencing. A new way of thinking is required to
understand presencing independently of such a reference. The new way of
thinking can again be expressed in terms of 'sense'. Heidegger says for
instance that in the contemporary age "there reigns a *sense* in all technical
processes which lays claim to what man does and leaves undone: a sense
that man has neither invented nor fabricated in the first place."[43] What
does "sense" mean here? Certainly something temporal since its injunctions address us in the midst of "technical processes" rather than in pre-
industrial processes. The temporality of sense, however, is no longer ecstatic and located in man. It is destinal and located in the epochs of history.
"Sense" now designates the direction followed by "sudden epochs of
truth,"[44] their bearing.

The shift from consciousness to being-there was already accompanied by
a new understanding of truth. In *Being and Time* truth is no longer construed from intentional acts as the structural unity *ego-cogito-cogitatum*.
Truth is "resoluteness."[45] This transcendentalism answers the question of

the conditions for the possibility of our being in the world by disengaging the revelatory structures from *Dasein*, which is thus the "locality" of truth.[46] In that way, the origin of the 'world' is understood as the *there* of the possibilities for disclosure. This indicates a remarkable continuity between the phenomenology of intentional consciousness and the phenomenology of being-there: the possibilities of disclosure are always *ours*. That continuity becomes apparent only in retrospect. From the standpoint of *Being and Time* Heidegger has good reasons for not speaking of 'man' in that work. Compared to his later anti-humanism, however, being-in-the-world, just like eidetic knowledge, is constituted by the unfolding of characteristics proper to man. Being-in-the-world, just like knowing, belongs to the domain of our own potential. It is our ownmost potential. To be sure, intentionality of consciousness is but a figure derived from being-in-the-world, and the self but a modification of existence.[47] Nonetheless, in either phenomenology, that of the subject and that of *Dasein*, the question of truth leads back to man. Truth arises, respectively, from the effective and founding structures of consciousness or from projection. In either case its origin, however desubstantialized, is man. This is not to say that, according to *Being and Time*, we create truth by our projects. Being-there is always 'thrown', preceded by its facticity, located in the midst of limited historical possibilities. Nor can there be anything solipsistic in *Dasein*. However, the projects are indeed ours. Both the Husserlian and the early Heideggerian phenomenologies consider what Heidegger later calls "the preeminence of man"[48] to be constitutive of the origin of truth. For both, truth is accomplished by us.

After the discovery of destinal history the happening of truth runs in the reverse direction: no longer truth made, but truth in the making (the 'constitution of truth' no longer as *genitivus obiectivus*, but as *genitivus subiectivus*). Always and everywhere we respond and correspond to a truth "that has already happened."[49] It is no longer man who 'opens up' a clearing, who 'projects' light over entities, who 'resolves' the world by revealing it, but historical *alêtheia* which constitutes man by situating him. This sharpened anti-humanism requires a vocabulary more explicitly in accord with history. Each collectivity, each *Menschentum*, finds its locus of truth assigned to it. Its destiny consists in having to respond to the constellations of presence instituted by an epoch. A *Menschentum* is an epochal type of man.[50]

The shift of 'sense' toward the directionality inherent in the history of *alêtheia* preserves in transcendental philosophy the search for the conditions that make manifestation possible as well as the quest for an a priori. But these conditions and the a priori henceforth are not situated in man. As long as things present are called true because they enter into a project of disclosure, it is *Dasein* that circumscribes what is true (i.e., unconcealed because it is *bedeutsam*, meaningful). Aletheiological phenomenology, on the other hand, shifts from such circumscription to prescription. All its attention goes to what the historical constellations of truth prescribe through 'sudden epochs'. Heidegger thus undertakes a transcription of the contours of truth. Its horizon is no longer drawn by existential acts such as anticipatory resolution (nor, of course, as Jacques Derrida repeats after him, traced by some figure of the other[51]), but by the *epochē* which precedes all our initiatives as their historical condition. What we can do is made possible by our epochal inscription. If, after such displacements of the a priori, we still speak of transcendental thinking, it can only signify a post-subjectivist, post-modern transcendentalism, "a transcendentalism without a subject."[52]

'Sense' is to be understood now as historical and destinal bearing. Does this not restore a linear conception of time? Is not time—the horizon for the understanding of being—again the chain of the ages? Not at all. The epochal a priori is still more discontinuous than the ecstases in *Being and Time*. The expression 'sudden epochs of truth' points to this new discontinuity. In the context of the existential analytic, destiny (*Geschick*) means "*Dasein*'s coming-to-pass [*Geschehen*] in being-with others," "the coming-to-pass of the community."[53] After the turning, however, destiny is no longer anchored phenomenally in 'being-with'. A collectivity *receives* its destiny, it no longer accomplishes it. 'To destine', then, means "to prepare, to order, to put everything in its place." The 'destiny of being' is a setting in place of epochal phenomena by sudden rearrangements in the order of things. These intermittencies of destiny shatter linear time. "In the destiny of being, the history of being is not thought as some coming-to-be that could be characterized by development and progression."[54] Rather, destinal history "unfolds" itself.[55] The epochs (as retold by Michel Foucault) are as little continuous as the surfaces of a geological fold.

As a consequence of the distinction between the epochal reversals and the turning beyond the epochs, 'sudden epochs of truth' can no longer occur past the contemporary threshold. That is the very content of the hypothesis of closure. What has to be retained from the discovery of epochal history, however, is the notion of truth as historical order in which things, actions, and words are rendered mutually present. *Alētheia* is to be understood in terms of economies of presence. 'Economy' is the generic term here of which the *epochal* constellations (with their reversals) as well as the *anarchic* one (after the turning), constitute specific instantiations. The event of economic coming-to-presence, of presencing, which after the turning becomes the very issue of phenomenology, requires a still more neutral vocabulary than the inquiry into epochal types of man. The corollary of the epochs is '*Menschentum*', that of the event, 'thinking'.

Aletheiological economies are still treated as transcendental conditions, namely of the metaphysical ('conformity') and critical ('certitude') concepts of truth. This transcendentalism itself is however neither metaphysical[56] nor critical. As the constellation of what is veiled and unveiled in an economy of presence, truth furthermore is neither made by verification, nor projected. It dispenses itself to *thinking* which corresponds to it by abandoning itself to such constellations. The unity of this double 'letting', dispensation through economies and respondency through thinking, is called releasement.[57] The mutations of transcendentalism lead from metaphysics to fundamental ontology, to the history of truth, to topology; from substance or subject to being-there, to epochal human types, and then to thinking or letting. They may be more easily understood by examining the matching attitude at each stage: making, projecting, corresponding, and letting.

If Aristotle's *Physics* is indeed the "foundational" book of Western philosophy, not only its themes and methods, but especially the guiding attitude from which it springs, must have set the tone for the tradition. What is the posture in which becoming and its causes can arise as issues for inquiry at all? It is ποιεῖν, human making. That attitude predominates until the Husserlian consciousness as 'productive' of essences. The Aristotelian analysis of sensible substance and the changes that affect it provided ontology with its basic vocabulary. This is so because the understanding of being had come to be determined by a very particular experience, the astonishment of the classical Greeks before things produced by man, before his capacity to lead into being, to fabricate tools or works of art.[58] The *projective* is but a late formalized offspring of this *productive* posture. The poietic understanding of being quite naturally translates itself into the double concept of origin (1) as *archē* of fabrication, then of change, and (2) as 'principle' of doctrines for understanding both making and becoming. Knowledge results from such recourse to the origin as *archē* and as principle, as the focal point for constructing and for conceiving. "Where there is no first term, there is no explanation at all."[59]

Compare this to the economic notion of origin in the later Heidegger: the origin that lets all that is present be present makes nothing *known*. It merely gives us the emergence of entities in our constellation of unconcealment to think. The attitude it requires of thinking is neither poietic nor projective; it is releasement.[60] Releasement is the first and final answer to the question, What is called thinking? It is the first answer, for thinking can be learned only if we let ourselves be, if we abandon and give ourselves over to the economic dispensation that assigns us our place. It is the last answer, for to think is to gather up presencing which in itself is nothing but releasement. Presencing *lets* everything that is present be present. "Letting" is therefore the identical essence of thinking and being.[61] To think is to think presencing. To learn to think is to learn releasement. Far from connoting any carelessness or inaction,[62] releasement is the essential structure of both thinking and presencing.

The mutations of phenomenological transcendentalism thus lead to Heidegger's event-like Parmenidism: 'to be' and 'to think' are one in the event that is releasement. This unique event—coming to presence—assigns everything its location, including man. Because it is economic, it is an anti-humanistic Parmenidism; and it will be necessary to try to understand presencing itself in its terms. It is clear, in any case, that with the One as an economic event[63] Heideggerian phenomenology steps outside the philosophy of subsistent being and linear time. What is one is the process of *coming to* presence. Through the event-like and economic One, the 'very issue' of this phenomenology is definitively severed from all ties to subjectivity and consciousness.

The Kantian quest for universal and necessary conditions of appearance is thus reformulated in terms of processes not centered upon man: on one hand, the process by which any *economic* unity (whether 'epochal' or 'anarchic') arises, enclosing for a while all possible phenomena in one mode of presence; on the other, the unitary process called *event* of presencing. These are two temporal conditions that must be met if appearance is to be possible at all. The temporality of the one resides in the history of *alētheia;* that of the other, in the ahistorical *phuein* or showing-forth.

As has been shown, several mutations of phenomenological transcendentalism must be distinguished: from the subject to *Dasein* (from Husserl to *Being and Time*); from there to the 'destiny of being' which ascribes to any given collectivity or type its historical locus; and finally to the 'event'. To develop this ultimate phenomenological potential, it will be necessary once again to take up the guiding thread of time. Setting apart these two temporal conditions, that of economic history and that of the topology of the event—of presencing—is the later Heidegger's way of working out the ontological difference *as temporalized.* This difference will be developed below as the difference between the 'original' and the 'originary'.

This much should be retained at this point: with the mutations that have been traced we touch the withering away of the last in the series of epochal principles, subjectivity. From Husserl to Heidegger the a priori transforms itself from consciousness into being-there and then into an unfolding that is no longer in the least human: the diachronic, historical, 'original' unfolding called *Geschehen,* and the synchronic, ahistorical, 'originary' unfolding called *Ereignis.* The withering away already announced itself in *Being and Time* with the radical notion of *Dasein.* It comes to fulfillment, however, only when the very issue of phenomenology turns into the rhizomatic economies that situate presencing. The later Heidegger still sometimes calls an economic locus '*Da-sein*', but the transcendental step back toward that topos no longer reaches any origin as referential. The transcendental move then consists in the difficult retrogression in which thinking does what presencing does—let all present things rest in themselves, without manipulation and in accordance with the conjuncture in which they arise. Such respondency is what Heidegger calls "thanking."[64] It is an arduous task in which there is no room for resignation or quietism. It entails, on the contrary, a new concept of acting. An acting totally in compliance with presencing as it occurs economically would equally have to be described as 'thanking'.

In the age of the turning, however, the most we can do may be to prepare topological and economic thinking and acting. "Thinking begins preparing the conditions for such an entrance" into the economic 'there', into the place provisionally assigned to us by the way things come to presence. Acting, likewise, has a preparatory mandate to fulfill.

V

DECONSTRUCTION OF THE
POLITICAL

Prior to the question that alone always seems
to be the most immediate and urgent, What
ought we to do? we must ponder this: *How
must we think?* Thinking is indeed the proper
acting insofar as to act means to comply with
the essential unfolding of being. . . . This
original correspondence, carried out for its
own sake, is thinking.

"The Turning"[1]

If the claim is at all defensible that in today's culture subjectivity is
withering as the last in a long series of ultimate referents, then the
possibility of construing a ground for action also disappears. The deconstruction of practical philosophy is one accompanying feature of the transition from the late modern issues of consciousness and its acts to the issue
of closing modernity: "the being of entities in its unconcealedness and
concealment."[2]

What may begin to hold one's attention in that transition are the many
ways, changing with time, in which things enter into mutual relations.
There is nothing stable in this 'unfolding'. Nor is there anything that would
allow for a normative discourse, legitimating action, to be construed. We
think by 'complying' with the economic mutations of presencing. We *act* in
the same way. In the epigraph above, it is apparent that thinking does
retain a priority for Heidegger. We act as we think: permeable or im-
permeable to the ceaseless renewal of presencing-absencing. But for the
deconstructionist project, the two questions—"What ought we to do?" and
"How must we think?"—remain distinct only as components of the heritage
we have to assume. Working through that heritage reveals the common
essence of thinking and acting: corresponding to 'the essential unfolding of
being', 'thanking'.

I will spell out briefly what for Heidegger are the constitutive parts of
the phenomenological potential, and then see what becomes of them with

his discovery of the economies of presence. Heidegger lists three "fundamental elements" of phenomenology: *reduction, construction,* and *destruction*.[3] Later, when his focus shifts from past ontologies to past modalities of
presence, he speaks of "deconstruction" rather than "destruction." Nevertheless, the three elements survive—although in a new guise—the discovery of the economies of presence.

Their new guise dissociates them from any reference to the I. Their
severance from egology allows transcendentalism to move from the priority
of one present entity (the ontic precedence of *Dasein*) to the priority of
presencing. This metamorphosis of the a priori introduces history into the
transcendental conditions. Husserl could not recognize such historicity,
which is "essential in being," because of his subjectivist bias.[4]

Through the *reduction*, the phenomenology of intentional consciousness
traced the objects of natural perception back to experiences of my "pure ego
in the pure current of my cogitations."[5] For Husserl, the reduction led to the
discovery of the transcendental ego as the origin of perceptions. The phenomenology of being-there, on the other hand (early Heidegger), discovers
quite a different origin through the reduction: occurrences in the world are
reduced to the opening of regional projects through which being-there discloses those occurrences.[6] Finally (later Heidegger), to examine entities for
the sake of their historical modality of presencing is to practice yet another
type of reduction. Such a modality institutes and preserves an epoch. Here
the reductive gaze passes from the epochally present to epochal presencing.
This kind of transcendentalism operates under another pre-understanding
and another preliminary question than did the reduction to 'phenomena' in
the strict sense, whether phenomena for consciousness or for being-there.
As directed against the primacy of consciousness, the later form of reduction
is anti-humanist. Through the new pre-understanding, unconcealment is
established as prior to any act of consciousness and any project. But as a
quest for conditions, the reduction remains transcendental. Unconcealment
as the a priori—an aletheiological economy—arranges everything that can
become a phenomenon into an order of presence, which may last decades or
centuries.[7]

Phenomenological *construction*[8] consists in explicating the pre-understanding that guides first the intuition of essences, and later the projection of
entities for the sake of their being.[9] To construct is to grasp a horizon of
intelligibility, be it (a) the world for acts of the ego or (b) temporality for
being-in-the-world. With (c) the discovery of the economies of presence, "to
construct" does not mean to constitute either formal egological ideas or
existential structures. Here to construct, then, is to open up the *epochal*
horizon where a principle reigns and to trace the law that it imposes, from its
ascension through its withering away. The historical modalities of presencing
remain as unthinkable for the young Heidegger as they were for Husserl.
However, whether of universal ideas (a), existential structures (b), or ep-

ochal fields (c), phenomenological construction always does violence to the empirical, ontic, historical manifold. Construction establishes a preliminary from which interpretation proceeds: in the case of the later Heidegger, the modes in which an entity comes to presence within a given epochal order. Therefore, the description of the reversals within history is continuous with hermeneutic phenomenology, for which "interpreting is not acquiring information about what is understood, but elaborating the possibilities projected in understanding."[10] The three types of construction—(a) theory of intentional acts, (b) fundamental ontology, (c) economic topology—formally resemble each other insofar as no research can dispense with a preliminary grasp of that which it seeks. All three are phenomenological and transcendental: whether the preliminary is human or aletheiological, construction determines its function, each time, through a question. It is only a way of asking questions.[11] The preliminary that is "constructed" by the phenomenology of economies is the three-tiered difference between entities present, their historical field of presence, and the event of their presencing. *Meanwhile, there is presencing*. To construct that difference is thus to say 'meanwhile' and to say it temporally: while the Inca reigns over Precolombian Peru, words, things, and deeds are 'presencing' to one another according to the decimal system. . . .

The *destruction* is first of all a methodological consequence of the return to 'the things themselves'. Already for Husserl, the task of liberating the objectively given from the theoretical overlays and prejudices amassed by the tradition entailed a dismantling of philosophies in order to attain the pure intentional experience hidden under non-scientific theories. But neither the phenomenology of subjectivity nor that of *Dasein* can proceed with what Heidegger calls the "critical *deconstruction* of transmitted concepts toward the sources from which they have been drawn."[12] Since these "sources" are intentional experiences for Husserl and being-in-the-world for the early Heidegger, the deconstruction of transmitted concepts remains distorted—incomplete and entangled in metaphysics—as long as the sources are sought in man, that is, as long as these experiences and this being-in-the-world are not situated in a history of modalities of presence.[13] The phenomenological deconstruction of the history of ontology is complete and disentangled from metaphysics only as a phenomenology of epochal economies. The 'thing itself', the very issue that the deconstruction frees, consists in the numerous ways entities have of rendering themselves present, of presencing. These numerous ways result from the concrete shifts in our history. Wherever philosophers inquire merely about entities as present, analyzing for instance their composition, that coming to presence and its route remain implicit, 'always already' operative, but unthought. The *destruction* wrests from inherited systems presencing as a rare thinker may have experienced it. The concepts from his writings are 'destroyed' as doctrine, and they are reconstructed to reveal how he may have acknowledged, even if obliquely, being as a temporal event. The destruction is the positive appropriation of the tradition[14] because it recaptures what has always made us think, but has remained masked by metaphysical dogma.[15] The *deconstruction,* on the other hand, wrests from past established orders the event of presencing that happens always and everywhere in each entity that becomes a phenomenon. The successive orders are 'deconstructed' as they form a culture and reconstructed to reveal the event that gathers entities into historical constellations. Deconstruction differs from destruction by its disinterest in past authors, but it is identical with destruction in its quest for an understanding of being as time. From destruction to deconstruction, the text analyzed shifts from writing to epochal history.

The task consists, then, in thinking being as presencing and as differing from its economic modalities. This task for thinking will be completed successfully only through a deconstruction of the principles that administer an age. That is where phenomenology, now radicalized, encounters the problem of acting. As I have said, the political is situated in the confluence of words, things, and deeds. How are we to act publicly, how do we participate in common affairs, if this precarious confluence is the sole a priori legislator we can heed or 'thank'? A legislator more than a little inconstant.

There is no more irrevocable finitude than that of the epochal regimes as they prescribe what we can do; and no more transient norm than that of those principles whose arising opens and whose foundering closes an era. The representation of something ultimate which, because it objectivates presencing, matters most in any temporary public order is necessarily a finite a priori.[16] Epochal principles are always ontic givens. Each of them opens modalities of possible interaction and forecloses on others. An epoch, then, is "reduced" to the way things, words, and actions are mutually present in it; it is "constructed" out of the difference between present entities and their presencing; and it is "deconstructed" so as to let presencing as such become accessible to our inquiry. But if it is true that the event of presencing founds nothing, that it cannot even be understood as long as the very search for a foundation is not renounced,[17] the critique of grounds and reasons amounts indeed to deconstructing action: taking it out of its seemingly natural embeddedness in doctrine and meaningful order, and examining it as *one site where presencing occurs.* To the question "What ought we to do?" the answer is, then, the same as to the question "How ought we to think?" Love the flux and thank its economic confluences. . . .

The consequences of this deconstruction are most obvious in the political domain. We will trace them through the birth and the decline of referents for action: from the Aristotelian substantialist pattern for political philosophy, to the substitution of the 'event' for any ontic standard for practice.

§11. Deconstructing the Substantialist Patterns

> —You speak incessantly of a 'letting'. This
> gives the impression that what is meant is
> a kind of passivity. [. . .]
> —Perhaps a higher doing is concealed in re-
> leasement than in all deeds of the world
> and in the machinations of
> collectivities . . .
> — . . . which higher doing is however no
> activity.
> —Accordingly, releasement lies—if one may
> speak of lying here—outside the distinction
> between activity and passivity.
>
> "Conversation on a Country Path about
> Thinking"[18]

In order to understand how Heidegger uproots action we have first to make sure in what sense *Handeln* ("acting"), while as irreducible to activity in a narrower sense as to passivity, still remains a political category. Acting, like thinking, is a surrender to the economies of presence. Action is thus absorbed in releasement, the highest deed. At first sight, there is nothing very political about this. That impression may change, however, if we can clarify how action allies itself with speech and with things—the alliance I have used to describe the political. The key distinction will be one between an acting *opposable* to thinking and an acting *akin* to thinking. This elementary distinction will make it possible to grasp exactly which notion of the political the Heideggerian critique uproots. By definition, the metaphysical quest for an ultimate foundation seeks a *hupokeimenon*, a 'substrate'. Metaphysics is a fundamentalist quest. Therefore it should not be surprising that the substantialist notions of the political, inherited from Aristotle, are the ones that the deconstruction undoes before all others, and that all others are undone by means of the substantialist notions.

1. Heidegger does not always appear to distinguish clearly between *acting* as opposed to πάσχειν—being acted upon, suffering, 'passion'—and *doing* as opposed to being inactive. The 'highest deed', inseverably one of thinking and of acting, is sometimes called *Handeln* and sometimes *Tun*.[19] There is thus a broader concept of acting that transcends traditional antonyms such as action-passion, doing-not doing, acting-thinking, theory-practice, and even πράττειν (to act, *tun*)-ποιεῖν (to make or fabricate, *machen*). This broader concept is releasement. *Gelassenheit* is indeed poietic in an anti-humanist sense, it 'produces' the economies. Heidegger makes Parmenidean formulations his own in saying that *noein*, the act in which thinking receives economic presencing, and *einai*, an economy's self-production, are one and the same 'letting'.

The clearest way of disentangling Heidegger's restricted concept of action from his broader one consists in separating them by the 'turning': man until now (*der bisherige Mensch*), that is, until the metaphysical closure, "has for centuries acted too much and thought too little." Here we have the traditional, restricted concept of action opposed to contemplation. But "from now on" (*fortan*), that is, beyond the closure and as a result of the turning, action will mean something else. To act will be "to bring something where it belongs and henceforth *leave* it there." Here we have the broad notion, which joins acting and thinking in releasement. So that there can be no misgivings about the anticipatory character of this broad notion, Heidegger adds: "None of us will claim to carry out, however remotely, such a thinking, or even a prelude to it. At the very most, we may succeed in preparing for it."[20]

The other acting, which has remained unthought, will necessarily differ from action as conceived by the tradition issuing from Aristotle. It cannot be confused with the *praxis* assigned its goal by reason and sustained by the will. The representation of a goal to be attained—if not the construction of a human faculty, the will, aiming at it—dominates the concept of action from the very opening line of the *Nichomachean Ethics:* "Every art and every inquiry, and similarly every action and pursuit, is thought to aim at some good."[21] The question is: are τέχνη and μέθοδος, πρᾶξις and προαίρεσις "similarly" dominated by an end to be attained? Theoretical teleocracy seems rather to be born from reflection about *technē* alone, so that we 'aim at' something, strictly speaking, only in the domain of fabrication. From there the rule of end has imposed itself on reflection about "inquiries," and finally on each and every form of acting, each and every form of choice. The rule of end has constituted the concepts of scientific investigation as well as those with which we account for moral decisions.

The broad notion of action, one may say, situates the restricted notion as a genus situates a species. Teleocracy provides the specific difference that determines not only *poiēsis* and *technē*, but also praxis. It demarcates the phenomenal region where an end reigns. From this *regional* preeminence follows the very telling kinship between Aristotelian *Ethics* and *Politics:* the patterns of analysis in each are not home-grown. They are taken neither from ethical nor from political phenomena. Grasped at their birth, in their home territory, teleocratic representations refer to the substantial changes *artisan man* is capable of effecting. From there Aristotle extends them to all philosophical disciplines. Teleocracy, however, reveals its total sway over thinking and acting only when examined in its historical outcome, contemporary technology. Considering the birth and the apotheosis of teleocracy, Heidegger can say that "the essence of technology" has "remained unthought until now." It will be thinkable only in virtue of a broader, non-teleocratic concept of action. "That all this has remained unthought until now is due primarily to the fact that the will to action, that is to make and be effective, has overrun and crushed thinking."[22]

An acting other than "being effective" and a thinking other than strategical rationality is what Heidegger puts forward under the name of releasement. It is unthought and unthinkable for metaphysics, which remains captivated by teleocratic design. But if such captivity results initially from *technical* phenomena, extrapolated—that is, from a *metabasis eis allo genos*—then it could be said that Western philosophy (and perhaps not only philosophy) has remained the captive of Aristotle's *Physics*.

At what price can substantialist patterns be applied to political phenomena at all? To be sure that a price is involved, let us first see with what right these phenomena can be characterized by the interdependence of actions, words, and things. Let us see, in other words, how politics ceases to be pervious to special, 'disciplinary' discourse when studied through the economies of presence.

An economy is a system. In it, certain variables group themselves and function for a time according to a *nomos*, a law. Since this law is one of interaction, all epochal variables are essentially public. Now the public variable *par excellence* is language. Its primacy was emphasized by Heidegger from the beginning, when his guiding question was that of the meaning—better, the 'sense'—of being.[23] It was restated in another way after his discovery that systems of presence are not unvarying, a discovery that directed his guiding question toward the epochal truth of being.[24] However, the variability of language in accord with epochal systems, as well as the primacy of language in the manifestation of being, was enunciated expressly only in the last writings, when the guiding question had become that of the topology of being: "Man's relation to language could transform itself in a manner analogous to the change in his relation to being."[25]

Language, in its synchronically public and diachronically variable character, is not sufficient to constitute the political domain. By itself, deprived of other speakers whom it addresses and of things that form its subject matter, language opens a phenomenal domain that is not that of the political, but, as I have said, of the text.

Actions in the narrow sense, too, may occur in isolation, without reference to speech and things. The deeds that constitute the highest forms of 'being-with' tend perhaps to remain deprived of speech and performed because of nothing.

Things, finally, can remain non-public for centuries. Theirs is then an ontic absence, excluding them from a given economy.

But when words, actions, and things conjugate in an always provisionary network, an economy of presence comes about. As so constituted, it is public. And since it is the locus where a plurality of agents participate in the discourse and affairs epochally within their reach, an economy so constituted is furthermore political. Understood this way, the political domain excludes none of the variables that form an epoch. It also is in no way discretional, subject to option. Such is at least the case if it is agreed that Heideggerian 'being' is best transcribed as mutual 'presencing', i.e., as the event of phenomena entering into interdependence.

From the topological viewpoint, relative to the loci of presencing, the political is the transcendental opening in which words, things, and deeds find their site, it is the 'locality' (*Ortschaft*) of linguistic, pragmatic, and practical loci. So understood, it obviously escapes disciplinary analysis. It is not a field for one of the traditional branches of philosophy or one of the social sciences. And yet Heidegger does not leave us entirely unequipped for dealing with the organization and exercise of power, the issues handled by political philosophers. This kind of organization and exercise constitutes *ways of responding to historical 'stamps' on presencing*. What the social sciences study are the modes in which a given era corresponds to its epochal principle. The price one pays for such a disciplinary treatment of politics is that the ontological difference—here between 'locality' and 'locus'—disappears from sight. Heidegger understands action entirely in terms of that difference: "All effecting rests in *being* and is directed toward *entities*."[26] All possible efficacy is prescribed by the predominant modality of presencing. Action in the strict teleocratic sense, then, shows itself to be born with the principial economies over which a supreme end reigns. But when the representations of some ultimate end fade, action as the pursuit of goals appears as a 'humanist' delusion. With the withering away of the principles that generate *telē*, action metamorphoses along with the economies. That is the hour when releasement can come into its own—the hour of closure—the hour when principial dispositions yield to anarchic ones. All political efficacy rests in the coordination, which can be either principial or anarchic, of words, actions, and things.

If this phenomenological conception of the political is granted, can one seriously go farther and oppose it to one metaphysical conception, which would in addition rely on a group of premises foreign to their domain of application? For Heidegger, every beginning contains within itself the fullness of the phenomena that will issue from it; thus if political substantialism could be traced to the founder of metaphysics, one might indeed suspect that it holds sway over the entire subsequent era. The opposition between a phenomenological and a metaphysical conception of the political would then boil down to the question: Where does the substantialist framework that Aristotle imposes on his *Politics* originate?

2. Heidegger's attitude toward Aristotle is ambiguous. This holds not only for the notions of *phusis* and *alētheia*.[27] From *Being and Time* onward, Aristotle appears like one whose philosophical breath has been sustained by the question of being, but who has also given to the elaboration of that question a turn that has proved ill-starred. At stake in this ambivalence is

the notion of *hupokeimenon*, of substrate. That, after Aristotle, the question of being "subsides as a thematic question for actual investigation,"[28] is
a consequence of his substantialist conception of being. Aristotle is the first
to have asked explicitly, *ti to on*, what is being? In this sense, Heidegger
claims constant kinship with him. But Aristotle is also the first to have
answered that question by pointing to sensible substance. His ontology is
lodged within the domain *Being and Time* called *Vorhandenheit*, subsistent
being. In this respect, Aristotle instead prefigures and inaugurates the long
errancy that includes even Husserl.

Aristotle's ambivalence transpires in his political philosophy. On the one
hand, he has the merit of criticizing the utopian rigorism of Plato's *Republic* by attacking its source, namely, the conception of an abstract and universal political *eidos*. Aristotle formulates this critique for the sake of a
more empirical doctrine of the city. This fidelity to the phenomena, to the
tode ti, makes "Aristotle's thinking more Greek than Plato's."[29] On the
other hand, however, Aristotle has, as it were, betrayed his own sense of
the phenomena by imposing on the *Politics* the cadre of the four causes,
the principles of natural movement and analogy.[30]

How does the causal theory of nature arise? Could natural causality
impose itself on the mind because before all else man experiences *himself*
as a cause? He fabricates works. Beside these, he observes things that grow
and that he does not fabricate. Nature is a *cause, too*. Could his causal
conception of nature then arise out of his experience of human fabrication,
as a transposition of it? For Heidegger, only because there is a cause of
artifacts—namely, man—has "*phusis* been taken from the outset as
'cause',"[31] as the *other cause*.

There is, then, in Aristotle a double transference of method from the
doctrine of technical motion to that of physical motion and from there to
politics. The affairs of the city are treated genetically, in a manner analogous to natural growth, and in the last analysis, to human fabrication. In all
three domains the question is always one of analyzing the appearance of a
substance. But the imposition of technical and physicist schemata makes it
impossible to say what the political substance is. Here we have the other
Aristotle—the non-Greek Aristotle, the schoolmaster of the West—at his
best. He does not raise the question of the being of the city. At least when
he sets out to apply the four causes to the *polis*,[32] his fidelity to the
phenomena seems to abandon him.

Furthermore, this transference illustrates beautifully how being-moved
becomes "the fundamental mode of being" for Aristotle.[33] He distinguishes
among kinds of entities according to the corresponding kinds of movement:
natural things, τὰ φύσικα (plants, animals, elements), are moved by themselves, whereas ποιούμενα (artifacts) are moved by another.[34] Between the
two, πράγματα (human 'affairs', especially political ones) somehow take up
the middle ground, sometimes approximating the former, sometimes the

latter. In Aristotle, physical kinetics obstructs the phenomenal understanding of what political life is, just as the logic of definition through genus and species—'living' and 'endowed with speech'—obstructs the phenomenal understanding of what man is.

Beneath movements and causes lies the enduring substrate, which Aristotle often confounds with substance.[35] From substance he gains that decisive schema of thinking with whose help the political is made to resemble the physical, the *pros hen* schema.[36] Individual ends and actions are ordered to those of the city, as accidents are to substance and, in general, predicates to the subject. From this 'ontological' priority of the body politic spring the common stereotypes of politics—*Gemeinwohl geht vor Eigenwohl*, public welfare first, private interests next—as well as all corporatisms. The *polis* 'is' in the highest degree, it is 'naturally prior' to the household and the individual. But its supremacy and priority result from the application of general principles borrowed from the *Physics*, among them, the principle of the whole and its parts: "What is posterior in the order of becoming [the city] is prior in the order of nature [the individual]."[37] Correlatively, only what is naturally prior to its parts in this way is self-sufficient. The autarchic individual would have to be either an animal or a god. Now autarchy is precisely the chief trait of substance: "Nothing else is independent [χωριστόν] but substance, for everything is predicated of substance as subject."[38] The legitimation of the city in relation to its constituents is gained by substantialist criteria that belong properly to the analysis of fabrication. It is in *making* things that all acts of the artisan, all materials and 'accidents', must be directed 'toward the one', that is, the finished work. Only on this condition is there technical movement, and only then can the work be complete, independent, 'autarchic'.

Since the very beginning of politics as a branch of philosophy, its basic patterns have been aligned with the branch that studies technical production. The substantialist notion of politics in Aristotle confirms his *Physics* as "the foundational book [*Grundbuch*] of Western philosophy."[39]

Substantialism in politics and the ascendancy of the *Physics* over European philosophy also confirm, indirectly at least, the scope of the 'turning' in Heidegger. As the offspring of Aristotelian substantialism and physics triumph and reach completion in the guise of technology today, a partitioning becomes possible. Like *Sanctus Ianuarius*, thinking can then look forward and backward at the same time. It turns toward the anarchy it prepares, without turning away from the substantialism it deconstructs. The spirit of technology is the god Janus, the spirit of the *ianuae* and the *iani*, doorways and thresholds. The 'turning' traces the line of demarcation between the *pros hen* economy and the manifold economy, between archism and anarchism.

§12. Deconstructing the Ontic Origins

All *poiēsis* always depends on *phusis*. . . .
Human bringing-forth depends on *phusis* as
arising prior to everything else and coming
toward man. *Poiein* takes *phusis* as its
measure, it is *kata phusin*. [It] complies with
phusis and follows its potentials. . . . He,
then, is knowing who brings forth with an
eye on that which emerges out of itself, that
is, which discloses itself.

Heraklit[40]

No reconciliation or synthesis is possible between the *pros hen* economies and the economy that takes *phusis*—the event of *phuein*, presencing—as its only measure. If in "bringing forth" we are simply to follow
"that which emerges out of itself," all archaic constructs have to be deconstructed. More specifically, if in acting we are to espouse only the potential
of "that which discloses itself" as it discloses itself, the epochal principles
must wither away.

Understood through the *pros hen* economies of presence, the political
appears as the domain where the integrative force of one metaphysical
referent—e.g., "the suprasensory World, the Ideas, God, the moral Law,
the authority of Reason, Progress, the Happiness of the greatest number,
Culture, Civilization"[41]—becomes apparent in the conjunction of words,
things, and deeds.[42] An epochally ultimate principle is the *ontic origin* of
such a conjunction. It assigns to 'politics' the extent of its possible efficacy,
the sum of what is achievable in a given moment. What happens when the
lineage of these mortal principles itself becomes extinct? When these principles exhaust their force and when only the potential of *phusis* remains for
us to follow? What happens when man becomes "knowing"?

Action becomes free. What is its freedom? Let us look once more at the
last of the principles, the 'ego' as the final offspring of anthropocentrism or
'humanism', and see how it withers away.

When faced with the task of justifying political phenomena, all the phenomenology of intentional consciousness can do is reduce them to public
interaction of the 'ego'. This is an awkward solution. For Husserl, the
fundament of political phenomena is to be sought in the plurality of the
'ego', in intersubjectivity. It is true that this investigation was actually of
little interest to him;[43] nevertheless, in his view intersubjectivity completes
phenomenology. Only the experience of the alien ego makes the social
world conceivable. That world is properly the objective one for Husserl.
Any association remains impossible unless social constitution emanates
from the transcendental subject. The reduction, applied to another subject,
discovers that it, too, constitutes a unified world of objective meaning; it

discovers it, too, as a transcendental ego. Whatever the inherent difficulties in the constitution of the *alter ego* for Husserl,[44] his avowed goal is to show that the ego ceases to be a monad and phenomenology a monadology if the experience of the other is understood not merely as physical 'presentation', but also as psychic and transcendental 'appresentation'. It must be added, though, that if for Husserl intersubjectivity grounds the specifically social acts through which diverse communities are formed, these acts are, so to speak, purified of any imperative traditionally associated with practical reason.[45] They are no longer acts through which the ego gives itself laws. They are not free in the Kantian sense.

The difficulty in grounding the political is even greater within the parameters of existential phenomenology. The transition from intersubjectivity to the being-there of others (*Mitsein*) amounts to stepping back deliberately from the issue of how collectivities are constituted. In *Being and Time,* this double transcendental regress disarms practical reason. Any *subiectum* that abides below the exchanges within social formations is set off side. Freedom as reason legislating for itself becomes inoperative. The heterogeneity among phenomenal regions—*Dasein*, described by the existentials, and non-*Dasein,* by the categories—makes it impossible to grasp the ego reflectively and establish it as the objective substrate of an organization of the social non-ego, which would itself also be objective. Since existential phenomenology is not a philosophy of reflection, it dislocates the unity of the ego and the self: "I" am eventually someone other than myself, namely "everyone."[46] An egological and reflective phenomenology could still treat the ego as a given fundament for the constitution of a social world. However, for existential phenomenology, the I is never given; therefore it cannot be put to work like an available fundament on which one might rest a theory of civil society and, in the last instance, one of the state. Such theories would provide ontic instantiations of the ontological phenomenology of *Mitdasein*. But there is nothing normative about this phenomenology. It can actually 'ground' opposed political theories, for example, one that exalts the state as the ultimate "ethical substance conscious of itself" (Hegel) as well as one that promotes its dissolution. To say that the existential analytic grounds the political domain can mean only that it exhibits the formal structures obtaining in that domain. But these remain indifferent to the problems of legitimation. Fundamental ontology "founds" only regional ontologies.[47]

The phenomenology that seeks to understand the origin through the breaks in our history discovers no ground of the political in either intersubjective constitution or in existential resolution. When the transcendental a priori is dissociated from subjectivity and being-there, any ground capable of legitimating action is lost.[48] The phenomenology that understands the origin through the ontological difference between presencing and epochal presence has good reason to find itself incapable of assuring the legitimacy of public institutions.

The first of these reasons is methodological. It results from separating the two questions of ground and of origin. As 'presencing' the origin is not a ground, not a fundament. What can function as a basis for the political is a temporary principle (like the 'puma', coupled with the decimal system), but for the phenomenology of presencing, such a fundament is a locus that is not necessarily part and parcel of all economies. Methodologically, anarchy then appears in the transition from fundamental ontology to topology, that is, with the very elaboration of Heidegger's sole question.

The second reason concerns the ontological difference. An epochal principle is something, an inner-worldly entity[49] that has its era. But grounding one inner-worldly entity, for example, the state, on some other inner-worldly entity, an epochal principle, amounts to grounding historical entities upon historical entities, which is to ground nothing at all. To be sure, in many respects what is epochally ultimately present is incomparable to everything else epochally present. The one major referent and the many minor ones are of unequal 'force' (whereas "power" belongs to presencing alone[50]). But in its positivity any datum is ontic, whether it is an object for science,[51] God,[52] a vision of the world,[53] or some other entity. Epochal principles such as "the authority of God or the magisterium of the Church," "the authority of Conscience," "the authority of Reason," "the social Instinct," "historical Progress," "Civilization," "Business,"[54] are ontic referents that can be depicted; and they therefore differ from ontological conditions of possibility.

The third reason phenomenology has to abstain from any discourse about problems of legitimation stems from Heidegger's reformulation of the traditional quest for grounds. He understands any ground as grounding—as a verb, not a noun. A poetic project, to give his favorite example, is "a ground-laying foundation," a deed *ex nihilo*.[55] But such a gesture becomes sterile when successors refer to it as to a principle, claiming: This is how our founding fathers have willed it. . . . The "deed of founding a political state,"[56] too, is a happening without ascendants, perverted by the piety of descendants.

The ground of the political that is to be deconstructed proves to be the *archē* commanding an era, as well as the principle—the first in authority and intelligibility—disposing that era according to an order of coercion. The *archē* as commanding is the *archē* as commencing, but *perverted into a referent*. It is the ontic origin against which the turning works. With the *Kehre*, assuring a fundament for political action becomes literally unthinkable. In this way, topology uproots politics since the soil in which activities are implanted is no longer being-there but historical *alētheia*.[57] The fundamental traits (the categories) that the deconstruction generates are traits of presencing insofar as it is thought of "without regard to its groundedness in entities."[58] The deconstruction allows one to understand *archē* as the happening in which an order, until then buried, hidden, inconceivable, and even unrealizable, comes about. Whenever this happens, the former referent loses its ground-providing, normative force. Once its time is gone by, such a referent vanishes into concealment.[59] It moves out of reach again and loses its force, although in its slow death it remains with us as one ontic principle that once exerted its authority and its coercion.

The deconstruction of the ways presencing has been objectivated into epochal principles so as to serve practical legitimation yields a history of successive ontic fundaments that have "withered away"[60] and have become nothing. Within the course of history, such an absence of any principle of legitimation has at times invaded the political field and for brief lapses, before one ontic origin could replace another, has set action free. To mention some examples that are not Heidegger's: the citizens' unions in North America around 1776, the 'popular societies' in Paris between 1789 and 1793, the Commune of 1871, the soviets of 1905 and 1917, the Democracy of Councils in Germany in 1918—each of these modern efforts to free the public domain from coercive force (analyzed by Hannah Arendt in reference to the American model)[61] marks the end of an epoch. At these moments, the *princeps*—governance—and the *principium*—the system governance imposes and on which it reposes—are suspended for a time. In such caesurae, the political realm appears as the revealer of what the origin that connects words, things, and deeds truly is: not an entity (subject, being-there, or object), nor an *archē* that rules because it begins, nor a principle that dominates a society by organizing it, but the simple event in which all that happens to be present comes to presence. These breaks in our history reveal that the origin 'establishes' nothing: the pair of notions *archē-telos* does not comprise the entire phenomenon of origin, for at these reversals of history the decision is made "to eternalize the absence of a final goal" in action.[62] From such moments of breach it is also clear that the origin grounds nothing, that it is not a supreme reason, an indubitable 'why' from which one can derive maxims: the pair of notions 'principle-derivative' does not exhaust the phenomenon of origin either. The practical abolition of *archē* and of *principium* is the consequence of an understanding of origin that Heidegger refuses to render explicit, since he cuts off after his remark about the rose and life "without why": "We cannot however pursue this thought any further here."[63]

To deconstruct the ontic origins of the political would mean to recover some of the conditions of the Greek *polis* prior to the classical age,[64] that is, before the origin as *phusis*, presencing, came to be objectivated as *archē*, the instituting of what is present. The 'deconstruction' of the political field and the principles established over it at the reversals of history convert into a task for living what the 'destruction' of metaphysical ontologies suggested as a mere task for reading, namely, to prepare a thinking that renounces ultimate referents and "to anticipate the former dawn in the dawn to come."[65]

When it is said that in the age of closure acting becomes free, what is being claimed is not only that action liberates itself from 'principles', but more decisively that it then espouses economic fluctuations expressly as "its highest law." "This [law] is the *freedom* that frees toward the all-playing conjugation of never-resting transmutation,"[66] that is, toward the changing arrangements of historical *alētheia*. Action has always been free in this kind of freedom, in this obedience to the economies. But as long as the economies are principial and epochal, it remains necessarily inconceivable that freedom could be of the same essence as unconcealment, *alētheia*. We have already encountered the name of this strange freedom that gives us little to choose, to will, to legislate, to ordain. It is releasement. To be free is to do what presencing does: let everything be. "Freedom now discloses itself as the letting-be of entities,"[67] as entry into an aletheiological constellation. This freedom has nothing to do with Aristotelian deliberative 'choice', Augustinian 'will divided against itself', Kantian causality and 'moral self-determination', or Sartrian 'fundamental choice in which I decide my being'. All these concepts lodge freedom, if not in a faculty of the mind, at least in man. Such humanist concepts are best summarized by Matthias Claudius: "Free is not he who can do what he wants, but who can will what he ought to do." The anti-humanist concept, on the other hand, grafts freedom within the economic summons (*Geheiss*—more about this later): "The summons sets our essence free. . . . Freedom, therefore, is never something merely human."[68]

Here we have a new form of Parmenidean unity: freedom is the freedom 'of' presencing, in both senses of the double genitive. Seen from the side of *einai* (in modern terms, the object) freedom consists in 'self-disclosure'. Seen from the side of *noein* (in modern terms, the subject), it consists in "hearing" (*hören*) and "belonging" (*gehören*): "The destiny of unconcealing always holds complete sway over man. But it is never the fate of some coercion. Indeed, man becomes free precisely only insofar as he *belongs* to the realm of destiny and thus becomes a *hearer*."[69] The 'turning' can now be described as a retraining of hearing and therefore of allegiance. Under the *epochal* regime, within the metaphysical closure, what we lend our ear and allegiance to is the sway of principles. Beyond that closure, under the *anarchic* regime (if that can be called a regime . . .) we would abide by presencing without recourse to ultimate representations. To become free is to so shift one's attention. For contemporary man, this means discovering that the principles themselves come and go with the "destiny of unconcealing." On the borderline of the closure, allegiance can turn to the withering principles *as withering*.

Where does this opportunity arise from? From technology, double-faced, Janus-like. The text just quoted continues: "Once we open ourselves properly to the *essence* of technology, we find ourselves unexpectedly taken into a liberating claim."[70] The Heideggerian concept of freedom thus denotes more than the "free opening" which is the essence of *alētheia*.[71]

Already in the years of *Being and Time*, Heidegger was saying that "freedom is, and can only be, in liberation. The sole adequate relation to freedom in man is the self-liberating of freedom in man. . . . This liberating of being-there in man must be the sole and central point that philosophy as philosophizing can accomplish."[72] The open field of manifestation—first called *Dasein*, then "epoch of truth"—is that in which any phenomenon 'always already' appears. But it must be expressly set free, which requires certain conditions. They are fulfilled only with the closure. What, then, has obstructed the self-liberating of freedom? Any representation of a metaphysical first. It follows that deconstruction is complete only as a struggle against epochal principles, the *principes* that reign and the *principia* that order.

As a category of identity, freedom is reconciled not only to releasement, but to thinking. "Said plainly, thinking is the thinking of being. What the genitive says is twofold. Thinking is of being insofar as [a] thinking, appropriated [*ereignet*] by being, belongs to it. At the same time, thinking is the thinking of being insofar as [b] thinking, belonging [*gehörend*] to being, listens [*hört*] to it."[73] Likewise, freedom is the freedom 'of' presencing. It is such since (a) "liberation alone is the proper event [*Er-eignis*] of freedom."[74] At the same time, freedom is the freedom of presencing insofar as (b) it belongs to the economic mutations and does not cease to comply with them.

Presencing plays its economies freely, in a "free sequence."[75] Acting is called upon to become free by just that same playfulness, although in the boundary age called technology, to enter the play of freedom means to struggle. It means to liberate the constellations of the political (words, things, and deeds) from any arch-present referent whose rule would freeze them into constant presence.

As it locates the representations of supreme entities within the closure, the deconstruction of the political completes the *assignation to a site,* the 'situation', that the destruction of transmitted doctrines meant to achieve for philosophical texts. Each constellation, like each received ontology, is to be "set free into the freedom of its own essential richness and thereby left to the site to which, of itself, it belongs."[76]

The practical impact of the question of being, its consequence for the question of acting, can be described in terms of origin: if we are to understand being as mere presencing, we will have to turn our allegiance in action away from ontic origins and towards *phuein*, presencing, as what alone is originary. A knowing actor, according to the epigraph to this section, is one who takes his sole measure from what discloses itself. To prepare the terrain for the struggle against all pretensions to arch-presence we have to ask: Precisely which origin is freed by the repeal of epochal principles?

Part Three
The Origin Is Said in Many Ways

Here is what is needed: a new carefulness for language; not the invention of new terms as I once thought, but a return to the original richness of our own language, a language that is constantly dying away.

"An Interview"[1]

A possible answer to the *practical* question, What is to be done? appears, as we have seen, to depend on a preliminary answer to the *economic* question: How do things, actions, and words enter into mutual presence today? Heidegger is more assertive about this preliminary question than about its practical corollary. He suggests that the contemporary mode of economic interrelatedness is one in which the origin as pure presencing can be delivered from the origin as rule; that it is one in which aletheiological freedom can be delivered from our liberties under principial surveillance. Whether as presencing or as principle, the origin is what gives rise to thinking and acting inseverably. But *as presencing* and *as principle* it does not give rise to them in the same way. Anticipatory thinking, which Heidegger hopes merely to prepare, could answer the question, What is to be done? by pointing toward releasement: What is to be done is what presencing always does, let entities be. However, the economic context today does not yet allow for such a serene answer to the question of acting. The phenomenology of technology has to be more modest, or more combative. What is to be done at the age of closure? Set presencing free, prepare releasement, actively liberate ourselves from epochal principles, and make sure that fewer and fewer of them will prevail (see below, Part V).

If Aristotle's *Physics* has indeed remained the "foundational book" of philosophy, then his concept of *archē* is the one that teaches us how the origin has been understood by the mainstream tradition in the West, a tradition which today climaxes in technology. Secondly, once this continuity has been revealed, the origin Heidegger contests—*princeps-principium*—will be more easily described. Lastly, the representations that are to be resisted (like so many obsessions or bad habits) will have to be opposed to *Ursprung*, the origin that is to be retained and set free. These three guiding terms, *archē, principium*, and *Ursprung*, do not translate into one another. In each of the tongues in which it has articulated itself, the origin has been heard differently.[2] It may be a Heideggerian *idée fixe* to trace such πολλαχῶς λέγεται (the many ways something is spoken of) in order to understand presencing as freedom and the deconstruction as the liberating of that freedom. His etymologist *idée fixe*, however, has its advantages. The pair ἄρχειν-ἄρχεσθαι, to rule and to be ruled, expresses quite clearly which thought pattern is bound to wither away at the end of metaphysics. The pair *princeps-principium*, the authoritative and the rational first, exhibits how metaphysics integrates both the organization of life and the order of reasons into a concept of origin in which time is forgotten. And nothing better indicates the "event" than the word *Ursprung*, 'primordial springing forth', which tells us how time is reintroduced into the origin.

VI

ARCHĒ
THE KINETIC PARADIGM OF ORIGIN

> The Greeks usually hear two things in this
> word: on the one hand, ἀϱχή means that
> from which something takes its egress and
> inception; on the other it means that which,
> *as* such egress and inception, at the same
> time reaches beyond whatever emerges from
> it, thereby dominating it. Ἀϱχή means both
> inception and domination inseparably.
>
> "On the Being and Conception of *Phusis*"[1]

The word ἀϱχή seems to have entered philosophical language only with
Plato and Aristotle. Aristotle is the one who explicitly joins the more ancient sense of *inception* with that of *domination*. From the time of Homer,
the common meaning of the verb ἄϱχειν had been "to lead," "to come
first," "to open," for instance, a battle or a discourse.[2] In the epic tradition,
ἀϱχή designates what is at the beginning, either in an order of succession
in time, like childhood, or in an order of constitutive elements, as flour is
the basis of dough or as the organs are the elementary parts of the body.
The other meaning, that of command, of power, of domination, although
absent from Homer,[3] is found in Herodotus and Pindar. Aristotle also uses
the word in this sense.[4] But the Aristotelian innovation consists in uniting
the two senses, inception and domination, in the same abstract concept.[5]
Until the end of antiquity[6] ἀϱχή remains a technical term for designating
the constitutive, abstract, and irreducible elements in being, becoming,
and knowing. The metaphysical concept of ἀϱχή expresses that abstract
structural element in entities which, in their analysis, is *unhintergehbar*,
insurpassable. It is a concept thoroughly linked to the metaphysics of sensible substance and its 'theory'.[7]

§13. The Causal Concept of *Archē*

The concept ἀρχή is probably not an 'archaic'
concept, but one subsequently read back into
the beginnings of Greek philosophy by
Aristotle and later by the 'doxographers'.

"On the Being and Conception of *Phusis*"[8]

Anaximander is said to have taught that "the origin [ἀρχή] and element
of things is the boundless" (or the indeterminate, or the infinite).[9] Identifying the origin with the ἄπειρον, he would have reformulated the debate
about what is primordial in nature. With this innovation, the Aristotelians
opposed Anaximander, it seems, to the other Milesian and Pythagorian
'philosophers of nature'[10]: these others are said to have held that the primordial element composing all things is water, fire, air, or earth, whereas
Anaximander would have claimed that it is the boundless. The philological
issue is: did the Aristotelians present Anaximander as the first thinker of
the ἀρχή or rather as the first thinker of the ἄπειρον? Did Theophrastus
wish to say that Anaximander "was the first to call 'ἀρχή' the substrate of
the opposites,"[11] or rather that he was "the first to name the substratum of
the opposites as the material cause"?[12] If the second reading is correct, it is
not certain that Anaximander used the word ἀρχή at all. It then would
belong properly to the Aristotelian vocabulary. If ἀρχή is therefore the
metaphysical concept of a beginning that simultaneously 'commands', what
then do the Aristotelians have Anaximander say? First of all, they make
him a philosopher. Indeed, according to Aristotle the task of the philosopher is to investigate the ἀρχαὶ καὶ αἰτίαι,[13] commonly translated as "the
principles and causes." Then they attribute to him claims about the genesis
and corruption of things, that is, about becoming. They read him as a
philosopher of nature. His concept of *archē* would be physicalist. Things
come to be, they say, out of one constitutive element that Anaximander
calls the boundless. This element is an *archē* because it is the permanent,
irreducible substrate of things: they emerge from it, and they remain ruled
by it. For a mind schooled by Aristotle, *archē* means both that out of which
becoming develops and that which rules it.[14] All of this teaches us a great
deal about the classical idea of *archē* but may render Anaximander nearly
inaccessible.[15]

What now is the guiding meaning of *archē* in the three domains—being,
becoming, knowing—in which, according to Aristotle, it is operative? In
being, it is substance that begins and commands everything 'adventitious'
to it. Aristotle explicitly establishes the equivalence between *ousia* and
archē.[16] In becoming, the *archai* are the causes.[17] Finally, in knowledge
they are the premises on which cognition depends. If first philosophy is to
be possible it has to proceed from a prescience of the universal conditions
from which syllogisms draw science. All knowledge supposes a more origi-

nary knowledge. All demonstration starts with a hypothesis. What then is the ultimate presupposition? The origin of first philosophy would be the science of the universal, a science that is sought for but impossible to establish.[18]

However, in Aristotle the analysis of being, as well as that of knowledge, derives from the observation of change in sensible substance. As we have seen, what strikes the mind in the Greek classical age is that there is becoming, and first of all a becoming of which man is the author and master. Both metaphysics and logic derive from the astonishment before what our hands can make out of some material. In Heidegger's view, the guiding meaning in Aristotle's concept of origin results neither from speculation about being nor from the logic of knowledge, but from the analysis of becoming that affects material things. This is why in the *Physics*, the *Grundbuch*, previous thinkers could appear only as physicalists. "Aristotle himself is properly the author of the process which consists in seeking the metaphysical way of thinking—which begins only with Plato and himself—earlier in the thought of the pre-Platonic thinkers."[19]

The formulations of the Milesians and the Pythagoreans now appear as so many groping attempts to discover the notion that hylemorphism could finally identify in appropriate terms: the science of nature henceforth is able to term 'material cause' that origin of things that Anaximander had called 'boundless'. That way it also becomes understandable that Simplicius could speak of the *apeiron* as *hupokeimenon*:[20] the doctrine of the origin, as the Aristotelians believed they had found it in Anaximander, is the doctrine of a material substrate from which things arise in order to return to it as to their primordial element. This same substrate rules them for as long as the 'boundary' lodges them within the 'boundless'. Such is the double Aristotelian sense of *archē*, inception and domination, as the tradition applies it "forward and backward" from Plato and Aristotle.[21] It is decisive for our general concern to have established that the *concept* of *archē*—the philosophical technical term—is not more ancient than Attic philosophy.

How much of genuine attention to the phenomena and how much metaphysical construction is there in the Aristotelian notion of *archē*? If the origin immediately appears as ἀρχὴ τῆς κινήσεως, origin of movement, then it essentially designates the trait common to the four causes. The alliance between the notions of inception and domination is possible only *once the metaphysics of the causes is constituted*. Once it is understood that phenomena as a whole are knowable from the viewpoint of causality, then it can be said that a true cause is only that which begins its action "and never ceases to begin it,"[22] that is, a cause that also commands. In this way Heidegger links the fate of the concept of *archē* to the constitution of the metaphysics of causes.[23] It is true that in developing a threefold causality in being, becoming, and knowing, parallel to the theory of the four causes, Aristotle recognizes a diversity of phenomenal regions. Nevertheless, it is always the *archē,* says Heidegger, that constitutes "the internal link between the triple and quadruple division of the *aitia,* as well as the reason why the foundation of these different divisions fails to appear."[24]

What is the field of phenomena to which causality is appropriate, what is its home territory? What is the purview of causality? As I have said, with Heidegger the category of causality is germane for making *things in motion* intelligible, whether they are moved by man or by nature. In the terminology of *Being and Time,* the field of phenomena to which the scheme of causality is applicable is that of subsistent entities, of objects. But there are other fields: tools, people, works of art, etc. The phenomenology born of hermeneutics tells us that all of these let themselves be 'interpreted', but not 'explained' by causes. Causal explanation is one mode of understanding among others, although this mode has maintained its hegemony over Western philosophy. Liberating the phenomenological nucleus from the Aristotelian conception of the origin will require that inception and domination be understood otherwise than as the essential traits of the causes and of causality. It will require that the *archē* be disengaged from causal representations.

To deconstruct phenomenologically the received concepts of origin means first of all to dismantle the discourse about *archē* as a quest for causes. At the same time, the deconstruction of Aristotelian physics will make Anaximander's thought appear in a problematic that is not physicalist. If such deconstruction were to reveal that Anaximander, Heraclitus, and Parmenides did not think the origin as *archē*—as *incipit* and *regimen* of observable movement—a first hint of a non-metaphysical thought of origin would be gained. Situating the causal concept of origin will make it possible to recapture indirectly the primal elements fused in the classical concept of *archē.*

According to Aristotle's *Physics,* material things in becoming are of two species: those that bear the origin of their movement in themselves and those that are moved by another. The former are 'natural' in the strict sense, the latter are man-made. But where does such a distinction come from? What is the disjunctive factor between 'moved by themselves—moved by man'? The *tertium comparationis* is movement, change, as such. As such? Is it some ideal representation that has made the quest for origin into a quest for causes? Or is it rather one very precise experience, namely, that of the movement and change initiated by us, which switched classical thought onto the track of causal explanations? In that case, it is only because man first grasps himself as archi-tect, as initiator of fabrication, that nature can in turn appear to him as moved by the mechanisms of cause and effect. Growth, *too,* "begins" and "makes."[25] Because the artisan experiences the origin of production as indigenous to himself, he finds another such origin in nature, concordant with although allogeneous to his own. The experience that guides the comprehension of origin as it is operative in the 'philosophy of nature' is paradoxically the experience of fabricating tools and works of art, the experience of handiwork. In this way the Aristotelian tradition divides the totality of things into those moved by human hands and those moved by themselves.[26]

The most viable way of conducting the deconstruction of Aristotle's physics so as to return back beyond his concept of *archē* is to examine the scope of his 'kinetic' understanding of nature. It does not appear to be coextensive with his concept of *phusis*. A residual factor remains once natural things are opposed to man-made things, and once these two species are combined under the common genus 'moved things'. The specific differences, 'physical' and 'technical' movement, do not exhaust the phenomena that Aristotle calls natural. What is that residual factor that makes *phusis* in the strict sense—as complementary to *technē*—remain a derivative notion in Aristotle? He owes this residual factor, Heidegger says, to his speaking Greek: in spite of the predominance of manipulable and manufactured objects in his understanding of being, he occasionally still takes *phusis* in the sense of its verbal root as coming forth, presencing. In those cases the fabricative viewpoint of 'making present' recedes behind emergence into presence—behind the presencing of plants as well as of handiwork. In such texts the distinction between two types of *archē* disappears because the kinetic pre-understanding of nature disappears. The word *archē* does not occur in the passages where *phusis* recalls the verb *phuein*, 'presencing' or 'coming to presence'.[27]

The origin as inception and domination is derived from that more primal 'verbal' understanding, which is preserved even in Latin (*oriri*—origin; *nasci*—nature). As a speaker of Greek, Aristotle cannot but keep alive, as if in spite of himself, a trace of the Presocratic understanding of the origin as the event of *phuein,* with its connotation of showing-hiding.[28] But this intermittent allegiance to his predecessors fades in the texts and more so in the tradition, to the advantage of the link between physics and the search for causes. The cognitive interest expressed in the question Why? ties the philosophic career of the concept of *archē* to the science of things constantly present. "Ἀρχή is not a guiding concept for being. Rather this term is derived from the originary Greek determination of being."[29]

§14. The Teleocratic Concept of *Archē*

Ὁ τέκτων is the pro-ducer, the one who
brings forth and who brings into position—
'forth' toward unconcealment and 'into' the
open. This pro-duction that brings forth is
what man accomplishes, e.g., in building,
carving, shaping. In the word 'architect' lies
ὁ τέκτων. From the architect as the ἀρχή of
a τεκεῖν something emanates like in a project, and it remains guided by him: for
instance, the pro-duction of a temple.

Heraklit[30]

Another way of conducting the deconstruction of the kinetic notion of *archē* is to locate its antonym, *telos*. In which region of phenomena do we speak of ends to be realized?

As the text cited in the epigraph indicates, *archē* and *technē* (or the corresponding verb, *tekein*) belong together. The *telos*, the end in which a process reaches completion, primarily determines neither our relations with others, nor those with a work of art—except, precisely, in its production. Here again the 'technical' character of the problematic of *archē* is obvious since the *telos* is what the architect perceives before setting to work and what guides him throughout the construction. A craftsman possesses *technē*, know-how, if he does not lose sight of the initially perceived idea and if he is an expert in conforming the material at hand to it. The notion of *technē* is therefore a "cognitive concept."[31] It indicates that one knows how to render present in the product an end seen in advance. Ends of fabrication are realized with manipulable stock. Anything, to be sure, may turn into such manipulable stock, and it may well be that, because of the exclusive emphasis on fabrication since the beginnings of Western metaphysics, everything has in fact become just that. However, the notion of *telos*, like that of *archē*, has its legitimate purview only over things given for handling. 'Technical' knowledge is that which fixes an *eidos*, which lays hands on it. With the pair, *archē* and *telos*, 'pro-ducing' definitively ceases to mean 'bringing forth into the open' and henceforth coincides with 'fabricating', with the work of leading an *eidos* to complete visibility.

"The εἶδος must stand in view beforehand, and this appearance selected in advance—εἶδος προαιρετόν—is the end, τέλος, that of which τέχνη has know-how."[32] When the product is 'finished', it will be visible, set before the gaze that first was set on the idea. In this way, the end of becoming is its incipience: marble will not become a temple unless at the outset the architect grasped the appearance, the shape, to be conferred on it. When the artifact presents itself 'in its end' (ἐν-τελέχεια), when it stands fully 'in work' (ἐν-έργεια), the εἶδος will have reached constant presence.

Aristotle understands becoming as the process by which the *eidos* is rendered entirely and durably visible. A thing is in becoming to the extent that its *eidos* is en route toward constant presence. The why or wherefore (οὗ ἕνεκα) of any becoming is the completed piece of work: "the end is the work."[33] The end of the architect's craft is the finished building. In the metaphysic of origination it is quite natural that, as Aristotle holds, the finished piece of work is better than the activity through which it was produced. The good is the product, not the production. To commit a thing to becoming is to commit its 'idea' to exposure: it is led to exhibit permanently what it is in itself, its 'form'. This visible availability of the *eidos* or the *morphē* is the good toward which manufacturing tends under its numerous guises. When it has reached visible permanence, the thing has taken full possession of its *eidos*. "This is why the word ἐνέργεια is derived from 'work' (ἔργον) and refers to full possession of the end (ἐντελέχεια)."[34]

When the product has its 'final aspect', it is a work, it stands firmly and constantly in its end.

In this way Aristotle's identification of *archē* with *telos* loses some of its oddity. "Everything that comes to be moves toward an ἀρχή, that is, a τέλος; in fact, that for the sake of which a thing is, is its ἀρχή, and becoming is for the sake of its τέλος."[35] Considered in itself, movement does not yet possess its end. It is *a-teles*, "it appears as a kind of standing-in-the-work, but as not yet come to its end."[36] Like the Platonic *eros*, becoming is the child of poverty and invention: it is deprived of its end, and it invents the *energeia* to reach it. But if the end is not already given at the starting point as *hou heneka* (the 'wherefore'), there will be no becoming at all.

The language in which Aristotle treats the 'end' in the *Metaphysics* lends itself to confusion since *energeia* sometimes designates the entelechy,[37] sometimes the progress toward the entelechy. This ambiguity is lifted in the *Nichomachean Ethics* by the distinction between *poiēsis* and *praxis*.[38] In *poiēsis* (making), setting to work precedes the work as constructing precedes the edifice. But in *praxis* (acting), setting to work is itself the end. Therefore there are two sorts of *telē*: "some are activities (*energeiai*), others are works (*erga*) distinct from the activities that produce them."[39] The latter lie outside the maker, and thus the *energeia* is incomplete. Only the former are in the agent itself, and the *energeia* there is 'autarkic', self-sufficient. But even though Aristotle considers acting superior to making,[40] the vocabulary of end as well as the word *energeia*, coined by him, show that here again the paradigmatic scheme for understanding *archē* and *telos* is production. The notion of *archē*, then, proves to be generally kinetic and more specifically technical. The primacy of production appears clearly in the texts where the distinction between the end extrinsic to fabrication and the end intrinsic to action is not yet drawn:[41] the view set on the *eidos* is 'dominated' by the *telos* for as long as the latter is not achieved, as long as it lies ahead to be pursued. But once Aristotle, as he does in the *Nichomachean Ethics*, draws the distinction between practical and poietic ends, then the element of domination is no longer decisive for praxis, and the end of an action becomes immanent to that action.[42] *Telos* 'reigns', 'commands', and therefore exercises the function of *archē* only in the case of sensible substance. Aristotle's discovery of teleocracy is native to the field of fabrication. And that is where it should stay. That magistrates, kings, and tyrants are named under the same rubric as the architectonic arts can confuse only a modern mind. For Aristotle, political domination is but one instance of the domination that appears "especially"[43] in the know-how of the architect. The teleocratic frame of reference applies to action to the extent that action is still seen as a becoming: magistrates 'move' the city because they are themselves 'moved' by the idea that is its end. This is why architecture is the paradigmatic art: the anticipation of end through which Aristotle comprehends the origin is observed most clearly in construction. The finished building is the achieved end, and achievement as process is ruled by the 'foreseen' end, by the finished aspect of the product as precognized. How, then, does *archē* dominate? In anticipating *telos*. Fabrication is the case κατ' ἐξοχήν in which anticipation of the end rules over becoming. The gist of Western philosophy is thus a metaphysics of handiwork (literally, of manufacture, of *manu facere*, making by hand) that traces the displacements of the idea. 'Archically' beheld in the vision of the artificer, the idea is then imprinted on available material, and lastly it offers itself to everyone's inspection in the finished artifact. The *telos* "does not put an end to the thing; rather out of [the *telos*], the thing *begins* to be what, after production, it will be."⁴⁴

Before Aristotle conceived of the origin as what begins and commands production—whether human or natural—the Greeks do not seem to have understood the origin as located in the phenomenal region of the maneuverable. The fragment from Anaximander cited above speaks of *genesis*, 'generation', and of *phthora*, 'decline'. If in these words Anaximander meant to say something about *phusis*, one may doubt that he wished to compare the generation and corruption of living things to the process of fabrication. And if, in writing about generation and decline in 'nature', he had in mind the origin of that process, he can hardly have thought of it on the model of causality. Having escaped the obligatory training in the *Grundbuch* of Western philosophy, his mode of thinking in all probability was far from 'archeo-logical' and may rather have been 'an-archical'. Compared to Aristotle's understanding of origin, that of the Presocratics did not amount to conceptually fixing an *eidos* that initiates and rules sensible substances. For the pre-Attic mode of thinking, it seems, the origin appeared as simple presencing, as coming to presence, and in that sense as an-archic. If 'presencing', 'coming about', 'emerging' (*genesis*) are the words that best describe the origin in its pre-metaphysical sense, it can only elude all representations connected with the *archē* of things in motion. It is dislodged from the site of maneuverable objects. Regarding its two classical features, inception and domination, the first can be seen as an echo of presencing; but with Heidegger's return to pre-classical thinking, the notion of domination loses its central place in philosophy.

The Aristotelian concept of *archē* proves to be as ambiguous as that of *phusis*.⁴⁵ The example of the artisan is paradigmatic for both. And yet Aristotle is far from identifying *archē* with *homo faber*. *Archē* designates what man must never lose sight of when he fabricates, and only in that sense does it prelude what will become metaphysical humanism.⁴⁶ What dominates becoming in fabrication and even in public administration is not man, but the idea. In all phenomenal domains—art, science, becoming, being—some universal starts off and commands a concrete process. The *archē* is not an entity, human or divine; in this, as I have said, Aristotle remains faithful to his predecessors. Nor is the notion of *archē* onto-theological yet;⁴⁷ it does not designate a supreme being that creates and governs change, but only the common trait of the different types of causes.

Is metaphysics then the generalization of modes of thought appropriate to only *one* region of phenomena—artifacts? Is it ultimately by such an unwarranted extrapolation that Aristotle answers the question, 'What is being?' Does his answer, the science of the composition of sensible substances and of the changes that affect them, arise from such a sweeping *metabasis?* It would seem so, inasmuch as 'to be moving', 'changing', 'becoming', mean for him first of all 'to be fabricated'. In this way, we glimpse how the reversal of history sets in which will place first a divine, then a human constructor in the position of origin. What anticipates onto-theological and onto-anthropological doctrines, in which the origin figures as the predicate of one entity, is the novel concept—if not the word—*archē* in Aristotle.

VII

PRINCEPS AND PRINCIPIUM
TIME FORGOTTEN

> We do not give a thought to find out where
> something like axioms, principles and first
> propositions may occur at all, where they
> dwell, where they stem from. Principles—
> that seems to be a matter of reason.
>
> *Der Satz vom Grund*[1]

Principium translates the Greek ἀρχή into Latin. From Cicero[2] to Leibniz,[3] the Latin term is an integral part of the metaphysics of causes and in this respect faithfully renders the orientation provided by Aristotle's *Physics*. But from Cicero to Leibniz, the meaning of this word does not remain invariable.[4] More puzzling, the 'principle of sufficient reason' formulated by Leibniz[5] itself contains a remarkable difficulty. In the phrase *principium rationis sufficientis*, it is not the word *principium* that translates ἀρχή; it is the word *ratio*: "nothing is without reason," *nihil est sine ratione*. The "principle of reason" then seems to amount to a simple tautology: "principle of the ἀρχή," "principle of the principle." From the ἀρχή as primordial element constitutive of sensible substances, we have passed to *principium* as evident proposition[6] from which other propositions derive that are not evident themselves. Leibniz is telling us of a proposition about the *archē*: everything, he says, has a principle (understood as *archē*), such is my great principle (understood as first and evident proposition). If this ambiguity is confronted clearly, it will suggest a transition of quite different dimensions than the shift from the Greek to the Latin cultural world. The embarrassment of translating one metaphysical notion by another metaphysical notion may reveal an *embarment*, an enclosure within bars, in which the metaphysics of origin remains confined in general. The overdetermination of the Latin concept *principium*, if it is topologically deconstructed, will reveal something about the manner in which the origin manifested itself in the epoch of Latin philosophy. At the close of that epoch, the *principium* becomes a law of the mind. The 'first from which' things arise and are ruled is then a first truth conceived by reason and formulated as a premise. The overdetermination that progressively restricts the *archē* until it finally appears as a self-evident law indicates a history of presence, a history of the origin as presencing. Things come to presence otherwise when the *principium* is God[7] than when it is a proposition.

The phenomenological deconstruction of this history aims at 'reducing' the rule of principles to modalities of presence. As far as Leibniz's principle is concerned, we can then "hear the principle of ground in a twofold way: either as the supreme proposition about entities, or as an address from being"[8]—that is, either as logical principle or as epochal principle.

§15. From the Principle of Essences to the Principle of Propositions

> The ground demands that it be manifest
> everywhere in such a way that in the domain
> of that claim everything appears as a sequent,
> that is to say, that everything must be
> represented as a consequence.
>
> *Der Satz vom Grund*[9]

The complementary notion to *archē* is *telos;* that to "principle" is something entirely different, namely, the sequent, the consequence, the derivative, the "issue."[10] As the concept of origin changes its linguistic milieu, it also changes its strategy. Origination still means inception and domination; no longer, however, of a becoming, but of a hierarchical order. To be sure, the model for such an order is found in Aristotle himself.[11] But to say *principium* instead of *archē* is to extend the order of derivatives beyond the simple case of substance and accidents. In this way, the 'principle' comes to designate the supreme cause of all things.[12] Therefore, there are innumerable instantiations of an order constituted by a principle and its derivatives: a law of reasoning is called principium,[13] and so are the foundation of a science,[14] a norm for conducting life,[15] a law of the collective or individual unconscious,[16] and still many other variations of the modern "principle of all principles," namely, "absolute subjectivity."[17]

These are just so many "punctuations"[18] in the phenomenological deconstruction of the doctrines of the origin. Two key texts especially testify to the transition toward order: the first paragraphs of Duns Scotus's *Treatise on God as First Principle* and a few short paragraphs in Leibniz's *Monadology*. At the medieval apogee of Latin thought in Scotus, the order derived from a first is an order of entities receiving their cohesion from the divine substance; at the close of the Latin epoch in Leibniz, it is an order of propositions receiving their coherence from human subjectivity.[19]

What do we call a consequence, an 'issue'? Surely an effect, a resultant, something that comes after. After what? Precisely after the *principium*—

after that which, as the word indicates (*id quod primum cepit*), took hold or 'caught on, first'; after that which 'comprehends' eminently and which, in this way, occupies the first place in an order of ranks or grades.[20] The features of the medieval notion of *principium* relevant for the phenomenological deconstruction of the metaphysics of origin are not proper to the Scotist school. But in Scotus this notion, because he understands it as reciprocal to order and dependence, appears as the very model of the medieval understanding of origin in which time is negated, left out, forgotten.

The treatise begins with an invocation: "May the first principle of things grant me to believe, to understand and to reveal what may please his majesty."[21] It could not be clearer: the origin is his divine majesty. But why does Scotus call God 'principle'? Certainly there are the Johannine tradition and Arabic resonances[22] in this term; but the properly philosophic reasons for conceiving the origin as principle only appear in the way Scotus puts this concept itself to work. In the lines that follow, he defines the "principle" by its correlate, "essential order."[23] As it was for the Greeks, the origin is origin 'of' something. Becoming follows *archē*, but order follows *principium*. The eclipse of time occurs with the replacement of the Greek term for 'origin' by the Latin.

The order as understood by Scotus has its model in Aristotelian metaphysics, not as a metaphysic of becoming, but rather one of predicamental analogy.[24] Wherever there prevails an order, the manifold is referred to a first. Analogy in predication excludes pure and simple diversity. The order *begins* when a principle *commands*. This is the way substance imposes its order on accidents and God, in the metaphysics of Scotus, his order on entities. For there to be an order in the manifold, its constituents must not only be referred to one focal point, but that focal point must also be heterogeneous to the components. Otherwise there would not be any ordering at all. Strictly speaking, when the manifold is related to a first in this way, only the derivate should be called an order. Hence the following subdivision: "The primary division of essential order appears to be . . . into the order of eminence and the order of dependence."[25] What is the criterion for such a disjunction? "The prior according to nature and essence can exist without the posterior."[26] The relations of accident to substance can be applied to the created and its cause—a widening of perspective that would undoubtedly have plunged Aristotle into deep perplexity—inasmuch as in both cases, the pole of ordination subsists by itself, and what is ordered toward it subsists only through that pole. If the language of order also applies to the "first principle of things" *in itself*, this can only be in a sense unknowable for us, properly pre-eminent. To speak of order will be, for us, to speak of the order of dependence: the world is ordered toward God, but God is not a part of that order. He is not ordered toward the world. He is eminent, that is, heterogeneous to the order whose principle he is. The concept of *ordo dependentiae* in Scotus is therefore more rigorous than that of *ordo essen-*

tialis, which represents the principle and its derivate, the world, as two members placed in relation within one and the same set.

To speak of an "essential" order is to say that the relations ruling it are neither accidental nor unreal. Every metaphysical order is a system of relations; and every metaphysical relation consists of a 'subject', a 'terminus', and a 'foundation'. The change in firmness undergone by a piece of wax in my hand is 'essentially' ordered toward the warmth of my palm. The wax remains soft only as long as it is exposed to my body heat. An accidental relation is, for example, a son's dependence on his father. If the father dies, the son can nevertheless continue to live. In the first case, the subject and the terminus are linked by a *real foundation,* warmth; in the second case, by a *foundation of reason,* descent, even though the son is 'posterior' to the father and owes his existence to him.[27]

An essential order, now, is a system of relations with their starting points in numerous subjects, referring them all to a single terminus and based on a real foundation. Scotus calls this foundation a *res,* a thing.[28] It is not a third term, but the *ad* that inclines the subjects toward the terminus. The foundation, the viewpoint common to the subjects and to the terminus, is located in the form[29] and "naturally"[30] orients things to God. The Aristotelian metaphysics of relation was limited to the πρὸς τί by which a property is referred to a substance.[31] In the theistic speculation of Scotus, on the other hand, entities are related to something that precedes them as substances, either because it is their cause,[32] or because it is more universal and more simple.[33]

It is true that in Aristotle the ten categories, taken together, form an order. Substance is a principle of order: as the cause of accidents, it fulfills one and the same role in regard to them, that is, to maintain them in being; substance is furthermore part of their order since it functions as the first of the categories, and it transcends their order since they do not in turn cause it to be; it also orients and gives coherence to all predicaments; finally it founds an order that is not only logical but real, based on observation. Nevertheless, Aristotle's empiricism does not allow one to conceive a relation grounded in *ousia* itself. This is precisely the leap taken with the Scotist notion of essential order.

In an essential order the three constituents of relation are, then, introduced, as it were, into the very core of entities: the subjects are substances; the principle, as we just saw, is their cause, one and simple; and the reference itself is rooted, not in some secondary element of things, but in their being. If that element, the being that things have in common with their principle, were not identical everywhere—although differentiable— the order would lack unity. If that element were identical without being differentiated in the subjects and in the terminus, each subject would play the role of terminus, and there would be no unity either. That element is therefore the analogical foundation of the order, its common ground as it is encountered both in things and in the principle. Being analogical, it is by the same token the disjunctive criterion between the principle and the constituents: the latter possess it only partially, while the principle possesses it infinitely. It is true that Scotus conceives the essence, the ultimate foundation of order, as univocal. This univocity applies however only to the logical concept of essence. Heidegger observes that "unlike the domain of reality, that of logic is not analogical, but univocal."[34] Essence is logically one, but ontologically graded.[35] As such it is the milieu where things refer to God as to their principle and where the principle terminates that reference. In other words, all things are diverse modalities or states[36] of the essence that properly belongs to the principle alone. We need no more than the notion of principle together with its complement, the order of dependence, to see what understanding of the origin results from such creationist metaphysics. It is a concept of origin that clearly stresses the element of domination over the element of inception,[37] or constant presence over time: the enduring principle 'makes' the order.

In Aristotle, where the origin is understood in the context of *human* making, the elements of inception and of domination in *archē* balance each other. Production is a becoming over which *telos* reigns, perceived from the start as *archē*. But medieval problematics like that of essential order immobilize creative becoming, fixating it as *gubernatio mundi*, divine world-government. With the stress on order, the *Pantocrator* gets the upper hand over the Creator. The metaphysic of principle and of its derivative, the essential order, instates as supreme ruler the *archē* discovered in movement. Such a metaphysic invests the origin as a *princeps*, prince and governor. For Aristotle, analysis of change had to turn into a discourse on origin because changing meant approaching full possession of the idea. In the Middle Ages the origin is still construed from the perspective of change, but as its opposite. The origin is the absolute opposed to all contingents. To be sure, from *archē* as the anticipation of *telos* to 'principle' as the anticipation of 'terminus', the form of thought remains the same. But notice the implications of the transition from Aristotle to medieval Aristotelianism as enunciated at the start of the Scotist treatise: speculation on the world-order and on its divine principle displaces the question of origin. Aristotle spoke of *archē* in three domains: being, becoming, and knowing. In truth, however, as I have said, he applied to both being and knowing a notion of origin belonging strictly only into the domain of becoming. The analysis of becoming, Heidegger writes, was "the most difficult task for thinking in the entire history of Western metaphysics,"[38] precisely because it freed the ground for metaphysical developments until our own day, laying the foundations for the still predominant understanding of truth. But Duns Scotus—and in this respect he is representative of medieval philosophy as an epoch—grasped the kinetic analysis not only as having become metaphysical, that is, embracing all phenomena, but also as enriched by the dogma drawn from Exodus.[39] The transition from the categorial order, in which the principle is sensible substance, to the essential order, in

which the principle is divine substance (even though in itself unknowable[40])
is therefore not simply some innocent expansion of the πρὸς ἓν λεγόμενον.
Seemingly continuing the schemes of thought derived from observation, it
amounts to a new epochal position. This displacement further reifies the
origin. It also elicits "the illusion that the transformation proceeding from
the essential beginning of metaphysics preserves its genuine assets while at
the same time progressively developing them."[41]

If by the genuine assets is meant the metaphysic of causality, then the
transmutation of thought patterns declares itself magnificently in Duns
Scotus. Measured by that metaphysic, the essential order appears as an
order of causes. It is a network of secondary causes which are connected
more or less closely to the first cause, the principle, and which receive
from it their causal character. Here again Scotus makes use of a revealing
term: *primitas*, primacy. He introduces this term when attempting to reduce the different types of causes to the first nature, from which they
emanate as the 'producible' emanates from the 'productive'. Whereas the
principle is productive without being produced itself, the causes are *pos-
terius effectivae*—both produced by the principle and productive of effects
more remote from it. "In the threefold essential order, the threefold primacy of efficacy, finality, and eminence inheres in some one and the same
actually existing nature."[42] From the producibility of things, the medieval
mind passes to the idea of productivity; then, from the multiplicity of what
is productive—from the many secondary causes—to the unicity of an entity
that is productive by itself. From an Aristotelian starting point—all that
moves is moved either through itself or through another—Scotus and his
fellow scholastics conclude with a first that is not only a mover, but the
cause *omnimoda*. The essential order joins two types of causes: the many
'essentially ordered causes' and the one 'cause in itself'. The principle is
therefore one that has primacy in the causal order. This is why, in his
reasoning about origin, Scotus must speak of *primitas*. The principle has
causal primacy insofar as it empowers everything capable of causation.
With Scotus, the metaphysic of causes thus undergoes a transmutation, a
displacement from substance to creation. Nonetheless, it remains confined
within the phenomenal region of subsistent entities. Still more, in identifying the origin with what is most productively present, scholastic metaphysics settles within that region more resolutely than any other.[43] From the
origin as *archē* in bringing about constant presence, to the origin as *principium* in ordering the constantly present, *absence* disappears from
thought. Aristotle may not have thought absence as *lēthē*,[44] but he at least
recognized the absence of *eidos* in becoming. For him the very essence of
becoming is inducing an absent *eidos* to render itself present according to
"the number of motion in respect of before and after."[45] The forgetting of
absence and of time in the later metaphysic of order shows with great
clarity what the medieval understanding of the origin neglects when compared to its Greek understanding and what it retains from it: it neglects

inception for the sake of retaining pure domination. It loses sight of the origin as *incipit,* as the event of nascency, in order to fix its speculative gaze on the origin as pure *regnat,* as rule and dominion by a 'prince'—in Scotus's words, by "his majesty."

This is so because, in spite of the rediscovery of Aristotle in the thirteenth century, the locus where the origin can show itself as both inception and domination—human fabrication—has lost its paradigmatic role in the constitution of knowledge. Another site now functions as the center of things knowable and renders fabrication and know-how secondary, derivative. The domain from which the medievals understand the origin is no longer man-made change, but *gubernatio mundi,* the government the supreme entity exercises over things.

In such a representation of a first, what is to be retained is how the idea of a *primum* or a *princeps* (the Pantocrator of the Christians, or the 'puma' of the Incas) is linked to the idea of *principium* (the metaphysic of relation for Duns Scotus, the decimal system for the Incas); how the speculative mind passes without any apparent break from the hierarchy of entities to the hierarchy of propositions; how, at the close of the Latin era, the origin can appear, no longer primarily as substantive, a supreme agent, but as rational, a supreme proposition; how, in short, the passage from Duns Scotus to Leibniz only illustrates the double phenomenal content of the origin understood as principle—rule of a sovereign entity and rule of an evident truth.

§16. From the Principle of Propositions to the Epochal Principles

> It is only about to occur to man that he
> stands and moves in the wake of the principle
> of reason.
>
> *Der Satz vom Grund*[46]

The new reversal in history, by which the essential order dominated by a *princeps* is replaced by the logical order dominated by a *principium,* is best reflected in Leibniz's *Monadology.* Henceforth, to speak of a principle no longer means to follow the course of a kinetic trajectory nor to follow the lead of a religious transmittal. Rather, it means to confine oneself to the realm in which human knowledge is the principal, the principial, problem. This is not to say that, for Aristotle or the medievals, knowledge did not arise as a philosophical issue. However, the displacement of paradigmatic fields becomes obvious if we inquire about the manner in which, prior to modernity, knowledge was an issue for itself. In Aristotle knowledge becomes problematic insofar as know-how, τέχνη, 'accuses' (κατηγορεῖν) the visible traits of a present entity; after Leibniz, on the other hand, it be-

comes problematic through an examination of judgments and their forms.[47]
If for Aristotle the exemplary region from which the guiding intuitions of
philosophy emanate was physics, and for the Medievals religion, for Leibniz and those after him it is logic. Principles are henceforth something
posited by the mind. A principle is the starting point, the origin, of an
argument. As a 'premise' (*prae-mittere*, to send on ahead) it is 'put before'
other truths which impose themselves as consequences. Modern subjectivity posits principles and so sets the foundation for everything knowable.
The phenomenology of the reversals of history is capable of describing the
epochal *horizon* within which the subject can thus turn back upon itself.[48]

Leibniz, too, certainly means to establish that the world, such as it
exists, has its origin in God. But how does the mind assure for itself the
principial function of that first? God is the sufficient reason of this world, its
explanatory *ratio*.[49] Materially, the *Monadology*, like medieval ontotheol-
ogy, remains quite theocentric. Formally, however, it is centered on an
order other than that of essences. Leibniz clearly states that without his
principium magnum, without the principle of sufficient reason, we would
never be able to demonstrate the existence of God. To answer the question, What is the origin? it is no longer enough simply to point to the *ens
originarium*. An overarching principle is needed that leads the mind to that
primary entity. The difficulty might be settled by claiming that the principle of sufficient reason is first in the order of discovery, but that God
remains first in the order of foundation, or of the possible; in other words,
that God supremely realizes this principle, that as the living God he is this
principle which is only the abstract formulation of his concrete being. But
the turn toward modernity is more incisive. The domain that gains priority
with the rationalists is that of propositions and their legitimacy. In a sense
the principle of sufficient reason rules over God himself. The origin, as
understood by Leibniz, is a statement, a law articulated in words, an
assertion. Leibniz also calls this an "axiom."[50]

If the paradigmatic region of phenomena is, for Leibniz, that of the
principles which order truths—truths of innate ideas or truths of the senses
and of consciousness—then a displacement occurred at the close of the
Latin age and at the beginning of the modern age. The origin has been
transferred from the field of essential causes to the field of causes that
regulate representation. The principle articulated by Leibniz determines
the manner in which things are rendered present to the mind; it is a law,
the one imperative law that must be obeyed by all extended things so as to
appear before the thinking thing. A proposition is indubitable if it *renders
reason* for what it states, that is, if it "renders" it correctly present to the
representing subject. The principle of reason is therefore a law applicable
to proofs (*ratiocinationes*[51]). A logical deduction is well made if it can
provide (*reddere*) the grounds of what it states. And the ultimate logical
ground beyond which the mind cannot go is, on one hand, this very principle of sufficient reason, and on the other, the principle of non-contradic-

tion. In Leibniz, these two principles guarantee all knowledge. The over-determination of the concept of origin is apparent here. The notion of *archē* was, in Aristotle, generally physicalist and specifically kinetic. It designated either the material cause or the system of all causes insofar as they founded movement and rendered it intelligible. *Archē* is a technician's concept, whereas *principium* is primarily a logician's concept. In order to account for any fact of experience Aristotle investigates the laws of its 'genesis'. Leibniz investigates the laws of its representation by the mind. The concept of principle could receive this new sense—after two millenia of incubation, says Heidegger[52]—only if beforehand entities in their totality had been objectified *vis-à-vis* man as spectator. When the world turns into a spectacle, laws for becoming turn into laws for representation. And the supreme principle requires that all representable things find their ground in human subjectivity. The reference to subject is expressed by the verb *reddere:* "render," give back, reasons—namely, to the knowing subject.[53]

The course of what has been held to be first, from Aristotle to the moderns, seems to have been marked by few major punctuations: sensible substance, divine substance, human subject. But each of these epochal punctuations (a tautologous phrase, anyway) establishes a focal point whose *primitas* exhibits complex traits: it precedes all arguments, otherwise it could not found them; it is self-posited, otherwise it would be derived from a more original position; and it abides beneath entities, which otherwise could not be derivates. The impossibility of an infinite regress for principial thought always brings the metaphysical quest back to one form or another of ὑποκείμενον. It is precisely the "substrate" that unites the three characteristics of the referent just mentioned: being already in position (*das schon Vorliegende*), self-positing (*von sich her*), and providing a sup-position (*unter- und zugrunde liegen*). These traits of the ὑποκείμενον, literally translated as *subiectum*, suggest how, throughout the epochs, the origin has been conceived as pre-sup-position.[54] In spite of the proliferation of ways in which philosophers have come to view the "first out of which," deconstructionist analysis shows that any quest for principles is a quest for an ultimate ontic referent. Aristotle directed that inquiry toward "natural" things because "moved by themselves" (although he conceived nature from the standpoint of artifacts, things "moved by another"). Duns Scotus and his age redirect it toward God. With Descartes and Leibniz, the quest for a ground is aimed at the last of the three great regions of entities—world, God, man—and thereby exhausts the resources of metaphysics. To the phenomenology of the reversals of history, man is the last genetic field, the last possible *Ursprungsfeld*[55] where the origin can be apprehended as presupposition.

What happens, then, when Leibniz formulates his "great principle"? The presupposition, after having been ousiological and theological, becomes logical. It provides the sufficient condition on which judgments may be true. To think, for Leibniz, is to form propositions about necessary or factual truths. These propositions require grounding. The first in the order of foundation will be a rule for the conduct of the mind. There are two candidates for this supreme function, (a) the rule that, of two contradictory propositions, one must be true, the other false, and (b) the rule that one must render reasons for any proposition that relates one fact or truth to another.[56] The first of these two rules is subordinate to the second—this is Leibniz's *principial* discovery. A proposition is not yet legitimated when it is shown that it does not imply a contradiction. A statement's sufficient reason is provided only when it is established "why it is so and not otherwise."[57]

Leibniz departs from Aristotle not only in that for him, as a modern, the presupposition is of a logical order and that he therefore has to articulate the principle in an "aphorism" or a "maxim";[58] he distances himself further from the ancients by his very comprehension of logic, which changes its nature.[59] In Heidegger's words, it becomes the "exposition of the formal construct of thinking and the establishment of its rules."[60] It becomes transcendental logic, something other than a pure analysis of cognitive processes. It is invested with tasks that formerly fell to first philosophy. Consequently, the logical principle of sufficient reason must be understood in another "key":[61] no longer as a rule for correctly ordering propositions, but as the rule of "enframing" things through representation. It is a *principium* in the strongest, ontological sense. As such, this principle, which explicitly governs the principle of non-contradiction, is itself governed implicitly by another—that of subjectivity as the giver of objective being. "The I, as 'I think', is the ground upon which is based, hereafter, all certitude and all truth."[62] In Leibniz, the principles of non-contradiction and of sufficient reason are capped with a third principle, which is truly ultimate, the *Ichsatz* or principle of transcendental ego.[63]

Whether it is the *eidos,* God, or the subject that is first in the order of presuppositions, the origin always appears as "preceding" and "empowering" (*ermöglichend*). But even within metaphysics it is not always reified,[64] not always identified with one *res* that is privileged among all others. As long as Aristotelians still speak Greek, inception and domination cannot become the act of one particular being. In the *Physics,* the *archē* is the *eidos* of becoming, not of a thing. Nor is the origin any more reified— although about to be just that—in the *Metaphysics,* where substance is the *archē* of accidents, or in the *Ethics,* where happiness is the *archē* of action, or in the *Politics,* where the perfect state is the *archē* of free men, or in the *Logic,* where the concept is the *archē* of the categories. On the other hand, in the medieval universe where analogy reigns, the first analogate is *principium* in that it makes and governs all other entities. The continuity with Aristotle is quite legible. Not only are the domains of being and knowing secondary in comparison with that of becoming, but, further, becoming is conceived according to human making. The metaphysics of created things remains faithful to the "technical" understanding of being. However, the discontinuity with Aristotle is legible, too. When the origin is posited among entities, be it in the greatest, inception and domination come to signify something other than the trait common to all *pros hen* schemata. They come to signify the spontaneous creation and the design of ruling. For the *archein* to be sacred—a 'hierarchy'—the first has to be adorned with an arsenal of real attributes. In keeping with the regulatory role devolved upon language, in Heidegger, the reification of the origin seems to coincide with the transition from Greek to Latin. It hardens with the moderns. When Aristotelian physical *energeia* becomes medieval divine *actualitas,* and later, with Leibniz, subjective *vis,*[65] what "precedes and empowers" turns into something given, an entity. The passage "from Greek thinking to Roman representation"[66] results in an anthropologized origin. Under the principate of man, 'to begin' (inception) signifies the legislative spontaneity of reason, and 'to command' (domination), the will's design of enframing. The ultimate hardening of this concretization occurs, in Heidegger's view, with contemporary technology. Objects have definitely seized power and their domination has engulfed the very possibility of thinking inception. The illusion of durability has made the temporality contained in the original sense of *archein* unthinkable.

This history—which, after all, relates in its way "how the 'true world' finally became a fable"[67]—teaches us at great length about the humanization of the origin. This process has been at work ever since Aristotle turned toward human *technē* in order to know the multiple phenomena of genesis and corruption in nature; but it triumphs when Leibniz declares *perception* to be the unifier of the manifold. "The passing state which enfolds and represents a multitude in unity or in the simple substance, is merely what is called perception."[68] Here is how the subject rules: by perceiving, by effecting unity through its reflective acts, by reducing the manifold to simple substances. Leibniz expresses the rule of the ego-principle unambiguously. The manifold receives its being from reason. "As we think of ourselves, we think of being."[69] The break with traditional logic could hardly be more apparent. Perception is reduced to *representation* as the act of bringing the manifold before the unifying, legislative reason—as the act which bestows being. We are far from the principle of reason as the ultimate proposition. By its reflective acts, by 'consciousness', the subject constitutes itself as the origin of objective being. "The 'ground' and 'principium' is now the *subiectum* in the sense of the representation representing itself."[70] Representation is the conferral of being, supplanting creation *ex nihilo*. The being of entities, or the substantiality of substance, resides in the efficacy of representation.[71] No object 'is' unless it 'renders' reason to the subject: that principle means not only that objects are referred to the self, nor that such reference opens the domain where they can at all appear. More radically, the reference to the subject makes the principle of reason, "as fundamental proposition of knowledge, the principle of whatever *is*."[72] In a logical guise, that principle enunciates the fundamental fact of "the metaphysics of the modern age,"[73] namely, that entities are constituted as objective by perception *qua* position.[74] The consequence for the understanding of the origin is obvious: as egoical, as anthropomorphic,[75] the logical *principium* proves to be an epochal principle.

Where, then, does the change in tonality, the principle of reason heard in "the other key," lead? Phenomenal being is being that is rendered present to the mind, presented for the sake of the representing ego, set opposite it.[76] The change in tonality thus leads to "the other thinking," that of the reversals of history and of the epochs dominated by an ontic principle—here, the representing ego—which "gives, each time, the measure."[77]

At first sight, the origin appears in the *Monadology* as a logical rule. That was our point of departure. Then the origin seemed to shift toward the subjectivity of the knowing ego. Finally, it appeared that it must rather be sought in what Leibniz calls perception and what Heidegger understands as the very content of the *rationem reddere:* to render reason is to render an extended thing present a second time, namely to the ego. In order to learn what the epochal principle of modernity is, it seems that we would have to hold together the original essence of propositional logic, that of transcendental subjectivity, and of representation as bestowal of being. But it is clear that these are only three aspects of the same original establishment through which, at the beginning of modernity, the *principium* is brought back to man. The *locus* where the origin, understood in this way, obtains is the region of logical entities; the *locality* of that locus, the being of those entities, is subjectivity; and the *foundation* through which logical entities, henceforth held as paradigmatic, are anchored in their being, the method of founding them, is representation. The phenomenological deconstruction reveals the historical site where a philosopher can teach that the soul draws from its own ground all its thoughts and actions. Leibniz's quest for evident laws from which statements spring and are ruled is to be seen as identical, on one hand, with the quest for the subjective ground as inception and domination of objects and, on the other, with representation as a method. To understand this unthematized link within rationalism between objective evidence, subjective foundation, and representation would mean to understand the origin in its specifically modern guise. An indubitable proposition functions as a principle only to the extent that it anchors representations in the thinking subject. The proposition and the subject can both be 'first' because, for modern man, *archein* is to represent. A principle is always what is 'seized' before something else. The subject seizes itself before seizing objects, for which it then serves as unshakable ground ('subject' understood as translating *hupokeimenon*), and it seizes a certain propositional truth (the principle of reason) before seizing the derivatives for which that truth provides the premise.[78] That *capere*, seizing, as such is nothing other than representation.

We now know where entities such as principles in the sense of Leibnizian logic can be encountered at all[79]—in representation. But the history of philosophy has seen other principial concepts of origin, other ways of immobilizing inception and domination. Representation is one historical site among many where thought has sought to vanquish time. Neither for the Greeks, nor for the medievals, did truth lie in subjectivity as the scene where objects render themselves constantly present. Prior to the modern age, truth was a matter of adequate judgments, founded on a 'technical' understanding of nature in Aristotle and on its 'creationist' understanding in the medievals. As the epochal foundation of the metaphysics of representation, the concept of principle is modern.[80] The two 'keys' according to which the principle of sufficient reason is to be heard are then: as the first truth for representation and as the ultimate foundation for an epoch.[81] It marks that epoch for which the temporal dimension, not only of *techne*, but also of Creation, has ceased to be measure-giving.

As an epochal first, the principle of sufficient reason governs one of the successive fields of intelligibility that have arisen since the dawn of our history. We know that these fields cannot be integrated in some linear development.[82] Still, there are characteristic traits of this history that have remained the same: since the Presocratics, each of the guiding words of philosophy has had a posterity, a 'history of efficacy', by which it has been transformed nearly beyond recognition. Thus, the λόγος of Heraclitus[83] remains alive, although disguised, in modern 'cogitation';[84] φύσις,[85] in the modern 'extended thing'; ἀλήθεια,[86] in modern 'perception';[87] man as μέτρον, measure or standard, in modern 'subjectivity.'[88] Therefore, beneath the epochal differences something shows forth that remains the same. "Only, in the trait most proper to it, we see this 'same' with difficulty and rarely in its fullness."[89]

To speak of an epochal principle is to speak of a double retainment or withholding: not only does *the principle* of any provisional economy hold itself back in the order that it establishes with a 'halting' (*epochē*), but holding back is essential to *presencing*. The first mode of self-refusal is historical. Thus, in the modern age, representation does not appear as such, although it is what marks out the avenue—the 'method'—through which all that is present can enter our economy. The second mode is anhistorical; the entry into presence as such can only be read indirectly in the order of things present. "*Epochē* does not mean here a span of time in occurrence, but rather the fundamental trait of sending—its holding-back, for each while, so that what it gives may be received."[90] Neither presencing, which sends an economy, nor this economy which is sent, are easily thematized. What is too close eludes examination, although it demands to be observed. An epochal principle makes itself felt like an address, a requisition. It requisitions a community of men for a finite mode of thought and of action.

The origin of the political has always been such a principle. The origin of our own twentieth century so understood makes it "an epoch of history stamped by the atom."[91] The concrete order of what we call the atomic age is the manifest response to the hidden call of the principle through which this age is born and ruled, just as the hierarchy of essences and the subordination of truths to first propositions were the manifest responses to the principles ruling the Middle Ages and the modern age respectively.[92] So set to reason—first divine, then human—the origin has for two millennia repudiated time.

To redress that age-old repudiation, Heidegger seeks to gain an understanding of the ontological difference as a temporal difference.

VIII

ANFANG AND URSPRUNG
THE TEMPORAL DIFFERENCE

§17. The Vocabulary

Originarily [*ursprünglich*] and inceptively
[*anfänglich*] speech 'gathers' (collects) the
unconcealed as such by disclosing it. That is
why gathering as saying becomes the
distinctive *legein*—why from early on, as
gathering, *legein* also means saying.
Originarily [*ursprünglich*]—as well as
beginningly [*be-ginnlich*]—thinking and
poetizing are, although in fundamentally
different ways, the same: being bringing itself
forth into speech, gathering itself into
speech.

Heraklit[1]

To say *Anfang* or *Ursprung* instead of *archē* or *principium* is to abolish
the patterns of command and rule that accompany the Classical Greek and
Latin representations of origin.

Heidegger's writings may be read in their entirety as a quest for the
origin. They can never be read, however, as a quest for a *fons et origo*, a
mythical source of all things. The word *Ursprung* (literally "primal leap")
recurs at each stage of his itinerary. Toward the end it comes to designate
the pertinent trait of the 'event': not an occurrence or an incident, nor a
feat (*Ereignis* never connotes these), but coming about, coming to presence, 'presencing'. Since this is the phenomenon that Heidegger seeks to
grasp as 'being qua being', it will be no surprise that in this matter his
vocabulary is somewhat complex. I start therefore by trying to clarify the
contours of meaning between the different words for 'origin' used in the
lines quoted above.

In plain language, what Heidegger seems to say in those lines is that
there exists a pre-linguistic sense of *legein* and a more narrowly linguistic
one. In the pre-linguistic sense, speech does not differ essentially from
other activities in which man "gathers" something up (for example, twigs to
start a fire or arms and armors after battle). Gathering, then, is the *originary* sense of speech. And here is the first apparent slippage: gathering is

also said to be the *inceptive* sense of speech. "Originarily and inceptively speech 'gathers.'" Then, still plainly stated, Heidegger seems to explain why the linguistic meaning of *legein* has nevertheless prevailed over its broader meaning since a very ancient age—possibly Homer's. What constitutes the prepotency of 'saying'? Precisely its relation to being. Poets and thinkers give utterance to being and have done so since the beginning—probably of Greece. Hence, the second apparent slippage: poetry and thinking are said to be the same in their *origination* as in their *beginning*. It is not easy to untangle these relationships between beginning, inception, and origin in Heidegger. And yet, the task is crucial if acting—life—is to be disengaged from teleocratic as well as principial frameworks; if deconstruction is to set free from beneath *archē* and *principium* an origin less compromised by command and domination; and if in the final analysis the question of acting comes down to complying with that more elusive origin. It is as elusive as anything best designated by *verbs: beginnen, anfangen, springen.* The principles, on the other hand, bear *names* since, as we have seen, during the metaphysical age "being receives its essential stamping each time from *one measure-giving entity*."[2] First the three terms derived from those verbs have to be clarified. I shall translate *Beginn* as 'beginning', *Anfang* as 'inception', *anfänglich* as 'inceptive', 'initial' or 'incipient', *Ursprung* as 'origination' and *ursprünglich* as 'originary'. Then I shall try to show why and how presencing is inseverable from the reversals or breaks in history—how, in other words, the 'thinking of being' cannot dispense with deconstruction. In all this my ultimate purpose is to understand what acting would be like when freed from epochal principles.

1. The semantic extension of the three terms in the epigraph is not clear-cut. Would origination be identical with the beginning (of Western civilization or at least philosophy)? And would the latter not then be reckoned in centuries elapsed (approximately twenty-five)? Or conversely, would origination fall under the law of temporal distance? Is the originary contemporaneous with *us,* in us or around us, or is it contemporaneous with the poets and thinkers of '*the dawn*'? And what of inception? Is this a historical notion, or perhaps an existential one? Or is it ontological?

Of these three words the easiest to clarify is *Beginn*, beginning. In Heidegger it usually designates the birth of metaphysics in Plato and Aristotle.[3] However, Heidegger also speaks of the "unique and incomparable beginning of Western thinking," and here he means "pre-metaphysical thinking."[4] Obviously, the guiding idea is that of a moment when a new age arises, an auroral, inchoate moment. Our own era also constitutes a beginning. With the turning, being "has begun (*begonnen*) to come back to its truth. Being turns silently . . . in order to give humans the beginning (*beginnlich*) of their unique dignity."[5] Recognizable here are the three great inaugural moments in the history of presence, according to Heideg-

ger: the pre-metaphysical dawn, the classical reversal that founds metaphysics, and the transition, which has become possible today, toward a
post-metaphysical age.

However, by 'beginning' Heidegger understands yet something else. He
says: "Whoever has thought only *begins* to think and only then thinks."[6]
There is still something of an inchoate movement implied, namely, the first
steps (which one perhaps never relegates behind oneself) in thinking. But
the historical-epochal sense of 'beginning' seems to become entirely untenable when one reads, for example: "Man begins and conceals his essence
with being, he waits and beckons with it, keeps silent and speaks with it."[7]
These lines are not as enigmatic as they appear. They deal with the historical modalities of presence. They state that in his way of being, man always
follows these modalities, that historical truth appropriates him, makes him
its own. The event of appropriation is described here as something that
begins. Are we then to think of it as a perpetual birth, as something ever
new? If that is the case, even this last sense of *Beginn* cannot be separated
completely from the historical-epochal one. Are we to presume that *the
'beginning' which is the event can be grasped only through the 'beginnings'
which are the epochs?*

By *Anfang*, too, Heidegger designates a certain point of departure. And
here again his uses of the word shift from a historical sense to one pertaining to the event.

'Inception' is first of all a matter of experience. The so-called Presocratics
are *anfängliche Denker* because they experienced presence as pure
presenc*ing*, which is what made them think. As they are initially experienced, they initiate philosophy. The historical sense of incipience is thus a
result of the sense one might call experimental. *Inception* is to be distinguished from the "later *beginning* of metaphysics,"[8] that is to say, from the
forgetting that, with Plato and Aristotle, descends over the initial experience. What is that experience whose loss has gone unnoticed for so long?
The words *Anfang* and inception (just like *principium*[9]) mean that which
seizes, catches, takes hold first. The pre-Classical Greeks were seized, "that
is why they found the inception of authentic thinking."[10] Such finding comes
from being seized. By what? By something to which one can or must respond
and correspond. "This initial corresponding, carried out for its own sake,
is thinking."[11] The Presocratic experience is initial less by virtue of its
antiquity than of its responsorial character. The correspondence that initiates everything obviously cannot consist in the conformity between a judgment and its object. What is initially gripping is so elementary that responding to it amounts to something like perplexity. *Anfang* strongly resembles
θαυμάζειν, the wonder that Plato tells us is the *archē* of philosophizing.[12]
Philosophical thinking remains authentic—historically, with the Greeks, and
very personally in the Heideggerian 'repetition'—only as long as "the perplexity of not understanding the word 'being' "[13] remains alive and incipient.

Such is the initial experience of thinking—the always inceptive experience that is thinking—as it addresses concrete existence.

It is as an address, then, that inception has the characteristics of speech. For philosophy to remain authentic much more (or much less) is required than confessing perplexity before the many senses of one word, the copula. The starting point of thinking is something simple. A certain sense for word-like claims on man needs to be aroused, a sense for the injunctions that inaugurate every act of thinking. "At the inception of thinking" is an "initiating soundless word."[14] It is an exacting word (*Wort*) to which thinking is the response (*Antwort*); an in-ceptive word (*an-fangen*) that listening ac-cepts (*ent-fangen*).[15] The initiating claim laid on man is moreover so encompassing that it addresses itself to sight as well as hearing: thinking "sees being itself, imageless, in its initially simple essence as a constellation."[16] To be seized and called upon inceptively is, then, to find oneself inserted into an aletheiological constellation.

That thinking will be *anfänglich* which echoes such a disposition or such an economic presence-absence. '*Anfang*' is a historical notion only because, at the close of over twenty centuries of metaphysical principles, we will never regain the simple starting point of thinking—namely, heeding 'being' as a temporal constellation, without any suprasensible alibi—except by returning to the pre-metaphysical experience in order to take from it the cue for our post-metaphysical potential.

The commemoration-anticipation (*Andenken-Vordenken*) so described is the very content of the 'turning'. Obviously, under '*Anfang*', Heidegger thinks, in part, the same traits as he does under '*Beginn*': "If the incipient holds sway beyond all its consequents and prior to them, then it is not something lying behind us, but rather the One and the Same that comes before us, toward us, in a mysterious turning (*Kehre*)."[17] Something is mysterious which manifests itself while hiding (*alētheia*), or which emerges into presence while remaining absent (*phusis*). The reason Heidegger takes up the fundamental words of the Presocratics is that they enable us to think what comes toward us, what already grasps (*fängt*) us and in that sense is *anfänglich*. Not just any economic disposition that embraces and situates man is inceptive, but one definite historical-destinal disposition: ours, as stamped by global technology. "For us, what is wanted . . . is an inceptive reversal (*eines anfänglichen Wandels*)."[18]

What, then, is it that already holds us? Nothing other than the post-principial economy made possible by technology as the completion of metaphysics. What holds us is the *possibility* of "thinking 'appearance' in the Greek way, i.e., of experiencing it as being."[19] Pure appearing is the incipience to which the Greeks knew how to respond and correspond. It remains for us "to listen initially,"[20] to "put aside personal opinions and to think what is inceptive about incipient thinking really as if we were 'initiates', and that is to say, with simplicity." Indeed, "there is inception only in initiating, *Anfang ist nur im Anfangen*."[21]

It should be quite apparent how the historical notion of inception is linked to the experimental one: in both cases it is a matter of responding to the claim that *alētheia* addresses to us, that is, of entering into history as the conversation *alētheia* holds with itself. The Greek inception as well as the turning toward "the other inception" opens a historical destiny only insofar as we know how to experience the aletheiological mutations and give ourselves over to them.

Here, then, is how the experimental-destinal topos shifts toward the topos of *event*. If another *Anfang* is about to take shape around us in our contemporary world, its *primary* locus is not thinking, nor is 'to initiate' equatable with 'to think'. It is rather "*phusis* that has its constant inception in such a way that, *prior* to anything else that may appear, that is, prior to any entity that may be present for a while, emergence [as such] has already appeared."[22] In other words, if thinking is essentially a response, an echo, a reverberation of appearing as such, then it can hardly be initiating, taking initiatives. What, then, is it that catches hold first and thereby precedes any entity? The text says: *phusis*, "emergence," and that is to say being qua being. "That free inchoation is the inception itself: the inception 'of' being qua being."[23] In this way, *Anfang* comes to be situated in the ontological difference. Being precedes all and any entities. It ceaselessly "initiates" their unfolding. The difference between being and entities is "the initial difference itself."[24]

One may of course wish to add that, in this new focus, man is not at all marginalized since the difference 'initiates' appearances *for him*. And indeed, Heidegger writes that pure appearing, *phusis*, is "seen initially," prior even to the phenomena that appear.[25] But in what way is coming-to-presence *for man?* "The essence of inception" declares itself in the ambiguity of *phusis*, i.e., its locus is the conflict between hiding and showing;[26] or it declares itself in the ambiguity of *alētheia*, i.e., its locus is the conflict between veiling and unveiling.[27] Inception makes 'use' of men by *situating* them in a constellation of presence and absence. What road, then, is to be followed if we wish to understand the *Anfang* fully? None other than the road of deconstructing the sequence of these constellations, of "meditating on our position, the position of the West in relation to its historical inception,"[28] so as to wrest from this sequence 'emergence as such'. Our position within history is our good luck and our distress. It is our good luck, for "that mittence (*Geschick*) of being into its truth is *being itself* as initiating."[29] But our position is also "the unfolding of an initial distress," of the obfuscation that marks our entire course since the Greeks.[30] As with *Beginn*, access to the origin as inception is provided by the phenomenology of the reversals in history; access to the ontological difference as initiating ages is gained by the deconstruction of initial historical moments. But the difference as initiating is the 'event of appropriation', *Ereignis*. Access to the event is thus through history. "What is initial happens properly [ereig-

net] ahead of all that comes. . . . Recalling history is the only viable road toward what is inceptive."³¹

Ursprung, 'origination', first of all also expresses a certain destiny and its point of departure. Here are two examples of this use, one concerning the start and the other the end of the metaphysical itinerary: "In the equation between thinking and *logos* is hidden the origination of a Western destiny."³² "[To conceive of] man's thought as that of a 'subject' . . . is to fulfill an errancy that comes from far away and that originates in a misunderstanding of the essence of reflection."³³ When the essence of *logos* falls into oblivion, a long errancy sets in—"originates"—at the end of which man comes to understand his own thought as subject opposite his objects. However, origination as the starting point of the European itinerary is not the proper locus of the concept of *Ursprung* in Heidegger.

That proper locus is better approached by examining the function of thinking prior to the Socratic turn toward man. Insofar as Presocratic thinking does not pursue ultimate entities, it is "essential thinking." "If common opinion represents entities and only entities, and if essential thinking thinks being . . . then the cleavage between originary thinking and essential thinking must originate in the difference between being and entities."³⁴ This ontological difference makes the hiatus between thinking and opinion possible. Prior to the humanist and logical reversal, to think is "to correspond, by disclosing [phenomena], to *phusis*." Correspondence so understood is the locus of the origin. "In the essence of *phusis*, as in the essence of those that, in disclosing, correspond to it, *alētheia* sways as the originarily unifying ground."³⁵ *Ursprung*, then, is the "originary compliance"³⁶ through which man gives himself over to unconcealment.

Ursprung harks back to unconcealment as the identical trait of both *phusis* and man, to their 'freedom' as one and the same opening. This is a more essential origination than the rise of an age in history. On the other hand, as long as the imperative of logic to "think correctly" predominates, "the ground and origination of correct thinking, and even of thinking as such, still remain hidden from us."³⁷ Concealment, *lēthē*, remains hidden.

Heideggerian recollection has the consequence, infelicitous to some, that seen in light of *alētheia* the contrary of correctness, error, is as much thinking's originary "dowry" as is correctness.³⁸ Some have indeed been scandalized by Heidegger's statement, "Who thinks greatly must err greatly."³⁹ Whether scandalous or not, this consequence is inevitable once 'man' and 'nature' are traced to their common origination in unconcealment. So understood, the origin is irreducible to everything born of it, notably to *technē* and science.⁴⁰ It is an origin, however, that can "come back." In these "times of reversal" which are ours, "the essential stamping" under which "the originary essence of *logos* has been lost" for twenty-five centuries can be placed in question. Could "this want of the originary sense of *logos* . . . then be the inconspicuous foretoken of a long return?"[41] What is possible or to come, reaching beyond everything actual, is the return of the simple consent to the ever changing flow of *alētheia*, of unconcealment. In that potential of our era the *historical* and the *aletheiological* concepts of origination come together.

But their alliance is still far from the proper locus where *Ursprung* can be grasped. Its proper locus remains incomprehensible as long as *legein*, 'gathering', is considered to be something man undertakes. The proper locus of origination can be glimpsed—but still only glimpsed—when we think the agreement between the *legein* performed by man and the *Legein* which is presencing. Their agreement, Heidegger writes, is a "relation between relationships, that is to say, a pure relation, originating nowhere."[42] The gathering performed by man (for the moderns: by the subject) is already a relation, namely, of man to the things that he selects and retains from the mass of present entities. The gathering which is *phusis* (for the moderns: nature) also constitutes a relation, namely, between presence and absence. The relation between these two relations, Heidegger says, "originates nowhere." There is nothing more originary, it seems, than the *homolegein* between man and presencing. "Being itself cannot be experienced without a more originary experience of the essence of man, and conversely . . . Only the relation between these two, as their origination, [is] the true."[43] This clearly recalls Heidegger's *The Essence of Truth*: the essence of truth is the essence of freedom—the opening in which man 'ek-sists'. However, the 'ecstatic' opening cannot disown its antecedent, transcendental subjectivity. The event of origination, on the other hand, proves to be as unthinkable in terms of existence as it is in terms of subjectivity. Hence Heidegger's recourse to the Presocratic "basic words." Furthermore, origination remains equally unthought in its simplicity when it is construed as the "relation between the two *logoi*,"[44] as if presencing and human doing were two processes to be coordinated. In the foreword to the lecture course on the doctrine of *Logos* in Heraclitus, Heidegger introduces the task he assigns himself as the search for "the originary logic." This requires that the idea of homologizing human projects and given situations be renounced and that *a single Logos* be discovered: " 'Logic' as the thinking 'of' the *Logos* will be originary only when the originary *Logos* is thought."[45] The conjunction of thinking (which includes acting) and presencing must be reexamined, then, if the simple origination of all phenomena is to be found. This cannot consist in some rudimentary version of the conformity theory of truth.

Heraclitus could only point to simple origination from a distance, but he could not think it. If it is "being as time," then the Greek fundamental words, "each of which utters the originary essence of the initial thinking,"[46] can only serve as guideposts for "the other thinking" and the other inception. We must think "even more originarily than Heraclitus." Thus Heidegger's reading of Heraclitus is expressly dictated by "the other thinking."[47] In order to understand simple origination, post-metaphysical thinking cannot dispense with pre-metaphysical *Logos*, with "*Logos* in the sense of the gathering that preserves originarily";[48] but neither can it dispense with the epochal temporality discovered through metaphysics. The simple event that is origination can be attained only through the many complex junctures that have initiated new economies throughout the ages. This unavoidable detour through history will be fully understandable only when the *difference* between what I will call the original and the originary has been established. This difference will be developed below.

To conclude this survey of the vocabulary and to see what issues it raises, it should be clear that the historical-epochal notion of 'beginning' (*Beginn*), with its overdetermination of event, and the experimental-destinal notion of 'inception' (*Anfang*), with its ontological overdetermination, are fully intelligible only in conjunction with the notion of 'origination' (*Ursprung*) as the event proper, itself historically overdetermined. The natural locus of 'beginning' is epochal history; that of 'inception' is thinking; and that of 'origination' is the event of appropriation. The question is not: Which is more fundamental, history, thinking, or being? but rather: How is origination identical with both inception and beginning, yet nevertheless different from both? "*Originarily*, as well as beginningly," poetry and thinking are the same, said the text cited in the epigraph to this section. On the other hand, "*initially* being makes itself known as *logos* and thereby discloses itself as what is to be thought *originarily*."[49] If it is possible to see how, for Heidegger, the origin is linked to history, it will also be possible to overcome (while retaining it) the opposition between diachrony and synchrony—or between left-wing Heideggerians, who read in him only deconstruction, and right-wing Heideggerians, who read in him only the Poem of Being. The project Heidegger pursues after his *Kehre* crystallizes in the question, *How does presencing become history?* How does it, as event, condition all that can occur?

The event to which the Heideggerian notion of origination points is always a showing-forth. Its most familiar instances are the "rising up" of speech and of an artwork. "To make something rise up with a leap, to bring it into being from provenance in an enabling leap: that is what the word origination means."[50] This description suggests perfectly the event-like character of origination, but it reveals neither its anti-humanist impact nor its connection with history, nor in which (non-dialectical) sense the origin is both one and many. To retrieve the full sense of *Ursprung*, a double route has to be followed: asking the question of ontology more originarily (section 18) in order to attain the one issue of radical phenomenology, being as time, and asking the question of origin ontologically (section 19) in order to attain the anti-humanist solution to that issue, presencing as 'event'. *Ereignis* and history will thus appear as the terms of the *temporal difference*.

2. The first of these two routes is traced by the project of the young Heidegger in *Being and Time:* from the initial fact of immersion in entities, from being-in-the-world, existential analysis steps back to progressively more elementary conditions of such facticity. The phenomenological project of a transcendental *construction*[51] discloses, if not in fact, at least by right, the temporality of being. Being as time is its guiding pre-understanding.

Later, the second route is traced by the phenomenological project of epochal *deconstruction*. The focus is on those entities that have been held as ultimate rulers in the course of our culture because they institute and command a given economy. Presencing is then no longer only adumbrated, it is reached by an "enabling leap."

The constructive task of raising the ontological question more originarily is historical in the sense that the problematic of an a priori is inherited directly from Kant and indirectly from Plato.[52] The deconstructive task, on the other hand, of raising the question of origin ontologically is historical in an entirely different way. It is historical as a working through, thus an overcoming, of that problematic of the a priori inaugurated by Plato—as the retrieval, therefore, of an understanding of presencing to which the philosophy of *archai* and *principia* could hardly do justice. For Heidegger, to raise the ontological question originarily (before the *Kehre*) meant to ask again, after the Greeks, τὶ τὸ ὄν, and to do so by analyzing being-in-the-world. Later, to raise the question of the origin ontologically (after the *Kehre*) meant to transgress Plato so as to recover presencing from Presocratic thought, and simultaneously to transgress the ultimate referents so as to recover presencing as a possibility[53] for thought today.

This rather complex structure of the repetition of presencing—repeating the question of first philosophy, exhibiting the existential structures, returning to the Milesian and Eleatic beginnings, and retrieving the non-static at the core of everything present—must be preserved intact if the origin is to be understood in the full sense of *Ursprung*. The first task mentioned, i.e., raising the ontological question more originarily and making it "fundamental,"[54] cannot be pursued independently. Inquiring into more and more originary conditions would lead to the illusion of a hierarchy of grounds—the very fallacy that Heidegger denounces in the metaphysical quest for *principia*. It is true that at the same time he seems to outline just such a hierarchy when he sketches a transcendental retrogression that leads from the question, What is being? to that of 'being qua being', then to that entity who asks such questions, and finally to the very structure of the understanding where these questions are articulated. At a first reading of Heidegger's early writings, then, to think the origin 'originarily' means to step back from the τὶ τὸ ὄν to the ὄν ἦ ὄν, to *Dasein*, to *Verstehen*.[55] Many of the misunderstandings concerning Heidegger are explainable by the exclusive attention paid to his effort to raise the ontological question originarily, without noting his simultaneous effort to think the origin ontologically. By seeing only the "originary rootedness" (*ursprüng-liche Verwurzelung*)[56] of the being question in human existence, one ends up inevitably reading Heideggerian transcendentalism as yet another sequence of degrees that still lead to an ultimate condition of possibility and therefore a principial referent. The *Kehre* would then only push the search for ultimacy further back beyond *Dasein* and *Verstehen* into what the later Heidegger calls the "clearing,"[57] which he says "is being."[58]

To the extent that the "clearing" is a field of epochal economy constituted prior to all human projects, this term does designate an a priori to the existential structures. But to understand Heidegger is to understand that with him philosophy has rid itself of all ultimate a priori referents. That the clearing is not one such referent appears from his ontological notion of origin, without which the search for transcendental conditions of possibility would continually rebound. In the last text published during his life, Heidegger, as if the ultimate instance of the question of being had still not been reached, suggests one step further in "the attempt, undertaken ever anew since 1930, to shape the question of *Being and Time* in a more initial way."[59] He asks: "But whence and how is there the clearing?"[60] On the final page of his work, he thus seems to inquire about the horizon that encloses the opening in which entities "presence," the horizon that makes their mutual presencing possible and in which "there is [*es gibt*] being." What *seems* to be ultimate, then, is the "there is" itself—capitalized, moreover.[61] The "There is" makes the clearing possible, which makes understanding possible, which in turn makes *Dasein* possible, which alone allows one to ask what is being qua being, from which degree of derivation one might finally ask what beings are. . . .

But the stages that lead to the "there is" do not constitute such "a gradation in the sense of an ever greater originariness."[62]

The originary pursuit of the ontological question, then, must be supplemented by the ontological pursuit of the originary. The *ontic* question of origin has received plenty of answers throughout history. Sensible substance, later the first nature at the top of the essential order, then the principle of reason that orders reasoning, are just so many ways of designating a particular entity that institutes and commands the totality of present things for a time. The *ontological* question (in the sense of the *Seinsfrage*) of origin has shown itself to be tied to the deconstruction of the economies and the reversals through which principles rise and wither. It is obvious, then, that presence 'comes about' in two ways: according to phenomenological *construction*, as the emergence of entities constituting a world, as their synchronic 'there is'; and according to phenomenological *deconstruction*, as the instituting of an order of entities on the threshold that separates diachronically one world from another.

Raising together *the ontological question of origin* and *the originary question of ontology* is to reformulate the debate about transcendental conditions from the double viewpoint of the ahistorical, synchronic *Ereignis*, which is at issue in the construction, and of the epochal, diachronic *Geschehen*, the issue of deconstruction. One may see here an aporia comparable to that in *Being and Time:* in that earlier work, Heidegger set out to retrieve the question of being qua being, but he only reached the being of *Dasein;* likewise in the later context: the outset is the same, but again, he only reaches the being of history. The impression of an aporia vanishes however as soon as the systematic tie is seen that links the 'event' to the epochs. Heidegger therefore alludes to a historical-ahistorical dialectic.[63] It imposes a transmutation on the transcendental method such that this method can no longer yield any regulatory focal point by which philosophy becomes an edifice and reason, architectonic. The 'very issue' of phenomenology that Heidegger's transcendentalism sets free is *not one*. It is the twofold advent of presence: the epochal institution *in illo tempore* and the event-like manifestation *hic et nunc*. This double advent determines any possible discourse on being in the later Heidegger.

Due to this double coming to presence, truth itself appears in its unsurpassable *contingency*. How could there remain room for one canon of truth, one ideal of truth, if the origin is so essentially polymorphous? *Alētheia* is the self-manifestation in which anything thinkable and livable emerges from concealment (*lēthē*). Whether historical or ahistorical, coming to presence is an essentially precarious a priori.[64] The modesty of such a thinking, which remains riveted to contingency, appears in what one might naively be tempted to take as the ultimate Heideggerian referent, namely, the *there is* understood as the origin, *oriri*, of being. To the traditional philosophical wonder, Why *is there* being rather than nothing? Heidegger answers with the simple *there is*. Such an answer not only flies in the face of any quest for explanation, but it amounts to an option for the fortuitous, for the unstable. Explanations operate by recourse to some immutable referent, a cause or a condition; but to say 'there is' presencing amounts to espousing what is mutable in its shifting constellations.

A great many *ontic* origins have run our life world through the ages: "the suprasensory World, the Ideas, God, the moral Law, the authority of Reason, Progress, the Happiness of the greatest number, Culture, Civilization."[65] They regulate a given economy, each time, and they are always replaceable in that function. The *ontological* concept of origin proved to be linked to the phenomenon of setting into presence. This phenomenon is twofold: setting into presence as the rise of an order that will prevail for a while in history (the deconstructive moment), and setting into presence as the ahistorical, always instantaneous emergence of presencing (the constructive moment). In the later Heidegger the guiding issue for establishing the ontological difference is: how is the origin as a historical-ahistorical happening to be understood once its ontic representations have withered away?

We saw that the three key terms—*Beginn, Anfang, Ursprung*—all share a *historical* meaning. Certain features of Greek culture were called "the beginning," "the inception," and even "the origination" of Western civilization. But all three terms also share an ahistorical meaning. In one way or another, they all imply the event of appropriation. To articulate this ambiguity in the origin as both an empirical (*Geschehen*) and a transcendental (*Ereignis*) happening, a slightly different convention in vocabulary is required. I will call the phenomenon of *historical* beginning/inception/origination the 'original' and the phenomenon of *ahistorical* beginning/inception/ origination the 'originary'. This distinction emphasizes most sharply Heidegger's method in trying to understand being qua being, the method of reaching the (originary) event of presencing through the deconstruction of (original) epochs.

We also saw that the *metaphysical* concept of ontological difference rests on the mutual exclusion of ontic representations and their common fact of being. Understood *phenomenologically*, that difference sets apart the epochally determined fact of being (*die Seiendheit*) and the to-be (*das Sein*): from the viewpoint of the phenomenological difference, the 'original' and the 'originary' are the mutually exclusive and jointly exhaustive notions of the origin. One could continue speaking instead of 'history' and 'being', but then their kinship as the two types of *oriri*—of phenomenal showing-forth—would get lost.

These two notions of 'original' and 'originary' (to which the following sections are devoted) may be viewed as the result of Heidegger's critique of metaphysics: he criticizes the *archē* in order to recover its pre-philosophical sense of pure 'commencing', *archein;* and he criticizes the *principium* in order to recover its sense of pure 'showing forth', *phuein*. This double repetition restores historicality to the original and temporality to the originary. The outset of an era is the 'decisive' instant in which a new way of being-in-the-world substitutes itself for a previous one; the showing-forth or rise[66] is the now-'event' in which presencing appropriates absencing.[67] This appropriation will turn out to be the temporality of being, which had remained the sole issue for Heidegger since *Being and Time*.

The distinction between 'original' and 'originary' helps to spell out Heidegger's answer to the old question of the many and the one. There are many cases of new beginnings (although the leading instance of 'commencing' is undoubtedly borrowed by Heidegger from the German Romantics: what is original *par excellence* is ancient Greece), our history is made of many ruptures in which a new arrangement breaks through. Each of these breakthroughs has a date. But there is only one event of 'showing forth', one essence of manifestation, one originary origin. This is the conjunction, the coming together, of phenomena into such an arrangement—their mutual presencing. To understand the 'originary'—Heidegger's "being"—we first have to grasp the 'original'.

§18. 'Original' Origins, or How the New Comes About in History

> Before being can occur in its original
> truth . . . the world must be forced into ruin
> and the earth must be driven to desolation,
> and man to mere labor. Only after that
> decline does the event take place in which,
> in a long span of time, the sudden abiding of
> the original occurs.
>
> "Overcoming Metaphysics"[68]

These lines, written during the war,[69] indicate the conditions under which it would be possible to retrieve what Heidegger considers the initial issue of Western philosophizing. They especially show the sense in which such conditions are historical. The retrieval of the 'original' would require an occurrence, a happening (*Geschehen,* therefore both *Geschick,* a 'mittence' always beyond us, and *Geschichte,* the history in which we respond to such sendings), of the same scope as the reversal of history from which metaphysics was born after the Peloponnesian War. Deconstruction thus evinces how the new can appear in history, it points out the origin as a sudden break in which something unforeseeable, a new 'problematic', sets in. Furthermore, since "the inception already contains the end latent within itself,"[70] such a problematic has its cycle of development. An archaeology, to borrow Michel Foucault's term, would isolate regularities in a given problematic so as to read in it the *discursive* formations that govern *knowledge.* The phenomenology of the original, on the other hand, lays bare formations of *presencing* that govern *being in the world.* It can achieve this since, as I have indicated, its method consists (a) in raising the ontological question originally: "The beginning of the West is that in the Greek age, the being of entities becomes worthy of thought."[71] But such a phenomenology departs further from the archaeology of human sciences inasmuch as its method also consists (b) in raising the question of the origin ontologically: "The sudden abiding of the original" designates the possibility that after the devastations being-in-the-world "enter into the event of appropriation,"[72] an entry which would bring the initial question of metaphysics to completion. Overcoming metaphysics would therefore require taking up the pre-metaphysical inception. Even if, on the threshold where we find ourselves, such a return to the original is still bound to thought patterns inherited from ground-seeking ontologies, deconstructing the epoch issuing from Socrates and Aristotle at least allows one to confine those thought patterns to their one legitimate phenomenal domain, that of fabrication. The quest for an origin as a ground or foundation, the waning of which we seem to be witnessing with our own eyes, marks out an eventually closed field in history.[73]

The concept of the 'original' as it arises from the deconstruction of the epochs is understandable only within the context of an anticipatory retrieval. "Our thinking today is charged with the task of thinking what the Greeks have thought in an even more Greek manner."[74] Original thinking—the thinking in which the origin is understood as inception—proceeds on two fronts, retrospectively as well as prospectively. It recalls the ancient beginnings, and it anticipates a new beginning, the possible rise of a new economy among things, words, and actions. The wonder before that potential of our age displaces the traditional θαυμάζειν. It directs wonder or perplexity toward the temporal essence of presencing and thereby obliges us to "think through still more originally what has been thought initially."[75] This is the first ambivalence, metaphysical/pre-metaphysical, of what Heidegger understands to be original about the being-question.

From *Being and Time* onward, however, an incipiency in a quite different sense keeps mingling with the Greek original to be retrieved and thereby (possibly) anticipated. The book, *Being and Time*, not only *thematizes* the original in the context of such anticipatory retrieval, it *begins* with the retrieval of the Western beginnings—a quote from Plato about our ignorance concerning "being."[76] What Heidegger sets out to retrieve is indeed the beginning of metaphysics, the gigantomachia between the Academy and the Sophists on behalf of "being." What, then, does it mean to repeat the being-question originally? Does it mean to re-enact the gigantomachia, the original origin *of metaphysics?* Or rather to reclaim the *pre-metaphysical* original?[77] Neither of the two, according to this description of the task of retrieval: "Do we have an answer today to the question of what we properly mean by the word 'being'? Not at all." The ignorance to which the Eleatic Stranger confesses in the *Sophist* displaces what is held to be original: "Are *we today* even perplexed at our inability to understand the expression 'to be'? Not at all."[78] To be sure, the being-question originally appeared in the time of Parmenides, then later at the time of the Academy; but to raise this question anew is not to repeat the battle of the Schools. It is rather to confess ignorance and to experience perplexity. Why perplexity? Because this ignorance concerns something we ought to know and, in a way, do know. For the entity that we are, the relationship to being itself is always understood prior to any reflection and conception: "We do not know what 'being' means. But as soon as we ask, What is being? we remain within an understanding of the 'is.' "[79] This acquaintance with what nevertheless we do not know is the incipience of thought. The perplexity of not knowing while already having an understanding may be alleviated by a return to the Ancients which would be simultaneously a return to our own pre-understanding. Such is at least the double return with which *Being and Time* opens.

Unless the historical inquiry is so tied to the existential inquiry, the question formerly approached "in so general and ambiguous a fashion" can never be raised suitably. Heidegger's starting point is however still more complex. To "struggle for the question of being which in the [Greek] gigantomachia has not yet been worked out"[80] confers indeed a threefold temporal structure upon the retrieval: renewing the (past) Greek problematic, elucidating our (present) own pre-understanding, and anticipating a possible (future) thought of being. This last point is the guiding issue throughout, although it is clearly stated as such only in later writings. If the very problematic that has shaped the West "has not yet been worked out," the original origin must be construed out of the *future*. Phenomenological reduction and construction cannot do without an anticipatory deconstruction. As Heidegger works out the *Abbau*, the role of the future changes. From that of the primary sense of existentiality it shifts to that of a possible economic reversal. As was the case for the existential analytic, the time-dimension that guides the deconstruction is not the past at all. Deconstruction anticipates the possibility, "in a long span of time, [of] the sudden abiding of the original," i.e., of a thinking entirely given up to its sole issue, presencing. The condition for phenomenology to so take up its very issue is not only a post-technological economy, but also an attitude.

When Heidegger speaks of the origin as inception, it is not enough to read him as referring to the Greek "dawn," nor to "the epochal lighting of being"[81] in the subsequent reversals as testified to by the philosophers. Before as after the turning, incipience of thought consists first of all in an attitude: a Socratic confession of ignorance or an availability for a reversal to come in the aletheiological constellation of our age. Only when the 'existential' espouses the 'economic' do we have novelty in history. Inception is the "instigation of the strife of truth" by an "unmediated bestowal and foundation"; it is essentially the "setting-into-work"[82] of an order of presence-absence. The original, then, consists in a making, *poiēsis*, which is not purely man's. René Char spoke of "the poet, great Beginner."[83] This must be understood in the sense that every commencement is itself of a *poietic* nature. To initiate something new is to make truth by instigating an aletheiological struggle. "The poietic project comes out of nothing in that it never takes its gift from the ordinary and the transmitted."[84] Bringing about truth in acting has no other prerequisite than this attitude of readiness through which our projects, without the shackles of what has been transmitted and become current, turn into echoes of truth in presencing,[85] of networks of unconcealment setting themselves up.

In the texts on language, the poietic essence of an original inception is said to call for a way of "dwelling": a way of lodging ourselves in a given constellation of truth. As a practical a priori for thinking presencing, "we must first learn how to dwell."[86] And just as on the exordial page of *Being and Time* a confession of ignorance was demanded in order to retrieve the being-question, so these texts on dwelling demand that, as a condition for such a retrieval, we make the preconceptual Greek way of inhabiting language our own,[87] a way less obsessed with the architectonic of propositions and their foundation.

In the texts on Hölderlin, the original, although then situated within the "holy," is again described by the threefold temporality of the retrieval: the 'original', *das Anfängliche*, "remains as what was formerly," adumbrated by the poets. "Their adumbration points to what is forthcoming and breaking forth."[88] Thanks to the poets, the breaking-forth of presencing, *phusis*, becomes thinkable now, whereas it was "formerly perceptible only in a first glimmer, as the initial and original rise of what, since then, has become present in everything."[89] The original is not *phusis* itself, but the "first glimmer" of *phusis*, formerly recognized at the dawn of Western culture, set to work today by those we therefore call poets, and anticipated by thinkers.

The retrieval of the being-question is anticipatory *because* it is poietic. This results from the very way in which the original question of ontology is traced back by Heidegger beyond the "battle of giants" among schools and doctrines. The first historical gleam of being as *phusis* (in Heraclitus) was a happening in which a measure was set: "What was thereafter to be called 'being' was set into work, setting up a measure."[90] But this "happened" (*geschah*). No master-mind, human or not human, set any standards. Heraclitus only responded to "the claim of being as a whole."[91] The same holds for the other question, the ontological question of origin. It is answered always by a *poiēsis* that precedes any possible human doing. The arrangement of concealing-unconcealing "produces itself" for every age. It institutes itself without an agent or actor. Because it is poietic in this non-humanistic sense, it is also anticipatory: "A genuine inception is always a leap ahead (*Vorsprung*),"[92] incalculable and unforeseeable. To "dwell as a poet," then, means to espouse the aletheiological mutations strictly, 'sticking' closely to their folds. The decisive thinkers knew how to give themselves over to the "releasement of the original" (*Gelassenheit des Anfänglichen*)[93] which implicates us in its folds, so that the great philosophers do not really know what is given them to think.[94] The actual starting point of their thought is the dawn of an economy. This essential implication in the poietic fabric was acknowledged only by thinkers like Heraclitus. In retrospect we can learn from them that any order of presence locates, and in this sense even precedes, pre-understanding. Such a dependence of *Verstehen* on its economic situation, which becomes obvious in transition periods, tells us something about how a potential of thought is *one* with the order of its age.

The situation in which thinking finds itself at the reversals of history is indeed characterized by a remarkable kind of oneness, reminiscent of Parmenides. It results from the amphibology of the original just described. As a new *age* dawns, the starting point of *thought* shifts in such a way that the unthematized understanding of presence renovates itself. In the reversals of history it becomes plain, down to the vertigo seizing civilizations, that the 'economic' original, the world's *legein*, and the 'existential' original, the noetic *legein*, share one and the same starting point.[95] This essential dependence of thought on economies remains masked as long as thinking is described simply as a predicate of the subject 'man' or as the faculty for producing statements about him. From the viewpoint of the deconstruction of past historical fields, the incipience of an epoch and the incipience of its noesis are one and the same rise. This identity constitutes the full phenomenon of the 'original'.

The Parmenidean figure of unity, according to which thought begins where an *epochē* begins, should dissipate a frequent misunderstanding about what Heidegger calls *das Anfängliche,* the 'original'. Contrary to what some have claimed is implied in a few text segments, the initial setting into work of truth—in a work of art or in the establishment of a community, for example[96]—in no way entails praise of the heroic leader, of the great man as founder, of genius. On the contrary, "the creators, poets, thinkers, statesmen" are charged with what one's aletheiological constellation renders present, in the mode it is brought to presence. Their action follows in the closest possible way the struggle between what is epochally within reach and epochally out of reach. It follows the *polemos* (Heraclitus) of hiding-showing as it stamps an age. This polemics, and not man's initiative, is said to "project" what formerly remained "unheard of, unsaid and unthought." It is what inaugurates, what initiates the new. Men come and take it up "thereafter."[97] Their doings and dealings begin with what *alētheia* prescribes. Such an insurpassable priority, through which the dispositions of presence precede all thoughts and actions, gives an 'epochal' face to the identity between thinking and presencing. In the identity between *noein* and *einai,* being "claims and determines" all apprehending[98] like a transcendental condition. In this sense, it anticipates *noein,* although by itself, separated from what men think and do, an economy of presence is nothing. It "uses" men (Anaximander's *chreōn*). Only when the inception of thoughts and actions remains dissociated from epochal inception do they become 'humanistic', without locus or history. Such dislocation is what ideologies produce. Whether in the name of human dignity or any other 'standard', they separate discourse and practice from their embeddedness in a concrete aletheiological order.

The establishment of an order may be called poetic,[99] or rather, poietic, since the epochal struggle between the concealed and the unconcealed is itself a setting into work, *poiēsis*. The poet makes a given disposition of present and absent entities appear in speech. But, to quote René Char again, "in your essence you are constantly a poet."[100] Why? Because in his essence—which no hubris can swerve from the course of aletheiological orderings—man keeps responding and corresponding to what projects itself and sets itself in place around him; to "being" as it "sends itself" to him, "sets itself up" and "is a mittence";[101] in a word, to the original as it *sets in* around him. Man is not the measure of all things, but the identity between the birth of an epoch and the birth of a mode of thought is. It alone allows one to understand how "thinking changes the world": "The word of thinkers knows no authors."[102] Finally, this identity alone makes, for instance, Hölderlin's fear understandable when he writes: "Formerly I could rejoice in a new truth or in a better vision of what is above us and around us; now I fear that my fate will be like that of the ancient Tantalus, to whom the gods gave more than he could digest."[103] Thinking occurs as the truth, the epochal *alētheia*, institutes itself. As an order of presence-absence gathers itself, most articulately in those called thinkers and poets, the new comes about in history.

If the original is the identical rise of a *lex* of things and of its *logos* in thought, then what Heidegger holds to constitute the phenomenality of phenomena must be understood as twice anti-humanistic:[104] "The beginning reversal of the inherited position toward things"—that is, the beginning of an epochal *lex* (*legein* in the economic sense)—arises of itself; and the thought that gathers it (*legein* in the noetic sense) is in turn only the self-manifestation of that new law, that "changing fundamental position in the midst of relations to entities."[105] Phenomenality is constituted, not in reference to one source of forms, but by the systemic regime in which phenomena appear. Hence also Heidegger's claim that thinking is neutral with regard to the moral law, values, and the like.

One has to see the extent to which Heidegger's kinship with Parmenides in this domain upsets common sense. If he professed a relation of antecedent and consequent between an epochal order (*lex*) and thinking (*legein*), his claim would be less difficult. Such a relation may indeed suffice to account for the possibility of regional theories.[106] But one *logos* that spells itself out in two loci, the 'world' and 'thinking', is another matter. Again, common sense might admit that the opinions and convictions of men *depend* on the constellations of truth in history, on their cultural worlds; that a medieval may well be held in an order of presence such that the *mathēsis universalis*, or a critique of pure reason, or a genealogy of morals remain for him projects that are epochally out of reach. But is it not good sense to add that when a Duns Scotus writes about the order of essences or a Thomas Aquinas about analogy of being, all the same it is *authors* who conceive such views? Likewise, is it not good sense to say that the rise of an epochal regime is at most the necessary empirical condition of our thinking, however situated we may be; that the law of hiding-showing is perhaps a concrete a priori of thought, but that an identity between *legein* as economy of presence and *legein* as thought amounts to yet another version of monism—the opposite of ever-changing presencing?

By so reducing the phenomenology of reversals to a mere theory of *Sitz im Leben*, what gets cancelled out is the unitary happening of *epechein* and thinking: they are one in the way they come to pass. An epoch is not the other of thought, neither its empirical antecedent, nor its matter. Both are 'original' in the process[107] in which they occur, in their *oriri*. This identity of occurrence is what Heidegger at first called transcendence. "Being is the *transcendens* pure and simple"[108] because, following Kant's discovery, the structures of *Dasein*'s stepping beyond itself and those of the world into which it transcends itself are the same. Later, "thinking" explicitly designates the process character of the identity between being and life. In the epochs, when novelty unites differently phenomena and thought, their structural identity is most evident. If the decisive philosophers do not know what, literally, comes upon them, this is because they find themselves in the midst of a sudden phenomenal reversal whose latencies are still unknown, nameless and impossible to name. In these breaks there are few actually new things to be known, but there is much potential to be thought. For their investigation, Heidegger borrows from Kant the distinction between knowing and thinking,[109] or between "explanatory thinking" and "the other thinking."[110] Thus the original identity between a phenomenal constellation and the discourse about it entails no knowledge claims, it is not an issue for knowledge.[111] It is, on the contrary, the issue for a thinking that is *"besinnlich,"* the thinking compliant with the "sense" (*Sinn*) of the reversals: the historical directedness of their destiny.

The transcendental legacy in the description of original inceptions is ultimately preserved by the difference between a knowable ontic order and its thinkable historical rise or coming-about. Transcendental inquiry steps back from an *established* fact (*Vorhandenheit des Vorhandenen*), to disclosedness as the universal and necessary condition for such a fact to appear (*Entdecktheit des Vorhandenen*),[112] that is, to the *establishing*, the coming about of the economic functions that insert it in a play of unconcealment. The *Anfang* that regulates what Heidegger calls entities in their totality is the identity between *epechein* and *noein*. The identical coming-about of epochal being and thinking imprints its rule on all phenomena that become knowable for a time. Clearly transcendentalism has come a long way from thought as regulating the knowable through subjective *principles* to thought as regulating the knowable through epochal *inceptions*. Nevertheless, it is still according to the model of the a priori that epochal disclosure, the initial unity of unconcealment, becomes understandable at all. The other thinking, that which is other than knowledge, has no assignable content except this initial identity as it structures any aletheiological constellation. That identity determines in advance the modalities in which a proposition will be conformable to a given; it determines what will be 'true' in the sense of adequate judgments. The original identity between 'objective' *epochē* and 'subjective' *logos* (life) is the source of any and every law, whether it regulates cultural functions or reason.[113] "The inception is always what is greatest,"[114] but as the inception of both an order of presence and the response to it in thought, it also contains an inner complexity. It is "greatest" since it precedes everything knowable and doable as its condition, and it is complex since it dictates the rules for everything knowable and doable. In an entirely different context Heidegger thus preserves Kant's discovery that what we can only think regulates what we can know as well as what we can do.[115]

To commence is not to accomplish mighty deeds. And if the inception of thought bears the names of Heraclitus, Parmenides, Plato, it is only insofar as these names designate the decisive, critical reversals in the order of presence. Any inception is a disclosure of a new aggregate of entities. "But disclosure is *alētheia*. This and the *logos* are the same."[116] Truth institutes itself in presence in one stroke, "abruptly, in an instant."[117] Understood as the rise of an order, the original regulates the totality of existence, "its gods, its art, its polity, its knowledge."[118] Truth qua *alētheia* precedes all instances of truth qua *adaequatio*, it is their transcendental condition. This implies that such instances remain essentially contingent, provisional. The history of being becomes the issue for phenomenology when *the conditions of pre-understanding*, discovered by the existential analytic, are in turn examined and *show themselves to be the original shifts in history*. These put in place the coordinates that determine the modalities of pre-understanding for a while.

The epochal beginnings indeed yield an anti-subjectivist notion of the transcendental *because* they are occurrences. They exhibit the historical 'sense' of presencing. It is therefore a misapprehension of the *Sinn des Seins* to construe the 'sense' as 'meaning' for reflection and to advocate a 'return to the subject' as the hermeneuts do who claim kinship with Heidegger. Even in *Being and Time,* 'sense' implied direction as much as meaning: time is the sense of being as one would say that a body moves in one *sense* or another.[119] This antihumanistic thrust of the vocabulary of sense in Heidegger is confirmed especially in his ontological comprehension of the original. The *epochē* is to be understood as inception since it imparts a new orientation to phenomena. The temporal bearings of the being question are thus due to the fact that it has always been 'stamped' epochally. In deflecting the issue of time from the three ecstases toward the sudden epochs in history, this phenomenology definitely ceases to be centered on man as the bestower of meaning.

Three conclusions should be retained:

1. The difference between the *original* comprehension of ontology and the *ontological* comprehension of the original amounts to a radicalization of the difference between the empirical and its transcendental conditions. Something new (ontic) can happen in history only because thinking belongs to the (ontological) displacements called 'epoch' as *Dasein* belongs in the world. There could be no lived history if thinking did not essentially comply with those displacements. Heidegger uses the Kantian understanding of the a priori—a set of conditions—to retrieve the Parmenidean understanding of identity: the economical *legein* and the noetic *legein* are one insofar as they make novelty in history possible. Concretely, their identity allows for the shifts from pre-classical antiquity to the classical age, to Rome, to the Middle Ages, to modernity, and to the contemporary era.

2. What is original in history is the identity between two non-identical beginnings, between a novel disposition of phenomena and the new starting point it provides for thought (i.e., for existence). But if this is so, the

epochs cannot merely be understood as the sequence of the ages just enumerated. The epochs introduce a fluidity into any given economy. The constellations of truth must be thought of as broken by incessant internal rearrangements.

3. The original in the sense of "the earliest dawn" (*die früheste Frühe*), Heidegger says, is an object of piety—that is, of "compliance"[120]—for us to the extent to which its return, "the other dawn" (*die andere Frühe*), becomes a possibility.[121] That possibility assigns us our locus in the flux of economies. The *topology of the epochal constellations gives us our location:* near the original which remains what is "initially familiar,"[122] but which also reserves itself while it grants itself.[123] In speaking of piety and of the possible dawn of another order of things, Heidegger indulges neither in secularized religion nor in utopia. To be pious (*fromm* as *fügsam*) is to heed (*sich fügen*) the junctures (*Fugen*) of concealment-unconcealment.[124]

§19. The 'Originary' Origin, or How Presencing Comes About

> *Phusis*, the originary mode of appearing. . . .
>
> *What Is a Thing?*[125]

The *original* modes of appearing are countless; they are as numerous as the disjunctive moments in history. The *originary* mode of appearing, on the other hand, has no history. With the originary concept of ontology and the ontological concept of the originary we leave the phenomenology of reversals (needless to add that this is not to return to an ontology of full presence, to a predicative conception of origin in which presencing would be the predicate of an *ens originarium*, an entity out of reach for our understanding but considered constantly present to the phenomena within our reach). Rather, presencing itself is to be understood as originary, as emergence in the economic fabric, as pure coming-about. Thought of *originally*, this coming-about articulates itself through the epochs in the past history of being; thought of *originarily*, it "puts an end to the history of being."[126]

The originary origin, "the rise that presences at the same time as it withdraws into itself,"[127] is always implicated in what we live and understand. But it is rarely grasped for its own sake. Whence the necessity of a phenomenology which attempts to "wrest" it from present entities; which disimplicates the *presently* given, its epochal entrance into *presence*, and *presencing* as such, i.e., as temporal (although ahistorical) coming about.[128] The identity between thought and the *original* origin referred human initiatives back to the aletheiological constellations which consolidate and dissolve and which a thoughtful man lets come to pass. The identity between thought and the *originary* disarms man in another way: it deprives thinking of all references to entities. The description of the reversals in history teaches us nothing about the *Ursprung*. It has to be *ersprungen*, attained by a leap.[129] Only as a step back from referential constructs does "philosophy belong to the most originary of human efforts."[130] The Parmenidean figure of an event-like identity takes on its radical form here: at the root not only of the metaphysical notions of the origin (*archē* and *principium*), but also of these same notions under deconstruction, being and thought are one in their *phuein*, their identical arising. Entities become phenomena when they appear, united with others, in a finite constellation which is their truth. To think is to follow this appearance and this gathering. It is to adhere to the movement through which present entities emerge into presence, by an 'originary leap' (*Ur-sprung*). Originary thinking heeds such emergence for its own sake and not for the sake of these entities. To advocate a 'leap' in thinking is therefore not to plead some form of the irrational, but to disentangle the two levels of the temporal difference: that of the 'original', in which the coming-about of presence is described as the birth of a more or less short-lived network of present entities, and that of the 'originary', in which that coming-about is described without reference to entities.[131]

But what does it mean to say that this event-like identity (*ursprünglich*, not *anfänglich*) is essentially ahistorical?[132] It means that it resists reiteration, that the return to the ancients is not enough—although as a means of constituting the phenomenality of the originary, that return is indispensable.[133] As soon as it has occurred, the originary identity between presencing and thinking is lost. It remains the great absentee in all reflection on history. That is why we will never comprehend from within what Delphi meant for the Greeks, Sacsayhuaman for the Incas, or the proclamations of Jesus for the Jews. Indeed, how could the mutual emergence of things, actions, and words be repeated once their interdependence has changed its mode? The origin as entering into presence is instantaneous, the extreme finitude, it has no history—which is why we remain forever mute when we would like to know what the 'puma' was before the conquest of Peru, how the trans-Andine routes, the decimal system, the works and sacrifices, the ornaments, the solid metal statues, the temples of Cuzco, the caciques and the emperor, and death were mutually present.

Phuein has no history, no destiny. But this is not to say that it is atemporal. If it were, how could acting ever be *kata phusin*, following the coming-about of presence? The temporality of this coming-about may be understood through the corresponding notion of nothingness. The 'original', i.e., an epochal beginning, is a rise out of *ontic* nothingness, out of all those (possible) entities that remain absent for an age. The 'originary' is a rise out of *ontological* nothingness, out of the pull toward absence that permeates presencing to its very heart. This presencing-absencing is originary time: both approaching (*Angang*)[134] and departing (*Abgang*);[135] *genesis* and *phthora*, rising and declining;[136] being and non-being.[137] The mutual emer-

gence of phenomena, in which non-being temporalizes being, is the 'originary' origin, *Ursprung*.

The togetherness of hiding and showing can be thought of as temporal only
in regard to the future. Heidegger has always held the possible, the not-yet,
to "stand higher"[138] than the actual. But the anticipatory character is not the
same in the case of the 'original' and the 'originary'. At the beginning of an
era, new components enter the economy of words, things and deeds. The
gold of the conquistadors, the theses nailed to the doors of the church at
Wittenberg (if that gesture ever took place), the insurrections of the peasants
following Thomas Müntzer, are just so many new elements that compose the
economy of emerging modernity. But the gold, Luther's theses, and the
Peasants' Revolt were absent, economically impossible, until that epochal
reversal. At the breaks in history, then, certain entities withdraw ("At the
end of the Middle Ages, leprosy disappeared from the Western world"[139]),
fall into oblivion, and others reveal themselves. Such is the structure of *ontic*
hiding-showing as the deconstruction—the "overcoming of metaphysics"—
allows it to be read at the moments of transition. The *ontological* structure of
hiding-showing does not involve entities. It is the interplay of *lēthē* and
alētheia, "without regard to the relation of being to entities. . . . What
matters is to let all 'overcoming' be and leave metaphysics to itself."[140] Why
does the originary hiding-showing remain unthinkable as long as the question of being remains tied to the project of overcoming metaphysics? Because that project is aimed at dismantling the ontic economies, at dethroning
ultimate referents, at subverting the principial constellations of which our
history consists, whereas presencing as such is to be thought "prior to the
[ontological] difference . . . and therefore *without* entities."[141] What then is
the futurity due to which presencing appears as a temporal, although not a
historical, event? Heidegger's answer is: the appropriation of absence. But
this is meant to suggest no more than a feature in the essence of manifestation. For manifestation to be a temporal event, the absence which lies at its
heart has to be seen as possible presence. In any phenomenon, what is
future-oriented is indeed the *possibility* that belongs to it: the most tenuous
element, as it were, in any aletheiological constellation. Heidegger tries to
suggest this ahistorical temporality through the German phrase *"es gibt,"*
"there is."[142] The *es* ('it') designates the utter anonymity of presencing, and
the *gibt* ('gives'), its temporal nature.

Needless to add that the 'originary', the *phuein* which is manifestation,
remains irreducible to the ancient *existentia* or the mere *dass* (the fact-of-
being), and the 'original', the *epochē*, to the ancient *essentia* or the mere
was (quiddity). The epochs do not add whatness to being as they would in a
metaphysics of real composition. If *phusis* were just another name for
actuality, living "according to *phusis*" would be a rather abstract en-
deavor—divine, perhaps. But as thoroughly temporal, being has lost all
divine connotations. It renders the economies—and thereby, any modalities of action—possible by the way it retains absence. The differentiating

factor in the economies, which determines what can be done and thought, is the temporal rapport of *alētheia* and *lēthē*.

In *Being and Time*, the 'originary' was already recognized as the temporal condition of all that can be done and thought. Entities "arise," Heidegger wrote then, within the horizon opened by our project of being, according to the way we relate to them.[143] But since it remained construed out of our death, temporality could not yet be retained as mere presencing. What is 'originary' in *Being and Time* is the opening, projected by ourselves, in which entities *are* insofar as they appear to the entity that *we* are. The Kantian model is obvious. The continuity between transcendental criticism and existential analysis appears nowhere more clearly than when Heidegger finally links the *Ursprung* to transcendental apperception.[144] So understood, the 'originary' is *finite* in that it manifests some entities against a background of others that are not manifest. The necessarily selective character of such gathering signifies that the unlimited manifestation of everything potentially present is impossible.[145] This has some consequences for the understanding of truth. The existential structures by which we discover entities in their many ways of being present also "manifest the most originary phenomenon of truth." Truth is understood as the disclosure opened up by our being-there. The 'originary', in *Being and Time*, is thus both an homage to, and a denial of, subjectivist transcendentalism. A homage, since "uncovering is a mode of being-in-the-world," and even the relationships of reciprocal belonging that constitute the world are construed from the standpoint of human being-there: "the world . . . is a character of being-there itself."[146] And yet subjectivist transcendentalism is denied by the equiprimordiality of *Dasein* and the world. All of this certainly does not mean that in *Being and Time* what is originary about truth and the world is conceived "humanistically" in the sense of humanism, that "circulatory movement around man, approximating him more or less" in his metaphysical essence.[147] Rather, in being-there we "let [the world and truth] spring forth" (*Ursprung* as *entspringen lassen*).[148]

The tendency toward anti-humanism in the understanding of the originary—and consequently of truth as disclosure and of the world as the network of phenomenal interconnectedness—becomes reinforced after *Being and Time*. Most revelatory in this respect is the coupling of 'originary' and 'original': in the history of philosophy, "the essence of truth could not be retained and preserved in its original originariness" (*in seiner anfänglichen Ursprünglichkeit*); whence the necessity of "retrieving it more originarily in its originariness."[149] Heidegger now no longer understands truth as a disclosure constituted by man. It does remain located in one privileged entity, however: in "the work of the word, poetry; the work of stone, the temple and the statue; the work of the word, thought; the work of the *polis*, the historical place in which all this is grounded and preserved."[150] What "opens up a world" is no longer the human entity, but a "work."[151]

The originary is thus displaced from being-there to works. That shift clearly reveals the anti-humanist thrust of the *Kehre*, but it also shows how the originary is thought in relation to the original. This link appears for instance in the opposition between the "world," understood as manifest arrangement, and the "earth," as sheltering and hiding (*bergen*). A work of art "sets up a world . . . and lets the earth be earth."[152] The struggle between hiding and showing, the originary essence of truth, finds itself displaced from existential transcendence to an "originary conflict"[153] between earth and world. What is not immediately apparent in these metaphors is that they refer to the history of presence: the works, especially communities, of which our history is made, each time open a domain for life and thought. Setting to work *differs* from coming to presence. They are distinct as the phenomenology which describes historical constellations is distinct from the transcendental phenomenology of ahistorical presencing. What, then, is substituted as originary for the quasi-humanist 'projection' in Heidegger's early writings, after he has turned away for good from all remnants of subjectivist transcendentalism? It is the anonymous historical happening in which a work imposes itself on a fabric of exchanges among phenomena.[154] Besides communities and works of art there are few classes of entities that so institute a world.[155] Even though, in these writings concerning the history of being, the locus of the originary is no longer the entity that we are, *it is still one entity that institutes a world* and that sets off the struggle between the closed and the open, the aletheiological struggle. That reference to entities and their regions disappears as Heidegger's phenomenology comes into its own: he no longer seeks to understand the originary through its ontological difference from entities, but through its temporal difference from the original.

Once so thematized in itself, the *Ursprung* proves to be irreducibly manifold. This is the decisive discovery. It shows that prior to the binary struggle between veiling and unveiling, presencing de-centers the process of manifestation. When Heidegger speaks of a fourfold struggle,[156] it is not the number four that is important, but the *fragmentation of the originary*. Presencing then appears as the appropriation, "out of an originary oneness,"[157] of the multiple dimensions of the world.[158] This event of multiple appropriation "cannot be retained either as being or as time"; it is rather their mutual coming to presence, "the neutral '*and*' in the title *On Time and Being*."[159] Presencing has lost its center. The "originary oneness" allows for no henology. Heidegger never conceived of presence according to the *pros hen* model, as "presence to" man, to a work, or to some other entity. But if indeed he understood the field of presence as opened 'by' man or an artwork, even these phenomenal referents lose their codifiers' prestige. Originary oneness is no more than the simple event of any phenomenon's 'coming-about'. This event has its own temporality, its "motility,"[160] which no longer has anything to do with the ecstases or with the epochs. The event is the most ordinary trait, that most common to any experience: the appearance of the 'there'. To speak of the fourfold is then not without polemical overtones, directed against representations of a 'universe', that is, of a world turned toward one, be it a substantive (metaphysical), formal (transcendental) or phenomenal (e.g., the artwork) 'one'. Nothing is gained—on the contrary, everything is lost—when the event of presencing is interpreted, as some commentators have done, from the viewpoint of the Aristotelian difference between *dynamis* and *energeia*,[161] or from that of the Hegelian dialectic of recognition.[162] In both cases, coming to presence or presencing remains oriented toward man, centripetal, not truly a manifold play. The event of appropriation is *one* only as it directs dimensions of manifestation (such as "the earth and the sky") into an "essential mutual relation."[163] These dimensions of the fourfold have little in common with phenomenal regions besides their multiplicity. They are as multiple as Dionysus torn to pieces.[164]

The way presencing comes about differs from the way something new comes about in history. This difference between the originary and the original is the *temporal difference,* the ontological difference radicalized. Heidegger establishes it in three successive approaches:[165] (1) the originary is the a priori of the original; (2) to think the originary is to bring the history of epochal beginnings, that is, of original origins, to its end; (3) the concealment that belongs to the essence of the original is cancelled, superelevated, and preserved in the originary.

1. The event of coming to presence is the a priori of any epochal beginning. We have seen that *Ursprung* does not designate a new historical stamp, not yet another mark in the sequence of Western configurations. The versions of the original, as they have left their imprint on the way something new has been capable of coming about in history, all "belong to" and are "reabsorbed in" the originary. The a priori so understood certainly cannot be construed according to the traditional model inaugurated by Plato (as ideal cause) and taken up by Kant (as subjective condition). And yet, as a priori, it can only function as preceding any experience. The ahistorical event in which presencing comes about must "(in one way or another)" be recognized as the condition for the possibility of the historical occurrence in which something new, a new order of things present, appears. We understand 'being' as the synchronic emergence of such an order, which situates everything knowable as well as doable. As emergence, it determines not only presence but also and identically, absence, out of which emergence takes place. To discover the determinative function of the temporal difference, it suffices to wonder that in each instant *there is* such an event-like distributing of presence-absence, that presence 'comes about'. In its ultimate phenomenal content, then, the difference appears as that between the *there is* and the epochal stamps that arrange an order of things present and absent.[166] Presenc*ing*-absenc*ing* is the a priori event that makes it possible for any such order to spell itself out in history.

2. The entire intent of Heideggerian phenomenology is toward this emergence of presence, thought of in itself and for its own sake. That is what is meant when he claims that the lineage of epochal inceptions has come to an end. "Thinking then stands in and before 'It' which has sent the various shapes of epochal being."[167] But "It" is always understood by each and every one, prior to any empirical content. When an entity like the city of Cuzco was inhabited solely by the descendants of the emperor, to the exclusion of any other clan, the web of being was pre-understood otherwise than when Pizarro had churches and convents built on the partially razed Inca dwellings; and Cuzco "is there" still differently as it turns quietly into a commodity on the international tourist market; differently again when, sooner rather than later, "the air which is so pure that corpses don't rot," in the words of a Spanish chronicler, surely will have become unbreathable even for the monoliths, when UNESCO will decide to protect them, too, under plastic domes. At each stage of this history, certain *entities* are present, others absent. Today, Atahualpa is no longer in that valley and modern industry, not there yet. The absence of what is gone and the absence of what is to come demarcate the field of ontic[168] presence. At each stage, too, there is *beingness*, the foundational beginning of an order that articulates an aletheiological constellation for thought. Lastly, at each stage there is the *there is* itself, the event of coming-about by which presence rather than pure absence is possible. But to become attentive to this last origin, to the bare springing forth, the philosophic gaze must be diverted from the series of the constellations of beingness over the course of the ages. What is it precisely then that is seen as drawing to a close?

3. "With the awakening into the event of appropriation, the forgottenness of being is cancelled, super-elevated, and preserved."[169] Forgottenness is what draws to a close. But is this to say that to think presencing beyond "apprenticeship" and "preparation,"[170] would amount to capturing it at the high noon of a univocal 'there is', beyond all absence? No, for as we have seen, in its advent presence withdraws into itself; it is *essentially* "a bestowal in withdrawal."[171] Inasmuch as the event is both appropriation and expropriation in one, the concealment that characterizes the epoch of metaphysics is *aufgehoben*. To be sure, this allusion to Hegelian dialectic does not make it easier to understand how the ('originary') event is linked to and differs from history (the 'original'). What can be said, though, is that a shift in standpoint occurs: historical time is no longer merely described through the reversals, but transcendentally construed as different from primordial time, the event. In that sense, the original, along with the concealment that mingles with all beginnings, is indeed *cancelled*. As deconstruction, then, attains its aim, as it sets free a springing forth entirely other than the original, it also *preserves* historical time in the always nascent coming about of presence that founds nothing. Lastly, it has *super-elevated* concealment, namely, from *epochē* to *lēthē*, and so introduced absence, the not-yet, expropriation, the *ad* of the future, into "*appropriation*," into presencing as

*ad*vent. "For the thinking that enters the event of appropriation, the history of being as what is to be thought, is at an end."[172] The allusion to dialectics— a *hapax legomenon,* single occurrence, in Heidegger—concerns exclusively the step back from 'epochal' forgottenness of being, to *lēthē* and its temporal figure, 'expropriation'. The allusion in no way entails any reconciliation of opposites, nor the constitution of any universal. If the history of being comes to "an end," Heidegger's negation of principles remains non-dialectical.

Such is the 'step back' from the original to the originary, by which Heidegger attempts to overcome the epochal principles that have governed the constellations of present-absent things. The 'It gives', or better: the 'there is' (*'Es gibt'*), is to be grasped in such a way that it accounts for the possibility of these concrete constellations and their principles. But the issue of phenomenology lies beyond them. What, then, is at issue in the overcoming of metaphysics? It is the effort to forestall the relapse from an understanding of the origin as *event* into its *principial* comprehension. The transmutation through which presencing institutionalizes itself into principles that rule and justify action is the ill fate of the origin. As pure emergence, the originary is essentially fragile, finite, no sooner recognized than ready to turn into a principle. Heidegger may have done a disservice to his own radical phenomenology by surrounding 'It' which 'gives' presence— i.e., its self-giving—with an aura of mystification. *'Es gibt'* means: appearance occurs. Transcendental philosophers since Kant have stressed that *what appears* is beyond the reach of knowledge. As Heidegger displaces the transcendental conditions from the subject to originary presencing, he radicalizes this apophatism, too. He urges us to be silent before the mystery of that which 'gives'. What is at stake is the impossibility of speaking of absence as absence. The "expropriation" at the very heart of appropriation "includes the question: expropriation toward where? Of the direction and the sense of this question nothing more was said."[173] Unknowability, too, is then taken "a step back," namely from the Kantian noumenon as absent, to absencing as such. In any principial order, absence is one distinctive feature of the supreme referent. The medieval God and the Kantian noumenon can only impart their measure on our living and thinking because they escape our grasp. To fulfill their normative office, both must rule from remote and impenetrable heights. Radical phenomenology, on the other hand, not only brings principial history to an end, but it takes away from absence the aura of authority by showing its *temporal* "direction and sense." The price paid, in the metaphysical quest for a distant father, is the abandonment of the temporal essence of presencing. Any ultimate referent always governs, fully and timelessly present in its absence. Not so 'It'.

The annihilation, in Heidegger, of philosophy's legitimating, justificatory function results from the link he establishes between the 'original' and the 'originary'.[174] If the history made of "stamps" of being (*Seinsprägungen*) comes to an end,[175] the one issue for philosophy—for thinking—will be the event of presencing as such. The original is then opposed to the originary as the last epochal principle, the technological, scientific, industrial complex (*Gepräge*[176]) is to the possibility of a turning. This would be a reversal entirely other than those separating the epochs. The phenomenology of the originary *It* "does not wish and is not able to predict a future"; but it wishes indeed and is also able to demand "that man be ready for a determination which, whether it is heard or not, always speaks in the still undecided destiny of man."[177] What is clear, at least, is that this originary determination sustains, authors or authorizes nothing. *It* is neither present nor absent, nor another "stamp." It differs from the two forms of rule, *archē* and *principium*, as well as from the original, in that it fails to stand in league with duration. Any ultimate referent that would legitimate human activities would have to subsist, remain constantly present and available, ready to be called upon as a norm wherever action is taking place. But if *Ursprung* is indeed a determination that is heard everywhere and always by man, it by no means determines praxis by referring it to one founding term. It is a "broken foundation," and we have only manifold modes of emerging within a "temporal play space" by which to measure our actions.[178] Compared to the quest for foundations, and viewed as restoring innocence to radical multiplicity, the originary can only appear as play.[179] The manifold *Ursprung* commits "thinking to the play with that in which being qua being rests, and not with something on which [being] would repose as on a foundation."[180] *It* is the time factor in that play.

The inquiry into the epochal beginnings already amounted to de-humanizing, so to speak, the phenomenon of origin. A 'project' of truth was seen as springing, not from existence, but from the aletheiological struggle. The inquiry into presencing consummates that anti-humanistic impact. An original project (*Entwurf*)—Inca civilization or modern technology—is possible only due to the always preceding originary coming-about (or throwing-toward, *Zuwurf*) which is presencing. The difference that impels Heidegger's thought more and more exclusively is that between the pro-jective original and the ad-jective originary. From the origin as an existential project to the origin as an epochal project, the *regions* of presence were displaced from our own being to that of history; but with the step back to the mere event of presencing, phenomenology ceases to be regional.[181] As Heidegger comes to recognize presencing as the one issue for thought, the structure of springing forth turns from a making (or 'setting' into work) to a receiving (or 'letting'). In this way, the poietic element appears as secondary in comparison with *phuein*, originary springing forth. Once the primacy of 'letting' (*entlassen*) over 'making' (*poiein*) is recognized, that is, once *archē* and *principium* are unmasked as ontic substitutes for the originary, metaphysics has found its location: as the sum of the attempts to objectivate the *Ursprung* under the guise of arch-present entities. Their reign, be it divine, logical, or human, functions as a pretext that obfuscates the texture of presencing.[182] Little would be gained if deconstructing that pretext were only a matter of revoking metaphysical representations, without laying bare the 'forgotten' texture. In asking what is genuinely originary among phenomena, Heidegger's whole point is to free that texture of interconnectedness; to rehabilitate, in other words, the essentially non-objectifiable, multiple event of phenomena *entering* into mutual presence. From this rehabilitation nothing is gained for the lofty problem of securing an underwriter who guarantees truth, and much is lost for the systems of authority articulating their legitimation on the *pros hen* relation. This reference to a first showed itself to be the conceptual pivot that has allowed metaphysicians since Aristotle to translate a first philosophy into practical philosophy. Radical phenomenology, on the other hand, will never allow propositions or public and private acts to be referred to the originary as accidents are referred to substance; or, in the most recent attempt at legitimating praxis through a first philosophy, as Critical Theory refers rational propositions about emancipation to an ideal community of undistorted communication.[183]

At the end of an epoch, when its principle expires, thinking is in the unique position of *reverting* to the issue of presencing (to 'the question of being'); but it can seize that possibility only by *subverting* all ultimate referents. The post-modern age, inaugurated by Nietzsche,[184] is the one in which the availability of referential truth for purposes of legitimation becomes suspect. Indeed, when not only one or another epochal principle, but the *pros hen* itself which in metaphysics sustains all firsts, gives way, it becomes urgent to ask how the origin could ever come to be conceived on the model of juridic justification and architectonic underpinning. The difference between the 'original' and the 'originary' then tells us something about presencing as such, as opposed to its predominant modes in the West: namely, that it is without principle, an-archic, and that in an age of transition the origin as pure *phuein* is all there remains to be thought for those who look for truth . . . very little, to be sure, to justify and sustain any economic referent. But as long as one seeks to revert to the initial question of Western philosophy without also subverting the focal points into which that question has crystallized, it will remain unintelligible why Heidegger can claim: "finding the way into the truth of being" presupposes that we renounce "instituting rules."[185]

Heidegger's progressive discovery of the origin as essentially an-archic is traceable by following his usage of the phrase *Es gibt* ("There is," literally "It gives"). At first it refers to the phenomenon of understanding, that is, to ourselves as discovering things in the world and thereby rendering them true.[186] "Only as long as *Dasein* 'is' . . . 'is there' being."[187] Later (second period), Heidegger interprets passages such as the line just quoted from the perspective of the history of presence: 'being' is given differently at each epochal reversal.[188] The sudden advent of an order 'gives' a new modality of presence. 'It' which 'gives' originally sets itself to work in an epochal order. To seek truth then means to preserve the novelty of this setting to work:[189] for Freudianism or Marxism, to seek truth would mean to keep alive the insurrection among 'entities as a whole' as it bears the names of Freud and Marx; it would mean to safeguard (*bewahren*) their aletheiological (*wahr*) constellation not in its doctrinal fixity, but in its incipiency. The dogmatisms that have been born from these new beginnings, with their retinue of individual or collective oppression systems, show to everyone's satisfaction how easy it is for the original to be perverted into a principle. Then the uniform rules: 'in principle', men belonging to one epoch all do the same things. Finally in Heidegger's writings where the "There is" (third period) designates the simple springing forth of presence, "It" which "gives," not only bears no human name,[190] but it is operative in language in such a way that it forbids thinking of the origin otherwise than as an an-archic, non-principial, manifold: this neuter "It" is neither being[191] nor time.[192] And if it "is" speech, "all standards are still lacking in every way for determining it."[193] "It," the coming-about of presence, is nothing, as the visibility of the visible is nothing. At the same time, that coming-about is everything: it is the monstration of the visible, and in this sense, its truth. Here there is no risk of dogmatism and no room for administration and surveillance, whether over thinking or doing.

The link between Heidegger's late form of the ontological difference and deconstruction is easily stated: the 'original' is the deconstructed *archē*. To grasp an entity by its form, or a case of generation or corruption by its causes, that is, to grasp metaphysical being or becoming, means to respond in one way or another to the question: where does this come from? The origin as *archē*, even critically articulated in epistemology, is still conceived in view of a mediate, genetic production of knowledge. To explain substance and becoming, or to explain our knowledge of them, is always to trace substantial being, becoming, or knowledge to *an entity* that 'gives' them: *forma dat esse*, "the form gives being." But in the 'original' as deconstructed *archē*, no such causal, entitative giving occurs. Phenomena are seized in the rise of an epochal order, which incipience produces no science. The original is only thinkable. In this deconstruction knowledge loses its essence, at least if to know is essentially *scire per causas*, knowing through causes.

Likewise, the 'originary' is the deconstructed *principium*. A principle governs beyond time. It manifests itself in its effects. But the originary manifests nothing; it is manifesta*tion*, the temporal event of manifest*ing*. Understood originarily, an entity is true as it enters into presence. Its manifestation is its truth. In this way, the deconstruction of the 'principle' leads to a differential understanding of truth: the field in which 'there is' truth is the difference between a modality of presence and presencing, or between the given and the giving. This differential, phenomenological understanding of truth precedes all of its causal, metaphysical conceptions. It is also prior to—indeed, more originary than—economic arrangements and their description. Heidegger's retrieval of the originary entirely abolishes whatever could have survived, in the guise of remembering founding deeds, from the old genetic method in his program of returning to the original.[194]

The origin is said in many ways: metaphysical *archai* and *principia,* and phenomenological 'original' and 'originary'—the original rise of a mode of being (*Seiendheit*,[195] "beingness") and the originary rise which is the event of being. The gist of Heidegger's deconstructive method is this difference between mode and event, the temporal difference. It puts out of function any notion of origin as first referent. It thereby renders possible a phenomenology of being that is not a first philosophy. In order to show, then, how claims to both theoretical and practical ultimacy are annihilated by Heidegger's dismantling of the *pros hen* model, it is necessary provisionally to separate two questions: How is multiple presencing thinkable ('theoretical' question)? and: What arc its consequences for practice ('practical' question)? The separation of these two questions is provisional since the *question of being* and the *question of acting* are not two different questions for Heidegger.

The temporal difference will allow us first to establish the categories of presencing (Part IV) and then to show their practical implications (Part V). Neither question could be raised without a preliminary understanding of being as time. This has been worked out through the two senses of origin and can now be put to work.

Part Four
Historical Deduction of the
Categories of Presencing

> Wherever the thinking of the Greeks pays
> heed to the presencing of what is present,
> the following traits of presencing are stressed:
> unconcealedness, the rising from
> concealedness, the entry into it, the coming
> and going away, the lingering, the gathering,
> the shining-forth, the resting, the hidden
> suddenness of possible absencing. Through
> these traits of presencing the Greek thinkers
> thought of what is present.
>
> *What Is Called Thinking?*[1]

If Western philosophy—and for Heidegger "there is no other, neither Chinese nor Indian"[2]—was set on its way by the Presocratic experience, the originary can be gathered from the original only by examining how the Presocratic traits of presencing have been 'varied' over the course of the centuries, that is, how factors of discontinuity have determined this continuity without disrupting it. At the contemporary stoppage on the "way enjoined" the West, "the other traits of the being of entities" appear, such as "the objectivity of the object, the reality of the real."[3] Between these two complex clusters of aletheiological modalities, neither of which cancels the other, stretches the history of epochal reversals. Without recounting here how the economic configurations are connected from break to break—how for example, from ἀλήθεια, unconcealment became ὁμοίωσις, then *rectitudo* and *adaequatio,* then certitude, justice, domination[4]—in unframing these successive frameworks it is a matter of setting free what pervades them all (*etwas Durchgängiges*),[5] of liberating the identity running through these differences, of seeing how they are articulated on what is so all-pervading. The unity across time does not rest on any ground, endowed with permanence, be it substantive or subjective. It is nothing that endures beneath appearances, not a suppositum. If it is possible, then, to show that the element pervading the epochs is of a merely *categorial* kind, the absurdity of coopting Heidegger's notion of presencing will leap to the eye. It can be put to use neither as a quasi-divine noumenon nor, at the other extreme of interpretations, as a poor disguise for historicist relativism "locked in the squirrel cage" where "the raw existent nauseates. . . ."[6] For the understanding of the originary—of presencing—the categories trace the middle way between the noumenal and the empirical.

Starting from the raw existant, the *empirical*, clearly no proposition, whether descriptive or prescriptive, can be formulated about praxis. The particular is an object of desire or need, but it yields no discourse. Such was Kant's crucial experience: without a noumenon—or, from the viewpoint of the deconstruction, without some epochal principle—there can be no practical philosophy. Since Heideggerian phenomenology dismantles all noumenal constructs, one may rightly expect that the very project of a *categorization* of presencing cannot remain without consequences for understanding praxis. Heidegger cuts through the received opinion according to which theories that focus on systems (functionalism, structuralism, *et alia*) stand in irreconcilable opposition to theories that focus on praxis. The deduction of categories indeed yields a systemic concept of the 'history of being', in which the epochs are self-regulated like an ecosystem. But at the same time, the hypothesis of withering principles tells one what is to be done at the end of metaphysics as it entails a call to intervention: to the politics of "mortals" (as opposed to the 'rational animal') which consists in "removing" all lingering principial representations (Part V).

IX

TABLE OF THE CATEGORIES OF PRESENCING

§20. The Categorial, the Noumenal, and the Empirical

> A reversal in the meaning of words . . . is no
> mere affair of linguistic usage; it is a reversal
> in being-there—that is, in the clearing of the
> being of entities such that the foundations
> crumble.
>
> *What Is a Thing?*[1]

To the philosophic legitimation of ultimate representations and their rule Heidegger opposes the concept of originary presencing as the (non-dialectical) negation of any such rule. Whence can his subversion be legitimated in its turn? To be sure, the subversion of all sovereign referents is at stake when, late in his writings, he answers the being question in terms of *Ereignis*, the event of appropriation. With that event discovered at the core of every phenomenon, "the foundations crumble," it is *grundstürzend*. The practical consequences to be pointed out later all result from that discovery as it yields the imperative of conforming acting to polymorphous presencing alone. It thus frustrates the very desire for an unshakable ground of theory and action—for a ground, especially, of a theory of action. But what is the preliminary, the prior limen, that bars archic constructs? What delimits the phenomena among which Heideggerian anarchy finds its locus and insinuates itself? It would disconcert any phenomenological rigor if one were able to invoke as a criterion only "the experiences which Heidegger himself has had with Being."[2] The lines cited in the epigraph above point toward the class of phenomena among which anarchy is at all thinkable: the "reversals in being-there."

In the writings after *Being and Time*, the concept of being-there (*Dasein*) signifies less and less the individual and increasingly collectivities and peoples—for example, "the historical being-there of the Greeks."[3] The term designates the situatedness of a *Menschentum* or a community.[4] In the recurring phrase "historical being-there in the midst of entities as a whole," it is synonymous with "fundamental position," and in that sense with "epoch."[5] Heidegger's very idiom thus places the issue of legitimation within anti-humanistic parameters. In the "legitimation of the being of entities," being-there "is in no way human."[6] Where is the network of phenomena to be sought that justifies dissolving all representations of sovereignty and letting any call for standards get lost in the void of the place they have deserted? It is to be sought in questioning the history of being-there about the traits of presencing (objective genitive).

This is not to say that Heidegger expects any legitimation from a *narrative* (as is the case in myths). The history of being-there is narrated only for the sake of discovering the categories of its unfolding. Those categories, the conditions for history, are gathered in a second-order discourse which, although called *Seinsgeschichte*, history of being, no longer tells any story. It is a discourse *about* that unfolding and its story. Nor is the categorial investigation speculative as if it reflected the narrative, the first order discourse, on a more universal level. The difference between the narrative and the inquiry into its general traits is the same as the difference between descriptive and transcendental phenomenology.

In his abandonment of any origin that commences and commands—of any standard as stander-before, as θέσις or position—Heidegger proceeds as in an annulment. His revocation of the titles of rule so generously dispensed by metaphysics follows *criteria*, ways of *krinein,* sorting out and discerning, but not *standards,* postures of measurement.[7] To cancel the juridic instruments of power having passed as legitimate for too long is again to bring legal jurisdiction to bear. Two instances or stages (in the juridical sense) of legitimation must therefore be distinguished: the constructive, which establishes the legitimacy of a regulation of obedience,[8] and the deconstructive, repealing the principial representations on which inherited forms of regulation have rested. To pursue the Kantian metaphor of reason as a tribunal: radical phenomenology acts like a deconstructive higher court cancelling the justifications of authority issued by the constructive lower court of metaphysics. The constructive sentences have been shown to be rooted in the Aristotelian *pros hen*. What is at issue now is the deconstructive sentence, the *legitimation of delegitimizing*. This is possible on the condition that the factors of 'all-pervasive' unity in history not be derived from some in-itself, not even the unity of reason, but be constituted as a network of categorial functions from what in the epigraph above was called the positive "reversals in being-there."[9]

The focus on legitimation through categories, along with the quasi-juridic preoccupations that accompany it, mark the birthplace of transcendental philosophy. For Kant, legitimation designates the procedure whereby *Rechtmässigkeit,* lawfulness, is assured in the usage of a priori concepts. This quest is the pivot on which his critical enterprise revolves. To be sure, in moving from a constructive to a deconstructive use, that method is dissociated from subjectivity, rendered 'anti-humanistic'. But Heidegger never repudiates the attempt to establish legitimating categorial conditions for 'the very issue' of thinking. From Kant to Heidegger, the mechanism of a priori regulation is taken out of the domain of subjectivity, disengaged from the speculative and practical interests that, in Kant, culminate in the question: "What is man?"

In Kantianism the transcendental apparatus legitimates knowledge and action, whereas the Heideggerian retrieval of originary presencing, twin to the delegitimation of regulations of obedience, produces neither scientific knowledge nor any moral law. Rather, it divests thought of all founding power regarding knowledge and action. Stated positively, it invests thought with a new mandate: that of pointing out the historical unfolding of being-there, each configuration of which has been produced by its epochal economy. That historical *description* allows the phenomenologist to gather 'originary' presencing from the 'original' reversals and to ask the *transcendental* question of how the originary differs from the original. If the a priori so discovered is radically poorer than in any German philosophy prior to Heidegger, his way of laying it bare is still a deduction in the Kantian sense. To deduce is to establish the claims of a power (*Vermögen* as well as *Macht*) by sorting out what is "by right" (*quid juris*) from what is "in fact" (*quid facti*).[10] The legitimation of the anarchic origin requires a deduction. This is both feasible and inescapable since presencing can only be thought economically; since the originary appears only in differing from the original; since the event of appropriation (*Ereignis*) can be thematized only through the reversals in historical destiny (*Geschehen*) —inasmuch as it is their condition. It should not be objected that in his last writings Heidegger seeks to think presencing precisely without recourse to orders of presence, the originary without the original, *Ereignis* without *Geschehen*, and that the ontological difference is then no longer his 'leading idea'. Such is indeed the case, but that last project presupposes the cumulative result of the early 'destruction' and the later 'deconstruction'. Furthermore, when in his very last essay Heidegger addresses himself to the issue of legitimation, originary presencing is again situated as different from original epochs: thinking the event of unconcealment is *verbindlich* because such thinking is the counter-move to the epochal transition from Parmenides to Plato and Aristotle.[11] Asking the being question remains essentially inseverable from taking the long detour through the historical or 'destinal' modes of being-there. The temporal difference remains essential to Heidegger's thinking until the end.

To see that essential link, it is sufficient to reflect on one curious consequence of the *Kehre:* in the first writings the transcendental traits of being were gathered, not, as in Aristotle, from the many ways in which we speak of it, nor, as in Kant, from the "covert judgments of common reason,"[12] but from our daily ways of being in the world. It is in the ordinary relationships with what surrounds us that we understand 'always already' what being is. But the reference to daily experience becomes inoperative with the *Kehre*. There is a good reason for this. If presenc-

ing—'being'—is grasped only through its difference from epochal presence, then our everyday experience of being is *lost forever* as soon as a
new fold unfurls presence in a new constellation. Everydayness gives us
immediate access to presencing, but that access remains momentary. To
retrieve it historically is to recover the event of presencing only *medi-
ately*. Heidegger never denies the key discovery made in *Being and
Time*, namely, that we are implicated in the play of presencing and absencing through everydayness. But if 'being' has a history, we can only
recall the everyday originary through the distant original. Past presencing
is mute. That is why we will never know what the Incan monuments and
jewels truly meant for their users. Above all, that is why, once history has
become the guiding issue, a discourse on presencing can no longer be
construed from the "characteristics of being proper to being-there," understood as "that entity which we are always ourselves."[13] *The existential
analytic ceases to be a viable path as soon as everydayness is understood
to have a history*. It is not as if after 1930 Heidegger lost interest in the
'existentials' and in everyday existence. Rather, their analysis until then
supposed 'care' and 'being-in-the-world' to denote presencing beyond historical contingencies (while grounding these—but that is another problem). Everydayness designated the locus of trans-historical presencing.
Now, if henceforth presencing is seen as articulating itself epochally, and
the difference, temporally, then being can be retrieved only indirectly by
a return to its reversals. What is mine, possessed, in everydayness can
now be repossessed only as deferred, that is, by the long detour through
the concrete beginnings of the ages in Western history.[14] If one wishes to
speak of holism in Heidegger, after the 'turning', that can no longer be
done in terms of *Dasein*'s "potentiality for being a whole,"[15] but only in
reference to epochs as whole "fundamental positions."[16] An *epoch* is a
broken whole, however, since the word designates the witholding of presencing. The three-tiered difference (entities-beingness-being or present-
presence-presencing) confines totality to the *ontic* —beingness makes entities complete—which entails the impossibility of construing being as
"belonging" or "maintaining."[17]

This new mediation for a discourse on presencing—no longer through
existential characteristics, but through epochal reversals—contributes at
least one element, and an essential one, to the problem of legitimation in
Heidegger, namely, the deduction of the categories of presencing from the
moments of historical inception.[18] The *Verbindlichkeit* for delegitimating
the rule of epochal principles is obtained by formalization of those beginnings which, although they never introduce any entirely new 'trait' into
history, produce empirical newness within categorial oldness. The issue of
legitimation must therefore be broached by an analysis of the concrete
sequence of original beginnings—by an analytic that will be neither no-
tional nor existential, but epochal. The legitimating material is taken from
the finite slice of Western history. Needless to add, this method does not

stop at a mere account of "the raw existant," for it does not raise the question of what is originary in the original *ontically*, and its question is not answered by enumerating a sequence of facts, to be explained by other facts. Heidegger's is not a positivist account. In his epochal analytic, the ontological question is raised historically or originally, which allows him to ask simultaneously the question of the originary *ontologically*. The sequence analyzed is not one of facts, but one of *economies of facts*. It is obvious how Heidegger remains faithful, even while transposing it, to the Kantian project of "unveiling analytically the totality of a structure."[19] Such a structural whole is now an epochal economy, that is, the historical deployment of beingness as presence. It will come into view once its own formal determinants or conditions have been analyzed. That is what it means to deduce the categories of presencing.

The categories and their status are decisive for understanding the purport of the Heideggerian project and notably of 'the history of being'. Commentators have read that project as a quasi-theology of history or, at the other extreme, as a kind of historical positivism. These two readings are equally unacceptable. Between them, the domain of the categorial stakes out the intermediary ground.

On one hand, some interpreters, perhaps more interested in proselytizing than in conceptual *ana-lyein*, claim to have detected a "theological a priori in the historical progress of Western thought" according to Heidegger;[20] to them being appears as a noumenal "not-I," the "overpowering partner" of man, "a power toward which one can adopt personal attitudes as toward the Christian God."[21] On the other hand, the 'history of being' has appeared as the triumph of empiricism and historical relativism. Here Heideggerian 'philosophy' would oppose, point for point, all that the theologizing readings praise in it: instead of a Subject of history, the raw positivity and the irreducible contingency of facts; instead of a Doctrine, inventory; instead of a Law of Being, "the pragmatic comprehension of being," "bound by no normative or methodological attachment."[22] Heidegger took adamant exception to both renditions: "Being—that is not God";[23] and "historicism" arises from the embarrassment of "wanting to arrange the history of being in accord with the *historiographical* representations current today."[24]

Nevertheless, it is not difficult to draft the route between these two extremes, between the Scylla of a noumenal Subject and the Charybdis of positivist historicism. It follows the intermediary line of the functional determinations which, over the course of epochal reversals, have structurally stamped the economic orders. To speak of categories is to focus on the network of traces that are medial to the noumenal and the empirical, a network made of the totality of relations among phenomena as they are epochally possible and which are in that sense both historical and formal. To categorize is to gather the rules for interaction by which the successive fields become at all comparable. Since these rules originate in a given constellation of the *temporal difference,* they are a priori. Gathering them is the task of a phenomenology in which, as I believe I have established, the 'very issue' is no longer any subjectivity that gives sense (or signification) but the history of presencing and its shifts in sense (or direction). Due to the a priori role of the categories, reconstructing 'the history of being' is a project, not of descriptive, but of transcendental phenomenology. If it is understood that the traditional term 'category' is here shorn not only of all ousiological and subjectivist connotations, but also of all references to phenomenal regions—human (*daseinsmässig*) and non-human (*nicht daseinsmässig*)[25]—if it is understood, in other words, that κατηγορεῖν, "to accuse," no longer means "to address oneself to entities as such or such,"[26] but to address presencing and its manifold ways of differing from the economies of presence, then nothing prohibits rehabilitating this venerable word. Categorial phenomenology does not seek to formalize an object or some representable content. It seeks to set free the continuities according to which the many networks of epochal presence have differed from presencing. When the material to be so formalized turns from human life, in the early Heidegger, to the history of being, the meaning of κατηγορεῖν changes accordingly. The 'existentials' are replaced by 'fundamental traits'. Nevertheless, both *Existenzialien* and *Grundzüge* are modifications within the one categorial problematic.

Instead of speaking of *categories* of presencing, it could be objected that it is rather a matter of schemata, of transcendentals, or of *topoi.*

Following Heidegger's interpretation of Kant, the schemata are operative in the formation of finite transcendence. They render 'ontological knowledge' sensible in an image and thereby constitute the pure dimension of encounter called being-in-the-world. In that role, their function is a transcendental one. The schemata are the literally radical acts of the imagination: through them the imagination, the common root of intuition and understanding, forms the temporal horizon of any possible phenomenon.[27] In the critical sense, the schema is an a priori unity of heterogeneous elements which makes a concept applicable to experience. In the ontological sense, the schema is an a priori unity of homogeneous elements which is formed by the imagination and which makes it possible for the ego to transcend itself toward what stands opposite it. In the first sense, defined by the relation between pure concepts and intuitions, the schema vindicates too little—a simply intermediary role in knowledge—to be applicable to the phenomenology of the reversals of presence. In the second sense, defined by the a priori constitution of transcendence, it claims too much, for then there is only one single form of all schemata, time.[28] The multiple determinations of the economies that we are seeking must assuredly be applicable to the sensible, to empirical history; but the question of this application and its forms remains distinct from the question of the functional traits to be applied, and the latter is precisely the categorial question. In other words, the schematism does not seem to provide a viable transition from a phenomenology of *Dasein* to that of 'the history of being', whereas the categories round that cape very well.

The *transcendentals* warrant an analogous remark. They do not make it possible to round the cape that separates a realist ontology from a phenomenological ontology. The 'fundamental traits' with which the latter operates, just like the 'existentials', often appear *convertible* into one another. In reading that Heidegger translates, for example, *phusis, eon,* and *logos* by the same word *Anwesen*, presencing, one cannot help recalling medieval doctrines of the convertibility between the transcendental perfections of being. And yet, those Greek words translated as *Anwesen* assuredly do not designate real perfections. Those traits are not qualities of things, but operational rules for 'destinal' articulation. By this operational character of the categories, the deconstruction of epochs remains a transcendental enterprise in a sense derived from Kant. To speak of categories is precisely to take exception to the ontological realism implied in the neo-Aristotelian usage of "transcendental."

The word *topos*, lastly, would be perfectly suitable as a title for the identical elements pervading the mutations of presence if it were not indispensable precisely as a designation for the punctuations in the history of being, that is, for the stops or stays which, within the metaphysical closure, are called epochs. Non-epochal (non-principial) economies are obviously *topoi* of presencing, too. The concept of *topoi* is thus to be retained for the synchronic stampings (*jeweilige Prägungen*) as the loci[29] of the temporal difference, but not for the traits of its diachronic unfolding (*Austrag*). The economies, as well as the nodal points that both link and separate them, are the *topoi* in which presencing assumes its guises. The first instance in which Heidegger uses the term 'topology' links it to *Dichten* ("poetizing," but more literally, "rendering dense"—*dicht*[30]—perhaps 'crystallizing' or 'coagulating'). The topology, the 'gathering of places', designates the coming-together of presencing in a finite order of presence. Only secondarily does the term refer to the reading of such an order, also called "site," "abode," "dwelling," "fatherland" by the phenomenologist. But to call *topoi* the formal 'all-pervasive' invariables of the historical folds would be to immobilize them. These invariables, as functionally identical but differing topologically, are appropriately called categories.

As such a baring of traits, the verb κατηγορεῖν recovers its pre-philosophical sense, "manifesting." To 'categorize' is to prosecute: to stand above (κατά) the market place (ἀγορά) on a platform and to 'accuse' someone by declaring straightforwardly that his deeds have been such and such. It is to manifest the various features of what is the case.[31]

To deduce the categories of originary presencing from the concrete sequence of the original modes of presence is to bring into view "a stretch of the way of the authentic history which is always the history of the revealedness of being; but this way remains necessarily hidden from the ordinary eye."[32] The natural, ordinary attitude can only be overcome by a gaze that sweeps the course of metaphysics in more than one motion. What is literally decisive in that history are the slidings: moments of distress and danger for the era that is departing, but inaugural, auroral moments for the one arriving. The reversals thus disclose themselves to a bifocal analysis which progresses toward the threshold of transition by following the expiring economy, and regresses toward that same threshold by looking back from the economy about to appear. This progression and regression are movements of the analytic gaze. The categories it deciphers are therefore *prospective* and *retrospective*. But two eyes are not enough. In order to seize the phenomenon of reversal as such, a third class of categories is required, the *transitional* categories. It is to these that Heidegger has devoted his greatest effort of analytical phenomenology.

What is to be attempted, then, is a threefold reading of the 'history of being': forward from its Presocratic inception which yields the prospective categories (*eon, phusis, alētheia, logos, hen, nous*); backward from its late modern conclusion, which yields the retrospective categories (will to power, nihilism, justice, eternal recurrence, transmutation of values and death of God, overman); and finally from the turning that closes this history and which yields the transitional categories (ontological difference/world and thing; 'there is'/favor; unconcealment/event of appropriation; epoch/ clearing; nearness/fourfold; corresponding/thinking).

The pages that follow attempt to show how this table of three times six categories enables one to wrest originary presencing from the original shifts in presence. Whereas the three classes of categories seem exhaustive to me, the number of categories in each of them certainly is not. The reason lies in the very nature of their deduction: not an a priori construction, but a historical analytic along the leading thread of what I have called the temporal difference. This is the table:

Prospective categories	Retrospective categories	Transitional categories
eon	will to power	ontological difference/ world and thing
phusis	nihilism	'there is'/favor
alētheia	justice	unconcealment/event of appropriation
logos	eternal recurrence	epoch/clearing
hen	transmutation of values, death of God	nearness/fourfold
nous	overman	corresponding/thinking

But is it not a monstrosity to draw categories, a system, a table even, from what Heidegger called "thinking" precisely to oppose it to "philosophy"?

Thinking's "good and therefore wholesome danger is the nighness of the singing poet." But its "bad and therefore muddled danger is philosophizing."[33] A monstrosity indeed: the one that I have tried to encapsule in the phrase 'anarchy principle'. It inexorably stamps our age as hyper-ordered, oversystematized, and yet perhaps as capable of another birth, "still unnamable, but which announces itself—and cannot but announce itself as is necessary each time a birth is in progress—in the species of a non-species, in the formless, mute, infant and terrifying form of monstrosity."[34]

§21. A Reversal Undergone by the Puma-Shaped City

> In what seems like a confused variety of
> representations when gathered up at random
> and telescoped by historiography, a sameness
> and simplicity of the destiny of being comes
> to the fore and, accordingly, a solid
> steadiness of the history of thinking and of
> what it has thought. However, seeing in its
> ownmost trait what so remains the same is
> difficult for us and seeing it in its fullness,
> rare.
>
> *Der Satz vom Grund*[35]

No epochal break has been more incisive than that undergone by the American civilizations at the time of the Spanish conquest. Before examining the fundamental traits that are needed in general to read reversals between eras, let us see empirically how many *types* of such traits—how many categorial classes—are required to render intelligible the scission of 1531 from which 'the new world' was born.

This is how a chronicler describes that novelty: "The good Christians arrived here with the true God; but that was the beginning of our wretchedness, the beginning of tribute, the beginning of alms, the cause of the misery from which hidden discord came, the beginning of battles with firearms, the beginning of offenses, the beginning of despoiliation, the beginning of enslavement by debt, the beginning of debts affixed to our shoulders, the beginning of continual brawling, the beginning of suffering."[36]

In order to understand what changed in Peru when within a few weeks Pizarro and his troops made themselves masters of an empire as vast as Spain, France, Germany, and ancient Austria-Hungary combined, it may seem enough to relate the events. But having stated the facts of arms, ruses, and alliances, we would still not know what mutation the Inca principle—supreme cacique and decimal system—underwent, how a new principle established itself, how the substitute apparatus took root, and how it was agglutinated on the preceding order. Therefore, a more complex perspective is called for.

A first scrutinizing sweep consists in following the salient traits of the pre-Columbian state of affairs and in examining how these traits are transformed with the Christian conquest. The most visible trait of the Inca civilization is the *princeps*, the Inca himself. What did the autocracy become after August 29, the day Pizarro had Atahualpa garroted?

The arrival of the Spaniards had been preceded by baleful omens and soothsayings. The eighth Inca had predicted that strange men would invade and destroy the Empire. This prophecy was expressed once more by means of the decimal system. The Inca calendar was divided into units of ten. The bygone ages had each lasted a thousand years. Ten legendary emperors had reigned, each for a hundred years. Hence the agonizing question: would the present age expire at the end of a similar cycle? Now according to these calculations, the last Inca would reign in the sixteenth century A.D.[37] The eighth Inca had even erected a statue in honor of the god to come: it represented a man of great height, bearded, dressed in a long tunic, and holding a fabulous taloned animal by a chain. Pizarro, one might say, had indeed been expected. The Indians perceived his arrival as the fulfillment of a prophecy announcing the return of a civilizing god. The great riddle prompted by the conquistadors was: are they gods or men? On one occasion, Pizarro's soldiers intercepted a message carried by couriers from one Inca general, Callcuchima, to another, Quizquiz: "Callcuchima had sent them to inform Quizquiz that they [the Spaniards] were mortal."[38]

However, Pizarro does not inherit the status of *princeps*. It becomes fragmented among the local Indian chiefs, the vestiges of the separatist Inca state,[39] and the viceroy of Lima. Once the last Inca has been baptized, forty years after the conquest, only to be immediately beheaded, the ancient Inca autocracy splits into two parallel systems: the indigenous caciques, often exercising their power in secrecy, and colonial centralism. The first, that of the vanquished, preserves no more than regional holdovers of the ancient principial power. The second, that of the conquerors, has its center in the remote person of Charles the Fifth and remains foreign to the Indians. During his lifetime the Inca had embodied the center of the universe. That center assassinated, chaos ensues: "the sun, castrated, the father, forsaking his children, utter grief and solitude." "Everything vanishes into hiding, everything fades in suffering," a popular elegy says.[40] With the disappearance of its chief, Cuzco is no longer what its name signifies, the cosmic navel.

What becomes of the rational Inca *principium*, the decimal system? The social organization it supported can hardly maintain itself in the face of the demographic catastrophe that the conquest inflicted on the groups of 10, 100, 1,000, and 10,000 men. The ravages caused by smallpox, measles, and influenza in that unimmunized population are well known. The natural ally of diseases is the violence which "characterizes colonial society like a fact integral to its structure."⁴¹ The documents show Indians driven to suicide: "Some hang themselves, others let themselves die of hunger, others ingest poisonous herbs, women kill their children at birth, 'to free them from the torments their mothers suffer.' "⁴² Before the close of the century, the population has decreased by four-fifths. However, social networks paralleling those imposed by the new masters continue to take shape around the ancient decimal units. Throughout the colonial period, people will speak of the Republic of the Indians and the Republic of the Spaniards.

In addition to these two most striking features of the fast-vanishing age, the autocracy and the decimal system, the expiration can be read by numerous other traits. For example, the use of coca. Under the Inca, only the priests and dignitaries were entitled to it. Offering the leaves or chewing them ritually was part and parcel of all ceremonies. After the conquest, it turned into a stimulant used to neutralize hunger and fatigue. Its production increased accordingly. As a need-depressing nutrient, it is a major factor in the new tableau. Even today, the poorer a Peruvian village, the more shops one finds in it filled only with bales of this bitter shrub. It continues to play a part in ceremonies, but the main purpose of its consumption is to make days of work possible practically without food. "Without coca, there would not be a Peru."⁴³

These descriptions have followed a first perspective. All factors cited have been taken from the economy that precedes the reversal, and I have suggested what has become of them in the grip of expropriation. Their description has been prospective. A second type of factors is to be examined: everything truly new that the conquest brings, never seen before on American soil. The description of this second ensemble will have to be retrospective.

Here is how a chronicler of Cuzco describes these unseen sights: "They say that they had seen arriving in their country beings quite different from us, as much in their customs as in their clothing: they resembled the 'Viracochas', a name by which we formerly designated the Creator of all things. . . . And they gave that name to the beings they had seen, on one hand because they differed so much from us in looks and dresses, on the other, because they saw them astraddle very large animals with silver feet: this because of the sparks flying from the horseshoes. They also gave them that name because they saw them speak at leisure by means of white sheets, as a person speaks to another: and this because of their reading of books and letters. Lastly, they called them 'Viracochas' because of their remarkable faces. There were great differences between them: some had black beards, others, red ones. They saw them eat from silver plates. And they possessed 'Yllapas', a name we give to thunderbolts: this because of the harquebuses, which they believed to bring thunder down from the heavens."⁴⁴

Here the new 'traits' mix diversely with the ancient ones. Some continuity is obvious, but it does not preclude a radical transformation. In the

domains of production and distribution the new features amalgamate with
the old through the forces of need. The most striking example is the
monetary economy imposed by the conquistadors. In the market which
results, the Indians and their institutions quite naturally come to play the
role of exploited work forces. We have seen that under the Inca, on the
contrary, state distribution rendered market exploitation impossible. In the
areas of clothing and food, such an amalgamation of traits is less successful.
The Indians resist the consumption of wheat and, to a lesser degree, the
adoption of pants and hats. However, the ancient and new 'traits' remain
entirely disparate in the religious domain. The pre-Inca cults, holding fast
to life, subsist parallel to the Catholic institutions. Clandestine rites are
practiced, for example, around a mummy from the time of the Inca. Often,
as if in defiance, they are carried out near churches or even behind the
altar. Llamas are sacrificed right in front of the parish priest's door. When
the Creole authority strikes, the Indians yield, but only for a while. The
missionaries compel them to bury their dead instead of disposing of them
in nearly inaccessible cavities in the lofty mountains. The Indians comply,
but at night they go to the cemeteries to dig up the corpses—"out of pity
and out of compassion for our dead, so that they are not fatigued by the
weight of the clumps of soil."[45]

The market economy, ecclesiastical burials, writing, horses, firearms: it
is no exaggeration to say that these have 'made' colonial and modern Peru.
They are indeed traits that, given their role since the conquest, can be
recognized retrospectively as more salient in the tableau than, for example,
the beards of which some were dark, others red. This second ensemble of
aspects can therefore be deciphered only backward. They do not simply
substitute themselves for the ensemble made up of the theocracy, the state
economy, the decimal system, the Inca; rather they overdetermine and
thereby transmute it.

The reason why these two classes of indexes, prospective and retrospective, do not sufficiently comprehend the reversal undergone by the puma-
shaped city is that they do not address this reversal itself. What is still
required, then, is an ensemble of viewpoints relative to the transition as
such. Here the terms will necessarily be more abstract. What happens in
the transition from the pre-colonial to the colonial era is primarily a
dispossession.[46] The Indians are deprived of their gold, their goods, their
land, their peace, their means of production and consumption, their sites,
their rites, their administrative and spriritual organization, their progeni-
ture, their life. Dispossession says more than annihilation, it indicates the
passage of one's possessions into other hands. Colonial dispossession is,
however, incomplete. It is accompanied and counteracted by many ways of
surreptitious reappropriation. The Indians develop the art of camouflage.
For example: "the dissimulation of the traditional cults under Christian
veneer."[47] To understand a historical break, *pairs* of categories are required. The Spaniards bring upon the Indians a deculturation, but one that

is only the reverse of a project of acculturation (that this acculturation has, on the whole, run aground deplorably is another matter: except in isolated cases, conversion to the imported culture never took place). "Deculturing was never followed by real acculturing."[48] Stated otherwise, the destructuring proceeds without real restructuring.[49] Since assimilation was to remain a wish, since none of the attempts at acculturing the Indians and restructuring their society penetrated the real apparatus, the most appropriate term for describing the epochal transition in question is perhaps that of disjunction. The disappearance of the Inca, guardian and guarantor of social and, it was believed, cosmic order, disjoins the *princeps* from its dependents. Moreover, his disappearance entails a disjunction between the new lords and the Indians. Ultimately, the Earth itself is disjoined from the Sun.[50] On the surface, the disjunction opens a rift that sets apart two eras; in depth, it tends to give autonomy to life strata that hitherto formed a whole. Heidegger will speak of "decision," *Ent-scheidung*, in addressing such phenomena of systemic disruption.

To understand at all what a reversal or a crisis is in history, a threefold perspective is required. The *prospective* categories reveal the received traits as they undergo a transmutation. The *retrospective* categories reveal what comes about as new, original, in such a crisis and what, although as yet hidden, determines the new order of phenomenal interconnectedness. We cannot speak of such epochal novelty except after it has already grown old. Lastly, the *transitional* categories are to reveal, in the crisis, the χρίνειν (separating) itself. The mutations, the displacements, the continuities, the ruptures, the overdeterminations become intelligible only when examined from these three viewpoints. The new distribution of powers, truths, expectations (e.g., in the Indian Messianism) are graspable in their novelty only through this threefold approach whereby the Spanish variables invest their future in the Incan variables, thus transposing the phenomenal network in its entirety. In this way, the dividing line that separates the Incan apparatus from its colonial displacement appears as traced by a tactic of reinterpretation.

X

AT THE PRESOCRATIC INCEPTION

THE PROSPECTIVE CATEGORIES

> The basic words are historical. That is not
> merely to say that they have various
> meanings for various ages, meanings which,
> since they are bygone, we survey
> historiographically; it is also to say that, in
> accordance with the interpretation of them
> that comes to prevail, they ground history
> now and in the times to come.
>
> *Nietzsche: The Will to Power as Art*[1]

It is one of Heidegger's persistent convictions that the traits of presencing understood as event must be deciphered, in the first place, from the "basic words" (*Grundworte*) out of which Western philosophy was born. However, a fair exposition of them encounters a crucial difficulty. In each of the six Greek words that will be treated here as "basic," the meaning lent by Heidegger will have to be separated from the meaning or meanings with which they have been transmitted. The purpose of such demarcation is not to renew philological debates, but only to circumscribe what is at stake in Heidegger's 'retrieval'. At stake is not some imaginary remigration to a lost Greek fatherland, but only and exclusively the *differentiation of the originary ('being') from the original ('history')*. In this chapter, then, I wish to show what becomes of Heidegger's strategy concretely. I have already described it formally above (Part III) in relation to the deconstruction of our past: the strategy of setting free the one event of appropriation as it *differs* from the many epochal inceptions.

The Presocratic basic words are few in number. In order to garner from them their ways of *katēgorein*, of accusing presencing, we must de-nature what the tradition has made of them, alter their received nature, and de-naturalize them, deprive them of their unquestioned citizenship in "representational quarters that have become common for us."[2] Without such an effort of de-naturing and de-naturalizing, how they can "ground history" will never be apparent. And yet, even with that effort we will not be able to conclude: here is what the Greeks meant by *eon, phusis, alētheia, logos, hen, nous*.[3] In order to answer questions pertaining to the 'history of being', Heidegger's retrieval shakes off the representations that have been agglomerated with those words throughout the ages. Do the *Grundworte* allow us to sort out something formal, all-pervasive in history? If so, in what sense are they fundamental and founding? With what right can it be claimed that they will retain that function even "in the times to come"? In other words, what makes them *categories for the entire history of being*?

The starting point of a historical deduction of the prospective categories of presencing is therefore the temporal difference, which shows how the 'originary' becomes accessible through that 'original' from which the course of Western philosophy unfolds. That original is the Greek inception (*Anfang*). "What is *That* which enjoins and arranges the fundamental traits of what *thereafter* unfolded as Western, European thought?"[4]

Heidegger provides a first answer to that question, and a sweeping one: "The history of being is solely being itself."[5] It is a sweeping answer since, so equated with being, history remains unintelligible in its capacity for novelty, for beginnings, which *differ* from being. Its equation with being indicates, however, that it is useless to seek the articulation of being anywhere outside of history, for instance, in an unvarying life-world. All categories, then, manifest the historical self-articulation of being as presencing. This is a remote application of Dilthey's tenet, "*Das Leben legt sich selber aus,*" life interprets itself, or, better: life lays itself out.[6] If this tenet is severed from the double preoccupation with a philosophy of life and a hermeneutic of the human sciences, it suggests what is to be understood by 'ontology', namely, the *legein (auslegen) tou ontos*, of being; the laying-out in which being structures itself. 'Onto-logy' designates literally presencing as it articulates itself. This compound word—although coined only in the seventeenth century—divides the prospective categories into two groups, one clustered around the key word *on* (or the archaic *eon*), the other around the key word *legein*. Together, they suggest a pre-metaphysical understanding of 'ontology': not the doctrine of a perfection common to all entities, but the self-display of presencing. *Auslegen* would be a human doing, an act of the mind, only derivatively; and the *logos* would be discourse only as 'accusing' that self-display through basic words and the propositions made of them.

Let us take up, then, these basic words of Heraclitus and Parmenides and try to detect with Heidegger what they revealed, what has become of them subsequently, and what they are capable of revealing once again.

§22. Eon

The basic word *par excellence*, the standard of all metaphysical configurations to follow, is the word 'being' itself. Parmenides, historians tell us, was the first to oppose it to the moving multiplicity of things given in experience. He was the one, they add, who forged '*eon*' as a *singulare tantum*. He is also said to have opposed the present participle, 'being', to things multiple that, as multiple, amount to not-being.[7] But if Parmenides indeed discovered a radical difference concerning being, this may not lie in its opposition to not-being. Grammatically, the present participle itself indicates a difference. To say, for example, that a surface is 'shining' is to say that it is neither dark nor dull, but, of course, that it shines. In this way, the word participates in the *verbal* form. At the same time, it designates the surface itself—sea, metal—that shines. The word thus participates also in the *nominal* form.[8] 'Shining' means: something that *shines*, and *something* that shines. Likewise, 'being' means: *to be*, and *a being* or entity. When Parmenides precedes the present participle with an article (τ' ἐόν: a construct that marks the transition from epic to philosophical language) and follows it with the infinitive (ἔμμεναι),[9] he sets apart the noun and the verb. He thereby 'accuses', makes explicit, the duality contained in the present participle.

Exactly what Parmenides intended in so juxtaposing the nominal participle and the infinitive of the verb 'to be' is not easy to tell. It seems safe, however, to say that as participating in the verb, *eon* contains a motility that has nothing to do with 'things in motion'. For something 'to be', it must occur: enter upon the stage of presence, linger, and then withdraw. The verbal form emphasizes this entrance into presence and the possible exit. In the epic and the tragic traditions such intrinsic motility is sometimes expressly rendered by two verbs, παρεῖναι and ἀπεῖναι,[10] *anwesen* and *abwesen*, "presencing" and "absencing."[11] So understood as occurring, entities come out of concealedness, abide for a lapse of time in the unconcealed, and retire into the concealed. The noun 'presence', on the other hand, stresses the fullness, the roundness,[12] of availability and accessibility, the givenness of something, its being the case. *Eon* is the name of that twofold play, presencing on the horizon of possible absencing, and the present entity standing fast in its presence. It is the name for the duality (*Zwiefalt*), "to be—entity."[13]

Neither of the two elements so set apart, the verb 'to be' or the noun 'entity', points to some maximal entity, some ultimate reason for being. The duality is properly called unconcealment: the emergence from concealedness (which stays with the unconcealed as its shadow) and the self-imposition in unconcealedness (whose light is never epiphanic, never total). It is a duality permeated with time, with movement, with chiaroscuro—but not the duality of the more and the less evident, the more and the less great, powerful, certain, or reliable. Yet the verb-noun duality of

eon was soon bent to designate that latter difference between a fundament and its dependents. Parmenides' discovery prefigures and renders
possible what was later represented as the analytical distinctness of *on*
from its *ousia,* of *ens* from its *entitas,*[14] or of entities from their beingness
(*Seiendheit*). The difference between a given entity and its self-giving
comes to be displaced first as the difference between the given entity and
the cause of its givenness, and from there, without much difficulty, as the
"separation between a supra-sensory and a sensory world."[15] The progressive slippage of the differential sense on the threshold of classicism has to
be understood as a categorial modification.

The first of the categories contains traits that the others will also exhibit,
although accentuated in different ways. All prospective categories will
prove to reveal the same characteristics of presencing, namely, "unconcealedness, the rising from concealedness, the entry into it, the coming and
the going away, the lingering, the gathering, the shining-forth, the resting,
the hidden suddenness of possible absencing."[16] But *eon* remains the leading category of originary presencing since in 'presencing' it addresses motility and in '*oriri*', temporality—the two traits of the 'verb' connotation in
the participle. *Eon* remains the hidden guiding category for philosophy, its
forgotten space, until the publication of *Being and Time.*[17] Correctly understood, *eon* means the ensemble of structures that allow one to grasp both
being's genuinely temporal nature and its metaphysical 'reification'. Seen
from the vantage point of *eon*, metaphysics is properly described by the
forgottenness of the intrinsic motility and temporality of being. Through
the Aristotelian question, *ti to on,* and its concomitant restriction of the
participle to the noun, this category "has placed subsequent European
thinking on its enjoined itinerary."[18]

§23. *Phusis*

This second category, which has already helped us disengage the originary
from the original, emphasizes presencing as self-manifestation. Prior to the
physicists' distinction between things man-made and natural, prior even to
the distinction between man and things, *phusis* designates "what blooms
forth *of itself* (for instance, the blooming of a rose)."[19] *Phuesthai*—dehiscing
or, more simply, rising—is the name of originary presencing inasmuch as
entities "manifest and maintain [themselves] and endure."[20] It is therefore a
second way of addressing the entrance into the play and its moments: arrival,
staying, withdrawal. This is the sense in which *phusis* belongs to the group of
categories focused around *eon*. Moreover, it makes it possible to think time
otherwise than as the number of movements according to the before and
after in the genesis of entities—otherwise, too, than as memory, intuition,
and expectation in the experience of consciousness.[21] Arrival, staying, and
withdrawal are not three episodes succeeding one another. They are media-

tions for thinking the identity of the non-identical, the event-like identity of concealing and unconcealing: originary time.

Heidegger's interpretation of the fragment by Heraclitus usually translated as "Nature loves to hide"[22] may help clarify this identity. The interpretation proceeds by a number of exclusions. To understand the temporality operative in Heraclitean *phusis* is to understand the impossibility of confining time to manifest phenomena (facts of 'nature' and facts of 'consciousness' alike); the impossibility of seeking to account for time as originary, while ignoring the absence, the hiddenness, from which this category bespeaks emergence; the impossibility of some zenithal manifestation without concealment; as well as, lastly, the impossibility of occultation without appeal, of a fall outside time, of forgottenness without return. These exclusions thematize the temporal difference in terms of a twofold *absence*. The stage of any order of presence is drawn by the peripheral (or *ontic*) absence of entities excluded from it by an original *epochē*. But at the center of that stage occurs the (*ontological*) pull toward absencing which makes for the motility of originary emergence.

What is decisive in the categorial function of *phusis* is that the self-manifestation of the variables in an epochal order is nothing but the event of their very conjoining, their coming together, as differing from such an order's (present or absent) components or constitutents. During the paradigmatic economy[23] before the classical age, this "appearing out of hiddenness" received the name *phusis*.[24] From the viewpoint of the fields whose succession makes up the 'history of being', *phusis* is the *differential* factor in the indefinite multiplicity of ways things enter into the play of interaction. Originary presencing differentiates itself according to synchronically as well as diachronically adjacent territories.[25] On Platonic terrain, for example, the self-manifestation of entities in general is narrowed down to the proper 'aspect' of this or that specific entity.[26]

Before Parmenides "uttered *eon* as the basic word for Western thought," the basic words were *phusis, logos, Moira, Eris, alētheia, hen*.[27] However, *Moira*, the 'destiny' of the difference between presencing and the present, and *Eris*, the 'wrestling' between arrival and withdrawal, are both names that designate *phusis*.[28] They do not constitute categories since they add no trait of their own.

Later, when Aristotle declares: "Among things that exist, some are by nature (*phusei*), others by other causes,"[29] *phusis* ceases to be the name of originary presencing and comes to designate one species of substances, namely, those that grow by themselves, opposed to substances moved by another or fabricated. With the Academy, this second category in turn becomes operative subterraneously, not only in Aristotle's *Physics*, but also when the Medievals oppose the natural to the supranatural, when the moderns define nature as the thing extended or as "the connection of appearances determining one another with necessity according to universal laws"[30] or lastly, when in "the atomic age," "what presences no longer holds sway, but rather the assault reigns" over nature which has become an energy reserve.[31] *Phusis* is a *category* of presencing because, from Heraclitus to the technological era, "being lightens, although in various ways, according to the characteristics of shining-forth, of lingering in appearance, of presencing, of opposition and contrariety"[32]: these are all characteristics pertaining to *phusis*.

§24. *Alētheia*

This word has oriented Heidegger most consistently throughout his writings since it addresses the 'struggle' at the heart of the difference disclosed by *eon*, the struggle between truth and untruth. The last century has seen—in Hegel as well as in Nietzsche—concepts of truth in which its affirmation stands in an essential relationship to its negation; concepts of truth as struggle, therefore, which were either dialectical or sharply anti-dialectical. But what is (perhaps) new with Heidegger is that the struggle between truth and untruth is situated outside of man, on the turf of the economies where dialectics is rendered inoperative because man is only one variable in the play of originary presencing. As a result of that displacement, truth becomes unrecognizable to philosophers. The category *eon* underscores the difference between the noun and the verb, between an entity and being, or between the present and its emergence from absence, thereby altering all received notions of 'being'; that of *phusis* designates presencing as self-manifestation, which amounts to transmuting 'nature'; whereas that of *alētheia* places presencing on the battlefield of the economies, de-naturing and de-naturalizing 'truth' as well.

The anti-humanistic, categorial sense of this third perspective on presencing can best be shown in connection with the two preceding ones. If presencing differs, on one hand from present entities, as stressed by *eon*, and on the other hand from absencing, as stressed by *phuein*, then the negation contained in the privative prefix (*a-lētheia*) can be seen as differential, too: presencing negates substance-like permanence and it negates absencing. This category thus signals the dual movement in being: the *giving* of whatever happens to be unconcealed, and the undertow *back* toward concealment. It shows presencing as binomial, under the double law (*nomos*) of giving and of taking back. Heidegger describes the play of unconcealment as a violent struggle: the struggle of light against darkness, and then *alētheia* appears as "clearing"[33]; the struggle of the lightness of world against the weight of earth, and then *alētheia* appears as "lightening" or "alleviating"[34]; the struggle of "the untrembling heart of well-rounded unconcealment" against the "opinions of mortals," and then *alētheia* appears as the "free space of the open."[35] But this category is not

properly understood if these various figures of struggle are not recognized
in their non-human essence. Darkness, the weight, opinions and errors,
in short, *lēthē* in its many guises, are affairs of economies before eventually becoming human affairs. *Lēthē* belongs to *alētheia* "not as shadow to
light, but rather as the heart of *alētheia*."[36] To understand the play of
presencing-absencing as non-human is to understand the *economic* notion
of *alētheia*. Such a notion of 'truth' has departed from all referents, including the Hegelian *concept* as reality-creating and Nietzschean *life* as
lie-creating. Inasmuch as it emphasizes the double pull toward presencing
and absencing in any economy, the notion of *alētheia* is a category. It
undergirds all subsequent concepts of truth. These concepts, however,
are 'humanistic': just as, with the beginning of metaphysics, man enters
the scene of phenomena and sets himself up as the criterion for *phusis*—
which then designates the sum of everything not produced by his hands—
so at a later stage, he institutes himself (immediately, or through the
mediation of one supreme entity 'true in itself') as the measure and
standard for *alētheia*.

That "reversal in the essence of truth," making truth henceforth "a
mark of human comportment toward entities,"[37] occurs with Plato. The
transference toward anthropomorphism does not preclude, but rather requires, that truth be identified with a supreme entity, *ontos on*. For truth
to be located in man, a supremely true referent is needed from which
man can take his bearings, to which he can assimilate and adjust himself.
In its turn, that representation guards and guarantees the truth—the
perfection of things—to which the mind can then conform in 'accurate'
propositions. The various theories of truth that have seen the light of day
after the birth of Greek classicism—first and foremost among them, the
conformity theory—could develop only to the extent that the conflict
between presencing and absencing remained tacitly operative, even
though philosophers had ceased addressing it. The aletheiological struggle
provides the background for the 'humanist' notion of truth as the agreement between a statement and a state of affairs, a notion unfolding from
Plato to Aristotle, to Thomas Aquinas, to Descartes, to Nietzsche.[38] In the
contemporary age where the true coincides with the accuracy or pertinence of technological devices, that is, with appropriate solutions to the
problems of mastery over nature, *alētheia* may well seem to be muted
under the yoke of *archai* of all kinds.[39] Nevertheless, "it never fades
away."[40] A trait that so continues to determine presencing throughout
history, but which has lost access to speech and has in that sense been
forgotten, is what I call a category.

Alētheia belongs to the categorial group of *eon* because it 'accuses' the
struggle between presencing and absencing, just as *eon* accuses the difference 'to be—entities', and *phusis* accuses presencing as self-manifestation.
With the help of these first three "traits of the history of being,"[41] originary
being can be gathered from the original reversals as what pervades them.

§25. *Logos*

A second categorial group is constituted around the verb *legein*. This denotes more than the phenomena in language. In the Homeric tradition, *legein* primarily signifies 'laying [something] down' in its proper place, 'collecting', 'bringing together' what lies scattered, like twigs for a fire or pieces of enemy armor before Troy[42]—in short, 'gathering'. In its reflective usage it means settling down in order to find rest. Gathering, so understood, is a kind of ordering that encompasses speech and memory only as two particular, even transposed, cases. In general, *legein* in the epic tradition signifies that one turns toward something, gives it one's attention and thereby selects it from other entities present, which are not worthy of being so singled out. What is notable, and what Heidegger's interpretation endeavors to rescue from a more philosophic usage of the term in Heraclitus, is that this diacrisis has nothing to do directly with a distinction between man and things. The thrust of the discriminatory *legein* opposes a sum of entities, regardless of whether they are human 'subjects' or 'objects', to the magma of what does not fall under attention.[43]

The explicit disposition of an ensemble of factors before one's eyes, their becoming accessible, is, then, 'logical' in the original sense. The verb *legein* addresses the movement through which such a disposition comes about, the movement by which a certain combination of entities is rendered present. The opposition between what is said and what remains unsaid, that is, the more special program of making entities accessible *to speech*, is only one case, the most eminent, of discerning between matters dealt with and the rest. Speech is only the most explicit 'gathering'. Essentially, *legein* means letting come to presence something that previously was present as absent: like the scattered twigs or pieces of armor which, as long as they are still scattered about, are present to the concern of all *as to-be-gathered*. Even though such collecting is something done by men, and even though since Homer *legein* of course also signifies 'saying' and 'speaking', this verb nevertheless stresses the 'letting'—letting come to presence—over anyone's act, whether in speech or otherwise.[44] In Heraclitus, as read by Heidegger, such coming to presence, such presencing, is not change effected by man. It is an economic event, occurring prior to anything humans can do or say. That priority—of a condition, not of a sequential moment—is best expressed by the middle voice *legesthai* and perhaps best translated as (intransitive) 'laying-out'.[45]

So understood as economic 'layout', *logos* specifies the three preceding categories, that is, *eon* and its derivatives. Its specific emphasis is on the passage from *lēthein*, hiding, to *alētheuein*, showing. It addresses the very movement suggested by the privative prefix of *alētheia*. In that sense, it can be held that *logos* and *alētheia* "are the same": *logos* bespeaks the emerging from absence and *alētheia*, the constellation or conflict of presencing-absencing.[46]

As the event of an economy's self-display, *logos* also provides the condition for what humans can and cannot undertake. It does so by gathering their activities into the finite order of phenomena it discloses. Heidegger sometimes writes "the *Logos*" (capitalized) to underscore its a priori character and to point out the relation between condition and conditioned. "The *Logos* preserves man's obedient belonging to being, that is to say, by its measures it grants [such belonging] and by its measures it simultaneously denies it."[47] Such gauging, which inescapably situates all our doings, is what Heraclitus called *homologein:* homologizing in the sense of "setting the human *logos* in its proper relation to the *Logos.*"[48] The hardest apprenticeship is that by which man learns how to hear and heed no imperative other than that relation. There is, then, a practical wisdom that Heidegger seeks to preserve from the Greeks and to prepare anew. It consists in speaking and acting (human *legein*) by attending solely to the layout of presencing (economic *Logos*).[49] Acting as homologizing is nothing other than acting *kata phusin:* following the coming-about of phenomena, giving oneself over to the movement of presencing-absencing. Understood that way, the verb *homologein* may be read as Heidegger's own last word on the question of acting. Indeed, "human *legein* is in itself at the same time *poiein,* 'leading forth' "; now, *homologein* means to conform human *legein* to "the *Logos* as *Alētheia* as *Phusis*"—to act, therefore, is to homologize with the aletheiological constellations as they come about.[50] This entirely precarious, uncodifiable conformity, which may have been the *nomos* of the pre-classical Greek *oikos,* the archaic economy, is erased by subsequent codes of theoretical adequation and practical normalization. Yet the original sense of *homo-,* keeping the economic layout in all human leading-forth, never ceases, as it were, shining through the erasure. Original wisdom, *sophia,* never ceases shining through the dogmas of sapiential metaphysics. "The *sophon* consists in *homologein.* Proper knowing comes about as the soul's *legein* corresponds to 'the *Logos.*' "[51] What, then, does someone do who is properly or authentically knowledgeable? He looks nowhere else for guidelines than to the way things render themselves present in his everyday life, and he complies with the mutations in their presencing. Although there is nothing optional about such compliance since it is the very mark of our finitude, express homologizing occurs "not always, perhaps even only rarely."[52] Originary knowledge is thus something to be gained, conquered by the 'logical' measure over hubris, the lack of measure.[53] This is a practical conquest, the birth of practical wisdom: "The issue of logic understood more originarily is such a 'doing', which is at the same time a 'letting.' "[54]

More than the categories connected with *eon, legein* addresses the event character of presencing. Heidegger emphasizes this at the risk of blurring the distinction between originary and original. A case in point is his questionable translation of *sophon* as "destinal" (*geschicklich*).[55] With this most artificial of his etymological constructs, *legein* finally signifies not only the originary emergence from concealment but also the incipience of Western thought, its original display in Greece. In this way, *Logos* would be the name of both the rise from absence into presence and the rise of history. What is blurred are the two senses of *proteron*, of 'priority': according to condition or according to sequence. The *historical* antecedence of an era would be linked to the *structural* antecedence of an a priori by a double use, ontic and ontological, of the same category. But such equivocation fogs up the very contours of the categorial. How can the essence of *logos* be the event of presencing which, as primordial time, makes all other time concepts—among them, history—possible and yet also be "properly destinal"?[56] In the first, and indeed genuine, of these two senses *legein* would be the condition of what, in its second sense, is conditioned. How can this or any category designate the "hidden source" of Western history?[57] The deduction establishes the way one fundamental trait, here *logos*, enters into various successive epochal fields: the way "the *logos* unfolds," after Heraclitus, so as to signify the proposition,[58] then the cosmic or dialectic order,[59] the principle of reason,[60] the concept, *Begriff*, and finally the assault, *Angriff*, by cybernetics and "logistics," "that form of planetary organization."[61] Truly innovative in Heidegger, this is the proper usage of a category in tracing the history of being. At each of those stages, *logos* designates a particular modality in which entities gather together (become phenomenal), emerge from absence, lay themselves out and thereby become accessible. But it is more difficult to follow Heidegger when *legein* stands not only for such presencing within any given economy or structure, but also for that *historical* occurrence in which "what still endures" today, namely, "Western destiny," came about. One hesitates to accuse Heidegger of a category mistake. At the same time, it is difficult to avoid the impression that there is a confusion between a category and its application, between the originary and the original, between the structural and the historical. *Legein* is a "leading word" when it denotes the presencing of what is present, but not when it connotes any datable reversal in presence.[62] We retain this word as the category that focuses on the irruption of unconcealment in concealment, of life in death, of day in night,[63] in short, that focuses on presencing as event.

The two final categories, *hen* and *nous*, depend directly on the category *legein*. They are comprehensible only in relation to it. One could superimpose the triad dependent on *logos* to that dependent on *eon* so as to illustrate graphically the pre-metaphysical unity of 'onto-logy'.

§26. Hen

As a category of presencing, the Heraclitean *hen* designates the unity of what *logos* lays out in presence, the unity of what I am calling *an economic field*. Understood that way, *hen* is a deficient category: it does not address the dynamism proper to *legein*, the dynamism of unconcealment, of light-ening, of the play of presencing, of the pull toward absencing. "It is from the essence of *logos*, thought in this way [as gathering together], that the essence of being is determined as the unifying One: *hen*."[64]

Not that *hen* in Heraclitus is static itself. It is described as lightning, sun, fire, thunderbolt, the seasons—all so many ways of saying how *hen* unites or unifies multiple things, *ta panta*.[65] *Hen* is the global unity of the rela-tions that present entities maintain with one another. As such, it is to be distinguished from the divine *hen*, Zeus. "*Hen* is twofold: on one hand, the unifying One in the sense of what is everywhere primal and thereby most universal; on the other hand, the unifying One in the sense of the All-Highest (Zeus)."[66] Only the former, the economic One, is a category of presencing. That One seems to be thought in terms of *logos* when Heracli-tus says: "Lightning is the pilot of all things."[67] The One sets all things in place—not as supreme agent, but the way a flash of lightning does. The One is the "self-lighting of being."[68] It is apparent in what way *hen* can be called non-static: as the sudden rise, ever-new, of the order of things present. It says the *phainesthai* without also saying the simultaneous *krup-testhai*. Indeed, the setting in place is 'one' as *already gathered* into the arena of epochally given entities. This category is deficient when compared to the preceding ones because, by itself, it does not address the undertow toward *lēthē*, hiding or concealing. *Alētheia* stands only in the background of Heraclitean henology.[69]

Absencing is also accused by the *hen*, although not directly, but only in the conjunction of *hen* with *logos* and *alētheia*. One additional sense must therefore be distinguished: not specified by the other categories, *hen* desig-nates the global order of a field of given entities, but specified by *logos* and *alētheia* it designates the unity of presencing-absencing, of unconcealing-concealing, the agonistic unity of giving what is the case and retaining what can economically not be the case. An *agonistic* notion of the One, then, needs to be added to its *economic* notion. *Hen* "in the sense of the oneness of two domains," the oneness of day and night—that "originary form of the difference"—needs to be added to *hen* as the "counter-word to *ta panta*."[70] Neither of these two notions, economic and agonistic, opposes the One to the many as immortal Zeus is opposed to the things that perish. The economic One and the agonistic One unify the manifold in two connected ways. The economic One spells out the manifold in a visible, livable order, intact as it is given, so that "the totality of innerworldly things comes to appear in the *hen* thought of as sunlight."[71] The agonistic One spells the innerwordly manifold out in its opposition to what does not appear. "As *logos*, the *hen panta* is the letting-presence of all that is present."[72] In this second sense, which is properly aletheiological, the *hen* designates "the reciprocal intimacy of revealing and concealing,"[73] their conflict, their join-ture, their mutuality, their oneness.

As agonistic, *hen* is a temporal category. "Time, a child that plays": time

is the simultaneity of *phuein* and *kruptesthai*, of breaking forth into presence and of retreating from the sunlight, of letting-be and annihilating,[74]
"of unconcealing-concealing, of their gathering."[75] This agonistic play—
whose historical unfolding is called *Austrag*[76]—designates the intrinsic motility of the One. Perhaps it is of this simultaneous arrival in presence and
departure toward absence that Heraclitus is reported to have said: *panta
rhei*. In any case, the temporality of presencing-absencing, understood as a
play, means that the One founds nothing. It is "without why," "only play."
"But this 'only' is All, the One, the Unique."[77]

Lastly, it is easy to show how "*hen* pervades all of philosophy,"[78] how it
functions categorially: the One as the most manifest entity in Plato,[79] as
ultimate and supreme in the Medievals,[80] as transcendental apperception
in Kant,[81] and as the totalitarian reign of technology[82] are all so many
instances where the categorial signification of *hen* is verified diachronically.
They are also examples illustrating the forgotteness of the agonistic sense of
hen: all these later acceptations vary the economic One—when it is not
Zeus—whose temporality is constant presence.

§27. Nous

This last category is convertible with *logos: noein* means to 'heed' the
things gathered together in an order of presence. Furthermore, like *legein*,
noein, too, has traditionally been understood in relation to the human
faculty of reasoning: philosophy is 'noetic' when it examines that faculty as a
receptive organ, and it is 'logic' when it examines reason's acts. But here
again a deconstruction of the transmitted representations—from the Aristotelian ἀπαθὴς νοῦς to Anglo-Saxon 'philosophy of mind'—reveals a
broader sense: "νοεῖν heeds presencing."[83]

Nous is the only category that makes express reference to man.[84] Like all
categories, *noein* addresses presencing from a certain angle. Here, that
angle is defined by man's attending to what is present. To attend, in this
sense, is "to notice something present, to take it discerningly before oneself, and to accept it as present."[85] One always notices, takes on, or accepts
an *entity;* noticing, taking on, accepting are verbs that address the way
present entities concern *man*. This category is therefore less originary.
Legein "precedes" it. For entities to be at all noticed and accepted, they
must first show themselves. *Legein* "requires" *noein*.[86] Prior to being the
faculty coordinated to the intelligible and its grasp, *nous* is what makes
man the "guardian" of the ontological difference between things gathered
and their gathering: "When we pay heed to something laid out before us,
we heed its being laid out."[87] *Noein* is to heed the layout (*logos*) before
man. It is presencing for man.

What is 'convertible' with the leading category, *eon*, is then, strictly
speaking, the pair *legein-noein*. *Noein* indeed leaves absencing and con-

cealment unsaid. "Its essential weight [is] to linger within the unconcealed."[88] The dependence of *noein* on *legein* results from the manner in
which this category addresses presencing: *sub specie hominis*. It is not to
be construed 'humanistically', however, for man is not understood here as
an entity endowed with certain attributes; he is characterized by a function:
ver-nehmen, "per-ceiving," or "noting, taking before oneself, accepting."
What is decisive in accounting for this verb as a category is that it is
operative only *within* the domain of whatever happens to be present, unconcealed. *Noein* turns out to be secondary, it follows upon the other
categories, because to heed and attend the present is to endure it as
already-there. This category is therefore deficient. Heeding and attending
do not bespeak the entire phenomenon of being. Not that any of the verbs
by which Heidegger translates *noein* designate an act or faculty of passive
reception, opposable to some act or faculty endowed with spontaneity (an
agent intellect, or pure legislative reason). But what is paid heed to, in
noein, is the present as given, without reference to its coming-about and its
potential going-away. To say that *"noein* and presencing are one" supposes,
then, that *noein* is tacitly conjoined with *legein*, which addresses not only
laying-out, but also possible laying-away. *Noein* is a "basic trait" only as so
linked to *legein*.[89] Its poverty appears twice: to speak of presencing this
category has recourse to man, and to speak of absencing it has recourse to
legein. Under that twofold restriction, *noein* is an economic category. Its
specificity as well as the anti-humanism it indirectly entails appear when
that double dependence is understood as a single reference to being as
originary emerging. In no Presocratic writer does it serve to establish some
distinctive property of the human species; if it points toward man, it does
so not for the sake of defining his nature but for the sake of confining him
to the realm of presence opened up by the event of presencing.

For the entire subsequent history of *noein*, this relationship remains
inverted. Metaphysics is born when *nous* no longer serves to describe
man's attention to presencing but to label what is distinctive about his
own species. The corollary of *nous* is then the *noēton*, understood as an
entity and as non-sensory.[90] The *nous* itself comes to be conceived as an
entity: as that which is capable of representing the intelligible by an "act
of elevation."[91] Such is the Platonic moment. *Noein* means to see the
permanent in the changing, it is *idein*.[92] Later in that history, the permanent turns into something to be declared by an act of judgment and a
sentence. *Nous* becomes the "tribunal of reason"[93] which submits to laws
everything that can appear—laws decreed by that same reason as supreme legislator. When *noein* passes from ordinary *vernehmen* to the
intellect and to *Vernunft* as the faculty of a priori laws, it no longer finds
the 'matter' it addresses among entities in general, but in selected ontic
regions: first in the transcendent region, then in the region immanent to
the subject. At this last stage, that of Kant, the pre-metaphysical sense of
noein—*vernehmen*, receiving, heeding—is divorced from its metaphysical

sense, regulating. (Kant's very project consists in bridging that gap between receptivity and spontaneity, each understood as the act of one of
the mind's radical faculties; Heidegger however does not read this partial
return of *noein's* original meaning, in Kant, as an incipient overcoming of
its age-old reification.) Transcendental formalism engenders a concept of
Vernunft, Heidegger maintains, entirely dependent on *logos* as the "logic
of things."[94] Kant's guiding concept of *nous* remains the divine intellect:
"the transcendental ideal goes together with the *intuitus originarius*" of
the supreme entity.[95] The reification of *nous* culminates in "technological
and scientific rationalization."[96]

XI

AT THE TECHNOLOGICAL END
THE RETROSPECTIVE CATEGORIES

> The world age in which metaphysics reaches
> completion—which we descry when we
> think through the basic features of
> Nietzsche's metaphysics—prompts us to
> wonder how we can at all gain access to the
> history of being and, prior to that, how it is
> that we must experience history as the
> release of being into machination.
>
> *Nietzsche: European Nihilism*[1]

Two things should be clear from the outset: (1) the following exposition of Nietzsche's six 'basic words' is not an exposition of Friedrich Nietzsche's thought; (2) as Heidegger makes Nietzsche's basic words his own, he substitutes, within the 'history of being', the contemporary technological moment for the Nietzschean moment.

The first of these two points goes without saying since what is at stake here is Heidegger's deduction of the categories of presencing. As for the second point, the evidence for it is to be found throughout Heidegger's texts on Nietzsche: they speak *formally* about Nietzsche, but *materially* about technology; they describe technology as the closing field in the history of presence, as "the release of being into machination," but they do so with the help of a vocabulary taken from Nietzsche. The soil where the retrospective categories are formed and from which they let themselves be gathered is not Nietzschean. Is it the philosophical muteness of technology that accounts for this game of substitution? Or is it the exhaustion of the concept, turned into machine and machination? Would Heidegger's refusal even to attempt seeking the retrospective categories in their proper locus, contemporary technology, prove that despite his proclamations to the contrary there is an inability in his thinking to emerge effectively from the philosophic tradition? Could this be a sign that the 'history of being' is contained for him ultimately only in philosophical texts? In any case, the *quid pro quo* is flagrant: technology is metaphysics come to fulfillment;[2] it is the supreme danger for "that history of being called metaphysics,"[3] a danger in which "a reversal comes to pass in being, that is, in the essence of enframing [*Gestell*]"; a beneficial danger, for "with *this* turning" and no other, the originary origin emerges from forgottenness.[4] There can be no doubt that Heidegger is describing the economy of the twentieth century: "These days" when we "possess tanks, airplanes and telecommunications equipment," when we live the "machine economy," "metaphysics has turned into the unconditioned."[5]

In Heidegger's usage of "*Machenschaft*"—machination as well as mechanicalization—one has to hear, ringing through that term, the Greek μηχανή (machine), the Latin *machinari* (to machinate) and the German *machen* (to make). The term covers the systemic links between industrial mechanization, attitudinal manipulation, and the generalized project of fabrication in the contemporary economy. In the epochal strategy called enframing, Heidegger thus suggests features that account for its global reach. As mechanical, cunning, and productional, technology stands opposed to the connotations of *phuesthai:* coming about by itself, letting-be, and growing naturally.

Why then ask Nietzsche to make that reversal understandable where 'metaphysics' is drawing to a close and where 'the other beginning' is opening up? One must see the option—for it is one—that unifies Heidegger's Nietzsche interpretations, namely, that Nietzsche's basic words bespeak the closing of the era opened with Greek classicism; that as a terminal figure, he is the "anti-Platonist" *par excellence* so that his "metaphysics" makes it possible to cast a regressive and encompassing look over all previous metaphysics; in short, that he is the "last thinker of metaphysics."[6]

The terminal constellation of that history—be it only for the worldwide triumph of its 'principle'—is, however, situated beyond Nietzsche: it is the technology of the twentieth century. One might wonder by what conversion game the spokesman of technology could have preceded it, through what anticipation the 'thinker' of completed metaphysics speaks for a language net that belongs to a subsequent aletheiological economy. The question has nothing to do with chronological calculus. But notice how the closure is described: by a technological disposition named after atomic energy;[7] by the total state;[8] by the struggle for planetary power;[9] by "functionalization, perfection, automation, bureaucratization, communications."[10] It would be difficult to claim that the epochal economy detailed by these factors is the site of that fundamental historical position from which the Nietzschean discourse speaks. Besides, Heidegger says pointedly that Nietzsche's metaphysics occupies "the penultimate stage" in the unfolding of the "will to will."[11] The switch between the epochal economy and its alleged discourse could not be more evident. It results in a crucial inadequacy of the retrospective categories: the will to power, nihilism, justice, the eternal return, the transmutation of values (and the death of God), as well as the overman will speak of technology only with the help of massive overdetermination and interpretation. Heidegger does not provide us with categories taken directly from the "machine economy" which he describes as the last in metaphysics.[12]

The substitution of the Nietzschean discourse for the technological economy clearly appears in the double relation that, according to Heidegger, technology maintains with metaphysics. Technology does not only complete metaphysics, it is itself a metaphysics, the metaphysics of our age. In it, presence turns into provocation. The law that gives coherence to the technological order is the challenge to nature, treated as a stock of resources, and the challenge to man to exploit it.[13] The natural sciences and their so-called applications[14] constitute one systematic realization of this latter-day metaphysics. Historiography, which aims at rendering the past available to knowledge, is another. Likewise theology, whose function it is to prepare access to the Supreme Being. Physics, psychiatry, philology, all enter into that strategy whose aim it is to place entities at our disposal.[15] Consequently, it is one thing to call Nietzsche the last metaphysician, but quite another to call contemporary technology the last metaphysics. The economic loci held by each are distinct and should not be confused. Take the category of the will: if man is inescapably challenged today to challenge entities in their totality; if that destiny is inescapable because it is rooted in the two-thousand year old 'will' to submit entities to reason; and if technology is the full and therefore final implementation of that will—then this retrospective category, the will (to power), is formally taken from Nietzsche, but materially it denotes the economy Heidegger calls 'atomic'. The same is true of all the retrospective categories: they only look Nietzschean. Their actual content is "the technical interpretation of thinking. Its inception reaches back to Plato and Aristotle."[16]

The 'destinal' analytic, then, traces "Nietzsche's metaphysics backwards, following the uniform tracks of modern metaphysics,"[17] which, in turn, is "borne historically by Platonic-Aristotelian metaphysics and moves, despite the new beginning, within the same question: 'What is an entity?' "[18] From one end of the metaphysical age to the other, that analytic clears the strategical tracks (*Bahnen*) along which the epochs unfold. The tracks bared by the retrospective gaze do not differ essentially from those discovered by the prospective analysis. However, no one's imagination nor any prophecy could have anticipated, before the reversal undergone by Cuzco, that the Inca principle would turn into the colonial principle, although retrospectively the schematic continuity leaps to the eye; likewise, in retrospect, persistencies appear throughout the West's concatenations. To speak only of the two guiding categories, Heidegger draws a proportion, on one hand, between *eon* and the "will to power," and on the other, between *logos* and the "eternal return of the same." "The will to power is the fundamental characteristic of entities as such," it is "the 'being' of entities" for the age of closure;[19] and "the eternal return is the most stable stabilization of the unstable," a function assigned to *logos* since Aristotle.[20] The will to power responds, then, to the retrospective question: what is? and the eternal return, to the question: in what way is it?[21] What is? The retrospective answer: the forces under the law of 'always more'. How is it? The retrospective answer: constantly present under the law of the circle. The regressive analytic shows that the will for 'always more' has been at work in Western thought since Plato. That determination of metaphysics as a whole becomes thinkable only in its terminal phase when its reach has spread worldwide. The enterprise of stabilizing presence also appears ancient: to the gaze back through the epochs, it occurs first in Platonic thought, in which the Good is established and fixed so as to maintain itself above the transient. It occurs also in Aristotelian thought in which the substratum is established and fixed so as to maintain itself beneath the transient. A more immediately technological vocabulary would doubtlessly have rendered the epistemological status of the retrospective categories less ambiguous. Nevertheless, as Heidegger uses the will to power and the eternal return, these terms succeed in making the traits of 'onto-logy' since Plato explicit as well as in bearing out the hypothesis of metaphysical completion and closure.

Heidegger gives two lists of the regressively applicable "basic words" in Nietzsche: "nihilism, transmutation of all values until now, will to power, eternal return of the same, overman";[22] and " 'Will to power' is the word for the being of entities as such, their *essentia;* 'nihilism' is the name for the history of the truth of entities so determined; the way entities are in their totality, their *existentia,* is called 'eternal recurrence of the same'; 'overman' designates the human type required by that totality; 'justice' is the essence of the truth of entities as will to power."[23] Where the first enumeration places "transmutation of all values until now," the second lists "justice," to which must be added another phrase from Nietzsche, "which has always been spoken in Western history without having ever been uttered":[24] "God is dead." Here the two meanings of *hen* that remained predominant after the agonistic One had fallen into forgottenness are easily recognizable: the economic One becomes "all values until now" and the divine One, "God." Their destiny in the epoch of metaphysics' closure is to undergo a "transmutation" and "death." As for "justice," since it is said to be the essence of truth, it pertains to *alētheia.* "Nihilism" signifies that "all entities, *in their totality,* must become other,"[25] that their "nature" must change. As a category, nihilism descends from *phusis.* "Overman," lastly, descends from *nous,* the one prospective category directly addressing man. These summary parallels suggest, at least schematically, the cogency of the number of the six retrospective categories as well as the place assigned to them in the table. Their signification and position with respect to the Greek categories will have to be established separately for each.

For the project of a historical analytic, it is essential not to confound (as I have indicated regarding *logos*) the application of a category with that category itself. In other words, will to power, nihilism, justice, eternal return, transmutation, and overman do not designate *incidences* in the contemporary epochal economy of the categories *eon, phusis, alētheia, logos, hen, nous*. On the contrary, the retrospective categories just like the prospective ones apply in every epoch. For example, the Middle Ages: If *eon* for the Medievals takes the form of the difference between *ens* and *esse*, both said of the Christian God, and if *logos* is the order He imposes as Creator (cosmic *logos*) and as Savior (filial *logos*), then these are applications or incidences of two Greek categories (although that understanding of being "never again attains the *esti [eon] gar einai*,"[26] nor that understanding of the Word of God, the *logos*). But the same epoch, the Christian Middle Ages, must also be read according to the technological categories: then will to power appears as "securing [one's] salvation." Upon this medieval figure follows the modern reversal through which "the will releases itself in truth as certitude."[27] Correspondingly, the eternal return in its pre-modern shape gives permanence to the Guardian and Guarantor of that salvation, it applies as the *nunc stans*, the form of solidity and stability, which prefigures the modern identification of reason and ground.[28] Stated otherwise, in a prospective reading, the Medieval understanding of being shows itself as an impoverished version of *eon*, and the understanding of the Son-Word as an equally poorer version of *logos*. But retrospectively, 'being' in the Middle Ages means to be sure of one's salvation, and then Medieval being is an incidence of the will to power; likewise, '*logos*' in the Middle Ages signifies the fixity that makes the supreme entity worthy of faith, and then the Word is an incidence of the eternal return.[29] Medieval 'onto-logy' is not the same in a prospective and a retrospective reading. This may illustrate the fact that the basic words borrowed from Nietzsche are categories, not applications of categories. Those words are therefore to be carefully distinguished from what Heidegger calls the "superimposition of a new beginning upon received metaphysical thought."[30] Such superimposing occurs notably with Descartes, where "all entities are seen from the viewpoint of Creator and creature, and the new determination of man through the *cogito sum* is, as it were, merely inscribed into the old framework."[31] The key terms of Scholasticism and Cartesianism are only *applications* of the two categorial nets, prospective and retrospective. The technological basic words, on the other hand, since they are gathered from the moment of closure, constitute a *determinant* categorial ensemble. Through them the history of metaphysical thought is counter-invested (as in an anticathexis) by significations that become manifest only at the moment of its technological deployment.

The counter-investment of the epochs by the technological categories has the curious status of an a priori that operates regressively; an a priori that, while appearing at one precise moment in history, nonetheless functions as a transcendental determination "pervading" all epochs; an a priori that requires a given epochal constellation, our own, in order to be at all thinkable. With this dependence of the phenomenology of presencing on two economies, on two givens—the economy of inception and the economy of closure—the Heideggerian enterprise does not dissociate the a priori from the transcendental (as is for instance the case with Michel Foucault's 'positive' a priori). Heidegger redefines the relationship that the transcendental and the a priori entertain with the empirical: The Greek "dawn" of thought and its technological "night" (Hölderlin) reveal the structuring elements which 'make the day' of the epochs in between and which thereby transcend both the inaugural and the closing moments. The deduction of the retrospective categories obviously moves in a circle: they are categories and not categorial incidences because they are gathered from technology, metaphysics' terminal economy; conversely, technology is the terminal economy of metaphysics since in it the regressively determinant categories become explicit and show themselves to prevail finally. But the apparent argumentative circle only indicates that the deduction of the categories, just like the construction of the closure, depends on a more fundamental project: the repetition of the being-question. It is made possible and necessary, as stated in the first sentence of *Being and Time*, by the deconstructionist observation that "this question has today fallen into forgottenness." Deduction and construction depend on deconstruction as the method of repetition. The two categorial sets, prospective and retrospective, appear when the repetition of the being-question takes as its starting point the *fact* of the technological break and places it in correspondence with the *fact* of the Socratic break. No deduction is possible unless that one question is put to this twofold fact. The deduction, "in raising the fundamental question of philosophy, seizes the inception and the end of Western metaphysics in their antinomic [*gegenwendig*] historical unity."[32] Our history is thus permeated with ambiguity from one end to the other.

§28. The Will to Power

The will to power denominates "the fundamental character of entities," "the reality of the real," that is, "the being of entities."[33] These equations speak primarily of the technological epoch. They signify that it is the will which sets up subjectivity as the unassailable metaphysical principle. They bespeak the triumph of totalitarian anthropocentrism over presencing as self-manifestation. Those equations signify moreover that the technological subject wills something. It wills power. This marks the triumph of *teleology* over presencing, the 'play without a why'. Lastly, they signify that what the will wills is 'always more' of itself; it is the 'will to will'. In this they address the triumph of *reduplication* over the difference contained in presencing as *eon*.

To understand the *Heideggerian* concept of will to power is to view that threefold technological triumph—of subject, goal, and reduplication—as the outcome of the direction taken by metaphysics from its start. The triumph of subjectivity lies in the will to power's establishing its own conditions, called values. "Value seems to express that, in positing a relation to it, we ourselves accomplish what is most valuable."[34] The will to power posits values in order to overcome itself ceaselessly. That necessity in each existent of constantly going beyond itself is not a mere consequence of 'being' now settled as 'will to power'; it is rather the very essence of that settling. Power is power only if it always pursues more power, only if it posits the conditions of its own preservation *as* conditions of its enhancement, and vice versa. "Power enhancement is, then, in itself at the same time also the preservation of power."[35] With presencing so given over to the conditions of willing—not only in its configurations but in its very possibility—the will becomes properly the *subiectum* of all: "standing by itself and lying underneath everything."[36] The retrospective scope of this category is easily seen. Through it, the technological project appears as one of placing being under the narrowest criteria. Only what is posited by the will and enhances it qualifies as an entity. This voluntaristic pre-understanding allows for an oblique reading of transmitted doctrines, laying bare the work of a counterforce in them: "Comprehended from the standpoint of the will to power, the Ideas must be thought as values"; read prospectively, however, "the Platonic Ideas are not values."[37] Likewise with Aristotle: when read retrospectively, *hupokeimenon* is a positing that anticipates the self-positing of the *subiectum* as willing subject.[38] If the will to power is indeed to be considered the ground of metaphysics in its last phase, then the self-positing of "subjectness"[39] has deep roots. They feed on an interest operative in metaphysics since its beginning, namely, that the reality of the real be set up by the willing ego.

The will wills power, hence it has a goal. With Nietzsche as the spokesman for technology, the teleocracy introduced into philosophy with Aristotle's *Physics* reaches the very being of all entities. But in its fulfillment, finality also cancels itself. Teleocracy does not signify here some ontic process of unlimited accumulation, but the very structure of accumulation or transformation into stock which Heidegger describes as the basic law of technology. The economy of metaphysical closure is permeated by the law of self-overcoming toward whatever the subject has posited as its object. In that sense, one may speak without contradiction not only of the triumph of 'subjectness' (*Subjektität*), but also of reification, the triumph of objectivation. "Indeed, the essence of subjectivism is objectivism insofar as for the subject everything turns into an object."[40] In that sense, Kant's discovery of the co-constitution of subject and object in a subjective act becomes radicalized when translated and displaced into the terms of will to power and value: the will to power posits itself as its own condition in positing all things as values, that is, as its own objects; in striving after 'mastery over the earth', in willing that everything become its object, what it wills is thus itself; it wills the totality of possible objects as its immanent goal. The boundless reach cancels its own goal-directedness. The law that makes the will aim at limitless appropriation thereby dissolves teleocracy, so that "entities in their totality are goalless and, as such, will to power."⁴¹ The will to power internalizes every end or purpose since these are what it posits. It sets out to make everything its own; its very aim, as so unlimited, therefore requires the overcoming of all aim. Every *telos* of the will to power turns into its obstacle: erected by the will itself, but for the sake of being over-come. The background against which the will to power displays its mo-ments of erecting and abolishing aims is the spectacle of global submission to Western culture. It implants itself everywhere and in order to abide, it must surpass itself without respite and without mercy. This second func-tion, too, is thus traceable back to the dawn of our culture—not only back to the Cartesian *cogito* understood as *co-agitatio*, as an "objectification that masters,"⁴² but further back to the Aristotelian *kratein*.⁴³

Lastly, this is the triumph of reduplication over difference. *Eon* spoke of presencing in its difference from the present. The retrospective cate-gory opposite *eon* preserves that duality only under the guise of a redupli-cation: what the will to power wills is—as its condition and its object—always itself. "The will to power counts only on itself." Since the law of technology is so bent back upon itself, it is best called "the will to will."⁴⁴ From the difference between an entity (nominal) and being (verbal) to the reduplication of the will, the 'verbal' connotation disappears from pres-ence: the will as the self-assertion of present entities in their beingness (*Seiendheit*) covers the self-manifestation of presencing with the thickest obfuscation. Entities are not only what is willed; their totality—their economy—wills itself, wills itself present. The Greek name for such unrestrained self-imposition is *hubris*.⁴⁵ This 'I-I', of present entities—'I', an entity, and 'I', its beingness or economy—simulates the ontological difference. I am what is willed, and I am that which wills. The reification and objectivation with which Heidegger so frequently characterizes the strategy of the retrospective categories⁴⁶ are to be understood less by the mechanism of representation than by that of reduplication. The subject-object representation is the Cartesian penultimate phase before the law which has articulated from within the metaphysical difference since Plato and Aristotle made itself known as the reduplication will-will.

My purpose here is neither to explicate the Nietzschean concept of will to power, nor to criticize its Heideggerian use, nor even to show how Heidegger applies it to technology, but only to indicate the way that con-cept functions as a retrospective category when read through the techno-logical economy. From this viewpoint, the scope to be given to statements like the following becomes clear: "The essence of technology *comes to the light of day only slowly*. This day is the world's night converted into a merely technical day." As a slow arrival of night, the moment of closure is for each epochal economy its utmost danger. "It is not only the totalitarian character of willing that is the danger, but willing itself, in the guise of self-assertion within a world admitted only as will."[47]

§29. Nihilism

In order to establish the categorial significance of nihilism, it must be shown how *phusis* gets overdetermined throughout epochal history; this is accomplished by a regressive strategy that traces this notion backward from technology. Here again, the beginning of metaphysics and its entire course prove to be animated, at first unnoticeably, by a force that becomes patent only in the age of closure: "The metaphysics of Plato is no less nihilistic than the metaphysics of Nietzsche."[48]

Pervasive nihilism appears in a first layer of evidence: "metaphysics as metaphysics is nihilism proper,"[49] because *phusis*, the originary phenomenon of being, has remained forgotten. In that sense, *nihil* designates the historical or destinal negation of that phenomenon. "The unfolding of nihilism is the history in which there is nothing to being itself."[50] The destinal *nihil* unfolds, triumphs with technology, and in this triumph reveals itself. Nihilistic overdetermination is therefore more than forgottenness; it is an organizing economic force leading to the obfuscation of being as *phusis*. The presencing of the present is 'nothing' since it is conceived in terms of other present entities—causes, principles, values—and identified with them. Nihilism is, then, the name for presencing as it has articulated itself concretely from the Platonic turn onward.[51] The essence of metaphysics is nihilistic, for its very project forecloses understanding the historical folds and backfolds as successive modalities of *phuein*. *Nihil* signifies the dissimulation of the *phenomenological* difference between the present and its presencing.

There is a second layer of evidence. Here, it is not *phuein* that is nothing because epochally forgotten; nihilism is that epochal *phuein* where even the *metaphysical* difference—in short, the difference between the here-below and the beyond—is nothing anymore. Heidegger asks: "In what does that appearance of nihilism proper which is of immediate historical concern to us, namely its completion, have its ground?"[52] In other words, in what does it become flagrant in the twentieth century that the philosophy with which the West has grown has exhausted itself by construing schemes of ultimate foundation upon one supreme entity, principle, or value after another; but that it has not been *in a position* to think those constructs themselves as so many inflections of presencing? Eighteenth and nineteenth century critics of metaphysics answered questions prefiguring this one by pointing toward progress and scientific rigor and by demarcating critical rationality from the dogmatic slumber of the School philosophies.

Heidegger, on the other hand, traces "the appearance of nihilism proper" precisely to the identification between rigorous thinking and foundational rationality, an identification in which the traditions of 'slumber' and of critical 'wakefulness' concur. *Jointly* they have led to the collapse of all after-worlds. That collapse, "of immediate historical concern to us," marks the "completion" of nihilism. He thus opposes the beginning of metaphysics in Plato to its end in technology as he opposes latent nihilism to manifest nihilism. At issue throughout that course or deployment (*Wesen*) is the growing integrity and integrality in exposing reason's self-incurred illusions. "Nihilism proper" then means: the epoch of closure is nihilism's proper site; it is in its essence (*Wesen*) nihilistic, for it proclaims aloud that only entities and goods are worth anything, that their 'difference' from being or the Good is worth nothing. Here *nihil* stands for the soberness of the technological economy according to which there is nothing to look for behind the visible and manipulable. As the final sentence passed on illusions, nihilism designates the way things come to presence today. It denotes that epochal determinacy according to which *phuein* remains operative when even the difference between the visible and the invisible is eclipsed.

In order to grasp the categorial import of nihilism, it is sufficient to hold together these two senses of difference as they appear in the two senses of '*Wesen*': destinal (*geschicklich*)[53] unfolding of the metaphysical difference and event-like (*ereignishaft*) essence of the phenomenological difference. Technology is only the "final stage"[54] of the former insofar as it is the proper locus of the latter. Technology is "inverted Platonism"[55] because in its *epochē* it has dismissed the world of the beyond, declaring it vain, as the shadows in the cave were once declared. When read diachronically as "a history," nihilism is "the basic trait of Western history," "its 'logic.' "[56] But nihilism may be read this way because synchronically *it is* phusis *itself laid out in a technological economy.* The epochal economies in which presencing has counted as worthless can be spelled out retrospectively the moment presencing shows itself explicitly as worthless, as securing no beyond. At that moment, "metaphysics divests itself of its own possibility of unfolding."[57] *Retrospectively,* one can say that metaphysics has completed its cycle and has collapsed, since *synoptically* one must say that contemporary man, "dislodged from his essence, compensates his homelessness by the organized global conquest of the earth."[58] As decidedly one-dimensional, such conquest is the most revelatory manifestation of the technological *phuein*.

The category "nihilism" is "a concept of being." As such it designates the tendency in the Western epochs toward a fundamental position where the nothingness of being "not only *cannot* be understood but also *will* no longer be understood."[59] Even in its form of a metaphysical duality between more and less actual entities, that no-thingness is cancelled. The force at work in nihilism is then none other than the will to power, whose self-affirmation entails here the negation of being, in the guise of negating any transcendence. Once that position has been reached, metaphysics is closed, and its history lets itself be explicated according to one more of its basic traits: the eclipse of presencing first in its objectivation as a supreme referent (the birth of nihilism in Plato) and then in the devaluation of that referent as worth nothing.

§30. Justice

The categorial usage Heidegger makes of the Nietzschean concept of justice is comprehensible only in connection with "the calculative importunity" with which technology "objectivates nature."[60] The line of ascendency, then, is clear—at least etymologically: from technological calculus (*Rechnen*), Heidegger goes back to Nietzschean justice (*Gerechtigkeit*) and to logical rightness or accuracy (*Richtigkeit*); from there to *reor, rechtfertigen* and *Rechenschaft* as acts of predication and judgment, to the *ratio* which is their faculty, and lastly to the verb εἴρω, 'to speak', but also 'to join'.[61] Under the etymological cast is hidden a regressive reading of the epochs following the guiding thread of 'calculation'. "Man is the calculative animal. All this holds true, in various transformations and yet unanimously, throughout the entire history of Western thought."[62]

In its effort to secure a stock of available resources technology reveals yet another trait that has been operative all along in the history of presencing. The categorial concept of justice tells how human life and the totality of entities have come to be mutually adjusted by technical procedures. To render justice to that totality is to "level and insert human life" into it. Doing justice to it is an act of *conforming* man to what he has been able to place at his disposal, himself included. Such universal equalization throws a new light on the traditional understanding of truth as conformity: retrospectively, "as *homoiōsis,* truth must be what Nietzsche calls 'justice'. . . . Here 'justice' is the metaphysical name for the *essence* of truth—for the way in which the essence of truth must be comprehended at the end of Western metaphysics."[63]

As a category, justice has nothing to do with juridical or moral considerations. If, late in the metaphysical day, the essence of truth appears as 'justice', understood as technological equalization, it is the theory of adequation rather than that of virtue which is placed in new contexts. Following the structural-historical parallel, which has already proved itself workable in the deduction of the preceding categories, one can say that the structural or synchronic essence (*Wesen*) of truth appears only when its epochal or diachronic unfolding (*Wesen*) draws to an end. Technological equalization tells the truth about truth, namely that "*alētheia* had to remain unthought in its essence" for the sake of various mechanisms of adjustment and conformation. Adjustment is the enduring pattern on which the versions of truth have been modeled since "the forgetting" of *alētheia*. Retrospective categorization, then, reveals the "ground for the possibility" of the most traditional notion of truth.[64] In the light of technology, 'justice' specifies the transcendental trait that underhangs the various instances of conformity born from the Platonic notion of 'assimilation' to the Good. Man is the calculative animal insofar as in all metaphysical economies—whether Greek or technological—the relations that link entities have been fixed in reference to him and therefore remain, more than ever, equalizing. So understood as adjustment to man, justice "is the condition of the being of what is living, that is, of entities in their totality." It is "the basic trait of life."[65] The truth about truth is that, as correspondence ('predicative' for Aristotle, 'eidetic' for Plato, 'transcendental' for the Medievals, 'pro-positional' or 're-presentational' for the Moderns), it has remained the chief tool for equalization throughout the epochs. The elevation of the theoretical gaze toward the sun of the Good, the soul's road to God, the image of the world in the *cogito*, synthetic a priori judgments, are so many incidences of the one categorial trait which becomes full-fledged in contemporary standardization and normalization and which Nietzsche addressed as 'justice'.

It should be obvious now how this category depends on the will to power: 'justice' is the conversion of everything, without remainder, into values for the will; it is the willful transformation into stock (*Beständigung*). Willful homogenization is part of the very project of preservation and enhancement which defines the will to power. The category of justice declares itself in that epochal economy which reaches for "unlimited domination over the earth,"[66] that is, which completes the adjustment of entities in their totality to man's hold. Such universal adjustment through and to the will is the retrospectively evident kernel in the ancient constructs of assimilation, for example of ϑέωσις, deification, ἔνωσις, unification, or ἅπλωσις, simplification.

From the vantage point of technological standardization, the relation of the retrospective category, justice, to the prospective category, *alētheia*, seems to be one of mutual exclusion. Truth, it seems, is either unconcealment or global uniformity. Adjustment, and even before that, adequation and assimilation, seem to deny their origin located in unconcealment. "But denial is the contrary of overcoming." Beneath the retrospective strategy, the prospective one continues to be at work, "always already [*immer schon*] and always still [*immer noch*], even though transmuted, inverted, obstructed, and thereby misunderstood." Justice stands not only for the countermove to metaphysical assimilation and adequation; it is "the extreme counter-deployment of the initial [pre-metaphysical] determination of truth."[67] The bi-millennial course of the quest for truth shows itself to be set, here again, on two undeflectable tracks: forward from the Presocratics, *alētheia*; and backward from technology, justice.

§31. The Eternal Return of the Same

If the will to power is "the being of entities" for the era of metaphysics'
closure, the eternal return of the same indicates "the sense of being" for
that technological era. Here again, 'sense' is not to be understood as 'meaning', but as the structural orientation of *legein:* the directionality of the
Selbstauslegung, self-interpretation or self-display of presencing. The will
to power lays itself out, displays itself, interprets itself in the circle of the
eternal return. Only such an understanding of sense as directedness makes
it possible to say that the eternal return is, for the will to power, "that from
which and on the grounds of which being in general can become manifest
as such and can *come into* truth."[68] The eternal return is the order in which
everything present in the contemporary epoch *comes about,* the tendency
it follows in entering our economy. It is the law according to which things
'come into' the rigorous arrangements of *Gestell* (technological en-framing
or im-posing).

The sense of presencing called eternal return has been prepared for a
long time. It is "the thought that, although concealed, pervades the whole
of Western philosophy as its proper driving [force]." With this motive
now in the open, the onto-logical structure of all economies can be addressed by correlating their commencement with their epochal consummation: Nietzsche's basic words bring us "back to the inception of Western philosophy"[69]—beyond the Platonic reversal where *eon* turned into
the difference between *to estin* and *to ti estin,* and where *logos* became
the doctrine of that difference. The hypothesis of closure stands and falls
with the proportion

'will to power' : 'eternal return' :: *eon* : *logos.*

When 'onto-logy' becomes equatable with 'eternal return, sense of the
will to power', the solidification of presencing is no longer only a matter of
propositions and their faculty in the mind; with technology, *logos* leaves
the 'logical' domain and comes to fix the system of technical regulations.
This ultimate stabilization appears from the peculiar way the will to power
and the eternal return 'repeat' *eon* and *logos: there is no difference* between will to power and eternal return. Viewed from the technological
economy, where entities are framed so as to be constantly accessible to
'machinations', being (the will to power) and its sense (the eternal return)
are identical: both designate the depthless surface where the rational animal operates, henceforth deprived of its proper transcendence once bestowed by 'reason' and the 'true world'. Now only 'animality' and 'brutality'
are left. They unroll in our century, unbound by any limits assignable by
reason, since they have made rationality—a certain rationality—their essence. "After the liquidation of the 'true' and the 'apparent' world, a single
flat surface is all that remains. It reveals itself as the identity of eternal
return and will to power."[70]

Here, then, is the criterion that makes it possible for Heidegger to treat the eternal return as a category of closure: with the negation of 'depth', that is, with the reduction of the pre-metaphysical difference (*eon*) as well as of any metaphysical transcendence (sensory-suprasensory worlds) to sheer planarity, being's intrinsic motility is reduced to zero. Without the connotations of process contained in both the grammar of participles and the praxiologies of transcendence, being becomes literally 'sense'-less. The doctrine of the eternal return is "the *last* 'metaphysical' fundamental position in Western thought."[71] With that doctrine, then, the verbal-nominal difference and its laying-out (*legein*) collapse into one. So do all constructs of otherness, such as ground-appearance, beyond-below, etc. They are rendered *epochally impossible*. 'Real distinctions' were however the backbone of metaphysics just as the participial difference was the backbone of pre-metaphysical thought. With the reduction of those distinctions and that difference to technological one-dimensionality, being and entities (*eon*), being and its 'layout' (*logos*), as well as being and essence (*hoti-ti*) are all one.

This is so because, with the eternal return, being and time are all one. *Legein* was the category that stressed the emergence of the present from absence. As such it was a temporal category. The eternal return, which corresponds to it, likewise addresses temporality: the directedness of the will to power, its accession to the regularity of the circle. But since the time-dimension of technological products resides in their unvarying availability itself, being and time are the same in the eternal return. The constancy that, as a category, it imparts to those products is thus the temporal mode of presencing in the era where all received dualities collapse. The eternal return stabilizes becoming in the geometric permanence of the circle. But more radically—retrospectively—it stabilizes coming-to-presence; it immobilizes the event of presencing. To think the eternal return is "to keep oneself essentially within the true as within what has been made fast; in this way, the thought of the eternal recurrence of the same makes fast the eternal flux."[72]

But if the signification of *logos* pertaining to speech disappears with technology, does *logos* not, overdetermined as eternal return, recover its original sense, namely, the orderly emergence into presence? Is technology not the triumph of *logos* as systemic self-display? If so, how is such recovery reconcilable with the pretended 'humanism' of the epoch of closure? Answer: the eternal return is the anti-*logos*, its late but complete and therefore symmetrical inversion, because in it a more radical humanism comes to light than anything born from the classical Greek turn of *legein* toward *dialegesthai*. That first turn, from which sprang metaphysical anthropocentrism,[73] encloses *logos* in speculations about the specific difference of human nature: man is ζῷον λόγον ἔχον, the living entity endowed with speech, with reason. But 'humanism' reaches its apogee when *logos* is displaced from the context of defining human nature and comes to designate instead "the basic determination of the world-all," that is, "the supreme humanization of entities in one with the extreme naturalization of man."[74] Eternal return is the proper name of this *Vermenschung*. It means that man, a certain epochal type of man, poses as the hub around which entities are arranged in a circular disposition, immobilized. Viewed retrospectively, this literally exorbitant humanization tells us something about *logos* that the prospective reading, which traces its slippage toward the orbit of speech and logic, had no way of discerning: the type of man who thinks that the eternal return is the truth "*posits himself* within that truth of entities in their totality; hence, by the simple fact that there are some who think that way, entities are already transmuted in their totality."[75] When read *prospectively*, from the Platonic to the technological turn, the transmutation of *logos* indicates the humanization of presencing in and through discourse; but when read *retrospectively*, the eternal return indicates its humanization in and through a project of the will, in and through a positing of the self that sets to work all the resources of domination accumulated by technology.

Regarding the necessity of such a two-way reading, the Cartesian new beginning is again illustrative: prospectively, the *cogito* is of obviously 'logical' descent, but retrospectively, it appears as *co-agitatio*, the forebear of technological en-framing and im-posing.

The two last categories place the technological economy under two complementary viewpoints directly dependent on the eternal return. The first answers the question: what is the condition of *entities* in their totality, their mode of presence, if the 'sense' of technology, its presencing, is the eternal return? The second answers the question: who is the type of *man* around whom everything in that economy is arrested in the fixity of a circle? The transmutation of all values answers the first question; the overman, the second.

§32. The Transmutation of All Values and the Death of God

The rigorous symmetry between the opening and the closing phases of the metaphysical era according to Heidegger appears best in the transmutation—or rather the permutation—of the echelons within the ancient hierarchy of the Good.

That overturn implies more than the modern identification between what is real and what is empirically verifiable; it goes beyond transcendental criticism with its opposition between the intuitable and the merely thinkable "to which no corresponding object can be given in sense-experience."[76] Located as it is in the late modern economy, technological metaphysics "must direct itself against the supreme values posited in philosophy," be they ancient or modern. Technology therefore functions as the counter-movement against "the whole of Western philosophy inasmuch as that philosophy remains the formative principle in the history of Western man."⁷⁷ The contemporary economy produces a transformation *of* values, then, but one that is only the most vivid consequence of a much older transformation *into* values. Seen from our hypothetically terminal site, the ancient echelons, the Ideas, as well as the modern rules, the categories, appear not at all as pure concepts, but as illusions valued by, and therefore valid for, the type of life called Western man. Metaphysics opens with that type constituting itself through transforming phenomena into values; it closes with that type undoing its own estimations through the transvaluation of all values until now.⁷⁸ To the retrospective gaze, Ideas and degrees of being prove to have been always already posited by man. Such positing of the worthy and worthless begins with Plato and includes Kant who esteems most highly what is formally synthetic and empirically applicable. The technological transvaluation, first understood by Nietzsche, *inverts* the high and low established at the beginning of metaphysics—and thereby renders it the greatest homage, permuting from within, from bottom to top, the valuative game. That game is thus lodged more decidedly than ever within the Platonic scheme. The "counter-movement against metaphysics is, as its mere turning upside-down, an inextricable entanglement in metaphysics."⁷⁹

Compared to its counterpart, the prospective category *hen*, the transmutation—the inversion or permutation of values—signifies first of all that what was most elevated, the divine *hen*, is to be found at the bottom of the scale where matter and non-being were once located. That is what makes this a transvaluation. But from the regressive viewpoint, the 'death of God' is only one instance, although the most striking, of such transvaluation. Technological metaphysics, as the contemporary mode of presence, inverts the entire order of the economic *hen*. Through 'machination' and 'equalization' on the depthless surface, presence—the constellation of being—is confined to the manipulable and the manufacturable, reducing whatever will not so fall into our hands to a shadow of the real relations. Of that estimation by which whatever was formerly high turns into nothing, and which affects the entire order of the economic *hen*, Heidegger can say: the decision "whether or not God is God comes to pass from out of the constellation of being and within it."⁸⁰

At issue in the *trans*mutation of values, understood as their *per*mutation within the enduring Platonic constellation, is its categorial scope. For the manipulable to inherit the prestige of the ancient Good, the representation of an ideal hierarchy must have contained its fatal agent within itself ever since its conception. From the genealogy of principles we know that such is indeed the case. The phrase "God is dead" "has always been spoken in Western history without ever having been uttered."⁸¹ The technological evacuation of the suprasensory is the consequence of man's oldest and boldest claim—to crown the creation. That evacuation, too, can be stated in the double meaning of '*Wesen*': the *essence* of the technological era is that the divine defaults; but that waning of the suprasensory is only the outcome, the self-revelation, of a historical *unfolding*. As a synchronic concentration, the default of the highest values is only the outcome of a diachronic process: "Because Nietzsche's basic metaphysical position is the end of metaphysics, the greatest and most profound concentration—that is, the completion—of all the essential fundamental positions of Western philosophy since Plato occurs in it, and it does so in the light of Platonism."[82] In terms of the transvaluation: since the fundamental position called technology concentrates and unites the valuations of all previous fundamental metaphysical positions in their extreme, it is terminal.

From this, the categorial scope of the transmutation becomes evident: the *chorismos* between a world of being and a world of becoming has, at the outset, introduced estimation and valuation into the speculations about entities. Inasmuch as one world is estimated more valuable than another, entities in their totality have been placed, and are so more than ever, in a situation of obligation to estimating man. The fatal agent contained in metaphysics since its beginning is such estimation, the preference for one region of entities over others, the attribution of rank. In this way, ever since the classical reversal the economic *hen* has included degrees of eminence, which is to say, it has been an order of *values for man*. But that dependence on man, that evaluative humanism, appears only when estimations get inverted. "All values," the entire economic field as centered on man, then flips from the positive to the negative, and "this inversion in which the opposition between being and becoming is extinguished, constitutes its completion proper."[83]

The birth of the great ladder of being from an act of human evaluation also suggests how transmutation, as a category, depends on the preceding category: the stabilization of becoming addressed by the eternal return occurred long ago, in the cradle of idealities. It is by declaring values, whatever they may be, that man places himself in the center of the circle described by the eternal return. The metaphysical arrangement that gathers entities in their totality, *on*, the supreme entity, *theos*, and the law of their stabilization, *logos*, into an 'onto-theo-logical' order is thus the most ancient instance of the categorial convertibility between the eternal return and the transmutation of all values.

With the forgottenness of the differential One and with the institution of man as principle over the economic One, entities turn into values. When a new constellation displaces the highest of those values, the divine One, the "conviction shared with Platonism" does not change; only, henceforth "the true is the sensory."[84] In the 'counter-position to Platonism' one entity, one region of entities, is still being singled out as permanent and supremely real. The real is now lodged in what is apt for technological treatment, but the new locus only confirms that "in its essence, truth is an estimation of values."[85] The category of transmutation indicates that, from one extreme to the other in this history of the slow perversion of Platonism, it is man who has bestowed the titles of real-unreal, high-low, true-apparent, valid-

invalid, simple-derived, immutable-changing, ὀντῶς ὄν-μὴ ὄν. The category of transmutation tells how entities are epochally arranged around the
valuating 'hub' called man.

But does technology not *abolish* all those opposites just mentioned? How
can Heidegger describe the contemporary economy both as one-dimensional
and as inverted Platonism? One-dimensionality signifies that the formerly
low, the sensory, has annihilated, as Nietzsche saw, what was formerly high,
and that dichotomies have been effectively rendered inoperative: "With the
true world we have also abolished the apparent one."[86] For Heidegger—
here again turning Nietzsche against himself—the permutation of values
preserves the distinction between a true and an apparent world.[87]

The paradox is less disturbing if placed under the hypothesis of metaphysical closure. According to that hypothesis, what is it that was formerly
high? The epochal principles. They still determine presence in the twentieth century, even though they have long fallen from esteem. Transvaluation as a trait of essentially ambiguous technology thus points to the task (to
be elucidated below) of removing the remnants of self-incurred fictions
which have already lost most of their efficacy in stamping our age. The
abolition of the true and the apparent world is still incomplete on the
borderline of technology, when, *for all practical purposes*, 'anarchy' has to
be turned into an operative 'principle'.

§33. The Overman

If the transmutation describes how entities fit into the age-old epochal
economy centered on the human subject—namely, as values—the category
of overman points to *evaluating man* himself in that economy. The transmutation reveals the subjectivization of the world by the act of estimation.
Once this link between anthropocentrism and the transformation of the
world into values is seen, the question cannot be avoided: "In which subjectivity is the 'subjectivization' of the world grounded?"[88] The category of
overman answers that question. It can be viewed as the final consequence
of the 'Copernican revolution' through which the world is arranged around
the axial figure of the self-affirming subject.

Just as the category of *nous* remained unintelligible without reference to
logos and *eon*, so the category of overman is pertinent only in conjunction
with the will to power and the eternal return. "That man is called overman
who, in the midst of entities, is related to entities which, as such, are will
to power and, in their totality, eternal return of the same." Consequently,
just as with *nous* man explicitly entered the table of categories, so the
overman indicates "the anthropomorphism necessary in the completion of
metaphysics."[89] Anthropomorphism indeed: man *informs* the order of present things. Anthropomorphism is necessary for the completion of metaphysics inasmuch as man no longer encounters anything but himself in

entities; the 'meta-', the reference to a reality other than sensory, has been engulfed by the reduplication of the will. This triumph of anthropomorphism not only requires that the will will itself, it also presupposes that entities be stabilized in the immobile stricture of the eternal return. The human type that the Western *epochē* has instituted as master over presence is therefore the one that essentially wills itself and wills itself in steadying concentrically around it all that there is and can be. The overman is the counter-category to *nous* as well as to its most traditional metaphysical trope, *animal rationale*. Its opposition to *ratio*, reason, does not signify any irrational project; 'overman' is the name of a figure that speaks for a peculiar kind of rationality. It is the name for the double agent behind the esteem in which the West has held reason, the double agent that the will to power is in its sense or directedness, the eternal return. The overman is the agent of the rationality of dominion.

As the subject willing itself exceedingly—exceeding all measures not originating from it—the overman legislates that he ought to legislate, commands himself to command, wills himself to will. Such is his "self-stamping" (*Selbstprägung*).[90] Stamping himself willfully as commander and transmutating entities into the eternal return around him, he "institutes unconditional dominion over the earth" through the "simplification of all things and men."[91] These two traits, the will and the return, show how in the era of metaphysics' closure, to be is to will; being is subjectivity. Retrospectively, the slippage toward being as subjectivity clearly begins with the moderns, when *noein* turns into perception and "interrogation" before the tribunal of reason, "which decides the being of entities." It is already under way, although less clearly so, with the ancients: "Since the beginning of metaphysics, re-presentation (*noein*) is that perception which does not receive entities passively, but lets the present be given as such to a gaze raised actively."[92] But what was indecipherable for a prospective reading from the viewpoint of *noein* is that such representational activity should culminate in the unconditional enframing of the globe and thereby reveal an essential trait of Western culture. Here again, then, *Wesen* as essence reveals itself only at the end of *Wesen* as historical unfolding.

The category of the overman depends, moreover, on that of transmutation. The prefix 'over-' indicates the overcoming of the human types prior to the final metaphysical reversal. What type of man is to be overcome so that the whole of entities submit to the overman? It is the type that underestimates. In the will willing only itself and its one dimension, there can be no place for underestimation. What is it, then, that the type prior to the closure has learned to underestimate most? Why can he not will himself without hesitations and without restraint, without mediation, and without delay? It is the underestimation of the body that has inhibited the consummation of the will into will to power, an underestimation that reverses the overestimation of the soul or the spirit over the body. As Heidegger traces this category, the overman appears when the double control over the self (will) and over the world (its stabilization in the eternal return) abolishes the preëminence of representational reason over the body. At the moment of closure, that abolition can only happen as an inversion: the economic strategy which exalts the spirit thereby declares that the body is inferior—nothing; whereas the strategy which dismisses such an estimation and abolishes the superior, thereby declares that the spirit is nothing, that I am entirely body. The overman commands with his body understood as a form of the will to power in "unconditional and, since inverted, for the first time complete subjectivity."[93] The era of metaphysics can be considered closed if technology can be shown to permutate spirit and body, or if technological man is shown to 'estimate' with his body. Of this last permutation of the Platonic terms, Heidegger sees an indication in the violence with which technological man subjects the globe or 'entities in their totality'. Because of the physical nature of that submission, the turn toward *animal rationale* retrospectively proves to be a turn toward "the metaphysical fixation of man as animal."[94]

Man, as he existed prior to the transvaluation of all values, is 'overcome' toward animality by the training of a stronger race thanks to the inversion of the metaphysical poles, the sensible and the intelligible. But for that inversion to be effective, it must eventually undo the very distinction between those poles. On the borderline of an economic transition beyond valuative thinking, to overcome metaphysics is, then, to advance toward the uniform and to will it. To overcome metaphysical man means to will 'mechanization': "Discipline is the accumulation and purification of forces toward the univocity of a strictly masterable 'automatism' in all action."[95] When read from the perspective of technology, what Nietzsche calls the overman's *Zucht und Züchtung*, discipline and breeding, comes to stand for the process of planetary standardization. The overman is in no way a *goal* fixed by men and for men. It is an epochal trait in our economy of presence: "Man erenow has not yet been at all prepared in his essence for the being which, meanwhile, has come to permeate all entities. Yet the *necessity* reigns in them that man go beyond man erenow."[96] What necessity? The economic necessity according to which the humanist cycle of metaphysics is closed only when entities have been 'humanized' worldwide, without remainder. Retrospectively, this is nothing new. The breeding of the overman is as old as the metaphysics of the soul.

Heidegger's interpretive violence in reading Nietzsche is perhaps most glaring in the context of this last retrospective category.[97] In *Was heisst Denken?* (*What Is Called Thinking?*), however, he situates the overman differently. His new site is determined by the second meaning of that German book title, *What Tells [Us] to Think?* If it is the event of presencing that tells us how to think as well as to act, a name other than *animal rationale* is necessary to describe man obeying the event. That name is 'overman'. Heidegger's shift in emphasis is meant less to redress his earlier reading than to place the figure of the overman clearly on the boundary line that closes and encloses metaphysics; to give him the two faces of Janus. Looking backward from that line he is the inverted 'rational animal'. But looking forward, that figure prefigures a locus outside the "machinery" of "remote-controlled public opinion and the stock-exchange of the culture business," a locus outside technology,[98] *outside the struggle of estimations* and therefore outside the rationality of dominion. With high and low gone—with technology having successfully abolished all representations endowed with ultimacy—man can follow the arrangements and rearrangements in presence as they come and go. That is what the overman's other face looks toward. In the words of a commentator, he is "a figure that announces letting-be and meditative thinking."[99] Meditative (*be-sinnlich*) indeed: following the *Sinn*, the direction, of the depthless folding and unfolding of the economies. Following pliant being with compliant acting.

XII

AT THE "TURNING"
THE TRANSITIONAL CATEGORIES

> In technology, that is to say, in its essence, I
> see man standing under a power that
> challenges him, over and against which he is
> no longer free. In this predicament I see
> something announcing itself, namely a
> relation of being to man. I see that this
> relation, which is concealed in the *essence* of
> technology, might some day come to light in
> its unconcealedness.—Whether or not that
> will happen, I do not know!
>
> "An Interview"[1]

In order to grasp the phenomenon of transition from one economic order to another, the prospective and the retrospective categories do not suffice. Those two sets of traits—'guiding' traits, providing a direction, rather than 'founding', providing a base—while allowing the phenomenologist to apprehend the sequence of the economies, leave him unequipped for his diacritical task, that of describing the shifts or crises which set eras apart. How can breaks be accounted for as such? It will not do to proclaim with Michel Foucault "the break that separates us from what we can no longer say" and be content with this "diagnosis": the archaeology "deprives us of our continuities; it dissipates that temporal identity in which we [. . .] exorcise the discontinuities in history."[2] Not even in Foucault's archaeology are discontinuities and differences thinkable without corresponding forms of continuity and identity.[3] The question is: in what domain are these forms applicable, competent? If one does not wish to abandon the transcendentalist search for conditions along with its subjectivist casings, there is no other candidate for continuity and identity than such a set of guiding traits. Their attempted rejection marks off French deconstruction from its Heideggerian antecedent.[4] To address directly the issue of identity and difference in history, Heidegger gathers into a third class of categories all those characteristics that articulate the thresholds, catastrophes, commotions, breaks in the history of presencing—thresholds, catastrophes, etc., which, even though they set up a new historical world, need not be conspicuous. This third series of features thus deals directly with the phenomena of passage from one site to another. They assign our own times the uncomfortable locus of an end, *eschaton*, in which a new beginning, an original origin, is taking shape: the end of the economy of epochs as well as of their principles, and the beginning of the economy in which manifold presencing might no longer be obstructed. "Are we the precursors of the dawn of an entirely different world age, which has left our contemporary historicist representations of history behind?" If so, the phenomenology of reversals is *eschatological*. The epochs, then, run toward their end, and "the long-hidden destiny of being takes its departure." "Since it is thus fateful, being itself is in itself eschatological." "A different destiny of being" would set in.[5] The categories of transition articulate the crises of the *same* and the appearance of the *other*. Only these categories allow us to hold together the entire system which organizes, on one hand, the concepts of *archē* and *principium* as well as their phenomenological 'truth', the original and the originary, and, on the other, the oppositions accompanying the distinction between metaphysical and non-metaphysical thinking, such as modern/post-modern, subjectivism/anti-humanism, making/letting, constant presence/presencing, consciousness/site (*topos*), etc. The transitional categories bring into view the phenomena that account for the 'turning' as perhaps the most complex historical reversal known—not, of course, the cultural changeovers as they are actually occurring today, but their conformation, their formal identity. Synchronic and diachronic transitions between economies allow us to apprehend the same and the other in the 'history of being'. If historical identity and difference are situated in these transitions, they remain unintelligible except through the discovery of formal invariables in the reversals. Only a systematization of the traits exhibited by historical crises will, then, yield a play of identity and difference that is purely categorial without ceasing to be ontological. From Kant we learned that what is formal supplies no answer to the ancient question, What is being? Transcendental formalism only answers the question, How is *experience* possible? With Heidegger, on the contrary, the formal does not serve to dismiss the ontological, at least if it is understood that 'being' designates neither some noumenal in-itself nor the mass of raw sense data, but the event of presencing. To attempt a deduction of transitional categories is to advance no farther than to the edge of metaphysics. Here as in its two previous parts, the deduction must borrow its parameters from the history of the beginnings it deconstructs. But this advance, the cutting edge of the enterprise, is not nothing. It is the sting that unnerves all archaeo-teleological desire, the presumed need for an archaeo-teleocratic origin. The call for such an origin sounds *edgy* as it rings across the edge of the closed field policed by representations guaranteeing satisfaction to that desire and that need.

Here more than in its two previous parts, the deduction has to proceed obliquely. The whole understanding of the transitional categories, which constitute what is most Heideggerian in Heidegger, depends upon the way they are untied from the metaphysical edifice. They grow upon that edifice but at the same time fissure it, threatening to disjoin its most established evidences and, through an oblique split, making room for a "thinking yet to come."[6] This set of categories by no means allows Heidegger to escape from the onto-theological economy. Functioning on its fringe, however, they draft its closure as any border line consititutes the loci it sets apart. Each of these transitional categories thus bears Janus' face: looking back, it faithfully mirrors the articulations of the metaphysical field in its entirety, while looking ahead, it outlines *a possible rule for a possible non-principial play of presencing* to come—or perhaps already begun.

The bifocal functioning of this categorial class—in one focus recapitulating the guiding traits of past transitions, traits of "errancy," and in the other focus anticipating those of a contemporary potential, traits of "homecoming"[7]—is enacted by the double functioning of technology, according to the way Heidegger reads it in these lines from Hölderlin:

> But where there is the danger, there grows
> Also what saves.[8]

"Technology is a modality of unconcealment," he writes as a commentary on these lines, and in this sense it preserves, protects, safeguards things and humans in their aletheiological essence; but "the unconcealment that rules in modern technology is a provocation," it is the threat of the "supreme danger,"[9] a threat to *alētheia*. The provocation negates the "free essence"—another name for *alētheia*.[10] Insofar as technology ends a development that started with the Aristotelian notion of *technē*, we would thus be living today the ultimate metaphysical danger; but since technology, *as* the culmination of that deep-rooted danger, may put an end to the obfuscation of presencing by 'principles', that which saves already announces itself within technology. Hence its two faces. With the one that looks ahead, technology begins to "loose, set free, woo, spare, shelter, safeguard, preserve" presencing.[11] The face that looks back sees the world "forced into ruin, the earth into desolation, and man into mere labor."[12] Together they suggest that the principial rationality may have come full circle, that an economic transition may be taking shape, and that with the might of the possible, a non-principial constellation of presencing makes itself felt. At that moment in history, one eye is not enough. The diagnostician has to look with both eyes and speak of the *one* phenomenon of transition with a *double* vocabulary: a vocabulary addressing the subverted as well as the subversive collocation, but not in the same words. The words will not be the same since one can only speak of a situation of simple contiguity from the adjacent fields, of which there are two. In order to grasp the transitive essence of technology we shall thus have to establish a list of terms relating both to the "danger" and to the "salvation" it is capable of providing. The frontline where these two terminological strategies collide, the locus of their impact, is one and simple. The two sets of terms are legitimated by the transcendental phenomenology of technology (it is transcendental since it exhibits the aletheiological, and in that sense universal and necessary, conditions of technology). The recapitulatory and the anticipatory set meet at the line that demarcates life under the rule of *pros hen,* the rule of the first, from life in what will be called the 'fourfold'.[13] *Janus bifrons*.

With this last class of guiding traits, Heidegger tries to indicate the step from the actual to the potential, or the transition to *the other* arrangement that may begin with the technological turning. Construed from the simple phenomenon of bifrontality—and no longer from the beginning or the end of the closed era—they will have to allow for a formal account of the dawning constellation in which presencing would be deprived of the string of referents whose prestige has brought us where we are.

Each transitional category bears two titles. The first makes it a category of closure, and the second, a category of opening, of 'the other beginning'. Each category strikes twice, it has two angles of incidence, recapitulatory and anticipatory. The transitional categories are the ones that combine recapitulation, *Wiederholung,* with anticipation, *Vorläufigkeit*.[14] Either title limits the extension of the category under discussion. Thus the first category's title of closure, 'ontological difference', is connected with *eon* and 'will to power'; but that title is not applicable beyond the post-modern threshold. This threshold draws the final line under all economies that may be conceived with the help of the ontological difference between entities and their being. The opening title of the first transitional category, 'world and thing', likewise limits its extension: in this case, the post-modern threshold functions as the initial trait, as the first lineament outlining a non-principial economy. The structuring of history, its self-regulation, results from the phenomena of breaks which determine the scope of a category's applicability. For the second leading category, the one that is connected with *logos* and 'eternal return', the title of closure is *epochē,* but its title of opening is 'clearing', *Lichtung*. Technology brings the epochs—the economies in which presencing 'withholds' itself—to a close and inaugurates the 'clearings'. In epochal history, the hypertrophy of one arch-present entity allows being only to be thematized as *chiefly* (literally) that entity's being. In the play of clearings, on the other hand, what will have to be treated as 'being' is an ever-shifting, event-like network of relations. The same bifocal incidence applies to all other transitional categories.

For each category, the title of closure and the title of opening—historical recapitulation and anticipation—have 'o be read as the two sides of one and the same guiding trait. To understand Heidegger otherwise would mean to advocate either utter equivocity between epochal and non-epochal history, utter discontinuity and heteronomy, or, on the contrary, plain univocity, homonymy. The first amounts to utopianism, the second, to historicism. Both make change unthinkable, the one by losing sight of continuity because of a fascination with novelty, the other by losing sight of novelty due to an obsession for continuity. Only the play of categorial identity and difference accounts for economic *contiguity* without levelling it into sheer continuity. If the categorial texture persists beyond the breaks, it follows that the anarchic economy cannot be sharply demarcated from the principial. The dividing line becomes blurred. From one terrain to the other we find economic novelty as well as continuance. From the field structured by technological enframing to the field structured by the future-oriented titles of the transitional categories, there is "no mere sequence"; rather, "there is always a passing by and simultaneity,"[15] contiguity. The very persistence of the categorial text throughout the economic breaks compels one to maintain predicative identity, but also difference in scope, regarding each of these transitional traits.

The epigraph above indicates, once again, the source which legitimates these transitional categories and from which emanate, consequently, the prospective and retrospective categories as well: that source lies neither in the solitary experience a certain Martin Heidegger is said to have had of Being,[16] nor in the simple return to Presocratic experiences,[17] but in a phenomenology of the double-faced essence of technology.[18] To the extent that technology *essentially* "threatens" and "saves" at the same time, it locates for our epoch the play of categorial continuity and discontinuity. From the viewpoint of what I have called the temporal difference, it is the violence in the way technological presence differs from presencing that makes a threshold appear in the contemporary economy.

This entire effort at laying bare the historical categories of presencing will entail consequences for political praxis. But such consequences will arise from an angle quite unlike the one that might be expected. Especially in the context of the transitional categories some commentators have imagined they caught Heidegger dreaming of a better world, a world to come, and waiting for it.[19] This amounts to confusing the categorial and the empirical. Heidegger does not draft tomorrow's world, but he outlines the formal features which, for better or for worse, apply when ultimate referents lose their credibility. Should the "relation of being to man" "some day come to light in its unconcealedness," nothing guarantees that life would for that reason be more livable. The 'saving essence' of technology does not hold any automatic salvation in stock for man. It designates a modification in unconcealedness such that no standards are reliable any longer in private and public life—most of all, public—and that life has nothing else to conform itself to but the event of presencing. It is that event which is 'saved'.

In the interview quoted in the epigraph above, Heidegger indeed goes on to say: "I see in the essence of technology the first brightening (*Vorschein*) of a much deeper mystery, which I call 'event.' "[20]

Heidegger's disinterest in our concrete future (which we shall have to examine in greater detail) runs quite deep. If the anticipatory incidence of all transitional categories entails a modification in unconcealedness, and if that modification consists in the withering away of ultimate representations, then it is useless to look for any authority capable of deciding whether such a decline will be to our advantage or disadvantage. For that, we will have to rely on the thoughtfulness of present and future actors. Any other reference game would constitute pure speculation, pure dogmatic construction. In a phrase that is not Heidegger's, it would amount to "German ideology."[21] From the transcendental 'subject' of Idealism, to the *Dasein* of the Existential Analytic, to the 'thinking' of the Topology of being, the discourse on man progressively deprives itself of the very possibility of approving or condemning, and especially of commending, concrete behavior, whether individual or collective. And if the hypothesis of metaphysical closure nevertheless leads eventually to a certain discourse on action, this will be devoid of any criterion other than the 'plurification' of presencing. That discourse on action futhermore remains entirely confined to the situation—ours—described by the contiguity of 'principles' and 'anarchy'. The solution radical phenomenology brings to bear on its assignment of deconstructing the normative principles—the solution obtained through the historical deduction of the three categorial classes—does not therefore consist in predicting any reconciliation of the antagonisms that rend our century, but in examining *concrete economic sites* in history (Presocratic, Platonic, and technological) so as to gather from them the features that have 'always already' been operative throughout Western history. The lineaments of transition thus emerge and become legible only with technology: read backward from that turning, they manifest a recapitulatory incidence on each reversal since the Greeks; read forward, they exhibit an anticipatory incidence on a contemporary *potential*, which it is the task of thinking to set free. "Preparatory thinking does not wish and is not able to predict any future."[22] Having ascertained and shown the conditions of the technological turning, it cannot shift from the ontological to the ontic and describe what the political, economical, social, technical or scientific facts will be: "Neither the political, nor the economical, nor the sociological, nor the technical and scientific, nor even the religious or metaphysical perspectives are adequate to think what is happening in this age of the world."[23]

What is happening is that a new set of categories is becoming thinkable which sheds an entirely formal light on both the past and the future. As the site from which one class of categories manifests itself, technology is thus 'ecstatic' in its own way. *Dasein*'s three temporal modes of being 'outside itself' turn out to be derivative of "the epochal essence of being," which in turn is dependent on being as the event.[24] One may presume that the transition from *Dasein's* temporality to that of being, which remains unthinkable in *Being and Time,* consists mainly in this transmutation of the ecstases. They persist in the later context but are no longer reducible to a self, to any aspect of man. To dismiss the categorial novelty as it appears in that turning would amount to "killing the being of entities."[25] In order to articulate the reversal wherein the principles decay, one must find words which, as said earlier, are no longer 'fundamental', but only 'guiding'. They guide thought through its inventory of the possible accents of a possible economy. The point in drafting these guiding words—the transitional categories—is to think a mode of presence that may substitute itself for the one Heidegger calls 'enframing'. Such a substitute economy, whose first guiding words are 'world and thing', announces itself with the technological age inasmuch as "in the destiny of being there is never a mere sequence: now the enframing, then world and thing; rather, there is always a passing by and simultaneity of the early and the late."[26]

§34. Ontological Difference/World and Thing

The first prospective category, *eon,* indicated how the difference between present entities and their presencing could become an issue at all and how it could give way to the distinction between entities and their beingness. From its inception, that problematic has indeed been 'ontological': present entities were conceived in relation to what is other than they, transcends them, and is one. This has been called "being."[27] From Parmenides through *Being and Time,* although in many guises, the ontological difference has been operative in the model of transcendence: "Being is the *transcendens* pure and simple."[28] "We surmount entities in order to reach being."[29]

The first retrospective category, the will to power, revealed how the transcendental essence of the difference has worked to the advantage of knowledge, of explanation, of mastery over entities, in short, to the advantage of man; how an interest in quite another overcoming has been operative under the guise of a sought-for 'science of being' or science of the metaphysical difference, namely the interest in man's self-overcoming; how, consequently, from the Socratic turn onward, the difference could lapse into a simple reduplication affecting man; and how this forgetting of the phenomenological difference culminates in the technological reduplication of the 'will to will'.

The transitional category corresponding to *eon* and will to power reveals the many ways in which, at each reversal in the history of metaphysics, the difference has articulated transcendence—the ways it has articulated itself *as* transcendence. Furthermore, this category is the first to point out a strategy at work today which denatures the law of 'humanist' overcoming and transforms it into an 'economic' overcoming: into the transition, this time, beyond the metaphysical field in its entirety. As it opens a breach in the internal regulation of that field, this category equips one to think the transgression of the very domain of principial competence. Under the hypothesis of closure, 'ontological difference' becomes the general title for the oppositions between the One and the many, being and entities, being and thought, all oppositions inherited from Parmenides. Since these oppositions are so many forms of transcendence, a radical phenomenology of simple presencing will have to renounce the ontological difference. For the principially bound play of entities and their being, it substitutes the free play between thing and world.

Here is the key text in Heidegger showing his dismissal of the ontological difference (the category of 'event' will be taken up later): "With the event of appropriation, it becomes necessary to free thinking from the ontological difference. From the perspective of the event of appropriation, this relation now shows itself as the relation of world and thing, a relation that could, in a first approximation and in a certain way, still be understood as the relation between being and entities; but then its proper characteristics would be lost."[30] In order to grasp at their core the various breakdowns by which social scientists describe the twentieth century it would thus be necessary to lay bare one radical transmutation: that in which the difference between being and entity turns into the difference between world and thing. If this transmutation is indeed radical, it will enable us not only to unfold past epochal folds, but more decisively to free ourselves for another foldure.

What is so innovational about speaking of the 'world' in its relation to 'thing'? What do these words mean if the age-old treatises concerning *ousia* and *on, esse* and *ens*, being and entity bespeak the "loss" of world and thing? "What, then, is the thing as thing, that its essence has never yet been able to appear?"[31] A formidable question in what it affirms, what it denies, and what it asks: (1) it affirms the old *on hē on*, entity qua entity, but by substituting for it the phrase "thing as thing"; (2) it denies that the essence of the thing has ever yet been *able* to appear; and (3) it asks what the thing may well be *in order* for its essence to have remained obscured ever since Aristotle set out to investigate the entity qua entity. Here is where that threefold questioning leads Heidegger: "If we let the thing unfold its essence in its thinging from out of the worlding world, then we think of the thing as thing."[32] With its overwrought verbs (both in German and English) and its deliberate tautologies, this phrasing is perhaps more complicated than the situation it describes. Implied, it seems, is that the question of presencing has been raised originally as that of a difference. That difference soon came to stand for transcendence (*on* and *ousia*) and reduplication (*on hē on*). In order to dispel the illusion of prehension in these two representations of the difference, being is to be understood again as a *process*—hence the verb coinages—of a *self*-display: hence the tautologies. With the category 'world and thing', the *qua* is transmuted. Heidegger's entire effort here consists in trying to suggest that the world, or contextuality, announces itself in the "as"—the thing "as" thing. This deals a blow to transcendence, since the world is not elsewhere than the thing, as well as to reduplication, since the thing is not just reaffirmed in its flat givenness. The category 'world and thing' is Heidegger's ultimate effort to protect the being question from "trivialization."[33] What motivates it is the desire for a gaze freed from any dogmatic blur. A phenomenon is taken as what it is only when we understand it as gathering its context, as 'worlding'. And the context is taken as such only when we understand it as gathering the phenomenon, as 'thinging'.

The weakness of this paraphrase in terms of context and phenomenon is that it tends to neutralize Heidegger's anti-subjectivist thrust. No anthropocentrism can be construed from 'world and thing'. Indeed, the understanding of world here abolishes all structures of self-transcendency. This concept no longer relates to "being-in-the-world" as the "a priori necessary constitution of *Dasein*."[34] Since it is anti-transcendental in that sense, it operates without any reference to man. The anti-humanism of radical phenomenology is thus only the most striking aspect of the step from *Dasein*'s being—the '*transcendens* pure and simple'—back to its de-centered or ex-centric condition, the interplay of 'worlding' and 'thinging'. If Heidegger emphasises 'the thing' as it emerges, accedes to presence, conjointly with 'the world' it establishes, his strategy is to suggest an interplay deprived of its center, man. Therefore the 'world' can no longer designate here "worldliness," "itself an existentiale." The world is no longer discovered as "equi-originary" with the self and others.[35] The moment the world ceases to be seen as the structuring element of *Dasein*, men—'the mortals'—find themselves, as it were, marginalized. They only enter as one of the elements into the 'fourfold', the *autonomous play of the world*. How is such a play, the self-structuring of the world, thinkable if it cannot be thematized in terms of the *kosmos* transcending the *onta*, nor the *mundus* transcending the *res*, nor even of the world as *Dasein*'s 'transcendental' being?

The world continues to be thought of as structuring the thing a priori and, in that sense, as constituting it. The essence of a thing lies in its gathering temporally, that is, 'staying', the four dimensions of the world. "Each thing stays the fourfold into a gathering in which the simplicity of the world lingers for a while."[36] As it provides a context, 'worlding', for the thing, the world makes it come to pass, conditions (*be-dingt*) it. But such translation into the idiom of a priori constitution, too, sheds only partial light on this leading category since appearance and cognition are precisely not at issue in it. Nor is the world to be conceived spatially as exceeding the thing (the way a galaxy exceeds a star by encompassing it and thereby fixing it in its place). If the double unfolding of the world and of the thing is a mutual staying, *Verweilen*,[37] then Heidegger's thought schema is more

temporal than spatial. In the thing, the world is there for a while. Nor does
the self-structuring of the world precede the thing as its transcendental
horizon. How could a thing transcend itself? Heidegger's shift from man's
transcending to the thing's 'thinging' puts an end to all construals of hori-
zons, a construal that remained still tacitly operative when he called the
world as set up by the artwork, "more fully in being," *seiender*, than any
object present.[38] With the gradual reformulation of his understanding of
the world—first 'world and being-there', then 'world and earth', finally
'world and thing'—Heidegger effaces the horizon of transcendence. Its
place and function are assumed by the economic "injunctions."[39]

   This replacement marks the *dis*placement from inside to outside the metaphysical arena. The step from 'being-there' to 'the thing' amounts to an
egress, a transgression of the closure. It is Heidegger's decisive yet complex
move toward unfolding the anti-principial potential in technology. As such,
it is misread as long as one seeks anything less in it than an economic
passage, affirming and cancelling—that is, transmuting—the ancient *on hē
on*. That passage, which after subjective transcendentalism tempts thinking
and is attempted in thinking, can be spelled out according to the three
observations made earlier. (1) Of the difference between "the entity for
which being is always at stake" and "that being itself" (the transcendental
difference of *Being and Time*), only the features of identity in difference are
preserved formally in the new locus: before the dislocation, those features of
identity in difference are the existentialia that unite being-there and its
world; after, they are the dimensions of the 'fourfold' that unite the thing and
its world. (2) The economic concept of injunction or address—"the constellation of being addresses us"[40]—allows Heidegger to argue that the phenomenological essence of the ontological difference was never *able* to appear as
long as 'being' continued to function, overtly or tacitly, as a principle of
transcendence, and, as such, a principle of causal explanation, of moral
betterment, in short, as a principle of epochal arch-teleocracy. At the moment of a possible transition from the technological economy (the terminal
effect of metaphysics, just like the book, *Being and Time*) to the economy of
the 'fourfold', the *res* becomes the 'thing' whose "essence has never yet been
able to appear,"[41] "the world all of a sudden (*jäh*) worlds as the world,"[42] and
"the living entities endowed with reason must still *become* mortals."[43] The
'injunctions' are nothing but the forms of economic regularity, they convey
to us "the *way* in which everything renders itself present."[44] When Heidegger is asked to account for the injunction his own thinking obeys, he can
therefore do no more than point to our historical site by which it is "bound to
the essential destiny of being," *bound by* "the turning (*Kehre*) of the oblivion
of being, the turning that announces itself in being's destiny."[45] (3) Lastly, it
becomes clear why the thing has never yet been able to appear in its essence. To understand the thing otherwise than as a piece of the world, a
practical condition has to be met: one must first let it be. This requirement,
letting-be as the properly phenomenological attitude, is irreducible to the

earlier laying of foundations and the opening of transcendence, that is, to any quest for a philosophical science. A specific practice (whose nature remains to be examined) thus imposes itself with the discovery of pliant economic regularities. As the post-metaphysical a priori it replaces all theoretical frameworks of ground and of transcendence. The 'rational animal' seeks both to ground and transcend the given; but the 'mortals', complying solely with the fourfold, let the given be.

The ontological difference—the recapitulatory incidence of this first transitional category—is constituted by an act of overcoming, of 'stepping beyond' entities. The difference between world and thing, on the other hand, that is, its anticipatory incidence, is constituted by a "step backward."[46] To 'overcome metaphysics' thus amounts to a displacement of 'overcoming', namely, from transcendence as construed in metaphysics to transgression as articulated by the anticipatory incidences of these categories. Working toward the site indicated by the hypothesis of closure requires, then, giving up transcendence and letting oneself be determined by the things alone and their mode of presencing. With the substitution of the anticipatory for the recapitulatory incidence of this category, certain economic factors—the collusion between *pricipium* and *princeps*, between an epochal referent of presence and centralized power—would fall into forgottenness; others, such as the ancient proofs for the existence of a supreme entity, would sink into indifference; and yet others, the very principles toward which the rational animal transcended the world, would simply become impossible. That substitution would not only allow, as all reversals in history do, for new things to emerge from forgottenness, indifference and impossibility; it would furthermore free them from the universalist overdeterminations with which the Western mind has covered up radical finitude. The double incidence of the first transitional category allows one to think of things not according to their unchangeable essence, but in their singularity, unheard-of since the Greeks. The identity of the fourfold dimensions of the world and the difference in 'thinging' set the coordinates for what both Aristotle and Hegel have held to be impossible and what non-phenomenological critics of technology can only do selectively, for instance, through an aesthetics: think the particular as particular.[47]

When so read as Heidegger's attempt to dare unshielded finitude, his replacement of the ontological difference with the difference between world and thing can obviously not be confused with the gesture of some Great Refusal, as if he wished to "reject the old, decrepit world, Christian, metaphysical and bourgeois."[48] The substitution works rather on the level of the a priori: "The a priori is the title for the essence of the thing. According to how the thingness of the thing and the being of entities is understood, so also is the a priori and its priority interpreted."[49] Philosophy, to be at all able to think the manifold things, has traditionally stabilized them by transcending the *res*, the *ens*, the object toward their reality, entity, objectivity, and by terming "being of entities" what it has so ascertained.[50] Such ascertainment produces the metaphysical difference. Each way of transcending the given responds to one historical modality of presence. With these modalities a new difference appears, namely, between reality, entity, objectivity, and other versions of 'beingness' on one hand, and presencing as an event—'being' as emergence—on the other. What so appears is the phenomenological difference. It operates like a corrosive and disjoins the jointings by which entities have been colligated into being as particulars are into a universal or as the transcended is into the transcending. It is, then, not enough to wrest the phenomenon of singular emergence, of 'thinging', from the economic surfaces of history; that phenomenon would have to be thought of otherwise than in terms of inherited distinctions. What conceptual language cannot achieve, the distinction between world and thing can at least suggest: heeding this pitcher, this bridge, for its own sake as its world comes to pass in it. It then becomes apparent that the metaphysical difference overdetermines the thing, does not take care of it, and is forgetful of the world as it comes about in the thing. The phenomenological difference between beingness and being reveals that obscuration of the particular by the universal; but only the difference between world and thing can 'accuse' finite emergence as such.

When raised in terms of the category 'world and thing', that is, in terms that address the originary as an event, the question of presencing is no longer merely adumbrated by the deconstruction of metaphysics. It is taken out of the perimeter that has defined metaphysics. From its new site, one can recapitulate the traditional answers brought to bear on that question and observe that "the received determination of the 'thingness' of the thing, that is, of the being of entities"[51] conceals rather than reveals the thing. In its stead, the received constructs direct our gaze to the thing's nature or its essence. No answer can fall outside the premises set by the question; if it does, it ceases to be an answer to the question. Thus the metaphysical question of being receives the answer it prepares, beingness; the phenomenological question, being; and the question that anticipates another site, the answer, "thingness of the thing."[52] If 'thingness' here is to be understood as 'thinging', as an event, then this answer comes closer to the new site. Constructs of transcendence, on the contrary, "skip over the things surrounding us and over the interpretation of their 'thingness'."[53] The deconstruction of the onto-theological era therefore cannot give up that era's premises, which is why the category of ontological difference is applicable only to a recapitulation of the epochs. At the extreme of that era, technology's "constellation of being is the denial of world, in the form of injurious neglect of the thing."[54] The full category of transition must complement the recapitulatory title with an anticipatory title. The difference that points to a non-metaphysical site appears when the question of being is addressed to the *oriri* as such: it is the difference between world and thing, their juncture understood as an always particular occurrence.

§35. 'There Is'/Favor

Under the hypothesis of the metaphysical closure, the 'denial of world' and 'the injurious neglect of the thing' have had their time, namely, the era in which the difference has taken on the form of transcendence, in which it has been ontological. On the other hand, it will be recalled that the second prospective category, *phusis*, indicated the impossibility of unshaded presencing. It implied an essential concealment, of which that denial and that injurious neglect are the epochal features. From the recapitulatory perspective of the difference between entities and their being, *phusis* bespeaks a twofold absence, at the periphery and at the heart of any past order of presence: the peripheral, ontic absence of the entities excluded by the *epochē*, and, at the heart, the ontological absence of presencing as event, as *phuein* or *oriri*.

The question now is: Does this corresponding transitional category indicate a possible, thinkable cancellation of obfuscation and concealment, of forgetfulness of each and every movement of withdrawal proper to *phusis?* The peripheral, ontic absence of entities in the anticipatory categorial modes will have to be examined later in the context of *legein* and the 'clearing'. Here we need to know whether with the transgression of being as articulated by the ontological difference concealment, too, becomes inoperative. What exactly does it mean to say that with the (possible) post-technological reversal 'the denial of world' and 'the injurious neglect of the thing' come to an end? The following argument indeed seems unavoidable: in the 'destinal' constellations of the difference, brought into relief by the recapitulatory category "there is,"[55] presencing as event—or being qua *phusis*—withholds itself (*epechein*); but with the transgression of the metaphysical closure, "the being that rests on destiny is no longer the proper issue for thought."[56] Would the anticipatory title that corresponds to *phusis* then eliminate its most originary trait, the conjunction of presencing and absencing in one *katēgorein?* Would the essentially ambiguous Presocratic experience of presencing lose its paradigmatic character with the anticipatory title of this transitional category? If the ontological difference is to become inoperative with the turning, will presencing no longer imply even the possiblity of denial and neglect? Quite as happiness for Plato is the *possession* of the subsisting Good, does "authentic thinking, assuming that one day it will be granted someone,"[57] consist in the full *possession* of presencing, in a total presence that stills all desire and all absence?

That way of arguing can avail itself of the retrospective category that corresponds to *phusis*, nihilism. Inasmuch as presencing has remained concealed behind unconcealed entities, nihilism pervades the entire onto-theological arena. Nihilism means that presencing is worth nothing for man. But—and this is where Heidegger's attempt to help us extricate ourselves from nihilistic metaphysics by "thinking of being" can be misconstrued—"as oblivion turns about, the safekeeping of being comes to pass."[58] With the ontological difference transmuted into the difference between world and thing—with 'world' torn from nihilism—being would not fall into forgottenness any longer. This is a good reason, it seems, for Heidegger to give the second transitional category the anticipatory title of "favor," *Gunst*.[59] It also makes it look plausible to speak of "the favor *as yet ungranted*" that "the world comes to pass as world and that the thing things."[60] 'Favor' is that one of the two faces of technology which looks toward the future. To understand whether, for Heidegger, there is indeed full light ahead of us it is necessary to show how this category joins the two Janus perspectives into an event.

The 'there is', the incidence of technology upon the epochs behind us, works as the phenomenological lever for deconstructing those epochs. In that sense, 'there is', *es gibt*, is a phrase that speaks of destiny: the epochs 'give' themselves, they reach us each time in a finite constellation of presence. To say *es gibt Sein*, "there is being," and *es gibt Zeit*, "there is time"[61]—and this point has not always received sufficient attention—is still to speak of the era read through the ontological difference. Beyond the line that demarcates anarchic from archic presence one can no more say *es gibt* than one can speak of being and time. "Does the name for the task of thinking then read, instead of *Being and Time:* clearing and presence?"[62] (One would have expected, "clearing and presencing.") Heidegger's "attempt to think being without regard for its groundedness in entities"[63] amounts to dismissing the English 'there is' and the German *es gibt* since both entail "the relation to man."[64] As the anticipatory categorial incidence, 'favor' is a trait which is in no way 'humanist'; which is no longer epochal and therefore also not destinal; which speaks of no transcendence, nor of any figure of the ontological difference; and which, lastly, is irreducible to the hidden problematic of metaphysics, the relation between being and time. In Heraclitus, *Gunst* translates as *philia*, which is a predicate of the pre-metaphysical notion of *phusis*.[65]

Favor is said to come about with the reversal whereby the preservation (*Wahrheit* in the sense of *Wahrnis*, safekeeping) of presencing replaces forgottenness.[66] But this is not to say that with the exit from the era of the ontological difference and of the 'destiny of being', all denial and all concealment are henceforth eradicated. The leave taken from principial thinking does not lead us to full possession, to the proper and to inalienable property. Such is not the meaning of *Ereignis*, event of appropriation. It will be remembered that *phusis* was also the most explicitly temporal prospective category. In the corresponding transitional category, this temporality reintroduces withholding and denial into the favor, although the withholding is no longer an *epechein*, and the denial no longer a denial of world. The word *Gunst*, favor, derives from a verb (in modern German, *gönnen*) which, just as *geben*, "to give," signifies "to grant, to bestow." The break between destinal giving ("there is," *es gibt*) and eventful giving ("favor," *Gunst*)—between presencing within and outside the closure—

operates via the respective modalities of time: "One may speak of denial and withholding even in the event of appropriation, insofar as they concern the way in which there is time."[67] The temporality of the historical fields instituted by constellations of the ontological difference is *epochal:* this word designates precisely the scansion of being through successive reversals in which 'being as such' denies and withholds itself. The anticipated temporality, on the other hand, is no longer epochal. It is a finite temporality, not thought of in relation to any form of transcendence. It "is no longer thought in terms of the relations to infinity, but rather as finitude in itself: finitude, end, limit, the proper"—this last term understood as the *proper site* established by the topological analysis, *Erörterung* ("situation").[68]

The problematic of transition must thus be followed up in two directions: the direction of the concealment-unconcealment operative in 'world' and 'favor', and the direction of the specific finitude which, under those same anticipatory titles, takes over from the 'epochs'. The anticipated concealment-unconcealment and the associated finitude will indicate in what sense the discourse on presencing must, after 'the other beginning', remain an *economic* one. The next two categories follow those two directions.

§36. Unconcealment/Event

The prospective category *alētheia* designated a play of hiding and showing whose variations make the epochs. Each reversal articulates anew what remains hidden or concealed and what is shown or disclosed, so that a crisis in history appears as a redistribution of shade and light, as a rearrangement of the 'clearing' within which life and thought are possible for a while. The corresponding retrospective category, justice, shows conformation to have been an anthropocentric undertaking since the Greeks. Such notions as *homoiōsis, adaequatio,* 'justice' have had the effect of committing *lēthein* and concealment to oblivion and of restricting unconcealment to a human comportment: assimilation to the Good, assertion of correct judgments, and finally justice done to chaos.

Under the anticipatory incidence of the transitional category which corresponds to *alētheia* and to justice, the hiding-showing can be neither epochal nor humanist.[69] Indeed, what is the 'favor' that announces itself in the danger of transition and thanks to which the 'world' can appear as a self-regulating play, as the 'fourfold'? "In the essence of the danger a favor dwells and prevails, namely, the favor that the oblivion of being turn about into the truth of being. . . . We have thought the truth of being in the worlding of world as the mirror play of the fourfold of sky and earth, mortals and divinities. When oblivion turns about, when world as the safekeeping of being's essence turns in, then there comes to pass (*ereignet*) the lightning stroke of world."[70] As if to point out the threshold upon which the *Ereignis,* event of appropriation, starts coming into play, Heidegger adds: "The lightning stroke is the event in which the constellation of the turning [comes about] in the very essence of being, and that in the epoch of enframing (*des Gestells*)."[71] The categorial transition from 'unconcealment' to 'event of appropriation' is datable: it occurs with contemporary technology.

What is called 'the event' of appropriation here would thus be *setting in* with technological enframing. Technology is "the liminal appearance of the event of appropriation," the limen of a possible era determined solely by surface fluctuations. "Between the epochal formations of being and its transformation into the event of appropriation stands enframing."[72] The most pertinent description the phenomenology of reversals can give of this turning is that it is "the entry into dwelling in the event of appropriation."[73] These threshold metaphors must not hide the fact that the event of appropriation has been operative 'always already', although it emerges from the rubble of principles only with technology.[74] Also, if principial constructs could foul its recognition, this indicates that the event of appropriation is simultaneously an event of expropriation. The very possibility of 'denial' and 'neglect' must be traced to this ultimate, although radically finite, condition of the self-structuring designated by the categories of world and of favor. Expropriation, *Enteignis*, accounts for the tendency toward negativity in a given economy—all and any negativity in all and any economy. It accounts for concealment (*lēthē*) in unconcealment, which in turn accounts for withholding (*epechein*) in the epochs. It is the undertow in all surface fluctuations. "The event of appropriation is in itself an event of expropriation; this word takes up, in a manner commensurate with the event, the early Greek *lēthē*, in the sense of concealment."[75] The play of appropriation and expropriation conveys something *alētheia* cannot say. This shows once again how mistaken one would be to place Heidegger in the company of the German Romantics and to read in him a ploy for reviving experiences inspired by pre-classical Greece.

The anticipatory incidence of this transitional category, 'event' as the play of appropriation and expropriation, thus reveals a 'motility'. This is opposed to the 'destiny of being' as the anticipatory incidence is to the recapitulatory incidence: "The absence of destiny from the event of appropriation does not imply that it lacks all 'motility.' "[76] In Anaximander, we saw that the early Greek understanding of *alētheia* indicates in entities a movement of arrival from absence, lingering in presence, and withdrawal back into absence. This is no longer the way hiding-showing is thought of here. Heidegger suggests two paths toward understanding 'expropriation': the event supersedes epochal-destinal unconcealment in such a way that, firstly, "it can be retained neither as being nor as time; it is, so to speak, a *neutrale tantum*, the neutral 'and' in the title 'Time and Being.' "[77] The motility of appropriation and expropriation is secondly thematized in relation to the fourfold. These two paths are however no more than suggested. The seminar dealing with this 'motility' cuts short the discussion of the "expropriation that belongs essentially to appropriation. This includes the question: expropriation whither? The direction and sense of this question were not discussed any further."[78] The event of appropriation-expropriation is the thought of the most tenuous issue for philosophy ever and therefore a tenuous thought, only to be hinted at. It is the thought of the phenomena's simple entering, always particular and precarious, into intercourse.

One can nevertheless attempt to follow three ways of access. (1) If the event of appropriation is to be understood along the lines of the neutral 'and' as well as of the 'fourfold', the concealment which, as expropriation, is operative in it cannot be broached through questions either about man or about entities that are epochally present or absent. Such arrival and with-drawal of entities within the arena where man is co-present to them was precisely stressed by the recapitulatory incidence, 'unconcealment'. But neither the 'and' nor the 'fourfold' refers to entities or man. The concept of event (if it can be called a concept) is, in a sense, the one most devoid of content that is conceivable. It carries less beingness than Aristotle's cate-gory of relation. Indeed: (2) To think being and time "is to think of the most difficult thought of philosophy, namely, being *as* time."[79] The play of appropriation and expropriation seems to address this '*as*' prior to, and without regard for, being and time. In the most difficult thought of philoso-phy—since it entails breaking with philosophy—being "disappears."[80] This 'as', always finite and always other, would be permeated with a motility of its own. It would be the locus of the motility that hides and shows. In these hints one should see primarily a way of stating that the moving constella-tions of presencing continue to operate beyond the metaphysical closure: no longer (as indicated by the next transitional category) in an 'epochal' fashion, but acknowledged as inconstant, transient. (3) The 'fourfold' does not signify anything other than the constellations—no longer of entities, nor even of presence and absence—of the event in which the particular 'presences'. In the idiom borrowed from Hölderlin, it signifies the cease-less newness with which 'the earth and the sky, the gods and the mortals' determine 'the thing', each thing.

Heidegger describes that newness as so radical that one wonders whether it is still possible to speak of things in terms of species and genera. Manifestly, the movement of expropriation accuses extreme finitude. The category of 'event' complements that of 'world and thing' in pointing out the process character in that finitude. It brings into focus, not the present particular, but *a particular presencing as particular*, that is, as permeated with its unique negativity. While 'unconcealment', the recapitulatory inci-dence of this third category, indicates general constellations of presence endowed with a certain duration, its anticipatory incidence, the 'event', scatters the general, disregards even the particular thing, and fragments any thought-content other than this or that presencing singularized by its distinct absencing. Such plurification is impossible to transcend and think-able only as a movement of 'rising' or 'clearing'.

§37. Epoch/Clearing

Legein, it will be recalled, was the second guiding category among the prospective ones, and the 'eternal return', the second among the retrospective categories. Both addressed the self-structuring, *Selbstauslegung*, of presencing into a field of presence. They described how presencing 'interprets itself', renders itself explicit, unfolds. From the transitional viewpoint, it appears that presencing articulates itself in 'epochs' only inside the closed field of onto-theology. *Epechein*, it will also be recalled, signifies the self-withholding of presencing throughout the ages of metaphysics, the 'forgottenness of being'. The danger which grows as metaphysics tightens its grip in the form of technology is nothing but this *epechein*. "The danger is the epoch of being."[81] But since the category 'world and thing' as well as the two that depend on it, 'favor' and 'event', are traits of presencing independently of its groundedness in present entities, under the hypothesis of metaphysical closure one can no longer speak of *epochē*. Expressions such as "epoch in which being qua being withholds itself," "epoch of the withdrawal"[82] have then something pleonastic about them. Instead of 'epoch', the phenomenology of the turning has to speak of *Selbstlichtung*, "self clearing."[83]

The hypothesis of withering epochs may seem to cancel what has just been shown regarding the 'event', namely, that the transitional categories do not in any way anticipate a total self-giving of presencing, its shadowless reception, its possession without expropriation. And it is true that their function is not to break the seal of concealment and let daylight in on full presence. World, favor and event remain shot through with denial and retention. They remain finite. These titles even indicate the extreme consequence of the modern discovery of finitude. The second guiding category now brings precisely the modality of such radical finitude into relief. The decay of the epochs will not seem incompatible with the persistence of concealment in unconcealment, once it is understood that with the transgression of the closure presencing is not finite the way the epochs were. If, as has been shown, the *legein* gathers being and entities diversely according to the epochs, then 'epoch' designates the irruption of a new constellation of the ontological difference into entities such that its verbal-nominal function (*eon*) itself does not appear. To think the *eon* freed from principial overdeterminations—to think it, not in its Greek, but in its post-technological constellation, hence not as *eon*—means to think a double *legesthai*, double like Janus's face. The trait of 'gathering' has to be traced through two sites, separated by the closure. Looking back, one would see the epochs of philosophy extending from Plato to that "site in which the whole of its history *gathers* itself in its most extreme possibility."[84] This first site, the extreme of the history of metaphysics, is technology. Looking forward, "thinking may, *one day*, no longer shun the question whether the clearing, the free opening, is not the site in which alone pure space and ecstatic time, as well as everything present and absent in them, are *gathered* and sheltered."[85] This second site, the extreme of the old problems of time and space as well as of the entities appearing within them, is the locus toward which the technological threshold is to be transgressed.

In the first locus of gathering, technology, philosophy "comes to an end." It follows that its second locus, the "clearing" (*Lichtung* in the active sense), operates beyond the consummation of philosophy as that constituted discourse whose essence is the same as technology's: "Of the clearing, philosophy knows nothing."[86]

The clearing remains akin to the *epochē*, which it replaces, by the sudden revealings of presencing, as if by lightning strokes. The metaphor of clearing must thus not be taken to suggest a patch of light, be it conceived as *lumen naturale*[87] or as a "fixed stage with a permanently raised curtain,"[88] but a fulguration; not an open field, but the opening up of a field; not a glade in a forest, but (to pursue the sylvan metaphor dear to Heidegger) the very felling of the wood. It must be taken to evoke a setting-out, but not an arrangement settled-in; an event of 'standing out' (*herausstehen*) from concealment, but not the opposite of concealment. So metaphorized, the event of clearing explicitly links the process of absencing to the process of presencing. It also links the peripheral absence of certain entities to the presence of those given by a clearing. This anticipatory title addresses the "bolt" (κεραυνός) of gathering both as it includes entities in the realm of presence and as it excludes others that remain absent.[89] The concept of clearing differs from that of *epochē* in that it makes explicit the absencing within presencing. In the movement of emergence, of coming into the light of day, in the dawn, it greets both the night that holds back the nascent clarity, and the day that tears the brightening from it. The concept of clearing negates the *epochal* negation of absencing within presencing, it negates the forgottenness of concealment. To think of presencing as an event of clearing means to think of it in itself and in such a way that absencing is 'retrieved' in it. The clearing literally imparts, gives to present entities their share of presence and to absent entities their share of absence. Its categorial stress, however, lies not on (ontic) availability or unavailability, but on the imparting and the giving, or the alleviating and lightening, the lifting-off from oblivion.

The prospective category of *logos* already functioned as the dispensation of a place or a site, as situation. The *logos* divided the sum of entities into those present to and those absent from a given economy. It emphasized the arrival of entities in presence and thus, too, 'accused' the path from absence to presence. But strictly speaking, *legein* is not the event of presencing. Rather, it is, as will be recalled, the setting apart, the factor of differentiation that accounts for economic inclusions and exclusions as well as for the sequence of historical epochs. *Logos* is what allows Heidegger to think being as history of being, as destinal time. But for that very reason, *logos* is not sufficient for thinking the end of the "stampings of being,"[90] nor, put positively, "the *possibility* of a path toward presence."[91] This question of the possibility of wresting entities from absence points beyond the epochs. What responds to that question is the event of clearing. Under the name of 'clearing', the economies, which are ontic and *describable*, are explicitly thought of as a function of ontological and *transcendental* presencing. 'Clearing' is a category of a transcendental phenomenology that can dispense with the 'history of being' as the systematic link to descriptive phenomenology. The retrospective category, the eternal return, was unfit even for suggesting such a condition of possibility, so exclusive was the reference to man around whom technology orders all things into a circle of availability. The fixity of that circle makes concealment in general unthinkable. It makes it even impossible to understand how entities can remain shut out, absent, from any economy. The pretense to total presence thus proceeds under the trait of eternal return, not of clearing.[92] If 'clearing' is the word by which Heidegger seeks to think presencing independently of its epochal scansions, this category stresses precisely the movement of absencing in presencing, the undertow away from constant presence, and thereby originary time or the event. "Time . . . is the clearing of being itself."[93]

It is not the least of ironies that such a transgression of the epochal regime in its entirety should be made possible by the technological danger or peril: "The essence of the danger conceals the possibility of a turning in which the forgottenness of being's essential unfolding so turns about that, with *this* turning, the truth of the essence of being properly turns in—turns homeward—into entities."[94] When, with technology, the thought of the event of appropriation and of the clearing becomes *epochally possible, the epochs wither away*. This decay provides thought with what will henceforth be its sole issue: "instead of 'Being and Time,' " "clearing and presenc[ing]." "The task of thinking would then be to relinquish all thinking until now to the determination of [that] issue for thinking."[95] Under the reign of epochal principles the absence that characterizes the event remains unthinkable. To work through the philosophy born under their aegis, to surrender the *epochē* to the 'clearing', is to espouse the precarious in place of the principial, the phenomenal surface in place of unshakeable foundations; it is to permeate presencing with absencing.

§38. Nearness/Fourfold

The prospective category *hen* designated, on one hand, the supreme entity, the divine One, and, on the other, the unity of a phenomenal constellation, the economic One. However, these two notions, while they were mutually exclusive, in no way exhausted the categorial scope ensuing from the conjunction of *hen* with *logos* and *alētheia*. This conjunction revealed the differential One as the henological category proper. The recapitulatory incidence of the transitional category corresponding to *hen* will have to stress the motility of inclusion-exclusion as it has shaped all differential constellations: the nearness-farness of entities in each era marked by the Western destiny of being. Only to the recapitulatory gaze, then, does presencing appear as the "world-play" of near and far.[96] The point of this category is missed altogether if one sees in it no more than a "metaphorization" of the old metaphysics of presence.[97] What is thereby missed is the one issue of these transitional categories, the shift from the recapitulation of the actual to an anticipation of the possible.

'Nearness' recapitulates the three senses of *hen:* on the threshold of the metaphysical closure, the divine One is both near and far;[98] the economic One, the order that "lies nearby" (*das Naheliegende*), escapes us all the more since we are inserted in its constellation;[99] while the differential One which, as the ownmost issue for thinking, is closest to us, has ceased even to be a question at the moment of the closure and is thus farthest removed.[100] But if, in the possible transition to post-modernity, the ontological difference is to be given up for the sake of a difference that *plays otherwise*—for example, between 'thing' and 'world'—then these networks of nearness also change their strategies: the 'near-and-far' of God, of the epochal principles and of being must yield to a modified play of determinations. Whether the new play is called "the fourfold"[101] or something else, what counts is that nearness has ceased to play. The new play's terrain does not entirely coincide with that of metaphysics. With that dislocation the nearness modelled after the Presocratic *hen* becomes inoperative.[102]

This necessity of a categorial displacement becomes even clearer with regard to the retrospective category, 'transmutation of all values' and 'death of God'. These Nietzschean titles in Heidegger underscore the extreme anthropocentrism produced by the *hen*. In 'world and thing', 'favor', 'event', and 'clearing', on the other hand, man has hardly been at issue.

In every economy, words, things and actions are 'near' each other according to a given constellation. In the metaphysical era, their mutual proximity is regulated by a principle. In the modern era, technology lays them out near man. In the era anticipated by the transitional categories, their nearness or proximity is groundless, without foundation and without why, without either *archē* or *telos*. Nearness is disentangled from the *pros hen* relation. To suggest relations, no longer to one term but among a number of terms within an economic net, a category is needed that stresses the plurification of *hen*. That category is 'the fourfold'.

Hence the relational metaphors used to describe the interaction among the earth and the sky, the gods and the mortals: "play," "mirror-play," "ring," "ringing," "roundel."[103] The four constituents, taken from Hölderlin, matter less than the way in which they transmute the *hen*. Their "simple onefold" (*Einfalt*) lies in the unicity of the economic fold (*Falte*) which they determine. The one and the many—the onefold and the fourfold—are here thought together as the differential law according to which presencing *un-*

folds outside the metaphysical closure. How is such unfolding to be understood? As "nestling, malleable, pliant, compliant, nimble."[104] Not an easy thought. What is clear, however, is that in quadrupling the poles of reference Heidegger seeks to disjoin the economic One from the divine One—from foundations and principles, from the entire arsenal of archic and telic representations—through transmuting the differential One. When difference is grasped as a playful exchange between world and thing, and no longer as transcendence, the age-old collusion between economies and principles has lost the space in which it can prevail.[105] With the 'fourfold', the economies lose their affinity to epochs and epochal stampings. The transmutation of *hen* into *Geviert* does more than de-center man: one would have to speak, not even of an eccentric core, but of eccentric cores. This plurification shows that the entire idiom of core, center, focus, chief, primacy, is incompatible with the thorough transmutation of values. The anticipatory incidence of this transitional category renders impossible the principial arrangements which its recapitulatory incidence not only tolerated, but called for ceaselessly from Heraclitus through the technological age.[106] In keeping with the categorial "passing by and simultaneity,"[107] the 'fourfold' is not exactly substituted for 'nearness'.[108] From attributive—nearness of many terms to one—it turns systemic: nearness of many terms to each other. This can be shown regarding the content of the four words, earth and sky, divinities and mortals. The first pair of these responds indeed to *eon* and the second to *logos:*[109] earth and sky (or heaven) express the way the post-metaphysical 'being and entities'—world and thing—enter that play of systemic nearing, while the divinities and the mortals thematize how in that play the 'gathering' comes to function as 'clearing'. Unfortunately for conceptual clarity, this is where Heidegger's language follows Hölderlin's most closely.

In the commentary on Hölderlin's poem "Remembrance," the poet—hermeneute, half-god—is called the Incomparable. His utterances, those of a messenger between heaven and earth, are neither celestial nor terrestrial. He is "the Incomparable both to the sky and the earth. . . . Here conciliation does not mean equalizing into indifference, *but rather letting the differentiated hold sway equally in its difference*."[110] What the poet says arises from the in-between. He lets the differentiated prevail as differentiated, without returning to the Greek site—to *eon*—which is lost, but also without subjecting the differentiated to the metaphysical scheme of explanation, to the 'ontological' difference which is becoming inapplicable. The in-between makes "the sway (*das Walten*) of the difference" thinkable. "What we call that way directs our thinking into the region which the guiding words of metaphysics—being and entities, ground and grounded—are no longer apt to utter."[111] The word pair 'world and thing', on the other hand, reaches that region inasmuch as it bespeaks the perpetual newness of the differentiated terms. The pair 'sky and earth' addresses the same difference but by specifying how far the distinct foci lie apart—as far apart, precisely, as heaven and earth. If the poet lets "the differentiated hold equal sway," he achieves what no philosopher can achieve: standing, or bearing, irreducible otherness as irreducible.

As to the 'divinities' and the 'mortals', they, too, are essentially apart. In Heidegger's reading of Hölderlin, this word pair suggests the interplay that the difference intitiates as 'clearing', which is the anticipatory trait inherited from *legein*. What the divinities do to the mortals is alleviate, lighten, clear their lives. The clearing, it will be recalled, designates not only the emergence into presence, but also the function of assigning entities their place, of situating. To presencing that category joins absencing, and to things present or absent it assigns their respective sites. For Heidegger, to speak of divinities is to denote lightness, the movement of emergence, and to speak of the mortals is to point to extreme finitude, to the variations in situatedness. These somewhat forced connections are suggested by Hölderlin inasmuch as for him the "messengers" "brighten up" and "greet" the mortals, thereby opening their access to presence. The divinities are thus rather angels: "The essence of those who, elsewhere, are called 'the divinities' is addressed in a purer fashion through the name 'the angels'. Indeed, the divinities are those who brighten up. . . . What belongs properly to the divinities is that they bring greetings in which serenity greets."[112] "To brighten up" or "lighten up," *aufheitern*, is yet another way of designating the sudden irruption in which a constellation of presencing and absencing situates everything anew. The fourth constituent, 'the mortals', furthermore indicates the impossibility of total disclosure. Death is the pull toward absencing in every situation. In that sense it *is* situation.[113] The very concept of 'mortals' indicates that entities disclosed to us, situated in our vicinity, are, as it were, selected; that total presence is out of reach; that finitude ruptures the immediacy or the face-to-face with what is originary. The 'mortals' are so named because for them it has never been full presence that is originary. As 'gathering' entities into presence, they are the locus of absence. They 'belong and do not belong' to what is present. To be mortal is to hear, *legein*,[114] the present in a certain way, namely, so as to heed absence in it also. For us, to so become what we are—the arena of presencing-absencing, or of appropriation-expropriation—a new self-understanding is required: the 'rational animal' has yet to become mortal.[115] This is but another way of stating that referential thinking has yet to become systemic, which for our age means that technological representation, clasped to available stock, has yet to remember absencing.

The category of fourfold thus indicates how the two guiding categories of 'onto-logy', *eon* (presencing-absencing) and *logos* (gathering), become transmuted at the end of metaphysics: as humans find themselves *played by* the gathering or self-lightening of the difference between world and thing, they appear as carriers of absence more than as builders and masters of the present. The closure which technology may bring about will be crossed only when we thus have learned to be mortals.

§39. Corresponding/Thinking

With the principial sense of 'nearness' and the anti-principial sense of the 'fourfold', the last of the transitional categories becomes discernible.

Epochal principles have always demanded immediate compliance since their *Anspruch*, their claim or address, is so near that no room is left for mediations of any kind. Our *Entsprechen*, responding or corresponding, to any figure of an epochal First, due to the fateful nearness of their dictates, has been and is so urgent that whatever humans can do or not do, say or not say at a given epoch, "rests in the destiny of being" (which is therefore what "is nearest to us"). In that sense, we have little choice, little distance from those dictates. Without intentional, cultural, sensible or rational intermediates, the epochal requisitions fill our ears and eyes: "Receiving and accepting now have the sense of a correspondence that hears and sees."[116] That these dictates should appear as essentially linguistic is no surprise if one recalls that, phenomenally, listening does not require the distance demanded by sight. We do no see what lies too close. But, as observed earlier, the nearer a sound is, the better we hear it. Destinal history claims us without exemption, like an authoritative call. That is what is 'metaphysical' about it: the fantasy of an arch-present ordering agent. The last of the transitional categories thus recapitulates the history of reversals from the viewpoint of those inescapable injunctions which, as the linguistic modality of the *epochē* and hence without mediation, make an age.

This recapitulatory incidence agrees with the last prospective category, *nous*, as well as with the last retrospective category, 'overman'. *Noein* signifies 'to receive', *vernehmen:* not to perceive by noetic acts, but "to accept something as present."[117] The category of 'correspondence', now, concerns man's reception and acceptance of the *epochal* orders in which he lives. Their principles do not tolerate questioning, nor can their claims be objectified, examined, and evaluated as legitimate or not, their competence accepted as binding or rejected as spurious. One does not probe their validity. One does not even speak about them. It is they who speak. But that epochal truth of *noein,* the immediate reception of principial injunctions, becomes thinkable only when examined from the site, technology, where the history of principles appears as the self-incurred illusion of perfect presence and where it therefore comes to an end. Here one can say: in their words, their actions, their things, humans have not ceased to respond and correspond to the requirements of what happens to function as an ultimate ground in their epochal economy.

Technology also allows one to situate the 'overman' within the recapitulatory strategy of *Entsprechen*, corresponding. The subjectivization of the world through the figure of overman can succeed only by an inversion of *noein* which is as old as metaphysics: it is not man who responds and corresponds to the rule of epochal referents, but these referents are what we have declared to rule epochally, they are representations. Hence the

identification between metaphysics and humanism. The one epochal referent, then, that has governed the West is man understood as *nous* and *ratio*.
All else has been placed in a position of accountability to him. Still latent in
antiquity, but manifest in modernity, 'correspondence' therefore means: all
entities are answerable to subjective reason. The cogito, the Kantian 'tribunal of reason', and 'overman' render explicit the dictates that *man* voices
over the totality of entities, namely, that they conform to the pure laws
emanating from the subject. Following the recapitulatory reading, only
what is rational, *vernünftig*, because received, *vernommen*, by the subject
is real.

Man can appear in the posture of a legislator over entities only epochally:
such is the paradox this phenomenology of economies reveals. He is epochally summoned to summon entities so that they conform to his reason. By
so doing, he guards one aletheiological constellation. *Man responds* to the
destinal injunctions by ordaining *entities to be answerable* to him. The
subjective command over objects has been the predominant form in the
West of responding to the principial command over the economies. However, the subjective and the epochal summons do not operate on the same
level. For metaphysical, and a fortiori, technological man to set himself up
as 'master over the earth' is still no more than his response to the claim that
governs Western destiny in its quasi-totality.[118] With the "end of being's
destiny" an altogether different form of human response to economies appears. Principial or archic economies enjoin us to master all that there is
and can be, while an-archic—post-metaphysical, post-destinal—economies
enjoin us 'think' in the sense of 'thanking', of submitting to economic
mutations.[119]

In Heidegger's writings subsequent to the existential analytic, 'thinking'
takes over the role of *Dasein*[120] as the locus of possible inauthenticity or
authenticity, expropriation or appropriation. Epithets such as "authentic,"
"originary," "essential"[121] not only aim at opposing thought to the sciences,
to metaphysics, to philosophy in its entirety, including rationalism as well
as irrationalism, but they also indicate a shift in the locus of response or
respondence: "Essential thought is an event of being," which "claims man
for the safeguard of being."[122] The respondence structure (not to be confused with anything about conformity theories of truth) as such has not
changed: thinking is "the echo of being's favor"; it is "man's answer to the
word of the soundless voice of being"; "this thinking responds to the claims
(*Anspruch*) of being."[123] But the respondence structure has been taken a
step back from the conditioned to the conditioning: thinking's response is
no longer understood as the preservation of an epochal order, but as the
'guardianship' of presencing, with the absencing that permeates it. This
transmutation of response only parallels the step back from the epochs of
presence to the event of presencing. On the threshold of the closure, that
step entails the possibility of putting our allegiance where our *Wesen*, our
essential unfolding, occurs: in the fluctuations of presencing-absencing.

'Thinking' is Heidegger's word for that possibility of a novel allegiance: "The thinking which obeys the voice of being" "heeds the slow signs of the incalculable and recognizes in this the unforseeable coming of the ineluctable."[124] What is both incalculable and ineluctable? The inconspicuous passage from the technological economy into one determined solely by the play of presencing-absencing. For our age, then, to think means to respond and correspond to the precursory signs of an economy determined only by the favor, the event, and the clearing. But if 'thinking' is the name of a mere possibility, does this not imply that actual thinking is something yet to come, still out of reach for us?

Indeed, and since "we are still not thinking,"[125] the phrase 'thought to come' has something pleonastic about it just as the phrase 'epoch of withdrawal' does (the two are mutually exclusive as are compliance with anarchic presencing and compliance with principles). At the end of all these categorial determinations, and, in particular, with this last of the anticipatory titles, the question arises, "What task still remains reserved for thinking at the end of philosophy?"[126] That question would be more easily answered if the issue for thinking were something noumenal, for it would then suffice to establish laws of history through which thought might once again master becoming and predict future stages of a Subject. The answer would be simpler, too, if that issue were merely empirical: its task would then consist in waiting for events to occur and in recording them. But since the issue for thinking is of a categorial nature—investigating the history of reversals so as to discover the traits of being—the answer can hardly be more than a series of negations: thinking, as it results from the play of the transitional categories, will be "neither metaphysical, nor scientific"; anticipatory thinking is "less than philosophy"; "its task is only of a preparatory, not of a founding character." "It is content with awakening in man a readiness for a possibility whose contour remains obscure and whose advent, uncertain."[127] What is the task of thinking? Raised at the end of an era, that question can only be answered by pointing to the possible exit from all monisms and dualisms, that is, by pointing to thinking as the agent of transition toward a polymorphous economy.

The categories of *nous* and 'overman' were the ones that contained the most explicit reference to man. Since 'thinking', as a category, situates man (either within, or on the threshold of, or outside the metaphysical closure), it allows one to speak of thought *types*. The site determines the type. On the threshold of the closure, thinking is of an anticipatory type. Given our locus in advanced technology, the anticipated thinking, on the other hand—outside the closure—arises as a "possibility whose contour remains obscure." Deconstruction is anticipatory in its entire thrust. Radical phenomenology 'prepares' for another, a possible, economy. Most of the determinations Heidegger ascribes to the thinking he anticipates apply in fact only to his own anticipatory thinking: it would be "meditative" instead of "calculative";[128] through it, we would "let the technical objects enter our daily world and at the same time leave them outside";[129] we would pass "by the sciences without despising them."[130] These are unmistakably features of the potential *within* technology. What, then, would "the other thinking" be, the one which is hardly adumbrated by the phenomenology of technology as the era of closure? This is much more difficult to describe. It would have left behind the Janus-like ambiguities of calculating-meditating, science-thought, etc., and would have turned Proteus-like. The difficulty of describing it led Heidegger for some years into the vicinity of Hölderlin's poetry. To think, he would then say, is to "dwell poetically."[131] To be sure, Heidegger claims anticipatory thought as his own, but just as surely he does not claim for himself the thinking he seeks to prepare or anticipate. For that, deconstructive phenomenology is still too closely bound to academic traditions, not yet simple, *schlicht*, enough.[132]

In addition to the dependency of man—of thinking—on our economic site, that is, on the double-faced line of closure, this category shares the poverty of all last categories in the table: like *nous* and 'overman', the category of 'corresponding/thinking' needs the preceding ones to be fully operative. Anticipatory thinking remains flush with 'things' emerging in the 'world'; its proper issue is no longer the 'ontological difference', but multiple presencing as multiple. It responds to the 'favor' that bestows upon us ever varying economic constellations. It gathers 'the event' and lets those constellations be as they arrange and rearrange themselves, always transitory. It keeps itself exposed to the ever new 'clearing'. Lastly, it discovers itself to be mortal, drawn into the 'fourfold' flux and cast in a role it has neither created nor produced, and where it does not play the lead. The anticipated thinking can only go very far in the dispersion which already characterizes anticipatory thinking: the unceasing newness mandated jointly by all the other categories renders it host to an irreducible plurality of meanings.[133] If the state of affairs this thinking anticipates is an economy deprived of principles, then the noetic drive to oneness will have to remain content with merely categorial unities within economic multiplicity. As 'thanking', thinking will comply with systemic diffractions despite and against all *archai* and *principia:* "Only a multivocal thinking attains an utterance that responds to the issue of such a state of affairs," a state of affairs which is itself "intrinsically manifold."[134]

Part Five
Action and Anarchy

> More essential than the institution of any
> rules is that man find the way into the truth
> of being so as to dwell there. This abode
> alone yields the experience of what he can
> hold onto. It is the truth of being that
> dispenses the hold for all conduct.
>
> "Letter on 'Humanism' "[1]

According to received philosophies, the 'hold' (*Halt*) for all conduct (*Verhalten*) was 'dispensed' by various species of the genus 'rules'—norms, standards, measures. In these lines, Heidegger offers an alternative to the inherited metaphysics of mensuration. The normative experience, he claims, is man's dwelling in 'the truth of being'. The way this is to be understood emerges from the preceding analysis of the categories: 'truth' not as that to which the mind gives its assent by conforming propositions to a state of affairs, but rather as an arena for ever-shifting constellations, that is, as a historical era; 'being' not as that which fills the senses or fulfills the mind, but as an economy of presencing describable only through the traits read off the reversals from one order of presence to the next. This historicized notion of truth in the later Heidegger completes and prolongs what he had described earlier as the 'sense of being', a phrase in which 'sense' (*Sinn*) was not to be taken as signification, meaning, or semantic unity, but as temporal directedness. What we can hold onto in action, what 'measures' it, is the economy dispensed to our era. Such a hold is not open to challenge, it is the injunction that assigns us our very dwelling place. If this new understanding of measurement takes the issue of action and its norms out of metaphysics, out of even the deconstruction of metaphysics, then it must be asked: What happens to the question, What is to be done? at the end of metaphysics?

The way Heidegger displaces the received issues of norms, standards, and commands for action—'rules', 'holds', and 'injunctions'—is the most striking proof that his thinking has indeed moved beyond the mere deconstruction of transmitted referential edifices. It had already gone beyond deconstruction with the anticipatory incidences of the transitional categories. From their deduction it appeared furthermore that what deconstruction prepares is not some reconstruction. Contrary to many of his commentators, Heidegger does not look for a few valuable pieces of the tradition worth preserving. Nor does he declare anything valueless. What he prepares is more modest than any value assessment, more modest, too, than building and rebuilding: it is what he calls simple dwelling. It has to be 'simple' since it consists in espousing economic transmutations in their precariousness, and it is 'dwelling' since it brings to completion the modern project of rendering to man what is his own, of assigning him to his finite economic site.

The method of Heideggerian phenomenology results directly from the understanding of the 'truth of being' as our historical abode. As it follows the temporal course of those successive arenas and eras—the *hodos,* path or itinerary of the economies[2]—that method is *besinnlich* in the literal sense: not 'meditative', but adherent to the time route that is *Sinn.* As it strives to attend to the sequence of past aletheiological contexts, wresting them from systematic constructs, it is both commemorative and deconstructive. It also strives to attend to the emergence of a new reversal in history, to the 'turn'; as such it is preparatory and has gone beyond deconstruction. The transitional categories—'ontological difference/world and thing', ' "there is"/ favor', 'unconcealment/event', 'epoch/clearing', 'nearness/fourfold', 'corresponding/thinking'—in their bifrontality are all commemorative as well as preparatory.[3] In each of the pairs, only the first term is deconstructionist.

The practical impact of Heideggerian phenomenology, too, results from his understanding of the truth of being as our abode. Just as, for the methodological reasons mentioned, thinking (*Denken*) is to become a resolutely accompanying, attentive thinking (*Mitdenken*), so action, too, is to turn resolutely attentive, obedient (*hörig*) to the constellations and their succession. The transformation of acting and thinking called for by Heidegger's turn must be 'resolute' not in the sense of the will's contraction, but literally: resolved into their essential constituent. In acting and thinking we have always belonged (*gehören*) to the aletheiological order of the epoch. In the age of closure, that implicit belonging can and must be made explicit through a turn from constructive philosophy to a more elementary attention paid to the truth of being, our abode. Attentive thinking is also resolute in dissolving such overdeterminations of economic injunctions as those established by eidetic intuition and, more primordially, by the intellectual vision of the Good. With being understood as time, all such ideative overdeterminations lapse before the hearing (*hören*) of the economies to which acting and thinking are to yield. Hearing has indeed proved to be that one of our faculties that is most attuned to time. With the turn from building to dwelling, from seeing to hearing, from referential to systemic legitimation, few inherited 'holds' remain, many are to be let go; few 'rules' are to be instituted, many to be heard to fade away; fewer and fewer arch-present standards to be observed and ideals to be contemplated, many new injunctions—ever new injunctions—to be listened to. These injunctions are neither visible nor invisible, but audible to an ear as yet to be sensitized to them.[4] With a greater or lesser degree of deafness, more resolutely or less resolutely, we have always given allegiance to them. They are unforseeable injunctions but their kind is not exactly unheard of. The threshold where stable norms give way to economic injunctions, the threshold of post-modernity, introduces anarchy into action. What happens at the end of metaphysics to the question What is to be done?, then, is that the figures of *archē* from which any answers could be drawn give way to mobile determinations. To belong fully and *for all practical purposes* to our age, we are to follow that giving-way as well as to take up the struggle against whatever remnants of archic representations can still be shown to "linger unjustly" (see below, Heidegger's understanding of *dikē* and *adikia*, justice and injustice.)

Such is the result of the two types of displacement, now to be examined, that happen when the economies of presence become phenomenology's 'very issue'. On one hand, this *Sache selbst* inverts the traditional relation between thinking and acting and makes action—a type of action—the transcendental condition for thought. On the other hand, it entails several concrete negations and transformations in the realm of the doable. Thinking, which is action in the broadest sense, will show itself to be flanked by action in the narrow sense as both thinking's condition and its consequence.

XIII

ACTING, THE CONDITION
FOR THINKING

> Only so far as man, ec-sisting in the truth of
> being, belongs to being can there come from
> being itself the assignment of those
> injunctions that must become law and rule
> for man. In Greek, to 'assign' is νέμειν.
> Νόμος is not only the law, but more
> originarily the injunction contained in the
> dispensation of being. Only this injunction is
> capable of inserting man into being.
>
> "Letter on 'Humanism' "[1]

The *nomos* or injunction always and everywhere determines the *oikos*,
the abode of man. The eco-nomy of presence has always and everywhere
already situated us. Heidegger endeavors to make us belong explicitly to
the aletheiological constellations that 'always already', *immer schon,* enclose us. The explication of our site, he trusts, will dissipate the darkness
we ourselves have incurred in endowing certain representations with ultimacy. That radical twist he gives to enlightenment is to make us belong to
presencing. Such belonging, which is however never achieved once and for
all like a state of affairs, is the sole issue for thought. But it is not a given.
Just as economic "insertion" repeats and transforms the notion of *Geworfenheit,* thrownness, in *Being and Time,* so "belonging," which designates a
doing, repeats and transforms the earlier notion of *Entwurf,* project.
Thrown into the economies, man, according to Heidegger, can retrieve
them in taking them as his sole measure for acting. Thinking is thus made
dependent upon a practical condition: the injunctions, he says, reach us
"only so far" as we "belong" to being. Exactly which relation between
antecendent and consequent is implied here?

Thinking is a consequent inasmuch as it does not arise without preparation. On this crucial point—still more than on the two topics of *Gelassenheit,* 'releasement', and of *Anwesen* understood as a verb, as 'presencing'—
Heidegger belongs to the tradition initiated by Meister Eckhart. At the
beginning of one of his sermons on poverty, Meister Eckhart says: "So long

as you do not equal this truth about which we now want to speak, you cannot understand me." And at the close of that same sermon: "Those who cannot understand this speech should not trouble their hearts about it. For, as long as man does not equal this truth, he will not understand this speech."[2] At the end of another sermon, this one on detachment, he repeats: "There are many people who do not understand this. That is not surprising to me. Indeed, whoever wants to understand this has to be very detached and raised above all things."[3]

To understand poverty one must be poor. To understand detachment one must be detached. In Heidegger, to understand the turn, one must oneself turn about. To understand authentic temporality, one must exist authentically. To understand the directionality, *Sinn,* of being, one must become *besinnlich,* meditative. To understand the fourfold's play without why, one must live without why. To understand releasement, one must be released. To understand the primordial leap (*Ur-sprung*) which is the originary, one must take a leap.

§40. The Practical A Priori

> Thus a leap is needed in order to experience properly the *belonging* together of man and being. This leap is the abruptness of the unbridged entry into that belonging which alone can grant a matching of man and being, and thus the constellation of the two.
>
> "The Principle of Identity"[4]

Here is how Heidegger explains these lines: we must "leap away from grounds" (*vom Grund abspringen*), "let go" (*loslassen*) of them. This is the practical imperative for understanding the other releasement which is non-human and through which presencing tenders its economies. Through *our* releasement and on its condition alone, we are "let into" (*eingelassen*) that other releasement—both identical to and different from ours—which is the event of presencing. Only such a practical a priori will allow the phenomenologist to make presencing explicit in its "coming to pass" (*an-wesen*).[5] The relation of antecedent to consequent is, then, not only that of implicit to explicit belonging; it is moreover one of doing to thinking.

The relation between implicit and explicit understanding, hence the characterization of the phenomenological method as explication, is found even in Heidegger's earlier texts. In *What Is Metaphysics?* he wrote that in its essence, by its fundamental but implicit process of transcendence, *Dasein* is always "metaphysical." The task is to bring into view that essential occurrence. "Going beyond entities occurs in the essence of being-there. But this going beyond is metaphysics itself. . . . Metaphysics is the fundamental occurrence in being-there. It is being-there itself."[6] This notion of metaphysics, not yet related to the history of being and its epochs, designates the movement through which being-there goes beyond itself toward the world. Therefore, being-there is "metaphysical" inasmuch as it always already implicitly transcends itself. Phenomenology wrests this movement, which "belongs to the 'nature of man,' " from ontic obfuscation. As Heideggerian anti-humanism develops, the program of explication only changes its content. After the 'turn', the issue to be expressly retrieved is the "belonging together of man and being" as it varies from epoch to epoch. As a method of procedure, this is still an explication.

The practical a priori, when compared to the earlier writings and understood as a procedural antecedent for thinking, contains nothing new either. Indeed, according to *Being and Time,* on what condition can explication succeed at all? On the condition that man first tear himself from what obfuscates his 'nature'. And what is it that conceals the transcendence called *Dasein?* A certain way of behaving, a certain attitudinal way of being in the world—inauthenticity. The practical a priori required for phenomenology is by no means a belated discovery in Heidegger. As to the content, that is, the concrete comportment required a priori, after the turn it bears many names, of which authenticity is no longer one and releasement only the most prominent. Throughout, a mode of thinking is made dependent on a mode of living. Let us see how this dependency is articulated before and after the turn.

The systematic priority of comportment and the determination it imposes on thinking appear clearly in the verdict Heidegger brings against all of his predecessors since Aristotle. According to *Being and Time,* the classical ontologies, whose insights just as much as their fallacies only reinforced the obfuscation of finite transcendence, spring precisely from inauthentic existence. A rash charge, perhaps, on the part of the young Heidegger, but one whose bearing must not be misunderstood: it indicates first and foremost that the retrieval proper of the being question is bound to fail unless it is preceded by what he then calls an existentiell modification. This requirement is less a summary condemnation of the Ancients than a statement of method unlike almost any ever made by philosophers—apart, doubtless, from Plotinus and Meister Eckhart.

And Socrates. I have said that the quotation from the *Sophist* that opens *Being and Time* refers to *thaumazein,* wonder, without mentioning it by name. The practical a priori enters phenomenological ontology as Heidegger steps from his first to his second query following that exordium. First query: "Do we today have an answer to the question of what we properly mean by the word 'being'? Not at all." This query concerns something to be known or thought, an issue for philosophy. It meets with ignorance. Second query: "Are we today even perplexed at our inability to understand the expression 'to be'? Not at all."[7] This query is no longer cognitive, concerning knowledge and ignorance. It is not even philosophical anymore.

In it something entirely different is demanded, the response to which must *precede* the very question of what we mean by the verb 'to be'. From the outset of *Being and Time*, Heidegger's strategy consists in awakening first (*vordem*) a pre-philosophical perplexity and only then raising the question of the meaning of being. A practical modification of existence has systematic priority over its 'philosophical' analysis. First comes an appropriation of existentiell possibilities, then existential ontology. More than a priority of expediency is at stake in this order of precedence. It goes to the heart of what Heidegger has to say about praxis. His usage of 'authentic', *eigentlich*, and 'inauthentic', *uneigentlich*, he says, must be understood "strictly terminologically."[8] To exist authentically then means to act with regard to my being in the way that is most proper (*eigen*) to me; to seize my being as it is concretely mine. Inauthenticity means acting with regard to my being in a way that is not proper to me; a way which follows that of everyone else.[9] Since these two possible modifications of being-there determine all the existentials, their differentiation remains operative throughout the fundamental analytic (Part One of *Being and Time*). However, it becomes comprehensible as such only with the repetition or retrieval carried out in Part Two, "Being-There and Temporality." Authenticity and inauthenticity are modifications of temporality. In their opposition, these terms "signify the 'ecstatic' relation, hitherto hidden from philosophy, between the essence of man and the truth of being."[10] To exist 'properly' is to make the temporal possiblity of anticipatory resolution (*vorlaufende Entschlossenheit*) one's 'own'. Not to exist properly is to reify the past in forgottenness, the present in retentional presentation, and the future in expectation.

Why call the practical a priori a priority of method? This must not be taken to mean that the temporal character of the existentiell modifications, authenticity and inauthenticity, amount to mere stages in reflection.[11] That would be saying too little. The *hodos* of the 'method' (or the *cedere*, 'going', in the 'procedure') is one that leads from a way of living to a way of thinking. Inauthentic existence produces ontologies that remain forgetful of being. It follows by implication that the sense of being can become an issue only in an authentic existence. It follows moreover that to satisfy the practical a priori it is not sufficient to write books about 'Being'. Nor can that a priori be satisfied through some individual practice. If Heidegger is able to elicit a hint of the being question from almost any text, read separately, in the history of metaphysics, the charge against the very project of philosophy, the project of securing foundations, remains intact: it amounts to a quest for one preeminently solid entity. Philosophers have therefore consistently and, as it were, professionally "passed over" the problem of inauthenticity,[12] and the being question has fallen into oblivion. The path of our history has been one of errancy, of a 'methodical' errancy that has spared and spares no one. But that errancy has resulted from an error on an entirely different *hodos*, path, which leads from life to thinking: the error that Nietzsche called "the absurd overestimation of consciousness,"[13] the *methodical* retrenchment of life or of praxis so that mind may speak solely to mind.

Far from ceasing to be operational after the turn, the requisite analogue to authenticity for thinking divests itself of any existentialist overtones. It grows civilization-wide as it finds its place in the phenomenology of the economies.[14] It undergoes a threefold transmutation: (1) the mode of practice required for the 'thought of being' (*Seinsdenken*) is more and more expressly linked to the withering away of the principles; (2) the 'proper', or an existent's 'own', loses its paradigmatic role for behavior; (3) the undeniably individualistic implications of the practical a priori as conceived before the turn recede behind political ones. As economic, non-appropriative, and political "the terms 'authenticity' and 'inauthenticity', used in a preliminary fashion, do not signify any moral or existentiell discrimination."[15] *Ereignis*, the successor to *Eigentlichkeit*, makes thinking depend on a type of acting, which is in that sense neither moral, that is, grounded on an ought, nor existentiell, grounded on my own potential.

1. The practice required for thinking presencing is dictated by the withering of the epochal principles. Their self-emptying entails an imperative—releasement. "We can say 'yes' to the unavoidable use of technical devices, and we can at the same time say 'no' inasmuch as we deny them the right to lay exclusive claim on us and thereby distort, embroil, and finally obliterate our being (*Wesen*)."[16] What is noteworthy in this description of the practical a priori is first that the imperative springs up against modern technological devices. Releasement thus has its hour in history. That hour is the moment when objects, as 'devices', have achieved their strongest grip on us, the moment when constant presence has become technological and hence hegemonic. It is furthermore noteworthy that they lay their exclusive claim on *Wesen* ('essential unfolding'), which is another word for originary presencing in Heidegger. The constant availability in which technology secures all things as objects and devices overdetermines the event of a thing's entering its world, the event of presencing. Objects are forced into constant presence opposite a subject. This split world turns deadly with the confrontation between 'devices' and *Wesen*. Technology, the ultimate figure of the subject-object split, tends to distort, embroil and obliterate the one process the Greeks thought of as *phuesthai*, coming to presence. To say both Yes and No to technology therefore means to heed the common phenomological origin of technical objects and of men who have become technical subjects. In this return to the origin as presencing, "our relation to the technological world will become wonderfully simple and still," and the objects or devices come to "rest in themselves."[17] The confrontational dualism can be set to rest only by laying bare the *essence* of the conflict, by 'essential' thinking. This has nothing to do with a supposed reconciliation of man with nature, but much to do with a reconciliation of action to the chaotic fluctuations in presencing. The twofold rest of 'devices' remembered as things and of men remembered as mortals is think-

able only when constant presence, or the very principle of constancy, has forfeited its prestige. If, as has been held since Aristotle, 'rest' signifies the full possession of one's own, and if on the other hand for Heidegger a 'thing' has no substrate to rest on, then this repose is far from immobility and inaction. As born from a simultaneous Yes and No, as non-cooptable, therefore, for any form of full possession, it is perhaps not much of a repose at all.

2. This points to the second transmutation of the practical a priori after the turn. If a doing is required to prepare "the *belonging* together of man and being,"[18] and if such a requirement is indeed reminiscent of the earlier call for authenticity, *Eigentlichkeit*, the issue is nevertheless taken out of the context in which *eigen* in any way designates the proper. It is not an issue of owning or appropriating one's self or one's other, nor of possessing being. It must be recalled that in the event, *Ereignis*, appropriation is permeated with expropriation. Not only is being to be understood as a process, man, too, as the 'mortal', is desubstantialized. And if, as has been shown, belonging (*gehören*) is a matter of hearing (*hören*), hence of listening and complying, then Heidegger, with this a priori, is breaking the old concurrence between θεωρεῖν and κατέχειν, beholding and holding.

3. Lastly, the practice required to think presencing is non-individual. I have said that the term *Dasein*, in Heidegger's writings after the turn, designates a people or community rather than the self. I have also said that the political realm is phenomenally constituted by the public interchange of words, things and actions. Now historical being-there—Greek, Latin, Medieval, modern, contemporary 'atomic'—must each time learn the practice destined to it. It will correspond explicitly to its destiny solely on the condition of such a collective apprenticeship. Heidegger is quite clear about this public dimension of the practical a priori. He spells it out for each of the three factors, words, things, and actions.

We have yet to learn the syntax of the *words* corresponding to the destinal fold that is our own. Heidegger speaks cautiously, questioningly, of the language through which we would be wholly the inhabitants of our transitional era: "Each in its way, our Western languages are languages of metaphysical thinking. It must remain an open question whether the essence of the occidental languages is metaphysical in itself and thus stamped once and for all by onto-theo-logy, or whether these languages offer other possibilities of utterance."[19] If such different utterances are possible, they will free natural language from onto-theo-logy. Language, to be emancipated, will have to rid itself of the grammar dictated by metaphysics. The tongue to be learned would then have to extricate itself from that fundamental *pros hen*, the subject-predicate attribution. If we knew how to speak in such a way as to correspond to the Janus economy, an inconstancy as unsettling as the decline of the epochal principles would creep into words. Such inconstancy would give that decline its very extension and comprehension. The apprenticeship that may render our relation to technology 'simple and still' will then, be it only for its linguistic nature, necessarily be collective. Responding and corresponding to the essence of technology cannot be an individual affair. How could a natural language be private? If, in its essence, technology is still principial in stature but already anarchic in germ, how could words free themselves from their metaphysical order without subverting the most basic speech patterns of our civilization as it discovers itself relocated, by that germinal power, outside of onto-theo-logy? And if, in order to experience the 'limits' of technology, our being-there is to open itself up to that bifrontal essence, how could *Dasein* in any way designate the individual subject?[20] That it is still impossible for us to string words together in an order other than *pros hen*, should say something about the time it may take to free the post-modern economy of any principial overdetermination, about the time necessary to prepare an a-principial economy. Still more, it might be asked whether we are even prepared to learn the language of our own time, an *anti-principial* language, a double-talk as bifrontal as the anarchy principle. According to Heidegger, a transference, a setting-across, a translation is necessary for us even to enter the constellation of our own age. We must *über-setzen* toward the economy of the twentieth century the way one sets over to another shore.[21] In general, "in a given epoch of the destiny of being, an essential translation corresponds each time to the way a language speaks within that destiny."[22] Either we learn to speak as the contemporary economy of presence speaks to us, or what is propitious in advanced technology will be lost. To put it negatively: either we unlearn the *pros hen* grammar, or the technological grip will be fatal for us. Either we listen and hear how the guiding word of Western philosophy, *eon*, speaks to us today, or the accumulation of *onta* will consolidate their assault (*Andrang*). "Whether or not we will get beyond talking about technology and attain a relationship to its essence may well depend on this 'either-or'. Indeed, we must *first* of all respond to the essence of technology in order to ask *afterward* whether and how man can master it."[23] Here, the either-or is a matter of hearing and speaking: hearing the injunctions of the age of closure or not hearing them; unlearning the grammar of the *pros hen* or not unlearning it. The question is one of syntax. There can be nothing private about that.

Especially with regard to poetry, Heidegger develops the conditions for our entry into destinal language. Through the "poematic project of truth" a historically given community responds to the potential "thrown toward" it.[24] Its every 'project' (*Entwurf*) corresponds to that economic 'casting forth' (*Zuwurf*). In Heidegger's writings on language, just as in those on deconstruction, 'being thrown' prevails over 'projecting'. For example: "To follow the essential unfolding of language, to say of it what is its own, requires a transformation of language that we can neither compel nor invent." This is because we are thrown into a tongue and more generally, languages, which are "determined by destiny," historical. When measured against that thrownness (*Geworfenheit*), any project is of little account: "At

the very most we can perhaps prepare, to a slight extent, the transformation of our relationship to language."[25] What is to be retained is the fact
that the bifocal essence of technology dictates the possibility of a double
way of speaking from which, eventually, a simpler speech may be born,
one freed of the grammar that has made the West. But these transitions
will be public or they will be nothing at all.

The *things* unfolded by the destinal fold which is ours demand to be
freed, too—freed from the principial reign that has turned them into objects and, more recently, devices. Objects must yet become things.[26] On
what condition? To be sure, that we 'let them be'. But is this, can this be,
an individual, private, 'subjective' affair? How could their setting-free be
subjective if it consists precisely in abolishing the subject-object cleavage?
And how could releasement be a purely individual task if, on the threshold
of the metaphysical closure, it signifies the struggle against epochal principles? Once these are recognized as obstacles to aletheiological freedom, the
way in which liberation and releasement are interconnected becomes more
apparent: for objects to become things again, a loosening of the reifying
hold is necessary on an economic scale. The thingness of things can only be
restored economy-wide, coextensively with the concrete community placed
under the principle of objectivity. To set presencing free can in no respect
amount to some inward attitude. If 'existence' pertains to the individual,
then releasement has nothing 'existentiell' about it. That term, like its
correlative, authenticity, is "obsolete"[27] in the later Heidegger *inasmuch* as
neither denotes the public realm in which alone things can at all be freed
from the principle of objectivity. Since this is none other than the principle
of representation, of *adaequatio* understood as subjectivization and subjection, one may also say that objects will become things on the sole condition
of a shift away from subjectivity toward the network of phenomenal interconnectedness that situates subject and object alike. The principle of subjectivity—of which that of objectivity is but a counterpart—can be fought
only in public, in political life. Unless the 'world' to which 'things' belong is
so freed from all references to the subject as the last epochal principle, our
century's economic turn will never become explicit or be recovered as
such. A political a priori determines thinking. Anarchic praxis restores the
thing beneath the object, presencing beneath principles, and truth as freedom beneath truth as conformation.

Actions provide the third constituent of the political as a phenomenal
region. I have distinguished between action in the strict sense, πρᾶξις
(including ποίησις) in opposition to θεωρία, and action in the broad sense.
This latter kind is of the same essence as thinking—the thinking which is
'other' than theory. The 'other' politics corresponding to it would arise from
a syntax that shatters the preeminence of the *pros hen* in the order of
words; from things entering the world out of themselves, not represented;
and from actions receiving their mensuration from the economic injunctions alone. To be sure, thinking enjoys a priority over action: it is thinking

that receives, hears, reads, gathers, unfolds the injunctions, notably the withering away of the principles. But there is a priority, too, that action enjoys over thinking. The apprenticeship of anti-principial, and eventually a-principial actions (in the narrow sense) is requisite for thinking as 'highest acting'. It is impossible to receive, hear, read, gather, unfold the anarchic economy as long as actions—assimilating to that economy, *turning* into a groundless play without why—do not precede thinking.

In any given age, everyone has a preliminary knowledge of what it is economically possible to do. This constitutes the practical character of pre-understanding, which Heidegger descried before discovering its historical character. Such knowledge comes to us primarily from our hands, for example, from the tools epochally at our disposal. No one in the Stone Age dreams of a stainless steel axe nor, conversely, of a wooden plough in the age of mechanized agriculture. No one in the Greek polis imagines organized lobbying in a federal legislature, nor is direct deliberation feasible in a mass democracy. The implicit understanding of an economy springs from what we make and do. The philosophical effort to render that understanding explicit will remain paralyzed unless preceded by poietic, political-practical modifications. The explicitation of what is economically given cannot succeed through pure acts of consciousness. This is not to say, with Sartre, that "man is what he does," but rather that man thinks as he acts (and not, as the metaphysics of legislative reason would have it, that man ought to act as he thinks). In *Being and Time*, Heidegger had stated: "Without an existentiell understanding all analysis of existentiality will remain groundless [*bodenlos*]."[28] This version of the practical a priori is still a hesitant one since the 'existentiell' remains a concern of the understanding. Similarly, without practical understanding, *without practice*, any analysis of the economies proceeds in a vacuum. The unhesitant version of the practical a priori makes it clear that without an-archic praxis the withering away of the principles is bound to remain 'only theory'.

If in *Being and Time* authenticity, as the existentiell condition of thinking, could still admit of individualistic implications, this is no longer the case in the later writings. Releasement, the key concept of the second period in this regard, dispels such implications. Its practice distorts (this is one literal sense of *verwinden*) the technology that stamps the entire atomic age. Now, if in the struggle against the technological principle, we can "say 'yes' to the unavoidable use of technical devices and at the same time say 'no,' " then it is already impossible to take releasement as an inner attitude chosen in heroic isolation. It must be the attitude of an age. Otherwise, the anti-principial struggle Heidegger calls for would be quixotic. But the supersession of subjectivist individualism becomes unmistakable in the third period of his writings. From there it has to be read backward. If the principles are to yield, and entry into the event is to occur, unprincipled praxis will either claim everyone that lives in the economy of transition or it will be nothing at all. That is what is meant when

ontological anarchy is called a potential. Due to the encompassing character of any destinal or historical 'stamp' of presence, a challenge to the
principles by marginal, individual actions cannot, by right, transfer us into
the economy of *Ereignis*. The scope of the imperative that requires us to
"open ourselves to the injunction"[29] is therefore societal. The 'stamps' situate everyone, without possible exception. Much more than intellectual fads
is at stake when holders of various -isms, inherited from the past, discover
themselves more or less suddenly incapable of reaching *statements* and
move in circles among quotes. It is impossible simply to say No to one's
economy. The mere negation of a fundamental position only "throws the
negator off the path."[30] The same holds for the praxis that renders the
deterioration of the epochal stamps explicit: sooner or later it must become
the praxis of everyone. What Heidegger says about the novelty of an artwork, namely, that it re-situates us, displaces us, and thus henceforth
suspends all current actions, applies eminently to economic novelty: "To
follow this displacement means to transform our ordinary relations to the
world and the earth and henceforth to suspend all current doing."[31]

At each stage, then, Heidegger's writings contain allusions to a practical
a priori required for thinking, although these are hardly ever developed for
their own sake. Perhaps Heraclitus's "child who plays,"[32] Meister Eckhart's
"life without why,"[33] Nietzsche's "eternal return" as it "eternalizes the
absence of any final goal"[34] are all so many prefigurations of the "existentiell
ground" for thinking. One would especially like Heidegger to have been
more specific about the precise actions that are to allow for an entry into
the event. It is however useless to examine his texts for further hints. Of
Being and Time an interpreter like Marcuse could still say that "this philosophy attains its supreme meaning as authentic practical science."[35] Confronted with the later writings, the same Marcuse came to indict the "fake
concreteness" of the entire Heideggerian enterprise.[36] But it is one thing to
show the deterioration of all foundations for answering the question, What
is to be done? and to show the conditions that result for our lives; it is
something else to draft a program of action or actions. From the "destruction of ontologies" through the "eschatology of being," to "the entry into
the event,"[37] Heidegger tackles the first task, leaving the second to others.

The practical a priori for understanding fully that deterioration and its
virtualities inverts the sequence of condition and conditioned in which the
tradition has placed thinking and acting. Once a practical consequence of
standards is established for it speculatively, action turns into a condition
that needs to be fulfilled *in concreto* for thought—the thought of being—to
be at all possible. The transcendental inversion does not rehabilitate humanism, this time under a practical guise. The economies of presence
unfold with little human control. Thinking may choose to remain enfolded
in its given fold, without raising a question about it, the question of being.
What it cannot choose is to dis-imply itself from its historical ply. But it can
free itself from mute implication. It can begin to question. In Heidegger,

the conditions for so emerging from the slumber of thoughtlessness are that action take explicit aim at all principial vestiges, that it challenge and subvert their sway, and that this subversion be collective.

§41. The Problem of the Will

> We are still far from thinking the essence of action *decisively* enough.
>
> "Letter on 'Humanism' "[38]

There is a common thesis concerning the problem of the will in Heidegger that can be summarized in three steps. (1) In *Being and Time*, the will is rooted phenomenally in care, and therefore in *Dasein*'s existential openness. The voluntary and the involuntary, then, are opposable as the authentic is to the inauthentic.[39] In this view the phenomenon of the will is linked to the existential determination called resoluteness or resolve. When being-there is authentically resolved it wills something: its own (*eigen*) possibilities. Its *Eigentlichkeit*, authenticity, consists in making these resolutely its own. In that way, the will is not a faculty but a phenomenon concomitant with the modifications through which I attain my ownmost, most originary truth. (2) But on the other hand, still according to that *opinio communis*, Heidegger deconstructs the very notions of truth that might function as regulative measures for resoluteness, namely, its normative notions. Truth deconstructed—unconcealment—yields no standards, no guide for the possible impulses of the will. These impulses shoot forth blindly, as it were, into the dark. Hence a certain underlying decisionism[40] in the young Heidegger. (3) After the 'turn', this decisionism would lapse into its contrary, 'letting-be'. Heidegger would no longer recommend that we will resolutely so as to exist authentically, but that we 'will not to will' so as to unlearn objectivation, representation, prehension—the entire mechanism of essentially technological thinking. The topical shift from resoluteness to releasement would, it may be added, not have occurred without difficulty. Thus in the essay "The Origin of the Work of Art" (1935), the two themes, voluntarist and anti-voluntarist, would curiously coexist, so much so that more than twenty years later, Heidegger would feel obliged to append an explanatory supplement to that essay. He would then strive, if somewhat tortuously, to reconcile the opposition between 'willing' and 'letting' by tracing both back to "existing man's ecstatic commitment to the unconcealment of being."[41] That he should have taken the trouble to state several times that "the resoluteness thought of in *Being and Time* is not decided action,"[42] would indicate precisely how artificial the retrospective harmonization of these two positions remains, how disturbing a problem it raised for him. In short, "the turn" would be accompanied by an "abdication of this will, of this self-assertion in the face of Being."[43]

All this may be plausible. But what that common opinion does not say is more telling with regard to action as the condition for thinking than what it does say.

To begin with the most elementary, it says nothing about the word *Entscheidung*, decision, itself. The German, like the English, derives from a verb that means 'to separate', 'to cut'. To separate and cut what? "Thinking has not yet risen out of the separation (*Scheidung*) between the metaphysical being question, which inquires into the being of entities, and that question which inquires more originally into the truth of being."[44] The separation here sets apart two types of questions. The first is "metaphysical," the second no longer is. It is therefore also a separation between two eras. These lines say clearly enough that questions invented by man do not decide anything essential at all; that two historical questions set themselves up as separate even before he can intervene; in other words, that the decision, understood as a separation, a cut, a break, is economic. It cuts out an age, a historical order of presence, a world. "The world is that opening which unlocks the broad tracks of the simple and essential decisions in the destiny of a historical people."[45] A decision is, then, first of all, a matter of collective destiny. It is the disjunction between two economic eras.

Every essential decision is not only economic, it is also aletheiological. "The world is the lighting of the tracks of the essential injunctions with which all decision complies. Every decision, however, bases itself on something unmastered, hidden, confusing; otherwise it would never be a decision."[46] An economic decision contains something hidden and confusing, inasmuch as every pre-understanding is confused and dark. But such a decision is also essential because it 'lights' concealedness, wrests 'world' from 'earth', *alētheia* from *lēthē*, and thereby opens the space where human decisions can occur at all and where understanding can articulate pre-understanding. A constellation of truth determines the tracks—the variables that structure an age—through which the economic injunctions reach us. Concretely, for example, the decision or disjunction from which the post-modern age was born (experienced by Marx in 1845, by Nietzsche in 1881, and by Heidegger in 1930) established technological breakthroughs, the very idea of progress—not in morality (Kant), but in the techniques of mastery—as the conveyer for our age of what is true and false, to be done and not to be done.[47] One could say that these injunctions produce the concrete and structured order of presencing-absencing, the aletheiological order that marks an age. Here, Heidegger designates that order as the set of 'tracks' (*Bahnen*) according to which a historical cut-off structures a given economy. The concept of 'track' underscores the systemic nature of *alētheia*.

As aletheiological and therefore systemic, any essential decision is neces-

sarily non-human. Here are a few examples of what Heidegger calls historically "decisive": "fundamental words" such as "truth, beauty, being, art,
knowledge, history, freedom"[48]; "a transformed fundamental position"[49];
"constructive thinking"[50]; "the thought of the eternal return."[51] In each of
these cases an economically disjunctive decision precedes all possible volitional decisions. The relation between the two types of decision, conditioning and conditioned, appears best in the following example: "For Marx it
has been *decided in advance* that man and only man (and nothing besides)
is the issue. Whence has this been decided? How? By what right? By what
authority?—These questions can be answered only by going back to the
history of metaphysics."[52] Hence philosophical humanism itself is also the
product of a prior decision which is economic, not human.

What I am calling economic decisions here, those which situate each and
every human decision, Hannah Arendt described in the following terms:
"We may very well stand at one of these *decisive* turning points of history
that *separate* whole eras from each other. For contemporaries entangled,
as we are, in the inexorable demands of daily life, the dividing lines between eras may be hardly visible when they are crossed; only after people
stumble over them do the lines grow into walls which irretrievably shut off
the past."[53]

Conditioning decisions set apart networks of interaction. Thereby they
both open up and restrict all possible voluntary, conditioned, decisions.
They enjoin or tell us ('condition' stems from *dicere*, to say) what is essential in our age. As indicated in the first line of the "Letter on 'Humanism' "
cited in the epigraph above, decisive thinking is therefore essential thinking: "We are still far from thinking the essence of action *decisively*
enough." If the essence of action consists in its compliance with the plies in
the history of being, with the economic decisions, then voluntary action
can or cannot be essential. At the turn which sets apart the modern and
the post-modern regularities, this means that action can choose to follow or
not to follow the disjunction that seems to be growing into walls today. It
can renounce the principles and adhere solely to the economic transmutations. This kind of action alone, possible only in the age of closure, would
be essential, originary. "Are we in our being-there historically at the origin?" This is, Heidegger adds, a question of "comportment," of "an either-
or and its decision."[54] The step back from the conditioned to the condition
is clear. Just as thrownness precedes every project, so an essential, disjunctive, historical-destinal, economic, aletheiological, non-human, systemic
decision precedes all human or voluntary decisions, all comportment.
These decisive conditions are always "confusedly" pre-understood by us,
and thus make every understanding and every deciding possible. Heidegger also calls the context-setting decision a crisis. "The thought [of the
eternal return] must not only be thought each time out of an individual's
creative moment of decision, it belongs to life itself: it constitutes a *historical decision*—a *crisis*."[55] The 'critical' decisions, in that sense, account for

the changing conditions of life itself. They differ from the 'creative' decisions as life differs from any momentary act. In Nietzsche all these terms are obviously heavily overdetermined. In Heidegger, the concept of decision is primarily topological. A crisis assigns us our site. The economic disjunctions that we may espouse or not espouse in praxis *situate* that praxis. It is this economic, topological, significance in Heidegger's usage of *Entscheidung* and related terms that makes the charge of decisionism difficult to sustain.

The will can follow the economic flow or not follow it, observe its own context or decontextualize itself. If, as has been shown, the last epochal principle, whose efficacy culminates in technology, is the subject reduplicating itself as will to will—if for our age being is willing—then the will, too, is primarily contextual and only secondarily behavioral. What does it mean, in our age of closure, to follow the economic modifications? It can only mean to follow the context-setting will in its epochal decline, to dismiss it as the last metaphysical stamp, as the being of entities, as the mark of our age. It means to "renounce willing voluntarily." Such is the practical condition for us to be, "in our being-there, historically, at the origin." It consists in saying: "I will non-willing."[56] This twofold notion of the will, economic and behavioral, shows once again the practical a priori for thinking: revoking the epochal principles.

But what would uncompliant comportment be, the one that abstracts itself from its economic context and aspires to consolidate the rule of principles? Is it even possible *not* to espouse the historical decisions as defining our condition? Hannah Arendt is probably not mistaken when she evokes Anaximander's *adikia,* injustice, in this regard. Heiddeger understands *dikē,* justice, as a harmony in presencing, as the jointure (*Fuge*) between arrival and withdrawal. *Adikia,* then, is disjointure. "Disjointure means that whatever lingers awhile becomes set on fixing itself in its stay, in the sense of pure persistence in duration." The 'unjust' entity disjoins itself from the finite flow of absencing-presencing-absencing and "holds fast to the assertion of its stay."[57] The present insists on its presence, consolidates it, persists against absence. It con-sists with other entities against the movement of originary arrival, which is ever new and conjoined with departure. This essence of the will by which it is set on constant presence stands in agreement with conceptual, i.e., 'grasping' thought, but it is opposed to 'thinking' in the sense of the last transitional category. When, in the closing age of philosophy, the human will becomes absolute, willing nothing but itself, it shows forth its insurrectional nature. "The will acts like 'a kind of coup d'état,' " Hannah Arendt wrote.[58] It is that force which seeks to establish the self as permanent and time as lasting.[59] If 'justice' means for each thing to arrive and depart in accordance with the economies, 'will' is the name for rebellion against that justice. Put in a simple correlation: constant presence is the very issue of willing, just as the event of presencing is the very issue of thinking. Willing and thinking are thus understood not as faculties of the mind, but as modalities of disclosing the world. If one recalls, now, that it is the epochal principles that claim constant presence most of all, it becomes obvious, too, that principial acting is hubris. The Greek word *hubris* stems from *huper*, 'beyond', 'across'. Principial acting is hubristic since it oversteps our finite condition expressed in the temporal difference between presence and presencing.

Heidegger seeks a counter-will to that absolute, rebellious, will. The mere possibility of "willing not to will" places action before the alternative either to let itself be carried by the economies or to rebel against them, thereby immobilizing the event of presencing on a fictitious mainstay. Of the two options, ecstatic transport or enstatic support, only the former is thoughtful. Voluntary decisions either abandon themselves to the epoch-making disjunctive decisions or they harden themselves against those decisions. Such hardening is the source of all thoughtlessness. Both Hölderlin and Nietzsche dared to 'let'—to abandon—themselves to the movement of transition in which the modern age, and perhaps the metaphysical age, comes to an end. However, the poet's craft yields greater lucidity than the thinker's. Unlike Hölderlin, Nietzsche "was not capable of discerning the historical rootedness of the metaphysical question concerning truth in general nor of his own decisions in particular."[60] Nietzsche's own decisions remain entirely, if unsuspectingly, inscribed within that other decision, the "decision not made by us but which, as the history of being, is made for our history by being itself." With Nietzsche, metaphysics "took a decisive turn toward the fulfillment of its essence."[61] This instantiates once more the poverty of the transitional thinkers: Nietzsche remained necessarily ignorant of the shift that articulated itself through him. But his *Mitdenken*, the thinking accompanying that shift, is telling. It reveals that practical decisions can approach, as it were, asymptotically, the historical decision. In that lies the advantage of transitional ages, when practical releasement becomes a concrete possibility; when action can retain as its sole measure the varying constellations of *alētheia;* when it is possible to will non-willing because for an entire civilization the hubris of principles has lost its credibility.

The concept of decision in Heidegger entails several answers to the problem of the will. (1) In the primary, essential sense, a decision is the historical separation, cut-off, or crisis between two economies of presence, their severance. The reversals within metaphysical history as well as the turn beyond metaphysics are such aletheiological, non-human decisions. (2) The contemporary crisis sets apart the economy of the final metaphysical principle, the will to will, and a possible economy, one deprived of any standard-setting principle. Economically speaking, the turn is that decision in which the will is given up as the increasingly exclusive stamp of Western civilization. (3) Individual and collective decisions, our voluntary acts, are always inscribed within the horizon of economic decisions. Humanity is 'used', 'utilized' (*chreōn*, Anaximander), for and by these trenchant incursions. (4) Within the transient horizon thus carved out, action is faced with an either-or: voluntary acts comply with economical transitions or they "hold fast to the assertion of their stay." The truly ultimate products of such holding-fast are the epochal principles. In temporal terms, that either-or means that being is experienced as constant presence or as event-like presencing. (5) The response to this either-or gives rise to 'philosophy' or to 'thinking' respectively. The willful quest for constant presence, then, is to be relinquished if, at the end of philosophy, the issue for thinking is event-like presencing. To will non-willing is the practical condition for "thinking of being."

Thinking springs from two forebears, two types of conditions. Its economic condition might be opposed to its practical condition as a conditioning is opposed to an a priori. Heidegger defines the condition qua conditioning as the setting up of a world. "Wherever the essential decisions of our history occur—taken up or foregone by us, misknown or retrieved by new inquiry—there the world worlds."[62] The setting up of a world, its 'worlding', is the *economic* condition within which we can take up or forgo, misknow or retrieve, the decisions that have made history. If a thinking is at all possible that transgresses its predominant conditioning, the stepping stone for such a transgression must again be provided by the economy. Such is the case with technology, whose 'worlding' is actually the most principled and potentially anarchic. The *practical* condition for such an other thinking to arise is best described by the transformation of the a priori, 'willing', into the a priori, 'letting'. This is a transmutation of one willing into another, of willing as absolute because it wills itself, into "that willing which, renouncing willing, lets itself be committed (*eingelassen*) to what is not a will."[63] The acting that eventually shatters metaphysical conditioning introduces us fully into what Heidegger here calls *die Gegnet* [*sic*], the "open expanse"—none other than the economy emancipated from principles. "When we let ourselves be committed to the releasement [turned] toward the open expanse, we will non-willing."[64]

Heidegger is not content with examining what happens to the question, What is to be done? at the end of metaphysics. He also asks: What is to be done at the end of metaphysics? In his answer, he does not urge decision for decision's sake. Neither does he advocate love in order to combat hatred, nor expropriation of the expropriators in order to combat injustice. He urges the express downthrow of the epochal principles that are already foundering economically. This downthrow of what is already falling must be understood otherwise than as a willful, 'decisive', 'resolute', "efficacious" (*tatkräftig*) enterprise. For Heidegger, non-willing and releasement are more subversive than any project of the will that "wills to actualize and wills effectiveness as its element."[65] Given our place at the end of epochal history, non-willing and releasement turn out to be more powerful than willing and hubris.

XIV

ANARCHIC DISPLACEMENTS

The event of appropriation grants, each time,
the span from which history takes the
warranty of an epoch. But that span in which
being gives itself to openness can never be
found in historically calculated time nor with
its measures. The time span granted shows
itself only to a meditation already capable of
presurmising the history of being, even if this
succeeds only in the form of an essential want
which, soundlessly and without consequence,
shakes everything true and real.

"Recollection in Metaphysics"[1]

These lines, which close Heidegger's two-volume work on Nietzsche, speak of the epochs that articulate history and of a silent upheaval in which a transition sets in that shakes everything. In order to follow the transition at stake and the displacements it entails, one has first to see what the understanding of time is which, in this text, allows Heidegger to hint at some consequences of the history of being.

The time of that history is made of 'spans'. Understood properly, this word (*Frist*) can help clarify what is meant by the end of epochs. 'Span' is here the generic concept that covers, on one hand, epochal time, and on the other, a time no longer epochal, one that we may already have begun to live. Heidegger's claim that the history made of epochal breaks is drawing to its close does not amount to reclaiming, after a heterogeneous past, homogeneity for an age to come. He does not rehabilitate linear time against its scattergram. It is true, with the contemporary turn time no longer spells itself out in epochs, in sudden foundings of eras in which being holds itself in reserve: no longer through the beginnings of economies in which presencing remains controlled by one arch-present. Still, after the silent exit from epochal articulation, time continues to articulate itself. This happens through a modification of the 'spans'.

The time spans, he says, arise from "the event of appropriation," from *Ereignis* understood as the entry into mutual relations of everything present to an age. If that entry into presence—presencing—"grants the spans," they necessarily remain incalculable. In meditating on them we are seized by an "essential want," the want of a hold on them. Heidegger is denying here any type of history or historical transition governed by laws and hence somehow predictable. The spans of the history of being are measurable neither by the historicist's yardstick nor by that of Providence, whether secularized or only metaphoricized. Rather, the event opens a kind of history one can only "presurmise," *ahnen*. This word is polemically anti-rationalist. If the modes of time that arrange presence for a while arise from the event, then history—epochal as well as non-epochal—is not only discontinuous but as such it remains alien to reason. No longer can it be said that throughout civilization reason supremely rules the world; still less that reason comes to itself in and through history, that reason recognizes in history its own aspiration to complete self-possession. Those tenets of a triumphant rationalism can no longer be sustained once the method for studying history has become phenomenological: once presencing has become the very issue that reveals and conceals itself in the finite fields it opens in arresting the aletheiological constellations at this or that configuration. To say that the time spans proceed from the event is to say that *no* historical time, no time, is continuous. The passages from one constellation to another are reason's distress, its want (*Not*).

Nor are the time spans, granted by the event, simple units of duration or time lapses. The text says that they grant in turn the units we can measure in years, decades, centuries. In other words, these spans fulfill a mediating role and must not be confused with historical periods. Heidegger is again thinking along transcendental lines. He is looking for conditions of possibility that, in agreement with the three-tiered temporal difference, have to be equally three-tiered: the sudden *spans* are the conditions that render possible the *periods* of history, but they are themselves conditioned and rendered possible by the *event*. Heidegger is thus playing out, from the viewpoint of history, the triadic difference whose non-temporal terms were (beginning with the middle term): beingness (*die Anwesenheit, die Seiendheit*), which renders entities (*das Anwesende, das Seiende*) possible (the metaphysical difference) and is itself rendered possible by being (*das Anwesen, das Sein*) (the phenomenological difference). The poverty of reason before history is such that no deductive argument can lead from the mediating function of beingness to the mediating function of the "spans": they appear only to a gaze "already capable of presurmising the history of being." This points once again to the 'impasse' of *Being and Time* and the necessity of raising the being question from a different angle. The juncture of the metaphysical and the phenomenological difference does not, by itself, yield access to the history of being. For that, another presurmise or pre-understanding is needed.

'Beingness' designates what metaphysicians have tended to hypostatize as the a-temporal being-itself. But now the 'spans', discovered through the pre-understanding that being has a history, bridge the hiatus between lived time and being-itself as time. They translate being into history and only thereby make it thinkable as event. In Heidegger's earlier vocabulary, they translate being's temporality (*Temporalität*) into *Dasein*'s (*Zeitlichkeit*).[2] From such radical temporalization, history "takes the warranty" of an age. The spans historicize being as event by punctuating it. Due to that transcendental priority, they cannot be measured "in historically calculated time." These mediating terms are phenomenologically indispensable inasmuch as they allow Heidegger to think of a history that is no longer epochal. An anarchic economy would comply with those spans without the principial over-determination that is the very nature of *epechein*.

Indeed, today the time spans that are granted by the event and that warrant our historical age open on something that is "already" ours, that now and henceforth is possible. Whereas the first lines of the opening quotation—which speak of time articulated in spans, of their provenance in the event, and of their transcendentally mediating function—apply to all reversals in history, the last lines speak of the one turning, the technological age. It is at the moment of metaphysical closure that "soundlessly and without consequence, everything true and real" overturns. "Here everything turns about," *"Hier kehrt sich das Ganze um."*[3] The closure is the moment of absolute distress. In the reversals of epochal history distress is relative—relative to the principle whose economic over-determination is fading. For example, when the medieval field of the creator-creature tension overturns and yields to the field of the modern subject-object tension, the distress is great. The arch-present God who says 'I am He who is' is no longer available for measuring the true. Man, who says 'I think,' is now arch-present. As a guarantee of the real, no hierarchy of participation but only an act of perception presents itself. To be sure, the want left by one vanishing principle "shakes everything true and real," but it is a want, a distress, relative to a *substitution* of referents. At the beginning of modernity, the principial office passes from God to man, but it does not pass away as an office. At the turn beyond epochal history, on the other hand, distress is absolute and "essential." The *dissolution* of referents signifies that with technology the cycle of supremely true and real entities—World, God, Man—is exhausted. They have withered "without a sound," but also "without a consequence," since no new representation of a supreme entity is there to take over. Where now is the measure of truth and the guarantee of the real to be sought? This is the essential distress; the crisis of reason is only its backlash. The displacements from one metaphysical epoch to another are principial. But if metaphysics is the ensemble of economies each governed by a shape of *archē*, then the displacements from the metaphysical to the post-metaphysical era are anarchic. Only with these do Hölderlin's words apply: "Is there a measure on earth? There is none."[4]

From the viewpoint of grounding any practical philosophy, the displacements that accompany the dissolution of referents affect the key notions through which philosophers have attempted to comprehend action. Here are five of those fundamental notions: goal, responsibility, function, destiny, violence. Their selection, manifestly arbitrary, results from the rank they hold either in traditional theories of praxis, or in Heidegger. To be sure, other concepts would be worth submitting to the trial of economic displacement. I have done so above with 'freedom' and 'will' or 'decision', and it appeared that with Heidegger's *Kehre*, these turn from moral into topological concepts. Regarding the five notions just mentioned, I wish to show what happens to them when the open field of presencing is no longer understood as occupied or possessed by a measure-giving first—what happens when all cathexis is withdrawn from that field.

It should be understood that this trial is in the first place a test. Like Kant[5] and Nietzsche,[6] Heidegger makes an attempt with thinking, a *Denkversuch*. The thought model to be tested in its practical consequences is the one I have called the hypothesis of closure, the hypothesis that with the technological turn the epochal principles wither away because all that there is—'the real'—shows itself without the illusory lid that has stabilized the incidence of the temporal difference.

§42. Practical Negation of Goals

> In the wood are paths which, mostly
> overgrown, end quite suddenly in the
> untrodden.
> They are called woodpaths.
> Each runs its separate way, but in the same
> forest. Often it seems as though one
> resembles the other. Yet it only seems so.
> Woodcutters and forest rangers are familiar
> with the paths. They know what it means to
> be on a woodpath.
>
> *Holzwege*[7]

To understand the bearing of the metaphor of woodpaths in Heidegger, it suffices to oppose it to a declaration of faith in teleology like Aristotle's in the first lines, already cited, of his *Nicomachean Ethics:* "Every art and every inquiry, and similarly every action and pursuit, is thought to aim at some good."[8] Using the concept of *Holzwege*, Heidegger attempts to think a certain abolition of finality or goal-directedness in action.

The observation that all our activities tend toward some good serves Aristotle as the point of departure for ascertaining which among the sciences has to be the 'architectonic' or first science. If such a science exists, it will govern all knowledge, just as the subject matter of which it is the science will govern all action and all choice. The master science would be the science of the master goal. It would be directive for the many sciences we might conceive just as the one end would be directive for the many practical ends we might pursue. Whether in the last analysis the guiding science turns out to be wisdom or politics[9] matters little compared to the totalistic sweep of the concept of end utilized in this way of raising the issue of praxis. With the medieval Aristotelians, the master science that treats the 'ultimate end' will be theology. It, too, will be born from a declaration of unqualified faith not only in goal-directedness as such, but in one particular goal: "Anything whatsoever tends in its operation toward the ultimate end."[10] No "woodpaths," here, that "end quite suddenly in the untrodden." Under the rule of end, all paths, theoretical as well as practical, lead somewhere, even if windingly: namely, to happiness. The idea of a master science supposes, first of all, that in each and every activity there is an end or goal to be attained. It supposes furthermore that the rule of end transcends the distinction between theory and practice. Lastly, it supposes the unicity of the ultimate end.

Within the Aristotelian edifice, structured as it is by the representation of ends and of one end, Heidegger begins by displacing the foundations. His deconstruction of Aristotle, it will be recalled, revealed that both θεωρία and πρᾶξις are systematically rooted in ποίησις. In actual fact and Aristotle's own professions to the contrary notwithstanding, the master science, from which spring the declarations of unqualified faith in finality, is neither wisdom nor politics, but know-how, *technē*. Goals are aimed at, first and foremost, in acts of production. As shown in the *Physics,* the changes affecting sensible substance and hence their causes provide the proper context where ends rule. Historically as well as systematically, only because fabrication is the key-experience from which metaphysics springs can the representation of ends, final causality, come to govern philosophy in general and each of its divisions in particular. It is in *making* things that the three other causes come into play once the end is given. Once an artifact has been conceived by an artificer, it becomes the end that 'moves' the efficient agent, form, and matter. One does not seek out a workman, draft a model, and select the appropriate materials without being guided by the idea of the final piece to be realized. For Heidegger, the preeminence of finality in philosophy results from Aristotle's raising the 'entelechy', the entity as completed, to the rank of being *par excellence*. The prestige of finality in "every art and every inquiry, and similarly every action and pursuit" rests on the representation of sensible substance as made, be it by man or by nature.

Before pointing out a second displacement traced by Heidegger, which affects the notion of *ousia,* a warning is in order concerning the qualification with which, under the metaphor of 'woodpaths', he challenges the declarations of faith in finality. That challenge obviously does not consist in an attempt at a blanket cancellation of teleological thinking. Rather, it circumscribes and thereby limits the domain in which such thinking rightfully obtains. What the possible end of metaphysics would cancel is the possibility of *metabasis eis allo genos*, the transposition of goal-directedness beyond the domain of making into those of acting and of thinking in general. As epochal history draws to a close, thinking cannot be the only doing that remains without ends, without any preconceived goal to pursue in a deliberate course, without linear discourse. Action, too, suffers the economic loss of finality, a component that applies to production alone. The possibility of closure thus entails a twofold impoverishment, goallessness in thinking and in acting. At least this is how Hannah Arendt understood the metaphor of woodpaths: "Of . . . this thinking one cannot say that it has a goal. . . . Even the laying down of paths itself is [not] conducive to reaching a goal sighted beforehand and guided thereto. . . . The metaphor of 'woodpaths' hits upon something essential." To mark clearly that we suffer the loss of goals not only in our mental acts but in praxis as well, Arendt adds that "the thinking so described can no more have a final goal—cognition or knowlege—than can life itself."[11]

The first displacement Heidegger traces in the beginning of metaphysics amounts to restricting the legitimate rule of ends. The second consists, not in a narrowing, but in a broadening of scope. It concerns the semantics of *ousia*. He shows that the pre-metaphysical meaning of this noun extends beyond sensible substance. Metaphysics, on the other hand, has constituted itself immediately, originally, as ousiology, and ousiology as teleology. "The word *ousia* was coined as a 'term' only as late as Aristotle. The coinage consists in his separating from this word's denotation something decisive which he retains as its sole meaning."[12] What is that single sense of *ousia* that Aristotle selects from an earlier and greater richness of the word? It can only be the one that predominates in his 'groundbook', the *Physics*, as that book's very issue. Aristotle's single sense of *ousia* can only spring from his "interpretation of motility, the most difficult issue to be thought in the entire history of Western metaphysics." Aristotle seizes upon the word *ousia* and sorts out from its denotative field what pertains to *motion* and its end. The movement of production terminates in substance. If the 'aiming' at some end comes to fulfillment with substance, then that is the ultimate ground out of which change as such becomes intelligible. Substance is ultimate because it, and it alone, contains its end in itself; it no longer aims at anything but itself. To have one's end in oneself is what 'entelechy' means. "This noun, coined by Aristotle himself, is the basic word of his thinking. . . . Only when something is in the mode of *entelecheia* do we address it as properly being."[13] A third coinage of Aristotle's designates the same completeness, *energeia*. Only substance stands fully 'in the work', in its own *ergon*. Whether it is by nature, *phusei on*, or as an artifact, *technē on*, substance is what all change aims at. This meaning of being—having one's end in oneself—remains paradigmatic throughout the metaphysical epoch. But what is it that this concept of self-possession as the universal standard for being omits from the initial semantic scope of *ousia*? What has that coinage cost?

"The other essential moment of *ousia*, coming into presence, is omitted. Now, that is the decisive factor for the Greek conception of being."[14] Heidegger's entire effort consists in recovering, at the other end of the metaphysical epoch, that broader sense of being as coming into presence (*Anwesung*) or presencing (*Anwesen*). As early as *Being and Time*, he understands *ousia* as presence (*Anwesenheit*).[15] Later on, once he has elaborated the three elements of the ontological difference (*Seiendes-Seiendheit-Sein*: entity, beingness, being or 'to be'), *ousia* designates the second term of the triad, the being of entities conceived metaphysically, as beingness. With the temporal difference (*Anwesendes-Anwesenheit-Anwesen*: the present-presence-presencing), *parousia*—that surplus Aristotle allowed to escape from his selective grasp—designates the third term of the triad, being as the event of presencing. The deconstruction of Aristotelian physics thus yields the triad *on-ousia-parousia*: present entity, its mode of presence, presencing.[16]

The disjunction between *ousia*, as made suitable for the account of physical change, and its surplus, omitted by Aristotle, reveals that the prestige of final causes in philosophy, with the attendant prestige, whether overt or covert, of the book, *Physics*, results from the systematic predominance of one phenomenal region over all others, that of production and the producible. This shrinking of perspective has engulfed acting and thinking in the finalist schema of making and has shaped an epoch. Teleocracy exacts a narrowing of the gaze which retains from *parousia* only *ousia* and from presencing, only the full presence of the end to substance. The lines from the *Nicomachean Ethics* cited above demonstrate the repercussion of that sweeping interest in goals upon the theory of action. As for Heidegger's own interest in this deconstruction of practical teleology, it should be obvious that he must restrict the rule of ends to the sole domain of fabrication *because* his interest is to widen the sense of *ousia* (as *parousia*) beyond the domain of sensible substance.

It is the subjection of thinking and acting to the representation of theoretical and practical ends, of goals, that Heidegger repeals by the metaphor 'woodpaths'. That metaphor is one way of undoing the telic boundaries imposed upon phenomena by Aristotle's coinages of terms.

The reign of goals is repealed first of all for thinking, as indicated by the opposition between thinking and knowing. In seeking knowledge we seek certitude about contents. In certainty the quest for knowledge comes to rest as in its end. Thinking, on the other hand, does not have any contents, properly speaking, to pursue. "Three dangers threaten thinking," says Heidegger. The "bad," and therefore most ominous one, is the philosophic pursuit, notably that of grounding conformity between propositions and given states of affairs. Thinking lacks any external end, then. "The evil and therefore most corrosive danger"—corrosive but not fatal—is thinking itself. What is evil about thinking is its trust that it can find within itself all it takes for its own satisfaction: for example, innate ideas. That is why "it must think against itself," against the ancient conviction that it provides its own contents, that it possesses its own end in itself. It also lacks any internally given end, then. "The good and therefore wholesome danger is the nighness of the singing poet."[17] A poet, we are to understand, "sings" for no end or purpose. He is of the family of woodcutters and forest rangers, a frequenter of woodpaths.

But how can that family be extended to include thinkers? Does Heidegger not untiringly insist on 'the issue', *die Sache*, for thinking? It seems difficult to understand thinking otherwise than as aiming at the complete possession of that 'very issue', its end.

The very issue for thinking is presencing as it differs from systems of presence. Heidegger can attempt to repeal the reign of finality in thinking only because he has first dissolved that reign in the play of the temporal difference. *Phusis* in the metaphysical sense seeks *energeia, entelecheia*, as its end. A rose that does not bloom, an adolescent who refuses to become an adult, a house that remains a building site are just so many instances of failure in the pursuit of a natural or a fabricative end. The verb *phuesthai*, on the other hand—*phusis* as "ever-rising: in Greek wording, τὸ ἀεὶ φύον"[18]—designates an emerging into presence without aim, for nothing. Goal-directedness sets Aristotle's concept of *phusis* apart from Anaximander's; it sets *ousia* apart from *parousia*, beingness from being, methods of inquiry from paths of thinking. "To understand this, we must learn to distinguish between *path* and *method*. In philosophy there are only paths; in the sciences, on the contrary, only methods, that is, procedures."[19] Inasmuch as everything present comes into presence for no purpose, the paths of thinking, too, lead nowhere. They are woodpaths since to 'think' is to espouse, to 'thank', the goalless showing-forth of phenomena. Such is the essential identity of thinking and presencing: it is their common essence to be 'without why'.

Lastly, the temporal difference repeals the rule of finality in action. This is a consequence of action's a priori status in the phenomenology of being as event. If, then, originary, *phuein* requires a mode of existence so as to become at all thinkable, the metaphor of woodpaths applies to this practical condition more than to anything else. The paths to which existence must commit itself in order to think the event of presencing "end quite suddenly in the untrodden." With being no longer conceived as substance, our practical pursuits lose their telic bearings. The existence that sets out on such paths is already misjudged when it is asked to produce reasons for its behavior. If it were possible to dismantle the machine of behavior, of goal directed action, of internal motivations and external determinations, if we could think action according to models other than purposive, life would begin to 'thank' that non-principial economy into which the technological turning has already introduced us. It would enter that post-modern clearing where each path "runs its separate way, but in the same forest. Often it seems as though one resembles the other. Yet it only seems so." The

metaphysical closure, that is, the end of philosophy or its *eschaton*, remains a hypothesis unless the technological turning and the phenomenological deconstruction overcome the end of philosophy, its *telos:* the representation that "every art and every inquiry, and similarly every action and
pursuit . . . aims at some good." Such is the truly decisive displacement
Heidegger traces concerning the ends of philosophy, an a-teleocratic, anarchic displacement.[20]

The normative concept of goal serves traditionally to regulate and eventually legitimate praxis. Any acceptable behavior is made dependent on the
establishment of ends considered to be good or desirable. But aspirations,
efficacy, and performance characterize existence only insofar as, prior even
to all practical theory, being is fixed, 'framed', within the causal schema, a
schema in which, as has been shown, final cause rules supreme. Action
displays a natural proclivity toward ends solely on the condition of such a
calculative pre-understanding of being as calculable. Once that preconcep-
tion is undone, the extended family of woodcutters, forest rangers, poets,
and thinkers comes to include all actors, to the dual exclusion of the
knowers and the makers. If there is a maxim to be gathered from this
deconstruction of teleocracy, it would be for literally thoughtful action, or
against thoughtlessness in action.

One may wonder whether the description of care in *Being and Time*,[21] as
well as the emphasis on projection and "that for the sake of which" being-
there projects itself,[22] is entirely disengaged from the teleocratic framework. Later, that disengagement is explicit, be it only in the way Heidegger makes the principle of ground formulated by Leibniz his own, even as
he restricts it. "Something, such as the rose, is not without a ground, and
yet it is without a why."[23] Like the metaphor of woodpaths, the "without
why" restricts the scope of phenomena to which final causality, the pursuit
of goals, is applicable. Once again, the practical negation of goals, on the
threshold of a non-principial economy, does not mean the all-out cancellation of any teleological representation, but the restriction of such representations to their native domain, production—here, the 'natural' production
of vegetal growth. To be sure, from the botanical viewpoint, a blooming
rose has an extrinsic end or entelechy, which is attained only when it
seeds. But its event of presencing is goalless. The rose flowers for nothing,
"it flowers because it flowers."[24]

Heidegger inserts his anti-teleocratic strategy more or less surreptitiously into his interpretation of Aristotle, Leibniz, and Angelus Silesius.
But it is most forcefully operative in his interpretation of Nietzsche. Heidegger cites the following declaration of faith by Nietzsche, which flatly
contradicts the Aristotelian declarations: " 'Goallessness as such' is the
principle of our faith."[25] The 'goal' as such, Heidegger comments, would
signify 'meaning' which, in turn, is understood by Nietzsche as 'value'.
Therefore, this is a nihilist declaration of faith intending to affirm, to will,
that the world have neither meaning nor value. Then Heidegger continues:

"However, we no longer think nihilism in a 'nihilist' fashion as a disinte-
grating dissolution into nihilating nothingness. Valuelessness and goallessness, then, can no longer signify a lack, mere emptiness and absence.
Those nihilist characteristics of entities in their totality mean something
affirmative, an essential process, namely, the *manner in which* entities in
their totality come into presence. The metaphysical term for this is: eternal
recurrence of the same."[26] Heidegger's 'metaphysical' interpretation of the
eternal recurrence as well as of the will to power is riddled by passages
such as this where the anarchic strategy, in which he sides with the non-
metaphysical Nietzsche, becomes suddenly obvious. Goallessness designates "an essential process," a "manner in which entities in their totality
come into presence"—in other words, an economy of presence. Anticipating an economy where no 'goal as such', no last meaning and no first value
reign, establishing the equality of forces, goals, meanings, values, and thus
abolishing them as forces, goals, meanings, values, the eternal recurrence
already translates the *economic* negation of goals into their *practical* negation. A 'metaphysics' of the eternal recurrence? Certainly not. A phenomenology, rather, of the temporal difference between the essential process of
presencing and the economic net into which it emerges for a while; and a
description of the practical a priori required for following the late modern
rearrangement in that net. Viewed from the most principial of all economies, contemporary technology, the practical negation of goals can only
appear as "the outbreak of a delirium."[27] And yet, what Angelus Silesius
says about the rose—"it flowers because it flowers"—Meister Eckhart had
already said about action: "If you were to ask a genuine man who acted
from his own ground, 'Why do you do what you are doing?' if he were to
answer rightly, he would say no more than, 'I do it because I do it.' "[28]

§43. Transmutation of Responsibility

It may happen unexpectedly that thinking
finds itself called upon to enter the
question, . . . What do you make of the
difference?

"The Onto-Theo-Logical Constitution
of Metaphysics"[29]

As complex as the problems connected with the phenomenon of responsibility may be (problems concerning its role in legal and moral philosophy,
the concept of freedom that determines the word's semantic scope, the
frequent identification of responsibility with imputability, etc.),[30] they rest,
in one way or another, on the recognition of a reciprocal commitment
between two parties. In Latin *spondere* (from the Greek *spondē*, 'libation'

or 'vow') means 'to promise', 'to pledge oneself to', and *respondere* there-fore means 'to commit oneself in return'. To be responsible is to be ready to give an account of one's acts and deeds to a tribunal before which—implicitly or explicitly, morally or legally, by nature or by contract—one finds oneself bound or has bound oneself. To be responsible is to be ac-countable. It implies a 'for' and a 'to': one is always responsible or account-able for actions to a competent authority. This may be a tribunal within man, like conscience, external to him, like institutionalized power or a communication community, or above him, like a deity. He is responsible if he is ready to render accounts and so to legitimate his conduct. Legitima-tion is the successful answering for one's acts to such a normative and justificatory agency. As legitimated, our acts 'come back' (*re-*) to us. The legitimating 'referent'—from *re-ferre*, to carry back—measures them and therefore necessarily transcends them. We are responsible actors if we take upon ourselves and claim like measurement. This return structure is the ground for imputation. Through it, our acts weigh on our account. *Rechen-schaft ablegen*, to give, make, or lay one's account for something, to call or bring to account, *rendre raison, rationem reddere:* in the main Western languages responsibility is linked to the rendering of a reckoning.[31] The reckoned return of the acts upon the actor and the normative tribunal or authority meting them back are the two dominant traits that characterize the phenomenon of responsibility.

Such at least is the result of Heidegger's deconstructing the received concept of responsibility. He abolishes neither of the two traits: neither the rendering of the reckoning, nor the authority before which accounts are to be rendered. But as deconstructed, these two traits find themselves dis-placed. Once humanistic, once corollaries of the dispositions of 'moral' faculties, they turn economic, corollaries of the dispositions of 'ontological' presencing. This twofold incidence of the turning strikes a twofold blow at freedom. Firstly, the *accounting for* occurs in a place other than the sub-ject. The discharge of conduct and the answering for it do not originarily emanate from freedom understood as the faculty of choice. Neither initially nor essentially does to render a reckoning mean to assume the conse-quences of one's choices. With the turning, moral freedom, the capacity for practical spontaneity, appears as a derived freedom. Secondly, the measur-ing can no longer be construed as transcending our acts. Originarily, re-sponsibility as an *accounting to* cannot mean to go before some authority that limits freedom understood as absence of constraint. As deconstructed, both the rendering of a reckoning and the reference to a mensurating tribunal are thus to be understood in terms of the economies.

Here again, putting to work the temporal difference, Heidegger shows the *originary* condition of responsibility by recourse to its *original* source. The guiding representation of counting and accounting then appears as born from the great reversal in Greek thinking that brought about the beginning of metaphysics. The very essence of that reversal consists in a steady reduction of *legein* to calculation. The reckoning of rights and duties, the computability of rights and wrongs, presupposes the obfuscation of presencing as an event, an obfuscation that manifests itself linguistically in the restriction of *legein* as gathering to the reasoning that is 'straight' (*orthos, orektos*—in Latin, *rectus*—'right', which Heidegger seems to link to *reor*, to reckon, count, calculate). The native sense of the Latin word *ratio* is calculative reason. That word stems in fact from the language of Roman merchants.[32] The very essence of reason consists, then, for Heidegger in "stating, holding, justifying,"[33] that is, in counting or calculating *on* something. Being as the ground one can count 'on' is the ontological condition for any accounting 'for' and 'to'. The entire *epochal* history of presencing "goes together with that destinal mark known as fundament, *ratio*, calculation, the account rendered." The calculative stamp originally impressed on presencing gets reinforced along the way. In modern times, reason "demands that an account be rendered of the very possibility of universal calculability."[34] Reason then has to produce a referent that accounts for reckoning as such—a ground to which an account of accountability in general can and must be rendered. At the heart of the metaphysical concept of responsibility lies a call for accountability. The climax, in moral philosophy, of this accountability is undoubtedly what is known as utilitarianism. Karl Marx had already mocked Jeremy Bentham, that Great Accountant.[35] If for Heidegger, ethics amounts essentially to an accounting enterprise, this is so on the same score that science is essentially technical and metaphysics, essentially rationalistic. These are but three shapes of one and the same *epochē*. The rendering of a reckoning as the condition of responsibility is one predominant mode of unconcealment. To propose for scholarly research a theme such as " 'physics and responsibility' . . . is but double-entry accounting."[36]

As for the other trait of the metaphysical concept of responsibility, the normative and justificatory tribunal, its deconstruction has been carried out above with the genealogy of the epochal principles.

What then would a non-metaphysical, non-calculative understanding of responsibility be? It must be one in which the debt of accounts and the referent to which it is discharged, are proved to be systematically operative only in those economies in which time has been 'forgotten'. The withering of the epochal principles would then entail the impossibility of accounting *for* actions *to* a referent since no a-temporal ground would be available to count *on*. Heidegger shows this impossibility by recourse to the same etymologies. If the Latin verb *reor* has furnished the English 'reckoning' and the German *rechnen*, then all has not been said about *ratio* once the connection with counting and calculating has been established. The English 'rightening' and the German *richten* or *ausrichten* signify an act of orienting: " 'To take one's bearings from something' is what our verb *rechnen* means."[37] To reckon is to righten. This allows Heidegger to step back from the phenomenon of calculation to that of directionality. Responsible acts, then, are those that follow the direction or grain of a given economy; that adopt the bearings of things in a given era; that 'thank' presencing in aligning themselves by the way things enter their world. "But such thanking is no paying-off."[38]

In the step back from accounting and calculating to complying with temporal directionality, something quite different is at issue than making "being-up-to-date the measure for the 'inner truth' of human action."[39] At issue are the modalities of presencing or freedom in the aletheiological sense, as the originary condition for action or freedom in the moral sense. With that step from the conditioned to the condition, to be responsible no longer means to 'answer for' one's actions before a tribunal but to 'respond to'—namely, to the aletheiological constellations, the modifiers of presencing, in which our acts are embedded. Such responsiveness or respondence is not something the phenomenology of being as time can in turn account for. If it were, the temporal difference would again be rendered null and void as the sole measure for thinking and acting. Displaced into the economies, responsibility means response. Response to what? To "the call of the difference" which is "the difference between world and thing."[40] A response to the ever new modality in which the world unfolds things and in which things give configuration to or "bear" (*gebärden*) the world. "Things bear world. World grants things." A response to their "intimacy," to "the between where world and thing differ," to the event of their mutual constellation. A response to the *Ereignis*, then, which, as 'appropriation', calls upon thinking and acting. The responsorial essence of responsibility removes it from the moral domain and turns it into a phenomenon akin to language. It is a response to "the injunction in which the difference calls world and things," a response to the event of appropriation which, as articulating itself silently, is "nothing human." "Such an appropriating occurs inasmuch as the essential unfolding of language, the pure call of silence, uses the speech of mortals."[41] This topological reimplantation entails that speech is always a response to the historical modifications of the event, but it does not entail that responsibility is reduced to a linguistic phenomenon in the narrow sense: appeal and response can only be conjoined in a way of being. The 'way to language' designates an on-the-way which is neither the mind's (it is not an *itinerarium mentis*) nor the individual's (it is not a *conversio*) alone. The event of presencing 'uses' men, it situates them in such a way that everything they undertake is but a response to the economy that calls upon them.[42]

Does this displacement of responsibility from the moral to the economic leave any room for a non-response, for irresponsibility? It should be clear that the displacement does not absorb project into thrownness. If the economic order 'calls' for our response, that order is a network of potentials rather than a frame of the actual. In that sense it calls as if from ahead of us, which should dispel any impression that the response is somehow automatic. If this were the case, then indeed no room would be left for

irresponsibility. For Heidegger, irresponsibility consists in what Anaximander called *adikia,* injustice.[43] So long as responsibility is construed as
the meting out of charges and discharges, irresponsibility amounts to an
infraction against one of the various principles of order: law, conscience,
custom, power, father, other, God, people, reason, progress, classless society, etc. The entities so represented summon another entity, the actor, to
render an account of his actions; not to answer that summons is to be
irresponsible. It is to depart from the given principial constellation of concealment and unconcealment. *Irresponsibility is always a breach of the
mode in which presencing occurs and calls upon us.* But that mode can be
epochal or non-epochal. At the hypothetical end of metaphysics, irresponsibility therefore does not consist in the same kind of breach as it does under
the sway of epochal principles.

That change in the nature of irresponsibility follows from the very hypothesis that there remains no *referential* order of presence to transgress. In
the age of closure, to be irresponsible is to contravene the network of *systemic* presencing. And what is it that so contravenes by definition the multiple event of *phuesthai,* of showing-forth? It is any entity and any act that
"becomes set on fixing itself in its stay," that seeks "pure persistence in
duration," that "holds fast to the assertion of its stay."[44] That description fits
anything that closely or remotely resembles an epochal principle. The hubris
of staying, of permanent presence, arises only under and through the rule of
those principles. They are what is irresponsible essentially. With Heidegger's step back to another time, a time other than duration, what is irresponsible for man is any practical a priori that calls for persistence against flux and
thereby contributes to the survival of the principial economy.

The break that appears with the (possible) end of metaphysics destabi-
lizes both that *for* which and that *to* which one can be held accountable. It
dissolves the former because it subverts the latter. With the turn, responsibility therefore undergoes a displacement not only toward the economies
but also toward anarchy. This radical shift lifts the phenomenon of responsibility out of the regency of ultimate representations and situates it in
another space, the in-between of presence and presencing. By the same
stroke, it situates existence within its originary locus where it lives by the
sole event of mutual appropriation among the things that make up a historical world. The shift of responsibility toward economic an-archy is the practical condition for thinking the difference between world and thing as
temporal. In an economy deprived of any epochal principle, responsorial
existence—responsible action—will be a response to the ever new modes
in which things unite in a world and differ from it. One answers the 'call of
the difference' by inscribing one's acts within the play of identity and
difference between world and thing.[45] Whatever the difficulties raised by
Heidegger's deconstruction of responsibility, one will always be able to
respond only through praxis to the question, What do you make of the
difference?

§44. Protest against "Busy-ness"

In busy-ness the project of the object-region
is primordially built into entities.

"The Age of the World Picture"[46]

The two anarchic displacements that I have traced, the practical negation
of goals and the transmutation of responsibility, impair the smooth functioning of what Heidegger calls "busy-ness" (*der Betrieb*). How, one must
wonder, could a society *function* if Meister Eckhart's 'life without why',
Nietzsche's 'eternal return of the same', and Heidegger's 'call of the difference' were allowed to subvert the project of objectivation? The word
"busy-ness" is meant to indicate that this project, while legitimate in its
own region (and legitimated by the Existential Analytic), is today extended
to the totality of entities. Technology is the factor that renders it so primordial. The action Heidegger urges as the practical condition for responding
and corresponding to today's constellation of the difference entails a certain
dis-articulation of that project which has made and still makes the technocratic universe. If the 'atomic' economy is effectively—actually and effica-
ciously—bi-frontal, if it is a threshold economy, its mere situation calls
into question the pertinence of the Aristotelian inquiry into the *function* of
man. By its historical locus alone, technology simultaneously pushes the
referential features of the economies to their extreme and hampers them,
corrupting the interest in the ordered functioning of communities, an interest that is perhaps the most evenly distributed commodity in the world.
Located on the boundary of possible closure, technology as the last 'stamp'
both produces and transgresses "uncanny" functioning.[47]

The concept of *Betrieb*, busy-ness, in Heidegger designates first of all
the decontextualization of artworks: even "if we visit the temple in Paestum
at its site and the Bamberg cathedral on its square, the world of these
works, henceforth objectively present, has perished." To say that their
world no longer is, and that in the contemporary era they are rendered
objectively present, is to say the same thing twice. Object is opposed to
work. "The object-being of the works . . . is not their work-being." What is
the criterion for that disjunction? A work institutes a world that is its own,
while an object, constituted by the mathematical project—the project of
generalized calculability and accountability—lacks a world of its own. A
work rests in its world, but an object results from an entirely different
project: the subject's scheme of placing everything at its own disposal. A
work that becomes an object is thereby torn out of its context, and that
decontextualization is irreparable. "World-withdrawal and world-decay can
never be undone." The work has changed into one item among others in
the isomorphic universe of calculation. 'Busy-ness' is the consequence of
the project of objectification, and bustle (*der Umtrieb*), the most glaring

symptom of such transformation into busy-ness. Heidegger thus places such phenomena as the art market and the art industry within the scheme of universal *mathēsis:* "The whole art industry, even if carried to its zenith and busying itself entirely for the sake of the works themselves, reaches only the object-being of the works."[48] Transformation into busy-ness extends, however, beyond the domain of artworks. It affects everything present in the contemporary economy. This is the critical charge pressed by Heidegger here. It can be spelled out by tracing the original and the originary origins of busy-ness.

Originally, busy-ness is that modern scheme of transformation through which 'things' lose their 'world' by becoming 'objects'. This scheme is imposing itself today on all entities as such, without exception. The logic of technology consists in building object-being into them. The logic of *mathēsis* and the (transcendental subjectivist) logic of object constitution have prevailed beyond Descartes' and Kant's fondest dreams, as the way of being 'objectively present' or 'given for handling' (*vorhanden*) gets built into everything, including the subject. This is a logic of implacable violence. "In busy-ness the project of the object-region gets primordially built into entities." 'Region' does not refer to regional ontology, which is an a-historical phenomenology. If the object-region arises from the modern subject asserting itself, 'region' is a term of a historical ontology, of the history of being. What is primordial for modernity is that only the empirically verifiable is present. Furthermore, if modernity originates with (although not from) experimental science, then the endless *et cetera* of hypotheses and their verification through experiment, yielding new hypotheses, is the original busy-ness. Under this concept, then, Heidegger exhibits one of the basic traits of science, namely, that the results of previous research prescribe the ways and means to be adhered to in new research. "This need to adapt itself to its own results as the ways and means of advancing its procedure is the essence of busy-ness as a feature of research." Busy-ness designates the process through which experimental sciences perpetuate themselves by feeding on their own products. But from the start the experimental sciences have been in the service of practical mastery over nature, not vice versa. Technology, the contemporary figure of that mastery, a figure "whose essence is identical with the essence of modern metaphysics,"[49] equally progresses and even maintains itself only on the condition of eating its own children, like Kronos. The "priority of procedure over entities (Nature and History)" means "science as research has, in itself, the character of busy-ness."[50] In the bustle of scientific research the omnivorous essence of technology shows forth, which in turn finally reveals the violence inherent in the fundamental position of metaphysics' boundary epoch.

Heidegger contests busy-ness as the ultimate and totalitarian shape of objectivation simply by asking what it is originarily, what its essence is. As with Socrates, raising the question of essence already means calling into question and protesting (except that the Athenian Senate perceived the danger in such essential questioning better than the German Chancelleries following 1935). Unlike Socrates, however, Heidegger raises the question of essence in historical terms. Essence is always a mode of unconcealment. That is why it is reached, not by an act of intuition, but by deconstructing the economies that it structures. *Betrieb* comes from *treiben*, to drive. I have said that this translates the *cogito*, as *co-agitatio*. But that original drive toward mastery has its originary condition, the 'drift' (*die Trift*) in presencing, i.e., the way being is time for modernity. A certain directionality of time, toward solid presence, is the essence of busy-ness. To so deconstruct our fundamental position and to retrieve the truth of its temporal essence is neither to condemn nor to countenance it. Busy-ness is no more a matter of condemnation for Heidegger than technology in general. Neither the modern drift in presencing nor the sequence of economies it has produced, leading up to the atomic age, harbor anything fatal: "I do not see the situation of man in the world of global technology as an inextricable and inescapable fate."[51] But if the essential questioning of busy-ness is—like 'thinking' in general—a doing, it definitely counteracts it by a practice impossible to co-opt.

To begin with, the thinking proper to busy-ness, a thinking that poses and disposes, has its corollary practice: imposing the project of objectivation on entities in their totality. 'The other thinking', the one that questions and calls into question, also has its corollary practice. It is non-attachment, *Abgeschiedenheit*. That attitude alone, Heidegger argues, opens us to a new ply in the history of economies by making us comply with it. He follows Georg Trakl in waiting for "a breed, not yet borne to term, whose stamp marks the future generation. The gathering power of non-attachment holds the unborn [stamp] beyond the deceased, and saves it for the coming rebirth of mankind out of the dawn."[52] This is a somewhat contorted way of linking, beyond deconstruction, the arrival of an age that bears the mark of the originary (presencing freed from the technological cathexis) to a return to the original dawn (ancient Greece). It is also a way of linking, beyond the epochs, the new stamp (economy, fundamental position) to a doing (the practical a priori). It is a way, in other words, of suggesting a transgression. The protest that hastens it does not act strategically, but rather through an apprenticeship in non-attachment. This erodes a boundary drawn since Parmenides. Heidegger describes that boundary as a certain conception of the "it is": its conception as ontological difference.[53] To take leave, *Abschied nehmen*, is what those detached always do. They are *abgeschieden*, departed. Non-attachment is the practical protest that may bear to term a breed detached from the ontological difference. *Abgeschiedenheit*, then, is the one praxis capable of undoing the principles that have run the age of ontological difference. The way of calling busy-ness and its essence into question is to be unattached to the epochal principles. Non-attachment contests the global technological enterprise just as 'the other thinking' contests the project of total objectivation. Both denature the epoch of calculation and by the same stroke denaturalize those who inhabit that epoch.

Several commentators have drawn attention to the protest against objectivation and calculative thinking as one of the rare "political elements" in Heidegger.[54] Still, the conditions on which such protest can be staged make it peculiar. Heidegger does not attempt to redress alienation. He does not come to the rescue of total man. If he indicts—both declares publicly or denounces (in Latin, *indicere*) and gives evidence against (*indicare*)—the conditions for indictment are provided by our economy of presence. Indeed, no polemic can be drawn from the temporal difference unless this difference first declares itself publicly in the evidence of an epochal break. The original locus of the polemics Heidegger engages, the locus of the original *polemos*, is the contemporary economy of presence. It *is* the confrontation of the principial constellation with the anarchic. Meditative thinking does not combat calculative thinking—nor non-attachment, busy-ness—in the way Don Quixote tilts at windmills. To raise the question of presencing and of the way a given constellation of presence differs from it is not to 'attack' the project of objectivation or its final shape, technology. Heidegger does not attack, but he asks where the type of deployment that he calls busy-ness comes from. This is, by the way, why there is not the slightest trace of an ideology in his writings, which have therefore resisted and confounded all partisan readings. His contestation puts into question, but does not take a position. 'Thinking' is not a position that one occupies like a fort and from which one launches out against the sciences and techniques. That 'the sciences do not think' does not amount to opposing thought to science as the negation to a position. Thought and science are not contraries within one genus. If the call to thinking in Heidegger meant, as has often been claimed, an escape from the technological age and a return to the Greek 'dawn', then the call would be ideological. But: "Never have I spoken against technology, nor against the so-called demonic in technology. Rather, I try to understand the *essence* of technology."[55] It is well known which ideology, at least in Europe, expresses itself today—and certainly not fortuitously—through the slogan of a return to Greece.[56] Heidegger, on the other hand, observes that we lack all models. "The renunciation of historically fabricated models—ages, styles, tendencies, situations, ideas—is the sign of the extreme distress we and those to come have to endure." Even if we wished, "that initial thinking cannot be 'renewed', nor even erected as a 'model'."[57] Lines such as these should put an end, once and for all, to the conservative readings of Heidegger which hold that for him thinking is a matter of preserving the "ever so few authentic things" bequethed by our ancestors[58] from being levelled by busy-ness. Inquiring into the essence of technology is neither a conservative nor a progressive undertaking. It is a search for the categories according to which presence has spelled itself out since the time of those figures known as the Presocratic philosophers. A quest for historical categories is hardly an ideological return to the Greeks.

Non-attachment to busy-ness is not an option placed before our free will. Heidegger distorts the tradition from which he takes the word *Abgeschiedenheit* by treating it as designating an economic possibility. As such, it points to a practical potential in the current era, the power "to bring an issue where it belongs and henceforth to leave it there."[59] Which issue? The one that, at the moment of economic transgression, most amply provides food for thought, *das Bedenklichste,* and is most worthy of question, *das Fragwürdigste.* Anything, then, insofar as it appears to the gaze of the anticipatory incidences of the transitional categories: any 'thing' in its relation to its 'world'. It remains for us to prepare the thinking capable of such non-attachment. If that word indeed designates a potential to be set free— the relation to things through which they are "left" to their world—then non-attachment amounts as clearly to a doing as does thinking. Essential thinking and unattached acting are inseverable as the *practical* reply to the *economic* ply in which the principles wither. That practice and that economy together form the condition for the transition toward *ontological* anarchy, pliant being.

In this way protest gets distorted, too. Heidegger does not directly *protest against* technology and the atomic age, but he *protests* directly the economy that produced them: he testifies to it. Quite as Nietzsche protested the innocence of becoming, Heidegger protests the possibility for thinking to become essential and for acting to become non-attached. 'Protestation' thereby recovers its primary sense, which is to declare, to attest to a truth. The way to challenge busy-ness is to protest non-attachment. The latter, in turn, by its very possibility attests to an economy without principle, to essentially anarchic presencing.

After the practical negation of goals and the transmutation of responsibility, non-attachment provides a clue for verifying which path is aberrant and which is viable in the contemporary bi-frontal order. The point of impact of Heideggerian dissent is situated neither behind nor ahead of us, it is a dissent out of neither nostalgia nor utopia. Its impact is on today's course as affected by a possible, thoroughly contingent declination. Even preparatory thinking—preparatory for 'the other thinking', which Heidegger hopes will become "efficacious" after all, perhaps 300 years from now[60]—first constitutes a challenge to the current hold of busy-ness. Non-attachment is necessary so that things may enter a mode of interdependence unattached to principles. Contingent pliancy in presencing must be affirmed *as contingent* for an entirely contingent aletheiological constellation to arise. Stated in Trakl's words: the hold of busy-ness is to be unloosened through non-attachment for a breed severed from ultimate grounds to be borne to term.

§45. Transmutation of "Destiny"

> By 'destiny' one usually understands what has
> been determined and imposed by fate: a sad,
> an inauspicious, a beneficial destiny. This
> sense is derivative. Indeed, originarily to 'des-
> tine' means to prepare, order, bring
> everything where it belongs.
>
> *Der Satz vom Grund*[61]

These lines describe the transmutation to which Heidegger subjects the notion of destiny. Commonly humanist or 'existentialist', it turns economic and topological.

To fashion one's destiny or acquiesce to it, to assume and carry it out or to meet it: such human doing is not the horizon in which these lines inscribe *Geschick*. Once the modalities of presencing have been recognized as the very issue of phenomenology, destiny can no longer designate an individual's or a collectivity's appointed lot and its reception. It designates, rather, the way the modalities address us, as if they were emitted. To be 'destined' or bound for a particular place is to have committed oneself to it. To commit, emit, transmit all imply a sending, *schicken*. *Geschick* has therefore been translated as "mittence."[62] At stake are the ceaseless arrangements and rearrangements in phenomenal interconnectedness that "bring everything where it belongs." To speak of destiny is, then, to speak of places and of placing.

In this transmutation two consequences must be seen which make it clear that humanity's lot is not what holds Heidegger's closest attention. The first is nothing new: destiny so understood—no longer as man's vocation, but as each thing's allocation to its locus, as its situation in its site— only instantiates the methodic anti-humanism that characterizes this phenomenology in its entirety. The second consequence is more incisive. It points to one result of the turning toward the anarchic economy. The arrangement of phenomena committed or 'sent' to us with that turn, situates us differently. The specific mittence of the moment of metaphysical closure enacts a change of place, a *displacement*. The end of metaphysics is a concrete possibility as the modalities of presencing—destiny—begin to place us otherwise and elsewhere. On that threshold Heidegger's generally anti-humanist notion of destiny becomes specified as anti-principial.

The economic tenor of *situation* only appears in the writings subsequent to *Being and Time*. In *Being and Time* Heidegger wrote: "By 'destiny' (*Geschick*), we understand the coming-to-pass (*Geschehen*) of being-there in being-with-others." He thus understood destiny as a collective process. Futhermore, it was understood as exhibiting the sense of being, its three-fold ecstatic directionality: destiny is grounded in "the anticipatory act of translating oneself into the 'there' of the moment."[63] We are bearers of destiny to the extent that future, past and present are united, not in individual *Dasein,* but in "the coming-to-pass of the community, the people." Destiny engages being-there ecstatically, "in and with its 'generation'."[64] It ties us to our heritage and becomes explicitly our own when we repeat, or retrieve, that heritage for the sake of new possibilities ahead of us. In *Being and Time* destiny designates man's lot, the allotment that befalls him due to his historical and social constitution. It is man's lot to have to suffer his past, his link to ancestors and contemporaries, and to assume the tradition into which he is born even as he fashions his future.

With his discovery of the epochal essence of situation, Heidegger's understanding of destiny shifts. That discovery—namely, that presencing itself has a history and concretely has had the history of metaphysics—makes it necessary for him to give up whatever words may evoke the philosophy of meaning with its attendant philosophy of the 'existent' for whom his lot has or does not have meaning. The move away from the search for a meaningful destiny is a move toward "the truth, the *alētheia,* of being." Truth so understood "is historical in its essence, not because to be human is to run through the temporal flow, but because mankind remains positioned (sent) in metaphysics, which alone is capable of grounding an epoch." The new understanding of destiny, after the turn, results from the fundamental positions whose genealogy Heidegger then traces. For us Westerners, to have a destiny means to be placed in a history of forgetfulness, under "the destiny of the default of being in its truth."[65] Paradoxically, the dehumanization of destiny in the later Heidegger is thus coupled with a new emphasis on history. But man is not the agent of that history. If in this second period Heidegger displays some preoccupation with the future which, given the accumulated heritage of concealment, will be ours, he can hardly counsel more than to wait and see: "Each time, being lets powers arise for a while, but it also lets them sink with their impotencies into the inessential."[66] There is nothing mythical in this way of speaking about being since it is not itself treated as some superpower. It does not 'make' the powers that be. No one nor anything—neither man nor being—has power over history. The 'destiny of being' re-issues neither God's Providence nor capital's 'invisible hand'. It is the most ordinary phenomenon known to everyone who says 'things are no longer as before', 'this is going to change', 'the time is not right', etc. Destiny is the ever moving order of presencing-absencing, the aletheiological constellation as it situates and re-situates everything in time.

What the later Heidegger calls destiny can best be described in terms of place or site. Tracing "the destiny of the default of being," he discovers the possibility of another destiny. The technological constellation may assign us to a site that is radically new, although at first imperceptibly so. That destinal break cannot be described in categories such as 'unconcealment', which address only the recapitulatory incidence of the transition. Having outlined *alētheia*'s history, Heidegger can draft a topology. The *topoi* of being are of two kinds: ruled by principles and ruled only by the event of presencing. The new site would differ from all received positions as nomadic differs from sedentary life. To speak of the end of epochal history and of the entry into the locus called event is strictly to speak about the same matter twice—of the boundary where one economy expires and another sets in, where an entire culture finds itself *displaced* and where "another destiny of being is released,"[67] "a different destiny, yet veiled."[68] With that break in its destiny, Western culture takes the shape of a heritage bequeathed without directions for use. "Our heritage is preceded by no testament" (René Char).[69] The displacement of culture felt by so many of Heidegger's contemporaries has perhaps been expressed best by Nietzsche's phrase 'God is dead'. For the topology, 'God' stands for all supreme ontic principles in metaphysics, for all archic *topoi*. Since Heidegger extends the impact of this phrase of Nietzsche's to the whole of epochal economies, the new, anarchic, *topos* has been in the making since the Greeks: "This phrase of Nietzsche's names the destiny of two millennia of Western history."[70]

The destiny of metaphysics is, throughout, the destiny in which principles wither away, and not episodically but essentially. That destiny of withering comes to completion with technology, "the last epoch of metaphysics."[71] But does this hypothesis of a new *topos* then not smack of reconciling us with what has been estranged, of humanity restored in its autonomy, liberated from the representations of the first entities under which it has been humiliated? Does Heidegger not re-issue Feuerbach's critique of religion and urge man to recapture the goods alienated for too long in heaven? Is the displacement beyond epochal destiny not a highly interesting thought, interesting man above all? Does Heidegger's thinking, then, not exhibit the utmost concern about a better future for mankind? And does he not go as far as to compare the overcoming of metaphysics to "what happens when one gets over grief or pain"?[72] Do not texts that proclaim a new era—and Heidegger's role in preluding it—abound? But what is the status of those texts? When he hints at a possible mutation in destiny, does Heidegger speak, like Nietzsche, in the capacity of a physician of culture? Is the future for him, as it was for Nietzsche, a curative, medicinal art?[73] Few misreadings of Heidegger would be more unsound. The diagnostic art of highlighting the contours of a closure has nothing to do with the therapeutic art of stemming a malady in order to recover from it. "All mere chasing after the future so as to compute its picture by extending what is present, although half-thought, into what is to come, although now veiled, itself still moves within the attitude of technological, calculating representation."[74] To want to close metaphysics in order to depart from it—to want to deconstruct it in order to construct the future— would amount to implanting oneself more firmly than ever in the attitude that counts and discounts, that takes into account rather than into custody.

The displacement "cannot be fabricated and even less forced."[75] The constructions of History entirely miss both the practical a priori required for anarchic displacement and its destinal nature, which is impossible to reckon up.

A certain disinterest in mankind's future is evident not only in this conception of place, but also in the conception of time required for understanding today's context as potentially anarchic. An anarchic economy would be one in which thinking and acting espouse the fluctuations in the modalities of presencing. It would be an economy in which the only standard for everything doable is the event of mutual appropriation among entities. It follows that the temporality of that event is no longer to be understood—can no longer be understood—from man's viewpoint. As a place, *Ereignis* is as irreducible to epochal stamps (Heidegger's second period) as it is to man's projected world (first period). As time, it is as irreducible to aletheiological history (second period) as it is to ecstatic temporality (first period). If 'destiny' is to designate no more than the epochal determination by retrospective categories—if, in other words, destiny is eschatological[76]—then the event itself has neither history nor destiny. It is "a-historical (*ungeschichtlich*), or better, without destiny (*geschicklos*)."[77] Not that the event is atemporal: its temporality is the coming-about of any constellation of thing and world. In such coming-about the preeminence of the future that characterizes ecstatic time as well as aletheiological-historical time is preserved (event as advent). But it is obvious that this originary coming-about of any relation between thing and world differs from the original coming-about of an age just as the 'soundless' play 'without consequences' differs from any inaugural founding deed. These are but two ways of stating the temporal difference between the event as condition and all economies as the conditioned. When Heidegger envisages an 'entry into the event', i.e., a post-modern economy whose only time structure is the originary, he trusts that the event could become our sole temporal condition, one without principial overdeterminations. The crisis he tries to think is not, then, a founding one. Today's destinal break is rather a disseminating crisis. In this sense, the temporality of the event puts an end to the effort to know and decide what the principles of the forthcoming human world on earth should be.

From the locus of the one to that of the many, the displacement in economy can only occur in a 'leap'. No progression, no evolution, links one destiny to the other. Summer does not 'become' autumn. Suddenly it is autumn, the eighties, old age. Suddenly there is another way of thinking ("From the moment the question 'What is metaphysics?' is asked, the interrogation proceeds already from another question domain"[78]). Suddenly the anarchic economy is ours. "The turning of the danger occurs and appropriates [us] suddenly. *Die Kehre der Gefahr ereignet sich jäh*."[79] Clearly the leap which Heidegger says separates thinking, *Denken*, from the understanding, *Verstand*,[80] refers to mental activities only secondarily. Primarily, that leap comes to pass as a break between economies of presence. Such disjunctive ruptures are in no way spectacular. They may go unnoticed for a long time. They are nevertheless sudden inflexions in the fundamental disposition of presence. To become thinkable, they demand of us an equally *decisive* leap. Western history appears as a closed destiny from the moment thinking risks placing itself resolutely where it is already situated, namely, outside the principles whose downfall technology consummates. "What is called 'destiny of being' characterizes the history of Western thinking so far, inasmuch as we look back upon and into that history from out of the leap."[81] A closed destiny makes for a closed thinking. In order to risk oneself beyond that enclosure, courage is not enough. Two conditions must be fulfilled, each of which, from its own angle of transgression, has priority over the other: priority of the economic break over the leap in thinking, but also a priority of the leap in thinking over the economic break. The turn toward an essentially new mode of presencing—"the reversal in our fundamental position in relation to being"—is the *economic a priori* for entering the *topos* or place of a new thinking: for entering the "essentially other realm of essential thinking."[82] But conversely, that other thinking is the *practical a priori* for bearing to term the other fundamental position already in place around us and in us. The leap freezes the understanding so as to unfreeze thinking.[83] The issue for the understanding is whatever is first in an order of foundation; the issue for thinking is being. Therefore the leap "sets out from the principle of reason as a proposition about entities over to the utterance of being qua being."[84]

It is first of all the modality of presencing that frees itself from epochal principles. Only then can thinking and uttering be freed from the proposition 'nothing is without reason'. Conversely, however, if we are already situated, be it inceptively, in another destiny, thinking and acting must first become 'without reason' so that our world may be freed from principial vestiges and idols and so that we may pass from the era of Janus to that of Proteus.

At the end of the "slumber of being,"[85] the *epechein*—that is, the destiny where presencing is granted only while also denied—can draw to its close. The new destiny renders possible and demands another way of thinking and uttering. It also renders possible and demands another way of acting. If Heidegger barely develops that 'other practice' which is to agree with 'the other thinking' and 'the other destiny', it is because the three displacements are truly inseverable. That much at least he repeats unequivocally. The practice that would agree with the other thinking and the other destiny is action in compliance with the ever moving constellations of presencing, thus introducing a great fluidity into the public domain. But under the anarchy principle, as yet only on the threshold of closure, thinking remains merely preparatory and the other destiny, a potential. Similarly, preparatory acting must be distinguished from the 'other' acting. The only action capable of preparing an economy without principles is that which contests their ves-

tiges in today's world and confines them to their site: as remnants of a closed
destiny. In the final state of epochal destiny, the state that is ours, nothing
can resuscitate those residua, "neither some patchwork of past fundamental
metaphysical positions nor some flight into a reheated christianism."[86] More
precisely, then, what would 'the other acting' be? That is to ask what the
absence of systemic violence would be.

§46. From Violence to Anarchy

> The ordinary concept of 'thing' . . . captures
> the thing but does not seize it as it unfolds its
> essence. It assaults it. Can such an assault
> perhaps be avoided, and how? This would
> probably succeed only if we grant the thing
> an open field, as it were, so that it may show
> its thing-like character immediately. Any
> conception and enunciation of the thing,
> which tend to place themselves between the
> thing and us, must first be removed.
>
> "The Origin of the Work of Art"[87]

These lines suggest a few traits of 'the other acting', which is to be one
with 'the other thinking' and 'the other destiny'. They allow one to say
what it is not, but also what it is. The other action is not "capture,"
"assault." It is "granting the thing an open field." Hence, the practical task
for our age: to remove everything that tends to place itself in front of the
emergence of things into their world.

In the philosophical tradition, the concept of 'thing' is coextensive with
that of 'entity': for the scholastics, *res* is one of the five transcendental
perfections convertible with being.[88] Heidegger rejoins that such an "ordinary" way of thinking, "captures the thing but does not seize it as it unfolds
its essence." Why? Because of the conceptual nature itself of that way of
thinking. *Begriff*, 'concept', derives from *greifen, capere*, to 'grasp'. To
conceive is to catch. By vocation and design, conceptual language places
itself in a position of attack. This aggressive essence of our language, both
philosophical and ordinary, is the result of complex references of condition
to conditioned: our "relation to speech for more than twenty centuries has
been determined by 'grammar'; grammar, in its turn, is based in what is
usually called 'logic'; logic, finally, is only one—but not *the*—interpretation
of thinking and saying, namely the interpretation of the essence of thinking
proper to metaphysics."[89] These relations of gradual priority among speech,
grammar, logic and metaphysics explain the ancient trust in the convergence
between modes of predicating and modes of being: between the subject-
predicate relation and the substance-accident relation. The 'ordinarily' held

convergence between language and being is an imposition, a mere corollary
to the position of man at the center of the knowable. Such 'bending together'
(*con-vergere*) thus turns out to be the violent act par excellence from which
Western civilization was born. It is the unmistakable stamp of the metaphysical economy. The imposition of grammatical forms upon what Heidegger calls 'entities in their totality' is blatant in Aristotle, who investigates the
many ways in which being is *said*, and from this learns the many ways in
which entities relate to substance. Again in Kant, the categories are deduced
from the structures of judgment without any justification or even a recognition of such a subsumption of being—if we admit with Heidegger that the
Kantian categories are "ontological predicates"[90]—under grammar. "To seize
speech, if only externally, in its essence of speech, we know as yet no other
route than that of grammar." It is not difficult to see where the attitude that
forces entities into convergence with words leads: "Words have become
instruments for hunting down and hitting, namely in the 'procedure' and the
'labor' of representing everything [as surely as] precision-firing. The ma-
chine-gun, the camera, the 'word', the poster—all have this same fundamental function of putting objects in retainment."[91] The violence of the concept,
devised by the classical Greeks, is reinforced in a decisive way with Descartes. Since the beginning of modernity, an entity is "what is held at bay
over against, what is ob-stant as an object." An entity is *gestellt*, just as game
is 'held at bay' by a hunter. "Representation drives everything together into
the unity of what so stands against [the subject]. Representation is
coagitatio."[92] The hunting metaphors are most pertinent to the violence of
the modern *cogito* by which objects are re-presented, i.e., forced into constant presence to the subject. As an act of conceiving (*begreifen*), representation already amounts to an act of attacking (*angreifen*).

Here again technology reveals a development that becomes evident only
to a retrospective reading. Technology attests that in its beginning and its
essence violence is actually more than a matter of concept, of theory. The
apparently inescapable hold of technology, leaving no possible refuge,
shows itself to be the delayed and perhaps terminal outcome of decisions
and directions taken since classical Greece. Even if, from that beginning
onward, it has been logic, the Greek heritage par excellence, that has made
thinking a captor, these decisions have been inseverably both 'theoretical'
and 'practical' and therefore neither one nor the other. Assault as a mode of
presencing is the offspring of logic, itself an offshoot of metaphysics[93]—
which in turn was born from decisions on the level of the 'fundamental
positions', that is, of the constellations of being. Reinforced at each subsequent step, those ground-laying decisions have led to universalized violence more destructive than war: "We do not even need an atomic bomb;
man's uprootedness is already there. . . . This uprootedness is the end
unless thinking and poetry attain once again to a nonviolent power."[94]
Faced with that threat of the end, long in preparation, Heidegger therefore
asks: "Can such an assault perhaps be avoided, and how?"

It is obvious that Heidegger does not oppose a counter-violence or at least not a violence of the same kind to institutionalized violence. He does not call for some counterattack. He does not seek confrontation and expects nothing from it. Since the modern subject-object split, confrontation has been everywhere, making violence the very heart of our fundamental historical position. Mounting yet another front could only solidify the universalized assault. Nor does Heidegger urge abandoning the public domain. His project of tracing the economies of presence abolishes, as we have seen, the oppositions between public and private, outside and inside, active and contemplative.

Heidegger is asking whether the 'assault' can perhaps be avoided. It is as ambiguous as technology. The violence of our potentially terminal position results from global control as it both closes metaphysics upon itself and renders the turning possible. Not that violence prompts its own negation. There is nothing dialectical at stake in the hypothesis of closure, only a double-faced fundamental position. The 'assault' simultaneously constitutes us natives and neighbors of the metaphysical terrain. In mounting ever new tactics in the offensive game, it also engages another *possible* play, that of the truth of presencing. "If the true as the only destiny is to come truly toward us and our descendants, everything must remain provisional, widely expectant, cautious: we could not yet calculate when and where and in what shape that event will occur."[95] How is an economy to be anticipated in which truth could be truly encountered? Heidegger responds clearly: Everything that "tends to place itself between the thing and us must first be removed."

But what can such a removal mean if it is to hamstring the assault? How could the specific mode of interdependence between words, things, and actions, which was born from logic and today dominates us through the most enslaving epochal principle our history has known, be at all avoided? To call for a removal can hardly mean to recommend some program calculated to neutralize the offensive of the will: such calculus would only enforce the offensive. To engage in the possible other play and to begin removing the remnants of the ultimate representations that are already losing their credibility, a space for action, for a certain praxis, is to be preserved from the onslaught and *can* be so preserved. For Heidegger, a single attitude is within our reach that allows us to prepare for crossing the closure and withdrawing public exchanges from the will's offensive: "Releasement does not belong to the domain of the will."[96] Releasement is the preparatory play that allows the true to come truly toward us and our descendants as the only destiny. It literally preludes the transgression. The violence Heidegger espouses before the institutionalized assault is the nonviolence of thinking. Indeed, what is thinking's "nonviolent power"? It is to do what presencing does: to let be. Heidegger opposes *lassen*, "letting," to *überfallen*, "assailing,"[97] as he opposes the "entry into the event" to the obstacles that "place themselves between the thing and us." Releasement is neither a benign attitude nor a spiritual comfort. It is the sole viable path that may lead from action as mapped by calculative reason to a praxis not conceivable in terms of calculative reason, neither as its negation nor as its dupe. Letting-be is the only possible way out from under the principles and into the event because (1) it displaces the conflict, (2) it is essentially a-teleocratic, and (3) it prepares an anarchic economy. The first of these points locates releasement on the level of the originary; the second identifies it as the practical a priori; and the third shows it to be the economic alterant needed for distorting and getting over (both senses of *verwinden*) metaphysics. For these three reasons—which must be examined individually—Heidegger can continue, in the lines cited as the epigraph above: "Can such an assault perhaps be avoided, and how? This would probably succeed only if we grant the thing an open field."

1. To grant the thing an open field first of all amounts to displacing the conflict incurred at the end of a long history. Heidegger opposes no dialectical Great Refusal to violence. Dialectic is but "the strongest power of logic to this day," and to philosophize against technology would amount to "a mere re-action against it, that is, to the same thing."[98] Heidegger does not negate technology; rather, he seeks to step back toward the conditions that render it possible as organized violence. This step back toward essence, toward the modes of interconnectedness between words, things, and actions, displaces the conflict; for instead of asking how to 'face' systemic violence, Heidegger inquires about presencing. The open field toward which his critique steps back is the field of phenomenal interdependence of which technology is but one possible modality. Originary—transcendental—openness is both wider and more elusive than one or another historical constellation to which it gives an original shape. The call to grant the thing an open field, a world, then displaces the question of systemic violence from the epochal disposition that rules our age to the event ('world and thing' understood as interplay). Raised as such a call and from such a site, the question goes more surely to the heart of technology than the search for alternatives to standardization and mechanization ever could. The very thrust of Heidegger's critique of violence is missed when it is recruited into the ecologist cause or some other remedial program. What is missed when Heidegger's recollection of being is turned into a parody of dialectics, is the change of level on which he discusses technology: not its pros and cons, nor his or our or anyone's or consciousness's 'for' and 'against', affirmation and negation, but technology's native site. Heidegger steps back to 'nature' understood as *nasci*, as the occurrence of springing from the interplay of world and thing from which springs any epochal disposition. Following this displacement of the question concerning technology, what is it that appears as "granting the thing an open field"? That granting, he adds, "happens all the time." It is the event of mutual appropriation between world and thing which always already lets phenomena be encountered (*begegnenlassen*) and so grants

them their open field. It follows that the practical a priori capable of subverting systemic violence will consist in doing what the phenomenological a priori does, "abandon (*überlassen*) ourselves to the unobstructed presencing of the thing."[99] The practical condition for raising the question concerning technology and the violence inherent in it can only consist in letting things enter their world in constellations essentially rebellious to ordering. The praxis that leaves things an open field can only be a polymorphous doing, 'homologous' to polymorphous presencing. Heidegger thus raises the question of violence not in terms of violence and counterviolence as Marx did, for example ("material violence can only be overthrown by material violence"[100]). Neither does he raise it, as Merleau-Ponty did, in humanist terms (is "violence capable of creating human relationships between men?"[101]). Heidegger asks, What constellation of presencing-absencing is capable of making technology an essentially violent historical fundamental position? He raises it in economic terms. Releasement as a possible praxis springs from that step back toward the temporal difference between presencing and one of its economies.

2. To grant the thing an open field means furthermore to free thinking from representations of an end. If technology is the triumph of telic rationality and if thinking that triumph requires a step back to its conditions, then thinking has no identifiable goal. It does not enter the telic network, either to enforce or negate it. The constitution, retention, possession and mastery of objects is not its task. In its essence and its activity it remains free from teleocratic dominion. Its essence is far too poor, and the task it accomplishes far too modest, to weigh on technology since to think is to follow things as they emerge into their world. It is to follow the emerging from absence into presence, i.e., presencing. Its poverty is nevertheless instructive. It instructs us about an origin without a *telos;* an origin that is always other and always new; on which one cannot count and which thereby defies the technico-scientific complex born from telic rationality. Heidegger's counsel to grant the thing an open field, then, also yields an imperative. Things that enter their world are other than products that enter a planning scheme. Products have a use. That operational purpose constitutes their very being. To speak of things instead of objects given for handling or subsistent as stock is to disengage entities from the frame of finality. How can such disengagement or dis-enframing be carried out? With the imperative contained in this question: "Are we in our existence historically at the origin?"[102] To be at the origin would be to follow in thinking and acting the phenomena's *oriri,* their emergence 'without why'. Concerning the "open field" into which things emerge Heidegger cites Goethe: "Seek nothing behind the phenomena: they themselves are the lesson."[103] Behind the phenomena would be the noumena, and only divine intelligence would know the role it has assigned them among the marvels of creation. In conversation, Heidegger also quoted René Char: "Look only once at the wave casting anchor in the sea." "Of all clear waters, poetry is

the one that dallies least in the reflections of its bridges."[104] Thinking and
poetry corrode teleocracy as rust from a gentle rain corrodes iron. Again, it
is Meister Eckhart who dared translate such corrosion into a discourse on
action: "The just man seeks nothing in his works. Those are serfs and
hirelings who seek anything in their works and who act for the sake of some
'why.' "[105]

3. From the viewpoint of the economies, lastly, granting the thing an
open field means to commit oneself to a transition, to the passage from
violence to anarchy. This translocation leads from a place where entities
stand constrained under an epochal principle to one where they are restored to radical contingency. It is a passage from 'substances' determined
by immutable first principles—*archai* and *telē*—to 'things' emerging muta-
bly into their equally mutable 'world'. Heidegger suggests the innocence
restored to the manifold and to mutability especially in his texts on the
work of art. His Heraclitean strategy broadens the scope of these texts
beyond what is called aesthetics. The work of art establishes a network of
references around itself and thereby produces truth as a contingent sphere
of interdependence. For Heidegger the artwork is the paradigm not of the
"founding deed,"[106] but of the non-principial way a thing opens up a world
and the world places the thing. However, for an economy to so restore all
things to their worlds—for economic anarchy to so displace the principles—the practical condition is the downfall of those telic phantasms that
have already "lost their constructive force and become void."[107] To the
question, What is to be done? when raised together with the question,
What is being? a radical phenomenologist can only respond: dislodge all
vestiges of a teleocratic economy from their hideouts—in common sense as
much as in ideology—and thereby liberate things from the "ordinary concept" which "captures" them under ultimate representations. In the ambiguous situation of a possible transition, that, then, is how Heidegger's
thought of the temporal difference enables one not to remain passive under
the technological "assault."

Inasmuch as the crises or reversals in history impose practical conditions
on thinking and acting, a phenomenology that attempts to understand being *as time* cannot remain content with a merely descriptive notion of
anarchy. Every mode of presencing—every constellation of the temporal
difference—reaches us as a call (*Anruf*), a demand (*Anspruch*). This prescriptive trait turns the imminent constellation into the measure for praxis.
It also turns the doing commensurate with the potential ahead of us, into
the condition for realizing that potential. If, then, technology 'voids' telic
referents and renders possible an essentially a-teleocratic constellation,
Heidegger indeed bares a measure for praxis today: it is the discontinuity
in the event of appropriation. He responds to epochal violence by revealing
the fissure that appears in fixed entitative constellations when we do what
Ereignis does, namely, grant the thing an open field. He has been cautious
on what it would entail for our institutions to break up constant presence,

but he has been explicit on what it entails for language to uncover the break that releasement introduces into the metaphysical structure of propositions. As has been shown earlier, the obstacle par excellence that screens off the event of appropriation stems from the "Greek metaphysical fundaments . . . of the sentence as a relation of subject to predicate." The potential of complying solely with the event of presencing appears in the realm of language as "the potential of saying 'There is being' and 'There is time' without understanding these as propositional statements."[108] Heidegger points directly to the ambiguity of our contemporary economic site—the ambiguity of the 'anarchy principle'—when he regrets that the conference "Time and Being" could still "speak merely in propositional statements."[109]

However allusory Heidegger's remarks about the practical implications of his thinking may be, and however obstinate his refusal to admit to any at all, there is no doubt that, on the linguistic level, his attack on the proposition and, on the ontological level, his interpretation of the temporal difference in terms of 'thing and world', demand the introduction of radical fluidity into social institutions as well as into practice in general. Given the bifrontal essence of technology, to legitimate practice can no longer mean to refer what is doable to a first ground or some supreme reason, to a final end or some ultimate goal. The principle of reason is overturned as it is not present entities (and acts inasmuch as they are entities, too) that call for a ground, but groundless presencing that calls upon existence and demands equally groundless acting. This is how we are to understand the complex link, mentioned toward the end of the epigraph to this section, between the grammar of the proposition, the difference between 'thing and world', and the removal of the principial obstacles as just so many conditions for compliance with the event of appropriation: "Any conception and enunciation of the thing, which tend to place themselves between the thing and us, must first be removed." Which are the conceptions and enunciations that most massively tend to place themselves between us and things emerging into their world? They are the conceptions and enunciations about essentially hubristic ('unjust', in Anaximander's words) representations— the epochal principles. These, then, are to be removed if the potential in our disjunctive era is to be seized and systemic violence transmuted into economic an-archy. Only on the condition of that removal does the "entry into the *Ereignis*" become possible in the strict sense of the word: the entry into what is *eigen*—not what is 'proper' or one's 'own' (property, appropriation, possession), but what is *oikeion* (from *oikos*, the 'house', hence 'eco-nomy'), pertaining to one's dwelling. The entry into the event is the homecoming from metaphysical errancy, which, for us children of technology, remains thinkable and doable only as the struggle against the injustice, the hubris, of enforced residence under prinicpial surveillance—whatever form it may take. Such removal would be the politics of 'mortals' instead of 'rational animals'. It carries out the answer to the question, What is to be done at the end of metaphysics?

CONCLUSION

§47. Economic Self-Regulation and Its Loci

> The plurivocity of utterance . . . arises from a
> play which, the more richly it unfolds, the
> more strictly it is *bound by a hidden rule*.
> Owing to this rule, the play of plurivocity
> remains in a balance whose oscillation we
> seldom experience.
>
> *The Question of Being*[1]

The argument I have tried to develop may be comprehended by the
distinction between *rule* and *principle*. Every economy of presence is self-
regulated, hence Heidegger's anti-humanism. But not every economy of
presence is self-regulated by one entity held to be its ultimate regulator—a
principle. Hence Heidegger's an-archism.

There is in Heidegger a peculiar fascination for 'functioning', for 'cybernetics'. On one hand he deplores the fact that "everything functions: this is
precisely what is uncanny."[2] And he flatly states that today philosophy has
been replaced by cybernetics.[3] But on the other hand he tells us that the
epochs in history establish themselves by and of themselves, that to think
is to correspond to a truth "already accomplished" in advance[4] by the
self-interpretation (*Selbtsauslegung*) of being, and that the economies unfold "bound by a hidden rule." Without a form of systemic self-regulation,
it would seem difficult to speak of identity and difference in history, that is,
to think change. Such a fascination appears even inevitable to me from the
moment one admits with Heidegger the withering away of principles while
still taking care not to plead the cause of anarchy in the ordinary sense of
pure and simple disorder.

At the risk of repeating here in conclusion a few points already made, I
would like to show how economic self-regulation works concretely in its
two loci—thinking and praxis.

I. Rules for the Direction of 'Thinking'

The play of internal regulation, as Heidegger understands it, is most
obvious in what he says of *history* and the modalities of presence whose
concatenation according to rules of transformation (the categories) history

is. But these original rules refer back to more originary rules, those of being as time, or of the *event* of appropriation (*Ereignis*). Understood as a temporal process without duration, as mere coming-about, 'being qua being' can indeed also be said to regulate itself. That self-regulation is less obvious—more hidden, Heidegger says—although it constitutes the very issue of phenomenology. We know what the rules are to which being conforms as Heidegger came to think of it in his last writings: they conjoin an *entity* that is present, the *modality* of its presence at a given moment, and *presencing* as such, i.e., as event.

How does this three-tiered play of the (temporal) difference regulate thinking by binding it (1) to epochal history, and more specifically (2) to technology, as well as—essentially—(3) to the event?

1. *First rule: The understanding of being as time cannot dispense with the deconstruction of the epochs.*
Throughout his writings, Heidegger raises only one question, that of the relation between being and time. "To head toward one star, only this."[5] However, the answers he brings to bear on it are several. (a) Time is the sense of being, he said first, and this answer made it necessary to investigate the characteristics of that entity we are ourselves. (b) Time is the truth of being, he said next, which necessitated an inventory of the fundamental traits of our history since the Greeks. (c) Being is event, he finally said, which was the only answer allowing him to understand being *as* time. Eventlike temporality was already recognized obliquely in the two earlier answers, in time as 'ecstasis' and as '*epochē*'. The obliquity is lifted as the event of appropriation turns out to be the condition not only of historical or destinal temporality, but of ecstatic temporality as well. Even more, *Ereignis* designates the phenomenological condition that has rendered possible all of the received time concepts, whether physicist, like Aristotle's, or mentalist, like Augustine's. The event of appropriation is being as originary time.

This trajectory generated by the *Seinsfrage* must be retained in its integrity. The discovery of time as event does not supersede epochal temporality any more than the latter supersedes ecstatic temporality. However, if a decisive reorientation—'the turning'—forced itself upon Heidegger as being-in-the-world proved to have a history, the third answer (c) to the being question is linked with the second answer (b) by a particularly close affinity. The event of appropriation presupposes the work on history and cannot forego it. In this regard Heidegger even speaks of *aufheben*:[6] the undertow toward expropriation in time as event preserves time as *epochē* while both cancelling and superelevating it. In other words, originary time can be reached only by deconstructing the historical orders of presence via the disjunctive moments from which they were born and in which they founder.

Deconstruction directly concerns the self-regulation of epochal economies. It is the method for uprooting the very event of *phainesthai*, of manifestation, from past manifest configurations of phenomena. It is the method by which the phenomenologist gathers presencing as the synchronic event—or advent—from the cultural fields of presence and their diachronic shifts. In Heidegger's words, deconstruction is the method for stepping back from the historical modalities of presence (*Anwesenheit*) to presencing itself as event (*Anwesen*). Such a step back to the conditions can be called transcendental as long as this does not imply any ultimacy of the subject. It is not a step into the blue, however, since it is bound by the rules within history which this step itself helps bring to light. Any reading method organizes the text it is meant to open up. As deconstruction remains the key method in Heidegger, its text, the 'history of being', is the most apparent domain of internal regulation in this phenomenology.

When Heidegger speaks of traits, categories, or rules in the text of our history, he understands by that the systemic features that *connect* its epochal disposition. These are rules of conservation as much as of transformation. Insofar as the economies of presence are self-regulating, the ruptures within history are never total. Neither the transitions *within* metaphysics nor the turning *beyond* it make for anything so utterly new that the old is simply blotted out. It is true, though, that if these rules "traverse"[7] history, this is to say that the originary traits of being appear in the effort of disengaging thinking from metaphysics. Hence the importance of a historical deduction of the categories of presence. It shows what happens in epochal breaks such as the arrival of modernity: a play of differences determines anew something that remains the same across the ages. But what remains the same is only a fabric of categories. This excludes any remnant of an in-itself, which would transcend becoming, as a candidate for what endures through history. The historical deduction of the categories of presence is essential not only for establishing that 'thinking of being' cannot outgrow the deconstruction of history, but also for insuring that 'being' is not conceived as something noumenal, as quasi-divine; that it is 'one' only formally, as a law of economic functioning. The first rule for understanding 'being' is to wrest from history the traits of *epochal self-regulation*.

2. *Second rule: The three-tiered difference appears in analyzing the contemporary modality of presence, technology.*

What is the given that radical phenomenology deconstructs? The arrangements among phenomena as they have had currency in the West— the economies of presence. Among these economies there is one that guides the entire enterprise of deconstruction, namely, contemporary technology. In Heidegger, the interpretations of both the Presocratics and the metaphysicians aim at illuminating that one *topos* which is our own. These interpretations do not in the least intend to lead us back to some Greek golden age beyond an alleged metaphysical interlude. The phenomenology of the reversals of history therefore proceeds retrospectively. The modali-

ties of presence are unfolded from the fold where we people of the twentieth century are lodged.

Just as transcendental criticism in Kant starts from a fact, that of experience, and asks the question of its a priori conditions, so does Heidegger's
historical criticism. Its starting point is the contemporary phenomenal
order, technology as the age without a beyond. The question this criticism
asks about its given is not that of subjectivist philosophy: What is man? but
that of ontology: What is being? Heidegger does not examine the contemporary site and its genesis in order to gain further information about man.
If he asks: How did we arrive there? it is not as a historian of culture. It is
rather to elucidate the complex structure of the being question itself. That
question is complex, for an economy of presence—for example, technology—is not an immediate given. It is the *Anwesenheit* of what is
anwesend, the modality of presence of what is present. Radicalized transcendental phenomenology consists in stepping back from this modality of
presence toward *Anwesen* as such, toward the event of presencing. A second rule for thinking results from this *differential self-regulation* by which
the present, through the modality of its presence, both hides and reveals
the event of presencing.

If it is admitted that the starting point of the deconstruction is one
particular economy, it becomes clearer why the ontological difference
unites the three terms I have just sketched and not two (e.g. *ta onta*,
"entities", and *to einai*, "the to-be"). The middle term is that order which,
following Heidegger, other authors have located in discourse and called
epistēmē or discursive regularity.[8] In Heidegger, the three-tiered difference is generally described as between 'entities,' their 'beingness' and
'being' (as a verb, as 'to-be'). This way of formulating it, however, passes in
silence over the decisive factor, time. In his last writings, he therefore
characterizes beingness and being with some subtlety as two moments of
'letting', as "letting-*be-present*" and as "*letting-be*-present."[9] Originary
time has 'letting' as its essence, which is to say that it remains unintelligible
within any metaphysical quest for ultimate causes, grounds, or principles.

The play of self-regulation among the three terms is the complex temporal condition of everything that can become a phenomenon. It is a condition that is *ultimate without being a ground*. From transcendentalism Heidegger thus preserves the search for an a priori, although dissociated not
only from subjectivity but also from any foundational problematic. Such a
problematic is incompatible with the *temporal* essence of the event as a
priori. The temporal condition functions as an a priori regulation without
any enduring principial referent. For nothing is more tenuous than this
'letting', or *phuein* (coming to presence, presencing). The permeation of
transcendental conditions with time carries finitude—together with the a
priori, the other discovery of critical philosophy—to its extreme. It is not
only *Dasein*, but being itself *as time*, that is finite.

3. *Third rule: To think is to follow the event of presencing, without re-course to principial representations.*

The responsibility traditionally incumbent on the philosopher, his true mission, consisted in securing ultimate referents or principles. Whether he analyzed substance and its attributes or consciousness and its intentional acts, he spoke as the expert on deep anchorage: an anchorage that guaranteed meaning in discourse, soundness of mind, objectivity of knowledge, value of life, if not possible redemption from infractions. Is it an overestimation of the contemporary era to read in technology the expiration of that mandate, to suspect that today the *principial play lapses out of order?* When Heidegger affirms "the end of philosophy,"[10] what is at stake is that expiration as the principial constellations of presence lose their credibility.

The end of philosophy as grounding and building entails a task for thinking. It is to *unlearn* its age-old reflex, the search for invariable standards, and it is to *learn* doing explicitly what it has always done, that is, heed the modality in which phenomena come about in any given economy. Such unlearning requires our questioning the referents we have made hegemonic over our history since the Greeks. And such learning demands that the economic mutations, giving shape to the event, be retained as the only measure for thought.

The loci to which thinking finds itself assigned when it renounces timeless ideals are always new and always different. A third rule for thinking is, then, to submit to *topological self-regulation*. This task is less grandiose than the ancient mission of guaranteeing reasons. However, it is a difficult task. It goes against the fiber of our cultural fabric, against the ingrained recourse to some measure-giving first, be it 'the cause' or 'the father'. The deconstruction undoes this fabric born from the *pros hen* relation, and the topology replaces it with a texture of ever changing unconcealment.

II. Consequences for the Direction of Life

These premises entail a few consequences for praxis. I will limit myself to indicating their points of incidence.

1. *The heuristic and the determinative priority of praxis.*

If in his last writings Heidegger's starting point is a particular economy— our own—in *Being and Time*, it is a particular praxis, namely, everyday activities. This starting point has, among other functions, a heuristic one. It provides access to fundamental ontology. At no stage in his work is Heidegger interested in praxis as the subject matter of the 'practical' disciplines, ethics and politics. Asking the question 'What is to be done?' in the context of *Being and Time*—as opposed to the context of later writings—would amount to confusing the ontic with the ontological. The confusion par excellence would be to expect *Seinsdenken*, thinking of being, to provide principles for action as Aristotelians sought to derive the principles of moral and institutional theory from a first philosophy, or as philosophers in early modernity divided general metaphysics into branches of special metaphysics.

For Heidegger, everyday praxis serves to retrieve the more ancient question, *Ti to on;* What is being? Consequently, the very thrust of his new beginning was mistaken when, shortly after the publication of *Being and Time,* he was asked: "When will you write an ethics?"[11] It was mistaken because the suggestion implied that the phenomenological *traits* of praxis could somehow be converted into *norms,* or descriptive categories into prescriptive ones.

However, there is another priority of praxis in Heidegger, which appears as early as in *Being and Time* and which remains operative throughout all of his work: to retrieve the being question from the point of view of time, a certain way of life is required. To understand authentic temporality, it is necessary to 'exist authentically'; to think being as letting phenomena be, one must oneself 'let all things be'; to follow the play without why of presencing, it is necessary to 'live without why'. Here the priority of praxis is no longer heuristic. It is a practical a priori without which thinking—in the strong sense of complying with the fluctuating loci of presencing—lapses into impossibility. According to the mainstream of the metaphysical tradition, acting follows being; for Heidegger, on the other hand, a particular kind of acting appears as the *condition* for understanding being as time. Here praxis determines thinking. In writings subsequent to *Being and Time,* it is suggested that this praxis is necessarily of a political nature.

2. The political character of the economies of presence.

As mentioned before, being can be understood as time only through its *difference* from history. The investigation into the concrete epochs and their regulation is what binds the later Heidegger's phenomenology to experience. Since this is, however, not an individual's experience, the issue of phenomenology proves to be political in a broad sense. An economy of presence is the way in which, for a given age, the totality of what becomes phenomenal arranges itself in mutual relations. Any economy is therefore necessarily public.

But an economy of presence is political also in a stricter sense. This is most obvious in the retrospective reading of the epochs, beginning with technology as the last 'mark' of Western destiny. Enframing (*Gestell*), as Heidegger calls this mark or stamp, is the inescapable determination of our era. It will not do, then, to describe technology merely as the contemporary *public* form of presence. As a willful posture, it pushes toward *domination*. Retrospectively, the trend toward global mastery can be read as far back as the epochal reversal that instituted metaphysics with Plato and Aristotle. It gains momentum with the Cartesian *cogito*, understood as *co-agitatio*, 'forcing together'. It triumphs with the Nietzschean will to power as the essence of the 'atomic age'—philosophers are the ones who

always respond most thoroughly to the phenomenal disposition that encloses them and situates them. For the deconstructionist, then, the notion
of the political covers more than the mere public character of an epochal
mark; but it covers less than the received notions of the political that
denote the sphere of the city (opposed to that of the household), or civil
society, or again a community based on the social contract. The epochal
marks in Western history have been political because, more evidently at
each stage, they have forced the network of things, words and actions of an
age into the logic of domination.

It is in this ensemble of things, words and (telic) actions that thinking
'acts' in a non-telic way and anticipates a possible post-technological economy not stamped primarily by institutionalized violence.

3. *The withering away of epochal principles.*

The practical a priori for working through generalized domination and
mastery, says Heidegger, consists in 'letting [technology] be'. What does
this mean?

From the standpoint of praxis, metaphysics appears as an enterprise of
legitimation. It refers the question: What is to be done? to a primary
discourse, whether about being, nature, God, or a supreme judgment of
reason. Because of this search for a justificatory fundament, metaphysics is
a system in which representations of a ground replace one another across
the ages. Heidegger enumerates a few: "Metaphysics is that historical
space in which the suprasensible World, the Ideas, God, the moral Law,
the authority of Reason, Progress, the Happiness of the greatest number,
Culture, Civilization, lose their constructive force and become nothing."[12]
These referents, which have served successively to legitimate the practical
disciplines, I have called the epochal principles.

The referent that could serve in this role today would be 'enframing'. It
could indeed be added to this list of ultimate representations. But what
becomes of such grounding? Since 'enframing' designates domination at its
apogee, as effectively global, domination has only itself to legitimate itself;
cybernetics, only cybernetics; the will and mechanization, only the will and
mechanization. With this collapse of an ordering referent—or of the *pros
hen*—metaphysics comes to a close. The hypothesis of closure results from
the *reduplication* 'will to will' substituting itself for the *difference* between
'being and entities'. Enframing, then, is not like any other principle. It is
transcendence abolished. Total mechanization and administration are only
the most striking features of this abolition and reduplication, of this loss of
every epochal principle; a loss that, as Heidegger suggests, is happening
before our eyes.

To let technology be would mean to follow the potential for bringing down
representations of transcendence, a potential contained in technology itself
as the culmination of the deep-fixed logic of domination. Under the hypothesis of metaphysical closure, technology appears as essentially bifrontal. Its

actuality, its Janus face turned toward the past, is the most violent principial grip ever. But because it is the rationality of control fully deployed at last, it also harbors, pointing ahead, the *possibility* of a turning toward a non-principial mode of presencing. "Higher than actuality stands possibility." It is this possible turning that letting-be, or 'releasement', prepares.

4. Poiein kata phusin.

The hypothesis of closure obliges us to understand the turning (*die Kehre*) as an occurrence that comes about in the twentieth century's economy of presence. The turning in Heidegger's thinking is, then, secondary, an echo of the turning in the contemporary arrangement of phenomena. Now if this turning, rendered possible today, completes a movement begun twenty-five centuries ago, it affects the domain of the doable as much as that of the thinkable. Furthermore, if this turning consists in an emancipation from epochal principles, we will no longer need to invest certain among us with a special mission, that of establishing reference points legitimating praxis. There will no longer be 'philosophers', but perhaps there will be 'thinkers'.

Philosophy and reason in general are in league with the epochal principles. Reason imprints, imposes, informs. Thinking, for its part, is essentially compliant with the flux of coming-to-presence, with constellations that form and undo themselves. To think is to follow the event of appropriation, to follow *phuein*. Therefore in the final analysis, there is only one rule for the direction of thinking: *phusis* understood as the movement of emergence out of absence into presence.

What would the acting be that would prepare an economy freed from ordering principles? It would be an acting following that same rule. Heraclitus described it as *poiein kata phusin*, "acting according to presencing."[13] Since an ordering principle initiates and commands, since it is the *archē* of an epoch, such acting preparatory to a post-modern economy would be literally an-archic.

§48. Objections and Answers

1. *Granted, Heidegger can argue that the technological turn yields the potential of a transition toward an anarchic economy of presencing. But if entities and their representations have indeed lost their mensurating power—if being alone is to provide the measure—does that turn not, on the contrary, risk preparing the terrain for a regime more 'archic' than ever? This danger should already be empirically evident: nothing produces its contrary more surely than lofty ideas about social relations at last freed from all coercion, especially when 'thinking' is to function as the sole thread of Ariadne toward freedom. More fundamentally, is the very argument for an end of principial economies not fraught with danger? It is not*

so difficult to transform anarchy itself into an apology for totalitarianism.
How could anyone fail to recognize that the disappearance of practical
standards leads unerringly to the anarchy of power?

—Economic anarchy is not an anarchy of power. What I called the
hypothesis of closure makes it impossible to conceive of public affairs according to the model of reference to the one, that is, according to the
principial model that founds the delegation of functions and the investment
of power in an ad hoc representative or titular. Economic anarchy is opposed to the anarchy of power as lawfulness is to lawlessness, as thinking is
to the irrational, and as liberty is to oppression.

First, lawfulness versus lawlessness or a-nomy: an eco-nomy, as the word
indicates, is a whole of laws for a dwelling, a synchronically closed set of
determinants in mutual relation. It is probably safe to assume that the
positive laws of nations have always quite faithfully reflected the economic
laws of presencing by which those nations lived.[14] The example of communal realizations mentioned earlier[15] should suffice to show that anarchy does
not mean anomy. When, in the few instances of direct democracy in modern history, laws arose from a deliberation renewed, as it were, every day,
positive legislation most closely followed the economic constellation shifting between eras. In those rare intervals, as perhaps again today with the
"turning," laws lose their permanence. The ideal of a time that endures has
sustained legislations from the Platonic republic to Condorcet's 'mathema-
tizable society' and even further to Max Weber's 'charismatic authority'. If
what is at issue in the possible transition toward an anarchic economy is a
new understanding of time, then the synchronically closed sets of determinants for dwelling are to be thought of otherwise than in solid diachronic
continuity. The new understanding of dwelling requires working through
(*verwinden* in the sense of *durcharbeiten*) the representations of constant
presence as the temporality of the law. It is one and the same deconstruction that breaks the prestige of referents and of constancy. Under the
hypothesis of closure, lawfulness can no longer be derived from one constantly present focal point, be it an entity, an order of entities such as
nature, or the act of an entity, such as consciousness. Deriving it from a
political leader constantly present to his people would constitute the most
blatant relapse into legitimation through recourse to an entity. Once it is
understood that the time continuum is the nerve of all relation to a leader
and the *pros hen*, the very muscle of the arm with which he governs, any
attempt to co-opt the concept of anarchic economy for such exceedingly
'metaphysical' regimes as the one in which Heidegger placed his hope for a
year or so remains bound to fail. Rather, what makes the law is *phuein*,
unstable presencing.

Next, thinking versus the irrational: the turn that may lead out of the
principial epochs (a redundant phrase anyway) is solely a matter of thinking. Heidegger repeats this often. On the face of it, this praise of *Denken* is
one of the most clearly Kantian elements in his later writings. The charge

that "the sciences do not think"[16] is a slightly more trenchant way of iterating Kant's disjunction between knowing and thinking. Furthermore, in many respects thinking in Heidegger remains the agent of enlightenment—not so remote from the way Kant understood it: "To think by oneself is to seek in oneself the supreme touchstone for truth (that is, in one's own reason); and the maxim always to think by oneself is enlightenment."[17] On what condition then will the economic principles perish? On the condition of learning to think by oneself.[18] Heidegger's phrasings are, however, more trenchant because for him thinking by oneself designates something more radical than verification in subjective reason. It means to follow expressly the event of presencing as it ceaselessly occurs anew around us. The locus of enlightenment is not the subject but an economy at one moment in history.

Lastly, freedom versus oppression: the impossibility of the latter is the very content of the hypothesis from which I have read the later Heidegger, namely, the withering away of the epochal principles. With that withering, oppression becomes an economic impossibility if it is at least admitted that the domination of man by man is only the result of the original hubris, domination of *phuein* by the *principia*. The possibility of the former, i.e., of freedom, resides in the conjunction, without that hubris, of being and thinking—of the event of appropriation and economy-wide enlightenment.

Heidegger can and, in my opinion, should be criticized for having treated the problems of so-called practical philosophy all too allusively. On a first reading, elementary distinctions seem so thoroughly lacking that one has the impression of advancing in a night where all cats are grey. And where political distinctions are lacking, the yearning for a leader is indeed not far: a leader who will make distinctions of his own kind. But once it is understood on a second reading that these problems find the beginning of their solution in an analytic of the economies of presencing (with the historical deduction of categories that is its keystone), it is no longer possible to hold that Heidegger becomes the witting or unwitting apologist for that peculiar reference to a first—the call for a leader. The analytic assigns that reference its expiration date: the technological era. The idea of a natural inequality of men, the theoretical apology for the strong individual on the basis of a belief in 'Man', in human nature, the idea of an elite that best incarnates that nature, the cult of certain individuals, 'archons' or place-holders of epochal principles—it takes a special bent for the absurd to hold that Heidegger smuggles these or other offspring of the metaphysics of degrees past critical customs without declaring them. On the contrary, he declares them. He calls them by their generic name, epochal *Prägungen* or *Gepräge* (stampings or stamps), and he relegates them under the hypothesis of closure.

The criteria that legitimate economic anarchy thus have nothing in common with those invoked by twentieth-century anarchism of power (superiority of a race, etc.), just as deconstruction has nothing in common with the metaphysical hierarchies it dislocates. Neither do these criteria resemble those used by Proudhon (the substitution of Science for the domination of man by man)[19] or Bakunin ("spontaneous life," "passion," the "revolt of life against science").[20] The criterion in question is rather technology itself and its bifrontal essence. Economic anarchy is therefore a concept of phenomenological ontology. It has nothing to do with the ancient debate about the best form of government: the three forms traditionally judged good, monarchy, aristocracy, and democracy, and their respective perversions, tyranny, oligarchy, and anarchy. To confuse the amalgam of these three perversions—the anarchy of power—with economic anarchy is to be mistaken about the starting point, the method, and the result of the phenomenology of reversals in presencing. Its starting point is the ambivalence of the technological age, not some valuation of human types; its method consists in tracing the economies that have produced that ambivalence, not in redistributing power among human types; and its consequence is a potential for freedom in our age, not the control of one type by another.

2. *You give such status to contemporary technology that it comes to close a culture. Does that not exaggerate the significance of today's transformations? Rather, let us say that for a century Western intellectuals have run out of ideas and that from the prescriptive that it was, philosophy must henceforth remain content with being modestly descriptive. This does not entitle one to claim a dramatic break in world history, still less to advocate some sharp political discontinuity. If Heidegger inflates the* Kehre *to such proportions, he can only end by asking for a total change, which amounts to rendering all change impossible.*

—It is true that the technological reversal is for Heidegger the most decisive in over two millennia. Its potential is therefore hardly skimmed when social scientists define it by the transition to advanced capitalism, the post-industrial era, the managerial rather than authoritarian disposition of power, post-liberalism, etc. All these traits pertain to one of the two Janus faces, the one whereby the age without a beyond, which is ours, calls in its very economy of presencing for something to stabilize its drifts. As absolute referents have lost their credit, the office of stabilizing passes over to administrative rationality. It is this rationality—which is not instrumental, as Weber would have it—that reaches its acme with the technological turn. It is the same rationality of total administration which becomes monstrous in totalitarianism. One has to see that these deliria indigenous to 'framing' are backlashes to the anarchism in the modality of presencing itself. The either-or that Heidegger suggests brings into play the other Janus face: we either learn how to comply with the drifts in the network of phenomenal interconnectedness, or we will witness and bring about more and more of those deliria—and truly global ones.

This is not to say that the transition beyond epochal constellations is anything extraordinary, a sharp, highly visible turnabout in public life. It consists in doing explicitly what we always do and cannot help doing:

conforming to presence as it comes about, to the event of presencing—but henceforth without the fiction of some ultimate stabilizing ground. In this way the technological reversal contains the opportunity to recognize and retain what is most ordinary in life, namely, that its context is never the same. Ever since Aristotle succeeded in solving the more ancient aporias about motion, becoming and change, *kinēsis* (except in astral theology) has stood opposed to being. Read in terms of the question *ti to on* the fact of the technological turning appears to be charged with a potential that shows how Heidegger works not only through, but also against metaphysics: leading the attributive modes of presencing—in which presence is primarily the attribute of God, nature, or consciousness—to their fulfillment, that turning opens up the possibility of a withering away of these modes. Such a decline would break the Aristotelian opposition between being and becoming and would allow action to conform, not to any principial regularities, but rather to each thing's arrival in presence, each event of presencing, as such.

This gives additional evidence that to speak of being inevitably also includes speaking not only of becoming, but furthermore of doing or acting. Action (in the strict sense of intervention in public life), just as much as thinking (in the strict sense of life of the mind), must become docile to the event of presencing—which, since the *kenōsis* of ideals in the Western world, it has already begun doing. The question of action, and more precisely of political intervention, enters this phenomenology from an entirely different angle than in any formal derivation—in which the middle term is 'goal' (*telos*)—of the schemes of πϱᾶξις from the schemes of θεωϱία. Heidegger does not hold that either thinking or acting is intrinsically telic. That is why practical doctrines cannot follow in any way from ontological ones: the argument of derivation has lost its middle term. As stated earlier, instead of an argumentative priority, he seeks a practical one. The ensuing inversion of the transcendental status of action permits him to suggest that public praxis in an economy deprived of any epochal principle can only be anarchic. The hinge on which this inversion turns again concerns the representation of goal: it is necessary to exist 'without why' in order to understand presencing as itself without *archē* or *telos*, 'without why'.

Praxis deprived of a goal or end is the concrete condition for thinking 'being itself' as deprived of an end. Although he renders the derivation 'acting follows being' non-operational, Heidegger is more explicit about the impossibility of deriving any philosophic disciplines from the thinking of being than he is about the practical abolition of teleology as the condition of that thinking of being. Anarchic praxis: this is the *topos* where the man Martin Heidegger undoubtedly would not so much have liked to see himself led.

3. *'Acting without a why': you will not escape the accusation of advocating the abolition of all practical norms. Your reverse reading of Heidegger's texts leads you to oppose a relativism without remedy to those who*

consider at least Being and Time *still compatible with moral formalism. If natural teleology is its target, the deconstruction leaves us with no more than mere descriptions of historical givens. "Truth on this side of the Pyrenees, error beyond . . ." (Pascal). Indirect givens perhaps, since this version of Pyrrhonism seems to describe not the mores and customs themselves, but their changing regularities. Empirical givens all the same. No transcendence, nothing but the facts and their concatenations. At the reversals of history the kaleidoscope of things is shaken, and a new configuration appears. It is doubtful that Heidegger understood the question of being that way. In sum, you confine him to what Kant might have called a cultural anthropology. Or rather, given the great case you make of modalities of exchange and the sequence of their arrangement, in a systematization of what Michel Foucault described as the order of things. Deconstruction so understood is perhaps broader, but no less positivistic, than the archeology of knowledge.*

—This might be so if the deconstruction exhibited only the beginning and end of the various economic eras, only the 'epochs' in the sense of reversals, only the historical folds and modes of unfolding. But the inquiry does not stop there. The *original* origins, the beginnings that set the stage for a while, are of no particular interest except in view of the *originary* origin, which is the simple event of presencing as such. It is easy to show that the originary is not a historicist or positivist concept. The phenomenology of the later Heidegger is indeed *descriptive* in that his argument steps back from historical givens or entities to the datable rise and while of their interconnectedness, i.e., to 'beingness' in the sense of an epochal way of things to be. But his phenomenology is *transcendental* in that it seeks to reach in turn the conditions of these historical orders and breaks between them. From the original and its principles it therefore steps back to the originary; from beingness to 'being'. The first step backward (which reveals, for example, how the Inca became the *princeps* of the Precolumbian empire and the decimal system its *principium*) is only the preamble— where one 'goes first'—to the second step which reveals the general traits according to which being can at all be 'principled'. Heidegger's history of being does not stop at narrating a sequence of epochal regularities since that twofold *Schritt zurück* leads from the given to the modes of giving, then to the 'there is' that gives. Any interpretation of Heidegger that would end by paralyzing that double movement would stall his train of thought at its crucial juncture.

As for practical norms, their source is equally twofold. On one hand, *material* obligations, such as what were once called estate duties, have their obvious source in norms that epochal orders alone can justify (thus with the Christian conquest of Peru, llama sacrifices cease to be a duty). Material norms are legitimized by recourse to the epochal principles of the day. They are displaced—for instance, from one side of the Pyrenees to the other—as the principles gain and lose their sway. *Formal* norms, on the other hand, have been held to entail necessary and universal obligation inasmuch as every rational agent found himself bound by them through his natural constitution—in whatever way this may have been construed. Whether philosophers located their source in a divine intellect or in practical reason, these were the norms capable of 'in-forming' human conduct and of guaranteeing virtue. If, now, by 'formal' one wishes to address such an imprint of an intelligible ought on sensible matter, these norms depend again on the epochal principles: not on this or that particular one of them, but upon their trail from Plato onward, since they are what has brought us such distinctions as those between sensible and intelligible, matter and form. But if by 'formal' one wishes merely to address the set of traits according to which men have in fact acted—traits which are generalizable beyond the epochs toward a possible transition—then these traits have their source not in the original, but in the originary. They are born from the self-differentiation of presencing, which is to say that they are no longer norms but rules.

Practical anarchy, then, requires no other method than the one that has produced the categories of presencing. Their identity results from the Parmenidean formulations in Heidegger according to which 'thinking' and 'presencing'—*noein* and *phuein* (*einai*)—are one and the same event. The formal identity of traits for thinking and norms for acting is also in keeping with what has been said above of moral evil: "If there is anything in thinking that can prevent men from doing evil, it must be some property inherent in the activity itself."[21] It follows that the categorization of *Ereignis* indicates at least the contours of a possible deduction of rules for action. What would the status of these practical categories be—categories which, for lack of any basis in Heidegger, I will refrain from hypothesizing? Their status would be exactly the same as that of the categories of presencing: read phenomenologically as an ensemble of regulating features that structure Western history. Their formalization would make it possible to escape moral relativism without, however, fantasizing yet again a human nature, a reason occupied by invariable laws with which to govern sensibility and instincts, and an "irrevocable morality" imposing itself on everything—as the anarchist Saurin put it,[22] following Kant—through logic alone. The unity in the 'destiny of presencing' makes it impossible for action to follow paths significantly deviant from the fundamental prospective, retrospective and transitional traits. In this unity of transcendental formalization we hold with Kant for whom the moral law did not require a special deduction since in his *Critique of Practical Reason* he could presuppose the general structure of transcendental arguments.[23] Furthermore, the practical incidence of the categories—of which Heidegger (against Kant, this time) says nothing, be it only to avoid any new dichotomy between theory and practice—confirms that anarchy means absence of rule, but not absence of rules.

Nor do the anarchic displacements spelled out above amount to deriving once more a praxology from an ontology. If the traits that determine action are to be won through the same method as the traits of presencing, it is because 'thinking' in the sense of complying with the event—in the sense of 'thanking'—includes action. "Thinking changes the world," "thought itself is a doing."[24] Heidegger renovates the transcendental problematic not only by dissociating it from that of the subject, but also by abolishing the methodological distinction between theoretical and practical inquiry. As 'thinking' is understood so broadly that it includes the way an entire culture lives and acts, subjective reason and its acts (knowing, willing, judging) can only disappear as issues within the more general investigation of the temporal difference: formal rules for knowing, willing and judging alike come to be sought on the side of presencing and its event, while material maxims for these acts appear on the side of the economies and their history.

We have seen that, at the moment of closure, action in the narrow sense turns into the practical condition for the exit beyond the epochal economies as well as for a phenomenology capable of exhibiting the road of that transgression. The inversion of roles whereby praxis ends up as a condition for philosophy is not incompatible with the formalism in question. The maxim concomitant with the 'turning', one that demands universal application, would then prescribe the struggle against any vestige of an epochal first—a *material* maxim and, as such, of course thoroughly provisional.

4. *There remains the objection of idealism. These 'epochal principles' look very much as if they were making history, directing the lives of men, in the received phrase, behind their backs. More surprisingly still, under Heidegger's gaze Western history since the Greeks seems to articulate itself with an intrinsic necessity. Does it not run toward the atomic age as its inescapable resolution? Whatever Heidegger's assurances to the contrary, is he so far from systematizing a process that remains unintelligible and unreal as long as it is not 'closed', a process that realizes itself in the medium of history according to strict laws of progression and that places us in a privileged, panoptic, eschatological position?*

—I have said how the categorial, the middle zone between the factual starting point and the question of being, makes it possible to avoid the two stumbling blocks of relativism and idealism. The issue is best broached through the temporal difference this question and the categories precisely seek to address, namely, the difference between presencing and history, or between *Ereignis* and *Geschehen*. If one speculates that full presence comes to itself in and through history, then, yes, the epochs and their end provide the framework for a panoptic system ordered by ideatable principles and in which the atomic age marks the moment of rational apotheosis. But it has been shown that the event of presencing escapes diachronic retrieval. Only economic modes of presence can be retrieved this way. The categories deconstruct access to the event, but they do not name that event itself. It is without temporal extension. The deconstruction of historical eras frees the matrix into which the event of presencing cuts synchronically, vertically. Furthermore, the reversals between economies do not concretize presencing as such. The event—the entry into mutual relations of everything that shows itself in one given moment—occurs *immediately*. It is what can be, and has always been, closest to us. Only the methodic access to it, the effort of wresting it from the phenomena and of introducing it into discourse, is necessarily *mediate*. This mediating function for the sake of a discursive retrieval is incumbent upon the categories. Strictly speaking then, these are only indirectly categories 'of presencing'—only in the sense of an objective, not a subjective, genitive. Heidegger seeks to recapture the *question* of being, but 'being itself' resists categorization and full grasp: the event joins presencing with absencing.

It follows that the closure is not in the least an ontophany. The 'end' of philosophy does not designate anything like the certitude that consciousness has at last made reality rational and appropriated it through the medium of history. It is on the contrary the hubris or injustice (*adikia*) of epochal principles to give the illusion of full intelligibility; but they are no agents, and their culmination or eschaton in technology universalizes nothing. Nor does full presence result from their disappearance, as if their withering led the event to complete possession of itself. We have seen that in spite of the awkwardness of the vocabulary the *Ereignis*, 'appropriation', is irreducible to the metaphysics of presence. To a phenomenology whose first step is descriptive, the principles appear rather like centers of gravity around which phenomena arrange themselves for a time. That excludes all speculation about progress. Since the starting point of this phenomenology is an entirely contingent fact, and since the unities it discovers are purely categorial, its endpoint cannot be anything noumenal. If Heidegger meant it as such, he would be committing the grossest 'undue transition' (*metabasis*) from the transcendental to the transcendent. Under the name of being, he seeks the condition of any entity in its entry into the economy where it has its place—not its natural, but its historical place. That name, being, which is a verb, therefore designates the self-manifestation of an entity out of and against absence. This is why it cannot be the name of a universal. There is entry into an economy, there is manifestation, only of this or that entity (which is not to say that the entry is also thinkable only in terms of entities; on the contrary, it is thinkable only in terms of the economies). *Alētheia* prevails over *lēthē* in the multitude of what occurs: multitude of this or that entity, of these or those entities, appearing, lingering, and withdrawing. What occurs is only the visible world, the network of relations between words, things, and actions, only the shifting affinities among phenomena as the folds are unfolded by critical reversals. Neither presence and its economies nor presencing and its event can be understood as anything but tenuous. If the epochal constellations as well as the self-manifestation on which they confer their momentary modality are always the constellations and the manifestation 'of entities', then to speak of presencing 'itself'—even without asking about its groundedness in those entities—is inevitably to speak of the transient.

Presencing—Heidegger's 'being'—is not present. All the more is it not omnipresent. Nor is it powerful or omnipotent. Although mysterious as hiding-showing, it is nothing divine. *It does not realize the theological idea.* And although it may be gathered from any and every entity, from every region or economy of entities, presencing is neither the total composite of things—extended with or without limits in time and space—nor the infinitesimal, simple part composing each thing, nor the cause of all things happening in the world, nor the first and necessary ground on which they depend. *It does not realize the cosmological ideas.* The problem of the whole and the parts, as well as that of causes and effects, is entirely linked to the question of the constitution—finite or infinite—of the world represented as an entity. Since the inner makeup of entities is not at issue, none of these antinomic ideas bears on presencing in any way. Lastly, although there is manifestation only for man, and although the non-cosmological concept of finitude has an 'existentialist' and therefore 'humanist' origin, presencing is nothing human and still less mental. It is a matter neither of consciousness nor of the will, nor of life, nor of the mind or one of its faculties, nor of any attribute through which philosophers have characterized the human entity. *It does not realize the anthropological idea.* Not legitimately reducible, even covertly, to any of the three traditional ideas from which metaphysicians have construed the infinite—God, World, Man—nor to their unity in the concept, presencing does not fall under the 'either-or' of the finite and the infinite. Together with the representation of the ideally infinite, its contrary, that of the really finite, also becomes unworkable. It would therefore be best not to risk suggesting a contrary to finitude in connection with presencing, but to deconstruct 'finitude', too, and to speak instead of what occurs—precisely of the event.

These reminders of the status of the categorial and of finitude are sufficient to refute idealism. But they are not enough to refute a last possible misunderstanding, the temptation to reduce 'being' to 'economy'.

5. *Heidegger's starting point and the question he puts to it—that is, the fact of technology and the* Seinsfrage—*may indeed be instructive concerning today's cultural situation in the West. But at what a price! You have certainly said that the sole issue Heidegger continually addressed was that of being. It is however all too obvious that the word 'being' is one you would rather avoid. Your stress on the 'economies' ends by altering that very issue. It substitutes the problematic clarity of a one-dimensional concept for a Heideggerian depth—as charged with ambiguities and obscurities as that depth may be. As far as we know, economies of presence have not prompted any battle of the giants, any gigantomachy. Your genealogy obfuscates once again the question intially raised by Parmenides and Aristotle. Instead of helping to overcome the forgottenness of being you aggravate it.*

—'Economy of presence' translates Heidegger's noun *Anwesenheit* and 'presencing' his verb *Anwesen.* The first is a set-concept, the second, an event-concept. Their difference is already contained in the duality of Hei-

degger's starting point and the question he puts to it. Phrasing that difference in terms of epochal economies allows one to bring out certain traits
that other words, too, may connote—but not as well. Positively, the concept of economy makes it possible to retrieve what some Presocratics and
Aristotle hinted at concerning being: the difference and the a priori. Negatively, it shows being's non-human and its mobile, non-stable character.

Difference. The economic order in which things are arranged at any given
moment is by definition transitory. Since these orders are discoverable and
definable only in relation to epochs, they come and go. Something present
receives a function and a place in them which vary epochally. For example,
an entity such as an academic institution is present in the economy of an age
in one way when it is situated at the intersection of a State bureaucracy,
ideological and political pressure groups, public funds, and national as well
as individual prestige. Such an institution betrays another function and
place, it is present in another way, when campus buildings bear the names of
the banker Mellon, of Rockwell armaments, Carnegie steel, and Westing-
house electronics. The first mode of presence is that of today's European
universities, the second, that of many American universities. A third mode
of presence would be the medieval, for instance, in which the university was
phenomenally located at the intersection of a migrant clergy, rural over-
population and poverty, the authority of one text and a dead language, and
the promotion of a single doctrine. These are just so many economies or
modalities of presence which *differ* from the entity they situate.

In the difference between entities and their beingness, 'being itself' does
not appear yet. Moreover, if the history this difference helps uncover is
indeed one of givens, it is a history of given strategies rather than of hard
data. The strategies—soft facts, because indissociable from interpretation—
have dates, which are those of the disjunctive moments that open and close
their viability. But the later Heidegger's starting point for the question of
being is not an entity. It is the predominance of a certain strategy today,
and in that sense a fact, for which he seeks the condition in the phenomenon of entry into presence: an ever-new entry, whatever the historical
arrangement may be into which it cuts. To speak of economies is not to
substitute structure for being but to set apart three levels in phenomena:
entitative, strategic, eventlike. This answer to the being-question, the
three-tiered temporal difference, is not then a one-dimensional concept
without depth.

To understand the difference in terms of the economies clearly does not
amount either to reissuing the ancient distinction between *ti* and *hoti*, or
essence and existence, as if modality of presence answered the question:
quid sit? what is it? and the event of presencing, the question: *an sit?* is it?
Economy does not add quiddity to event. If in itself the event that is *phusis*
were deprived of all economic-historical quality, if it were neutral in that
sense and stood in need of composition, then what Heidegger calls "the
entry into the event" could not put an end to epochal history, nor could

action become *kata phusin*, compliant with the event. The turning—the transition toward an economy whose *nomos* is only *phuein*—would lapse into absurdity, and the emancipation of the aletheiological constellations from principial rule, into impossibility. If the event designated the mere fact or act of being, Heidegger's decisive contribution to philosophy— namely, the understanding of being as time—would be done for. As developed earlier, he sought to reach that understanding first through ecstatic, then through historical-destinal temporality; but only the 'event' allowed him to answer the question: "What leads us to name time and being together?"[25] Only the 'there is'—literally, 'it gives'—allows for addressing time together with being. To speak of the temporality of being is therefore not to speak of the essence of an existent. The giving of the given, the simple 'there is', *differs* from the economies, but this difference is irreducible to that of *ti-hoti*, or *was-dass*. The originary duality cannot be a matter of composition. In discussing Parmenides and the noun-verb distinction contained in the participle, then again in analyzing the ontological difference, and lastly in connection with 'thing and world', each time it has appeared that retrieving an originary duality is rather a matter of thinking the identity of the non-identical. All the more is the event, although inseparable from the economies, both irreducible to and uncompoundable with them.

The a priori. The concept of economy of presencing repeats the a priori while dissociating it from cognitive issues. It had remained linked to these issues since its two births in antiquity and at the beginning of modernity. Its first birth occurred with Plato. In order to know that two wooden planks or two stones are of equal shape, we must possess a foreknowledge of what equality and identity are. Where does such preliminary knowledge come from (*Phaedo*)? Or again, where does knowledge of mathematical or geometrical principles come from so that simple maieutic questioning can make us discover it in ourselves (*Meno*)? Plato answers with the double speculative doctrine of the ideas and of recollection. The second birth of the a priori occurs with Kant. In order for us to know that, for example, all change follows the law of causation, we must produce in ourselves the concept of causality even before observing this or that incident of change. The judgment that links such an observed incident to its cause and categorizes it as an effect expresses a complex, synthetic knowledge. This knowing necessarily precedes experience, but it cannot be obtained by simple analysis of either the concept 'cause' or the concept 'change'. Such a judgment is not analytic, yet it is conceptual. It is not empirical, it is not generated from repeated experience, yet it amplifies our knowledge. The a priori results here not from a speculative but a critical construct of structures and their functions in subjectivity. From that apparatus arises a group of forms and notions whose pure conjunction renders these judgments possible. In Kant as in Plato, the a priori serves to give an account of how we can at all obtain universal and necessary knowledge. In antiquity as well as modernity, the a priori rests furthermore on the distinction—which it both justifies and bridges—between the sensible and the intelligible.

Third birth: even before handling a tool, examining a chemical compound, addressing others, we already understand that tools, objects, and others do not solicit the same type of behavior from us, that their modes of being are not the same. *Being and Time* analyzes the structure that makes such a pre-understanding of the regions of being possible. That pre-understanding is no longer a cognitive one. The first prejudice, the systematic precedence of knowing over all other activities, is thereby broken. Pre-understanding is now operative first and essentially in everyday comportment, which it diversifies according to regions and thus determines. With that focus on ordinary gestures falls, too, the separation between the sensible and the intelligible— the other unexamined assumption in all previous metaphysical investigations of the a priori. Later on, Heidegger discovers that pre-understanding has a history, that it articulates itself variously from one reversal to the next. In deconstructing the strategies of interaction, i.e., the epochal a priori that is an economy, the condition appears that in turn renders an epoch's pre-understanding possible: the event of presencing. The concept of economy therefore dissociates the a priori from any construct of intelligibles, whether one that constitutes a separate world or a subjective faculty. The analytic of economies locates the a priori neither beyond the visible realm in subsistent ideas nor underneath it in abiding concepts of the understanding. What determines a priori all relations among entities is their arrangement as it results from a crisis in history; the evanescent layout which is truth as *alētheia;* the mode of interaction in a given constellation of presence and absence—in short, an economy of presence. In Plato the a priori is a power of anamnesis and its condition, the separation between the two worlds; in Kant it is a power of synthesis and its condition, the separation between the two stems of knowledge. In Heidegger the a priori is economic and its condition no longer any separation, but the temporal difference between economy and event.

Just like its ancient and modern forebears, the phenomenological a priori is nothing in itself. An economy is only appearance, the fabric of relations according to which the ingredients of an era coalesce—not as givens for consciousness, but by acting systemically on one another. The concept of economy is crucial in order to exclude, with no appeal possible, not only any one-dimensional denotation of being in Heidegger, but also the lingering noumenal connotations whose seductive charms on many commentators, particularly in the United States, seem irresistible.

In his last public address, Heidegger assigned himself the task, already quoted, of "thinking being without regard for its groundedness in entities."[26] The temporal difference, hinging as it does on the economies and their categories, in no way contradicts that assignment. To understand being—event, *phuein,* presencing—via its economic traits is not to understand it in terms of any groundedness in entities, but in terms of beingness which, as a set of conditioning historical loci, 'grounds' nothing. If it should be objected that with "the entry into the event" "the history of being comes to its close"[27]—that with the discovery of the eventlike character of presencing the detour through the historical economies is no longer viable—the answer has to be that what draws to a close is *epochal* history. In the midst of what may be the technological turn, the requirement for thinking being as groundless remains, then, an anarchic economy.

This is, however, a requirement that has only indirectly to do with man.

Anti-humanism. Heidegger's equating metaphysics with humanism remains incomprehensible without the mediating concept of economy or some equivalent—mediating between the entity 'man' and the non-entity or no-thing 'being'. Man is the ordering principle whose representation has governed the modalities of presence ever since the Socratic turn, although representation as the mechanism of his ordering power was to become evident only later along the road. For a long period, that rule of man as well as that master device, representation, were able to remain hidden behind other shapes, notably those of a supreme entity whose attainment was the goal of Greek *paideia* as well as of the medieval *itinerarium mentis*. That rule and that device come unmasked with the modern *cogito* and triumph with the 'will to will' in the technological age. One should therefore not feel alarmed at risking the truism that man has been the epochal principle of all Western philosophy and civilization.

In a first sense, then, anti-humanism is a polemic stance which faces up to principial regimes so as to hasten their downfall and 'carry to term' a non-principial economy. Not that the methodic denial of man's master posture, for instance in the areas of today's social sciences in which anti-humanism was coined as a term, suffices to produce such a liberation. The theoretical turn away from anthropocentrism is only one condition for the possible thinking (being as time) of a possibility (anarchic economy). But one acts and thinks through possibilities, and no other concept suggests a radical, although perhaps inconspicuous, economic mutation as precisely as the concept of anti-humanism.

The polemic stance is however only the consequence, whether or not acknowledged by those social scientists, of the two possibilities mentioned. They are intertwined. If anti-humanism turns into a viable path for *thinking*, it does so by virtue of an *economy* whose turn that thinking echoes or responds to. The contours of the anarchic order of things which is today a possibility have been traced by the categories of transition. They do not delineate a safer dwelling for man, one in which everything beautiful and noble that men have created in history finally will be protected and preserved; but they do draft the end of the modes of presencing in which one referent reigns supreme. The ambivalence of technology—both climax and fulfillment of anthropocentrism, its fulfillment *because* its climax—therefore announces, at least to the gaze of deconstructive phenomenology, the destitution of man, the legislator of presence, that is, of man as representor. To say that metaphysics is essentially humanistic is to say that, with growing determination through the ages, representation is what confers on things their meaning, their place, their being. All that is or can be is there for representational man. The no longer polemic, but economic, concept of anti-humanism already subverts this distribution—which is inseverably theoretical and practical—by the master's hand. The possible shift in presencing would make masterly handling an awkward move.

The economic concept of anti-humanism takes root, however, in yet another one due to which the senses of anti-humanism come to parallel those of the three-tiered temporal difference. Indeed, presencing as an event is nothing human. To say a thing arrives in its world is not to say that man's initiative brings it there. On the contrary, as 'mortal', he is to be counted among the systemic constituents—gods/mortals/sky/earth or, following a different cut, things/words/actions—that come forth from absence. This is obviously neither to say that man is the author of nothing, that his ancient titles of demiurge through the goodness of the Demiurge, and of creator through the grace of the Creator, are 'false'. The categories of transition seek to retain something of phenomena that belongs to another problematic and that has nothing to do with human 'creativity', either by sustaining or contradicting it. The event is non-human, as time is in Presocratic *phuesthai*.

The polemic concept of anti-humanism, in social theory as well as in thinking, is conditioned by the economic concept and this, in turn, by the eventlike. Perhaps the term 'anti-humanism' should be reserved for the first of these three, while the second should be spoken of as negation of anthropocentrism, and the third as a-humanism.

Motility. It will be recalled that the economies, since they assign each thing its site or world, can be called 'poetic', or better, 'poietic'. They order the *topoi,* the places, where each phenomenon is what it is. Action, too, is to be understood in this topological sense. The universal and necessary conditions for action reside in the constellations as they come about and undo themselves. That literal sense of 'poetic', according to René Char, tells us what we are: "In your essence you are incessantly a poet."[28] In the age of transition—René Char would say: at the "ford"—this making, this *poiēsis* of modes in presencing, turns and becomes irreducible to any archic figure. To the question, What is to be done? the poet responds with another question: "Why should this ford of philosophy be a single stone?"[29] In the age of closure, economic *poiein* becomes multiple, mobile. As such, it precedes action and determines it: "Poetry no longer punctuates action; it moves ahead of action to show it the motile path."[30]

A HEIDEGGER BIBLIOGRAPHY, WITH ABBREVIATIONS USED IN THE NOTES AND INDEXES

I. Titles in German

(Note: Except for SdU, this list includes only the titles of Heidegger's works published prior to completion of the original French version of this book, i.e., 1981).

EdD   *Aus der Erfahrung des Denkens*. Pfullingen: G. Neske, 1954, 27 pp.

EiM   *Einführung in die Metaphysik*. Tübingen: M. Niemeyer, 1953, 157 pp.

FD   *Die Frage nach dem Ding*. Tübingen: M. Niemeyer, 1962, VII, 189 pp.

FS   *Frühe Schriften*. Frankfurt: V. Klostermann, 1972, XII, 386 pp.

Fw   *Der Feldweg*. Frankfurt: V. Klostermann, 1953, 7 pp.

Gel   *Gelassenheit*. Pfullingen: G. Neske, 1959, 74 pp.

GA 9   *Gesamtausgabe*, Vol. 9: *Wegmarken*. Frankfurt: V. Klostermann, 1976, X, 487 pp.

GA 21   *Gesamtausgabe*, Vol. 21: *Logik. Die Frage nach der Wahrheit*. Frankfurt: V. Klostermann, 1976, VIII, 420 pp.

GA 24   *Gesamtausgabe*, Vol. 24: *Die Grundprobleme der Phänomenologie*. Frankfurt: V. Klostermann, 1975, X, 473 pp.

GA 25   *Gesamtausgabe*, Vol. 25: *Phänomenologische Interpretation von Kants Kritik der reinen Vernunft*. Frankfurt: V. Klostermann, 1977, XII, 436 pp.

GA 26   *Gesamtausgabe*, Vol. 26: *Metaphysische Anfangsgründe der Logik im Ausgang von Leibniz*. Frankfurt: V. Klostermann, 1978, VI, 292 pp.

GA 55   *Gesamtausgabe*, Vol. 55: *Heraklit*. Frankfurt: V. Klostermann, 1979, XII, 406 pp.

Heb   *Hebel der Hausfreund*. Pfullingen: G. Neske, 1957, 39 pp.

Her   *Heraklit* (seminar held in collaboration with Eugen Fink). Frankfurt: V. Klostermann, 1970, 261 pp.

Höl   *Erläuterungen zu Hölderlins Dichtung*. Frankfurt: V. Klostermann, 1951, 144 pp.

Hw   *Holzwege*. Frankfurt: V. Klostermann, 1950, 345 pp.

IuD   *Identität und Differenz*. Pfullingen: G. Neske, 1957, 76 pp.

KPM   *Kant und das Problem der Metaphysik* (4th, augmented ed.). Frankfurt: V. Klostermann, 1973, 268 pp.

KR   *Die Kunst und der Raum* (bilingual ed.). St. Gallen: Erker, 1969, 26 pp.

MHG   *Martin Heidegger im Gespräch* (interview with Richard Wisser). Freiburg/Br.: K. Alber, 1970, 77 pp.

N I   *Nietzsche*. Pfullingen: G. Neske, 1961, Vol. I, 662 pp.

N II   *Nietzsche*. Pfullingen: G. Neske, 1961, Vol. II, 493 pp.

Phän   "Über das Zeitverständnis in der Phänomenologie und im Denken der Seinsfrage," in *Phänomenologie—lebendig oder tot?* Karlsruhe: Badenia, 1969, p. 47.

Rc   *Der Ursprung des Kunstwerkes* (Reclam edition). Stuttgart: Reclam, 1960, 125 pp.

SD   *Zur Sache des Denkens*. Tübingen: M. Niemeyer, 1969, 92 pp.

SAF   *Schellings Abhandlung Über das Wesen der menschlichen Freiheit*.
         Tübingen: M. Niemeyer, 1971, IX, 237 pp.
SdU   *Die Selbstbehauptung der deutschen Universität*. Frankfurt: V.
         Klostermann, 1983, 43 pp.
Sp   "Nur noch ein Gott kann uns retten" (interview), in *Der Spiegel*.
         Hamburg, May 31, 1976, pp. 193–219.
SvG   *Der Satz vom Grund*. Pfullingen: G. Neske, 1957, 211 pp.
SZ   *Sein und Zeit* (8th edition). Tübingen: M. Niemeyer, 1957, XI, 437 pp.
TK   *Die Technik und die Kehre*. Pfullingen: G. Neske, 1962, 47 pp.
US   *Unterwegs zur Sprache*. Pfullingen: G. Neske, 1959, 270 pp.
VA   *Vortrüge und Aufsätze*. Pfullingen: G. Neske, 1954, 284 pp.
VS   *Vier Seminare*. Frankfurt: V. Klostermann, 1977, 151 pp.
VwR   "Vorwort," in William J. Richardson, *Heidegger: Through Phenomenology
         to Thought*. The Hague: M. Nijhoff, 1963, pp. IX–XXIII.
WhD   *Was heisst Denken?* Tübingen: M. Niemeyer, 1954, 175 pp.
Wm   *Wegmarken*. Frankfurt: V. Klostermann, 1967, VIII, 398 pp.
WP   *Was ist das—die Philosophie?* Pfullingen: G. Neske, 1956, 31 pp.

II. Titles of English Translations

(Note: Abbreviations are given only for works quoted. These abbreviations are
arranged alphabetically. Works not quoted are also listed, alphabetized according to
the first noun in their title. This bibliography follows the one compiled by Keith
Hoeller in R. W. Shahan and J. N. Mohanty, eds., *Thinking About Being: Aspects
of Heidegger's Thought*, Norman: University of Oklahoma Press, 1984, pp. 221–
230. I thank both the compiler and the publisher for their authorization to make use
of it.)

AaS   "Art and Space." Translated by Charles H. Seibert. *Man and World* 6
         (1973):3–8.
         "The Age of the World View." Translated by Marjorie Grene. *Measure* 2
         (1951):269–284. See QCT.
BPP   *Basic Problems of Phenomenology*. Translated by Albert Hofstadter.
         Bloomington: Indiana University Press, 1982, 396 pp.
BT   *Being and Time*. Translated by John Macquarrie and Edward Robinson.
         New York: Harper & Row, 1962, 589 pp.
BWr   *Basic Writings*. Edited by David F. Krell. New York: Harper & Row,
         1977, 397 pp.
         "The Concept of Time in the Science of History." Translated by Harry S.
         Taylor and Hans W. Uffelmann. *Journal of the British Society for
         Phenomenology* 9 (1978):3–10.
         "The Course of My Life." Translated by Therese Schrynemakers. In
         Martin Heidegger: A First Introduction to His Philosophy. Pittsburgh:
         Duquesne University Press, 1965, pp. 1–2.
Disc   "A Discussion Between Ernst Cassirer and Martin Heidegger." Translated
         by Francis Slade. In *The Existentialist Tradition: Selected Writings*,
         edited by Nino Langiulli. Garden City: Doubleday-Anchor, 1971, pp.
         192–203.
DTh   *Discourse on Thinking*. Translated by J. M. Anderson and E. H. Freund.
         New York: Harper & Row, 1966, 93 pp.
EB   *Existence and Being*. Edited by Werner Brock. Chicago: Regnery-Gateway,
         1949, 369 pp.

"Editor's Foreword" to Edmund Husserl, *The Phenomenology of Internal Time Consciousness*. Translated by James S. Churchill. Bloomington: Indiana University Press, 1964, pp. 15–16.

EGT   *Early Greek Thinking*. Translated by David Farrell Krell and Frank Capuzzi. New York: Harper & Row, 1975, 129 pp.

Elucidations of Hölderlin's Poetry. Translated by Keith Hoeller. University Park: Pennsylvania State University Press, forthcoming.

EPh   *The End of Philosophy*. Translated by Joan Stambaugh. New York: Harper & Row, 1973, 110 pp.

ER   *The Essence of Reasons*. Translated by Terrence Malick. Evanston: Northwestern University Press, 1969, 144 pp.

"Eventide on Reichenau." Translated by W. J. Richardson. In *Heidegger: Through Phenomenology to Thought*. The Hague: Martinus Nijhoff, 1963, p. 1.

German Existentialism. Edited and translated by Dagobert D. Runes. New York: Philosophical Library, 1965, 58 pp.

"Hebel—The Friend of the House." Translated by Bruce Foltz and Michael Heim. *Contemporary German Philosophy*, vol. 3. University Park and London, 1983, pp. 89–101.

H   *Heraclitus Seminar 1966/67* (with Eugen Fink). Translated by C. H. Seibert. Alabama: University of Alabama Press, 1979, 169 pp.

HCE   *Hegel's Concept of Experience*. Edited by J. Glenn Gray. New York: Harper & Row, 1970, 155 pp.

"A Heidegger Seminar on Hegel's *Differenzschrift*." Translated by William Lovett. *Southwestern Journal of Philosophy* 11/3 (1980):9–45.

"Heidelberg Inaugural Address." Translated by H. Seigfried. *Man and World*, III(1970):4–5.

History of the Concept of Time: Prolegomena. Translated by Theodore Kisiel. Bloomington: Indiana University Press, 1985.

"Hölderlin and the Essence of Poetry." Translated by Paul de Man. *Quarterly Review of Literature* 10 (1959):79–94.

Ho   "Homeland." Translated by T. F. O'Meara. *Listening* 6 (1971):231–238.

IaD   *Identity and Difference*. Translated by Joan Stambaugh. New York: Harper & Row, 1969, 146 pp.

IM   *An Introduction to Metaphysics*. Translated by Ralph Manheim. New Haven: Yale University Press, 1959, 214 pp.

IPh   "The Idea of Phenomenology." Translated by Thomas J. Sheehan. *Listening* 12 (1977):111–121.

ISp   "Only A God Can Save Us Now" (interview with *Der Spiegel*). Translated by D. Schendler. *Graduate Faculty Philosophy Journal* 6 (1977):5–27. This interview has also been translated as " 'Only a God Can Save Us': *Der Spiegel*'s Interview with Martin Heidegger." Translated by M. P. Alter and J. D. Caputo. *Philosophy Today* 20 (1976):267–284.

IW   "Martin Heidegger: An Interview" (with R. Wisser). Translated by V. Guagliardo and R. Pambrun. *Listening* 6 (1971):34–40.

Kpm   *Kant and the Problem of Metaphysics*. Translated by James S. Churchill. Bloomington: Indiana University Press, 1962, 255 pp.

KTB   "Kant's Thesis about Being." Translated by Ted E. Klein and William E. Pohl. *Southwestern Journal of Philosophy* 4 (1973):7–33.

"Language." Translated by Thomas J. Sheehan. *Philosophy Today* 20 (1976):291.

"A Letter from Heidegger." Translated by William J. Richardson. In *Heidegger and the Quest for Truth*, edited by Manfred S. Frings. Chicago: Quadrangle, 1968, pp. 17–21.

"A Letter from Martin Heidegger." Translated by Zygmunt Adamczewski.
In *Heidegger and the Path of Thinking*, edited by John C. Sallis.
Pittsburgh: Duquesne University Press, 1970, pp. 9–11.

"Letter on Humanism." Translated by Edgar Lohner. In *Philosophy in the
Twentieth Century*, edited by William Barrett and Henry D. Aiken. New
York: Random House, 1962, vol. 3, pp. 270–302. See also BWr.

"Letter to Albert Borgmann." Translated by Albert Borgmann. *Philosophy
East and West* 20 (1970): 22.

"Letter to F. Joseph Smith." Translated by F. Joseph Smith. In his *Essays
on Heidegger,* forthcoming.

Logic: The Question of Truth. Translated by Thomas J. Sheehan.
Bloomington: Indiana University Press, forthcoming.

Mar   "From the Last Marburg Lecture Course." Translated by J. Macquarrie.
In *The Future of Our Religious Past*, edited by J. M. Robinson. New
York: Harper & Row, 1971, pp. 312–332.

"Martin Heidegger: A Recollection." Translated by Hans Seigfried. *Man
and World* 3 (1970): 3–4.

Martin Heidegger in Conversation. Edited by Richard Wisser, translated by
B. Srinivasa Murthy. New Delhi: Arnold Heinemann, 1977.

"Martin Heidegger's Zollikon Seminars." Translated by Brian Kenny.
Review of Existential Psychology & *Psychiatry* 16 (1978–79): 7–20.

"In Memory of Max Scheler (1982)." Translated by Thomas Sheehan. In
Heidegger: The Man and The Thinker, edited by Thomas Sheehan.
Chicago: Precedent Publishing, 1981, pp. 159–160.

MSC   "Messkirch's Seventh Centennial." Translated by Thomas J. Sheehan.
Listening 8 (1973): 40–57.

Metaphysical Foundations of Logic. Translated by Michael Heim.
Bloomington: Indiana University Press, 1984, 256 pp.

"Modern Natural Science and Technology." Translated by John Sallis.
Research in Phenomenology 7 (1977): 1–4.

N i   *Nietzsche I: The Will to Power as Art.* Edited and translated by David
Farrell Krell. New York: Harper & Row, 1979, 263 pp.

Nietzsche II: The Eternal Recurrence of the Same. Edited and translated
by David Farrell Krell. New York: Harper & Row, 1984, 289 pp.

Nietzsche III: Will to Power as Knowledge and as Metaphysics. Edited by
David Farrell Krell, translated by Joan Stambaugh. New York: Harper
& Row, forthcoming.

N iv   *Nietzsche IV: Nihilism.* Edited by David Farrell Krell, translated by Frank
A. Capuzzi. New York: Harper & Row, 1982, 301 pp.

"Nietzsche as Metaphysician." Translated by Joan Stambaugh. In
Nietzsche: A Collection of Critical Essays, edited by Robert C.
Solomon. Garden City: Doubleday-Anchor, 1973, pp. 105–113.

NOT   "The Problem of Non-Objectifying Thinking and Speaking." In *Philosophy
and Religion*, edited by Jerry Gill. Minneapolis: Burgess, 1968, pp. 59–
65.

OTB   *On Time and Being.* Translated by Joan Stambaugh. New York: Harper &
Row, 1972, 84 pp.

OWL   *On the Way to Language.* Translated by Peter D. Hertz and Joan
Stambaugh. New York: Harper & Row, 1971, 200 pp.

Pa   "The Pathway." Translated by Thomas F. O'Meara. *Listening* 8 (1973): 32–
39.

PDT   "Plato's Doctrine of Truth." Translated by John Barlow. In *Philosophy in
the Twentieth Century*, edited by William Barrett and Henry D. Aiken.
New York: Random House, 1962, vol. 3, pp. 251–270.

PG   "The Principle of Ground." Translated by Keith Hoeller, *Man and World* 7 (1974):207–222.

Phy   "On the Being and Conception of *Physis* in Aristotle's *Physics* B,1." Translated by Thomas J. Sheehan. *Man and World* 9 (1976):219–270.

PLT   *Poetry, Language, Thought*. Translated by Albert Hofstadter. New York: Harper & Row, 1971, 229 pp.

Pr   "Preface." Translated by William J. Richardson. In *Heidegger Through Phenomenology to Thought*, by William J. Richardson. The Hague: Martinus Nijhoff, 1963, pp. viii–xxiii.

PR   "The Problem of Reality in Modern Philosophy." Translated by Philip J. Bossert. *The Journal of the British Society for Phenomenology* 4 (1973):64–71.

PTh   *The Piety of Thinking: Essays by Martin Heidegger*. Translated by James G. Hart and John C. Maraldo. Bloomington: Indiana University Press, 1976, 212 pp.

QB   *The Question of Being*. Translated by William Kluback and Jean T. Wilde. New York: Twayne, 1958, 109 pp.

QCT   *The Question Concerning Technology and Other Essays*. Translated by William Lovitt. New York: Harper & Row, 1977, 182 pp.

     "On My Relation to National Socialism." *Semiotext(e)* 4, no. 2 (1982):253–254.

SA   "The Self-Assertion of the German University" and "The Rectorate 1933–34: Facts and Thoughts." Translated by Karsten Harries. *Review of Metaphysics* 38 (1985):467–502.

     Signposts: 1912–1976. Edited by Thomas Sheehan and Robert Crease. Totowa: Rowman and Allanheld, forthcoming.

ST   *Schelling's Treatise on Human Freedom (1809)*. Translated by Joan Stambaugh. Athens: Ohio University Press, forthcoming.

     "The Staiger-Heidegger Correspondence." Translated by Arthur Grugan. *Man and World* 4 (1981):291–300.

     "Thoughts." Translated by Keith Hoeller. *Philosophy Today* 21 (1976):286–290.

     "The Turning." Translated by Kenneth R. Maly. *Research in Phenomenology* 1 (1971):3–16. See QCT.

     "The Understanding of Time in Phenomenology and in the Thinking of the Being Question." Translated by Thomas Sheehan and Frederick Elliston, *Southwestern Journal of Philosophy* 10/2 (1979):199–201.

WCT   *What Is Called Thinking?* Translated by Fred D. Wieck and J. Glenn Gray. New York: Harper & Row, 1968, 244 pp.

WGM   "The Way Back into the Ground of Metaphysics." Translated by Walter Kaufmann. In *Existentialism from Dostoevsky to Sartre*, edited by Walter Kaufmann. New York: New American Library, 1975, pp. 265–279.

WNZ   "Who Is Nietzsche's Zarathustra?" Translated by Bernd Magnus. *Review of Metaphysics* 20 (1967):411–431.

WPh   *What Is Philosophy?* Translated by William Kluback and Jean T. Wilde. New York: Twayne, 1958, 97 pp.

WTh   *What Is a Thing?* Translated by W. B. Barton and Vera Deutsch. Chicago: Regnery, 1967, 310 pp.

     "Why Do I Stay in the Provinces?" (1934) Translated by Thomas J. Sheehan. *Listening* 12 (1977):122–125.

NOTES

Introduction

§1. Deconstructing Action

1. Sp 206/ISp 16. Although I refer in each citation both to the German edition and to the published English translation, I follow the latter only exceptionally. I use double quotes for all quotations, whether identified directly or only indirectly, single quotes for conventions, emphasis, etc.

2. SvG 123 f.

3. VA 25/QCT 18.

4. N II 428/EPh 25.

5. KPM 195/Kpm 206.

6. KPM 237 f./Kpm 253.

7. This concept enters even less here into the classical theories of the best State; cf. Plato, *The Republic* (558c), and Aristotle, *The Politics* (1302 b 28 ff.), who both characterized as ἄναρχος the unjust form of government that democracy was in their eyes.

8. Immanuel Kant, "What Is Enlightenment?" (A 481), in Lewis White Beck, ed., *On History* (Indianapolis, 1963), p. 3.

9. The two quotes are from VA 133 f./BWr 349.

10. Wm 245/QB 93. On "deconstruction," *Abbau*, cf. GA 24 31/BPP 22 f. and VS 133.

11. "Perhaps patient meditation and painstaking investigation . . . are the wanderings of a way of thinking that is faithful and attentive to *the world that is ineluctably to come and which proclaims itself at present*, beyond the closure of knowing," Jacques Derrida, *Of Grammatology*, trans. G. C. Spivak (Baltimore, 1976), p. 4 (trans. modified, emphasis added).

12. SvG 73.

13. SZ 39/BT 63 (emphasis added).

14. It is with reference to these epochal principles that I should like to read the lines from Novalis quoted by Heidegger: "Would the supreme principle contain, in the task it imposes on us, the supreme paradox? Would it be a position which never allows us any rest, forever attracting and repelling us, no sooner understood than always rendering itself unintelligible again? A position that ceaselessly prods our activity—without ever exhausting it, without ever becoming habitual?" (quoted SvG 30).

15. Wm 183/BWr 231.

16. VA 229/EGT 78. Cf. "Essential thinking is an acting" (Wm 106/EB 359).

§2. Theory of the Texts

17. VS 73. Cf. below, ch. 12, n. 24.

18. The two quotations are from EdD 23/PLT 12, a text written in 1947, the first in which Heidegger speaks of "the topology of being."

19. Understanding, *Verständnis*, is to be taken "in the originary sense of *Vorstehen*: to be standing before, to be on a par with, to be of a stature to sustain that before which one finds oneself" (VS 72, cf., SZ 143/BT 183).

20. VS 73.

21. SdU 15 f./SA 476 f.

22. SdU 18/SA 479. This reading of Heidegger is defended most coherently in the article by Karsten Harries, "Heidegger as a Political Thinker," *Review of Metaphysics* XXIX (June, 1976):642–669, repr. in *Heidegger and Modern Philosophy*, ed. Michael Murray (New Haven and London, 1978), pp. 304–328. That the structure of "resolve" in BT implies a need for authority appears highly debatable to me. Even those who find such a reading convincing would still have to acknowledge what in 1953 Jürgen Habermas called a transformation in the "quality

of appeal" between BT and IM. In BT, writes Habermas, "Heidegger still exalted the quasi-religious decision of the private, self-individuated existence as finite autonomy," while the praise of power and violence was only a momentary "fascist coloration" of the subsequent discovery of "the history of being," Jürgen Habermas, *Philosophisch-politische Profile* (Frankfurt, 1971), pp. 67–75, trans. Dale Ponikvar, "Martin Heidegger. On the Publication of Lectures from the Year 1935," in *Graduate Faculty Philosophy Journal*, VI, 2 (Fall, 1977):155–164. What makes for this tendency in reading BT is a voluntarist interpretation of *Entschlossenheit*. I will return later to the problem of the will (see below, sec. 42). But to convince oneself of the weakness of this starting point it is enough to see Henri Birault, for example, sustain with at least equal cogency that *Entschlossenheit* prefigures the later notion of *Gelassenheit*, *Heidegger et l'expérience de la pensée* (Paris, 1978), p. 519. This latter reading can at least avail itself of an explicit affirmation in Wm 94/BWr 138 as well as in the recently published lectures on Parmenides (1942–43), in which Heidegger opposes the conceptual cluster *Entschlossenheit/areta/alētheia/aidōs/Entborgenheit* to the cluster *Entschlossenheit/will/subject* (GA 54 111). Does the same concept in BT yield both the call to service and the call to letting-be?

23. Karl Jaspers, *Notizen zu Martin Heidegger* (Munich, 1978), p. 183. See also *Philosophische Autobiographie* (new ed., Munich, 1977), pp. 92–111. These two publications continue a debate formerly opened by Georg Lukács and Theodor Adorno and summarized by Beda Allemann, "Martin Heidegger und die Politik," in *Heidegger, Perspektiven zur Deutung seines Werks*, ed. Otto Pöggeler (Cologne, 1969), pp. 246–260. It has been taken up more recently in slightly different terms by Jürgen Habermas, who now opposes enlightenment to the "new right," a distinction which for him covers that between modernism (whose spokesman is Kant) and post-modernism (one of whose spokesmen is Heidegger). This typology becomes cruder still when rationality and communication are described as modern enlightened ideas, whereas today's "young conservatives" (Nietzschean, Heideggerian, French), "old conservatives" (Aristotelian, Straussian) and "neo-conservatives" (early Wittgenstein, late Gottfried Benn) stand accused of identifying modernism and nihilism, state intervention and totalitarianism, anti-militarism and sympathy for terrorism. . . . In writing he has formulated some of these criticisms in a summary treatment of the late Adorno and Heidegger, *Theorie des kommunikativen Handelns*, 2 vols. (Frankfurt, 1981)—for instance vol. I, pp. 516 ff. My earlier remarks about enlightenment may suffice at this point to suggest how untenable these facile disjunctions and amalgamations are.

24. Harries, op. cit., p. 669.

25. H. Birault, op. cit., p. 74.

26. "Firmness of the will" and "clearness of the heart" are the themes of the funeral eulogy delivered by Heidegger in 1933 for Leo Schlageter, G. Schneeberger, *Nachlese zu Heidegger* (Bern, 1962), p. 48.

27. Ibid., pp. 63 f. and 136.

28. The first position is more common; see, for example, Ernst Tugendhat, *Der Wahrheitsbegriff bei Husserl und Heidegger* (Berlin, 1967), p. 288. The second position, that of Gerold Prauss, *Erkennen und Handeln in Heideggers "Sein und Zeit"* (Freiburg, 1977), is undoubtedly more difficult to defend. In any case, Prauss presents it only as complementary to the first, ibid., pp. 30 f. The third is most in conformity with Heidegger's intention; see for example Otto Pöggeler, "Einleitung," in Pöggeler, ed., *Heidegger*, op. cit., p. 34.

29. Wm 145/BWr 193.

30. Cf. BT, sec. 69. The statements in this important section squarely contradict those made about "knowledge of the world," sec. 13. In this latter text, theoretical knowledge is the result of a suspension of *Besorgen:* "If knowing is to be possible as a way of determining entities given as objects by observing them, then there must first be a *deficiency* in our concernful dealings with the world" (SZ 61/BT 88). But this same conception of the genesis of ϑεωρεῖν from a suspension of manipulation is criticized in the other text: "It would be tempting to characterize the changeover from 'practical' circumspective manipulating, using and so forth, to 'theoretical' exploration in the following way: pure looking at entities is something that emerges when concern *holds back* from any kind of manipulation. What is decisive in the 'genesis' of the theoretical attitude would then lie in the *disappearance* of praxis. . . . However, the discontinuance of a specific manipulation in our concernful dealings does not simply leave the guiding circumspection behind as a remainder" (SZ 357/BT 409).

31. Wm 146/BWr 194, cf. VA 55 f./QCT 167.

32. SZ 358/BT 409.

33. The inauthentic project of existence is marked by a double reduction: coexistent beings, that is to say, others, become "objects" of concern (*Besorgen*) rather than of solicitude (*Fürsorge*, SZ 122/BT 159). Concern finds itself in turn reduced to the "mathematical project" as an existentiell a priori (SZ 362/BT 414). Through this double reduction, the three types of entities mentioned become undifferentiated, indifferent. The world is then the endless accumulation of the same, the addition of products detached from their context (*entweltlicht*, SZ 177/BT 221). Authentic totalization, on the contrary, "lets others be" and "shatters all one's tenaciousness in whatever existence one has reached" (SZ 298 and 264/BT 344 and 308). It is clear that inauthentic totalization here prefigures "calculative thinking," and authentic totalization the releasement (*Gelassenheit*) necessary to "meditative thinking" (Gel 15 and 25/DTh 46 and 54). Consequently, the later concept of technology does not have its root in the analyses of technique in BT, but in those of the inauthentic project of existentiell totalization. Technique still appears harmless here, whereas the traits that—dissociated from any existentiell project—later apply to worldwide technology, such as quantification, standardization, "one-dimensionality," etc., in BT characterize inauthenticity.

34. In BT there are two lines of reasoning about the "primordial" or "originary self" that once again contradict each other flagrantly. On one hand, "the originary phenomenon" (SZ 129/BT 167) is the "they," *das Man*. Authenticity can then only be the result of an existentiell modification of this primordial "they-self." But in other texts, the situation is exactly the reverse: "inauthenticity has as its ground possible authenticity" (SZ 259/BT 303). Here it is the authentic self that is originary, primordial. On this issue, one can even quote two literally contradictory statements: "The authentic self . . . can be only an existentiell modification of the 'they', which has been defined as an essential existential" (SZ 130/BT 168). Compare this with: "The 'they' . . . is an existentiell modification of the authentic self" (SZ 317/BT 365). The first type of argument is the one that predominates in BT (see also SZ 179, 267, 268/BT 224, 312, 313). On these difficulties as a whole, see the article by Joan Stambaugh, "Authenticity and Inauthenticity in 'Being and Time'," *Research in Phenomenology* VII (1977):153–161. For us, what counts is that in the period of BT, the question of the possibility of a technological domination of nature and its roots in *Dasein* not only remains unsolved but is not even clearly raised: is technological praxis the result of the techniques of scientific research, of the mathematical project as an a priori of inauthentic existentiell totalization, of the "they" as primordial existential structure, or again of a certain historical turn, the "decontextualization" (*Entweltlichung*) effected by Descartes (cf. BT secs. 6, 19–21, 43)? Whichever of these four answers is chosen, none of them allows one to say, as Heidegger later does, that "the modern natural sciences have their roots in the development of the essence of modern technique, and not the reverse" (MHG 72/IW 37). This is further evidence that the most decisive concepts, still fluid in BT, receive their precise denotation only when read in the light of the later writings.

35. EiM 152/IM 199. In 1966, driven to defend these lines, Heidegger opposes the concept of "technology" they contain to his later concept of *Gestell* (Sp 204 f./ISp 16). But these belated explanations raise more questions than they answer:
—Why was this passage not delivered orally although it stood in the manuscript of 1935? Because of "the imbeciles, stool pigeons, and spies" in the auditorium, says Heidegger. Does Heidegger want to give this parenthesis, thirty years later, an anti-Nazi ring that would have provoked an informer? Does the line contain a protest against National Socialism?
—In context, the parenthesis hardly sounds like a criticism: in 1935 Heidegger still trusts that if modern man can come to grips with technology it will be through National Socialism. Then how far did his disillusionment really go when he resigned from the university rectorate a year earlier? Does the line contain some form of allegiance to National Socialism?
—In 1935, technique, as I have said, is not yet seen in the context of Western metaphysics, but rather in that of authenticity. The later notion of *Gestell*, then, depoliticizes technology, since man's encounter with it is no longer thematized in the context of political forces. So, does the line perhaps hint at a relationship between technology and fascism which Heidegger would never take up again?
Protest, allegiance, and an implicit charge that technology is the hand of fascism cannot be meant at the same time. The basic ambiguity in Heidegger's comment on his earlier remarks lies in the understanding of technology. His attempt to make these lines express some amalgam of the three positions above is contradictory. One cannot praise National Socialism for allowing control of technology and at the same time equate National Socialism with "Americanism" and "the Communist movement" as being determined by "planetary technology." In

1935 National Socialism was said to possess an inner truth and greatness because of a potentiality that neither Americanism nor Communism could offer. The same line which in 1935 opposed National Socialism to planetary technology is used in 1966 to claim a fundamental identity between National Socialism and global technology.

36. EiM 34/IM 45. The description of what is happening in America and Russia recalls the very terms of the passage on inauthentic totalization in BT quoted above (note 33): "In America and Russia this development grew into the boundless etcetera of indifference and always-the-sameness—so much so that the quantitative took on a quality of its own" (EiM 35/IM 46).

37. Hw 102 f./QCT 152 f.

38. "Ways, not works." This epigraph is all that was left for Heidegger to formulate, shortly before his death, in lieu of a projected preface to the complete edition, GA.

39. SZ 263/BT 307.

40. "Possibility as an existential is the most originary and ultimate positive way of characterizing *Dasein* ontologically" (SZ 144/BT 183).

41. SZ 38/BT 63.

42. SZ 250/BT 294.

43. This opposition was first introduced by William Richardson, *Heidegger: Through Phenomenology to Thought* (The Hague, 1963), p. 22; see the reservations expressed by Heidegger in his prefatory letter, ibid., pp. xxii f.

44. SD 44/OTB 41.

45. N II 486/EPh 79. This extreme formulation should be tempered in the following way: what draws to a close in the technological age is the history of epochs, but not, of course, the history of presencing.

46. The first division of Henri Birault's remarkable work cited above—"Une introduction kantienne à la question de l'être" (pp. 45–353)—testifies, in its own way, to the continuity between Kant and Heidegger that I have been defending in this Introduction. It is regrettable, however, that for the most part Birault's book was composed prior to the publication of SD (this is suggested by, among other things, his observations about SvG and US, p. 394, and about the lecture "Time and Being," p. 452). This particular circumstance renders many passages in the second part obsolete from their very date of publication. Indeed, Birault uses expressions such as "ontico-ontological difference," "*Es gibt*," "unconcealment," "*epochē*," "proximity," "correspondence," *without ever even suggesting that with the lecture "Time and Being," these phrases cease to be applicable to the constellations of presencing incipient with technology,* and that other terms—"world and thing," "favor," "event," "clearing," "fourfold," "thinking"—must be substituted for them (see below, secs. 35–40, "The transitional categories"). Quoting SD only incidentally (pp. 476, 502 f., 506, 548—citations used only to illustrate points established from earlier writings), and not reading Heidegger backward, Birault seems to ignore the hypothesis of closure, although it was clearly adumbrated since 1946 in the concept of "eschatology of being" (Hw 301 f./EGT 18). This entails a confusion between the two senses of "concealment" in Heidegger: concealment as *lēthē*, an integral part of *alētheia*, is not clearly distinguished from concealment as *epochē*. Now, with the metaphysical closure, the second mode of concealment comes to an end; in this consequence lies the entire import, and possibly the sole content, of the hypothesis of closure. To speak, for example, of "the *epochē* as the draw and withdrawal of being" (the title of page 547, see the table of contents), is clearly to attribute to the *epochē* what belongs to *alētheia*. If, "for the thinking that enters into the *Ereignis*, the history of being is at an end" (SD 44/OTB 41), then it cannot be claimed that "the epoch of being is nothing other than the untruth, the mystery, the obscurity in being: a measure of darkness in the heart of the light" (p. 548). Since this confusion between the *epochal* withdrawal and the essential, *aletheiological* withdrawal of being is frequent in the literature, I want to stress the point here. Quoting a text from "On the Essence of Truth" about *alētheia*, Birault comments: "Untruth guarantees truth its essential origin and its essential element." Granted. But this does not entitle him to go on to say: "Untruth is therefore the *epochē* or suspension of truth" (p. 499). The first untruth designates the absence that abides *essentially* in the heart of presencing. The second untruth is entirely different. It is the "forgetting" or the withdrawal of being over the course of the metaphysical age. In regard to the first, it may be said indeed that "without ever lifting it, thinking unveils the veil of being." But it cannot be said that "because thinking of being is thinking of the forgetting of being, the true name for this thinking is remembering. '*Denken ist Andenken*' " (p. 550). Forgetting and remembering (Werner Marx had already established this in 1961; see

below, sec. 20, nn. 2 and 18) are terms that apply retrospectively to the history of metaphysics and are *canceled* by the hypothesis of closure. Therefore, to say that "the thought of being does not abolish the forgetting of being" (p. 551) is plainly ambiguous. The "thought of being" does not abolish *lēthē,* the essential untruth in the heart of truth, but it certainly abolishes the *epochē,* the forgetting or withdrawal of the truth of being since the Socratic turn. *Lēthē* is and remains the transcendental condition for error and errancy; but the entire effort of *Seinsdenken* is directed toward ending the concrete errancy that has been our own since the Greeks, and which Heidegger terms "epochal."

47. SD 44/OTB 40 f.

48. N I 28/N i 20.

49. SD 55/OTB 51.

50. Gel 37/DTh 62 f.

51. "The conditions of the *possibility of experience* in general are at the same time the conditions of the *possibility of the objects of experience,*" Immanuel Kant, *Critique of Pure Reason,* A 158, B 197.

52. SD 2/OTB 2, cf. SD 25/OTB 24.

53. According to GA 24, 29–31/BPP 21 f., the *construction*—"the central piece of the phenomenological method"—is the "free project" that brings itself into view. This construction or projection makes it possible to establish the structures of being (what later and in another context I will call the categories of presencing). The *de-construction* is the act complementary to the projection of those structures, the act by which they are dislodged from their casing of facticity. The *reduction,* finally, is the guiding back of the gaze from the naive natural grasp of entities to the question of their being. Heidegger calls the implementation of this whole program, *"durchkonstruieren"* (obviously another Kantianism in these early works, cf. the *"durchgängige Bestimmung,"* complete determination, e. g., *Critique of Pure Reason,* A 571, B 599). The complete construction "brings into light the pattern of foundations." Elsewhere, Heidegger speaks of "the 'dissolution' which loosens and lays bare the seeds of ontology" (KPM 39 f./Kpm 46).

54. Cf. SD 32/OTB 30. For the double step backward, see also below secs. 18 and 19.

55. VA 180/PLT 181, cf. SD 80/OTB 73 (emphasis added).

56. EiM 35/IM 46 and MHG 73/IW 37.

57. This in no way prejudges the nature of what I will call below the practical a priori, see Part V. As to the attempts to read outlines of theoretical anarchism or utopianism into BT, they "mutilate"—to say the least—the project of fundamental ontology as well as that of existential analytic, as Karsten Harries rightly remarks, art. cit., p. 651, n. 21, about the works of Graeme Nicholson, "Camus and Heidegger: Anarchists," *University of Toronto Quarterly* XLI (1971):14–23, and "The Commune in *Being and Time,*" *Dialogue* X, 4 (1971):708–726.

58. "The distinction, which is metaphysical in origin, between theory and practice, as well as the representation of a transmittance between the two, obstructs access to the understanding of what I call 'thinking' " (Sp 214/ISp 22).

59. About φρόνιμος as the "personification of the norm" in Aristotle, see Pierre Aubenque, *La prudence chez Aristote* (Paris, 1963), p. 41. The author also shows the "technical" and hence physicist origin of this normative relation: "In the *Nichomachean Ethics* ethical judgment is compared . . . to the know-how of the carpenter," p. 42. For the question whether in Aristotle's ethics actors are indeed related ideally to the standard of the "prudent man," see Hans-Georg Gadamer, *Die Idee des Guten zwischen Plato und Aristoteles* (Heidelberg, 1978), and below, sec. 11, n. 30.

Part One: Genealogy of Principles

I. Understanding History through Its Reversals

1. TK 42/QCT 44.

§3. The Puma-Shaped City

2. SvG 40, 42.

3. Bertrand Flornoy, *The World of the Inca,* trans.. W. Bradford (New York, 1965), pp. 111–112 (translation modified).

4. Friedrich Nietzsche, "The Genealogy of Morals," Preface secs. 2 and 7, trans. W. Kaufmann, *Basic Writings of Nietzsche* (New York, 1966), pp. 451 and 457.

§4. The Rise and Decline of Principles

5. SvG 192/PG 208.
6. Heidegger says "*Scheu*," see below, sec. 19, n. 194.
7. SvG 15, 96 f., 192.
8. The "reversal (*Wandel*) in being," understood as "reversal of its destiny," TK 38/QCT 39.
9. Quite a few phrases in Heidegger's texts concerning the history of being are openly reminiscent of Hegel's vocabulary: "eschatology of being" (Hw 302/EGT 18); the "identity and simplicity of the destiny of being" (SvG 153); "the essence of being hitherto declines into its still veiled truth" (Hw 301/EGT 18), etc. But in spite of these similarities, many of which should be explained by a desire for dialogue, Heideggerian phenomenology does not permit one to speak of a rationality underlying the reversals of history. For Heidegger, the essence of metaphysics is not itself metaphysical. About the dialogue, *Aussprache*, with Hegel see for instance GA 55 42.
10. Heidegger's characterization of all Western philosophy since its beginning in classical Greece as "metaphysics" (e.g., Wm 141/PDT 268) has attracted various criticisms. In *The Rule of Metaphor*, trans. R. Czerny (Toronto, 1977), Paul Ricoeur writes: "I regret the position assumed by Heidegger. This inclosure of the previous history of Western thought within the unity of 'the' metaphysical seems to me to express a sort of vengefulness" (p. 311). Jürgen Habermas, *Philosophisch-politische Profile* (Frankfurt, 1971), considers "this conception, on the whole unilateral" (p. 73), trans. D. Ponikvar, "Martin Heidegger: On the Publication of Lectures from the year 1935," *Graduate Faculty Philosophy Journal* VI, 2 (Fall, 1977):162. For Karl-Otto Apel, *Transformation der Philosophie* (Frankfurt, 1976), "his speculative efforts toward a philosophy that transcends metaphysics" cannot prevent Heidegger, in spite of himself, from objectifying the un-objectifiable (vol. I, p. 259). Many of these criticisms would collapse if their authors saw that what is at stake in the program of "deconstructing metaphysics" and the claim of an "end of philosophy" is an appreciation of the situation in which we find ourselves today, rather than a summary judgment on the past.
11. See for example N II 141–202/N iv 96–149.

II. Understanding Practice through the "Turning"

1. TK 40–42/QCT 41–43.

§5. Practical Philosophy and the Hypothesis of Closure

2. Hw 50/PLT 61 f. Several of the efforts to "extract" a political philosophy from Heidegger's writings are based upon this text. Alexander Schwan, *Politische Philosophie im Denken Martin Heidegger* (Cologne, 1965), has carefully traced the parallel between the essence of truth as it sets itself into work in art and as it unfolds itself in "the deed that founds a political state." But for Schwan, the apogee of such an unfolding of the essence of truth is the totalitarian state. Schwan's point of departure is undeniably correct: Heidegger's phenomenological deconstruction of metaphysics henceforth deprives political philosophy of its traditional foundation. But Schwan does not apply the regressive reading of history which alone would justify that starting point. In the words of Jean-Michel Palmier, *Les écrits politiques de Heidegger* (Paris, 1968), "for us, the question is to understand how Alexander Schwan, starting from correct principles, arrives at absurd consequences" (p. 152). These few lines from "The Origin of the Work of Art" provide a textual base that is extremely slender for developing a political philosophy out of Heidegger purely by exegesis. Otto Pöggeler, *Philosophie und Politik bei Heidegger* (Freiburg, 1972), qualifies such an attempt as "inadmissible" (p. 122) if it relies primarily upon that article on the work of art. Still, the reasons advanced by Pöggeler are hardly convincing either. This essay, he writes, "belongs to a 'romantic' position of Heidegger which he later abandoned" (p. 122). In the Introduction above I have tried to show on the contrary—and this is the only viable argument against those who believe they can read fascist tendencies into Heidegger's works—that a 'regressive' hermeneutics is the condition for

fully understanding Heidegger's itinerary, retained as a path and in its totality. If Schwan makes too big a case out of those sentences from *Holzwege*, and Pöggeler too little a case, Bernard Dauenhauer, "Renovating the Problem of Politics," *Review of Metaphysics*, XXIX (1976):626–641, is content to indicate merely a plan for working from this Heideggerian text. What is needed, he writes, is to achieve "the delimitation of the realm of politics from other realms of human expression" (p. 639). He sketches five elements that appear "if what Heidegger says about art is translated into the question of what the political is and is then conjoined with his reflections on meditative thought and technology." These five elements are: the historical, irreducibly manifold, speech-like, autonomous character of political action as well as the task of preserving tradition (pp. 635 f.). By virtue of their larger frame of reference, these remarks successfully correct Schwan and respond somewhat, implicitly at least, to the question posed by Palmier, but they are far from delineating even the contours of the terrain in which, after Heidegger, political thinking could take root. This terrain is the field of the history of Western metaphysics, and its contours are spelled out by the categories (see below, Part IV) of the phenomenological deconstruction of that history. Thus the preliminary for any reconstitution of political thinking after Heidegger is what I am suggesting as the genealogy of epochal principles.

3. There are four senses to be distinguished in Heidegger's usage of the German *Lichtung*, opening or clearing. The word is a translation of the French *clairière*, see SD 71 f./OTB 65. All four senses depend on the understanding of truth as *alētheia*, as unconcealment. The primary sense of "clearing" is that of the opening constituted by being-in-the-world insofar as the being that we are is the "there" in which entities can show themselves (SZ 133/BT 171 f., cf. Hw 49/PLT 61). A first slippage of meaning occurs when the location of truth is no longer thought of in reference to *Dasein* but to *logos*. The *logos* "yields" the opening in which presencing can occur. Now unconcealedness is understood as the difference between presencing and what is present (VA 247/EGT 93). As an event, the opening is seen as constituted by "nature," *phusis*, rather than by man (Höl 55–58). The third sense refers to the history of being. Here Heidegger speaks of "the history of the clearing of being" (IuD 47/IaD 51) or of the "epochal clearings of being" (SvG 143). The fourth sense, finally, is ahistorical: "the clearing is the opening for everything that is present and absent" (SD 72/OTB 65). This opening is thought of as the atemporal condition of history. It "grants being and thinking as well as their presencing to and for each other" (SD 75/OTB 68). In this last sense, *Lichtung* has lost all affinity with light metaphors and, as the translator observes, is rather "related to [the French] *lever* (i.e., alleviate, lighten a burden)," OTB 65, note. The sense that has priority in the genealogy of epochal principles is the third one. For the fourth, see below, sec. 37.

4. Herbert Marcuse, "Heidegger's Politics: An Interview with Herbert Marcuse by Frederick Olafson," in *Graduate Faculty Philosophy Journal* VI (1977):28–40, considers that due to his nearly exclusive focus on philosophical works Heidegger tends "to get away from the social reality rather than into it." He accuses Heidegger of a "fake concreteness." "Heidegger's concreteness was to a great extent a phony, a false concreteness" (ibid., pp. 29–31). Cf. H. Marcuse, *Negations* (Boston, 1968), p. 32. This general tendency, expressed a bit crudely by Marcuse, is confirmed perhaps by the two instances when Heidegger does leave the philosophical tradition: the poetry of Hölderlin and modern technology. It is confirmed there because Heidegger understands both instances in relation to his one philosophical issue, the question of being.

5. The manifest order is not *presencing*, understood as an event, but *presence:* the modality in which the totality of entities present epochally arranges itself.

6. To say that the political is the domain where an epochal principle is most apparent is not to claim that all other phenomena can only be explained politically, nor that phenomenology, as the deconstruction of metaphysics, ceases to be regional. The political is only that region (*Gegend*) of phenomena whose essential trait is to join publicly the theoretical and the practical. The analysis of 'regions' is given up only with Heidegger's discovery of *Ereignis*.

7. N II 421/EPh 19.

8. For Heidegger, the problem of the text usually comes down to that of poetic texts. As he wrote to the literary historian Emil Staiger, all speech is "that unconcealment which reveals something present," but the poem, in this instance a poem of Mörike, "brings to language that very mode of presencing" which belongs to language in general. Emil Staiger, *Die Kunst der Interpretation* (Munich, 1971), pp. 35 and 40. On the expression "bringing to language" see Beda Allemann, *Hölderlin und Heidegger* (Freiburg, 1954), p. 108.

9. Such an activity, described in SZ 66–72/BT 94–102, should not be confused with work as it is described in Wm 218–220/QB 42–68. The figure of the worker represents the reign of worldwide technology. See Palmier, op. cit., pp. 169–293.

10. Some of Heidegger's critics, particularly early ones, denounced the almost total absence of any reference to such elementary experiences as love and hate in his work. At least regarding the first period of his writing, their observations result from a misapprehension of the very task of existential analysis: to lay bare the ontological structures that compose, order, and determine the unity of the being that we are as well as its ontic possibilities (see SZ 13 f./BT 33 f.). Among these critiques, the most recent is Marcuse's "Heidegger's Politics," op. cit., p. 33. Love and hate are ontic "existentiell" forms of the ontological "existential" structure called "being-with," *Mitsein* (SZ 114–125/BT 149–163).

11. G.W.F. Hegel, *The Philosophy of Right*, Preface, trans. T. M. Knox (Oxford, 1952), p. 13.

12. Thus the "theater" is the fixed order of incipient modernity (Hw 84/QCT 131 f.) and technology as "*Gestell*," framing, that of closing modernity (VA 27 f./BWr 301 f.).

13. This premise of the "history of being," that there exists no primordial norm-giving order, marks the radical difference between Heidegger and the Frankfurt School. One of the preoccupations that indeed makes a 'school' out of this latter group is its attempt to construe forms of ultimate legitimation, see for example Jürgen Habermas, *Legitimation Crisis* (Boston, 1975), p. xxv: "the close connection between material questions of a theory of contemporary social formation and foundational problems . . . can be clarified within the framework of a theory of communicative competence." Cf. idem, *Erkenntniss und Interesse,* "Nachwort" (Frankfurt, 1973), p. 413.

14. Michel Foucault's description of "order in its very being," which he calls *epistēmē,* appears very much like the working out of a concrete instance of the history of being in Heidegger (the philosopher, he says, whom he has read most). This order, writes Foucault, shows itself in a region "anterior to words, perceptions, and gestures . . . more solid, more archaic, less dubious, always more 'true' than theories . . . ," *The Order of Things* (New York, 1973), p. xxi. But as an *archē* of knowledge, *epistēmē* is one of the regions where being gives itself, and the archeology of human sciences only one case of deconstructing modalities of presence.

15. SvG 123 f.

16. "Greek classic antiquity agreed that the highest form of human life was spent in a *polis* and that the supreme human capacity was speech. . . . Rome and medieval philosophy defined man as the *animal rationale;* in the initial stages of the modern age, man was thought of primarily as *homo faber,* until in the nineteenth century, man was interpreted as an *animal laborans,*" Hannah Arendt, *Between Past and Future* (New York, 1968), p. 63. Concerning the transition from the order prior to the *polis* to that of the *polis,* see idem, *The Human Condition* (Chicago, 1958), p. 26; concerning that from the Greek *polis* to the Roman *civitas,* ibid., pp. 23 f., and the entire second chapter, "The Public and the Private Realm," as well as *Between Past and Future,* pp. 120–135; on that from the Roman Empire to the medieval community, ibid.; on the rise of the nation state and the passage to imperialism, idem, *The Origins of Totalitarianism* (New York, 1958), pp. 123–302; on the transition toward the totalitarian state, ibid., pp. 305–479; finally, on the decline of the republican state, idem, *Crises of the Republic* (New York, 1969), pp. 3–47 and 201–233, as well as idem, *On Violence* (New York, 1970), *passim.*

17. This 'bottom', *Grund,* where the origin shows itself as neither *archē* nor principle (in an opposition to both which is not 'contradictory', but 'disparate') is the abyss, *Abgrund* or *Ungrund.* These terms borrowed from Meister Eckhart, are meant to negate the origin both as cause and as condition (SvG 71).

18. Arendt, *The Human Condition,* pp. 22–49.

19. It is in the sense of *eidos* and of *idea* as immediately graspable by sight that I call the political order of an epoch the "aspect" of whatever is present within it. Presencing itself, on the other hand, will have to be thought of otherwise than through the metaphor of visual perception, viz. through that of hearing.

§6. The Closure as the Withering of the *Pros Hen* Relation

20. SvG 73.
21. SvG 206/PG 219.

22. US 37/OWL 159; the translation omits the words *"Spitze des Speeres,"* point of the lance.

23. Wm 312/Phy 224 and SvG 111. Cf. H. G. Gadamer, *Die Idee des Guten zwischen Plato und Aristoteles* (Heidelberg, 1978), pp. 91 f.

24. Regarding medieval philosophy, Heidegger seems however to deny that the pre-understanding of causality which determines the representation of the world as created is of Aristotelian origin (Hw 19/PLT 29).

25. *Agere sequitur esse.* See the various formulations of this axiom in Thomas Aquinas, cited by Joseph de Finance, *Etre et agir dans la philosophie de Saint Thomas* (Rome, 1965), pp. 70–72.

26. Aristotle, *Posterior Analytics,* II, 19; 100 a 11 with the two commentaries by Hans-Georg Gadamer, *Truth and Method* (New York, 1975), p. 314, and, more specifically, *Kleine Schriften,* vol. I (Tübingen, 1967), p. 110. The *archē* to which the *pros hen* relation points in the last two books of the *Politics* is the perfect state; in the *Ethics,* it is happiness. Throughout the branches of Aristotelian philosophy the paradigmatic thought pattern remains that of ousiology, the doctrine of substance.

27. The special issue of the *Revue française de science politique* devoted to "Political Theory," Vol. XI, no. 2 (1961), contains several contributions illustrating this formal identity. See especially the remarks by Eric Weil, "Philosophie politique, théorie politique," ibid., pp. 267–294.

28. As I said, this concept of formal identity between the theoretical and the practical philosophies depends on the reading of *Metaphysics,* IV, 2; 1003 a 33 ("Being is spoken of in many ways, but always relative to one term") which remained predominant in Aristotelianism until Franz Brentano, *On the Several Senses of Being in Aristotle,* trans. R. George (Berkeley, 1975). Opposed to this reading based on the analogy of being stands that of Pierre Aubenque, *Le problème de l'être chez Aristote* (Paris, 1966), especially pp. 190–198. For Aubenque, the concept of the analogy of being is not authentically Aristotelian and consequently the One to which the *pros hen* relation refers is not, in the last analysis, substance: "the *pros hen* has nothing to do with a relation of attribution" (p. 194). Rather, it refers to being, as distinct from *ousia* and as a "residual" factor of the categories. Cf. Gadamer, *Truth and Method,* pp. 278–289.

29. *Nicomachean Ethics,* V, 6; 113 a 26 ff. This passage deals with political justice, that is, with justice as it applies to free men (which presupposes the existence of unfree men in the city, "unequals," toward whom relations are ruled by a mere semblance of justice, καθ' ὁμοιότητα). Justice among citizens is founded upon their "proportional or arithmetic" equality (κατ' ἀναλογίαν ἢ κατ' ἀριθμόν). Then Aristotle adds that this latter equality refers subjects, "not to a man, but to a rational principle." Thus justice and equality among citizens are understood in terms of the same reference to a first that provides the rational schema in the later theory of substance and accidents, see for example, *Metaphysics,* IV, 2; 1003 b 6–10.

30. This deconstruction, writes a commentator, has "in effect undercut all of what Heidegger would call the metaphysical theories concerning the relation between what is to be thought and what is to be done or achieved politically," Dauenhauer, "Renovating the Problem of Politics," op. cit., p. 629.

31. The metaphor of the body politic illustrates well the analogical relation between authority and subject. It has provided a semblance of legitimacy, based more on imagination than reflection, for enslavement to the state or to the "mystical body of Christ" as well as for the theories of a Hobbes (the state as "artificial man") or a Hegel (the state as "organism").

32. "What we call a site . . . is that which gathers in itself whatever is essential about a thing," SvG 106. Political action has its site just as a poem (US 52/OWL 172), or a thing like a bridge (VA 154/PLT 154), or, again, modern man (Hw 194/QCT 54), or God himself (Hw 235/QCT 100), or finally, each entity, present or absent (VA 222/EGT 72).

33. Here I am following a suggestion by Jean Beaufret: "Should we translate *Erörterung* as 'situation' then? Nothing indeed would be better if only the word 'situation' had not been so used and abused," *Dialogue avec Heidegger,* vol. 2 *Philosophie moderne,* (Paris, 1973), p. 148.

34. The distinction in BT between entities "given as present," *vorhanden,* and entities "given for handling," *zuhanden,* prefigures the topology to the extent that this distinction designates the sites where *Dasein* encounters entities in the world (SZ 132/BT 171). In subsequent writings, Heidegger understands a site no longer in reference to being-in-the-

world, but on its own terms, as a self-clearing, self-manifesting or self-alleviating (*Selbstlich-tung*, Her 189/H 117) of presencing. Thus in US 38/OWL 160 the "situation," *Erörterung* (and not "discussion" as the English translation has it), is the preliminary for elucidation, *Erläuterung*. This latter in turn makes it possible for clarity, *das Lautere*—unconcealed presencing—to show itself.

35. Sp 206/ISp 17.

36. "Essential space," *Wesensraum* (Höl 16) or "room for play," *Spielraum* (Hw 194/QCT 55).

37. SD 44/OTB 41. The act of thinking that retrieves the event of appropriation, Henri Birault correctly writes, "*opens up* a certain history, it *makes* history," *Heidegger et l'experience de la pensée* (Paris, 1978), p. 378. Strictly speaking, however, this cannot also mean that such an act "makes an epoch," as the author adds. Still to speak of epochs beyond the boundary of the closure amounts to a confusion between the "reversals," *Wenden*, within metaphysics and the "turning," *Kehre*, out of metaphysics. I therefore cannot agree with Birault when he adds: "The 'historical' thinking of being responds and corresponds to the epochal character of the destiny of being," ibid. It responds and corresponds indeed to the constellations of being, but these constellations are no longer "epochal." Birault however appropriately describes the several meanings of the word *Ereignis*, event or event of appropriation, in Heidegger: "Firstly, *das Ereignis* commonly signifies 'the happening'. Secondly, *das Ereignis* derives from the word *eigen*, which means 'proper' or 'properly'. From this sense come, for instance, *die Eigenschaft*, 'the quality' or 'property' in the sense of characteristic feature, and *das Eigentum*, 'one's own good' or 'property' in the sense of possession, as well as the currently somewhat obsolete philosophical notion of *die Eigentlichkeit*, 'authenticity'. Thirdly, in a more remote and hidden way, *das Ereignis* makes reference to the old German verb *er-äugen*, which is constructed from *das Auge*, 'the eye' or 'the look'," ibid., p. 41. I might add that Kant still says *eräugnen* for *ereignen*, e.g., *Critique of Pure Reason* A X and *Eräugnis* for *Ereignis*, ibid., A 199, 451, 543 f.

38. Letter to Peter Gast, August 14, 1881, Friedrich Nietzsche, *Werke in drei Bänden*, ed. Karl Schlechta (Munich, 1956), vol. III, p. 1172.

39. IuD 24/IaD 33. This text speaks of belonging as a constellation "of man and being." Belonging is therefore not something that happens in one domain or another, rather it occurs in that domain (*Bereich*) which in BT is called ontological (SZ 13/BT 34). However, this constellation of man and being, or the ontological essence of the entity that we are, is only the condition for the possibility of belonging to regions of phenomena: objects, tools, works, actions, etc. This transcendentalism is described, although in another language, in VA 158/PLT 157.

40. SvG 188.

41. Aristotle, *De Anima*, III, 4; 426 a 19.

42. René Char, *Le nu perdu* (Paris, 1971), p. 48; *La Parole en archipel* (Paris, 1962), p. 73; *Commune présence* (Paris, 1964), p. 255.

III. Genealogy of Principles and Anti-Humanism

1. Wm 176/BWr 225.

2. Wm 142/PDT 269.

3. Wm 141/PDT 269.

4. Louis Althusser, *For Marx*, trans. B. Brewster (New York, 1970), pp. 229 f. and *Positions* (Paris, 1976), p. 132.

5. Gottfried W. Leibniz, "New Essays on the Human Understanding," Preface, # 4, in *Philosophical Writings*, trans. M. Morris (London, 1934), p. 146.

6. Louis Althusser, "Reply to John Lewis," *Marxism Today*, XVI (1972), Part I:316.

7. Michel Foucault, *The Archaeology of Knowledge*, trans. A. M. Sheridan Smith (New York, 1972), p. 14.

8. Wm 153/BWr 202.

9. Claude Lévi-Strauss, *L'homme nu* (Paris, 1971), pp. 614 f.

§7. A Threefold Break with "Humanism"

10. Gel 37/DTh 62.

11. Althusser, *For Marx*, op. cit., p. 227.

12. Ibid., p. 67.

13. Ibid., p. 229.

14. Karl Marx, *Critique of Hegel's Philosophy of Right,* trans. A. Jolin and J. O'Malley (Cambridge, 1970), p. 137, cited in VS 125. Heidegger believes that "Marxism in its entirety rests on this thesis."

15. Friedrich Nietzsche, *Ecce Homo,* "Thus Spoke Zarathustra," 1, trans. W. Kaufmann, *Basic Writings* (New York, 1966), p. 751.

16. Friedrich Nietzsche, *The Will to Power,* trans. W. Kaufmann (New York, 1968), sec. 617, p. 330.

17. Ibid., secs. 485 and 490, pp. 269 f.

18. Ibid., sec. 715, p. 380.

19. Ibid., sec. 493, p. 272.

20. Ibid., sec. 574, p. 309.

21. Wm 159/BWr 208.

22. VA 180/PLT 181 (emphasis added). I translate *"das andenkende Denken"* as "the thinking that attends," namely the constellations of presence. *"An-,"* Latin *ad-,* indicates directedness, and "tending" (e.g., a flock), the attitude of the "shepherd of being." Cf. William Richardson, *Heidegger: Through Phenomenology to Thought* (The Hague, 1963), p. 294, n. 108.

23. Wm 176/BWr 225.

24. Wm 176/BWr 224.

25. Wm 160/BWr 209.

§8. A Threefold Break with Principial Origins

26. VwR XXIII/PrR XXII.

27. Marx, *Critique of Hegel's Philosophy of Right,* pp. 141 f.

28. Michel Henry, *Marx: A Philosophy of Human Reality,* trans. Kathleen McLaughlin (Bloomington, 1983), p. 69. I am well aware that this interpretation of Marx poses difficulties. Paul Ricoeur, "Le 'Marx' de Michel Henry," in *Esprit* (October, 1978):124–139, has brought them into relief with greater subtlety than, for example, François Guéry, "La division du travail entre Ure et Marx (à propos de Michel Henry)," in *Revue Philosophique,* IV (1977):423–444. Whatever the merits and shortcomings of Henry's transcendentalist picture of Marx may be, I am more concerned with the issues of metaphysical closure and plurification of the origin than with a literal interpretation of Marx.

29. Karl Marx and Friedrich Engels, *The German Ideology* (Moscow, 1976), pp. 36 f. (emphasis added).

30. "How the True World Finally Became a Fable," in *Twilight of the Idols;* trans. W. Kaufmann, *The Portable Nietzsche* (New York, 1954), p. 485.

31. *The Will to Power,* sec. 428, op. cit., p. 233.

32. Ibid., sec. 630, p. 336.

33. Ibid., sec. 462, p. 255.

34. Ibid., sec. 488, p. 270.

35. Ibid., sec. 715, p. 380.

36. Ibid., sec. 647, p. 344.

37. Friedrich Nietzsche, *Die Unschuld des Werdens,* vol. II, sec. 1332 (Stuttgart, 1965), p. 473.

38. *Ecce Homo,* "Thus Spoke Zarathustra," n. 3; *Basic Writings,* p. 757.

39. Wm 252/QB 107.

40. *"Ursprüngliche Verwurzelung"* (SZ 377/BT 429).

41. SZ 12/BT 32.

42. SZ 331/BT 380.

43. SZ 329 and 326/BT 377 and 374.

44. I borrow this term from Gilles Deleuze and Félix Guattari, *Rhizome* (Paris, 1976), pp. 17 f. Among the company of writers, notably in France, who today herald the Nietzschean discovery that the origin as *one* was a fiction, there are those who espouse the multiple origin with jubilation, and this is apparently the case with Deleuze. There are others who barely conceal their regret over the loss of the One, and this may indeed be the case with Derrida. It suffices to listen to him express his debt to Lévinas: "I relate this concept of *trace* to what is at

the center of the latest work of Emmanuel Lévinas," Jacques Derrida, *Of Grammatology*, trans. G. C. Spivak (Baltimore, 1976), p. 70. The article by Emmanuel Lévinas to which he refers announces in its very title—"*La trace de l'autre*," The Other's Trace—how far Derrida has traveled from his mentor. For Derrida, the discovery that the "trace" does not refer back to an Other *whose* trace it would be, is like a bad awakening: "arch-violence, loss of the proper, of absolute proximity, of self-presence, in truth the loss of what has never taken place, of a self-presence which has never been given but only dreamed of," ibid., p. 112. For Heidegger, neither intoxicated jubilation nor mourning—there is only sober attending to the πολλαχῶς λέγεται of the origin, "a thinking more sober than scientific technology" (SD 79/OTB 72).

45. "Thinking the most difficult thought of philosophy, means thinking being as time" (N I 28/N i 20).

46. I borrow this expression from Orlando Pugliese, *Vermittlung und Kehre. Grundzüge des Geschichtsdenkens bei Martin Heidegger* (Freiburg, 1965), p. 76.

47. According to Max Müller, *Existenzphilosophie im geistigen Leben der Gegenwart*, 3rd ed. (Heidelberg, 1964), p. 67, the third part (not published before GA 24) of BT should deal with a threefold "difference": "a) The ontological difference in the narrow sense, as 'transcendental': the difference between an entity and its beingness [*Seiendheit*]; b) the ontological difference in the broad sense, as 'quasi-transcendental' [*transzendenzhaft*]: the difference between, on one hand, an entity and its beingness, and, on the other, being itself; c) the theological difference in the strict sense, as 'transcendent': the difference between God, on one hand, and an entity, beingness and being, on the other." But even this third difference, a curious one to be sure, does not seem to have been intended to make God the subject of history. In any case, it is not to be found in GA 24, which is a "new elaboration of the third section of Part One of BT" (GA 24 1/BPP 1).

48. The rather puzzling remark that "the Marxist vision of history is superior to any other historiography" (Wm 170/BWr 219) clearly cannot in any way be read as the sign of an adoption by Heidegger of dialectical materialism, however understood.

49. Hw 311/EGT 26. Ἐπέχειν means to abstain from, to stop searching: the Stoic sage resigns himself to not possessing wisdom in the face of the multitude of doctrines about truth—and in this way he obtains wisdom, ἀταραξία, or ἀπάθεια, tranquility of the soul, equanimity. See the excellent article by P. Couissin, "L'origine et l'évolution de l'*epochē*," *Revue des études grecques*, 42 (1929):373–397.

50. "The epoch of being belongs to being itself" (Hw 311/EGT 26 f.) and: "Sheerly, out of its own essence of concealment, being appropriates its epoch in the event" (TK 43/QCT 44). In neither of the two senses "does epoch mean a span of time in occurrence, but rather the fundamental trait of sending," SD 9/OTB 9. Heidegger speaks of a "sequence of epochs in the destiny of being," ibid., dismissing both the theories of chance and those of necessity in history. Several texts enumerate epochal "stamps" of being, for example: "*phusis, logos, hen, idea, energeia*, substantiality, objectivity, subjectivity, will, will to power, will to will" (IuD 64 f./IaD 66 f.). See as early as 1916, FS 350.

51. Hw 54/PLT 66. This text directly recalls Cicero's advice to "withhold one's assent," *Academica* II, 59, as well as that of Sextus Empiricus, *Hypotyposes*, I, 232 f.: "to withhold oneself from everything," ἐπέχειν περὶ πάντων.

52. Hw 193/QCT 54. See also below, Sec. 37.

53. Karl Marx, *The Poverty of Philosophy* (New York, 1963), p. 115.

55. Wm 251/QB 105. After the "turning," Heidegger dismisses all root metaphors just as he dismisses the very question of political *systems* (see above, Introduction, n. 1). Instead of tracing phenomena to their "originary rootedness" (above, n. 40) in *Dasein*, he now says: "The concept of 'root' makes it impossible to say anything about man's relation to being," VS 127. Hence my loan from Deleuze and Guattari (above, n. 44).

55. Hannah Arendt, *The Life of the Mind* (New York, 1977), 2 vols., describes the lack of notable traits in Adolph Eichmann's personality, with one exception: "it was not stupidity but *thoughtlessness*," vol. I, p.4. She places the analyses in this first volume, *Thinking*, under an epigraph taken from Heidegger concerning *das Denken*. "Thoughtlessness is an uncanny visitor who comes and goes everywhere in today's world" (Gel 13/DTh 45). Arendt pursues the point: "Don't we all know how relatively easy it has always been to lose at least the habit, if not the faculty, of thinking?" (vol. II, p. 80). Heideggerian "thinking" stands not only at the antipodes of any apology for totalitarianism, the loss of one and the relapse into the other are

two sides of the same phenomenon. "If there is anything in thinking that can prevent men from doing evil, it must be some property inherent in the activity itself" (vol. I, p. 180).
56. Immanuel Kant, *Critique of Pure Reason*, B 472.

Part Two: The "Very Issue" of Phenomenology

1. Hw 67/PLT 80.
2. "Genuine knowledge of the history of being could not yet be reached in BT. This is the reason for the clumsy non-destinality (*Ungeschicklichkeit*) and, strictly speaking, the naiveté of the 'ontological destruction' " (VS 133).
3. VS 124 f. (emphasis added).

IV. Mutations of Phenomenological Transcendentalism

1. SD 90/OTB 82. The title under which Heidegger has collected his last essays, *Zur Sache des Denkens*, is obviously a word play on Husserl's slogan *"zu den Sachen selbst."* The terminological resemblance must, however, not hide the fact that in Heidegger the phrase designates thought "issues" rather than perceived or ideal objects, "things," that are directly given to experience. Heideggerian *Sache* recalls the Greek πρᾶγμα, as in Aristotle who said of his predecessors that "the very issue (αὐτὸ τὸ πρᾶγμα) marked out the way for them and forced them to investigate" (*Metaphysics* I, 3; 984 a 18).
2. SZ 38/BT 63. "*Möglichkeit*" means a possibility charged with power, *Macht*, which is seized upon because it is cherished, *mögen*. Therefore, it is also a "potential." It is true, however, that even in the period of BT, Heidegger writes: "When phenomenology is correctly understood, it is the concept of a method" (GA 24 27/BPP 20).
3. SZ 50 n./BT 490.
4. The remarks on Husserl that follow are based primarily on his *Cartesian Meditations*, trans. D. Cairns (The Hague, 1960), pp. 65–88, and *Experience and Judgment*, trans. J. S. Churchill and K. Ameriks (Evanston, Ill., 1973), pp. 58–68.
5. VS 124.

§9. From Subjectivity to Being-There

6. US 95/OWL 9, cf. Phän 47.
7. VS 111.
8. Hannah Arendt, *The Life of the Mind* (New York, 1977), vol. I, p. 241, cites a passage from Aristotle's scientific treatise, *On Sense and Sensible Objects*, one of the rare texts that accord primacy to the ear rather than the eye: "For the mere necessities of life and in itself, sight is the more important, but for the mind and indirectly hearing is the more important" (437 a 4 f.). She adds: "The point of the matter is that [Aristotle] seems never to have remembered this observation when he wrote philosophy."
9. Cf. ibid., pp. 110 f. Francis Bacon observed that "visibles require some distance between the object and the eye, to be better seen," *Sylva Sylvarum*, III, 272; *The Works of Francis Bacon*, ed. Spedding et al., vol. 2 (London, 1859), p. 431.
10. SZ 48/BT 74.
11. *Cartesian Meditations*, p. 67.
12. SZ 115/BT 151.
13. VS 110.
14. See the excellent article by Gérard Granel, "Remarques sur le rapport de 'Sein und Zeit' et de la phénoménologie husserlienne," in Vittorio Klostermann, ed., *Durchblicke: Martin Heidegger zum 80. Geburtstag* (Frankfurt, 1970), especially pp. 358–368.
15. SZ 38/BT 62 and VS 116.
16. VS 111, cf. SD 86/OTB 78. "Husserl himself who, in the *Logical Investigations*—especially the sixth—came close to the question of being proper, could not persevere . . ." (SD 47/OTB 44).
17. VS 113. For a more detailed commentary on these pages, VS 110–118, see Jacques Taminiaux, "Le regard et l'excédent," *Revue Philosophique de Louvain* 75 (1977), pp. 74–100, and Jean Beaufret, *Dialogue avec Heidegger*, vol. III (Paris, 1974), pp. 126–130.

18. E. Husserl, *Logical Investigations,* trans. J. H. Findlay (New York, 1970), p. 781.
19. Ibid., p. 780.
20. VS 115.
21. Hw 84/QCT 131. This remark is not aimed at Husserl in particular, but at the entire modern age.
22. Another way of describing this transition would be to contrast Heidegger's "hermeneutic" phenomenology with Husserl's "scientific" phenomenology, cf., SZ 397–404/BT 449–455. See also Hans-Georg Gadamer, *Truth and Method* (New York, 1975), pp. 214–234.
23. Rather than characterizing "the turning" in Heidegger's thinking as a renunciation of phenomenology, as Carl Friedrich Gethmann does in *Verstehen und Auslegung* (Bonn, 1974), p. 22, it should be read as "radicalized" phenomenology; cf. Ernst Tugendhat, *Der Wahrheitsbegriff bei Husserl und Heidegger* (Berlin, 1967), pp. 262–280.
24. Such is the way Husserl himself seems to have understood BT when, on the title page of his copy, he wrote these words: "Is this not anthropology?" His position has frequently been taken up since then, for instance by Erich Rothacker, *Philosophische Anthropologie,* 3rd ed. (Bonn, 1970), and more briefly, by the same author, *Gedanken über Martin Heidegger* (Bonn, 1973), pp. 23–28.
25. This reversal of the foundational relation between cogito and *Dasein* has been demonstrated most succinctly by Friedrich-Wilhelm von Herrmann, *Subjekt und Dasein* (Frankfurt, 1974), pp. 9–10.
26. It is only in the works subsequent to BT that Heidegger's terminology distinguishes clearly between being as the "beingness" (*Seiendheit*) of entities (e.g., Wm 329–331/Phy 237 f.) and being independently of entities (e.g., SD 2/OTB 2). These two meanings are still united in the determination of being as "the *transcendens* pure and simple" (SZ 38/BT 62).
27. Heidegger exposes a threefold preeminence of *Dasein:* ontic, insofar as "in its being, it is being itself that is an issue"; ontological, since "in its being, *Dasein* stands in relation to being itself"; and as "ontic-ontological condition for the possibility of any ontologies" (SZ 12 f./BT 32 and 34). This threefold preeminence implies that the subject is primordial neither in "existentiell" experiences, nor as an "existential" condition, nor as the starting point of past philosophical systems. Therefore, sentences like "ontology has an ontic fundament" (GA 24 26/BPP 19) must not be read out of context.
28. SD 67–69/OTB 61 f.
29. The phenomenology of BT remains a phenomenology of sight. It consists in "letting entities that are accessible be encountered unconcealedly" (SZ 147/BT 187). But it is not a phenomenology of evidence. Thus further on in that text Heidegger tries to set apart "intuition," "thought," and "phenomenological ideation" as three modes of understanding. It is true, however, that sight remains the model even of *Verstehen,* of which hearing is but one mode.
30. GA 24 23/BPP 17. In this text Heidegger speaks of the "science of being" and calls it "the transcendental science."
31. GA 24 69/BPP 50. This movement of thought is here called *Rückgang.*
32. In the Introduction to *What Is Metaphysics?* entitled "Regress [*Rückgang*] into the Ground of Metaphysics," Heidegger develops the image of Descartes' tree "whose roots are Metaphysics, the trunk Physics, etc.," and asks: "What is the soil in which the roots of the tree of philosophy have their hold?" That soil is *Dasein* (Wm 195/WGM 207).
33. SZ 34 f./ BT 58 f.
34. GA 24 3/BPP 3. In BT phenomenology is characterized as "scientific" (SZ 37/BT 61), but in the strict sense, the sciences are the project in which entities are thematized as *objects* in general (SZ 361–363/BT 413–415).
35. SZ 31/BT 54 f. Contrary to what one might believe, the first two senses do not, then, directly characterize the phenomenological projects of other authors like Husserl and Scheler, although this passage may well also contain such a polemic.
36. SZ 35/BT 59.
37. SZ 37/BT 61. A more detailed presentation of the three senses of φαίνεσθαι and of the corresponding types of phenomenology can be found, for example, in Jarava L. Mehta, *Martin Heidegger: The Way and the Vision* (Honolulu, 1976), pp. 98–104. The same author suggests that perhaps the training in phenomenological seeing recaptures the authentic sense of the Greek θεωρεῖν, ibid., p. 264. However, he does not corroborate his suggestion with the double etymology possible for that Greek verb: either θέα (aspect, appearance) and ὁράω

(seeing), in which case "theory" is the look that makes a present entity appear, or θεά (the feminine of θεός, god) and ὥρα (attention, respect, esteem), "and then θεωρία is the reverent paying heed to the unconcealment of what is present," that is, to *alētheia* (VA 52 f./QCT 163–165). If phenomenology recaptures *theōrein*, it is not in the Platonic sense of the vision of the Ideas, but in the sense—perhaps derivable from Parmenides—of "the beholding that watches over truth" (ibid.).

38. SZ 1/BT 19.

39. VS 73.

40. VA 68/QCT 180.

41. N I 28/N i 20, cf., Wm 205/WGM 215: "In *Being and Time*, 'being' is not something other than 'time', insofar as time is named as the first name of the truth of being." Gadamer says more bluntly, "Heidegger's thesis was that being itself is time," *Truth and Method*, p. 228.

§10. From *Menschentum* to "Thinking"

42. VS 128.

43. Gel 25/DTh 55 (emphasis added).

44. Hw 193/QCT 54.

45. "In resoluteness [*Entschlossenheit*] we have gained that truth of being-there which is most originary because it is authentically its own" (SZ 297/BT 343).

46. Wm 202/WGM 213.

47. Wm 204/WGM 215 and SZ 316–323/BT 364–370.

48. The "pre-eminence of man" is abandoned, Heidegger writes, once thinking understands itself as responding to what is historically "sent" to it, *das Zugeschickte* (VS 125). This however remains unthinkable in BT.

49. See above, the epigraph to this Part II.

50. As such, *Menschentum* (inexplicably translated by J. Barlow as "a race of man") is opposed by Heidegger to "mankind," "the individual," "a community," "the people" and "a group of nations" (Wm 142/PDT 269). Its sense as "epochal type" results from its link to the fundamental positions in the history of being (N II 421/EPh 19. Cf. Gel 35 / DTh 61, Hw 62 / PLT 75, N II 257).

51. See above, sec. 8, n. 44.

52. The phrase is Paul Ricoeur's, *The Conflict of Interpretations*, trans. K. McLaughlin (Evanston, 1974), p. 53.

53. SZ 386 and 384/BT 438 and 436.

54. SvG 108 f.

55. Heidegger describes the epochs of the history of being as the "folds" that Western destiny "unfolds" (for example, Wm 241 f./QB 87). In the context of the ontological difference, phenomenological thinking unfolds the "double fold" of the present and of presencing (for example, KR 10/AaS 6).

56. The metaphysical sense of the transcendental does not refer here to the medieval doctrine of the "transcendentals," universal and general qualities proper to created things, but to the Aristotelian πρότερον: being as substance is prior to all particular entities. It is their a priori, not πρὸς ἡμᾶς, but τῇ φύσει (cf., N II 213–217/N iv 159–161).

57. Needless to say, this "correspondence" or respondency has nothing to do with the traditional ὁμοίωσις or *adequatio*, the conformity between a proposition and a state of affairs, cf. below, sec. 39.

58. VA 166/PLT 168. The ambiguity of the concept of φύσις in Aristotle—"being" as simple presencing and "being" as the sum of things not made by man—reveals this poietic attitude in its incipiency (Wm 358 and 369 f./Phy 259 f. and 268). Jean Wahl, *Sur l'interprétation de l'histoire de la métaphysique d'après Heidegger* (Paris, 1951), p. 30, writes correctly that with Plato and Aristotle, instead of "general presence, we have as the starting point the idea of fabrication of objects or artworks."

59. Aristotle, *Metaphysics* II, 2; 994 a 19 f., op. cit., p. 713. The ἀρχαί, although more remote from our way of knowing (πρὸς ἡμᾶς), are more knowable in themselves (φύσει), Aristotle, *Physics* I, 5; 189 a 5 f. To know becoming in its *archai* or to know a reasoned argument in its principles is to give rise to science. "We say that we know a thing only when we think we recognize its first cause," *Metaphysics* I, 3; 983 a 25. The Scholastics say "*scire*

per causas": the intelligible principles, i.e., genera and species, allow us to define quiddities according to their degrees of universality. To know the absolutely first cause and principle would be to know everything indistinctly and absolutely—a doctrine that, in the Neoplatonists, Meister Eckhart, and the German Idealists, illustrates the progenitorship of the Aristotelian *Physics*. In a Heideggerian reading of these Aristotelian texts, and more so of his commentators, it is important to show the forgottenness of the earliest sense of the origin (contained in the word *phusis*) once the *archai* enter the context of fabrication, and then of science. This earliest sense even disappears from language when the Medievals translate πρὸς ἡμᾶς as *quoad nos* and τῇ φύσει as *quoad se*. Heidegger, on the other hand, makes a point of preserving the allusion to φύσις in Aristotle's parlance and translates τῇ φύσει by the paraphrase "according to the order in which being essentializes and an entity 'is' " (N II 217/N iv 161).

60. The word *Gelassenheit*, "releasement," does not appear in BT (although resoluteness is there called "the condition for letting the others 'be'," " '*sein' lassen*," SZ 298/BT 344). The later *zulassen*, "letting" in the sense of "permitting," is a translation of the Greek *parechein*, Wm 136/PDT 265. "Releasing," *entlassen*, properly designates the event by which presencing lets what is present appear. The correct understanding of Heidegger's notion of releasement requires that this event of presencing be seen as one with human *loslassen*, "letting go." For this oneness, see for instance IuD 24/IaD 32 (a text that is actually a commentary on Parmenides' fragment 3 on identity). Only when we disengage ourselves from the present is thinking *eingelassen*, "let in" or "left to," fitted into, that presencing, ibid.

61. WhD 86/WCT 126.

62. "Casualness," *Lässigkeit*, or "neglect," *Vernachlässigung* (WhD 114/WCT 187) or again "cessation," *Ablassen* (WhD 158/WCT 145).

63. The event of presencing is "what is purely and simply singular, what in its unity is unique and, as unique, is the unifying One before all number," Hw 318 / EGT 33. The Neoplatonic overtone is not fortuitous: Plotinus was the first to think of what is *ultimate* otherwise than as substance, idea, or any *entity*. See also below, sec. 26.

64. "Thinking is thanking" (WhD 91 f./ WCT 139f.). Much poetic, pious, or psychologistic ado about this assonance in the more lyrical Heidegger literature could have been avoided if *danken* had been clearly understood as receiving and heeding modalities of presencing. Thinking is thanking inasmuch as it cannot but respond and correspond to the way phenomena appear in a given order of unconcealment. But what it does *immer schon*, "always already," it has yet to learn to do expressly and for its own sake. "Thanking" then designates respondency to transient constellations of presencing, *as* transient.

V. Deconstruction of the Political

1. TK 40/QCT 40 f.

2. "Whence and how is it determined what must be experienced as 'the things themselves' in accordance with the principle of phenomenology? Is it consciousness and its objectivity or is it the being of entities in its unconcealedness and concealment?" (SD 87/OTB 79).

3. These three "fundamental elements belonging to *a priori* knowledge constitute what we call phenomenology" (GA 24 27/BPP 20).

4. Husserl cannot recognize that "what is historical is what is essential in being" (Wm 170/BWr 219 f.).

5. Edmund Husserl, "Pariser Vorträge," in *Cartesianische Meditationen und Pariser Vorträge* (The Hague, 1950), p. 8.

6. "The investigative gaze is led back from naively grasped entities to being" (GA 24 29/BPP 21).

7. Decades: e.g., those of the different epochs of modern physics (VA 61/QCT 172), or those of the atomic age (SvG 57–60); centuries: e.g., those of modernity, (SvG 99 f.); two millennia: the epoch of the "withdrawal of being qua being" (SvG 97).

8. This concept of construction must not be confused with the one originating in Kant and which has currency in logic and mathematics. In Kant, this term designates the synthetic process by which the forms of judgment are realized purely in the intuition of space and time. Only quantities, especially mathematical ones, are so "constructed," *Critique of Pure Reason*, B 742, whereas empirical judgments arise from reconstruction. A concept or a judgment that

receives a content of sensible intuition through "reconstruction" in this way is said to be "realized," B 185. It is this Kantian and Neokantian notion of construction that Heidegger rejects along with the distinctions between subject-object, interior-exterior, etc. (GA 24 90/BPP 64, cf. KPM 226/Kpm 241).

9. GA 24 30 / BPP 22.

10. SZ 148/BT 188 f.

11. In this, phenomenological construction differs from any metaphysical construction in the sense of a speculation on systems, cf. Hw 93/QCT 141.

12. GA 24 31/BPP 22 f. In the twenties, Heidegger does not yet distinguish between *Destruktion* and *Abbau*, cf. above, p. 10.

13. In BT the project of destruction "is still faulty" (Wm 187/BWr 235) because it "has not yet been thought according to the history of being [*seinsgeschichtlich*]" (N II 415/EPh 15).

14. SZ 23/BT 44. Cf. GA 24 31/BPP 23. The positive appropriation of the tradition is indicated in the phrase "*Verwindung* of metaphysics" (e.g., WM 242/QB 87 and VA 71/EPh 84): not "overcoming" (*Überwindung*) (and certainly not "restoration"!) but disengagement, or perhaps "enucleation," extraction of the nucleus. We disengage ourselves from something only in grappling with it, as a neurosis is grappled with by Freudian "*durcharbeiten*," working-through. "One cannot shake off metaphysics as one shakes off an opinion. One can by no means set it behind oneself as a doctrine no longer believed and defended" (VA 72/EPh 85). To "*verwinden*" means first of all "getting over" suffering: "This getting-over is similar to what happens when, in the human realm, one gets over grief or pain" (TK 38/QCT 39).

15. Not only does deconstruction avoid ridding itself of the concepts of the tradition, but it needs them as the very material for reduction and construction. As a result, Werner Marx rightly observed, in Heidegger "the basic words 'being' and 'essence' obtain a meaning so altered and opposed to the traditional," that their Aristotelian articulation becomes pointless; *Heidegger and the Tradition,* trans. T. Kisiel and M. Greene (Evanston, Ill., 1971), p. 6.

16. The principles men have retained throughout the centuries as, each time, the most real entity, from the Platonic Good to today's consumer goods, objectivate and reify entities as such (cf. Hw 76 and 79/QCT 123 and 126).

17. In his last writings, Heidegger attempts to "think being without regard to its groundedness in entities" (SD 2/OTB 2).

§11. Deconstructing the Substantialist Patterns

18. Gel 35/DTh 61.

19. In the "Letter on Humanism" the two formulations occur: "Thinking *acts* as it thinks," "*Das Denken* handelt *indem es denkt*" (Wm 145/BWr 193), and: "Thus thinking is a *doing*," "*So ist das Denken ein* Tun" (Wm 191/BWr 239; both emphases added). Thinking is called supreme "*Handeln*" (Wm 145/BWr 193), but also supreme "*Tun*" (Gel 35/DTh 61).

20. WhD 2 and 55/WCT 4 and 25; WhD 159/WCT 146.

21. Aristotle, *Nicomachean Ethics,* I, 1; 1094 a 1 f., trans. W. D. Ross, in R. McKeon, ed., *The Basic Works of Aristotle* (New York, 1941), p. 935. (Although the translation is always cited in this section [as *Basic Works*], I do not always adhere to the translations adopted by McKeon.)

22. WhD 55/WCT 25.

23. "Since discourse (*Rede*) is constitutive of the being of the 'there' . . . and since being-there means being-in-the-world, being-there . . . has always already expressed itself (*ausgesprochen*). Being-there has language (*Das Dasein hat Sprache*)" (SZ 165/BT 208). Language is public because it belongs to being-in-the-world. About the publicity of "world," see SZ 71/BT 100.

24. In "the saying that projects . . . the concepts of a historical people's essential way of being, that is, of its belonging to world history, are coined in advance (*vorgeprägt*)" (Hw 61/PLT 74). *Prägung*, "seal" or "stamp," designates the order of an era that manifests the epochal principle (cf. SD 44 and 67/OTB 40 f. and 60).

25. SD 55/OTB 51.

26. Wm 145/BWr 193 f. (italics added).

27. For *phusis*, see Wm 369 f./Phy 268. For *alētheia*, see Wm 138/PDT 266 (cf. below secs. 23 and 24).

28. SZ 2/BT 21.

29. N II 409/EPh 9 (cf. N II 228 / N iv 171).

30. Recent commentators on Aristotle seem divided about the status of his political and more generally, practical, writings. There is agreement that ethics is a part of politics and that both are concerned with prudence, φρόνησις. But for some, φρόνησις covers a domain of analysis essentially irreducible to metaphysics or even to knowledge. On this reading, Aristotle's practical philosophy proposes no "theory" ready for application, but rather an "interpretation" of concrete man and of what is good for him. This is notably Hans-Georg Gadamer's position in *Truth and Method* (New York, 1975), pp. 278–289 and 482–491, in *Kleine Schriften*, vol. I (Tübingen, 1967), pp. 186–191, and in *Die Idee des Guten zwischen Plato und Aristoteles* (Heidelberg, 1978), pp. 77–103. In this last work, Gadamer traces two concepts of "good" in Aristotle, one ontological, the other practical. The first "is inseverably linked to the problem of being" (p. 79) mainly because, as in Plato, it is established through mathematical metaphors: the supreme Good precedes all entities as the number One precedes all numbers (p. 81). As regards the practical good, no such "subsumption of the particular under the universal" is possible. Rather, like an archer, the φρόνιμος "fixes his gaze on an always particular goal" (p. 96) for the attainment of which "the idea of 'the Good' is 'practically' useless" (p. 89); Aristotle "accords some truth to that idea, but rejects it as irrelevant for politics" (p. 88). The non-ontological notion of "good" in Aristotle is actually genuinely Platonic, Gadamer adds. It is for reasons of polemic that Aristotle had to neglect all non-metaphysical traits of the ἀγαθόν and "insist particularly on the Good as χωριστόν" (pp. 79 f.; cf. p. 86). The practical good is irreducible to the theoretical Good because *subsumption* is of no avail in the know-how called prudence. What is at stake in politics is not "rendering universal knowledge concrete," but "rendering the concrete more general" (p. 97). Gadamer himself extends this understanding of the practical good, unyielding to subsumption, into Kant's moral philosophy (p. 99). A more developed treatment of that parallel, however, is to be found in Hannah Arendt, *Lectures on Kant's Political Philosophy* (Chicago, 1982). The φρόνιμος, she writes, has no ultimate measure to turn to in action, but only examples: "In the *Critique of Judgment*, i.e. in the treatment of reflective judgments, where one does not subsume a particular under a concept, the example helps one in the same way in which the schema helped one to recognize the table as table" (p. 84). For Arendt, who finds Kant's unwritten political philosophy (pp. 7, 19, 21, 31) in his third *Critique*, political phenomena are located neither within the reach of knowledge, compelling it to true statements, nor within that of the will, impelling it to appropriation; rather, their phenomenal site is akin to that of aesthetic objects in that praxis requires us to "think the particular" (p. 76). This can only be done through examples, as when we say that someone is "as brave as Achilles" (pp. 77 and 84). Φρόνησις is that kind of judgment that "enables man to orient himself in the public realm" (p. 104). At the other extreme of the spectrum, interpreters of Aristotle consider his theory of society to be based largely on his metaphysics. This was Wilhelm Dilthey's position, taken up and developed today by Manfred Riedel, *Metaphysik und Metapolitik* (Frankfurt, 1975). Riedel sees a systematic correspondence in Aristotle between political philosophy and metaphysics. "In its essential points," writes Riedel, "this correspondence rests on premises of a doctrine of principles, which reach beyond the domain of an originally political formation of concepts and principles" (p. 65). Pierre Aubenque's position, *La prudence chez Aristote* (Paris, 1963), is more nuanced. Like Gadamer, he is careful to separate the Aristotelian starting point—"a certain type of men we are all able to recognize"—from any essentialist starting point. "Here, recourse to portrait description is not a makeshift but a requirement of the issue itself." Indeed, "the existence of the prudent man is already implied" in any definition of the essence of φρόνησις. Therefore, such "logical" procedures as specification of a generic concept of virtue, that is, of subsumption, will never teach us what a prudent man is (pp. 35 and 39). Like Riedel, on the other hand, Aubenque considers "that Aristotle's ethical theory of prudence cannot be dissociated from his metaphysical doctrines" (p. 2). He maintains the phenomenal autonomy of prudence in Aristotle, but not the theoretical autonomy of his practical writing. This agrees with Heidegger's view of Aristotle as both "Greek" and "non-Greek."

31. Wm 315/Phy 226.

32. In the Second Book of the *Physics*, Aristotle introduces his exposition of the four causes by declaring that they are common to "coming to be and passing away and every other kind of physical change" (πάσης τῆς μεταβολῆς, *Physics* II, 3; 194 b 20 f./*Basic Works*, p. 240). This is a declaration of principle that seems to concern things that are "by nature"—"animals and

their parts, plants and simple bodies, like earth, fire, water, air" (*Physics* II, 1; 192 b 8 f./*Basic Works*, p. 236)—to the exclusion of those made by man. The definition of *phusis* at the beginning of that Second Book consists mainly in opposing *ta phusika* to things that originate from "other causes, viz., practical and poietic human activity." In texts like these, *phusis*, then, does not designate *ousia* as, for instance, in *Metaphysics* V, 4; 1014 b 35/*Basic Works*, p. 756.

As one reads the examples Aristotle provides for each of the causes one begins to doubt, however, that they are common to all phenomena of movement: "Bronze is the cause of a statue and silver of a cup." These are examples of material causes. "The man who gave advice is a cause, the father is cause of the child . . . health is the cause of walking" (*Physics* II, 3; 194 b 21–33, cf. II, 3; 195 a 15–26/*Basic Works*, pp. 240 f.). These are examples of efficient and of final causes, again taken from human fabrication or action. In this list only the example of formal cause, "the relation of 2:1 for the octave, and generally number and the parts of a definition," departs from *praxis* as well as from *poiēsis*, but here again without at all corresponding to the definition of *phusis* provided at the beginning of the Second Book.

Here is, now, how the four causes are applied to the city in the Seventh Book of the *Politics:* "*Just as a weaver or a shipbuilder or any other artisan* must have the material proper for his work . . . so the statesman or legislator must have the materials suited to him. First among the materials required by the statesman is population: he will consider what should be the number and character of the citizens, and then what should be the size and character of the country" (*Politics* VII, 4; 1325 b 41–1326 a 8/*Basic Works*, p. 1283, italics added). Such is the *matter* of the city-state. What is noteworthy are the examples that illustrate causality here, taken again from the technical domain. The *form* of the city is its constitution and its *end*, happiness: "The city is a community of equals, aiming at the best life possible. Since happiness is the highest good . . . the various qualities of men are clearly the reason why there are various kinds of states and many forms of government; for different peoples seek after happiness in different ways and by different means, and so make for themselves different modes of life and forms of government" (*Politics*, VII, 8; 1328 a 36–1328 b 2/*Basic Works*, pp. 1287 f.). Moreover, the identification of the formal cause with the constitution and with institutions entails this quasi-dogmatic result, which is indeed revealing of the technical model that presides over the description of the ideal state: changing the constitution amounts to changing the city-state. This surprising consequence is only understandable given the physicist premisses: to change the form of a statue is to make a different statue. The *efficient* cause of the city-state, lastly, is the natural impulse of human beings to live in common; this indicates by itself how close *pragmata* and *phusika* are in Aristotle's conception, it indicates his naturalist conception of the origins of community. But the legislator, too, is called an efficient cause: "To be sure, the tendency we all have to form a community of this kind is a natural fact, and yet he who first founded the state was the greatest of benefactors" (ibid., I, 2; 1253 a 29 f./*Basic Works*, p. 1130). For the transference of the causal schemata to the political domain in Aristotle generally, cf. Riedel, *Metaphysik und Metapolitik*, pp. 65–73. Riedel concludes that "politics, as a theory, works with concepts and principles that are not themselves 'political' " (pp. 58 f.).

33. Wm 314/Phy 225.

34. Cf. FD 53 f. and 63 f./WTh 70 and 81 f.

35. ἐστὶ δ'οὐσία τὸ ὑποκείμενον, *Metaphysics* VIII, 1; 1042 a 13/*Basic Works*, p. 812.

36. The *pros hen* schema is applied by Aristotle wherever something appears to be relative to something else. Terms relative to another are intermediary between synonyms or univocals and homonyms or equivocals. The former designate things identical in nature and pertaining to the same genus; the latter, things that have nothing in common but their name—for example, the bear in the forest and the Great Bear in the sky. Midway between synonyms and homonyms, the terms called *aph'henos* and *pros hen* are of things whose common name derives from one single "nature" they share. What they are, they are by virtue of this single nature. It functions as their principle of common determination. The case *par excellence* of such a relation to a single term is being: "There are many senses in which a thing may be said to 'be', but all that is is related to one focal point, to one common nature, and is not said to 'be' by homonymy" (*Metaphysics* IV, 2; 1003 a 33 f./*Basic Works*, p. 732). What is this one focal point? "Everything is predicated of substance as subject" (*Physics* I, 2; 185 a 31/*Basic Works*, p. 220). Substance is that to which all other terms refer, that to which they are either relative or inherent. Inherence is the mode of being of things essentially related to the

substantial One, and subsistence the mode of being of that One itself. The *pros hen* relation can be called an analogy, as long as this is not understood as a proportion. (In the *Nichomachean Ethics*, Aristotle calls ἀναλογία the proportion a:b::c:d—" . . . a unity by analogy: as sight is to the body, intellect is to the soul," I, 4; 1096 b 32 f./*Basic Works*, p. 940.)

In the Seventh Book of the *Politics*, Aristotle describes the ideal city. The description goes into the particulars, "for the perfect state cannot exist without a due supply of the means of life" (*Politics*, VII, 4; 1325 b 37/*Basic Works*, p. 1282). This due supply is spelled out in detail by applying the four causes: In the ideal city, what must the sum total of the population be and what the size of its territory? Who will be called upon to legislate? For which institutions? And, the decisive point, the final cause: If it is happiness that the inhabitants strive to have in common, in what way do they share it? Who will be happy "substantially" and who "accidentally," or only by analogy? The latter are the laborers, workers, and merchants. They play the role of means for the end which is the happiness of the whole. They are the instruments in the hands of free men. Between the class of laborers and the free city, "there is nothing that is common, except that the one receives what the other produces." Again a technical example follows: just as "the art of the builder is for the sake of the house," so the ideal city is the end for the sake of which some are like builders and others, the slaves, like tools. The happy city is the single focal point to which men are ordered analogically, *pros hen:* "Some attain it, while others have little or none of it" (*Politics* VII, 8; 1328 a 30, 32 f., and 39/*Basic Works*, p. 1287).

The transference leaps into view. From the *Physics* to the *Categories*, to the *Metaphysics*, to the *Ethics* and the *Politics*, the *pros hen* schema organizes phenomena so diverse that one cannot but ask: where does this schema stem from? I will take up this question again below, in connection with the concept of *archē*. The political triumph of the attributive schema is indeed reached with the relation ἄρχειν καὶ ἄρχεσθαι, to govern and to be governed. Within the context of the Seventh Book, the transposition of the *pros hen* schema to politics, its exile in that field, is obvious. It is at home in the domain of fabrication. From there, Aristotle expatriates the predicative model to the domain of the *polis*.

37. *Physics* VIII, 7; 261 a 13 f./*Basic Works*, p. 378. Cf. in the *Politics:* "The city is by nature prior to the family and to the individual," I, 2; 1253 a 19/*Basic Works*, p. 1129.

38. *Physics* I, 2; 185 a 31/*Basic Works*, p. 220. Cf. in the *Politics:* "the state is independent and self-sufficing," IV, 4; 1291 a 9/*Basic Works*, p. 1210.

39. Cf. above, sec. 6, n. 23.

§12. Deconstructing the Ontic Origins

40. GA 55 367. These lines are an interpretation of Heraclitus's frgm. 112.

41. Hw 204/QCT 65. Heidegger adds that the destiny of metaphysics consists in all these shapes "suffering the loss of their constructive force and becoming void." See a similar list in Nietzsche, *The Gay Science*, trans. Walter Kaufmann (New York, 1974), sec. 347, p. 289.

42. The critique Habermas directs at Arendt, viz., that taken by itself *praxis* yields a unilateral concept of politics, is certainly phenomenologically founded, whatever its sociological significance may be. *Praxis* is the conjunction of words and deeds, *poiēsis*, of things and deeds. To add "things," that is, work, to speaking and acting (or doing) is to enlarge the concept of *polis*, cf. Jürgen Habermas, *Kultur und Kritik* (Frankfurt, 1973), p. 366, and "Hannah Arendt's Communications Concept of Power," *Social Research* 44 (1977), especially p. 15.

43. Husserl never went beyond the position described in *Cartesian Meditations*, trans. D. Cairns (The Hague, 1960), pp. 106–36.

44. These difficulties have been pointed out for example by Klaus Held, "Das Problem der Intersubjektivität und die Idee einer phänomenologischer Transzendentalphilosophie," in Ulrich Klaesges and Klaus Held, eds., *Perspektiven transzendental-phänomenologischer Forschung* (The Hague, 1972), especially pp. 3–60, and Michael Theunissen, *Der Andere: Studien zur Sozialontologie der Gegenwart* (Berlin, 1965), pp. 35 ff., 51 f. and 102–155.

45. On this point I follow Jürgen Habermas, *Technik und Wissenschaft als Ideologie* (Frankfurt, 1968), p. 152: "At best, phenomenology grasps the transcendental norms according to which consciousness necessarily operates. It describes (in Kantian terms) the laws of pure reason, but not the laws of a universal legislation derived from practical reason and obeyed by free will." This is however only true of the phenomenology of the subject. What I wish to show of Heideggerian phenomenology is that the economies of presence indeed

produce injunctions or directives (*Weisungen*, e.g., VA 184/PLT 185): not universal ones, derived from reason, but epochal ones, derived from dispositions in "being." Furthermore, the practical injunctions that result from deconstructing metaphysics are not those of an "ideological whip" (*ideologischer Einpeitscher*), J. Habermas, "Martin Heidegger: On the Publication of Lectures from the Year 1935," *Graduate Faculty Philosophy Journal*, VI, 2 (1977):169, but the consequences, which grow more and more precise through the course of Heidegger's writings, of the concept of authenticity in BT (cf. above, Introduction, sec. 2, nn. 33 and 34). Helmut Fahrenbach, *Existenzphilosophie und Ethik* (Frankfurt, 1970), regrets that the sketches of concrete analyses in BT have not been pursued in Heidegger's later writings to show "how reflection, motivated by practical questions, leads back to praxis and guides it" (p. 210). To this Reinhart Maurer, *Revolution und 'Kehre'. Studien zum Problem gesellschaftlicher Naturbeherrschung* (Frankfurt, 1975), p. 56, objects correctly that such a search for a new link between reflection and practice misses the very meaning of the *Kehre*, but in my opinion, the reasons Maurer provides are not the appropriate ones. His aim is to rehabilitate "the *subjectivity of the totality of entities*," which requires "man to take back, to some extent, his own subjectivity" (p. 218, emphasis added). This is not a way of overcoming subjectivism as the late form of metaphysical humanism but only of moving in circles within it.

46. "It could be that the 'who' of everyday being-there just is not the 'I myself' " (SZ 115/BT 150).

47. The title "fundamental ontology" means two things: the discourse on the being of that entity that we are, and the discourse on the foundation of regional ontologies. In neither respect does it fulfill the task of working out the question of being as such; it only prepares it. The being-question receives appropriate treatment only through the topology.

48. The loss of foundations or grounds can be repaired only by reverting to some form of subjectivist transcendentalism. Witness transcendental philosophy of language: "critical theory" can base its rationalist utopia of undistorted linguistic communication only on a philosophy of the subject. In Karl-Otto Apel, *Toward a Transformation of Philosophy*, trans. G. Adey and D. Frisby (London, 1981), the problems of practical and political legitimation are solved by a "community of communication" that implies a new version of transcendental subjectivity, see especially the chapter "The A Priori of the Communication Community and the Foundations of Ethics," pp. 225–300. This subjectivity is called "transsubjectivity" only to defend "the argumentative representation of interests" against "the egoistic assertion of one's interests" (p. 277). The "poverty of critical theory" stems, then, from having to postulate surreptitiously an ontology of the subject. Günther Rohrmoser, *Das Elend der kritischen Theorie* (Freiburg, 1970, especially p. 80) sees this shortcoming in the proclaimed opposition, in Habermas, between ontology and criticism, while in their critical theory of rational consensus Habermas and his school have to appeal systematically and at every step, to an ontology of the subject. The other language approach, structuralism, suffers from the complementary defect. In dissolving political phenomena in "a vast semantic field," linguistic structuralism in fact presupposes an ontology of the object (see the text by C. Lévi-Strauss quoted above, ch. 3, n. 9). Indeed, one wonders whether in the end structure does not turn into a kind of *ens realissimum:* "In demonstrating the rigorous arrangement of myths and in thereby *conferring on them the existence of objects*, my analysis highlights the mythical character of the objects—universe, nature, man—which for thousands, millions, billions of years have done nothing but unfold their combinatory resources in the manner of a vast mythological system before folding up and annihilating themselves under the evidence of their obsolescence" (italics added), op. cit., pp. 620 f. Needless to add that the objective order thus "conferred" no longer has anything to tell us about the political or about action in general.

49. In BT, the ontological difference is meant to set apart "the ontic depiction of inner-worldly entities and the ontological interpretation of the being of these entities" (SZ 64/BT 92). This is not yet the *temporal* difference.

50. The coercive force of the state and institutions in general derives from the force of an epochal principle. But force is not power. Power is a potential (the German word *Macht*, power, just like *machen*, to make, derives from *mögen*, *vermögen*, to be capable of). In Heidegger, the understanding of this concept, too, changes radically in the transition from existential to aletheiological phenomenology. First, potential (*Möglichkeit*) as an "existential, is the most originary and ultimate positive ontological determinateness of being-there" (SZ 143 f./BT 183). Hannah Arendt, in her opposition between force and power, *The Human Condition* (Chicago, 1958), pp. 199–207, draws on these suggestions in BT. However, Arendt

emphasizes the "humanistic" character of power: "Power is what keeps the public realm, the potential space of appearance between acting and speaking men, in existence . . . so long, at least, as the interplay is alive," ibid. p. 200 f. For the Heidegger after BT, on the contrary, "it is being itself which empowers that potential. . . . Its essence is nothing human" (N II 377/N iv 232 f.). Cf. N I 392 f., where being's potential is described in the Nietzschean terms of eternal return (there remains however something "humanist" in Nietzsche when he founds "like all thinkers before him"—and one might add, like Hannah Arendt after him—the relation to others, to things and to oneself on the model of "mutual understanding," N I 577 f.). As the text of Hw 204/QCT 65 (quoted above, n. 41) indicates, an epochal principle exerts a coercive "force."

51. SZ 11/BT 31.
52. VA 175/PLT 176.
53. GA 24 15/BPP 12.
54. Hw 203/QCT 64.
55. "The poetic project comes out of nothing" (Hw 63/PLT 76).
56. Hw 50/PLT 62.
57. Heidegger develops the metaphor of soil in explicit reference to *alētheia* when he says that "truth happens in the struggle between world and earth" (Hw 38/PLT 50). "World" here signifies disclosure and "earth," "self seclusion." See also the notion of *Bodenständigkeit* (Gel 11–28/DTh 43–57).
58. See above, n. 17.
59. Concealment, *lēthē*, "earth," connotes the absence of an entity that is no longer present (Hw 323/EGT 37), but it denotes "the withholding of the twofold," i.e., of the difference (VA 256/EGT 100). Its connotation refers to entities, its denotation, to presencing. The retreat of an epochal principle is to be understood as a connotation of "absencing," *kruptesthai*. The point is that a connotation may cease, leaving the denotation intact (as happens when epochal principles wither away).
60. "*Verwesen*," Hw 204/QCT 65. In another enumeration of these principles, similar to the list in Hw 204/QCT 65 (n. 41 above), Heidegger mentions the Platonic Good, the Christian God, the moral Law, the authority of Reason, Progress, the Happiness of the greatest number (N II 273).
61. Hannah Arendt, *On Revolution* (New York, 1965), pp. 164–166. For the end of the Middle Ages one may add the movements of the Free-spirit: "It is this communal idea, pursued since the twelfth century . . . that triumphs on the 18 of March, 1871," writes a chronicler of the Commune, cited on p. 324.
62. N I 437.
63. See this text cited above in the epigraph to sec. 6.
64. The paradigmatic role of the *polis* is the key for understanding Hannah Arendt's political concepts, cf. *The Human Condition*, pp. 22–38, and *On Revolution*, pp. 21–25. However, I have said that from the perspective of the Heidegger after BT, the anthropocentrism in the classical Greek concept of power falls into historical impossibility. This concept, together with the paradigm of the *polis*, has been criticized in another light by Jürgen Habermas as "unimaginable for any modern society," "Hannah Arendt's Communications Concept of Power," *Social Research* 44 (1977), p. 15. But the other light that Habermas tries to shed on the phenomenon of power hardly makes it easier to circumscribe the rule of ultimate referents in history since there can be no legitimating of political action by a "universal and pragmatic reconstruction of discourse in general" (*Erkenntnis und Interesse*, 2nd ed., Frankfurt, 1973, p. 416, "Postscript" not translated in *Knowledge and Human Interest*, trans. J. J. Shapiro, Boston, 1971) without systematic recourse to a metaphysics of subject, be it the subject of communicative rationality. Transcendental-subjectivist reconstruction and phenomenological deconstruction are most sharply opposed in regards to norms for action. For deconstruction, the very project of "describing universal rules of a communicative ethics in terms of fundamental norms of rational discourse" (*Erkenntnis und Interesse*, p. 413), is but another variation on fundamentalist themes. Heidegger's unique position on practical imperatives will appear more clearly below, secs. 40 and 41.
65. Hw 302/EGT 18. In this text from 1946, under the concept of "eschatology of being," the first formulation is to be found of what Heidegger will later call the end of epochal history: "What once occurred in the [Greek] dawn of our destiny would then come, as what once occurred, to its extreme end (ἔσχατον); that is, the destiny of being, hidden until now, would

take leave. . . . The history of being is gathered in this departure" (Hw 301/EGT 18). The eschatology of being sets action free from the rule of principles. Henri Birault's book, *Heidegger et l'expérience de la pensée* (Paris, 1978), contains a long commentary concerning freedom as the essence of truth, to which nothing need be added (pp. 443–527). I will, however, address three questions to Birault from the passage of Hw just quoted: (1) If in "the turning" the history of being since the Greeks is gathered so as to take its departure (*Abschied*), this extrication from our metaphysical destiny cannot remain without consequence for our understanding of life in common, the political life. If it is foundational thinking that takes its leave— the thinking that grounds, first of all, action—can the "thinking of being" remain "in itself always indifferent to the ontic and practical forms of a historical or political commitment" (p. 378)? (2) Does the "departure" of the "destiny of being" not oblige us to distinguish between *reversals* and *the turning*, and correlatively between the epochal concealment (which is taking leave) and the aletheiological concealment (which is to be preserved and given emphasis) of being? If so, can it be said that "forgetting is always the forgetting of a forgetting" (p. 505), that "the thinking of being does not abolish the forgetting of being" (p. 551)? The *epochē* is the forgetting of *lēthē*, but does *Seinsdenken* not put an end to "the forgetting of this *epochē*"? Then, "any rise of a world" is precisely not held "suspended in the *epochal* essence of being" (pp. 553 f., emphasis added). It matters little whether this distinction between *epochē* and *lēthē* is expressed in terms of "principial economy" and "anarchic economy" or in another vocabulary. But does confounding the two not amount to missing the *Kehre*, purely and simply? (3) Is *lēthē* really "the initial non-essence of truth," substituting for "*Sinn*" in BT (pp. 504 f.)? In VS 133, Heidegger corrects himself about *lēthē*: it is not as he had said in SD 78/OTB 71, "the very heart of *alētheia*." Therefore it is not *lēthē* that takes the place of *Sinn*, but *eon* and its loci, the *topoi* of the temporal difference.

66. Wm 251/QB 105 (emphasis added).
67. Wm 83/BWr 127.
68. WhD 153/WCT 132 f.
69. VA 32/QCT 25 (emphasis added).
70. VA 33/QCT 26.
71. Wm 81–84/BWr 125–127, cf. N II 397.
72. KPM 257/Cas 197.
73. Wm 147 f./BWr 196.
74. N II 485/EPh 79.
75. SD 55/OTB 52.
76. WhD 22/WCT 52. These lines deal with the "destruction" of one transmitted philosophy, that of Nietzsche.

Part Three: The Origin Is Said in Many Ways

1. MHG 77/IW 40, cf. VA 148/PLT 148. The remark about the invention of new terms seems to allude to SZ 39/BT 63.
2. In Plato's dialogue, *Meno*, Socrates, before questioning a young slave about geometry, inquires about the boy's native tongue: "Is he Greek? Does he speak our language?" (81 b). It seems that the storehouse of forms on which recollection draws is first of all a natural language.

VI. *Archē:* The Kinetic Paradigm of Origin

1. Wm 317/Phy 227 f.
2. E.g., *The Iliad*, XXII, 116; *The Odyssey*, XXI, 4.
3. The German poet Johann Heinrich Voss (1751–1826), the unequaled translator of Homer, correctly rendered the verse of the *Iliad* at II, 494: "*Führer war der Boioten Penelos*"—'leader' and not 'commander', *Homers Ilias*, trans. J. H. Voss (Wiesbaden, s.a.), p. 32.
4. *Politics*, III, 13; 1284 b 2. Aristotle speaks of "nations whose spirit has been stirred by the recollection of their former power."
5. The list of the many senses of this word in *Metaphysics* V, 1; 1012 b 34–1013 a 17, is

hardly more than a lexicographical enumeration. It mixes the two meanings. Aristotle defines ἀρχή as that out of which something is or becomes or is known. The term therefore designates a source of being, becoming and knowledge beyond which it is useless to try to investigate: the source is ultimate in that it both begins and commands. Ἀρχή as inception, Pierre Aubenque remarks, "is not a simple beginning that is left behind by what follows, but on the contrary, it never ceases to begin, that is, to govern that whose ever bursting forth inception it is," *Le problème de l'être chez Aristote* (Paris, 1966), p. 193. The concept of ἀρχή is broader than that of αἰτία: "all αἰτίαι are ἀρχαί," *Metaphysics* V, 1; 1013 a 18, but all ἀρχαί are not causes (literally: all ἀρχαί are not 'guilty' of something, αἰτία designating "what is culpable for an entity's being what it is," Wm 315/Phy 227).

6. In Plotinus the hypostases are the constitutive elements, ἀρχαί, of the universe, just as created being and freedom are the constitutive elements of man, *Ennead* III, 3, 4, 1–7.

7. Θεωρεῖν "brings before [our] perception and exposition the ἀρχαί and the αἰτίαι of what is present" (VA 53/QCT 164).

§13. The Causal Concept of *Archē*

8. Wm 317/Phy 228.

9. H. Diels and W. Kranz, *Die Fragmente der Vorsokratiker* (DK), 8th ed. (Berlin, 1956), Fragm. 12 A 9: "ἀρχὴν τε καὶ στοιχεῖον εἴρηκε τῶν ὄντων τὸ ἄπειρον." Cf. G. S. Kirk and J. E. Raven, *The Presocratic Philosophers* (Cambridge, 1971), p. 105.

10. We owe this Aristotelian reading of Anaximander to the Neoplatonist Simplicius summarizing the Peripatetic Theophrastus. Heidegger mentions this filiation in Hw 299 / EGT 15f.

11. "Πρῶτος αὐτὸς ἀρχὴν ὀνομάσας τὸ ὑποκείμενον," quoted in Kirk and Raven, op. cit., p. 107. Their translation: "being the first to call the substratum of the opposites *archē*."

12. This is John Burnet's translation, cited in Kirk and Raven. Burnet takes ἀρχή in the most limited Aristotelian sense of 'material cause'. In any case, the point seems established that Theophrastus wanted to attract attention to the idea of ἄπειρον in Anaximander, and that he speaks of ἀρχή as an Aristotelian. Burnet writes: "The current statement that the term *archē* was introduced by [Anaximander] appears to be due to a misunderstanding," *Early Greek Philosophy* (London, 1930), p. 54. All this concurs with Heidegger, Wm 317/Phy 228, and conflicts with Bruno Snell, *Die Entdeckung des Geistes* (4th ed., Göttingen, 1975), p. 222 (chapter XIII, "Das Symbol des Weges," in which Snell treats the concept of *archē*, is not contained in the English translation by T. G. Rosenmeyer, *The Discovery of the Mind*, Cambridge, Mass., 1953).

13. *Metaphysics* I, 2; 982 a 6 f. Philosophy is an ἐπιστήμη, a science, because it poses the question of the ἀρχαὶ καὶ αἰτίαι, ibid. VI, 1; 1025 b 6.

14. "First philosophy" would then be the knowledge of the πρώτη ἀρχή, *Metaphysics*, VI, 1; 1026 a 21–30, that is, of "being as ground" (IuD 57/IaD 59 f.).

15. "The tacit standard for the interpretation and appreciation of the early thinkers is the philosophy of Plato and Aristotle. . . . But simply to disregard subsequent representations comes to nothing if we do not first of all examine how it stands with the matter [itself]" (Hw 297/EGT 14).

16. *Metaphysics* IV, 2; 1003 b 6 ff. See the commentary on this passage by Aubenque, op. cit., p. 192.

17. *Metaphysics* I, 3; 983 a 24–b 2; *Physics* II, 3; 194 b 16–195 a 3.

18. This impossibility of a "science that would possess universal sovereignty," *Posterior Analytics* I, 9; 76 a 16, has been pointed out by Aubenque, op. cit., pp. 206–219. The priority of first philosophy would make it the *archē* of all knowledge, but an *archē* that is inaccessible to knowledge.

19. GA 55 78.

20. See above, n. 11.

21. Hw 297/EGT 14.

22. See the quote from Aubenque above, n. 5.

23. SvG 182 f.; N II 431/EPh 28.

24. GA 9 124.

25. Heidegger sides with Nietzsche not only in denouncing the passion for causal explanations in the Western tradition as a symptom for an interest in manipulation (cf. Nietzsche, *The*

Will to Power, sec. 551, trans. W. Kaufmann, New York, 1967, pp. 295–297), but also in viewing the quest for causes as a thin disguise of what Nietzsche calls an anthropomorphic projection ("we derive the entire concept [of cause] from the subjective conviction that *we* are causes," ibid., p. 295). See in Kant, *Akademie-Ausgabe* (Berlin, 1902–1955) vol. XVIII, nb. 3921, and *Vorlesungen über die Metaphysik*, ed. K.H.L. Pölitz (Erfurt, 1821), p. 79.

26. See the analysis of *Physics*, 192 b 16–32, in Wm 320–328/Phy 230–236. In the Middle Ages the opposition 'moved by itself—moved by another' functions as the middle term in the proofs, other than the ontological and that from participation, of the existence of God.

27. Heidegger's remarks on the participle φύον (VA 267–273/EGT 111–115) should be read strictly parallel to those on the participle ἐόν (VA 242 f./EGT 88 f.). In both cases, the usage of the Presocratic key words is equivocal: they can be understood in reference to substance, and then the participle is nominal, or in reference to action, and then the participle is verbal. As nominal participles, φύον and ἐόν result in Aristotelian 'physics' and 'ontology'; but as verbal participles they produce expressions as anti-metaphysical as οὐσία φύσις τις, "the being of entities is something like an emerging" (cf. Wm 369/Phy 268) and τὸ τί ἦν εἶναι, "that which something was to be" (*Metaphysics* VII, 4; 1029 b 13–14, cf. KPM 233/Kpm 249, EiM 147/IM 193 and GA 55 56 f. and 73). At the close of his interpretation of *Physics*, B, 1, Heidegger opposes these two ways of understanding φύσις, the nominal and the verbal, as ἀρχὴ κινήσεως and κίνησις (in the primary sense of 'coming about', of γένεσις) (Wm 368/Phy 267).

28. "Γένεσις and φθορά are to be thought from φύσις, and within it, as a rising that alleviates and a decline" (Hw 315/EGT 30).

29. GA 9 124 (emphasis added).

§14. The Teleocratic Concept of *Archē*

30. GA 55 201.

31. Wm 321/Phy 231 and GA 55 369.

32. Wm 321/Phy 231. "*Telos* is not goal or purpose, but end in the sense of the completion by which the essence of something is determined," ibid.

33. *Metaphysics*, IX, 8; 1050 a 21.

34. Ibid., 1050 a 22 f. According to R. Hirzel, "Über Entelechie und Endelechie," *Rheinisches Museum, Neue Folge* 39 (1884):169–208, there are two possible etymologies of the word ἐντελέχεια: either it is composed of ἐντελές (or ἐντελῶς) and ἔχειν, 'to be fulfilled', or it is composed of ἐν, τέλος and ἔχειν, 'having the end in itself'. In both cases, however, if the entelechy is thought from the standpoint of the εἶδος, it means that becoming is accomplished in the fully constituted substance possessing its end and in that sense 'finished'.

35. *Metaphysics* IX, 8; 1050 a 7 f.; cf. *Nicomachean Ethics* VI, 2; 1139 a 32 f. and the commentary on this text (VA 53/QCT 164).

36. Ἥ τε κίνησις ἐνέργεια μέν τις εἶναι δοκεῖ, ἀτελὴς δέ, *Physics* III, 2; 201 b 31 f. translation by Heidegger (Wm 355 f./Phy 257).

37. "The standing-in-the-work is the work," ibid., 1050 a 22; τέλος δ' ἡ ἐνέργεια, "the end is the standing-in-the-work," ibid., 1050 a 9; as identical to ἐντελέχεια, ἐνέργεια (the scholastics translate it 'actuality') is opposed to δύναμις ('potentiality'), e.g., ibid., IX, 7; 1048 b 35 f. *Dynamis* is the 'not yet' of full presence; it is presence as about to become constant and visible.

38. *Nicomachean Ethics* VI, 4; 1140 a 2.

39. Ibid., I, 1; 1094 a 3–6.

40. Only action, and notably political action, renders one "self-sufficient," *Nicomachean Ethics*, I, 7; 1097 b 8–12.

41. These two types of ends remain intermeshed, for example, in the catalogue of the species of *archē* already cited, *Metaphysics* V, 1; 1012 b 34–1013 a 23, and ibid., IX, 8; 1050 a 7–15.

42. The Aristotelian theory of the immanence of the end in action has been summarized most succinctly by Hannah Arendt: "Acting is fun," *Crises of the Republic* (New York, 1969), p. 203. Action, she writes, has traditionally been described as pursuit of happiness; yet acting is already happiness. See also her "Action and the 'Pursuit of Happiness'." *Politische Ordnung und menschliche Existenz*, Festgabe E. Voegelin (Munich, 1962), pp. 1–16.

43. "Μάλιστα," *Metaphysics* V, 1; 1013 a 14.

44. VA 17/QCT 8 (emphasis added).
45. See above, n. 27, and Hw 298/EGT 14.
46. The different variants of humanism "all agree in this, that the *humanitas* of *homo humanus* is determined with regard to an interpretation of nature established in advance . . . what is peculiar to all metaphysics is that it is 'humanistic' " (Wm 153/BWr 201 f., cf. Wm 141/PDT 269).
47. In John the Evangelist it is onto-theological, since in his gospel *archē* designates God.

VII. *Princeps* and *Principium:* Time Forgotten

1. SvG 42.
2. "*Causam appello rationem efficiendi,*" *Oratoriae Partitiones*, n. 110, quoted in SvG 116. This should obviously be translated: "I call a 'cause' the reason [or ground] for achieving something." Heidegger, however, apparently to stress the prefix *ex-*, translates *efficere* as "to produce," *hervorbringen*, and *ratio* as "account," *Rechnung*. "I call a 'cause' what accounts for a production." His motive for that translation will appear below (sec. 16).
3. The *principium grande* reads: "*Nihil est sine ratione seu nullus effectus sine causa*" (quoted in SvG 43).
4. For example, "we accept without further examination that the proposition 'cogito sum', emphasized by Descartes himself as 'the first and most certain', is a supreme proposition and a 'principle' in the traditional sense: the ultimate premise, so to speak, for all conclusions. However . . . what is henceforth the 'ground' and 'principle' is [rather] the *subiectum* in the sense of representation representing itself" (N II 167/N iv 118).
5. L. Couturat, *Opuscules et fragments inédits de Leibniz* (Paris, 1903), p. 515.
6. Again it is Cicero who introduces the word *evidentia* into Latin philosophical language, translating ἐνάργεια, "clear, vivid presentation," a technical term of Greek rhetoric, *Academica*, ch. 2, n. 17. He is the one who opens the epoch of philosophizing in Latin.
7. The Latin versions of the New Testament quite naturally translate ἀρχή by *principium*, e.g., Jn 1, 1 and 8, 25. This last text especially ("Then they said: 'Who are you?' Jesus answered them: 'What I have told you from the beginning.' " But the Vulgate reads: "*Principium, qui et loquor vobis,*" "I am the Beginning, the Principle, that is speaking to you") gave way to patristic speculations identifying the *principium* with God. See for example, Saint Augustine, *De Trinitate*, Book V, ch. XIII, 14, where the three divine Persons are called a single principle: "Unum ergo principium ad creaturam dicitur Deus, non duo vel tria principia," with the commentary in M. Mellet and T. Camelot, eds., *Oeuvres de Saint Augustin*, "Bibliothèque Augustinienne," vol. 15 (Paris, 1955), p. 586, n. 37.
8. SvG 118.

§15. From the Principle of Essences to the Principle of Propositions

9. SvG 54.
10. In *Die Katagorien- und Bedeutungslehre des Duns Scotus* ("Duns Scotus' Doctrine of Categories and Theory of Meaning") Heidegger was already striving to trace the "differentiations of sense" of the concept of principle: just like "cause," he then wrote, "principle" "designates something from which something else *issues* and thereby receives consistancy" (FS 198, emphasis added). "Applied to logical relations, the word 'principle' means 'ground', but in the domain of natural reality, 'cause'," (FS 276).
11. *Metaphysics* VII, 1; 1027 a 31–34 where οὐσία is called the ἀρχή of accidents. In Aristotle himself, as well as in his reading of the Eleatics, ἀρχή may also designate one of the four causes (cf. Wm 336 f./Phy 243) or causality in general (Wm 316/Phy 227: "*das Urtümliche*").
12. Patristic and scholastic titles abound in which the supreme Being is called 'origin': for example Origen, Περὶ ἀρχῶν; Bonaventure says that the creature, "because of its imperfection, constantly needs its principle, and the first principle, because of its clemency, ceaselessly pours itself out into the creature," *Breviloquium*, V, II, 3.
13. See for example, the Analytic of *Grundsätze*, first propositions, in Kant's *Critique of Pure Reason*.
14. After Descartes, writing treatises on the 'principles' of a science became a veritable tradition: principles of philosophy (Descartes), of nature and grace (Leibniz), of mathematics (Russell), of political economy (Ricardo), of psychology (W. James), etc.

15. "To act according to principles," Kant; Hans Jonas, *Das Prinzip Verantwortung* (Frankfurt, 1979).

16. For example, Herbert Marcuse's "performance principle," *Eros and Civilization* (New York, 1962), pp. 81 ff.; E. Bloch, *Das Prinzip Hoffnung*, 2 vol. (Frankfurt, 1959).

17. SD 70/OTB 63.

18. This is how Nietzsche seems to have translated the Stoic ἐπέχειν, *The Will to Power*, sec. 715, trans. W. Kaufmann, New York, 1967, p. 381 (in one of his rare mistranslations, Kaufmann renders "Willens-Punktationen" as "treaty drafts of will"). Cf. sec. 639, where an "epoch" is called "a point in the evolution of the will to power," p. 340.

19. *Principium* has of course also always designated rules of thought formulated in propositions. But the propositional understanding of the principles did not predominate until the rise of modern subjectivity, to which it is intimately linked. The text cited in the epigraph above describes the relation between ground and consequent as the matter for representation: "everything must be represented as a consequence." The subject is the principle inasmuch as it *renders* everything *present* anew. In Heidegger, this connection to re-presenting subjectivity had found its first expression with the aid of Heinrich Rickert's philosophy of value, in his dissertation for habilitation on Scotus: a judgment, Heidegger then wrote (FS 212), just like a principle (FS 254), "obtains," "is valid," *gilt*. Later he writes that God himself "is pervaded by the *principium rationis*: the domain of validity of the principle of reason comprehends all entities, up to and including their existent first cause" (SvG 53). As Heidegger himself indicates in a letter, printed as the preface to Henri Mongis, *Heidegger et la critique de la notion de valeur* (The Hague, 1976), p. viii, throughout the three stages of its historical articulation—in Plato, Kant, and Nietzsche—the notion of value has been intimately linked to the question of being; it can therefore serve as guiding thread for the deconstructive trajectory, running through Western metaphysics since its beginnings. The root of the propositional understanding of principles—subjectivity—however, remains veiled until modernity. Before the reversal of history that institutes subjectivity as the tribunal over propositions, principles are not, and cannot be, 'evaluated', gauged explicitly according to their validity for the judge that we are. Subjectivity and value arrive on the philosophic scene together: "Value seems to express that, in the position we adopt in regard to it, we ourselves contribute what is most valuable" (Hw 94/QCT 142, cf. Mongis, op. cit., pp. 90–99). What has value first and foremost for subjectivity, once it is explicitly constituted as the tribunal for verification, is a principle formulated as a proposition.

20. Cf. SvG 35.

21. John Duns Scotus, *A Treatise on God as First Principle*, I, 1; ed. and trans. A. B. Wolters (Chicago, 1966), p. 2.

22. According to Etienne Gilson, *Jean Duns Scot, Introduction à ses positions fondamentales* (Paris, 1952), pp. 33 f., 158, 256, 327, the vocabulary of "*primum*" and "*principium*" in Duns Scotus goes back to Avicenna.

23. "I wish to start from the essential order as from the more fecund medium," I, 3; trans. p. 2 (translation modified). Since Heidegger in "Duns Scotus' Doctrine of Categories and Theory of Meaning" (FS 131 ff.) treats logical issues raised by the notion of order, he does not deal with the essential order.

24. Cf. FS 197–200.

25. Duns Scotus, op.cit., I, 6; trans. p. 5.

26. Ibid., I, 8; trans. p. 5. Scotus places this text under a reference to Aristotle, *Metaphysics* V, 11; 1019 a 1–4: "Some things are called prior according to nature and essence, namely all those that can exist independently of other things, whereas the others cannot exist without them—a distinction already employed by Plato." Pierre Aubenque remarks about this reference of Aristotle to Plato: "We do not know of Platonic texts that would expressly contain that definition of the prior," *Le problème de l'être chez Aristote* (Paris, 1966), p. 46. Scotus repeats, following Aristotle, that the priority of the principle is established "*testimonio Platonis*." But if the reference is obscure in Aristotle, it is doubtful in Scotus: priority "according to nature and essence," as it is operative within the representation of an essential order, presupposes a creationist perspective.

27. "*Relatio realis est simpliciter relatio, et relatio rationis secundum quid relatio.*" "Real relation is a relation purely and simply, whereas a relation by reason is only a relation in a manner of speaking," *Opus Oxoniense*, I, dist. 29, n. 1; "Editio Vaticana" vol. VI, 1963, p. 166. This distinction is complicated, however, by the fact that Scotus also calls a relation by reason a thing, "*res.*" See the following note.

28. Jan Peter Beckmann, *Die Relationen der Identität und Gleichheit nach J. Duns Scotus* (Bonn, 1967), pp. 69–74, has pointed out four meanings of the word *"res"* in Duns Scotus: it can designate the non-contradictory, the extra-mental, autonomous beings, or substance. Any relation is real in the first of these four senses, but the essential order is made of relations in the last sense only.

29. See the texts cited in Beckmann, pp. 44–47.

30. "Essential dependence terminates in nature," Duns Scotus, op. cit., IV, 91; trans. p. 150.

31. *Topics* I, 8; 103 b 20–25; *Categories*, ch. II; 1 b 25–2 a 3.

32. "It is clear not only what cause and caused are, but also that what is caused depends essentially upon the cause," Duns Scotus, op. cit., I, 10; trans. p. 6 (translation slightly modified).

33. See the argument to prove the unicity of the first nature, Duns Scotus, op. cit., III, 46–54; trans. pp. 62–66.

34. FS 223.

35. According to Scotus, the notion of essence cannot be comprehended by the opposition between universal nature and individual substance. Essence is indifferent to universality and singularity. As is well known in the history of ideas, it is with such an essentialist realism that the disciples of Duns Scotus challenged those of Thomas Aquinas. For Etienne Gilson's thesis on Scotist "essentialism" versus Thomist "existentialism," see, for example, his *L'Etre et l'essence* (Paris, 1948), pp. 121–140 and 297; *Being and Some Philosophers* (Toronto, 1949), p. 208.

36. In his thesis on Duns Scotus Heidegger expresses the concept of hierarchy again in terms of values: the principle is "what is of highest value," das *Höchstwertige* (FS 202). "Each object of natural reality possesses a determinate value (*Wertigkeit*), a degree of its being actual" (FS 203).

37. The thesis, Augustinian in origin, of the priority of will over intellect may well be, in Duns Scotus, the expression of a deeper necessity in which an ontology of order must represent the principle as 'power', as 'imposing' ordinance on entities, and in that sense as thetical.

38. Wm 353/Phy 255.

39. Ex. 3, 14: "I am He who is" (in the Septuagint translation).

40. On the unknowability of God as substance in Duns Scotus, see the texts quoted by E. Gilson, *Jean Duns Scot*, op. cit., pp. 218–234.

41. N II 410/EPh 10. This remark by Heidegger concerns the translation of ἐνέργεια as *actualitas*. It applies to medieval metaphysics as a whole, insofar as it is based on the causal analysis of movement.

42. Duns Scotus, *Treatise on God as First Principle*, III, 43, trans. p. 62 (translation modified). The expression *actu existens*, signifying the *primum effectivum*, the most efficient cause, illustrates the transmutation of ἐνέργεια as "standing-in-the-work" to *actualitas* as the "omnipresence" of the supreme cause (cf. N II 416/EPh 16).

43. The element of "construction" that best indicates this continuity between Aristotelian onto-physics and Scotist and medieval onto-theology, the one that Heidegger seems to have understood from the beginning as giving unity to metaphysics, is the principial role played by the four causes (FS 267).

44. GA 55 364; cf. Hw 324/EGT 38.

45. This reduction of the *archē* to rule—the result of "forgetting" time and absence (which were still implied in *Physics* IV, 11; 220 a 24)—indicates to Heidegger that one single region of phenomena continues to offer itself to thought, the region of subsistent (*vorhanden*) entities. Their constant availability is expressly affirmed by the notion of actuality. As the philosophical vocabulary changes from Greek to Latin, the understanding of origin slips from the activity of the artisan to the actuality of the Creator (cf. Hw 342/EGT 56 f., N II 410–420/EPh 10–19).

§16. From the Principle of Propositions to the Epochal Principles

46. SvG 14.

47. Commenting on the passage from the *Physics* II, 1; 192 b 16 f., Heidegger opposes the pre-terminological sense of the categories in Aristotle himself to their propositional sense. According to the latter, they "must" (in Kant) be deduced from *judgments* (Wm 320–323/Phy 230–232).

48. Therefore we will not have to pursue the two key lines along which Heidegger inter-

prets Leibniz, namely, the understanding of being as will (N I 45 and 68 f./N i 35 and 56; N II 342/N iv 205; VA 114/WNZ 421; Hw 226 and 256 f./QCT 90 and PLT 100) and the question: "Why is there something rather than nothing?" (Wm 210/WGM 220; N II 347/N iv 208; N II 446/EPh 42).

49. "The final reason for things must be in a necessary substance, in which the detail of the changes can be contained only eminently, as in their source. It is this substance that we call God," *Monadology*, # 38; G. W. Leibniz, *Philosophical Papers and Letters,* trans. and ed. L. E. Leomker (2nd ed., Dordrecht, 1970), p. 646. Cf. SvG 53 and 55.

50. In speaking of axioms, Leibniz intends to remain faithful to Aristotle. In the *Topics* VIII, 1; 155 b 29 f. and 159 a 3 f., ἀξίωμα designates an opinion from which an argument is initiated, a starting supposition that may eventually prove false. In the *Posterior Analytics* I, 2; 71 b 20 f., on the contrary, it more generally seems to designate a true, immediate, evident content of thought which founds the propositions of a proof. Axioms are κοιναὶ δόξαι, convictions common to all men or to all sciences (*Metaphysics* III, 2; 996 b 28) or κοιναὶ ἔννοιαι (cf. SvG 33). But for Leibniz, an axiom is a proposition, an "aphorism" or a "maxim," and not a general content of thought. That Leibniz appeals to Aristotle therefore "is not justified," Heidegger concludes (Wm 26/ER 17, cf. N II 159/N iv 112).

51. Cf. SvG 44.

52. SvG 15, 96 f., 192.

53. In this rendition different aspects of the ground become operative. The *reddere* is understandable only in light of the *Grundfrage,* the question of being; it indicates the *Grundstellung,* fundamental position, of modern man; it appears on the *Hintergrund,* the background, of the ontological difference and in the context of the *Grundlehre,* the fundamental teaching, of the epochal understanding of being. In this way Heidegger's *Gründlichkeit,* thoroughness, leads beyond the *Satz vom Grund,* principle of sufficient reason, as understood by Leibniz. On these different terms see Alexius Bucher, *Martin Heidegger, Metaphysik als Begriffsproblematik* (Bonn, 1972), pp. 190 f.

54. N II 141/N iv 96.

55. The phrase "field of origin" occurs already in KPM 20/Kpm 27, where, however, it designates finitude in a still non-historical sense.

56. Secs. 31 and 32 respectively of the *Monadology* treat the principle of non-contradiction and the principle of sufficient reason (Leibniz, op. cit., p. 646).

57. Ibid.

58. See above, n. 50.

59. Leibniz's logic is not "like" Aristotle's, Heidegger says; it belongs to the "same" mode of thinking according to *logos,* the "onto-theo-logical" mode inaugurated by Plato (WhD 103/WCT 165, IuD 68/IaD 70). The difference within this identity stems from the new concatenation of *on* with *theos* and *logos.*

60. EiM 92/IM 121, cf. Wm 25/ER 13.

61. SvG 75.

62. FD 82/WTh 106, cf. N II 24 f. and 298.

63. FD 84/WTh 108 f. Only through this ego-principle can the *logos* become, for Leibniz, "the activity of the subject" (US 249/OWL 119). The ego-principle indicates "a determinate idea of being in general," namely, as "the essence of the 'subjectivity' of the *subiectum,* understood monadologically" (Wm 32/ER 31).

64. In the texts dealing with the forgottenness of being, Heidegger tends to oppose "authentic thinking" (*das eigentliche Denken*) to "ordinary thinking" (*das gewöhnliche Denken*) as he opposes pre-metaphysical thinking to metaphysical thinking. Reification, then, is an epochal "stamping" or "seal." In a few texts on the Presocratics, however, reification is said to precede the turn toward metaphysics. Then the two modes of thinking are opposed as the ordinary opinions of the *polloi* to "the thinker's thinking," in particular Heraclitus's (e.g., GA 55 146).

65. N II 238/N iv 180 and N II 474/EPh 69.

66. SvG 210/PG 222.

67. See above, sec. 8, n. 30.

68. Leibniz, *Monadology,* sec. 14, op. cit., p. 644. Modern "perception," Heidegger observes, must not be taken as simple receptivity, but rather as "driving together," *co-agitatio,* and as "assault," *Angriff* (Hw 100/QCT 149 f.). See below, sec. 46.

69. Leibniz, *Monadology,* sec. 30, p. 646.

70. N II 167/N iv 118.

71. N II 439/EPh 35. Heidegger quotes two texts by Leibniz: "I say that substance is actuated by one entelechy without which it would contain no principle of true unity"; and: the unity of non-substantial being "stems from cogitation."

72. SvG 47.

73. SvG 65.

74. VA 234/EGT 82.

75. N II 452/EPh 48.

76. SvG 45.

77. During the age of metaphysics, "being takes its essential stamping each time from one being that gives the measure" (N II 421/EPh 20).

78. Leibniz calls principles necessary truths, as distinguished from contingent truths. Strictly speaking, however, principles are not truths but rules for truths. The principle of sufficient reason splits into a principle applicable to necessary truths, which stem from innate ideas, and another principle, applicable to truths that stem from sensibility. Heidegger's strategy, in *Der Satz vom Grund,* is to blur, it seems, this distinction between principles and truths so as to establish the principle of sufficient reason as the ultimate truth or referent for our era.

79. See the lines quoted above in the epigraph to this chapter.

80. Truth as representation constitutes the last narrowing of truth conceived as conformity between a judgment and a fact. The first such narrowing occurred in the transition from Platonic *homoiōsis,* moral assimilation to the Good, to Latin *adaequatio,* propositional adequateness to a fact.

81. According to the first "key," Heidegger emphasizes: "*nihil* est *sine* ratione," according to the second: "nihil *est* sine *ratione*" (SvG 75).

82. SvG 154, cf. above, sec. 10, n. 55.

83. Heidegger translates: "*Versammlung,*" gathering (VA 210/EGT 62).

84. *Cogitare* in the sense of *co-agitare,* driving together (Hw 100/QCT 150).

85. Heidegger translates: "*Aufgehen,*" rising (VA 271/EGT 113).

86. Heidegger translates: "*Entbergung,*" disclosure, VA 258/EGT 103.

87. Hw 100/QCT 149.

88. Hw 98/QCT 147.

89. SvG 153.

90. SD 9/OTB 9.

91. SvG 58. That we name our era after a source of energy indicates once again how exclusively thought has come to be determined by available stock and "oppressing presence" (*Andrang*).

92. The notion of principle does not designate here some in-itself realized progressively through the centuries—a construct that Marx has so sarcastically criticized in the Idealists; see his parody of Pierre-Joseph Proudhon quoted above, sec. 8, n. 53. A similar accusation is leveled against Max Stirner in the *German Ideology* (Moscow, 1976), p. 264. Marx there claims to "invert" idealism: "It is better the other way round: life has created the principle." However, this "reversal of metaphysics, already accomplished by Karl Marx" (SD 63/OTB 57) leaves the metaphysical quest for causes intact. To turn against idealism Marx reverses the causal relation between principles and life: the needs, the productive forces, in short, life, causes—"creates," he says—the principles rather than the latter creating the epochal forms of life. It is clear that this entire problematic of ultimate determination either by some in-itself, "ideas, categories, principles," or by material conditions, collapses the moment one is content to trace phenomenologically the internal ordering of epochs instead of searching for their ontic causes. The phenomenological notion of epochal principle does not designate a *cause,* but the most present, the most unveiled entity in a given aletheiological field.

VIII. *Anfang* and *Ursprung:* The Temporal Difference

§17. The Vocabulary

1. GA 55 370.

2. N II 421/EPh 20 (emphasis added).

3. E.g., GA 55 78. In the remarks about *Beginn, Anfang,* and *Ursprung* in this section, I follow especially Heidegger's 1943 course, "The Incipience of Western Thinking," whose subject is to a large extent the clarification of those terms. "Instead of the deliberately formulated title of this course, 'The Incipience of Western Thinking' ('*Der Anfang des abendländischen Denkens*')," Heidegger says in the introduction, "one could also say 'The Beginning (*der Beginn*)—or the Origin (*der Ursprung*)—of Philosophy in the West'. The reason we are retaining the other title will become clear as the course proceeds" (GA 55 3 f.).

4. GA 55 332.

5. GA 55 387. Thanks to the turning, "what the beginning of thinking has once (formerly) begun will once (at a time to come) come back toward man" (GA 55 288). On the insurpassable lead that the beginning in pre-classical Greece maintains over all Western history, see GA 55 383.

6. GA 55 211 f. (emphasis added). Elsewhere the *Beginn* designates the first step in questioning, which is the essence of thinking (GA 55 241).

7. GA 55 377 (emphasis added).

8. GA 55 78–80 (emphasis added).

9. See above, pp. 107.

10. GA 55 15.

11. TK 40/QCT 41. Here is how, in the course of a seminar, Heidegger connected the sense of 'correspondence' to the etymological sense of '*Anfang*': by "incipience" one has "to understand quite literally what . . . takes us and ceaselessly retakes us, what, therefore, holds us in a web. . . . This word does not so much mean 'announcing in advance something yet to come', but rather 'calling, provoking to respond and to correspond'," quoted in M. Heidegger, *Chemins qui ne mènent nulle part,* trans. W. Brokmeier (Paris, 1962), p. 60 n.

12. *Theaetetus* 155 d (quoted WP 24/WPh 79).

13. SZ 1/BT 19.

14. GA 55 27.

15. US 262/OWL 131.

16. GA 55 146.

17. GA 55 43. Cf. in the same sense: "We will never find the incipience of Western thinking by calculating backward through historical comparisons. We will find the incipience only by thinking forward through historical experience" (GA 55 80). "The transition toward the other incipience . . . [is possible only in] returning to the ground of the first incipience" (N II 29).

18. GA 55 175.

19. GA 55 25.

20. GA 55 125.

21. GA 55 93. In Heidegger, quite as in ordinary German, it is the substantivated verb, *das Anfangen* (or *das Unterfangen,* a word I have not found in his works) which designates the action of initiating something. In the narrower sense of human undertakings one would say "*das Beginnen*" (cf. GA 55 350).

22. GA 55 139.

23. GA 55 131. Concerning the experience of thinking, it may do to construe an equivalence between *anfangen* and "being-in-the-world," as C. F. Gethmann does in *Verstehen und Auslegung* (Bonn, 1974), p. 268. But that is insufficient for "the incipience 'of' being," i.e., the incipience which is being itself.

24. GA 55 150. "That which holds sway initially pertains to relatedness, it is neither a thing nor a state" (GA 55 133).

25. GA 55 143. This text, with its undeniable transcendental overtones, seems to make pure appearing a universal and necessary condition for all knowledge of what appears. The impression of transcendentalism is confirmed by the curious parallel that Heidegger establishes here with time and space: like them, *phusis* is always seen first, *gesichtet,* but also like them, it is never thematized, *erblickt.*

26. GA 55 159.

27. So understood, "truth is the initial essence of being, it is inception itself" (GA 55 175).

28. GA 55 128.

29. GA 55 345 (emphasis added).

30. GA 55 123.

31. N II 481/EPh 75.

32. GA 55 222.
33. GA 55 220. The editor of this volume, who formulated the section titles, put it more straightforwardly: "The Equation of Thinking and Logic as The *Origin of Western Destiny*" (GA 55 221, emphasis added).
34. GA 55 150.
35. GA 55 174.
36. GA 55 245.
37. GA 55 196.
38. GA 55 197.
39. EdD 17/PLT 9, cf. W. Marx, op. cit., p. 251.
40. GA 55 227.
41. GA 55 240.
42. GA 55 328.
43. GA 55 293. For *homologein,* see below, sec. 25.
44. GA 55 345.
45. GA 55 185.
46. GA 55 361 f. On the expression "being as time," see above, p. 18, 4.
47. GA 55 343 f.
48. GA 55 333.
49. GA 55 278 (emphasis added).
50. Hw 64/PLT 77 f.
51. GA 24 30; KPM 40/Kpm 46.
52. The "unrelenting pursuit of originariness" (*dieses unausgesetzte Drängen auf Ursprünglichkeit,* KPM 121/Kpm 133) in Heidegger is part of a long lineage: the Aristotelian quest for the πρότερον (πρὸς ἡμᾶς or φύσει) opposed to the ὕστερον, the Cartesian quest for *cur ita sit* opposed to *quod ita sit,* the Kantian search for the universal and necessary conditions of experience as opposed to its empirical conditions. . . . In every case the a priori is a "source" of concepts (see GA 24 31/BPP 23).
53. In BT the retrieval, *Wiederholung,* was already described as the repetition of a possibility: not only of the question of being as a possibility (SZ 2–4/BT 21–24), but also of authentic resolution (SZ 308 and 339/BT 355 and 388) and of existence as such (SZ 391/BT 443). Moreover, both before and after the "turning," the reference to Nietzsche is obvious in the context of the retrieval. "The authentic retrieval of a past possibility of existence—that being-there choose its hero—is grounded existentially in anticipatory resoluteness" (SZ 385/BT 437). This formulation is comparable to the description of "monumental" history in Nietzsche, that attitude for which "what is highest in one moment of the distant past be for me still alive, bright and great," F. Nietzsche, *On the Advantage and Disadvantage of History for Life,* trans. P. Preuss (Indianapolis, 1980), p. 15. Heidegger links his concept of retrieval or repetition explicitly to that of monumental history (SZ 396/BT 448). Later, the temporal mode of authentic retrieval, the instant (SZ 386/BT 438), is expressed in the vocabulary of the eternal recurrence. The Nietzschean phrase "collision of the future and past [in which] the instant returns to itself" (N I 312) then replaces the *Wiederholung* of SZ and KPM.
54. The inherited ontologies "take their rise" (*entspringen*) from fundamental ontology (SZ 13/BT 34). In more Kantian language, laying the foundations of metaphysics is to trace its origination (*Ursprung*) to the essence of knowledge in general (KPM 20/Kpm 26 f.) as finite intuition and dependence on the intuited.
55. KPM 216–219/Kpm 230–233.
56. SZ 377/BT 429. The allusion to Kantian transcendentalism and to the common root of the "two stems of our knowledge" (KPM 132 and 190/Kpm 144 and 201) is too evident for me to take at face value Heidegger's claim that BT enabled him to interpret that root as the "originary self," as opposed to Kant enabling him, in BT, to speak of "originary rootedness" (GA 25 394).
57. According to BT, the "clearing" is opened by human existence: "ecstatic temporality clears the 'there' originarily" (SZ 351/BT 402, cf. SZ 133 and 408/BT 171 and 460). After 1930, however, the clearing is understood out of being itself, as the opening of a field of presence. The word *Lichtung* then no longer signifies the natural light (SZ 133/BT 171)—disclosedness as man's ontological structure—but a "lightening": "to make something light, free and open" (SD 72/OTB 65, with the English translator's note). On this transformation of the notion of clearing, see the concordant remarks of Werner Marx, "Das Denken und seine Sache" in H.-G. Gad-

amer, W. Marx, G. F. von Weizsäcker, *Heidegger. Freiburger Universitätsvorträge zu seinem Gedenken* (Freiburg, 1977), p. 25; of Ernst Tugenthat, *Der Wahrheitsbegriff bei Husserl und Heidegger* (Berlin, 1967), pp. 275–277; and of F. W. von Herrmann, *Die Selbstinterpretation Martin Heideggers* (Meisenheim am Glan, 1964), pp. 61–63.

58. Wm 163/BWr 211.
59. SD 61/OTB 55.
60. SD 80/OTB 73.
61. SD 5/OTB 5.
62. SD 48/OTB 45.
63. Cf. the remark on *Aufhebung* below, n. 169.
64. As I have suggested above (sec. 7 and 8), in this refusal of all concepts of a necessary truth Heidegger's debt to Nietzsche is too evident to be masked by the violence of his interpretations in N I and N II.
65. See above, sec. 12, n. 41.
66. The exemplary sense of φύειν, *oriri, Aufgehen* is the rising of the sun (EiM 11/IM 14). On the double repetition see VA 267–276/EGT 111–118.
67. After Greek (*archein*) and Latin (*principium*), German, the third philosophical tongue ("*Sprache des Denkens*") according to Heidegger, seems more suitable for preventing and combatting the reduction of speech to conceptual language (*Begriffssprache*) because it is a more primary tongue than any other modern language. According to E. Schöfer, *Die Sprache Heideggers* (Pfullingen, 1962), the word *Ursprung*, along with its derivatives, is an exemplary case of "the vocabulary of German inwardness. . . . This vocabulary belongs to what is most German—*sit venia verbo*—in the German linguistic treasury and has always been keenly felt as the most genuine expression of the German soul" (p. 243; cf. the entire section entitled "*Das Vokabular der 'deutschen Innerlichkeit'*," pp. 243–247). Because it is less fixed, the German language would be particularly fit for "winning back the originary experiences of being in metaphysics through the deconstruction of representations that have become current and empty" (Wm 245/QB 93). Toward the end of the Latin age, Meister Eckhart was the first to designate the origin no longer by the noun *principium* but by the verb *urspringen*. This is not to say, however, as Schöfer does, that "since the German mystics the words of this derivation no longer appear in the philosophical texts" (p. 243). To mention only Kant, H. Ratke, *Systematisches Handlexikon zur Kritik der reinen Vernunft* (Hamburg, 1929), pp. 267 f., indicates eight different meanings of the word *Ursprung* in the *Critique of Pure Reason*. It is undeniable, in any case, that in Heidegger's view the German language, by its malleability, allows for a certain recovery of the initial experience of pre-metaphysical Greek thought: "I am thinking of the special inner kinship between the German language and the language and thinking of the Greeks. The French keep confirming this to me again and again. When they begin to think, they speak German" (Sp 217/ISp 24). In a letter to Jean Beaufret, Heidegger underscores Beaufret's remark, "the German language has resources, but the French has limits." Heidegger adds: "Here lies hidden an essential indication of the possibility of learning from each other," M. Heidegger, *Questions III*, ed. A. Préau, R. Munier, and J. Hervier (Paris, 1966), pp. 156 f.

§18. 'Original' Origins, or How the New Comes About in History

68. VA 73/EPh 86. I have translated *Anfang* as "original" and *ereignen* as "the event in which occurs. . . ." Cf. in the same sense GA 55 377.
69. The text continues: "The decline has already taken place. The consequences of that event are what has happened in the world history of this century" (ibid.). Elsewhere, however, Heidegger remarks on the contrary that "not even two world wars have been capable of tearing historical man away from mere business among entities and placing him before being itself" (GA 55 84).
70. Hw 63/PLT 76. It is from the standpoint of the end that any beginning even becomes thinkable as such: "The initial dawn (*die anfängliche Frühe*) shows itself to man only at the end" (VA 30/QCT 22).
71. VA 227/EGT 76.
72. SD 44/OTB 41.
73. Alluding to the poem of Parmenides on the way of truth (the first of the "only ways of inquiry that can be thought of" is the way of "it *is* and cannot not be," H. Diehls and W. Kranz, *Die Fragmente der Vorsokratiker*, 8th ed. [Berlin, 1956], frag. 2; G. S. Kirk and J. E.

Raven, *The Presocratic Philosophers* [Cambridge, 1971], p. 269), Heidegger describes this closure as "the event in which the farewell (*Abschied*) to all 'it is' comes to pass" (US 154/OWL 54). Cf. below, sec. 34.

74. US 134/OWL 39.

75. "*Das anfänglich Gedachte noch anfänglicher durchzudenken*" (VA 30/QCT 22). "What has been thought initially" is described by an implicit reference to a text from Aristotle: "Between what is prior by nature and what is prior for us there is no identity," *Posterior Analytics*, I, 2; 72 a 1 (trans. W. D. Ross, in R. McKeon, ed., *Basic Works of Aristotle*, New York, 1941, trans. modified). Cf. N II 215–217/N iv 160–162. By contrast, the other half of Heidegger's sentence, "to think through still more originally," refers to the dawn (*die Frühe*) before Plato and Aristotle. "Philosophy as metaphysics begins with Plato's interpretation of being as an Idea" (N II 226/N iv 170). Metaphysics begins with the discovery of the non-identity between what is prior and what is posterior in knowledge: "In this way the a priori enters into the distinction between what is prior and what is posterior in knowing" (N II 227/N iv 170). The pre-metaphysical beginning is nearly always called "*Anfang*": "At the inception (*im Anfang*) with Parmenides and Heraclitus . . ."(ibid). Cf. for example, Wm 370/Phy 268.

76. "For manifestly you have long been aware of what you mean when you use the expression 'being'. We, however, who used to think we understood it, have now become perplexed" (Plato, *The Sophist*, 244 a). These remarks are tendered by the Eleatic Stranger in order to confound a group of people who claim to know what a being is "by telling stories about it." The ignorance to which the Stranger confesses seems to signify the impossibility of gaining knowledge by story-telling. In the remarks on BT that follow I am indebted to the article by John Sallis, "Where Does *Being and Time* Begin?" in F. Elliston, ed., *Heidegger's Existential Analytic* (The Hague, 1978), pp. 21–43.

77. The distinction between the Presocratic inception of philosophy and the beginning of classical ontology remains implicit in BT (cf. the remark on Parmenides, SZ 100/BT 133). I agree with Werner Marx (*Heidegger and the Tradition*, trans. T. Kisiel and M. Greene [Evanston, Ill., 1971], p. 116) that the beginning to be retrieved in BT is that of Plato and Aristotle, and that in the subsequent writings *Andenken* differs from *Wiederholung* by its reach beyond the classical Greeks, i.e., by the "return to the [Presocratic] foundations of metaphysics." Similarly for the "end of philosophy": "the whole of the history of metaphysics" "lies between Plato and Nietzsche" (N II 226/N iv 170), whereas the problematic of the "there is," opened by Parmenides, would come to completion only with the closure, whose hypothesis alone can be formulated at present.

78. SZ 1/BT 19 (emphasis added).

79. SZ 5/BT 25. Post-metaphysical thinking would transform the Platonic discovery of the a priori, which inaugurates metaphysics. It is pre-*understanding* that comes to precede *knowledge* because it differs in kind from all conceiving: "We understand the 'is' . . . but we do not grasp (*begreifen*) it" (GA 24 18/BPP 14).

80. KPM 232/Kpm 248 (emphasis added).

81. " . . . *aus der epochalen Lichtung von Sein*" (SvG 143).

82. Hw 63/PLT 76 f.

83. René Char, *Fureur et Mystère* (Paris, 1962), p. 83.

84. Hw 63/PLT 76.

85. Cf. the text, which is paramount for my entire discussion of the question of acting, quoted above as the epigraph to sec. 12 (GA 55 367).

86. VA 162/PLT 161.

87. "The Greeks *dwelt* in this essence [the *legein*] of language. But they never *thought* this essence of language" (VA 228/EGT 77).

88. Höl 61 f.

89. Höl 63.

90. Hw 63/PLT 77.

91. Ibid. No phrase in Heidegger shows more clearly how far he stands from Sartre's "humanism." For Sartre, epochal constellations are brought about by the agency of millions.

92. Hw 63/PLT 76.

93. Höl 63.

94. Cf. the texts quoted above, sec. 1, notes 1–7.

95. See the use Heidegger makes of the Parmenides fragment 3 ("For thinking and being are the same"), Hw 83 f./QCT 130 f. and VA 231 ff./EGT 79 ff.

96. Hw 50/PLT 62.

97. "The [aletheiological] struggle first projects and develops what had hitherto remained unheard of, unsaid and unthought. Thereafter this struggle is carried on by the creators, poets, thinkers, statesmen" (EiM 47/IM 62).

98. Hw 83/QCT 130.

99. Hw 59/PLT 72.

100. Char, *Fureur et Mystère*, p. 205.

101. SvG 110.

102. VA 229/EGT 78.

103. Friedrich Hölderlin, Letter No. 236 to Casimir Ulrich Böhlendorf, December 4, 1801, 11. 73–77 (ed. Adolf Beck, *Grosse Stuttgarter Ausgabe*, vol. VI, 1 [Stuttgart, 1954–58], p. 427).

104. In order to think "more originally" [*anfänglicher*], it is necessary to go "counter to humanism" (Wm 176/BWr 225, cf. above, sec. 7, nn. 23 and 24).

105. FD 38/WTh 50. The anti-humanistic sense of 'economy' appears from the broader meaning of νόμος: "The νόμος is not only the law, but more originally the injunction contained in the dispensation of being. Only this injunction is capable of inserting man into being. Only such insertion is capable of supporting and carrying" (Wm 191/BWr 238 f.). Laws in a narrower sense, including Kantian laws of reason, are human responses to the eco-nomy of "being."

106. A theory, for example, one that maintained the determination in the last instance of things spiritual by the means of production, would thereby designate an *empirical* antecedent.

107. From frag. 3 of Parmenides to "the supreme principle of all synthetic judgments" in Kant (see KPM 114 f./Kpm 123 f.) to being-in-the-world, then to the phenomenology of the reversals, it is the process of identity that remains the same. It is best described by the ὁμολογεῖν of Heraclitus (see below, sec. 25).

108. SZ 38/BT 62.

109. It is rather curious that Heidegger, while making this distinction his own (see following note), nowhere recognizes its source in the *Critique of Pure Reason*, B XXVI, B 145, B 166 n., B 194–195, B 358–359, B 411 n., A 397, B 497, B591–592, B 799. Still more curiously, when commenting directly on the *Critique* (Kpm and WTh), Heidegger presents Kantian "thinking" as signifying indiscriminately both the activity of the understanding and that of reason.

110. VA 180/PLT 181. Under different designations, this distinction often recurs, e.g., Gel 15/DTh 46 f., Sp 212/ISp 20.

111. This confirms the regional character of the archaeology of knowledge as practiced by Michel Foucault. It is regional by the double restriction of the origin to *archē* and of thought to *epistēmē*. His archaeology cannot but describe the phenomenon of epochal beginnings—for example, the appearance of houses of confinement in the seventeenth century—in terms of knowledge, of "perception": "There must have formed, silently, and doubtless over the course of many years, a social sensibility, common to European culture, that suddenly reached a threshold and manifested itself in the second half of the seventeenth century. . . . It is this mode of perception which we must investigate." M. Foucault, *Madness and Civilization*, trans. R. Howard (New York, 1973), p. 45 (translation modified).

112. GA 24 68/BPP 50.

113. See below, sec. 47.

114. EiM 12/IM 15.

115. In his first book on Kant, this transcendentalism was not yet fully dissociated from subjectivity, but the interpretation of transcendental imagination as the common root of intuition and understanding aimed already at exhibiting *the originary as an event*, which explains the numerous comments on the literal sense of *Ursprung* in that book (KPM 20, 44 f., 190, 219/Kpm 26 f., 50 f., 201 f., 233). His second Kant book, with its emphasis on historical "fundamental positions" and the corresponding "reversals in being-there" (FD 74 f., 82, 143/WTh 95f., 106, 183), shows *the original as an occurrence* (*Geschehen*) which founds history (*Geschichte*).

116. VA 220/EGT 70.

117. VA 222/EGT 72.

118. FD 38/WTh 50.

119. See the conclusion to sec. 9, above, for this usage of 'sense'.

120. US 175/OWL 72.

121. Hw 301 f./EGT 18. When Heidegger calls questioning "the piety of thinking" (VA 44/QCT 35), the word πρόμος (Latin *primus*, German *fromm*) is to be understood out of the πίστις ἀληθής, "trusting [first] what is unconcealed," in Parmenides (SD 74/OTB 67, VA 42/QCT 34).

122. US 127/OWL 33.

123. What reserves itself while it grants itself is "the holy" (US 44 and 64 f./OWL 165 and 183). *Das Anfängliche* is holy in this double sense: through the ages, it opens up phenomena while obfuscating itself as the original phenomenality (cf. Höl 61). Its coming is adumbrated by the poet (Höl 62). Indeed, the holy "formerly smiled," whereas now it is "misknown" (Höl 63). As both hiding and showing, the holy is then the "trace" leading toward an imminent "reversal," toward the "return of the gods who have fled" (Hw 250/PLT 94). Hölderin called what is given and at the same time withheld "the fatherland" (Höl 14). *Das Anfängliche* is as antinomical as the *semainein* of Heraclitus ("The lord whose oracle is in Delphi neither speaks nor conceals but gives a sign," frag. 93) (cf. EiM 130/IM 170 and Wm 349/Phy 252).

124. To be "pious" toward the constellations of truth—"yielding" to them—is to anticipate a "brighter dawn" (*hellere Frühe*, US 70 f./OWL 188). For the "juncture" brought about by the changing context of *lēthē* and *alētheia*, cf. VA 272/EGT 118.

§19. The 'Originary' Origin, or How Presencing Comes About

125. FD 64/WTh 83.

126. SD 44/OTB 41. What Emmanuel Lévinas criticizes in Heidegger, it seems to me, is the *originary* Parmenidism, not *original* Parmenidism, the identity of being and thinking at the rise of an age. Lévinas attempts to save ontic thought as the "window on the Eternal" from ontological thought, "which fixes itself in the heart of the Same" at the expense of the Other, *En découvrant l'existence avec Husserl et Heidegger* (Paris, 1967), p. 89. The original is the identity of the non-identical: of *legein* and *epochē*. So understood, *original* Parmenidism does not prohibit saying that "Being is exteriority," Emmanual Lévinas, *Totality and Infinity*, trans. A. Lingis (Pittsburgh, 1969), p. 290.

127. GA 55 365.

128. Presencing, as temporal coming-about, remains "the very issue," *die Sache selbst*, of Heidegger's thinking throughout his writings (see SZ 35 f./BT 59 f. and SD 72–75/OTB 65 f.). This issue, being as time, is what the twofold transcendental step backwards is to attain which leads from ontic to ontological knowledge and from there to fundamental ontology; or in the words of KPM, from empirical to transcendental knowledge and from there to the foundation of metaphysics; or according to the last writings: from entities (*das Seiende*) to beingness (*Seiendheit*) and from there to being (*Sein*); or, in terms of time, from the present (*das Anwesende*) to its mode of presence (*Anwesenheit*) and to presencing (*Anwesen*, SD 75/OTB 68, or *Anwesung*, Wm 359/Phy 260); or finally from letting-be as an attitude to letting-*be* and to *letting*-be (VS 103 and SD 40 f./OTB 37 f.).

129. EiM 5/IM 6.

130. FD 43/WTh 57. In the absence of philosophy, "an originary relationship to things comes to be lacking" (FD 31/WTh 41).

131. SD 2/OTB 2. The "saltatory" *essence* of originary thought must be distinguished from the leap through which originary thinking is *entered*. The wordplay on *Satz* (both 'proposition' and 'leap') concerns the second meaning, the step back toward fundamental ontology or to the laying of the ground of metaphysics, i.e., to being or to coming-to-presence, to *letting*-be (see above, n. 128).

132. "*Ungeschichtlich, besser geschicklos*," "ahistorical, or better, without destiny" (SD 44/OTB 41).

133. For instance, the notion of *phusis* as coming-to-presence or presencing is worked out from the original usage of that notion in Aristotle (Wm 368–370/Phy 267–269).

134. SD 14/OTB 13, or *Anwesung*, Wm 369/Phy 268.

135. Or *Abwesung*, Wm 369/Phy 268.

136. Hw 315/EGT 30.

137. "What is purely other than all entities is non-being. But this nothing unfolds itself as being" (Wm 101 f./EB 353). In a subsequent edition of this text, Heidegger added two marginal notes: the 'absolute other' "is still thought [here] in a metaphysical fashion in terms of entities," and: 'non-being' here means "no-thing" (GA 9 306).

138. SZ 38/BT 63.

139. That is the first sentence of Foucault's *Madness and Civilization,* p. 3.

140. SD 25/OTB 24.

141. GA 9 306. During his middle period, in which the issue of phenomenology is the history of being through an overcoming of metaphysics, Heidegger thinks the ontological difference from the viewpoint of Anaximander's *chreōn,* as "the handing over to its while, in each case, of whatever happens to be present" (Hw 340/EGT 55). To the hiding-showing so understood refer such phrases as "distance and nearness" (Höl 138 and VA 108/WNZ 417), "danger and saving" (VA 36, 40/QCT 28, 32). During that period, the "difference" is the name for presencing insofar as it permits entities to appear as absent or present. When Heidegger later tries to think the difference without recourse to entities (whether present or absent) the double trait of appropriation and expropriation comes to belong to presencing as such (SD 44/OTB 41). This agonistic pull then no longer describes the "withdrawal of the essence of unconcealment, viz. of concealment, for the sake of the unconcealed, which appears as entities" (Wm 199/WGM 210 f.). Rather, concealment and unconcealment are traits of presencing itself, regardless of its difference from entities. After the discovery of the ahistorical event of *Anwesen,* then, the concept of *alētheia* is not the same as before.

142. "Denial and withholding obtain even within the event of appropriation inasmuch as they concern the manner in which there is time" (SD 58/OTB 54).

143. This "rise," *Ursprung,* is manifold, in accordance with the multiplicity of regions disclosed by existential projects. In order to understand what the 'originary' phenomenon in the Existential Analytic is, one has to see not only that the many regions coexist for the entity that we are, but also that an entity, e.g., the jug in the essay "The Thing," can pass from one originary region into another: it is present, it "arises" differently when used at the table, when photographed in a wine magazine, or again when analyzed according to its crystal composition. The entity that we ourselves are also 'arises' in more regions than one: *Dasein* for fundamental ontology, *vorhanden* as an object for medical science, *zuhanden* as cannon fodder.

144. According to BT, "Kant grasps the phenomenal content of the 'I' correctly in the expression 'I think.' . . . 'I think' means 'I bind together'." On the positive side, the "I" is therefore not a substance for Kant. On the negative side, however, it appears as *res cogitans* and as a logical "subject" that is *vorhanden,* and Kantian logic amounts to a "logic of things" (SZ 319 and 11/BT 367 and 31). In pursuing the direction indicated by Kant, Heidegger comprehends the *"ich verbinde"* as projecting a world. Care then takes the place of apperception as "originary unity of this structural whole" (SZ 232/BT 275). Werner Marx puts the continuity from Kant to Heidegger more squarely: " *'ursprünglich'* (transcendental)," op. cit., p. 90.

145. This impossibility is to be maintained against some ambiguous formulations in Heidegger himself, according to which the forgottenness of being could be "fundamentally and expressly overcome" (SZ 225/BT 268). See also Henri Declève, *Heidegger et Kant* (The Hague, 1970), p. 173, who suggests a double explanation for Kant's "recoiling" from temporality, by structural obfuscation (*lēthē*) according to BT, but for "historical reasons" (*epochē*) according to KPM. While *Seinsdenken* would eventually clear away *epochal* concealment, it would stress the concealment at the heart of *alētheia.* Later Heidegger maintains the impossibility of total disclosure against the pretense of universal explanation by modern science (e.g., VA 168/PLT 170).

146. SZ 64/BT 92.

147. Wm 142/PDT 269.

148. KPM 136/Kpm 148. The adjective *ursprünglich* corresponds to *"originarius"* in such Kantian expressions as *intuitus originarius* and *exhibitio originaria.* Needless to add that Heidegger leaves aside all speculation about intellectual intuition attached to these phrases and retains only what remains "bound to the phenomenon" (KPM 129/Kpm 141).

149. EiM 145 f./IM 190 f.

150. EiM 146/IM 191.

151. Hw 30 and 34/PLT 41 and 45.

152. Hw 35/PLT 46.

153. Hw 43/PLT 55.

154. See Hw 53/PLT 65.

155. "How does truth happen? We answer: it happens in few essential ways" (Hw 44/PLT 55). Some of the modalities of "originary setting-in of truth" are enumerated in Hw 50/PLT 61 f.

156. VA 150 f. and 171 f./PLT 150 and 173 f. See also "Hölderlins Erde und Himmel," in *Hölderlin-Jahrbuch* XI (1958–60):17–39. According to a remark in SD 45/OTB 42, all of OWL would treat the "fourfold."

157. VA 149/PLT 149. This originary unity is the synchrony of the fourfold: the four dimensions are situated, are "implicated," in the same "simple fold" (*Einfalt*, ibid.). Any diachronic perspective on the "folds" through which the destiny of metaphysics "unfolds" (*entfaltet*, Wm 241 f./QB 84) is in this way excluded from the "fourfold." On the diachronic *Entfalten*, see for instance SvG 182 f.

158. The "fourfold" is thus what presencing appropriates, *das Ereignete* (SD 45/OTB 42). It is not correct, then, to describe Heidegger's radicalization of finitude in typological terms, as Walter Schulz does: "Man knows himself to be conditioned by things [*bedingt*, as opposed to *unbedingt*, unconditioned], that is, integrated into the totality of entities which Heidegger designates as the 'fourfold' . . . the four prototypes of entities," *Der Gott der neuzeitlichen Metaphysik* (Pfullingen, 1957), pp. 55 f. The fourfold is not the totality of entities, nor are the earth and the sky, the divinities and the mortals types, even less prototypes. The "fourfold" is one term among many in Heidegger that allow him to think presencing as coming to presence, as the "play" of regions, without regard for entities that are present, be it to the senses or as archetypes.

William Richardson proposes two translations for *Geviert*, "Quadrate" and "four-fold polyvalence" (*Heidegger: Through Phenomenology to Thought* [The Hague, 1963], p. 570). While the second, taken up in PLT, is a happy choice not only for the metaphor of "folds" but also for the insistence on the manifold, the first is misleading. It is not the number four that is important, nor any hint at geometry.

"*Geviert*" designates first of all the essence of language insofar as it gathers (*dichtet*, *verdichtet*), i.e., as it is poetic. But Heidegger also says "*Vierung*," translated as "the fouring, the unity of the four" (VA 179/PLT 180). *Vierung* is a term from the history of architecture. It is the name for the intersection of the nave and the transept in a basilica. Their crossing gives light to the entire edifice since it is surmounted by a dome (*Vierungskuppel*) and a lantern. The four aisles meet there, so that it is also the point from which the whole interior can be seen. The *Vierung* or *Geviert* is the heart of the whole cathedral where it is good to stay: it is where the altar of the holy one (*der Heilige*) should be who heals (*heilt*) and who, by restoring integrity (*das Heile*), also grants salvation (*das Heil*). "Fourfold" is a happy translation since it suggests both the junction of enclosures and the bend or ply with which, in Heidegger, thinking and acting are to com-ply. A further connotation, both in English and German, has to do with the cardinal points: a *Gevierthof* is a yard surrounded by four buildings, forming a farm. The farmyard orients or situates the stable, the barn, etc., by placing them in relation to one another. It is this sense of orientation—traditionally established in reference to the earth's two poles and sunrise and sunset—that Heidegger retains in the word "*Geviert*." It suggests what is essential about a thing (VA 163 ff./PLT 163 ff.), namely, bringing the regions of the world near. The examples of the bridge and the jug (VA 152–155 and 164–172/PLT 152–154 and 166–174) are meant to indicate just that. Such "nearing" is the main characteristic of the fourfold (see also below, sec. 38).

159. SD 46 f./OTB 43.

160. "Bewegtheit" (SD 44/OTB 41).

161. Thomas Sheehan, "Getting to the Topic," *Research in Phenomenology*, VII (1977):299–316. The author wishes to interpret "Heidegger's so-called 'Being-as-such' in terms of 'sense-as-such' and his 'Being of beings' in terms of the 'meaningfulness of beings' " (p. 303). The price paid for such a return to a philosophy of meaning is that 'sense' as directionality remains a movement "which happens only in man's essential proper existence" (p. 313). Heidegger had renounced the vocabulary of meaning, shortly after BT, precisely to avoid understanding the event of presencing as what Sheehan calls "meaningful presence" experienced by man (ibid.). Cf. VS 73.

162. This reading has been put forth in several essays by Albert Hofstadter: *Agony and Epitaph* (New York, 1970), pp. 34–54 and 199–257; "Ownness and Identity," *Review of Metaphysics* XXVIII/4 (1975):681–697; "Consciousness, Thought, and Enownment," *Psychiatry and the Humanities* II (1977):85–109; "Enownment," in W. Spanos, ed. *Martin Heidegger and the Question of Literature* (Bloomington, 1979), pp. 17–37. The author opposes Heidegger's "*Ereignis*" (which he translates as "enownment") to Hegel's "alienation." Enownment comes to designate identification, recovery of self, self-consciousness, reconciliation. *Ereignen*

would then mean "making my own" what is at first other than I. Thus the "very issue" (*die Sache selbst*) of Heidegger's phenomenology would remain, after all, the self as a referent for consciousness.

163. *"Wesenhaftes Zueinander"* (Hw 250/PLT 93).

164. Ibid. The expressions that suggest the "originary oneness" of the fourfold—"play," "ring," "mirror-play," "ringing" (VA 178 f./PLT 179 f.)—may have to be read in connection with Dionysus, too.

165. All quotes from SD 44/OTB 40 f.

166. As I have indicated, the double step back toward the 'originary' parallels the one described in BT and KPM. The move from things present to their epochal order of presence and from there to presencing as such constitutes the three-tiered temporal difference (n. 128 above).

167. SD 44/OTB 41.

168. St. Augustine's time concept—"the presence of things past, the presence of things present, and the presence of things to come" (*Confessions* XI, 26)—is thus just as *ontic* as Aristotle's. See below, sec. 23.

169. "Die Seinsvergessenheit 'hebt' sich 'auf' " (SD 44/OTB 41). Heidegger's insistence on the notion of *Aufhebung* obliges translating it so as to retain the three Hegelian moments. On the historical-systematic locus of dialectics, however, see below, sec. 46, n. 98.

170. SD 66 f./OTB 60.

171. SD 44/OTB 41.

172. Ibid.

173. SD 46/OTB 43.

174. In the essay "The Origin of the Work of Art," this link is not entirely clear. The "originary event of truth" in a field of presence such as a community, a work, etc., seems to be the advent, the beginning, "the founding deed" that opens such a field (Hw 50/PLT 61 f.). This fusion of the original and the originary explains, to a large extent, the slanted readings of that essay (see above, sec. 5, n.2). To understand given historical fields of phenomena through their beginnings—e.g., to understand Marxism or psychoanalysis through their founders—is to trace what is *original* in them. The discourse on the originary will never yield any lineage of *principia,* justifying the reign of some *princeps,* or a lineage of *archai,* justifying an archon of some sort. Heidegger's focus on the founding deed, in "The Origin of the Work of Art," tends to blur the contours between *Beginn, Anfang* and *Ursprung.* This essay does not suffice therefore to understand that even recourse to *initial* deeds, e.g., those of some Founding Fathers, cannot legitimate *rule.* Heidegger's critique of such epochal figures and their sway appears only from his genealogy of principles and the hypothesis of closure.

175. SD 44/OTB 40 f.

176. SD 67/OTB 60. Heidegger suggests that the 'principle' of the contemporary era is atomic energy (SvG 199/PG 213 f.). In a 1962 seminar, he indicated the ambiguity of the *Gestell:* on one hand, this word stands for the last among what I call the epochal principles, and in that sense this notion does not allow one to "think being without entities"; on the other hand, *Gestell* is the anticipatory phenomenon of the event of appropriation ("*Vorerscheinung des Ereignisses*"). However, "the necessity as well as the possibility of this contradiction were not elucidated any further" (SD 35/OTB 32).

177. SD 67/OTB 60.

128. *"Fundamentum concussum"* (SD 34/OTB 32); *"Zeitspielraum* " (SvG 129 f.).

179. SvG 186. Eugen Fink has shown that a phenomenology which renounces construing ultimate foundations ("*Die Welt ist grundlos*") has to understand the world as a "play without players": *Spiel als Weltsymbol* (Stuttgart, 1960), pp. 233–239.

180. Ibid.

181. In some texts, Heidegger characterizes the *Ursprung* by the two traits traditionally ascribed to *archē:* "that out of which" and "that by which" something occurs; commencement and commandment. He integrates that Aristotelian pair in a regional phenomenology. "*Ursprung* signifies here that out of which and by which something is what it is and as it is" (Hw 7/PLT 17). Needless to add that the causal thought patterns, which, as I have said, determine the notion of *archē,* are left inoperative. That out of which and by which something is what it is, according to the essay "The Origin of the Work of Art," is its regional mode of presence. The work of art opens and institutes the region "art," and the political deed, "the political." This regional conception of the origin is entirely given up in OTB.

182. "According to the history of being, the origin (*Ursprung*) of the dominance of truth as certitude lies concealed in the re-lease (*Entlassung*) of its essence from the original (*anfänglicher*) truth of being" (N II 423/EPh 21). It is the most decisive contingent fact of Western history, according to Heidegger, that only the original thinkers formerly thought the originary truth. This truth has therefore to be gathered from the Presocratic key words. All subsequent forms of truth—the theories of conformity (Aristotle), of coherence (Leibniz, Spinoza), of identity (Hegel), of self-evidence (Husserl), or of pragmatic consensus (Peirce)—have been conceived from the standpoint of the knowing subject.

183. Karl-Otto Apel, *Toward a Transformation of Philosophy*, trans. G. Adey and D. Frisby (London, 1981), pp. 136–179, on *Letztbegründung*. Ultimate foundation grounds both theory and practice, it "does not allow maintaining the difference between theory and praxis . . . in order to set up the foundation of critical social sciences" (ibid., p. 145, trans. modified). All of Apel's work aims at establishing a transcendental philosophy of language as first philosophy capable of founding both critical theory and emancipatory practice. Even when the Aristotelian heritage (the reference to a first philosophy) in the theories of legitimation is less explicit, the very notion of legitimation includes the *pros hen* reference, the reference of subjects to a norm-bestowing authority. For the so-called Frankfurt School, this authoritative point of reference is the utopian voluntary and rational agreement of all members of society.

184. If post-modernity is to be characterized by the fragmentation of the origin, it is perhaps necessary to date its rise back to Marx's *German Ideology* (cf. above, sec. 7 and 8).

185. Wm 191/BWr 239. For Heidegger's understanding of "rules," see below, sec. 47.

186. "*There is* being only in the specific disclosedness that characterizes the understanding of being. . . . *There is* being only if truth, that is, if *Dasein* exists" (GA 24 24 f./BPP 18 f.).

187. SZ 212/BT 255.

188. "Being becomes destiny in that It, being, gives itself" (Wm 166/BWr 215, see also SD 46/OTB 43). Heidegger's self-interpretation is as violent as his interpretations of other writers on this point: "Is it not said in *Being and Time* (p. 212), about the issue of the 'there is': 'Only as long as *Dasein* 'is' . . . 'is there' being'? Indeed. That means: Being delivers itself over (*übereignet*) to man only so long as the clearing of being occurs properly (*ereignet*)" (Wm 167/BWr 216). Within phenomenological transcendentalism, the 'there is' has changed its sense. While in the early writings, the a priori is being in as much as it is mine, here the a priori becomes presence as it gives itself over to man, i.e., as it is pre-understood in any historical setting. The "Letter on Humanism," from which these lines are taken, has been aptly described as "the most important document of Heidegger's self-interpretation," von Herrmann, *Die Selbstinterpretation Martin Heideggers*, p. 7.

189. "In a work, truth is thrown toward (*zugeworfen*) . . . a historical human community" (Hw 62/PLT 75). The "adjectival" (from *ad-icere*, Latin, to "throw toward") structure of the 'original' is only a trait accompanying the "projection" of an order; in that it differs from the 'originary' *Zuwurf* that establishes neither work nor any order.

190. N II 377/N iv 233.

191. SD 19/OTB 18.

192. SD 18/OTB 17.

193. US 193 f./OWL 87 f.

194. This twofold retrieval has a curious corollary: If the original "repeats," in an entirely secularized way, the sacred, the originary properly forms the nucleus of Heideggerian "piety"—a piety that, like Nietzsche's, remains decidedly faithful to the earth. Just as the originary seems to have once been thought in words such as *phusis, logos, alētheia*, so man's attitude before pure presencing also found its denominations among the ancients: θαυμάζειν, wonder (WPh 24–26/WPh 79–85), ἦθος (Sophocles and Heraclitus spoke of "*ethos* more originally than Aristotle's lectures on 'Ethics'," Wm 184/BWr 232 f., cf. EiM 112 f./IM 146 f.) and above all αἰδώς, *Scheu*, awe. Awe is opposed, first of all, to what the will can accomplish: what inspires awe escapes our control. But awe appears in the face of what is most familiar, most intimate to us: "It clears and tends that site within which human being is at home" (Wm 103/EB 355). Still, this feeling indicates that what is most intimate also escapes us: "Awe is the knowledge that the originary does not let itself be immediately experienced" (Höl 124). It makes us hesitate to approach presencing directly, for in awe we know that presencing also means absencing. It is like the index for that duality of hiding-showing, which is why it is a feeling dear to thinking (Höl 137). But if it thoroughly animates thinking, it nevertheless

remains mute (EiM 115/IM 149). Since the notion of the *sacred* belongs in the context of the original, it keeps historical connotations: the sacred is "the trace of the fugitive gods," leading toward their possible return (Hw 250 f./PLT 94). On the other hand, *awe* and *piety,* since they accompany the phenomenon of the originary, direct thinking toward that event, presencing, which is not at all historical.

195. In the contemporary age, for example, beingness "becomes machination" (N II 486/EPh 80). For "machination," cf. below p. 183; for "beingness," sec. 34, nn. 50 and 52.

Part Four: Historical Deduction of the Categories of Presencing

1. WhD 144 f./WCT 237. Perhaps by mistake, instead of "concealedness" in these lines, the German text has a pronoun referring to "unconcealedness."

2. WhD 136/WCT 224.

3. WhD 145/WCT 238.

4. The "history of the epochs according to Heidegger" has been described, for example, by Peter Fürstenau, *Heidegger, das Gefüge seines Denkens* (Frankfurt, 1958), pp. 101–168; Jean Wahl, *Sur l'interprétation de l'histoire de la métaphysique d'après Heidegger* (Paris, 1952); and Katharina Kanthack, *Das Denken Martin Heideggers* (Berlin, 1959).

5. IuD 66/IaD 67.

6. These expressions are from Mikel Dufrenne and Paul Ricoeur, *Karl Jaspers et la philosophie de l'existence* (Paris, 1947), pp. 364, 372. I cite the authors' polemic against Heidegger and in favor of Jaspers to show that commentators as attentive as Dufrenne and Ricoeur simply do not seem to have noticed the new transcendentalism in Heidegger's thinking (see also ibid. pp. 327–333), a transcendentalism that Ricoeur was to describe later, but in a different context, as "a transcendentalism without a subject," Paul Ricoeur, *The Conflict of Interpretations,* trans. and ed. Don Ihde (Evanston, Ill., 1974), p. 53.

IX. Table of the Categories of Presencing

§20. The Categorial, the Noumenal, and the Empirical

1. FD 82/WTh 106.

2. Werner Marx, *Heidegger and the Tradition,* trans. T. Kisiel and M. Greene (Evanston, Ill., 1971), p. 190. W. Marx was the first to raise the problem of being in Heidegger in terms of categories. He distinguishes between two categorial classes: the categories of the "first beginning," that is, those that Heidegger repeats or retrieves from preclassical Greek thought, and those of "the other beginning," which he anticipates in today's "crisis" in history. Among the first are ἐόν, φύσις, ἀλήθεια and λόγος (pp. 125–159), and among the second, "world," "thing," and "speech" (pp. 183–207). Marx opposes these determinations of being in Heidegger to the "fundamental traits" of Aristotelian οὐσία and to the traits of being in Hegel. Marx's aim, although stated in a different vocabulary, is indeed to understand categorially the reversal in the history of being undergone in the twentieth century. But the distinction between *erstanfäng-liche* and *andersanfängliche* categories, if it enables one to "comprehend the unfolding of essence [*das Wesen des Wesens*] such that novelty can appear" in history (p. 9, translation modified), nevertheless deprives one of criteria for 'deducing' the second group of categories. Marx's distinction helps suggest how this second group is related to the first (pp. 173–179 and 205 f.), but it is unfortunate that he can only invoke Heidegger's alleged solitary experience of thought to justify the traits of "the other beginning." In what name can one postulate a shift in the categorial continuity that runs from the Presocratics through Aristotle and Hegel to Heidegger, the shift which is the post-modern 'turning'? That is the question to which the distinction between two beginnings, as W. Marx applies it to the problem of categories, does not contribute any response. The very polarity of a double beginning becomes yet another ideal construct. Instead of drawing them from two historical beginnings (from two 'original' origins), the categories of presencing have to be developed from a transcendental starting point if they are to account for a historical possibility: from the distinction between 'original' and 'originary'. This will not only allow for their justification or deduction, but will also yield a table of them much more developed than the indications provided by W. Marx.

3. EiM 131/IM 172 and Fd 38/WTh 50.

4. *Gemeinwesen*, N I 194/N i 166. About *Menschentum*, cf. above, Sec. 10.

5. N I 275; FD 38 and 143/WTh 50 and 183; Hw 311 f./EGT 27.

6. Wm 224 f./QB 55.

7. Many commentators have noticed the elimination of "standards" by Heidegger's early—and even more his later—project, see for example Peter Gay, *Weimar Culture: The Outsider as Insider* (New York, 1968), p. 82. Aside from the fact that a similar charge could be waged against both Husserl and Wittgenstein, it must be remembered that Heidegger in no way renounces *criteria* for setting apart principial hubris from economic obedience. On the practical consequences of this distinction, see below, Part V.

8. The expression is Max Weber's, for whom it designates the function of the ideal types or models that can motivate rational submission to one or another form of authority. See, for example, *Gesammelte Aufsätze zur Religionssoziologie* (Tübingen, 1920–21), vol. I, pp. 30–83, and *Wirtschaft und Gesellschaft* (Tübingen, 1921), vol. I, pp. 122–124. It is introduced here merely for reasons of conceptual convenience.

9. Ever since Otto Pöggeler's article, "Sein als Ereignis," in *Zeitschrift für philosophische Forschung*, XIII (1959):597–632, it has often been repeated that the '*Verbindlichkeit*' of Heidegger's thought comes to him "from the Western tradition which determines us all," cf. the conclusion of that essay. Still, the whole question is to know how this tradition "binds" us.

10. *Critique of Pure Reason* B 116. Whereas in his early writings on Kant, Heidegger denounces this distinction as a "slogan" having produced "a heap of misunderstandings" (GA 25 213; cf. KPM 66/Kpm 73), he later accepts it as what is "originary" in the first *Critique* (FD 94/WTh 121).

11. SD 75/OTB 68.

12. It is true that in BT Heidegger uses this Kantian phrase to express precisely the common understanding of being and therefore everyday existence (SZ 4/BT 23). But he himself recognizes the violence of such an interpretation (KPM 196/Kpm 207) and later abandons it.

13. SZ 44 and 7/BT 70 and 27. There has been much speculation on the reasons why "the attempt in *Being and Time* ended in a blind alley" (Wm 173/BWr 222). It has been said that in BT the question of being is raised from the standpoint of being-there, while after the *Kehre*, it is addressed directly, so that being-there can then be thematized only as a consequence; for example, Pöggeler, in "Sein als Ereignis," p. 621; James M. Demske, *Being, Man, and Death* (Lexington, 1970), pp. 87–91. This way of accounting for the unfinished state of BT draws only one methodological conclusion from the 'turning' (*Kehre*) instead of understanding the new perspective opened after 1928 as the discovery of aletheiological temporality (cf. VS 73).

14. One example that illustrates the impossibility of, as it were, purifying presencing of all empirical beginnings in the 'history of being' can be found in Heidegger's interpretation, before and after the Kehre, of the 'supreme principle of all synthetic judgments' in Kant. At first this principle provides Heidegger with one way of stating the finite transcendence of the entity we are, that is, of being-in-the-world (KPM 11/Kpm 123). Later that same supreme principle expresses, to the contrary, the original mode in which being is disclosed in the modern age: "Whoever understands that proposition comprehends Kant's *Critique of Pure Reason*. Whoever comprehends the *Critique* comprehends not only one book among the writings of philosophy but masters a *fundamental position* of our historical being-there" (FD 143/WTh 183, italics mine). While Henri Declève, *Heidegger et Kant* (The Hague, 1970), pp. 275 ff., reads these two passages without noting the radical shift in context, the transference accomplished by the *Kehre* is made perfectly clear by H. Hoppe, "Wandlungen in der Kant-Auffassung Heideggers" in Vittorio Klostermann, ed., *Durchblicke: Martin Heidegger zum 80. Geburtstag* (Frankfurt, 1970), especially p. 307. At any rate, Heidegger's recognition of the necessary detour through history takes the edge off Paul Ricoeur's polemic against his presumed "short route": "The short route is the one taken by an ontology of the understanding, after the manner of Heidegger," Ricoeur, *The Conflict of Interpretations*, p. 6.

15. "*Ganzseinkönnen*" (SZ 309 and 326/BT 357 and 374).

16. E.g. N I 455 f., 462–472 and N II 168, 174, 189, 421/N iv 119, 123, 136 and EPh 19.

17. Jacques Derrida describes Heidegger's "ontico-ontological difference" as an "intra-metaphysical effect of deferment" because it thematizes, he claims, "being" as "belonging" and as "maintaining," *Margins of Philosophy*, trans. Alan Bass (Chicago, 1982), p. 22. What is thereby obliterated for the sake of "*la différance*" is the temporal difference from which

Derrida, with an undeniable talent for gleaning catchwords from Heidegger, first developed his understanding of "deferment": "On a certain face of it, deferment is, to be sure, only the historical and epochal unfolding of being or of the ontological difference" (ibid.). The obliteration leaves Heidegger entertaining the sole questions of the "meaning or the *truth* of being" (ibid.), to the exclusion of the topology (cf. above, sec. 2, the epigraph) which articulates precisely the temporal difference.

18. In Werner Marx's interpretation (see above, n. 2), Heidegger speaks as an advocate of that "highly creative presence" which, he claims, characterized the age of the Greeks and in which man was a "violent co-creator" (Marx, *Heidegger and the Tradition*, p. 244, cf. pp. 139–141). His reading is humanist and romantic because it substitutes the distance between two instances of the original (*erstanfänglich* and *andersanfänglich*) for the *difference* between the original and the originary. While the two instances of the original—marking the beginning and the end of the metaphysical era—are mutually exclusive, the difference between original and originary applies throughout the history of being. As a result, the categories will have to be deduced, not from some anticipatory thought that has no locus of verification but itself, but from the concrete phenomena of transition in history. Therefore we need appeal, neither to some privileged experience of Heidegger's, nor to the violence of a "few really creative men" (Marx, p. 238), nor to the "ever so few authentic things" (p. 245). Nor need we follow Marx in his condemnation of technological "reification" more severe than anything to be found in Heidegger himself (pp. 244 f.). These simplifications can be avoided if one refuses to construe an opposition between two beginnings such that, when all is said and done, nothing really new has happened in the West during more than two thousand years.

19. KPM 73/Kpm 80.

20. This title is from Gustav Siewerth, *Das Schicksal der Metaphysik von Thomas zu Heidegger* (Einsiedeln, 1959), p. 28. See analogous formulations, to the point of identifying the Heideggerian "being" with "God," in Johann Baptist Lotz, *Das Urteil und das Sein* (Munich, 1957), pp. 181–200, and idem, "Denken und Sein nach den jüngsten Veröffentlichungen von M. Heidegger," *Scholastik*, 33 (1958):81–98.

21. These perplexing statements are from Reinhart Maurer, *Revolution und 'Kehre'* (Frankfurt, 1975), pp. 30, 35. But the champion of such metaphysical 'co-opting' of Heidegger is Walter Schulz. See especially "Über den philosophie-geschichtlichen Ort Martin Heideggers," *Philosophische Rundschau*, I (1953/54):65–93 and 211–232, reprinted in Otto Pöggeler, ed., *Heidegger* (Cologne, 1969), pp. 95–139. Schulz intends to show that Heidegger's thought is situated, not "counter to" modern metaphysics, but at its very heart. Heideggerian "being" is called a "principle of Christian origin" and is said to verify the "fundamental dialectical law" of metaphysics, namely, that finite subjectivity in its effort to grasp itself experiences that it is carried by its Other, divine Subjectivity. The same arguments have been developed by Schulz (to Heidegger's exasperation, it may be added) in *Der Gott der neuzeitlichen Metaphysik* (Pfullingen, 1957), pp. 48–58, and in *Philosophie in der veränderten Welt* (Pfullingen, 1972). In this last work, being is ultimately called the "Initiator of history" (pp. 531 f.), the "Subject of history" (p. 538). Hans Jonas, *The Phenomenon of Life* (New York, 1966), takes a similar stand: "Heidegger's statements about being are really, at least in part, ontic, not ontological, whatever his protestations. . . . For surely, a 'being' that acts must be; that which takes the initiative must exist . . . as vis-à-vis . . . some sort of subject" (p. 252).

22. Karl-Otto Apel, *Transformation der Philosophie* (Frankfurt, 1976), vol. I, pp. 270 and 40 (not included in the English translation). According to Apel, what he calls the "hypostatizations" in Heidegger's language—primarily "being"—would be purely metaphysical inasmuch as their criterion for meaning lies exclusively in praxis (ibid., p. 333). The project of the 'history of being', in abandoning transcendentalism (p. 43), would have to be content with tracing the positivity of past constitutions of meaning. Apel does recognize Heidegger's "step back" from propositional to aletheiological truth, but instead of acknowledging the genuinely transcendental quest for a priori conditions in that step, he dilutes it into a radical relativization of truth.

23. Wm 162/BWr 210. It is true that elsewhere in a disconcerting text he speaks, on the contrary, of "the god of being" (N II 29), which is however not the God of monotheism. The gods, it will be recalled, are not only one variable in the 'fourfold', they also come in the plural. "The" god of being is "a" god, just as only "a god" can save us (Sp 193/ISp 5).

24. VA 80/EPh 93. The rejection of historicism is a constant in Heidegger, although for different motifs, from the early to the last writings (cf. SZ 396/BT 448 and SD 69/OTB 62).

The deduction of categories, which establishes what remains "all-pervasive" in history, suffices to disprove the charge of historicism, particularly in connection with the perplexing additional charges of "individualism" and "metaphysical neutrality" as, it seems, Leo Strauss would have it in *Natural Right and History* (Chicago, 1953). According to one of Strauss's flock, indeed, that entire book was meant as "a response to radical historicism—to Heidegger." "It was only radical historicism that reconciled historical individuality and temporality, or 'being and time', by abandoning the plane of theoretical understanding" (Richard Kennington, "Strauss's *Natural Right and History*," *Review of Metaphysics* XXXV (1981):62, 65). All this lacks any base in Heidegger.

25. In BT, the characteristics of the first type are called "existentials," and only those of the second, "categories" (SZ 44 and 54/BT 70 and 79). It is obvious that this distinction establishes a division *within* the categorial problematic as such.

26. N I 529.

27. KPM 97/Kpm 106. On the role of the schematism in the constitution of "ontological knowledge" according to Kpm, see also Charles Sherover's exposition, *Heidegger, Kant and Time* (Bloomington, 1971), pp. 102–120.

28. KPM 100/Kpm 108 f.

29. The young Heidegger first speaks of "places" in a context of propositional logic, either to adopt that terminology (FSch 132) or to show the dependence of language and propositions on being-there (SZ 166 and 226/BT 210 and 268 f.). In the second period, he speaks of place, *Ort*, especially in the context of *Erörterung*, localization, of the epochal stamps of *alētheia* (for example, IuD 64–66/IaD 66–68). To "situate" the poet's word (cf. Höl 90–94) is another instance of aletheiological topology. Lastly, in the third period, the paradigmatic instance of "locus" is that of the reversals: "To localize the event of appropriation" is to prepare oneself for a possible imminent reversal (SD 58/OTB 54). As Heidegger describes the itinerary of his thinking through those three stages (VS 73), the difference between locus and locality, *Ort* and *Ortschaft*, remains non-temporal unless recast in terms of presencing (as in VA 255/EGT 99).

30. EdD 23/PLT 12. See also Heidegger's quotation from Aristotle, "it appears, however, to be something overwhelming and hard to grasp, the *topos*" in KR 5/AaS 3.

31. Whereas, in SZ 44/BT 70, Heidegger had translated κατηγορεῖν very literally by "to accuse publicly, to impute right in the face" (cf. FD 48 f./ WTh 63 f.), in commenting on early Greek thinkers, he translates the noun κατηγορία more freely by "suggestion, manifestation" (Her 261/H 162).

32. FD 82/WTh 106.

33. EdD 15/PLT 8.

34. Jacques Derrida, *Writing and Difference*, trans. Alan Bass (Chicago, 1978), p. 293 (translation modified).

§21. A Reversal Undergone by the Puma-Shaped City

35. SvG 153.

36. Nathan Wachtel, *La vision des vaincus. Les Indiens du Pérou devant la Conquête espagnole* (Paris, 1971), p. 63. In addition to this study, I have used the following works by George Kubler: "A Peruvian Chief of State: Manco Inca," *Hispanic American Historical Review*, 24 (1944):253–276; "The Behavior of Atahualpa," ibid., 25 (1945):413–427; "The Neo-Inca State," ibid., 27 (1947):189–203: "The Quechua in the Colonial World," *Handbook of South American Indians* vol. 2 (Washington, 1946), pp. 331–410; and lastly his essay, *The Shape of Time. Remarks on the History of Things* (New Haven, 1962).

37. Wachtel, op. cit., p. 131.

38. Ibid., p. 53.

39. Kubler (1947), pp. 189–203 and (1944) especially pp. 257 f.

40. Wachtel, op. cit., pp. 63, 60.

41. Ibid., p. 134.

42. Ibid., p. 146.

43. Cited ibid., p. 221.

44. Ibid., p. 49. Concerning the novelty of writing, the episode of Cajamarca is relevant: the Spaniards present the Bible to Atahualpa and tell him that it contains the word of God. Atahualpa opens it, presses it against his ear, but hears nothing. With disdain, he throws it to

the ground. Pizarro arrests the Inca and has his followers massacred. See Kubler (1945), op. cit., especially pp. 418 f.

45. Ibid., p. 210.

46. Ibid., pp. 55 and 64. All of the categories of transition from the Inca empire to colonial Peru that follow are borrowed from Wachtel. For the general concept of era, and to an extent that surpasses the Peruvian context, I am, however, indebted to Kubler's *The Shape of Time*. The author calls a "shape of time" "those durations which either are longer than single human lives or which, as collective durations, require the time of more than one person. The smallest family of such shapes is the annual crop of costume fashions. . . . The largest shapes, like metagalaxies, are very few: they dimly suggest their presence as the giant forms of human time: Western civilization; Asiatic culture; prehistoric, barbarian, and primitive society. In between are the conventional periods" (p. 99). From these distinctions, it is apparent that a "shape" of time is indissociably qualitative and quantitative. Its concept surpasses mere periodization as well as a simple opposition between synchrony and diachrony.

47. Wachtel, p. 235.

48. Ibid., p. 241. Cf. Kubler (1944), pp. 275 f.

49. "By the term 'destructuration', we designate the survival of ancient structures or of partial elements thereof, but severed from the relatively coherent context where they used to be situated: after the Conquest, fragments of the Inca State remain in place, but the cement that united them has disintegrated" (ibid., p. 134).

50. Ibid., p. 74.

X: At the Presocratic Inception: The Prospective Categories

1. N I 169/N i 144. The last words of this text directly contradict Werner Marx's distinction between *"erstanfängliche"* categories and *"andersanfängliche"* categories, cf. above, ch. 9, n. 2.

2. "What help are impressive-sounding epithets like 'basic word', if the bases and abysses of Greek thinking so little concern us that we cover them up with labels picked at random from representational quarters that have become common for us?" (VA 268/EGT 111).

3. George J. Seidel, *Martin Heidegger and the Pre-Socratics: An Introduction to His Thought* (Lincoln, Neb., 1964) examines Heidegger's use of most of these words. His exposition, although introductory indeed, has the merit of guarding the reader against confusing "Heidegger's own notion of being with the meaning of being which he finds among the Greeks" (p. 40), which is to say that "there is a theory of both history and language behind his historical exegeses" (p. 156).

4. WhD 140/WCT 232 (emphasis added).

5. N II 486/EPh 79.

6. Cited in Hans-Georg Gadamer, *Truth and Method* (New York, 1975), p. 199. In BT Heidegger described the being of *Dasein* as self-interpretation, *Selbstauslegung* (SZ 312/BT 360).

§22. *Eon*

7. For an example of that received opinion, see Werner Jaeger, *The Theology of the Early Greek Philosophers*, trans. E. S. Robinson (Cambridge, 1947): "True Being can have nothing in common with Not-being. Neither can it be many. . . . Thus there are no *onta* in the plural, but only a single *on*" (p. 102).

8. WhD 133/WCT 220.

9. χρὴ τὸ λέγειν τε νοεῖν τ' ἐὸν ἔμμεναι, Parmenides, frag. VI (cited in WhD 105/WCT 171). G. S. Kirk and J. E. Raven translate: "That which can be spoken and thought needs must be," *The Presocratic Philosophers* (Cambridge, 1971), p. 270. This translation obfuscates the duality that Heidegger wishes to stress in rendering τ' ἐὸν as *das Anwesende*, "the present," and ἔμμεναι as *anwesen*, "presencing" (WhD 141/WCT 233).

10. WhD 143/WCT 236. In Parmenides, these two verbs occur in the plural of the present participle (frag. IV). Kirk and Raven translate: "things present"—"things far off" (op. cit., p. 275).

11. The same experience of a dual motility is preserved in the words γένεσις and φθορά in Anaximander (Hw 315/EGT 30 f.). With Plato, Heidegger charges on the other hand, under

the domination of the 'idea' as pure visibility, φθορά, the movement of withdrawal, falls into forgottenness (Wm 135/PDT 264). With Aristotle, γένεσις and φθορά come to be restricted to the movement of the form, that is, to generation and corruption as analyzed in physics (Wm 358/Phy 259).

12. In 1973, Heidegger translates Parmenides' εὔκυκλος, on the contrary, by the difference "present-presencing," so that this word comes to equal ἐόν (VS 134 and 137).

13. VA 255/EGT 100.

14. These two distinctions do not entirely overlap. For Thomas Aquinas, the *entitas*, on one hand, "is divided into ten predicaments" (*Summa Theologica*, P. I, q. 48, a. 2, ad 2), and then this term appears to translate the Aristotelian *on;* but on the other hand, "there are various degrees of *entitas*" (*Disputed Questions on Truth*, q. 1, a. 1 c.), and then this term translates *ousia*.

15. Hw 162/HCE 107. What begins with that separation, Heidegger adds, "is only one specially adjusted interpretation of that early duality in the *on.*"

16. See above, the epigraph to Part IV and my remark in the accompanying note 1. Paradoxically, the reference to time in the Western understanding of being becomes explicit only with the beginning of metaphysics. When, "at the *end* of Greek philosophy, with Aristotle" (EiM 157/IM 206), substance is called τὸ τί ἦν εἶναι, "that which has always been" (KPM 233/Kpm 249), being's permanence is thereby stressed rather than a movement of arrival and withdrawal.

17. Cf. EiM 157/IM 205 f. "If the ἐὸν ἔμμεναι did not unfold as the presencing of what is present, Kant's thinking would have no space in which to utter even a single statement of his *Critique of Pure Reason*" (WhD 142/WCT 234).

18. WhD 145/WCT 238. Therefore, metaphysics only carries out "the hidden injunction [received] at the inception" (EiM 156/IM 205).

§23. *Phusis*

19. EiM 11/IM 14 (italics added). Heidegger recognizes that *Aufgang*, "blooming" or "dehiscence," is a poor translation of *phusis* (Wm 329/Phy 237). The botanical metaphor, precisely because it is only a metaphor, is however less misleading than Werner Marx's attempt to interpret the term as "creative occurrence" (*Heidegger and the Tradition*, Evanston, Ill., 1971, p. 139). The violence of the "creators" (EiM 47/IM 62) is indeed one way among many of *stopping* the free emergence called *phusis*. The praise of creativity presupposes "an essential reversal in the concept of *phusis*" parallelling its use in Aristotle's doctrine of motion (FD 64/WTh 83). As a category, *phusis* makes "the poets, the thinkers, the statesmen" (EiM 47/IM 62) appear as variables in a game of universal economic self-manifestation.

20. EiM 11/IM 14.

21. Of these two time notions, one Aristotelian (*Physics* IV, 11; 219 b 1) and the other Augustinian (*Confessions*, XI, 26), only the first is really overcome in BT. Augustine's text, on the other hand, serves as the point of departure for determining the temporal "ecstases" (SZ 427/BT 479f.). The temporality of *phuesthai* is more radical, not only than these received notions, but also than the *Temporalität* of being as it was to be worked out from the standpoint of the *Zeitlichkeit* of being-there (SZ 39/BT 63). The Augustinian background of the temporality of being as reached through that of *Dasein* is palpable, too, in Heidegger's identifying time and transcendental apperception (KPM 186/Kpm 197). Ecstatic temporality remains partly embedded in the tradition of the inwardness of time that runs from Neoplatonism to critical transcendentalism.

22. Frag. 123 (VA 270 f./ EGT 113 f. and Wm 370 f./Phy 269).

23. It is paradigmatic since, as I have said, every inception contains what will eventually emerge from it and to which it remains superior.

24. VS 69.

25. It is neither "for all time," nor everywhere "in the same way" that present things "presence" (WhD 143/WCT 235 f.).

26. *Phusis* is, "at the inception of Western thought, the rise of the concealed into unconcealment"; with Plato, on the other hand, a thing's aspect "determines what can then still be called unconcealment" (Wm 139/PDT 267).

27. Hw 324/EGT 38 f.

28. Hw 325/EGT 39. For *Moira*, see also VA 255/EGT 100.

29. *Physics* II, 1; 192 b 7 (cf. Wm 315 and 358 f./Phy 226 and 259 f.; FD 63–66/WTh 82–85).

30. Kant, *Critique of Pure Reason* B 479 (cf. N II 165 and 188 f./N iv 115 f. and 134; FD 175/WTh 225 f.).

31. Hw 100/QCT 149, cf. below, sec. 46.

32. SvG 154. The modern languages preserve something of the original sense of *phusis*—presencing—inasmuch as the word 'nature' derives from *nasci*, to be born. Thus, "even we, when we speak of the 'nature' of things, the 'nature' of the state, the 'nature' of man . . . we mean the being and the way to be of entities in general" (Wm 370/Phy 268).

§24. Alētheia

33. VA 258/EGT 103. This is not the place to trace the various senses of the word *alētheia* through Heidegger's writings and their stages (see the entry "*alētheia*" in the Index of Greek Terms in William Richardson, *Heidegger: Through Phenomenology to Thought* [The Hague, 1963], p. 728). Suffice it to recall that in BT it is being-there that constitutes unconcealment and, in that sense, the *Lichtung*, clearing (SZ 33 and 133/BT 56 and 171). In the early texts, *alētheuein*, to disclose, is even called "a basic comportment of the *psychē*" (GA 24 103/BPP 73; see also Wm 84 and 158/BWr 127 f. and 207). While it is generally admitted that *alētheia* is a 'privative' construct, its etymological opposition to *lēthē* seems less assured. Paul Friedländer (*Platon*, 2 vol. [Berlin, 1954], vol. I, pp. 233–242) had first criticized Heidegger's position on this issue, but retracted his criticism in the third edition of his book (Berlin, 1964), on which the English translation (3 vol., [Princeton, 1969]) is based (cf. vol. I, pp. 224 f.). Bruno Snell, *Die Entdeckung des Geistes* (4th ed., Göttingen, 1975), adopts the translation *Unvergessenheit*, "unforgottenness," but accepts also *Unverborgenheit*, "unconcealedness" (not included in the translation by T. G. Rosenmeyer, *The Discovery of Mind* [Cambridge, Mass., 1953]). Gerhard Krüger, "Martin Heidegger und der Humanismus," in *Studia Philosophica* IX (1949):93–129, on the other hand, considers the opposition *alētheia-lēthē* to lack any philological foundation. It seems to me that Heribert Boeder ("Der frühgriechische Wortgebrauch von *Logos* und *Alētheia*," *Archiv für Begriffsgeschichte*, IV [1958]) has put the issue in proper focus: "It is the 'transitive' *lēthein* that determines the sense of *alētheia*. . . . This eliminates any opposition between *alētheia* and *lēthē* . . . which indicates that the interpretation of *alētheia* as 'unconcealment' cannot genuinely rely upon the original sense of the word" (pp. 98 f.). The pertinent opposition would be between *lēthein*, to conceal, and "to grant *alētheia*," i.e., to show. In the epic tradition that opposition would be limited to the domain of speech (pp. 92 f.). It is evident that Heidegger shifts the very terms of the debate: "It is not for the love of etymology that I stubbornly translate the name *alētheia* as 'unconcealedness' "(SD 75 f./OTB 68).

34. Hw 38 f./PLT 50 f. and SD 72/OTB 65 (the translator notes: "The meaning Heidegger intends is related to 'lever' [i.e., to alleviate, lighten a burden]"). "Lightening means: to lighten, to weigh anchor, to clear. . . . What is so lightened is the free, the open" (Her 260 /H 161).

35. Parmenides, frag. I (cited SD 74/OTB 67), with Heidegger's commentary (ibid.).

36. SD 78/OTB 71. Later Heidegger retracted that interpretation of Parmenides: "What is said there [in OTB] is not correct" (VS 133). Werner Marx considers such belonging together of truth and error "extremely perilous," op. cit., p. 251. It may however appear less so if man as "co-creator" and *alētheia* are understood to be mutually exclusive from the viewpoint of the 'history of being': the unity of truth and untruth yields no apologia for wrongdoing.

37. The expression "*Wesenswandel der Wahrheit*" can be found in N II 430/EPh 27 (cf. Wm 109, 124, 136/PDT 251, 257, 265). For the displacement of truth from the economic struggle to human comportment, see Wm 137 and 270/PDT 265.

38. Wm 138 f. and 142/PDT 266 f. and 269. The last ten pages of Ernst Tugenthat, *Der Wahrheitsbegriff bei Husserl und Heidegger* (Berlin, 1967), pp. 396–405, suffer, it seems to me, from the absence of this historical perspective. I agree that the conflictual (*gegenwendig*) essence of *alētheia* "buries the very possibility of the question of truth" understood as the question of the "regulative idea of a measure" (p. 398). Truth is indeed rendered inoperative as a standard for "choice." But this is not to say the "question of truth need no longer emerge" in Heidegger's later writings (p. 399). On the contrary, the concept of truth as 'measure' has changed. "No formal rule is given" (ibid.). Not quite: for the era marked by the hypothesis of metaphysical closure, material rules are the epochal principles; for a possible economy after the 'turn', the formal rule can only be 'presencing', or *phuesthai* (see Part V). What Tugenthat does not see is that the "leeway (*Spielraum*) which is unconcealment" yields an economic

measurement because unconcealment has a history whose possible closure transmutes truth from ideal to event-like (*ereignishaft*).

39. N II 458/EPh 55.
40. N II 318.
41. *"Seinsgeschichtliche Züge"* (SvG 154).

§25. *Logos*

42. These examples are cited by H. Boeder, op. cit., p. 84. Cf. VA 208/EGT 60 and EiM 95/IM 124 f. For the etymological connection between *legein*, *legere* and *legen*, see WhD 121/WCT 198 f.

43. Since Karl Reinhardt, *Parmenides und die Geschichte der griechischen Philosophie* (Bonn, 1916), pp. 217 ff., it is generally admitted that the ordering enacted by the Parmenidean *logos* is irreducible to either some 'objective', world organizing principle, or any 'subjective' law governing discourse, education, thought. Heidegger has often underscored this contribution of Reinhardt's to the understanding of *krinein logō*, discriminating between unveiling and veiling (SZ 223/BT 494; Wm 38/ER 49; VA 275 f./EGT 117; EiM 82/IM 107).

44. "More originally than 'speaking', *logos* means 'letting presence' " (VS 70).

45. Klaus Held, "Der Logos-Gedanke des Heraklit," *Durchblicke*, op. cit., pp. 162–206, commends Karl Reinhardt and Heidegger for having cut short inherited debates of *logos* in terms of such alternatives as its 'objective' or 'subjective' sense (pp. 166 f.), but the translation or paraphrase he finally offers—"sprachlich sich darlegender Verhältnisvollzug," a "relational process laying itself out linguistically" (p. 198)—lodges *legein* within yet another classical either-or, namely, opinion and knowledge, *Ansicht* and *Einsicht* (pp. 191 f.). This is but one illustration of how difficult it is to dissociate the understanding of *legein* from essentially cognitive issues. To be sure, one need not speak, as I am suggesting, of economic layout, but some idiom should be reachable that helps to retain *logos* as *koinon*, all-pervasive (cf. the texts cited by Bruno Snell, *The Discovery of the Mind*, p. 19) while avoiding representations of both cosmic laws ruling natural processes and interlocutory laws ruling deliberative processes (for the latter, i.e., *logos* as the law of Socratic *dialegesthai*, see Gadamer, *Truth and Method*, p. 331).

46. VA 220/EGT 70. Heidegger's steady retreat from any "humanistic" understanding of *logos* becomes evident if one compares section 7 A of BT ("The Concept of *Logos*," SZ 32–34/BT 55–58) with the essay in EGT, "Logos." In BT it is still the Aristotelian standpoint that prevails: *logos* is located in discourse, it is "apophantic," it "lets something be seen by pointing it out" and as such "reveals what is 'at issue' in a discourse." In BT, this same disclosive function of speech also establishes the way *logos* belongs to *alētheia*. In the subsequent texts, when *logos* and *alētheia* turn into traits of presencing, they have for that very reason to be dissociated from human discourse.

47. GA 55 295 f.
48. GA 55 329 and 353 f., cf. VA 215/EGT 66.
49. GA 55 329 and 353 f.
50. GA 55 371.
51. GA 55 394, cf. 330.
52. GA 55 360.
53. "The present [*die Gegenwart*], usually unfolding as absent, of 'the *Logos*'—that is, of being itself—becomes one that is presencing [*zu einer anwesenden*]" against "hubris, [that is, against] our own potential, forgetful of being" (GA 55 356).
54. GA 55 279.
55. VA 217/EGT 68. The middle term of this acrobatic slippage is the German word *"geschickt"*—"skillful," but also "sent." In early Greek, *sophia* would designate the know-how that renders skillful, the experience through which "one knows the ins and outs, knows one's way about" things unconcealed. "Originarily *sophia* had the same signification as *technē*" (GA 55 247). Platonic *philo-sophia*, for example, would consist in knowing how to proceed so as to resemble the good, how to escape from the cave. Know-how is also the first sense of the German *geschickt*. The other sense, the past participle of the verb *schicken*, to send, has, however, no connection with the Greek *sophon*. The artifice enters this text from EGT when Heidegger describes practical knowledge as knowing one's way about the epochal arena in which things can at all be experienced. The know-how is then called *geschicklich* inasmuch as it consists in responding to a given order of presence "sent" by destiny. The emphasis on skill

in this description of *sophia* goes to the heart of the Heideggerian argument about Plato: *philosophia* is the knowledge of entities in their being which is the Idea and which is attainable through *homoiōsis*, assimilation. But if the word *sophon* has indeed a practical meaning— so that a captain or a charioteer can deserve this epithet (cf. Snell, *Die Entdeckung des Geistes*, p. 277)—the connection with "destiny" is devoid of all textual basis in either Heraclitus or Plato. The categorial slippage is prompted by the German, not the Greek.

56. "*Das eigentlich Geschickliche*" (VA 221/EGT 72).

57. VA 227/EGT 76. Whereas elsewhere Heidegger takes care to distinguish any 'occurrence' (*Geschehen*) that founds history (*Geschichte*), from *Ereignis*, 'event of appropriation' (which is therefore called *geschicklos*, "without destiny," SD 44/OTB 41), this text in EGT confounds the terms of that major distinction.

58. SvG 182; Wm 323 and 345 f./Phy 232 and 250; FD 121/WTh 155.

59. SD 7/OTB 7 and WhD 101/WCT 156. These two texts show the disjunction of what remained united until Heraclitus, namely, the law of the *kosmos* and the law of discourse.

60. SvG 184.

61. WhD 102/WCT 163 (cf. SD 63–65 and 79/OTB 57–59 and 72; N II 487/EPh 80). *Angriff* is the technological figure of the conceptual 'grasp' through the *Begriff*. (Cf. the text cited above, sec. 23, n. 31, and below, sec. 46, passim.)

62. These two senses are affirmed of *logos*, VA 227/EGT 76 f. It is called a leading word, *Leitwort*, SvG 184.

63. EiM 100/IM 131; VA 221/EGT 71.

§26. Hen

64. Hw 340/EGT 55.

65. See, for example, Her 203. *Ta panta* does not signify only "entities in their totality," but "each and every" entity, and more precisely, their opposites, a certain number of which Heraclitus enumerates (cf. K. Held, op. cit., pp. 177 and 190): cold-warm, night-day, upward-downward, good-evil, etc.

66. IuD 67/IaD 69. This is an explanatory comment by Heidegger on frag. 32: "One thing, the only truly wise, does not and does consent to be called by the name of Zeus" (trans. Kirk and Raven, op. cit., p. 204) (cf. VA 222–224/EGT 72–74).

67. Frag. 64 (cf. Her 29/H 15 and VA 222/EGT 72). Werner Jaeger, *The Theology of the Early Greek Philosophers* (Oxford, 1947), p. 233, comments: "That expression ['pilot'] is used frequently in a figurative sense of the activity of the wise ruler or king. The fire . . . takes the place of the divine ruler." This type of explanation levels the difference between the economic and the divine One. Among the most valuable results of the Heraclitus seminar held by Heidegger and Fink is the precision with which they disentangled these two senses (Her 77 and 188/ H 46 and 117). That was possible due to their notion of aletheiological temporality, which characterizes the economic *hen* (Her 193 / H 120).

68. Her 189/H117. On the double sense of 'light' and 'lighting'—'brightening' as well as 'alleviating'—see above, sec. 24, n. 34.

69. Her 203 and 219 / H 126 and 136.

70. Her 73 and 76/H 43 and 45. The difficulty with this agonistic notion of *hen*—or rather the necessity of distinguishing it from the economic notion—comes from the apparent grammatical inaccuracy of frag. 57. At a first reading, Heraclitus is criticizing Hesiod for not having seen that day and night are of the same essence. But the second reading proves to be more difficult: the verb 'to be' is in the singular: *esti gar hen*. This cannot be translated as "They are one." The problem can be skirted by paraphrasing: "night and day, which Hesiod had made parent and child, are, and must always have been, essentially connected and coexistent" (Kirk and Raven, op. cit., p. 190). The fragment could then be translated: "He did not recognize day and night: for that is just one" (my translation). But one may also surmise that "something entirely different is meant, which does not show itself at first sight" (Her 73/H 43): "not the coincidence of distincts, but the *hen* of the double region. There is the *hen*': *hen*, now, is the subject of the sentence" (Her 79/H 47). The unity of the "double region" (*Doppelbereich*) results from the conjunction of presencing and absencing. The agonistic notion of *hen* could then be described this way: There is the *hen*—the totality of the present (economic *hen*) against the totality of the absent. The strife mentioned in other fragments (πόλεμος, frag. 53; παλίντονος, frag. 51) would be expressed here by the movement of presencing against absencing.

71. Her 160/H 99.
72. VA 223/EGT 73.
73. VA 272/EGT 114. One of the fragments on "struggle" that can be read in this aletheio-logical-agonistic perspective is frag. 8: "Contrary is agreement; from discordances is born the most beautiful harmony, and everything develops in struggle."
74. Cf. Her 176/H 110.
75. N II 420 and 463/EPh 19 and 59.
76. For example, FD 143/WTh 183 and GA 55 272 and 318–321. As this last text indicates, *austragend* is Heidegger's translation of διηνεκῶς (Heraclitus, frag. 72)—"stretching out," "reaching far"—conjoined with the verb διαφέρειν, "carrying through."
77. SvG 188. The 'play' notion of time, as it addresses the motility in *alētheia*, is worked out in SvG from frag. 52 of Heraclitus: "Time is a child that plays, shifting the pawns: the royalty of a child." For this fragment and the πάντα ῥεῖ, see N I 333 f.
78. Her 38/H 21. In OTB, on the other hand, *hen* and *logos* seem to be treated as exclusively Presocratic names for presencing: "Presencing shows itself as *hen*, the unique unifying One, as *logos*, the gathering that preserves the All, as *idea, ousia, energeia, substantia*," etc. (SD 7/OTB 7). Read in this way, *hen* and *logos* are not categories any more than the other titles listed, since they then designate the traits applicable only to a single epoch.
79. *Phainotaton* (N II 458/EPh 55 and Wm 134/PDT 263).
80. FSch 157.
81. Her 38/H 21 (cf. N II 460 f./ EPh 57 f.). For other modern versions of *hen*, viz. in Leibniz and Hegel, see Hw 324 f./EGT 39.
82. N II 278. To view modern technology as the latest offspring of the Heraclitean *hen* is first to make evident technology's global character; then to dispel any instrumentalist concepts of it; and lastly to set apart technology and the essence (*Wesen* in the verbal sense) of technology (cf. VA 31/QCT 23).

27. *Nous*

83. Hw 162/HCE 107. Already in BT, *noein*—"simply receiving something present in its sheer presence"—helps to oppose Aristotle's "ontology" to "the interpretation of being" in Parmenides (SZ 25 f./BT 48. Contrary to the translators' footnote in BT, *Vorhandenheit* in this passage signifies "presence," and not, as further on in the book, "subsistence" or "given for handling," e.g., SZ 98/BT 130). As pure reception, *noein* is never liable to error. It matches *legein*, "letting something be seen" (SZ 33 and 44/BT 56 and 70), so that "any entity is encountered" in the junction of *noein* and *legein* (SZ 44/BT 70). The 'noetic' in the narrow sense coincides with the traditional preeminence of one region of entities, subsistent objects (SZ 147/BT 187). But in the larger sense, it designates the reception of what *logos* "appresents." In the subsequent works *legein* and *noein* are integrated in another context of thought, dehumanized, but their reciprocal relation remains fundamentally the same.
84. In a series of three remarkable studies, Kurt von Fritz has traced the development of the words *noos* and *noein* in the epic and Presocratic philosophic traditions: "Noos and Noein in the Homeric Poems," *Classical Philology*, XXXVIII (1943):79–93; "Nous, noein and their Derivatives in Presocratic Philosophy (Excluding Anaxagoras)," ibid., XL (1945):223–242, and XLI (1946):12–34. At each stage of this evolution, the reference to man predominates: in Homer, *noein* primarily signifies "realizing a situation" by grasping its implications. A person blunders into an ambush, and suddenly he understands the strategem to which he has fallen victim. Suddenly seeing what a situation is all about is the primary sense of the verb *noein* (von Fritz [1943], especially pp. 85 and 91). The distinction between an organ and its function is not found in the Homeric Greeks, "but if they had made this distinction, they probably would have considered *nous* to be a function rather than an organ" (ibid., p. 83). Already in Homer this word comes charged with numerous secondary significations: *nooi* as diverse as individuals and nations; "plan" or "project"; a "volitional element"; a "deeper understanding of things"; the unicity of *nous;* "imagination" (von Fritz [1945], pp. 223 f.). All of these deal however with man. In Heraclitus, *nous* "must" be coordinated to the divine law (a play on the words ξυν νοῶ—ξυνῶ, ibid., pp. 232 f.), which makes it "something humans possess only rarely" (p. 234). Lastly, in Parmenides *nous* displays, on one hand, a natural affinity to *eon* (and only from this viewpoint can *nous* "never be false," SZ 33/ BT 57) and, on the other, it is the capacity of spelling out the "logical deductions" through which that affinity becomes

articulated ([1945], pp. 238). Throughout these various senses, what endures is the reference to man. *Nous*, says Snell (*Discovery of the Mind*, pp. 11 f.) in summarizing von Fritz, is always both a human organ and a human function.

85. VA 140. The translation of Parmenides' frag. VIII, 34, which follows in VA 141, reproduces that of von Fritz (*noein* = "to perceive" [1945], pp. 237–42). Understood this way, *noein* suggests 'letting-be.' Indeed, to "perceive" an entity—to "be in touch with it," says von Fritz—is "to let it stand or lie before us, in whichever way it is standing or lying" (VA 140).

86. VA 242 f. and 245/EGT 88 f. and 91. When *logos* becomes the act of *nous*, this order of priority is inverted (cf. SZ 226/BT 269).

87. WhD 125/WCT 209.

88. N II 450/EPh 46.

89. WhD 128, 139, 145 f., 172/WCT 207, 211, 231, 239 f. A full understanding of Parmenides' frag. V on the identity of *noein* and *einai* can therefore be gained only in the light of frag. VI on *legein* and *noein*. Due to this conjunction, Parmenides "most often merely says *noein* instead of *legein te noein te*"(WhD 146/WCT 240).

90. Hw 162 and 193/HCE 107 and QCT 54. In Parmenides, *nous* is opposed to *doxa* as presencing is to the present. *Doxa* designates the various relations between present entities taken heed of and man heeding them as present, as 'laid out'. With the Platonic turn, that conjunction between *nous* and *logos* is replaced by the one between *nous* and *idea* (Wm 131 and 136 f./PDT 262 and 265 f., see also SD 49/OTB 46).

91. N II 295.

92. N II 474/EPh 69. Contrary to what Heidegger implies in this text, *idein* is already synonymous with *noein* in several Homeric passages (cf. von Fritz [1945], p. 233 and [1946], p. 31). It is true that in those passages it is a question not of a vision aiming at unobstructed *theōrein*—with the exteriority between contemplating and contemplated this term connotes—but of a vision that is not "the proper activity of the eye"; "the ego is not isolated, but a field of open forces" (Snell, *Die Entdeckung des Geistes*, pp. 23 and 296).

93. N II 295 and 320.

94. SZ 11/BT 31 ("*Sachlogik*").

95. Wm 57/ER 97.

96. SD 79/OTB 72.

XI. At the Technological End: The Retrospective Categories

1. N II 256/N iv 196.

2. "The name 'technology' is understood here in such an essential way that its meaning coincides with the term 'completed metaphysics' " (VA 80/EPh 93). It is curious that Henri Mongis, *Heidegger et la critique de la notion de valeur* (The Hague, 1976), should not have recognized this substitution. For Mongis, "the last metaphysical way station" of the truth of being is Nietzsche (p. 22), while elsewhere he describes that same "way station" in terms applicable to twentieth century technology alone (for example, p. 211).

3. N II 486/EPh 80.

4. TK 38–41/QCT 38–41; SvG 41.

5. N II 165/N iv 116.

6. Hw 94/QCT 142.

7. SvG 199/PG 213 f.

8. Hw 267/PLT 112.

9. VA 90/EPh 102.

10. IuD 48/IaD 51 f.

11. VA 81/EPh 93.

12. Heidegger makes his own the results Nietzsche had already reached in his deconstruction of epochs (although in a different idiom), only then to label Nietzsche the last metaphysician. It seems that today Jacques Derrida is engaged in a similar game with Heidegger. In *Margins of Philosophy*, trans. Alan Bass (Chicago, 1982), Derrida distinguishes between "two styles of deconstruction . . . the style of the first is mostly that of the Heideggerian questions, and the other, mostly the one that predominates in France today" (p. 135, trans. modified). Heidegger, then, "attempts an exit and a deconstruction without changing terrains," which

makes him risk "sinking into the autism of the closure." What the "French" style attempts—
an attempt presumably not foreign to Derrida himself—is "to change terrains, in a discontinuous and irruptive fashion, by brutally placing oneself outside and by asserting an absolute
break and difference" (p. 135, trans. modified). Asserting an absolute break and difference was
precisely what Derrida had done in saluting "the world that is ineluctably to come . . .
beyond the closure of knowing" (see above, sec. 1, n. 11). Heidegger reads Nietzsche "as the
last of the great metaphysicians," writes Derrida, only to add rhetorically: "Are we to understand *the question of the truth of being* as the last sleeping shudder of the superior man," who
"is *abandoned* to his distress in a last movement of pity"? (pp. 135 f., emphasis added). If
Derrida feels authorized to do (partially, cf. p. 123) unto Heidegger as Heidegger has done
unto Nietzsche, the price he pays is equally high: he must negate the difference between
presence and presencing in Heidegger (p. 132), reduce "the question of being [to] an intra-
metaphysical effect" (p. 22), turn Heidegger's quest for an understanding of the *verb* 'to be'
into a quest for "the ultimate proper name" (p. 27), to say nothing of tendencious translations
such as *"sceller"* (to seal) for *"prägen"* (to stamp or mark) which coopt what Heidegger calls
the "early trace" (of the ontological difference in Anaximander) and make it into yet another
version of full presence, of the "proper" in which "the very loss is sheltered, retained" (pp. 24
f., trans. modified). In *Writing and Difference*, trans. Alan Bass (Chicago, 1978), he is more
straightforward: "Nietzsche, Freud, and Heidegger proceeded within the inherited concepts
of metaphysics." After this summary confinement, Derrida seems to step outside the destruction game and watch "the destroyers destroy each other reciprocally—for example, Heidegger
regarding Nietzsche, with as much lucidity and rigor as bad faith and misconstruction, as the
last metaphysician." One cannot help thinking that Derrida steps back into that game and
speaks of himself when he adds: "One could play the same game with Heidegger himself, with
Freud, or with a number of others. And today no exercise is more widespread" (pp. 281,
trans. modified). Indeed.

13. VA 22–26/QCT 14–19.

14. Automation technology is not "the mere application of modern mathematical physical
science to praxis" (Hw 69/QCT 116).

15. VA 63 f./QCT 174 f.

16. Wm 146/BWr 194. It is not my purpose here to trace how Greek *technē* became
modern technology (cf., for example, Wm 321 f., 326 f., 359 f./Phy 231 f., 235, 260 f.).

17. VA 82/EPh 94.

18. Hw 91/QCT 139.

19. N II 264 and 232/N iv 176, and elsewhere.

20. N II 287. *"Logos* indicates the essence of the suppositum" as "permanence." "Metaphysics proper begins" with that *Gepräge* (N II 431 and 403/EPh 28 and 4). See, in the same
sense, GA 55 223.

21. N II 287.

22. N II 40/N iv 9.

23. N II 260 (cf., N II 329). I will not pursue the difficult parallels Heidegger draws
between the will to power and the metaphysical concept of essence as well as between the
eternal return and that of existence. These parallels are not rendered more intelligible when
Heidegger adds: "In Nietzsche's metaphysics the difference between *essentia* and *existentia*
disappears" (N II 476/EPh 70; see below, sec. 31). Furthermore, it is not always apparent if it
is the will to power that corresponds to *ti, was,* and the eternal return to *hoti, dass,* or the
reverse (see also N I 425 and 463 f. and N II 14–17, 345/N iv 206 f.).

24. Hw 196/QCT 57.

25. N II 277 (Heidegger's emphasis).

26. N II 459/EPh 56.

27. N II 132 and 467/N iv 89 and EPh 63. Elsewhere (for example, Hw 226/QCT 90), that
quest for sure salvation is described instead as a proper trait of modernity, beginning with
Luther.

28. On the sequence *logos-ratio-Grund-Vernunft,* cf., for example, SvG 177 f.

29. On the fixity of the *nunc stans* ("standing now") as a categorial incidence of the eternal
return, see N I 28/N i 20.

30. N II 163/N iv 115 (the translation of "impending" for *Überlagerung* misses the crucial
point, categorial over-determination).

31. Ibid.

32. N I 633.

§28. The Will to Power

33. N I 26/N i 18 and Hw 223/QCT 86.

34. Hw 94/QCT 142. "The epitome [of the will to power] consists in its *positing* its own conditions" (N II 324, emphasis added).

35. N II 268.

36. N II 272.

37. N II 273.

38. N II 141 and 435/N iv 96 and EPh 31; cf., Hw 98/QCT 147 f.

39. The term *Subjektität* (for example, Hw 236/QCT 100) signifies subjectivity inasmuch as it is "the being of entities" (ibid.) for the modern age.

40. N II 297.

41. N II 303.

42. Hw 100/QCT 150.

43. "The intellect must be free from all admixture to be able to dominate [κρατεῖν], that is, to know," Aristotle, *On the Soul*, III, 4; 429 a 19.

44. N II 272 and Hw 258/PLT 102.

45. Hubris (the act of applying a false measure, *"Vermessenheit"*) consists for man in "taking the measures (*Masse*) of his thinking and doing from the entities that impose themselves on him" rather than from "being itself, the sole measure" (GA 55 326). Etymologically, however, *hubris* stems from *huper*, 'beyond', and signifies a transgression, not a misapplication.

46. For example: "The willing at issue here is a pro-ducing, and this in the sense of an objectification purposely asserting itself" (Hw 266/PLT 110).

47. Hw 272/PLT 117 (emphasis added).

§29. Nihilism

48. N II 343/N iv 205.

49. Ibid.

50. N II 338/N iv 201, cf. Hw 239/QCT 104.

51. With the Platonic turn, *phusis* ceases to be understood (as it is in Heraclitus) "in its own essence" and starts to be conceived "in view of its relation to humans who either grasp or do not grasp it" (GA 55 140).

52. N II 342/N iv 204.

53. Nihilism is the *Grundgeschehen*—"that which happens at bottom"—of Western history (N II 275 f., cf. Hw 201/QCT 62). Metaphysics as such has a nihilistic historical essence: *"dieses nihilistisch-geschichtliche Wesen"* (N II 292).

54. Hw 193/QCT 53.

55. In terms of the history of being, only the commutation, described earlier, between the Nietzschean discourse and the technological economy gives coherence to Heidegger's frequent remarks that "Nietzsche's metaphysics" is "inverted Platonism." Therefore, in texts like the following, it is necessary to read "technology" wherever Heidegger says "Nietzsche": "The inversion of Platonism, according to which the sensuous becomes for Nietzsche the true, and the suprasensuous, the untrue world, remains lodged entirely within metaphysics" (VA 79/EPh 92). It is clear, at least, that the 'fundamental position', where all the historically earlier ones join as in an estuary because it exhibits most plainly the "danger" in the "forgottenness" of being, is technology: "The essence of enframing (*Gestell*) is the danger. As the danger, being turns about into the forgottenness of its essence, turns away from this essence, and in that way simultaneously turns against the truth of its essence" (TK 40/QCT 41; cf., Wm 221/QB 49).

56. N II 278.

57. Hw 193/QCT 53.

58. N II 395/N iv 248. The text continues by describing technological nihilism: "Needlessness (*Notlosigkeit*) in relation to being hardens in and through the increased demand for entities." Technology appears here as the effort to compensate by ontic accumulation the nothingness of transcendence.

59. N II 50 and 54/N iv 20 and 22.

§30. Justice

60. Hw 36/PLT 47.

61. N II 431/EPh 28 and SvG 167 and 193/PG 209. The Nietzschean concept of justice, *Gerechtigkeit*, says Heidegger, is best understood by looking at the subsenses suggested by

the word. " '*Recht*', *rectus*, is what is right," i.e., what fits; hence the connotations of "*richten*" and "*ausrichten*," adjusting, straightening, equalizing (N I 637). Justice, in Nietzsche, thus appears like a late version of truth as conformity.

62. SvG 210/PG 222. Heidegger expressly denies any kinship between Nietzschean "justice" and Heraclitean δίϰη. Nietzsche's concept springs from "the historical determination which the last metaphysician of the West obeys." The concept of justice translates "truth as ὁμοίωσις" for the age of closure (N I 632 f.).

63. N I 636 f.

64. N I 637. "Retaining ὁμοίωσις as the essence of truth and interpreting it as justice amount, for the metaphysical thought that effects such an interpretation [Nietzsche's], to fulfilling metaphysics" (ibid.).

65. N I 643 and 648. "Life" is here another name for "entities in their totality."

66. N II 320. In the same sense: "Justice is the attainment of self-mastery through the constructive ascent to the highest heights. This is the very essence of the will to power" (N II 323). "This highest will to power, the transformation of entities in their totality into stock, unveils its essence as justice" (N II 327).

67. N II 318 f.; cf., N II 325.

§31. The Eternal Return of the Same

68. N I 26/N i 18 (emphasis added). On the translation of *Sinn* as 'sense' (directionality), see above, p. 13.

69. N I 27/N i 19. Obviously this particular going-back to origins, no more than anything else said here about the eternal return, must not be understood in the Pythagorean fashion, as a cyclic process perpetually restoring the same events, entities or configurations throughout world history.

70. N II 23. This thesis of the collapse of rationality into animality entails an identification of existence and essence (cf. above, n. 23), analogous to the one construed in Scholastic speculations on the simplicity of the divine nature. Here it serves to describe the counterfeit of that simplicity, the technological homogenization of earthly nature.

71. N I 258 f.

72. N I 407.

73. About that turn from Heraclitus to Plato as the birthplace of anthropocentrism, see the text quoted above, n. 51.

74. N I 369 and 380. This allusion to the young Marx, whether deliberate or not, is all the more perplexing since the notions of "nature," "planet," "globe," retain a strong, if only occasional, romantic overtone in Heidegger himself.

75. N I 394 (emphasis added). "*That* truth of entities" designates here everything as stabilized by the thought of the eternal return: "What is the true according to Nietzsche's conception? It is what is made fast in the constant flux and change of things becoming" (N I 388). Needless to add that, for Heidegger, this stabilization by humanization is "the danger for truth" understood as unconcealment (N I 381).

§32. The Transmutation of All Values and the Death of God

76. Kant, *Critique of Pure Reason*, B 383.

77. N I 433 f.

78. "*Prior* to the transvaluation of all values until now, which Nietzsche takes on as his metaphysical task, a more originary reversal takes place, namely, that the *essence* of all entities is at the outset fixed as *value*" (N I 539).

79. Hw 200/QCT 61.

80. TK 46/QCT 49.

81. See above, n. 24.

82. N I 469.

83. N II 18 (cf., Hw 214/QCT 75). "The inversion is the transformation of the lowest, the sensory, into 'life' in the sense of the will to power"; it is "the transformation of metaphysics into its last possible form" (N II 16). Heidegger's texts on the transmutation as an inverted Platonism are numerous (see for example N I 177, 181, 231, 433, 464–469/N i 151, 154, 200). What is at issue for Heidegger in all these passages is to establish that the inversion of the "two world doctrine" is "the most hidden and extreme consequence of the first inception of Western thought" (N I 547).

84. N I 188/N i 160 f.
85. N I 547.
86. F. Nietzsche, *The Portable Nietzsche,* trans. and ed. Walter Kaufmann (New York, 1954), p. 486.
87. "The true world is the changeable, the apparent world is the solid and the permanent. The true and the apparent world have exchanged places, ranks and kinds; but in that exchange and inversion what is preserved is precisely the *distinction* between a true and an apparent world" (N I 617).

§33. The Overman

88. N II 305.
89. N II 291 f.
90. N II 308.
91. N II 308 and 166/N iv 117; cf. N II 310.
92. N II 295.
93. N II 300 f.
94. N II 307.
95. N II 309.
96. Hw 232 f./QCT 97 (emphasis added).
97. The distance between Nietzsche's and Heidegger's concepts of overman has been shown in some detail by Michel Haar, "Heidegger et le surhomme," *Revue de l'enseignement philosophique,* XXX, 3 (1980): 1–17. Haar also hints at the categorial dependence of the 'overman' on the 'will to power' and the 'eternal return': "It is only indirectly and as a consequence that the overman comes to represent [in Heidegger] completed subjectivity" (ibid., p. 6).
98. WhD 69/WCT 72. On the shift in Heidegger's understanding of the overman, see Haar, op. cit., pp. 15–17.
99. Haar, op. cit., p. 16.

XII. At the "Turning": The Transitional Categories

1. MHG 73/IW 38.
2. Michel Foucault, *The Archaeology of Knowledge,* trans. A. M. Sheridan Smith (New York, 1976), pp. 130 f.
3. To the four transcendentalist rules, "words and things," "pure form of knowledge," "ideality," and "fundamental [philosophical] project," Foucault opposes four classes of rules that regulate discourse: "the formation of objects,"of "enunciative modalities," of "concepts," and of "strategies" (ibid., pp. 40–70). If these "rules of formation" determine discourse in each and every shape, they are truly necessary and universal, and at least in that respect not foreign to the transcendental tradition.
4. See above, ch. 11, n. 12. To make good his promise to "change terrains, in a discontinuous and irruptive fashion" (quoted ibid.), Derrida had to arrive at "a new writing." Indeed, "the simple practice of language ceaselessly reinstates the 'new' terrain on the oldest ground." He had to "speak several languages and produce several texts at once" (Jacques Derrida, *Margins of Philosophy,* trans. Alan Bass [Chicago, 1982], p. 135)—more precisely, two languages, metaphysical and extra-metaphysical. He has attempted such "new writing" in *Glas* (Paris, 1974). The point is that discontinuity and abruptness are not easy if "metaphysics" is equatable with "our tongue" (*Margins of Philosophy,* p. 121). For Derrida, too, then, despite the desire to simply change terrains, natural languages and their grammar make it impossible to reject any continuity in "transgressing the closure of metaphysics" (*Margins of Philosophy,* p. 172).
5. Hw 300–302 and 309/EGT 17 f. and 25. Kostas Axelos has described Heidegger as an "indicator of future thought," *Einführung in ein künftiges Denken* (Tübingen, 1966), p. 3. This is in agreement with Heidegger's own understanding of *eschaton* as metaphysical closure, and of the task of thinking today. But Axelos goes overboard in his construction of a continuity between past and future thought since he conjoins the "new destiny of being" with its metaphysical destiny by way of a dialectic (ibid., pp. 16–35). Between utter dissemination and dispersion, as in "French deconstruction" and dialectical co-optation, the road most frequently

taken in the Heidegger literature is that of dismissing the essentially ambiguous nature of technology as the age in which the "turning" has become possible. Gerold Prauss thus denounces a "utopian backward orientation" in Heidegger's understanding of history. The latter amounts to "the extremest irruption of antiquity into the modern and contemporary world" (*Erkennen und Handeln in Heideggers "Sein und Zeit"* [Freiburg, 1977], p. 103). Thus the key feature of the *Gestell*, its bi-frontality, simply gets discarded.

6. It is Nietzsche's expression "philosopher of the future" that apparently accounts for Heidegger's phrase "thinking yet to come," *künftiges Denken*. In an equally Nietzschean vein, the deconstructive advance toward a non-metaphysical site of thought has the characteristics of a *Denkversuch:* an attempt at thinking another economy and, perhaps, a temptation. Leo Gabriel, "Sein und Geschichte; Martin Heideggers geschichtsontologischer Denkversuch" (*Wissenschaft und Weltbild,* IX [Vienna, 1956]:25–32) suggests such a reading of the "ontology of history" as a *Versuch,* as a trial in both senses of the word, a tentative and a test.

7. By *Heimat,* "home"—meaning 'dwelling-place' as well as 'native land'—and *Heimkunft,* "homecoming," Heidegger designates a possible fold in the unfolding history of being. These words, borrowed from Hölderlin, thus stand in opposition to the historical "errancy," *Irre,* subsequent to the Greek inception. The anticipatory incidence of the transitional categories brings home, back to our *oikos,* the *nomos* rendered foreign—estranged—under the sway of ultimate representations. This eco-nomic retrieval is ignored in the two best studies on the Heideggerian meaning of *wohnen,* "dwelling": Beda Allemann, *Hölderlin und Heidegger* (Zürich, 1954, especially pp. 119–161), and Walter Biemel, "Dichtung und Sprache bei Heidegger," *Man and World* II, 1969:478–514. As shown by the transitional categories, to retrieve a nonprincipial economy by no means amounts to reiterating the Greek mode of presence. The transitional traits are irreducible to the prospective ones. Only the polymorphous, Heraclitean, habitat is to be reclaimed and every edifice conceived as timeless, to be destabilized.

8. TK 41/QCT 42; VA 36 and 43/QCT 28 and 34; Hw 273/PLT 118.

9. VA 20, 22, 34/QCT 12, 14, 26.

10. VA 40/QCT 32. The "essential connection between truth and freedom" had been established since 1930 (Wm 83/BWr 127).

11. TK 41/QCT 42.

12. Quoted above as epigraph to sec. 18.

13. Heidegger only seeks to situate that line. He leaves it to the novelist Ernst Jünger to transgress it. However: "Your assessment of the state of affairs under the title *trans lineam* and my quest for its site under the title *de linea* belong together" (Wm 214/QB 37). Here is how situation and transgression belong together: "Where the danger is as the danger, there also thrives what saves. The latter does not occur incidentally. The very danger is what saves, when it is *as* the danger" (TK 41/QCT 42; for Heidegger's interpretation of Ernst Jünger's essay, *Über die Linie,* see Jean Michel Palmier, *Les écrits politiques de Heidegger,* Paris 1968, pp. 169–227). The point is that one cannot describe the line of closure as separating danger from possible salvation without having transgressed it already; without having "in a certain way left metaphysics behind" (Wm 197/WGM 208).

14. *"Vorläufig"* in the double sense of provisional and anticipatory (cf. SD 38/OTB 35).

15. See the text quoted below, n. 26.

16. Karl Löwith writes: "Heidegger will only be able to convince of the necessity of his thought those who believe, as he does, that his thinking has been destined to him by Being itself, that it is a 'sending' of Being, and that, as such, it tells 'the dictation of truth about Being'. Such a claim cannot be examined rationally." *Heidegger, Denker in dürftiger Zeit* (2nd ed., Göttingen, 1960), p. 59.

17. To illustrate a frequently held opinion, here is the assessment of one commentator who, in the end, finds in Heidegger no more than an "alternative" to technology "which amounts to an open regression": "In its return to the Presocratics, [Heidegger's thought] explicitly abandons reason and surrenders to the illusion that salvation from misfortune can only come from reverting to that primitive state," Winfried Franzen, *Von der Existenzialontologie zur Seinsgeschichte* (Meisenheim, 1975), pp. 163 and 150.

18. Wolfgang de Boer, "Heideggers Missverständnis der Metaphysik," *Zeitschrift für philosophische Forschung,* IX (1955):500–545, correctly remarks that Heidegger's interpretations of metaphysics and technology are "in no way presuppositionless" and that they "serve to prove the legitimacy of his being question." This legitimation can be gained, he adds, only

before "the forum of history" (p. 500). Here, then, the legitimating source of Heidegger's undertaking is acknowledged, but he stands accused of having denatured that source: "Has Heidegger understood or misunderstood Western metaphysics?" (p. 507). Answer: he has misunderstood it. As proof, the author points to "the radical ontological separation Heidegger establishes between human and divine being . . ." (p. 520). The interest that lies behind this criticism is the same that guided the postwar Neothomists, namely a rehabilitation of onto-theology. Only, in the Neothomists, that interest gave rise not to a critique but to co-optation; see: Max Müller, *Sein und Geist* (Tübingen, 1940), and *Existenzphilosophie im geistigen Leben der Gegenwart* (3rd ed., Heidelberg, 1964), especially pp. 95–139; Johann Baptist Lotz, "Das Sein selbst und das subsistierende Sein nach Thomas von Aquin" (in *Martin Heidegger zum 70. Geburtstag*, Pfullingen, 1959), especially p. 182; and Gustav Siewerth, *Das Schicksal der Metaphysik von Thomas zu Heidegger* (Einsiedeln, 1959), especially pp. 21–31 and 361–372.

19. To quote only two representatives of the "Frankfurt School": in 1928, Herbert Marcuse wrote that with BT "philosophy finally has come back to its original urgency. Henceforth it only concerns itself with existence alone, its truth and its fulfillment. . . . It is admirable to watch how, proceeding from there, all philosophical problems and solutions that have become rigid are *set into dialectical motion* and side with the concrete people who have lived and live in them" ("Beiträge zu einer Phänomenologie des historischen Materialismus," reprinted in H. Marcuse and A. Schmidt, *Existenzialistische Marx-Interpretation*, Frankfurt, 1973, p. 59, italics added). More recently, Karl-Otto Apel has spoken of a "new version of the belief in destiny" in Heidegger's philosophy of the history of being. This philosophy would, "in the end, like to deduce its own legitimation from the *kairos* of the destiny of being as it comes to pass" (*Transformation der Philosophie*, vol. I, Frankfurt, 1976, p. 41). The anticipatory structure of technology as revealed by the historical deduction of the transitional categories precludes dialectical constructs of a forward march since there is no entity, collective or single, that could function as the subject of such a march; and it allows one to speak of *kairos* only if that term is applied to what I have called the reversals in history—an application however in total contradiction with its original biblical sense, taken up in the 1920s by Paul Tillich and the Berlin "religious socialists," which always designates the irruption of the eternal into the temporal, of "theonomy" into human "autonomy." No such dualism is construable in Heidegger.

20. MHG 73/IW 38.

21. Since BT, Heidegger has kept denouncing "aprioristic constructs" in phenomenology (see for example SZ 16, 50 ftn., 302 f./BT 37, 349 f., 490). His terms recall Marx's labeling of Schelling as "traveling salesman for all constructors, *Musterreiter aller Konstruktoren*"(*The German Ideology*, Moscow, 1976, p. 146; trans. modified).

22. SD 67/OTB 60.

23. Hw 245/QCT 111.

24. "For us, the most readily experienced correspondence to the epochal character of being is the ecstatic character of being-there. The epochal essence of being appropriates in an event [*ereignet*] the ecstatic essence of being-there" (Hw 311/EGT 27). These lines sum up the three moments of Heidegger's itinerary sketched above in the epigraph to sec. 2. By implication, they also summarize the three-tiered temporal difference between things present, their historical mode of presence, and the event of presencing.

25. Hw 246/EGT 111.

26. VA 183/PLT 184 f.

§34. Ontological Difference/World and Thing

27. The following three fragments of Parmenides must be read conjointly if one wishes to see how he inaugurates the 'transcendental' (in the sense assigned to this term in BT) articulation of the ontological difference: "It is necessary to both say and think that being is; indeed, being is, but nothing is not" (frag. VI, 1; see above, sec. 22, n. 9); "the same is, indeed, both thinking and being" (frag. III; see above, sec. 18, n. 95); the third text would be the entire fragment VIII on the unicity of being. The first of these texts can be read as indicating being's self-sameness; the second, the transcendence of thought toward being; and the third, the unicity of being.

28. SZ 38/BT 62. Carl Friedrich Gethmann, *Verstehen und Auslegung* (Bonn, 1974), pp. 41–45, offers the most satisfactory exposition of the ontological difference in Heidegger. He

insists especially on the necessity of understanding the ontological difference as a synthesis of three terms: entity, beingness, and being; or *on, ousia,* and *einai.* However, he does not seem to think that after 1930 Heidegger abandoned the transcendental concept of being for an economic one. That substitution, which the first transitional category seeks to render explicit, escapes even more the attention of those commentators who construe the ontological difference either as an "alternative" between entities and being, an alternative that can only be resolved by a "pure belief" (Kurt Jürgen Huch, *Philosophiegeschichtliche Voraussetzungen der Heideggerschen Ontologie,* Frankfurt 1967, pp. 37 and 40), or as a clue "that being can exist without the human being" (Jean Wahl, *Vers la fin de l'ontologie,* Paris, 1956, p. 18; cf. Otto Pöggeler, "Jean Wahls Heidegger-Deutung," *Zeitschrift für philosophische Forschung XII,* 1958, p. 454), or as a regional linguistic formation (Johannes Lohman, "Martin Heideggers 'Ontologische Differenz' und die Sprache," *Lexis* I, 1948, especially p. 106), or, lastly, as a reminder of "the Wittgensteinian distinction between what can be said and what can only be shown" (Apel, *Transformation der Philosophie,* vol. I, p. 238). While all these interpretations may be viewed as acknowledging that the metaphysical difference functions inside the closure, they neglect the crucial fact that the three-tiered phenomenological difference in Heidegger serves to draw the line of that closure and that the function of *even that three-tiered difference is therefore limited to the recapitulatory task.*

29. GA 24 23/BPP 17.

30. SD 40 f./OTB 37.

31. VA 169/PLT 171. To understand this first transitional category I rely mainly upon the essay "The Thing." A more detailed analysis of this category can be found in Werner Marx (*Heidegger and the Tradition* [Evanston, Ill., 1971], pp. 193–198) always from the double viewpoint of the "first beginning" and "the other beginning." See also Heidegger's description of it in terms of speech which "calls upon the thing and the world" (US 22–32/PLT 199–209).

32. VA 179/PLT 181.

33. See the first paragraph of BT (SZ 2/BT 21).

34. SZ 53/BT 79.

35. SZ 64 and 146/BT 92 and 187.

36. "Jedes Ding verweilt das Geviert in ein je Weiliges von Einfalt der Welt" (VA 179/PLT 181).

37. VA 172/PLT 173.

38. Hw 33/PLT 44.

39. "*Weisung*" (VA 184/PLT 185).

40. TK 46/QCT 48.

41. VA 169/PLT 171.

42. VA 180/PLT 182.

43. VA 177/PLT 179.

44. VA 164/PLT 166.

45. VA 183 f./PLT 184 (cf. TK 40 f./QCT 41).

46. VA 180/PLT 181. According to OTB, this "step backward" does not only consist in acknowledging the condition of the conditioned, that is, the aletheiological fabric in which entities appear, but it "frees" them as phenomena so that they can show themselves in what makes them unique. "That step steps back before, gains distance from that which is only about to arrive" (SD 32/OTB 30). For such setting-free and the practical a priori in general, see below, sec. 40.

47. Certain similarities have often been noted between Heidegger's technology critique and that of the early Frankfurt school. Despite Theodor Adorno's polemics (*The Jargon of Authenticity,* trans. Knut Tarnowski and Frederic Will [Evanston, 1973]), this family resemblance between two modes of criticism, which popular wisdom still treats as extremes on the political spectrum, implies more than an agreement on the reification and objectification imposed on our entire culture by technology: it reaches the roots of that one-dimensionality, namely, conceptual thinking and its "identifying" nature as it has made the West since the Greeks (see T. Adorno and M. Horkheimer, *The Dialectic of Enlightenment,* trans. J. Cumming [New York, 1972], pp. 3–42). To that process of "repressive logic" the later Adorno opposes art as the one region of phenomena in which the particular cannot be repressed or suppressed (*Aesthetic Theory,* trans. G. Lenhardt [Boston, 1982]. But this opposition in Adorno between technical and aesthetic rationality (1) is obtained, not from within technology, but from its "negation," ultimately from a utopia; (2) seeks an inroad of the particular into

"reason" and "theory," the very agents of the universal, and thereby gives the particular over to dialectical cancellation and sublation; (3) rests on selected entities, works of advanced art, and thus abandons everything else—institutions of administration, production, culture, law— to the grip of reification; (4) arises from an interest in re-enchanting the world artistically, after its disenchantment through modern science. Heidegger's attempt at retrieving the particular, on the other hand, (1) results, as has been shown, from a phenomenology of technology itself; (2) calls not upon any form of *ratio*, but on 'thinking', understood as 'thanking', that is, as practical compliance with varying contexts; (3) is economy-wide and therefore not selective; (4) arises from an interest in the most "sober" (cf. above, sec. 8, n. 44) acquiescence to surface constellations. In a word, his first transitional category is not 'another world and a few beautiful things', but "world and thing."

48. Otto Pöggeler ("Sein als Ereignis," *Zeitschrift für philosophische Forschung* XIII [1959], p. 599) aptly denounces interpretations of this substitution according to which "the central theme of Heidegger's thought is not congealed and emptied being, but the 'world': the world as the 'true world', as the world which has left the whole of Western nihilism behind. Heidegger, we are told, rejects the old and decrepit world, Christian, metaphysical, bourgeois, and is awaiting the world to come, untouched and novel. In his last writings he supposedly even begins to proclaim its arrival. Read this way, Heidegger turns into a mythologist." Pöggeler does not ascribe these interpretations to anyone in particular, but their kinship with Herbert Marcuse's "Great Refusal" is striking. Elsewhere, Pöggeler stresses the continuity between the being-question, and that of 'world': "The world constitutes the proper issue toward which Heidegger's thought frees itself through the insight into that which is," *Der Denkweg Martin Heideggers,* (Pfullingen, 1963), p. 247.

49. FD 130/WTh 166.

50. Here is an impressive list, compiled by Gethmann in *Verstehen und Auslegung* (p. 42), of the reduplicating versions of the metaphysical difference: "reality of the real" (Hw 136/HCE 60), "subjectness of the subject" (Hw 122/HCE 34), "absoluteness of the absolute" (ibid.), "truth of the true" (Hw 172/HCE 125), "historicity of history" (Hw 141/HCE 67), "effectivity of the effective" (Hw 186/HCE 146), "worldliness of the world" (Hw 187/HCE 147), "thingness of the thing" (FD 8/WTh 11), "objectivity of the object" (SvG 46), "substantiality of the substance" (Wm 291/KTB 21), "egoness of the ego" (SvG 132), "appearance of the appearing" (Hw 144/HCE 73). I am not convinced, however, that these are all instances of the difference between beingness (*Seiendheit*) and entities (*das Seiende*), since in the context of this transitional category, 'thingness' is to be understood as 'thinging', as event (cf. the following two notes).

51. FD 137/WTh 175 (cf. FD 92/WTh 118).

52. "If things had shown themselves each time already *as* things in their thingness, then the thing's thingness would have become manifest. *It*, then, would have laid claim to thought. In truth, however, the thing remains denied, nil, and in that sense annihilated" (VA 169/PLT 170 f.). Here, as in WTh, it is obvious that Heidegger uses *Dingheit* not as an equivalent of *Seiendheit*, beingness, but of *Sein*, being.

53. FD 100/WTh 129.

54. TK 46/QCT 49.

§35. "There Is"/Favor

55. See especially SD 41–43/OTB 38–40. The deconstructive character of the "giving" in *es gibt*—in this case, deconstructive of the three traditional questions of *metaphysica specialis*— appears, for example, in Fw 7/Pa 39.

56. SD 44/OTB 41.

57. GA 55 372.

58. TK 42/QCT 43.

59. This term probably appears for the first time in the postscript to "What is Metaphysics?" (Wm 106/EB 359).

60. TK 42/QCT 43 (emphasis added).

61. SD 18 and 43/OTB 17 and 40.

62. SD 80/OTB 73. It is true that this text goes on to say: "But whence and how is the clearing given? What speaks in the 'there is'?" But this conjunction of the recapitulatory and the anticipatory is only the double language to be held on the threshold of the closure. At the moment of transition, one must affirm both "the farewell from being and time" and the "there

is" through which they "remain, so to speak, as the gift of the event of appropriation" (SD 58/OTB 54).

63. SD 2/OTB 2.

64. SD 42 and 43/OTB 38 and 40.

65. GA 55 127–139.

66. TK 42/QCT 44.

67. SD 58/OTB 54.

68. Ibid. Heidegger adds that "the new concept of finitude" is to be understood "from out of the concept of property" (ibid.). This remark, too, must be read as a reference to the topology.

§36. Unconcealment/Event

69. The transition under discussion breaks the conceptual concatenation by which *alētheia*, understood as truth, would be tied to some human comportment, which in turn—due to epochal errancy, *Irre*—would be inescapably prone to error. It is still in the name of an *ideally true* behavior that Werner Marx and others have been disturbed by statements such as this: "He who thinks greatly must err greatly" (EdD 17/PLT 9; cf. above, sec. 17, n. 39). Kostas Axelos has sought to articulate the transition from metaphysical to 'future thinking' as the transition from the pursuit of truth to the acceptance of its permeation with error: "Will some future thinking be enabled to experience 'truth' as 'errancy' and 'errancy' as 'truth', although not at all in that dichotomy?" *Einführung in ein zukünftiges Denken*, p. 19. This way of approaching the closure leaves the two chief *values* of metaphysics untouched, 'man' and 'truth'. It thereby deprives itself of all means to draft even the contours for the self-assigned problematic, that of transgressing the line of closure.

70. TK 42 f./QCT 44 f. For the many sense of the word *Ereignis* see above (sec. 6, n. 37) the quote from Henri Birault.

71. TK 44/QCT 46. See also the texts from IW quoted above (sec. 2, n. 34 and ch. 12, n. 20). Those quotes from TK suffice to oppose, point by point, the interpretation of *Ereignis* put forth by Pöggeler ("Sein als Ereignis," p. 621): "In its meaning or its openness and truth, being—the unmasterable destiny of being which is each time historical—shows itself as event. In this context, event no longer designates some particular occurrence or happening, as it still did within the terminology of *Being and Time,* but rather *Dasein*'s appropriation by being and being's self-bestowal upon authentic *Dasein.*" At least from the perspective of Heidegger's last writings, that raises four objections: (1) In OTB the event is precisely no longer understood as the historical-destinal reversal that establishes an epoch: "the entry into the event" (*Einkehr in das Ereignis,* SD 44/OTB 41) is the recognition of the temporality which makes epochal time possible. (2) The vocabulary of meaning is incompatible with that of event—it is at variance even with the vocabulary of the history of being, with destinal "openness and truth." (3) The event of appropriation in no way suggests a reference to *Dasein* nor any bestowal upon it: I have shown that under the title of the 'fourfold' the role of human *Dasein,* then called 'the mortals', is reduced to one of the four functions gathered together by the event. (4) As an economic notion, event a fortiori no longer concerns "authentic *Dasein.*" One must add, however, that in 1959 Pöggeler may not have been acquainted with the lectures "The Turning" (delivered in 1949, published 1962) and "Time and Being" (delivered 1962, published 1969), although he had consulted the "*Beiträge zur Philosophie*" and "*Das Ereignis,*" both still unpublished in 1986.

72. SD 35 and 56 f./OTB 32 and 53.

73. "*Einkehr in den Aufenthalt im Ereignis*" (SD 57/OTB 53).

74. In the lecture courses on Nietzsche (N i–N iv) given during the war, the event of appropriation is described only retrospectively, as what accounts for the epochs in the history of metaphysics (cf. the lines quoted below in the epigraph to ch. 14). There is no hint yet of a possible 'entry into the event'.

75. SD 44/OTB 41.

76. Ibid.

77. SD 46 f./OTB 43.

78. SD 46/OTB 43.

79. N I 28/N i 20 (emphasis added).

80. SD 46/OTB 43 (cf. VA 71/EPh 85).

§37. Epoch/Clearing

81. TK 42/OTB 43.
82. SvG 97 and 99.
83. Her 189 / H 117.
84. SD 63/OTB 57 (emphasis added).
85. SD 72 f./OTB 66 (emphasis added).
86. SD 73/OTB 66.
87. Ibid., cf. SZ 133/BT 171.
88. Hw 42/PLT 54.
89. In this same passage from PLT, the exclusion or the concealment, *Verbergung*, is opposed to *Lichtung* in two ways, which one could call ontological and ontic: as denial, *Versagen*, and as dissimulation, *Verstellen*. The denial indicates the 'absencing' in 'presenc-ing', the concealment from which everything present "stands out": "the inception of the clearing of what is lighted" (Hw 42/PLT 53 f.). Denial is co-constitutive of the tenuous movement, difficult to grasp, by which entities show themselves, come out of hiddenness. "Dissimulation" designates simply the cover-up of one entity by others, their superimposition or overlaying.
90. SD 44/OTB 41.
91. SD 75/OTB 68 (emphasis added).
92. This shows once more how unwarranted, at least in regard to the anticipatory incidence of these transitional categories, Derrida's attempt is to enclose Heidegger's understanding of clearing as event in the "epoch of the *logos*," in logocentrism and presence as total givenness (cf. Jacques Derrida, *Of Grammatology*, trans. G. C. Spivak, Baltimore, 1976, pp. 10–12 and 143).
93. Heidegger calls the clearing the fourth dimension of time. "Time is properly four-dimensional" (SD 16/OTB 15). To the three ecstases, or to the three dimensions of *epechein*, is added "a fourth: time as the forename of the region in which the truth of being projects itself. 'Time' is the ecstatic in-between (time-space), not the wherein of entities, but the clearing of being itself"; SAF 229; cf. Henri Birault, *Heidegger et l'expérience de la pensée* (Paris, 1978), pp. 34, 419, 485, 490, 536.
94. TK 40/QCT 41.
95. SD 80/OTB 73.

§38. Nearness/Fourfold

96. At the end of the essay "The Thing," Heidegger describes the "world-play" in terms of appropriation–expropriation, of nearness and farness, and of the fourfold (VA 178–181/PLT 179–182). The word pair 'near-far' is therefore not exclusively recapitulatory as the first inci-dences of the preceding transitional categories are (see below, n. 108). In BT, the pair "near-far" remained confined to the analytic of being-there. It was not a trait of being itself. *"The entity we are, in each case, ourselves is ontologically what is farthest*. The reason for this lies in care itself. What guides *Dasein*'s everyday interpretation and covers up ontically its proper being is our being alongside the nearest matters for concern in the 'world' " (SZ 311/BT 359; cf. SZ 15 f./BT 36 f.). Nearness functions here as an "essential tendency" in being-there: "*Dasein* is essentialy de-severant: as the entity it is, it lets entities be encountered near to it." De-severance, *Ent-fernung*, "in its active and transitive signification," unites the near and the far (SZ 105/BT 139). The word pair 'near-far', then, reveals the spatiality of being-in-the-world (it becomes operative again in the analysis of conscience, SZ 271/BT 316), but in BT it does not address the ontological difference. Later, "de-severance" signifies the step back that allows one to think of what is otherwise "too near" (SD 32/OTB 30).
97. Derrida writes that the topic of 'nearness', in Heidegger, "can only metaphorize the language it deconstructs" (*Margins of Philosophy*, p. 131), that is, the language of full presence. To enforce his claim he lumps together precisely the two terms this transitional category is meant to set apart, nearness and fourfold: "The presence of the fourfold is thought . . . accord-ing to the opening of propriation as the nearness of the near, as proximation, approximation" (ibid., p. 132 n.; cf. p. 64 n.). These lines, due to the role of 'presence' in them, miss even those texts in PLT (see preceding note) in which 'nearness' and 'fourfold' appear indeed side by side. To turn both into instances of full presence amounts to confusing Heidegger's deconstruction of the past with his preparation of a possible thinking to come, beyond deconstruction.

98. Höl 27 and 53.

99. SvG 16. Under the regime of *epochal* economies, what is closest to us are the principles. Thus the principle of reason, which stamps the epoch of modernity, is most remote for our grasp precisely because it clinches us so tightly (SvG 144 and 160).

100. In the writings subsequent to BT, *'Entfernung'* and the word pair 'near-far' mainly serve to spell out how "everywhere and at all times, we find in the issue of thinking what is called 'difference' " (IuD 61/IaD 63). The difference is near since it modulates the epochs; it is far since, as ontological, it has been forgotten and, as the difference between world and earth, goes unnoticed (Hw 61/PLT 74). The neglect of "what is nearest" amounts to "killing the being of entities" (Hw 246/QCT 111). Elsewhere, "what is nearest" designates "the truth of being" (Wm 163/BWr 212) or simply "being" (Wm 150/BWr 199; cf. Wm 334/Phy 241 and GA 55 61).

101. See the remarks on the word *Geviert* above, sec. 19, n. 158.

102. Inasmuch as it recapitulates the history of metaphysics, the category of 'nearness' points to the closure: "When the danger is" in technology, "the dawn of what has been thought" by the Greeks enters "the nearness of what is yet to be thought" (Hw 343/EGT 58). In two ways, following the bi-focal status of all transitional categories, the Greek experiences—for example, the experience couched in the word *chreōn*—come near to us in the technological age: *chreōn* determines "a history now racing toward its end," but within the *chreōn* there also lies hidden "an historic nearness of what has remained unsaid in it and what speaks out into that which is yet to come" (Hw 300/EGT 16). What *chreōn* thus already addresses across the closure *begins* with technology. To understand this anticipatory incidence, that is, to understand the 'fourfold', one can therefore no longer be content with a mere return to Presocratic categories—nor, a fortiori, with a return to the three topics of *metaphysica specialis*, God, man, the world, as suggested by William Richardson (*Heidegger: Through Phenomenology to Thought* [The Hague, 1963], p. 572). Richardson seems, however, to have been the only commentator who has seen the kinship between the fourfold and the *hen*.

103. VA 179/PLT 180 f.

104. Ibid.

105. Playful exchange, to distinguish it from that collusion, could be called 'allusion': *adludere*, to play in the direction of. . . . World and thing play *toward* each other.

106. This plurification of referential points is yet another way of describing extreme finitude. Such finitude is not a late discovery of Heidegger's. However, before the *Kehre*, it was thought of as man's finitude and later, as that of history. As Walter Schulz has shown ("Über den philosophiegeschichtlichen Ort Martin Heideggers," *Philosophische Rundschau* I [1953–54]:65–93 and 211–232; anthologized in Otto Pöggeler, ed., *Heidegger* [Cologne, 1969], pp. 95–139), BT radicalizes the nineteenth-century concept of finitude and thereby both completes and terminates the philosophy of subjectivity. Hegel had already 'de-substantialized' the human subject; but his 'subject' as dialectical *Vollzug* became unsublatably finite only with Schelling and Kierkegaard. Yet in these thinkers, the finite process that man is still occurred against an infinite, non-human process. *Geworfenheit* becomes radical only with BT. Here, no absolute becoming is possible any longer that would function as the backdrop against which man projects himself; no infinite subject that 'throws' him into the finite. Thrownness and projection are simple structural elements of being-there. The later writings give finitude the ultimate turn: as projection and being-toward-death are abandoned for another site— economic presencing—no totalization (*Ganzseinkönnen*, BT sec. 62, 65, 75) is constructable any longer. Finitude becomes radical as it is displaced from the world of man to that of history, to that of the thing.

107. See above, n. 26.

108. In the essays "The Thing" (VA 163–185/PLT 163–186), "The Turning" (TK 37–47/QCT 36–49), and "Building Dwelling Thinking" (VA 145–162/PLT 143–161), the essential way to be (*wesen*) of the thing and of the world is called nearing or approximation, *Näherung*: "Thinging is the nearing of the world" (VA 179 f./PLT 181). But such nearing is perpetually deferred: "pure nearness [is] the farness, *die reine Nähe—d.h. die Ferne*" (GA 55 18). Contrary to Jacques Derrida's claims (see above, n. 97), in Heidegger 'approximation' can never cancel distance. It is therefore the contrary of a passage toward full presence.

109. James M. Demske has shown—it seems, the first—how the 'fourfold' is related to the Greek categories of *phusis, polemos* and *logos* (*Being, Man and Death* [Lexington,

1970], pp. 152–55). The discovery of this filiation allows him to criticize Walter Schulz (*Der Gott der neuzeitlichen Metaphysik* [Pfullingen, 1957], p. 56) on one of his most glaring onto-theologisms, according to which the 'fourfold' would designate "four beings of an exceptional sort" (James Demske, *Sein, Mensch, und Tod* [Munich, 1963], p. 156; omitted in the English translation).

110. Höl 99 f. (emphasis added).

111. IuD 69/IaD 71.

112. Höl 19.

113. Demske (op. cit., p. 166) quotes the following two texts: "In death, there gathers the supreme *concealment* of being" (US 23/PLT 200, ital. added); "as the extreme potential of being-there [death] has the highest power of *clearing* being and its truth" (SvG 186 f., italics added). According to these passages, the mortals are called that way because, for them alone among all entities, concealment is joined to unconcealment, darkness to clearing.

114. Hearing what is present "is in a certain way the same as the *logos*" (VA 215 and 217/EGT 66 f.). In that essay, "Logos," the link between the 'mortals' and the prospective category corresponding to the fourfold, *hen,* is described as measurement: "Well-disposed to destiny are the mortals . . . when they measure the *logos* as *hen panta* and when they measure themselves to its measurement" (VA 226/EGT 75).

115. See above, sec. 34, n. 43.

§39. Corresponding/Thinking

116. All quotes taken from SvG 144 f.

117. See above, sec. 27, nn. 83 and 85.

118. The perspective of deconstruction thus sheds a new light upon Heidegger's linguistic approaches to the ontological difference: when he says (or has a Japanese say) that "man is essentially man insofar as he corresponds (*entspricht*) to the address of the twofold (*Zuspruch der Zwiefalt*)" (US 122/OWL 30), one can see there an indication that language, too, is epochal. The ontological difference, the twofold, is what articulates history. Such articulation institutes a language net which, each time, has its era (cf. SD 55/OTB 51).

119. About the connection between 'thinking' and 'thanking', see above, sec. 10, n. 64.

120. In BT, due to the preeminence of 'understanding', thinking appears as a derivative: " 'intuition' and 'thinking' are both already remote derivatives of understanding" (SZ 147/BT 187). Winfried Franzen, *Von der Existenzialontologie zur Seinsgeschichte* (Meisenheim: 1975), p. 216, rightfully observes that in BT the word "thinking" is "deliberately avoided." It is with IM and even more in the Hölderlin interpretations (called by Pöggeler "the other beginning" in Heidegger's path of thought, *Der Denkweg . . .,* op. cit., pp. 215 ff.) that a new acceptation of 'thinking' emerges, which locates thinking in the vicinity of poetry. That new notion of *Denken* is explicitly recapitulatory ("*Andenken*") and anticipatory ("*Vordenken*"): "Now there must first be thinkers if the poet's word is to become receivable. . . . In remembrance (*Andenken*) the first kinship with the homecoming poet begins, a kinship which for a long time is to remain precursory" (Höl 29). *Andenken* is anticipatory *because* it amounts to retrieving "what since long ago has not ceased to render itself present." The "other beginning," Hölderlin's, thus repeats the first, the pre-classical Greek beginning. " 'To think of' what is to come can only be 'to think of' what has been" (Höl 80). The double beginning marked by "this ambiguous *Andenken*" (ibid.) constitutes "thinking's homecoming," the return to the originary. The anticipatory incidence of this category—thinking of (*denken an*) what is to come, yielding to it—is thus one case of its *original* incidence, viz. "thinking of the originary," *Denken an den Ursprung* (Höl 124). This structure of *Denken* remains unchanged throughout Heidegger's last works, even though the theme of "thinking's neighborhood with poetry" (US 173/OWL 69) is soon abandoned. The issue of thought is the originary origin, but this issue can only be worked out through a return to the Greek original origin: like Plotinian *mnēmē* and Augustinian *memoria,* Heideggerian *Andenken* links the return to what has been to the return to what always is. However, to say 'thinking' instead of *Dasein* amounts to dismissing all reference, even remote, to subjectivity, to existence, to me who is thinking. After BT—from IM to OTB—the three guiding traits of 'thinking' remain the same: the originary as its issue, the original as the access to that issue, and anti-humanism as the condition for compliance with the economies (EiM 88–149/IM 115–196 and SD 61/OTB 55). Correctly understood, the title "The End of Philosophy and the Task of Thinking" sums up these three traits (cf. VA 83/EPh 96).

121. *"Eigentlich"* (WhD 4/WCT 7), *"echt und ursprünglich"* (EiM 93/IM 122), *"wesentlich"* (Wm 105/EB 357).

122. Wm 103 and 106/EB 156 and 159.

123. Wm 105/EB 358.

124. Wm 106/EB 359 f. Understood in terms of the economies, that is, as 'thanking', thinking's "proper attitude" is less the putting of questions than letting and listening (US 175/OWL 71). It is "to free itself and keep free for what is to be thought so as to receive its determination from that" (SD 38/OTB 35).

125. "Most thought-worthy in our disturbing times is that we are still not thinking" (WhD 3/WCT 6). "Not one of us would arrogate to himself [the capacity] of performing, be it remotely, such a thinking, nor even a prelude to it. At the very most, what may succeed is the preparation of such a prelude" (WhD 159/WCT 146).

126. SD 66/OTB 59.

127. SD 66/OTB 59 f.

128. Gel 15/DTh 46.

129. Gel 25/DTh 54.

130. Hw 195/QCT 57. "Science does not think" (WhD 4/WCT 8 and VA 113/BWr 349).

131. VA 187/PLT 211.

132. "The thinking to come will no longer be philosophy. . . . Thinking is on the descent into the poverty of its provisional essence. Thinking gathers language into its simple saying. Language is the language of being, as clouds are the clouds of the sky" (Wm 194/BWr 242). This simple thinking, described here in anticipatory terms, is not Heidegger's.

133. "Everything an essential thought truly thinks of remains multivocal, and this for essential reasons" (WhD 68/WCT 71).

134. Vw XXIII/PrR XXII.

Part Five: Action and Anarchy

1. Wm 191/BWr 239.

2. In Heidegger, 'method' (*meta ton hodon*) should be understood literally as the pursuit of a path. This has a threefold meaning in his work: first, the "path of thinking" is the one traversed by Heidegger himself from his university theses on psychologism and Duns Scotus through OTB (see SD 81/OTB 74; US 99 and 121/OWL 12 and 29). Next, this path designates "the course of the history of being" from the Presocratics through Heidegger himself (e.g., Hw 252/PLT 96). Lastly, it designates the originary arrival in presence, or presencing (US 197/OWL 91), that is, the avenue opened up among phenomena as being "claims" thinking (VA 242/EGT 89). The place Heidegger assigns to his own experience of thinking is fully understood only when these three 'methods' are comprehended as one (see EdD 19/PLT 10). More specifically, it will become clear that the 'method' consists in a certain *way* of saying: one thinks as one lives. This concrete *hodos* designates the birth of thinking from praxis. Since originary praxis is as anti-principial as presencing, it should not be necessary to warn anyone against construing its 'methodic' priority as some kind of Marxist resurgence in Heidegger.

3. It is therefore perplexing when Derrida, trying to establish a complicity between Heidegger and the metaphysics of presence, claims he can detect that complicity in, of all categories, 'nearness'—one of the economic traits precisely *put out of function* by the closure and its transgression. *"Beyond the joint closure* of humanism and metaphysics, Heidegger's thought remains guided by the motif of Being as presence and by the motif of the nearness of Being to the essence of man," *Margins of Philosophy*, trans. Alan Bass (Chicago, 1982), pp. 127 f. (trans. modified and italics added). Cf. idem, *Writing and Difference*, trans. Alan Bass (Chicago, 1978), p. 280.

4. "What 'being' means is something we cannot arbitrarily figure out by ourselves nor establish by decree. What 'being' means remains hidden in the injunction that speaks through the guiding words of Greek thinking. We can never prove scientifically, nor attempt to prove, what it is that this injunction says. We can hear it or not. We can prepare such hearing or leave that preparation unheeded" (SvG 121). For the topology, to hear or to listen is to receive a double echo: one from the Greeks before Socrates and the other from contemporary technology (VS 132). Already in BT, listening was that modality of understanding through which being-there received its possibilities. In listening, *Dasein* understands what it can be.

This link between listening and potential grows stronger from one text to the next in Heidegger. The setting-free of epochal possibilities is the act of a discriminatory listening: to hearken to a transmitted discourse and hear what rings through it. Each era of civilization announces itself as the disclosure of a potential that is first heralded, then occurs, and, after having made us its echo for a time, closes on itself again. The temporarily unfolded order is refolded. Henceforth, it will be present only to memory—present as absent. It is in this way that a sound lingers, and in lingering, induces the attention through which the ear retains it while letting it fade away. On this preeminence of listening, see in Hans Jonas, *The Phenomenon of Life* (New York, 1966), the chapter entitled "The Nobility of Sight," especially pp. 137 f. In Heidegger, listening is "the initial movement of thinking," even more primary than questioning (cf. Henri Birault, *Heidegger et l'expérience de la pensée* [Paris, 1978], pp. 396–98).

XIII. Acting, the Condition for Thinking

1. Wm 191/BWr 238.
2. Sermon "Beati pauperes spiritu," Meister Eckhart, *Die deutschen Werke*, vol. II (Stuttgart, 1971), pp. 487 and 506. Translation in my *Meister Eckhart: Mystic and Philosopher* (Bloomington, 1978), pp. 214 and 219 f.
3. Sermon "Praedica verbum," Meister Eckhart, *Die deutschen Werke*, vol. II, pp. 108 f.; trans. *Meister Eckhart, Mystic and Philosopher*, p. 185.

§40. The Practical A Priori

4. IuD 24/IaD 33.
5. IuD 24/IaD 32 f.
6. Wm 18/BWr 111 f. As Friedrich-Wilhelm von Herrmann points out in *Die Selbstinterpretation Martin Heideggers* (Meisenheim am Glan, 1964), the term "metaphysics" is to be understood literally here: "Because in concern (*Besorgen*) and solicitude (Fürsorge) man goes beyond (*meta*) entities (*phusika*), he is, as being-there, always implicitly already a metaphysician" (pp. 242 f.).
7. SZ 1/BT 19, cf. above, sec. 18, n. 78.
8. SZ 43/BT 68.
9. Cf. SZ 129/BT 167.
10. Wm 163/BWr 212.
11. That is Carl Friedrich Gethmann's position in *Verstehen und Auslegung* (Bonn, 1974). "Authenticity and inauthenticity primarily have the function of methodological stages" (p. 266). From that perspective, inauthenticity, just like the natural attitude in Husserl, is the initial stage of reflection. Only the second stage, authenticity, enables the phenomenologist to raise the question of being as the question of time, since for ecstatic temporality to become phenomenal "the everyday objectivistic self-understanding needs to be cancelled" (p. 387).
12. SZ 43/BT 68.
13. Nietzsche, *The Will to Power*, sec. 529, trans. p. 285.
14. It is difficult, therefore, to agree with Hans-Georg Gadamer that, for Heidegger, "to speak of the *Kehre* was to eradicate all existentiell meaning from the discourse on the authenticity of being-there and hence to eradicate the very concept of authenticity" (in Otto Pöggeler, ed., *Heidegger* [Cologne, 1969], p. 175). If with *Being and Time* one calls 'existentiell' the modifications *Dasein* is capable of undergoing, then *Gelassenheit* is at least analogous to the 'authentic' mode of existing.
15. Wm 163/BWr 212.
16. Gel 24 f./DTh 54. This simultaneous Yes and No to technological devices recalls Meister Eckhart's praise of Martha whom Luke depicts as busying herself with domestic activities (Lk 10:40): "You are *among* things, but they are not *in* you" (*Die deutschen Werke*, op. cit., vol. III, p. 485, 1. 2 f.).
17. Gel 25/DTh 54.
18. See the epigraph to sec. 40, above.
19. IuD 72/IaD 73.
20. "We are raising the question of technology, and in so doing we wish to prepare a free relationship to it. This relationship will be free if it opens up our being-there (*Dasein*) to the essence of technology. If we correspond (*entsprechen*) to that essence, we will be capable of experiencing the technological within its limitation" (VA 13/QCT 3 f.).

21. In a context less alien to this than it might seem, Heidegger states, for example, that in order to understand and translate Parmenides, we must first transfer ourselves, set over, to his language (WhD 137/WCT 226).

22. SvG 164. This attention to the destinal way of speaking is more than a "favorable nuance" that makes it easier to "correspond to the being of entities" (Reinhart Maurer, *Revolution und 'Kehre'* [Frankfurt, 1975], p. 212). The fact is that, according to Heidegger, we do not yet speak our destinal tongue. This would have to be a kind of double talk, still regulated by metaphysical syntax, but subverting it from within. Some twentieth-century poetry or fiction may have begun speaking that way.

23. WhD 142/WCT 235 (emphasis added).

24. Hw 62/PLT 75.

25. US 267/OWL 135 f.

26. See above, sec. 34.

27. Henri Birault, *Heidegger et l'expérience de la pensée* (Paris, 1978), p. 41. The reasons Birault provides for this *désuétude* have nothing to do, however, with a reflection on the public realm. Since Birault seeks in Heidegger "thought experiences," terms such as existence and authenticity are for him, on the contrary, not inner-directed, spiritualistic, enough.

28. SZ 312/BT 360. This is more than an "appeal to the reader that he reproduce in himself what he reads," Fridolin Wiplinger, *Wahrheit und Geschichtlichkeit. Eine Untersuchung über die Frage nach dem Wesen der Wahrheit im Denken Martin Heideggers* (Freiburg, 1961), p. 292. See, on authentic temporality in the same sense, ibid. (pp. 266–271). If Heidegger had simply proceeded according to a quasi-homiletic model of exhortation, one could *understand* first (ecstatic temporality, ontological releasement, anarchic economy) then *act* (anticipatory resolution, practical releasement, abolition of principles). Inasmuch as in this model action is to conform to an ideal type, it is essentially a moral model. But if, on the contrary, the existentiell is the ground (*Boden*) of the existential, no understanding will be possible as long as one does not act. The "existentiell understanding" of BT is practical, like our understanding of a tool, which comes to us from handling it.

29. "We must deliver ourselves properly to the injunction that enjoins us to think in the manner of *logos*. As long as we do not set out by ourselves, that is, as long as we do not open ourselves to the injunction and, with that question, get underway to the injunction—just that long shall we remain blind to the destiny that unfolds our essence" (WhD 103/WCT 165).

30. Hw 89/QCT 138.

31. Hw 54/PLT 66.

32. SvG 188.

33. SvG 73 f., cf. above, sec. 1, n. 12.

34. N I 437.

35. Herbert Marcuse, "Beiträge zu einer Phänomenologie des historischen Materialismus" (1928), reprinted in H. Marcuse and A. Schmidt, *Existentialistische Marx-Interpretation* (Frankfurt, 1973), p. 60.

36. See above, sec. 5, n. 4.

37. SZ 39/BT 63; Hw 301 f./EGT 18; SD 44/OTB 41.

§41. The Problem of the Will

38. WM 145/BWr 193 (emphasis added).

39. "Being-there *can* comport itself unwillingly toward its possibilities; it *can* be inauthentic; and factically it is that way, proximally and for the most part" (SZ 193/BT 237).

40. 'Decisionism' is opposed to 'normativism' in legal and moral philosophy. In this sense, although the concept dates from the twentieth century, Thomas Hobbes's principle "Autoritas, non veritas, facit legem," is the most succinct formulation of that doctrine. Karl Löwith, here again the champion of the 'existentialist' reading of Heidegger, labelled the content of BT a "philosophy of resolute existence," which satisfied all criteria of "decisionism." As Löwith uses the term, decisionism is the doctrine that "destroys" the transmitted normative systems in order to exalt "the pathos of decision in the name of pure resolution" (*Gesammelte Abhandlungen*, Stuttgart: 1960, pp. 93 f.).

41. Rc 97/PLT 84.

42. Hw 55/PLT 67. In other words, he is saying that *thesis*—*setzen* or *feststellen*, positing or establishing—is to be understood as "letting [something] lie forth in its radiance and presencing," not in its fixity as a fact (Rc 96/PLT 83; cf. Wm 159/BWr 207 and Gel 61/DTh 81).

43. Jarava L. Mehta, *Martin Heidegger: The Way and the Vision* (Honolulu, 1976), p. 337; cf. ibid., pp. 33, 74 and 352. Hannah Arendt, in her chapter "Heidegger's Will-not-to-will," *The Life of the Mind*, vol. II (New York, 1978), pp. 172–194, relies largely on Mehta, especially when she describes "letting-be" as an "alternative" opposed to the "destructiveness" of the will. She adds: "it is against that destructiveness that Heidegger's original reversal pits itself" (p. 178). One of her very premises in the two volumes, entitled respectively *Thinking* and *Willing*, is precisely that thinking and willing are "opposites" (ibid., p. 179).

On decisionism, in addition to Karl Löwith, see Ernst Tugenthat, *Der Wahrheitsbegriff bei Husserl und Heidegger* (Berlin, 1967), pp. 361 and 380, as well as Christian Graf von Krockow, *Die Entscheidung: Eine Untersuchung über Ernst Jünger, Carl Schmitt, Martin Heidegger* (Stuttgart, 1958), pp. 68–81 and 116–28. Herbert Marcuse takes up this common opinion about Heideggerian decisionism: in Heidegger, "the social-empirical context of the decision and of its consequences is 'bracketed'. The main thing is to decide and to act according to your decision. Whether or not the decision is in itself, in its goal, morally and humanly positive, is of minor importance," "Heidegger's Politics: An Interview," in *Graduate Faculty Philosophy Journal*, VI, 1 (1977), p. 35. See, in the same sense, Karsten Harries's article cited above, sec. 2, n. 22.

In the same spirit, Wiplinger (*Wahrheit und Geschichtlichkeit*, p. 270) calls attention to the "proportion" in BT: "The more authentically being-there decides [resolves] itself . . . the more unequivocally and unfortuitously does it choose and find the possibility of its existence" (SZ 384/BT 435). This quotation illustrates Marcuse's position according to which I must at all costs reach 'my' decision and then, without equivocation but necessarily, I will find my ownmost possibility of existence.

All these interpretations of resoluteness or resolve, of deciding and willing, are antithetical to the reading given by Birault: "Letting-be is what *Being and Time* called *die Entschlossenheit* and what the more recent writings call *Gelassenheit*. . . . The 'resolute decision' of *Sein und Zeit* does not have the 'heroic' meaning that was thought to be attributable to it, nor does *Gelassenheit* have the 'quietist' meaning that some wish to confer on it. . . . *Entschlossenheit* must not be thought of in terms of the traditional forms of willing; on the contrary, one must think of those forms themselves in terms of *Entschlossenheit* so as to elaborate a *non-voluntarist theory of the will*" (op. cit., pp. 519 f.). Even Gabriel Marcel, in a text otherwise crammed with untenable epithets (the most massive concerning the "substantivization of being" in Heidegger), writes: "Human decision can intervene only on a level where . . . the decisive initiatives do not issue from man," "Ma relation avec Heidegger," in *Présence de Gabriel Marcel* I (Paris, 1979), p. 31.

44. N II 293.

45. Hw 37/PLT 48.

46. Hw 43 f./PLT 55.

47. In the essay on "The Origin of the Work of Art," from which all these passages are taken, Heidegger can therefore ask: "Is it art still, or is it no longer, an essential and necessary way in which that truth happens which is decisive for our historical being-there?" (Hw 67/PLT 80). Perhaps art no longer functions as a decisive variable or 'track' for our existence. Religion, too, after having served as the conveyer of the essential injunctions throughout the ages, now has forfeited that role: ours "is the state of indecision toward God and the gods" (Hw 70/QCT 117). Indeed, "whether the god lives or remains dead is not *decided* by the religiosity of men. . . . Whether or not God is God comes to pass from the constellation of being and within that constellation" (TK 46/QCT 49, emphasis added).

48. N I 168 f./N i 143 f.

49. FD 38/WTh 50.

50. Constructive thinking must "constantly *de-cide* the sizes and heights [of its edifices] and consequently *ex-cise* [previous measures]. . . . Construction goes through decisions" (N I 641).

51. From that thought "spring the possibilities of decision and separation [*Entscheidung und Scheidung*] in regard to the being-there of man in general" (N I 393).

52. VS 132 (emphasis added).

53. Hannah Arendt, "Home to Roost," *New York Review of Books* (June 26, 1975), p. 5 (emphasis added).

54. Hw 65/PLT 78.

55. N I 415.

56. Gel 32/DTh 59.

57. Hw 328/EGT 43. With regard to the "fourfold," Heidegger states that, on the contrary, "none of the four strives to persist" (VA 178/PLT 179). Cf. Arendt, *Life of the Mind*, vol. II, pp. 193 f.

58. Arendt, *Life of the Mind*, vol. I, p. 213.

59. One may presume that this interpretation of *adikia* in Heidegger depends directly on his view of contemporary technology. It is indeed technological man who "struts (*aufspreizen*) in the posture of lord of the earth" (VA 34/QCT 27).

60. N I 633 f.

61. N II 98/N iv 59.

62. Hw 33/PLT 44 f.

63. Gel 66/DTh 85.

64. Gel 59/DTh 79.

65. Gel 60/DTh 80.

XIV. Anarchic Displacements

1. N II 490/EPh 83. In the first sentence of this quote, I am following the amendment ("epoch" for "time") which, according to the translator's note, Heidegger made to the text in a later conference.

2. Heidegger calls *"Temporalität"* "the determination of the sense of being by time," while he calls *"Zeitlichkeit"* "the constitution of *Dasein's* being" (GA 24 22/BPP 16 f.; cf. SZ 39/BT 63f.).

3. Wm 156/BWr 208.

4. Werner Marx (*Gibt es auf Erden ein Mass?*, Hamburg, 1983), takes that line from Hölderlin's poem "In lieblicher Bläue . . ." to head an inquiry into what he calls "a non-metaphysical ethics." It is worked out in constant debate with Heidegger, from whom he gathers various hints at a nonmetaphysical measure for action. Those hints are love, compassion, and respect as they may arise from the concrete experience of our mortality; the "clearing" freed from all traces of "errancy" (see above, sec. 24, n. 36); death as the mediator between being and nothingness; the relation between death and language; *"Ereignis"* as the measure for the history of being; *"Brauch"* (*chreōn*) as the measure for poetry. Marx criticizes Heidegger for not having shown any path for retrieving standards capable of guiding us in our actions. He concludes: "Against [that omission in Heidegger] we have shown in every essay in this collection that and how each of us, as he lets himself be transformed by the experience of his own mortality, is capable of gaining the measure of *brotherly love* as the measure for responsible action" (p. 153, emphasis added). Fortunately Marx makes it clear that this reconstruction of an ethics of brotherly love is his "own project" (p. xxi), not Heidegger's.

5. Especially in the preface to the second edition of his *Critique of Pure Reason*, Kant emphasizes the experimental character of that work (B XI, XVI, XVIII, XX, XXII, XXXVI, XXXVIII): the "Copernican Revolution" is a *Versuch*, an attempt, a trial.

6. *Human, All Too Human*, Preface, #4; *Thus Spoke Zarathustra*, Part III, "On the Vision and the Riddle"; *Beyond Good and Evil*, Part II, "The Free Spirit," # 42.

§42. Practical Negation of Goals

7. Hw 3/EGT 3f.

8. See above, sec. 11, n. 21.

9. According to the *Metaphysics*, A, 2; 982 b 2–7, this architectonic science of principles and causes is that of wisdom. According to the *Nicomachean Ethics*, I, 1; 1094 a 27, it is that of politics.

10. "Quaelibet autem res ad ultimum finem per suam operationem pertingit," Thomas Aquinas, *Summa Theologiae*, Part I, q. 62, art. 4. Aquinas even holds that wherever one thing causes another, the end "moves" the three other causes. The final cause is first in the causative process if not in the effect produced (ibid., q. 5, art. 4). Cf. Hannah Arendt, *The Life of the Mind* (New York, 1977), vol. II, p. 123.

11. Hannah Arendt, "Martin Heidegger at Eighty," *New York Review of Books* (Oct. 21, 1971), pp. 51 f. Cf. Arendt, *Life of the Mind*, vol. I, p. 197. Arendt's notion of thinking, opposed as it is to the *vita activa*, is however not Heideggerian, since for Heidegger thinking

comprises acting. To show the true bearing of goallessness according to Hw, she has therefore to add the reference to "life itself."

12. Wm 330/Phy 238; cf. GA 55 56 and 73.
13. Wm 352 f./Phy 255; cf. N II 404 f./ EPh 5.
14. Wm 342/Phy 247.
15. SZ 25 f./BT 48.
16. E.g., Hw 122/HCE 34.
17. EdD 15/PLT 8. In Kantian terms, the bad danger would be to conceive of thinking as synthetic, as the act of joining a predicate and a subject. The evil danger would be to conceive of it as analytic, as the act of extracting a predicate from a subject. The wholesome danger, lastly, would be to 'conceive' thinking not according to the form of judgment at all—or, for lack of that possibility, to conceive of it as a judgment whose predicate exactly repeats the subject. "I call the thinking that is demanded here tautological. That is the originary meaning of phenomenology" (VS 137). The task of phenomenology is "the explicit repetition of the question of being" (SZ 2/BT 21). It is safe to assume that in 1927, Heidegger did not yet mean that statement about repetition to be taken so literally. As tautological, repetition permits phenomenology to say hardly more than *"das Wesen west,"* "essence essentializes" (VA 38 f. and TK 42/QCT 30 f. and 43 f.). See also the other tautologies, equally untranslatable, such as *"das Ding dingt,"* "the thing things," *"die Welt weltet,"* "the world worlds" (ibid. and VA 179 f./PLT 181 f.).
18. VA 267/EGT 111.
19. VS 137.
20. To speak with Reinhart Maurer of an "ethic immanent to [Heidegger's] thought of being as a First Philosophy" (*Revolution and 'Kehre'*, Frankfurt, 1975, p. 41) would be to miss these displacements entirely. At least that author is consistent when he accuses Heidegger of "not having adequately grasped the role of teleology as the common ground for ancient theoretical and practical philosophy" (ibid., p. 218). The task is rather to grasp adequately how Heidegger undermines teleology or teleocracy as that ancient common ground.
21. Care is "being-ahead-of-oneself—in-being-already-in. . . as being-alongside . . ." (SZ 196/BT 241).
22. "By projecting its being upon that-for-the-sake-of-which (*auf das Worumwillen*) together with significance (world), being-there discloses being in general" (SZ 147/BT 187). The intrinsic *Worumwillen* renders all extrinsic purpose possible, but as a structure, "it always concerns the being of being-there, for which that being is at stake essentially" (SZ 84/BT 116 f.).
23. SvG 73.
24. Heidegger quotes this verse from Angelus Silesius (SvG 69):

Die Ros' ist ohn' warum: sie blühet, weil sie blühet,
Sie acht' nicht ihrer selbst, fragt nicht, ob man sie siehet.
The rose is without why, it flowers because it flowers,
Has no care for itself, desires not to be seen.

25. Nietzsche, *Werke in drei Bänden*, ed. Karl Schlechta (Munich, 1954), vol. III, p. 530 (WtP # 25; *The Will to Power*, trans. Walter Kaufmann [New York, 1968], p. 18; quoted in N II 283). On the absence of goal, *Ziellosigkeit*, in Nietzsche, see *Human, All Too Human*, Bk. I, ## 33 and 638; *Werke*, vol. I, pp. 472 and 730.
26. N II 283.
27. Pierre Klossowski, "Circulus vitiosus," in *Nietzsche aujourd'hui?* 2 vols. (Paris, 1973), vol. I, p. 101.
28. Meister Eckhart, *Die deutschen Werke*, vol. I (Stuttgart, 1958), p. 92, l. 3–6; trans. Matthew Fox, *Breakthrough: Meister Eckhart's Creation Spirituality in New Translation* (New York, 1980), p. 201 (trans. modified).

§43. Transmutation of Responsibility

29. IuD 61/IaD 63 f.; cf. GA 55 82.
30. For all these and many related questions concerning the concept of responsibility, see the veritable Summa by Hans Jonas, *The Imperative of Responsibility: In Search of an Ethics for the Technological Age*, trans. D. Herr (Chicago, 1984). Jonas's starting point is the observation that the premises of traditional ethics—(1) the immutability of human nature, (2)

evidence concerning the nature of what is the good for man, and (3) the conviction that the ethical realm is that of our proximate, as opposed to our distant, fellow men—have been invalidated (pp. 1 f. and 117–30) by technology, which (1) renders us capable of shaping man genetically, (2) plunges us into a certain state of ignorance about good and evil, and (3) bears its effects over a very long term and on a global scale.

Here, then, is an impact of the technological 'turn' on philosophical discourse such that this discourse finds itself more impoverished than by any previous reversal in history. What has compelled Jonas to reassess the foundations of ethics is his findings concerning the potentials of contemporary biology in general and the possibilities of artificial mutations in particular. He very appropriately observes that these concrete possibilities deprive, in effect, practical philosophy of the criteria and foci that first philosophy used to provide for it: "The movement of modern knowledge called science has by a necessary complementarity eroded the foundations from which norms could be derived; it has destroyed the very idea of norm as such" (p. 22). Jonas describes the many theoretical consequences entailed by that withering away of fundaments; by what he calls the contemporary "ethical vacuum." First among these consequences is anti-humanism: "The apocalyptic possibilities inherent in modern technology have taught us that anthropocentric exclusiveness could well be a prejudice and that it at least calls for reexamination" (pp. 45 f.). Another consequence: responsibility can no longer be conceived on the calculative model. Technological progress has put the very future of humanity at stake. Ethics can therefore no longer be construed according to "the received view of rights and duties" (p. 38). There can be no reciprocity of obligation, no accountability, binding human beings not yet born and the living. Technology, triumph of calculation that it is, by its success paradoxically eliminates calculation from the ethical domain. As a last consequence, the 'appeal' structure of being suffers a transmutation: "The immanent appeal" (p. 79) has so thoroughly changed its modality that today we find ourselves called upon to prepare "the openness (*Offenheit*) for the injunction (*Anspruch*), always uncanny and humbling, addressing us" (translated from the German original, *Das Prinzip Verantwortung*, Frankfurt 1979, p. 393, not reproduced in the English-language edition).

Whatever these descriptions of technology as the outcome of metaphysics may share with mine, Hans Jonas's argument points in the opposite direction since his aim is to restore the metaphysical bases of practical philosophy rather than to raise the question of action without recourse to such bases. His own "theory of responsibility" rests entirely on an "axiology [as] part of ontology" (p. 79), so much so that in the last analysis this book indeed re-issues the project of the *Summae:* deriving moral duties from a doctrine of being. It even provides a welcome illustration of my thesis that a 'normative ethics' cannot dispense with a first philosophy or metaphysics from which it derives its referents.

31. Cf. SvG 168.
32. SvG 210.
33. Logos "enters the interpretive sphere of the translation word *ratio* (ῥέω, ῥῆσις = speech, *ratio; reor* = to state, to hold, to justify)" (N II 431/EPh 28). To be sure, this is not to say that the meaning of *logos* as "calculation" appears only with that "reversal of metaphysics at its beginning" (ibid.), the translation of the Greek fundamental words into Latin. Prior to that reversal *within* early metaphysics occurs the very birth of metaphysics, the birth of *logizesthai* as 'calculating' (cf., H. Boeder, "Der frühgriechische Wortgebrauch von *Logos* und *Alētheia*," *Archiv für Begriffsgeschichte* IV [1958]:108 f.
34. SvG 169; cf. N II 319.
35. Karl Marx speaks of "Bentham's bookkeeping" (*The German Ideology*, [Moscow, 1976], p. 276).
36. US 210/OWL 102 f. Pöggeler comments appropriately: "Statements about 'Physics and Responsibility' are awkward: what is in question is precisely whether 'having responsibility' has not also been understood already for a long time in a purely technological and tactical sense" ("Hermeneutische und mantische Phänomenologie," in Pöggeler, ed., *Heidegger* [Cologne, 1969], p. 333).
37. SvG 167.
38. WhD 158/WCT 146.
39. Sp 206/ISp 17.
40. US 30/PLT 207.
41. US 24 f. and 30/PLT 202 and 207 f.
42. Ernst Tugenthat (*Der Wahrheitsbegriff bei Husserl und Heidegger* [Berlin, 1967], p.

383) criticizes the later Heidegger for eliminating "any leeway for various pre-given possibilities" for action. "Whereas in *Being and Time* and *The Essence of Ground*, being-there's freedom was thought in such a way that no link was possible to any referent for obligation, [in the later writings] on the contrary, freedom gets lost for the sake of obligation." It is clear—and he says so (ibid.)—that for Tugenthat the concept of freedom in BT is decisionist. It is also obvious that in the transmutation of freedom and truth into economic concepts, Tugenthat sees the elimination of the very possibility of alternatives, of choice. I have tried above to address that difficulty through the concept of a practical a priori. As for Tugenthat, the way he understands the notion of responsibility in Heidegger remains entirely dependent on that of freedom as faculty of choice (see ibid., p. 361, n. 36), which is why he ignores the two terms of the temporal difference—the economic order of presence and the event of presencing—and declares that Heidegger "posits the manifest [present entities] immediately as measure and thereby as binding" (p. 383).

43. See above, sec. 41, nn. 57–59.

44. See above, sec. 41, n. 57.

45. Unless responsibility is understood this way from the viewpoint of the temporal difference and its anticipatory incidence, 'world and thing', one will inevitably fall back from the potential of the metaphysical closure into principial constructs. Witness Reinhart Maurer, who seeks to place Heidegger's concept of responsibility in the context of what he calls "the ethic of awe," "das Ethos der Scheu." In spite of his reference to the Greek αἰδώς, Maurer ends up reducing Heideggerian 'awe' to a latter day version of the Kantian respect for the moral law: "In Heidegger, 'awe' . . . is the name for the readiness to recognize at all something measure-giving for subjectivity to which it can account for itself, but which it has not posited. The lack of such awe . . . is the ethical side of the 'forgottenness of being' " (op. cit., pp. 40 f.). In this way, awe would define our relation to precisely those justificatory referents that Heidegger exerts himself to deconstruct.

§44. Protest against "Busy-ness"

46. Hw 77/QCT 124.

47. "Everything functions. That is what is uncanny, that it functions and that the functioning pushes ceaselessly further toward still more functioning" (Sp 206/ISp 17).

48. All these citations are taken from Hw 30/PLT 40 f. Cf. Hw 56/PLT 69. The modern decontextualization of artworks has been described by Hans-Georg Gadamer (*Truth and Method* [New York, 1975], pp. 39–90).

49. Hw 77 and 69/QCT 124 and 116.

50. Hw 77 f./QCT 124 f.; cf. Hw 90/QCT 138.

51. Sp 214/ISp 22.

52. US 67/OWL 185.

53. "Then happens the farewell to all 'it is'," (US 154/OWL 54). The allusion is to fragment 2 (Diels) from Parmenides and to the first "way of inquiry": "that of 'it is' and 'it cannot not-be'." On the dismissal of the ontological difference see above, sec. 34.

54. Otto Pöggeler, *Philosophie und Politik bei Heidegger* (Freiburg, 1972), claims that Heidegger agrees with the "reform Marxists" on at least four points: "1. The critique of our time as that of great totalitarianisms. . . . 2. The thesis that it is precisely 'reason', as man's rise to mastery over nature, which has set in motion the process in which man himself is no more than object, a process to which Auschwitz belongs as well. 3. The critique of science and technology as an 'ideology'. . . . 4. The characterization of their own thinking as a 'theory'. . . ." These four points would show Heidegger's and the reform Marxists' "common protest against the manipulated world" (pp. 40 f.). I cannot help finding the first two to be truisms, and the last two, rather doubtful.

Karel Kosik, *Dialectics of the Concrete* (Dordrecht, 1976), seeks to establish "a fruitful dialogue between Marxism and existentialism" on the basis of their common denunciation of "manipulation" (p. 87). In the eyes of this Czech author, Heidegger described in BT only "the problems of the modern twentieth-century capitalist world" and not those of "the patriarchal world of backward Germany" (p. 86). "Care" would then designate "the subjectively transposed reality of man as an objective subject," as "manipulator and manipulated," caught "in a ready-made and fixed reality." The philosophy of care in this way would denounce "mystified praxis," that is, "the manipulation of things and people" (pp. 37–42). The price to be paid for this particular version of "dialogue" is obviously that the notion of care—to mention only this—

comes to stand for the opposite of what it means in BT: not the originary being of man, but "a derived and reified form of praxis" (p. 86), alienated praxis.

Lucien Goldmann, *Lukács et Heidegger* (Paris, 1973), has attempted to show that to a great extent, even if Heidegger never mentioned Lukács's name, BT consisted of a reply to the book by the early Lukács, *History and Class Consciousness* (1923). Aside from the extravagance of such a hypothesis, the two works perhaps share the same thrust against reification (*Verdinglichung*, SZ 437/BT 487). The early Heidegger and the early Lukács could be read as protesting against certain consequences of capitalist industrial civilization. To my mind, however, the parallel stops there. Goldmann, on the other hand, suggests an entire series of them: a parallel between the subject-object totality in Lukács and totality as the horizon of the existential project in Heidegger; the parallel between world-immanent meaning according to Lukács and Heideggerian being-in-the-world (pp. 65 f.); between the "category" and the "existential" (p. 68); between reification as well as false consciousness in Lukács and *Vorhandenheit, das Man* and inauthenticity in Heidegger (p. 72), etc. To claim, as Goldmann does, that Heidegger offers an ontological complement to Lukács's more historical and social analyses (p. 76) is to recognize the systematic difference, beyond all resemblances, in their outlooks.

Jean-Michel Palmier, *Les écrits politiques de Heidegger* (Paris, 1968), pp. 213-93, is both more modest and bolder than Pöggeler, Kosik, and Goldmann. He makes no attempt to detect in Heidegger some collusion or complicity with the Marxist critique of capitalism. Heidegger's taking objectification and calculative thinking to task is linked by Palmier to the "figure of the worker" as the locus of the confrontation with technology. This allows Palmier to show—and there lies his boldness—that active protest against the technocratic universe is the necessary corollary to "overcoming metaphysics."

55. MHG 73/IW 37. Contrast this with authors such as Wittgenstein and Simone Weil who do condemn science flatly: The atomic bomb offers "a prospect of the end, the destruction of a dreadful evil—our disgusting soapy water science," Ludwig Wittgenstein, *Culture and Value*, trans. Peter Winch (Chicago, 1980; inexplicably, the translator leaves out the word "disgusting"), p. 49. "In the indifference which science since the Renaissance has shown for the spiritual life, there seems to be something diabolical," Simone Weil, *Intimations of Christianity Among the Ancient Greeks*, trans. Elizabeth Chase Geissbuhler (Boston, 1957), p. 171.

56. The French acronym GRECE (Greece) stands for *Groupement de Recherches et d'Etudes sur la Civilisation Européenne* (Research and Study Group on European Civilization), an influential right-wing organization in France.

57. GA 55 68.

58. See above, sec. 20, n. 18, the citations from Werner Marx.

59. WhD 159/WCT 146.

60. Sp 212/ISp 21.

§45. Transmutation of "Destiny"

61. SvG 108.

62. This term was coined by William Richardson, *Heidegger: Through Phenomenology to Thought* (The Hague, 1963), pp. 20 f. and 435 n.

63. SZ 386/BT 438.

64. SZ 384 f./BT 436.

65. N II 257 and 397/N iv 249.

66. N II 482/EPh 76. This issue of waiting may illustrate Heidegger's distance from those philosophers of his day who longed for a political leader capable of perfecting both man and the city. Whereas nostalgics of "classical" authority such as Leo Strauss vest their "hope and prayer" in a wise man to unite law and virtue, Heidegger awaits, not an extraordinary guide, but an ordinary economy to come. Leadership ceases to be an issue in his political thinking as the modes of presencing appear as what "lets power arise." He thereby breaks with the two ideals of Western conservatism, the Greek law-giver and the biblical messiah, and avoids the absurdity of expecting men to become "awake to the highest possible degree" through "the absolute rule of the wise" (Leo Strauss, *Natural Right and History* [Chicago, 1953], pp. 127 and 185). Heidegger's much-quoted advice, "We are to do nothing but wait" (Gel 37/DTh 62), occurs precisely in the context of one of his strongest statements on anti-humanism (see the epigraph to sec. 7 above). Leo Strauss, on the other hand, sides with Machiavelli, who wrote: "To found a new republic, or to reform entirely the old institutions of an existing one, must be

the work of one man only" (*Discourses on Livy*, IX,1). As to the phrase "being lets powers arise," it obviously gives a secularized version of the Christian doctrine of Providence (cf. Augustine, *The City of God*, bk. V, ch. 21, and bk. XVIII, ch. 2, 1)—deprived, however, of the phantasm of any agent governing the course of events.

67. Hw 309/EGT 25.
68. Tk 37/QCT 37.
69. *Fureur et mystère*, op. cit., p. 106.
70. Hw 196 f./QCT 58.
71. Hw 234/QCT 98.
72. See above, ch. 5, n. 14.
73. Friedrich Nietzsche, *Die Unschuld des Werdens*, ed. A. Baeumler, 2 vols. (Stuttgart, 1978), v. 2, p. 308 (# 880).
74. TK 45/QCT 48.
75. "Standing in this reversal is something that can only be prepared historically in thinking, but it cannot be fabricated and even less forced" (GA 55 103).
76. "Being itself, as destinal, is eschatological" (Hw 302/EGT 18).
77. SD 44/OTB 41.
78. GA 55 98.
79. TK 43/QCT 44.
80. GA 55 119.
81. SvG 108.
82. GA 55 103 and 119.
83. "It is only when 'normal' understanding stands still that the other, essential, thinking can perhaps be set in motion" (GA 55 116).
84. The wordplay on "*Satz*," "proposition," but also "leap," is untranslatable: "Der Sprung ist der Satz aus dem Grundsatz vom Grund als einem Satz vom Seienden in das Sagen des Seins als Sein" (SvG 108).
85. SvG 97.
86. GA 55 84.

§46. From Violence to Anarchy

87. Hw 14 f./PLT 25.
88. These five perfections, as enumerated by Thomas Aquinas, are *res*, thing, *unum*, one, *aliquid*, something, *bonum*, good, *verum*, true (*Truth*, q. I, art. 1).
89. GA 55 70.
90. Cf. GA 25 167, 261, 291, 295 f.; KPM 52–54/Kpm 58–61; FD 137 f. and 144/WTh 175 f. and 184 f.; Wm 287 f./KTB 18 f.
91. GA 55 70 f. Just like the distinction between substance and accident, that between form and matter appears as a strategy of reason with a view to "putting in retainment" (*sicherstellen*). The form-matter distinction, says Heidegger, properly applies to the single region of equipment (*Zeug*). A piece of equipment is fabricated by the impression of a form on a matter, with a view toward its use. To extend the application of this distinction beyond the analysis of production, for example, to a 'hylemorphic' theory of being, amounts again to "making an assault upon the thing-ness of the thing" (Hw 19/PLT 25).
92. Hw 100/QCT 150. The identical roots (*cum* and *agere*) of both *cogere*, 'to drive together', and *cogitare*, 'to think'—the latter being the frequentative of the former—had already prompted wordplays in earlier Latin authors. Augustine writes of the triad—memory, intelligence, and will—that "when these three are drawn together (*coguntur*) into one, that conjunction (*coactus*) makes the result be called thinking (*cogitatio*)" (*On the Trinity*, bk. XI, 3, 6). As to *stellen* ('to set up', but also 'to hold at bay'), the early Heidegger had described the very goal of phenomenology as "pursuing a phenomenon and attempting to 'hold it at bay'" (SZ 72/BT 102)—a program expressly taken back in this text from QCT.
93. Cf. GA 55 113 f. and 199.
94. Sp 206–209/ISp 17.
95. GA 55 190.
96. Gel 35/DTh 61.
97. For example, GA 55 123, cf. 126.
98. GA 55 158 and 203. This confirms that when he speaks of *Aufhebung* (see sec. 19, n.

169), Heidegger does not intend to inscribe either thinking or acting in a system of negation and universalization.

99. Hw 15/PLT 25.

100. Karl Marx, "Contribution to the Critique of Hegel's Philosophy of Right," in T. B. Bottomore, ed., *Early Writings* (New York, 1963), p. 52 (trans. modified).

101. Maurice Merleau-Ponty, *Humanism and Terror*, trans. John O'Neill (Boston, 1969), p. xviii.

102. Hw 65/PLT 78.

103. Quoted in SD 72/OTB 65 f.

104. René Char, *La Parole en archipel* (Paris, 1962), p. 152 and *Poèmes et proses choisis* (Paris, 1957), p. 94.

105. Meister Eckhart, *Die deutschen Werke*, vol. II (Stuttgart, 1971), p. 253, l. 4 f., *Sermons and Treatises*, ed. and trans. M. O'C. Walshe (London, 1979), vol. II, p. 97. In Meister Eckhart, as in Nietzsche and Heidegger, the encroachment upon teleocracy is undoubtedly possible only because each of their economic sites is one of encroachment: of incipient modernity upon the scholastic Middle Ages (Meister Eckhart), of the end of modernity upon German idealism (Nietzsche), and of post-modernity upon metaphysics as a whole (Heidegger).

106. See the remarks on Schwan, above, sec. 5, n. 2.

107. See above, sec. 12, n. 41.

108. SD 43/OTB 40, see above, pp. 240–41.

109. SD 25/OTB 24.

Conclusion

§47. Economic Self-Regulation and Its Loci

1. WM 251/QB 105 (emphasis added).

2. See above, sec. 44, n. 47, and the texts cited in sec. 25, n. 61.

3. Sp 212/ISp 20.

4. See above, the epigraph to Part II.

5. EdD 7 / PLT 4.

6. Cf. above, sec. 19, n. 169. This is the only occurrence of so evidently a Hegelian term in his writings that I know of.

7. Cf. above, Part Four, n. 5.

8. Michel Foucault, *The Order of Things* (New York, 1973), p. xxii; and *The Archeology of Knowledge*, trans. A. M. Sheridan Smith (New York, 1972), pp. 19 ff.

9. Cf. above, sec. 19, n. 128.

10. SD 61/ OTB 55.

11. Cf. above, sec. 1, n. 15.

12. Cf. above, sec. 12, n. 41.

13. Cf. the lines cited above in the epigraph to Sec. 12.

§48. Objections and Answers

14. This has, couched in one terminology or another, been a basic insight of modern philosophy. Montesquieu was probably the first to articulate that derivation, casting it in terms of a collective physiological dependence of positive law on geography and history: "Better to say that the government most conformable to nature is that which best agrees with the humour and disposition of the people in whose favours it is established," Baron de Montesquieu, *The Spirit of the Laws*, Bk. II, 3, trans. T. Nugent (New York, 1949), p. 6. From the viewpoint of deconstruction, humor and dispostion are conditions that preserve ontically, while hiding ontologically, the dependence of positive law on economic law.

15. See above, sec. 12, n. 61.

16. See above, sec. 39, n. 130.

17. Immanuel Kant, *Was heisst: sich im Denken orientieren?* A 330. In this text, Kant opposes enlightenment to knowing as he elsewhere opposes reason, *Vernunft*, to understanding, *Verstand*. The maxim of enlightenment recalls the *koinos logos* (common reason) of the Stoics and their polemic against the proverbial *autos epha* ("he himself said so," the argument of authority first stated that way in the Pythagorean school), cf. Seneca, Letter to Lucilius

XXXIII, 7–11; trans. Richard M. Gummerie, *Ad Lucilium Epistolae Morales,* 3 vols. (New York, 1917), vol. I, pp. 239 f.

18. Kant concludes this same text on not so optimistic a note: "In this way it is quite easy to establish enlightenment through education in individual subjects; all that is required is to begin to habituate young minds early in this reflection. It is however a protracted and wearisome undertaking to enlighten an entire generation; for one then comes up against many external obstacles which partly forbid and partly hamper that kind of education" (ibid.).

19. Pierre-Joseph Proudhon, *What Is Property?* trans. Benjamin R. Tucker (Princeton, 1876), p. 28 and 34.

20. Michel Bakunin, *Oeuvres,* vol. III (Paris, 1908), pp. 82 f.

21. See the text cited above, sec. 8, n. 55.

22. Daniel Saurin, *L'Ordre par l'anarchie* (Paris, 1893), p. 18.

23. On this point, see Robert Benton's excellent study, *Kant's Second Critique and the Problem of Transcendental Arguments* (The Hague, 1977), especially pp. 7–25 and 105–11.

24. See the texts cited above, secs. 11, n. 19, and 18, n. 102.

25. SD 2/OTB 2.

26. SD 2/OTB 2.

27. SD 44/OTB 41.

28. See above, sec. 18, n. 100.

29. This question was addressed to Heidegger by René Char, see François Vezin, "Heidegger parle en France," *Nouvelle Revue Française,* no. 284 (August, 1976):85.

30. René Char, *Recherche de la base et du sommet* (Paris, 1971), p. 134.

SELECTED BIBLIOGRAPHY

The list below includes only the titles of works regularly consulted. For a complete bibliography of the literature on Martin Heidegger up to 1982, see the three volumes by Hans-Martin Sass: *Heidegger-Bibliographie* (Meisenheim am Glan, 1968; 2,201 titles); *Materialien zur Heidegger-Bibliographie 1917–1972* (Meisenheim am Glan, 1975; 1,566 titles); and *Martin Heidegger: Bibliography and Glossary* (Bowling Green, Ky., 1982; 6,350 titles).

Adorno, T. *The Jargon of Authenticity*. Trans. Knut Tarnowski and Frederic Will. Evanston, 1973.
Allemann, B. *Hölderlin und Heidegger*. Freiburg/Br., 1954.
———. "Martin Heidegger und die Politik." In *Heidegger, Perspektiven zur Deutung seines Werks*, ed. O. Pöggeler, pp. 246–260. Cologne, 1969.
Althusser, L. *For Marx*. Trans. Ben Brewster. London, 1969.
———. *Réponse à John Lewis*. Paris, 1973.
———. *Positions*. Paris, 1976.
Apel, K.-O. *Towards a Transformation of Philosophy*. Trans. Glyn Adey and David Frisby. Boston, 1980.
Arendt, H. *Between Past and Future*. New York, 1961.
———. *The Origins of Totalitarianism*, 2d enl. ed. New York, 1958.
———. *The Human Condition*. Chicago, 1958.
———. "Action and the 'Pursuit of Happiness'." In *Politische Ordnung und menschliche Existenz, Festgabe Eric Voegelin*, pp. 1–16. Munich, 1962.
———. *On Revolution*. New York, 1965.
———. *Crises of the Republic*. New York, 1972.
———. *On Violence*. New York, 1970.
———. "Martin Heidegger at 80." *New York Review of Books* 17/8 (October 21, 1971):50–54.
———. *The Life of the Mind*. Vol. I: *Thinking*; Vol. II: *Willing*. New York, 1978.
Aubenque, P. *Le Problème de l'être chez Aristote*. Paris, 1962.
———. *La Prudence chez Aristote*. Paris, 1963.
Axelos, K. *Héraclite et la philosophie*. Paris, 1962.
———. *Einführung in ein künftiges Denken*. Tübingen, 1966.
Beaufret, J. *Le Poème de Parménide*. Paris, 1955.
———. *Dialogue avec Heidegger*. Vol. I: *Philosophie grecque*. Paris, 1973; Vol. II: *Philosophie moderne*. Paris, 1973; Vol. III: *Approche de Heidegger*. Paris, 1974.
Beckmann, J.-P. *Die Relationen der Identität und Gleichheit nach J. Duns Scotus*. Bonn, 1967.
Biemel, W. "Dichtung und Sprache bei Heidegger." *Man and World* II (1969):478–514.
Birault, H. *Heidegger et l'expérience de la pensée*. Paris, 1978.
Boeder, H. "Der frühgriechische Wortgebrauch von Logos und Aletheia." *Archiv für Begriffsgeschichte* IV (1958): 82–112.
Boer, W. de. "Heideggers Missverständnis der Metaphysik." *Zeitschrift für philosophische Forschung* IX (1955):500–545.

Bourdieu, P. "L'ontologie politique de Martin Heidegger." *Actes de la recherche en sciences sociales* V–VI (1975):109–156.
Brentano, F. *On the Several Senses of Being in Aristotle.* Trans. Rolf George. Berkeley, 1975.
Bucher, A. *Martin Heidegger, Metaphysik als Begriffsproblematik.* Bonn, 1972.
Burnet, J. *Early Greek Philosophy.* London, 1930.
Couissin, P. "L'origine et l'évolution de l'epoché." *Revue des études grecques* 42 (1929):373–397.
Dauenhauer, B. "Renovating the Problem of Politics." *Review of Metaphysics* XXIX (1976):626–641.
Declève, H. *Heidegger et Kant.* The Hague, 1970.
Deleuze, G. and Guattari, F. *Rhizome.* Paris, 1976.
Demske, J. *Being, Man, and Death: A Key to Heidegger.* Lexington, 1970.
Derrida. J. *Of Grammatology.* Trans. Gayatri C. Spivak. Baltimore, 1976.
Dierse, U. "Anarchie." In *Historisches Wörterbuch der Philosophie,* ed. J. Ritter, vol. I, col. 267–294. Basel, 1971.
Fahrenbach, H. *Existenzphilosophie und Ethik.* Frankfurt, 1970.
Fink, E. *Spiel als Weltsymbol.* Stuttgart, 1960.
Foucault, M. *The Archaeology of Knowledge: Includes the Discourse on Language.* Trans. A. M. Sheridan-Smith. New York, 1972.
———. *Madness and Civilization: A History of Insanity in the Age of Reason.* Trans. Richard Howard. New York, 1965.
———. *The Order of Things: An Archaeology of the Human Sciences.* Trans. Don Ihde. New York, 1970.
Franzen, W. *Von der Existenzialontologie zur Seinsgeschichte.* Meisenheim am Glan, 1975.
Friedlander, P. *Plato.* Trans. Hans Meyerhoff. 3 vols. Princeton, 1964–70.
Fritz, K. von. "*Noos* and *Noein* in the Homeric Poems." *Classical Philology* XXXVIII (1943):79–93.
———. "*Nous, Noein* and their Derivatives in Pre-Socratic Philosophy (Excluding Anaxagoras)." *Classical Philology* XL (1945):223–242 and XLI (1946):12–34.
———. "Die Rolle des *Nous.*" In *Um die Begriffswelt der Vorsokratiker,* ed. H. G. Gadamer, pp. 246–362. Darmstadt, 1968.
Fürstenau, P. *Heidegger, das Gefüge seines Denkens.* Frankfurt, 1958.
Gabriel, L. "Sein und Geschichte. Martin Heideggers geschichtsontologischer Denkversuch." *Wissenschaft und Weltbild* IX (1956):25–32.
Gadamer, H.-G. *Kleine Schriften.* Vol. I. Tübingen, 1967.
———. *Truth and Method.* Trans. Garrett Barden and John Cumming. New York, 1975.
Gethmann, C. F. *Verstehen und Auslegung. Das Methodenproblem in der Philosophie Martin Heideggers.* Bonn, 1974.
Gilson, É. *L'Être et l'Essence.* Paris, 1948.
———. *Being and Some Philosophers.* Toronto, 1949.
———. *Jean Duns Scot. Introduction à ses positions fondamentales.* Paris, 1952.
Goldmann, L. *Lukàcs and Heidegger: Towards a New Philosophy.* Trans. William Q. Boelhower. Boston, 1977.
Granel, G. "Remarques sur le rapport de 'Sein und Zeit' et de la phénoménologie husserlienne." In *Durchblicke. Martin Heidegger zum 80. Geburtstag,* ed. V. Klostermann, pp. 350–368. Frankfurt, 1970.
Habermas, J. *Knowledge and Human Interests.* Trans. Jeremy J. Shapiro. Boston, 1971.
———. *Legitimation Crisis.* Trans. Thomas McCarthy. Boston, 1975.
———. *Protestbewegung und Hochschulreform.* Frankfurt, 1969.

Selected Bibliography

389

———. *Philosophical-Political Profiles*. Trans. Fred Lawrence. Boston, 1983.
———. *Kultur und Kritik*. Frankfurt, 1973.
———. *Toward a Rational Society: Student Protest, Science and Politics*. Trans. Jeremy J. Shapiro. Boston, 1970.
———. "Hannah Arendt's Communications Concept of Power." *Social Research* XLIV, 1 (1977):3–24.
Harries, K. "Heidegger as a Political Thinker." *Review of Metaphysics* XXIX, 4 (1976):642–669.
Held, K. "Der Logos-Gedanke des Heraklit." In *Durchblicke: Martin Heidegger zum 80. Geburtstag*, ed. V. Klostermann, pp. 162–206. Frankfurt, 1970.
Henry, M. *Marx: A Philosophy of Human Reality*. Trans. Kathleen McLaughlin. Bloomington, 1983.
Herrmann, F.-W. von. *Die Selbstinterpretation Martin Heideggers*. Meisenheim am Glan, 1964.
———. *Subjekt und Dasein. Interpretationen zu 'Sein und Zeit'*. Frankfurt, 1974.
Hirzel, R. "Über Entelechie und Endelechie." *Rheinisches Museum, Neue Folge* 38 (1884):169–208.
Hoppe, H. "Wandlungen in der Kant-Auffassung Heideggers." In *Durchblicke. Martin Heidegger zum 80. Geburtstag*, ed. V. Klostermann, pp. 284–317. Frankfurt, 1970.
Huch, K. J. *Philosophiegeschichtliche Voraussetzungen der Heideggerschen Ontologie*. Frankfurt, 1967.
Jaeger, W. *The Theology of the Early Greek Philosophers*. 2d ed. Trans. Edward Robinson. Westport, Conn., 1980.
Jaspers, K. *Philosophische Autobiographie*. 2nd ed. Munich, 1977.
———. *Notizen zu Martin Heidegger*. Munich, 1978.
Jonas, H. *The Phenomenon of Life*. New York, 1966.
———. *The Imperative of Responsibility: In Search of an Ethics for the Technological Age*. Trans. Hans Jonas with David Herr. Chicago, 1984.
Kanthack, K. *Das Denken Martin Heideggers*. Berlin, 1959.
Kaulbach, F. "Die Kantische Lehre von Ding und Sein in der Interpretation Heideggers." *Kant-Studien* 55 (1964): 194–220.
Klossowski, P. "Circulus vitiosus." In *Nietzsche aujourd'hui?*, 2 vols., ed. Centre culturel international de Cérisy-la-Salle, vol. 1, pp. 91–103. Paris, 1973.
Klostermann, V. *Durchblicke. Martin Heidegger zum 80. Geburtstag*. Frankfurt, 1970.
Krockow, C. Graf von. *Die Entscheidung. Eine Untersuchung über Ernst Jünger, Carl Schmitt, Martin Heidegger*. Stuttgart, 1958.
Krüger, G. "Martin Heidegger und der Humanismus." *Studia Philosophica* IX (1949):93–129.
Kubler, G. *The Shape of Time. Remarks on the History of Things*. New Haven, 1962.
Lévinas, E. *En découvrant l'existence avec Husserl et Heidegger*. Paris, 1967.
Lévi-Strauss, C. *The Naked Man*. Trans. John and Doreen Weightman. New York, 1981.
Lohmann, J. "Martin Heideggers 'Ontologische Differenz' und die Sprache." *Lexis* I (1948):49–106.
Lotz, J. B. *Das Urteil und das Sein*. Munich, 1957.
———. "Denken und Sein nach den jüngsten Veröffentlichungen von M. Heidegger." *Scholastik* XXXIII (1958):81–98.
Löwith, K. *Heidegger, Denker in dürftiger Zeit*. 2nd ed. Göttingen, 1960.
———. *Gesammelte Abhandlungen*. Stuttgart, 1960.
Luhmann, N. *Legitimation durch Verfahren*. Frankfurt, 1969.

Marcel, G. "Ma relation avec Heidegger." *Présence de Gabriel Marcel* I (1979):25–38.

Marcuse, H. "Beiträge zu einer Phänomenologie des Historischen Materialismus." *Philosophische Hefte* I (1928):45–68. Reprinted in *Existenzialistische Marx-Interpretation*, ed. A. Schmidt, pp. 41–84. Frankfurt, 1973.

———. *Eros and Civilization*. Boston, 1955.

———. "Heidegger's Politics: An Interview with Herbert Marcuse by Frederick Olafson." *Graduate Faculty Philosophy Journal* VI (1977):28–40.

Marx, W. *Heidegger and the Tradition*. Trans. Theodore Kisiel and Murray Greene. Evanston, 1971.

———. "Das Denken und seine Sache." In *Heidegger: Freiburger Universitätsvorträge zu seinem Gedenken*, ed. H. G. Gadamer, W. Marx, C. F. v. Weizsäcker, pp. 11–41. Freiburg/Br., 1977.

Maurer, R. *Revolution und 'Kehre': Studien zum Problem gesellschaftlicher Naturbeherrschung*. Frankfurt, 1975.

Mehta, J. *Martin Heidegger: The Way and the Vision*. Honolulu, 1976.

Merleau-Ponty, M. *Humanism and Terror: An Essay on the Communist Problem*. Trans. John O'Neill. Boston, 1969.

Mongis, H. *Heidegger et la critique de la notion de valeur*. The Hague, 1976.

Nicholson, G. "Camus and Heidegger: Anarchists." *University of Toronto Quarterly* XLI (1971):14–23.

———. "The Commune in 'Being and Time'." *Dialogue* X, 4 (1971): 708–726.

Offe, C. *Strukturprobleme des kapitalistischen Staates*. Frankfurt, 1972.

Palmier, J.-M. *Les Écrits politiques de Heidegger*. Paris, 1968.

———. *Situation de Georg Trakl*. Paris, 1972.

Pöggeler, O. "Sein als Ereignis." *Zeitschrift für philosophische Forschung* XIII (1959):597–632.

———. *Der Denkweg Martin Heideggers*. Pfullingen, 1963.

———. "Einleitung." In *Heidegger. Perspektiven zur Deutung seines Werks*, ed. O. Pöggeler, pp. 11–53. Cologne, 1969.

———. *Philosophie und Politik bei Heidegger*. Freiburg/Br., 1972.

Prauss, G. *Erkennen und Handeln in Heideggers 'Sein und Zeit'*. Freiburg/Br., 1977.

Pugliese, O. *Vermittlung und Kehre. Grundzüge des Geschichtsdenkens bei Martin Heidegger*. Freiburg/Br., 1965.

Reinhardt, K. *Parmenides und die Geschichte der griechischen Philosophie*. Bonn, 1916.

Richardson, W. *Heidegger. Through Phenomenology to Thought*. The Hague, 1963.

Ricoeur, P. *The Conflict of Interpretations: Essays in Hermeneutics*. Ed. Donald Ihde. Evanston, 1974.

———. *The Rule of Metaphor: Multi-disciplinary Studies of the Creation of Meaning in Language*. Trans. Robert Czerny with Kathleen McLaughlin and John Costello. Buffalo, 1975.

———. "Le 'Marx' de Michel Henry." *Esprit* (October, 1978):124–139.

Riedel, M. *Metaphysik und Metapolitik*. Frankfurt, 1975.

Rohrmoser, G. *Das Elend der kritischen Theorie*. Freiburg/Br., 1970.

Saurin, D. *L'Ordre par l'anarchie*. Paris, 1863.

Schneeberger, G. *Nachlese zu Heidegger*. Bern, 1962.

Schöfer, E. *Die Sprache Heideggers*. Pfullingen, 1962.

Schulz, W. "Über den philosophiegeschichtlichen Ort Martin Heideggers." *Philosophische Rundschau* I (1953–1954):65–93 and 211–232. Repr. in *Heidegger. Perspektiven zur Deutung seines Werks*, ed. O. Pöggeler, pp. 95–139. Cologne, 1969.

———. *Der Gott der neuzeitlichen Metaphysik*. Pfullingen, 1957.

———. *Philosophie in der veränderten Welt*. Pfullingen, 1972.

Schwan, A. *Politische Philosophie im Denken Martin Heideggers*. Cologne, 1965.

Sheehan, T. "Getting to the Topic: The New Edition of 'Wegmarken'." *Research in Phenomenology* VII (1977):299–316.

Siewerth, G. *Das Schicksal der Metaphysik von Thomas zu Heidegger*. Einsiedeln, 1959.

Snell, B. *The Discovery of the Mind: The Greek Origins of European Thought*. Trans. T. G. Rosenmeyer. Cambridge, Mass., 1953.

Staiger, E. *Die Kunst der Interpretation*. Munich, 1971.

Taminiaux, J. "Le Regard et l'excédent." *Revue philosophique de Louvain* 75 (1977):74–100.

Theunissen, M. *The Other: Studies in the Social Ontology of Husserl, Heidegger, Sartre and Buber*. Trans. Christopher Macann. Cambridge, Mass., 1984.

Tugendhat, E. *Der Wahrheitsbegriff bei Husserl und Heidegger*. Berlin, 1967.

Vezin, F. "Heidegger parle en France." *Nouvelle Revue française* 284 (August, 1976):85–86.

Wahl, J. *Sur l'interprétation de l'histoire de la métaphysique d'après Heidegger*. Paris, 1951.

———. *Vers la fin de l'ontologie*. Paris, 1956.

Weil, E. "Philosophie politique, théorie politique." *Revue française de science politique* XI, 2 (1961):267–294.

Wiplinger, F. *Wahrheit und Geschichtlichkeit. Eine Untersuchung über die Frage nach dem Wesen der Wahrheit im Denken Martin Heideggers*. Freiburg/Br., 1961.

CITATIONS FROM HEIDEGGER'S TEXTS IN GERMAN

Indexed here are citations of German editions of Heidegger's texts referred to in the Notes. Full titles corresponding to the abbreviations will be found on pp. 305-309.

CITATIONS FROM ENGLISH
TRANSLATIONS

Indexed below are citations of English translations of Heidegger's texts referred to in the Notes. Full titles are given on pp. 305-309.

AaS

3	354n.30
6	325n.55

BPP

1	322n.47
3	324n.34
12	332n.53
14	344n.79
16 f.	378n.2
17	324n.30,
	368n.29
18 f.	350n.186
19	324n.27
20	323n.2,
	326n.3
21	326n.6
21 f.	315n.53
22	327n.9
22 f.	311n.10,
	327n.12
23	327n.14,
	342n.52
50	324n.31,
	345n.112
64	327n.8
73	357n.33

BT

19	325n.38,
	341n.13,
	344n.78,
	375n.7
21	327n.28,
	368n.33,
	379n.17
21-24	342n.53
23	352n.12
25	344n.79
27	352n.13
31	332n.51,
	347n.144,
	361n.94
32	321n.41,
	324n.27
33 f.	318n.10
34	320n.39,
	324n.27,
	342n.54
36 f.	371n.96
37	367n.21
44	327n.14

48	360n.83,
	379n.15
54 f.	324n.35
55-58	358n.46
56	357n.33,
	360n.83
57	360n.84
58 f.	324n.33
59	324n.36
59 f.	346n.128
61	324nn.34,37
62	323n.15,
	324n.26,
	345n.108,
	367n.28
63	311n.13,
	314n.41,
	323n.2,
	333n.1,
	347n.138,
	356n.21,
	376n.37
63 f.	378n.2
68	375nn.8,12
70	352n.13,
	354nn.25,31,
	360n.83
74	323n.10
79	354n.25,
	368n.34
88	312n.30
92	331n.49,
	347n.146,
	368n.35
94-102	318n.9
100	327n.23
102	383n.92
116 f.	379n.22
130	360n.83
133	344n.77
139	371n.96
149-63	318n.10
150	331n.46
151	323n.12
159	313n.33
167	313n.34,
	375n.9
168	313n.34
171	319n.34,
	342n.57,
	357n.33,
	371n.87
171 f.	317n.3
183	311n.19,

	314n.40,
	331n.50
187	324n.29,
	360n.83,
	368n.35,
	373n.120,
	379n.22
188 f.	327n.10
208	327n.23
210	354n.29
221	313n.33
224	313n.34
237	376n.39
241	379n.21
255	350n.187
268	347n.145
268 f.	354n.29
269	361n.86
275	347n.144
294	314n.42
303	313n.34
307	314n.39
308	313n.33
312	313n.34
313	313n.34
316	371n.96
343	325n.45
344	313n.33,
	326n.60
349 f.	367n.21
355	342n.53
357	352n.15
359	371n.96
360	355n.6,
	376n.28
364-70	325n.47
365	313n.34
367	347n.144
374	321n.43,
	352n.15
377	321n.43
380	321n.42
388	342n.53
402	342n.57
409	312nn.30,32
413-15	324n.34
414	313n.33
429	321n.40,
	342n.56
435	377n.43
436	325n.53,
	382n.64
437	342n.53
438	325n.53,

	342n.53,
	382n.63
443	342n.53
448	342n.53,
	353n.24
449-55	324n.22
460	342n.57
479 f.	356n.21
487	382n.54
490	323n.3,
	367n.21
494	358n.43

BWr

111 f.	375n.6
125-27	333n.71
127	333n.67,
	366n.10
127 f.	357n.33
138	312n.22
193	312n.29,
	327n.19,
	376n.38
193 f.	327n.26
194	312n.31,
	362n.16
196	333n.73
199	372n.100
201 f.	336n.46
202	320n.8
207	357n.33,
	376n.42
208	321n.21,
	378n.3
209	321n.25
210	353n.23
211	343n.58
212	372n.100,
	375nn.10,15
215	350n.188
216	350n.188
219	322n.48
219 f.	326n.4
222	352n.13
224	321n.24
225	320n.1,
	321n.23,
	345n.104
231	311n.15
232 f.	350n.194
235	327n.13
238	375n.1
238 f.	345n.105

NAME INDEX

This index includes names mentioned in the Notes, pp. 311-85, as well as in the text.